Who's Who
in Greater Manchester

Golden Jubilee Edition

Her Majesty
Queen Elizabeth II

Prince Philip and I have been deeply touched by the many kind messages about the Golden Jubilee.

This anniversary is for us an occasion to acknowledge with gratitude the loyalty and support which we have received from so many people since I came to the Throne in 1952. It is especially an opportunity to thank all those of you who help others in your own local communities through public or voluntary service. I would like to think that your work will be particularly recognised during this Jubilee year.

I hope also that this time of celebration in the United Kingdom and across the Commonwealth will not simply be an occasion to be nostalgic about the past. I believe that, young or old, we have as much to look forward to with confidence and hope as we have to look back on with pride.

I send my warmest good wishes to you all.

ELIZABETH R.

6th February, 2002.

Colonel Sir John Timmins KCVO OBE TD

Lord Lieutenant of Greater Manchester
Byrom House
Quay Street
Manchester
M3 3JD

Tel. No.: 0161 834 0490

I am delighted that the Manchester Literary and Philosophical Society has been enabled to undertake the considerable task of producing a fifth edition of "Who's Who in Greater Manchester", as a consequence of a most generous gift.

The success of the first four editions has established the need for this excellent work of reference and I know that for some time the hope and expectation of a new edition has existed, not least amongst those involved with the many organizations across our County and City to whom it is a constant source of information. We are extremely fortunate that this expectation can be fulfilled in the Golden Jubilee year, as a consequence of the benefactor's wish to acknowledge this event.

The "Lit and Phil" has played a major role in the intellectual activities of the City of Manchester for more than 200 years. Now, sitting astride the largest University Campus in Europe, and in a thriving social and business community, it has the opportunity to go forward in the 21st Century. I am sure the Society will retain its unique position, and can look forward to future success.

John Timmins.

R.M. Willan

Great cities become great not by chance, but through the endeavour and vision of many people, and Manchester has perhaps been lucky to have more than its fair share of those visionaries, past and present, who have made it what it is today.......A vibrant modern city, proud of its historical eminence and yet facing its present day challenges with increasing confidence.

Manchester, whilst born out of Industry, has so much more to justify its place as one of the premier regional cities in Europe, but to list all its qualities would be merely stating the obvious.

My father had agreed to support this reference book and would have thoroughly enjoyed flicking through its pages. Sadly he passed away earlier this year and so this volume is but a small legacy from a man who gave so much to his friends and the city he loved.

The Manchester Literary & Philosophical Society, particularly Janet Evans, are to be congratulated for undertaking this sometimes thankless task with such efficiency and enthusiasm.

Robert Matthew Willan   October 1922 – May 2002

Madge Willan   March 1923 – December 2001

About the Society

The Manchester Literary & Philosophical Society, colloquially known as 'The Lit and Phil', is one of the oldest learned societies in Britain apart from The Royal Society in London. It was formally instituted on 28th February 1781 and in 1799 acquired No.26 George Street in Manchester, its home for nearly 200 years until its disposal in 1980.

Most of the original members were physicians, surgeons and apothecaries and by 1861 membership had risen to over 200. Always an outward-looking organization, the society, while retaining a major interest in both Science and Technology, has extended significantly its sphere of interest to include the arts and current social issues. There is also a Young Persons' Section which arranges lectures for students and is well supported by local schools. Today membership is over 400, including academics, professional people and others who enjoy widening their knowledge and interests.

John Dalton, 'Father of Modern Chemistry' and justly famed for his atomic theory, joined the Lit and Phil in 1794, became Secretary in 1800, and President in 1816, an office he held until his death in 1844. He and his gifted pupil, James Prescott Joule, were both scientists of international repute and other past members include Henry Roscoe, the chemist, Ernest Rutherford, the nuclear physicist, Joseph Whitworth, the precision engineer and P.M.Roget of Thesaurus fame.

The Lit and Phil is a registered charity and has an excellent programme of lectures to which entry is free to the general public. Members of the society and the speaker normally gather for refreshments after lectures. Annual Programmes are circulated to local libraries in Greater Manchester and newsletters are distributed to members throughout the season. The society also publishes the Manchester Memoirs, started in 1785, to record proceedings of the society and reproductions of certain papers presented. Extracts of news items and membership details can be found on the website www.manlitphil.co.uk or from the society: tel: 0161 247 6774.

Acknowledgements

Since 1996, the year of the last edition of this publication, Greater Manchester and particularly its City Centre have been transformed. The Lowry Centre, The Imperial War Museum North, Urbis, The Bridgewater Hall, and the extension of the City Art Gallery have all been completed. The construction of these public buildings has been matched by commercial, residential and retail projects such as The Printworks, No 1 Deansgate, Exchange Square, the rebuilding of the Marks and Spencer store and the Castlefield and Spinningfield developments. The regeneration plans for East Manchester were given a flying start by the overwhelming success of the Commonwealth Games this summer. Such projects demonstrate the prosperity and vibrancy of the area and reflect the character of the people who live and work there.

In preparing this edition we have endeavoured to identify people of influence, interest and achievement who contribute to the success and importance of Greater Manchester. We have tried to achieve this by researching broad areas of activity: arts, education, commerce, finance, health, law, media, public sector, sport and the voluntary sector. We have included an index based on these areas of influence, and though the degree of influence varies we hope that it will add to the value of the book as a work of reference. Most of the people appearing in the book have been nominated by others, and I would particularly like to thank all those individuals who have shared with me their knowledge of their colleagues, and have suggested names for invitation. We are very grateful to all who have responded. Inevitably there are many who, for a variety of reasons preferred not to do so and whilst respecting their reluctance we regret their absence.

Without the late Robert Willan this project to celebrate the Golden Jubilee would not have been possible. It is thanks to him that the idea was born and could be undertaken. I would like to thank Peter Willan, his son, for his encouragement and for the tribute to his father. Helen Beswick, the project coordinator, has been responsible for all the information processing, collation and typesetting, and to her and the staff of the Gaddum Centre much praise and thanks are due. I would also like to thank Claire Tindale, the cover designer, for her patience and creativity, as well as Andrew Caesar and John Liggett our printers for their good advice. Angus Yeaman has been unfailingly supportive and Faith Yeaman has helped with research. Throughout the project Michael Evans has been an invaluable source of wise counsel. It has been a privilege and a pleasure to discover the wealth of talent and creativity amongst the people featured in this book.

Janet E.Evans: Project Director

No acknowledgement would be complete without recognition of the hard work and enthusiasm shown by Janet Evans in this enterprise, and on behalf of the Society, my very sincere thanks to her and all others involved.

Angus G. D. Yeaman
President, The Manchester Literary & Philosophical Society.

First published in 2002
by
Manchester Literary & Philosophical Society
Registered Charity No. 235313

© 2002 Manchester Literary & Philosophical Society

ISBN 0 9024 28 24 1

Cover Design By Claire Tindale
Cover photographs by Claire Tindale and Manchester 2002 Ltd
Image of Queen Elizabeth II by Royal Images
Compiled and typeset by Helen Beswick, Gaddum Centre
Printed in Great Britain by
MFP Design and Print
www.mfpprint.co.uk

ABBOTT, John Noel, TD (1975), First Bar (1981), Second Bar (1993), Queen's Silver Jubilee Medal (1977), FCIT (1982), DL (1993), FPC (1997), FILT (2000)

Positions: Chairman, Marlboro' Properties (St Albans) Ltd; Deputy Lieutenant and High Sheriff, County of Greater Manchester (2000-01).
Areas of Influence: Commerce, Voluntary Sector.
Profile: *b*. March 10th, 1939; *m*. Janet Vivien; 1 son; 1 daughter.
Educated at Beech Hall Preparatory School, Macclesfield; Bradfield College, Berks; Manchester College of Commerce; Major (Rtd.), National Service, RASC (1958-60); Career profile: Royal Corps of Transport (TA); Royal Logistics Corps (TA); Engineer and Transport Staff Corps RE (TA). Student Medal, Chartered Institute of Transport (1965); Past President, Manchester Junior Chamber of Commerce (1972-73); Past Chairman, NW Section, The Chartered Institute of Transport (1982-83); Chairman, East Cheshire Branch, The Army Benevolent Fund (1983 - present); President, Manchester Royal Army Service Corps / Royal Corps of Transport Association (1992 - present); National Employers Liaison Committee (Greater Manchester). Clubs and societies: St James Club; Reserve Forces and Cadets Association; The Army Benevolent Fund; Movement Control Officers Club; Manchester Luncheon Club; Rotary Club, Manchester; Commanderie de Bordeaux a Manchester; Manchester Literary and Philosophical Society, Trustee, Spinal Foundation.
Interests: Travel, arts, country sports, needs of the disabled.
Contact details: Gilgo Cottage, Gore Lane, Alderley Edge, Cheshire, SK9 7SP (tel: 01625 582 720, e-mail.johnabb@gilgo.fsnet.co.uk).

ADAMS, Shirley Meri, BA, BA (Hons).

Positions: Chief Executive, Gaddum Centre (1996 - present); JP, Manchester City Bench; Chair, Executive Committee, VAM; Trustee, Manchester Relief in Need Charity, Manchester Children's Relief in Need, Manchester Girls Institute Trust Fund, Manchester District Nursing Institute Fund, Butterworth & Bailey Charitable Trust; Clerk to the Trustees, JT Blair Charitable Trust.
Areas of Influence: Voluntary Sector, Law.
Profile: *b.* May 10th, 1949; 1 son;
Educated at: Hunter College High School, New York (1961-67); Boston University (1967-71); University of Kent at Canterbury (1973-76). Career profile: Deputy Director, LANCE, a NACRO housing project (1976-78); Housing Development Officer, NACRO (1978-84); Housing Services Manager, NACRO (1984-87); Director, Wood Street Mission (1988-96);
Interests: Walking, crafts, gardening.
Contact details: Gaddum Centre, Gaddum House, 6 Great Jackson Street, Manchester M15 4AX (tel: 0161 834 6069, fax: 0161 839 8573, email: sma@gaddumcentre.co.uk); 20 Alexandra Terrace, Grane Road, Haslingden, Lancs. BB4 5EB (tel: 01706 220856).

AGARD, Caryl Edward, OBE (2002), MBA, DMS

Positions: Chief Executive, Progress Trust (1996 - present); Chair, Black and Minority Ethnic Sub Group of Compact; Member, National Working Group for Compact; Member, Minority Ethnic Advisory Group to the National Employment Panel; Neighbourhood Renewal Advisor, Neighbourhood Renewal Unit.
Areas of Influence: Voluntary Sector, Socially Excluded Groups, Public Sector.
Profile: *b.* March 11th, 1965; 2 sons, Nathan (19), and Kobe (1); 1 daughter, Melissa (13).
Educated at: Alexandra Park Junior School, Oldham (1972-76); Counthill Comprehensive School, Oldham (1976-81); University of Central Lancashire, Preston. Prior to his current position Caryl Agard was self employed in his own consultancy practice, Impact (1993-96). As a freelance consultant he undertook assignments for the Upper lee Valley Partnership, North London TEC, London Borough of Haringey, Barnet and Enfield, specifically on programme and project management of the Single Regeneration Budget, European Funds, Central Government Funds and TEC funded Initiatives. Before starting the consultancy Caryl was Chief Officer of Preston Caricom, which was a social and economic development agency for Black and Ethnic communities of Preston that he set up himself (1990-94). Prior to this and the initial starting point for his career in socio-economic programmes, Caryl worked as Project Manager for Age Concern, Preston and South Ribble, where he managed the first programme for developing services for elderly people from black and ethnic

minority communities in the organisation's history (1986-90).

Interests: Leeds United, squash, circuit training, weight training, reading Caryl Phillips.

Contact details: Progress Trust, Barclay House, 3rd Floor, 35 Whitworth Street West, Manchester M1 5NG (tel: 0161 966 0020, fax: 0161 906 0021, email: caryl.agard@progresstrust.com).

AHMAD, Riaz, FCCA, JP

Positions: Mayor, Oldham Council; Chairman, Oldham Primary Care Trust; Accountant, Riaz Ahmad & Co (1984 - present)

Areas of Influence: Health, Finance, Voluntary Sector.

Profile: *b.* June 13th, 1953; *m.* Safia Begum; 3 sons; 1 daughter.

Career profile: Fellow of Chartered Certified Accountants; Accountant, Co-operative Wholesale Society (1979-82); Accountant, British Telecom (1982-86).

Interests: Swimming, walking.

Contact details: Lord House, 51 Lord Street, Manchester M3 1HL (tel: 0161 835 9123, fax: 0161 839 9779); 157 Frederick Street, Oldham OL8 4DA (tel: 0161 652 3819, fax: 0161 284 0949, email: cllr.r.ahmad@oldham.gov.uk).

AHMED, Aaqil, BA

Positions: Deputy Editor, General Documentaries, BBC, Manchester; Chairperson, Bolton MELA Group which organises an annual arts festival in Bolton, Patron - Black History Monthly North West.

Areas of Influence: Faith Groups, Media, Voluntary Sector.

Profile: *b.* June 5th, 1969; *m.* Saima; 1 son; 2 daughters.

Educated at Wigan College of Technology and University of Westminster. Aaquil Ahmed is currently working on the 'Everyman' programme and has also been deputy editor of 'Islam UK', a high profile BBC Season of Programmes on Islam. Aaqil has worked in current affairs at the BBC producing shows such as *Here and Now* and *The Crime Squad* as well as working on major news stories such as the funeral of Diana, the Turkish earthquake and the UK floods. He received an EMMA (2002) for best documentary for the film *Islamaphobia*, and a prize from The Muslim Council of Britain for fostering a better understanding of Islam in Britain.

Interests: Sport, community work, a big lover of Bolton Wanderers Football Club, being involved in local Asian community activities.

Contact details: BBC, Oxford Road, Manchester M60 1SJ (tel: 0161 244 3501, email: aaqil.ahmed@bbc.co.uk).

AHMED, Iqbal, OBE (2001)

Positions: Chairman and Managing Director, Seafood Marketing International PLC, Seafood Marketing (Bangladesh) Limited, and Seamark (USA) Inc.; Senior Partner, IBCO Enterprises; Senior Partner, IQBAL Brothers & Co; Member, Competitiveness Council, DTI (1999 - present); Member of the Bond Scheme Board, The British Council.

Areas of Influence: Commerce.

Profile: *b.* August 4th, 1956; *m.* Salma; 1 son; 2 daughters.

Educated at Sylhet High School and City of Westminster College, London. Iqbal Ahmed joined the family business, Iqbal Brothers & Co (1976) and gave it new direction and impetus, pioneering the import of frozen fish and shrimps. He then formed Seafood Marketing International Plc (Seamark)(1991) to process shrimps for worldwide markets from a purpose built, state of the art, new frozen food factory in Openshaw, Manchester (1993). A second factory was opened in Manchester (1997), and a third in Cittagong, Bangladesh (2000). Seamark received the Queen's Award for Export Achievement (1998) and won 1st prize in Business in Europe Awards (1999). Iqbal received his OBE for services to International Trade, and has also been awarded Bangladesh - British Chamber of Commerce Businessman of the Year (1999).

Interests: Education, further education, music, history, tennis, badminton, swimming

Contact details: Seafood Marketing INT PLC, Seamark House, Edge Lane, Droylsden, Manchester M43 6BB (tel: 0161 355 5000, fax: 0161 355 5001, email: sales@seamark.co.uk).

AHMED, Kabir, MBE (1998)

Positions: Director, Hilal Restaurants Ltd (1969 - present); Vice President, Bursary Appeal Foundation, Manchester Grammar School (1997 - present); Member, Court of Manchester University; Magistrate, Manchester City Magistrate Court (1985 - present).

Areas of Influence: Commerce.

Profile: *b.* August 31st, 1940.

Education: Sylhet, Bangladesh; General Engineering, Stretford College of Technology; Electrical Engineering, Salford College of Technology; Current Affairs, St John's College, Manchester. Career profile: Council of Community Relations (1980-96); Member of former Race Relations Advisory Group, Manchester City Council; Member of Home Office's Working Party on Crime Prevention (1990-91); Member, Strangeways Prison Board of Visitors (1984-00); Founder Member and Chairman, Greater Manchester Bangladesh Association and Community Centre; Trustee, Guardian Society, Manchester; Director, Progress Trust and Chairman of

the Finance Working Group; Member, City College Corporation Manchester and Audit Committee; Non-executive Director, Christies Hospital (1996-01); Director of Manchester Enterprises; Chairman, Careers Partnership Ltd (2000-02); Chairman, Better Choices Ltd.
Contact details: Windy How, Broadway, Hale, Cheshire WA15 0PG (tel: 0161 904 0818, fax: 0161 904 8191, mob: 07771 747 831, email: windyhow@hotmail.com).

AINSCOW, Carol

Positions: Managing Director of Artisanan, an independent property development company and of a number of subsidiary property-based and leisure venues companies
Areas of Influence: Commerce.
Profile: *b.* 1962 Bolton.
Carol Ainscow has played a key role in the regeneration of the city, tackling challenging buildings in emerging locations and turning them into successful hubs of business and leisure activity. She began by converting derelict property in Bolton into nursing homes, and her first venture into Manchester was Manto cafe bar on Canal Street which opened in 1990. Further projects have included loft apartments on Sackville Street, a mixed use development in Regency House and the conversion of the Art Deco Buildings.
Interests: Passionate believer in urban living, hockey.
Contact details: Artisan, ExpressNetworks, 1 George Leigh Street, Manchester M4 5DL (tel: 0161 236 7385, fax: 0161 909 5312, email: info@artisanh.com).

AINSWORTH, Bernard, OBE (2000), FCIOB, FRSA

Position: Chief Operating Officer, Manchester 2002 Commonwealth Games (2001 - present).
Areas of Influence: Commerce, Construction.
Profile: *b.* October 6th, 1947; *m.* Rosemary; 1 son, Michael (18); 1 daughter, Charlotte (21).
Educated at St Joseph's Grammar School and Liverpool College of Building. Bernard Ainsworth has an unrivalled reputation in the understanding, management and timely delivery of large complex projects. With a career in major contracts spanning 33 years, the last 22 of these as a Team Leader, Bernard's experience has encompassed a wide spectrum of construction styles and types that has allowed him in turn, to develop his own personal approach to motivating and leading teams. It was this approach that served him well in leading the successful Millennium Dome Delivery Team whilst simultaneously playing a lead role in the management of the many complex media/PR issues surrounding this project. Previously, Bernard worked on a variety of Projects with John Laing and Laing Management (1968-95);

Fellow, Chartered Institute of Building; Fellow, Royal Society of Arts.
Interests: Walking, gardening.
Contact details: 16 Talbot Avenue, Edgerton, Huddersfield HD3 3BH (tel: 01484 453 1743, email: bernard@ainsworth16.fsnet.co.uk).

ALCOCK, Graham Paul

Positions: Director, Business Development, Royal Bank of Scotland PLC; Chairman, Pro Manchester; Director, Manchester Business School Incubator Ltd; Member, Lord Mayor's Charity Appeal Committee; Member, Institute of Fiscal Studies North West Committee; Member, Manchester Art Gallery Corporate Patrons Committee.
Areas of Influence: Finance.
Profile: *b.* December 27th, 1948; *m.* Joyce; 2 sons.
Educated at St Ignatius College, London. Career profile: Council of Stock Exchange, London (1966); Sydenden Snowdon Nicholson, Chartered Accountants, London (1967); Glyn Mills & Co, Bankers (1969). Various roles at RBS including: Area Manager, Yorkshire and North East England (1989); Manager, Mosley Street Office (1991); Regional Manager, Branches (1994). Clubs and Societies: St James Club, Manchester; Portico Library, Manchester; Artists Club, Liverpool; Northenden Golf Club.
Interests: Golf, gardening, theatre.
Contact details: Royal Bank of Scotland plc, 100 Barbirolli Square, Manchester M60 3NA (tel: 0161 242 1000, fax: 0161 242 1150, email: graham.alcock@rbs.co.uk); Beechwood, 15 Buckingham Drive, Knutsford, Cheshire WA16 8LH (email: graham@alcock43.freeserve.co.uk).

ALDERTON, Mark William, BA

Position: Editor, News and Current Affairs, Granada Television.
Areas of Influence: Arts, Media.
Profile: *b.* March 31st, 1965; *m.* Sarah.
Educated at: St John's College, Stoke on Trent (1976-81), Newcastle High School (1981-83) and Bristol University (1983-86). Career profile: Radio City Independent Radio Station, Liverpool (1988-90); Granada Television (1991 - present).
Contact details: Granada Television, Quay Street, Manchester M60 9EA (tel: 0161 832 7211).

AL-HAFEEZ, Mahmood

Positions: Civil Servant, Crown Court, Minshull Street (2002 - present); Executive Member, Manchester Council for Community Relations; Secretary, Trafford Ethnic Health Forum.

Areas of Influence: Education, Health, Voluntary Sector.

Profile: *b*. August 19th, 1947; *m*. Zuleikha; 2 sons; 3 daughters.

Education: Matriculation (1964); Safe Driving Diploma, Road Operators' Safety Council (1978); Business Study and Management Skills (1981-82); NVQ Certificate in Information Technology level 1 (1995). Career profile: Capstan Lathe Operator, Machine Operator, Booking Clerk (1964-74); Conductor and Bus Conductor, Greater Manchester Transport (1975-81); self-employed building contractor (1983-91); Volunteer Advisor, CAB and Community Relations (1991-92); Welfare Rights Advisor, Social Services, Manchester (1992-96); Co-ordinator, Old Trafford Rights Centre, Manchester (1996-01). With help from like minded people, Mahmood Al-Faheez has practically created Old Trafford Rights Centre as the first black and ethnic minority voluntary organisation providing advice, advocacy, and representation. The Centre has received recognition and a special M16 Community Award from Trafford Community Representative Group. Mahmood is also a member of the National Association of British Pakistanis and Old Trafford Muslim Society.

Interests: Reading about current affairs, watching documentaries, social events, playing cricket, watching football, tennis.

ALLAN, William Thomas, MA

Positions: Technician, University of Manchester (1970 - present); Member, The Court of the University of Manchester (1998 - present); Member, The Council of the University of Manchester (1999 - present); Secretary, The Committee of Assembly of the University of Manchester (1998 - present); Member, Manchester University Nominations Committee (2001 - present); Branch Secretary, Branch of MSF (1988 - present).

Areas of Influence: Trade Union Activities.

Profile: *b*. February 28th, 1950; div. Oloymatu; 1 son; 2 daughters.

Education: St Cuthbert's School; Wythenshawe College, South Manchester (1969); Postgraduate Diploma and MA in Industrial Relations with Labour Law, Manchester Metropolitan University. Career profile: Apprentice Electrical Fitter, General Electrical Company, Manchester (1965-70); Technician Representative, The Management Committee, The University of Manchester Superannuation Scheme (1986-95); Secretary, Manchester University Joint Campus Trade Unions Committee (1988-92); Branch Delegate, Stretford Constituency Labour Party (1990-94).

Interests: Dining out, swimming, current affairs.

Contact details: The Department of Physics and Astronomy, The University of Manchester, Oxford Road, Manchester M13 9PL (tel: 0161 275 4148); 3 Desford Avenue, Chorlton-cum-Hardy, Manchester M21 0TG (tel: 0161 861 0125).

ALLEN, Charles Lamb, FMCA

Position: Executive Chairman, Granada Plc (2000-02).
Areas of Influence: Media, Arts, Commerce.
Profile: *b.* January 4th, 1957.
Educated at Bell College, Hamilton. Career profile: Accountant, British Steel (1974-79); Deputy Audit Manager, Gallaghers (1979-82); Group Managing Director, Compass Vending (1982-85); Managing Director, Compass Group Limited (1988-91); Chairman, Granada Leisure and Services (1993-00). Honorary Doctorate in Business Admin, Manchester Metropolitan University; Fellow, RSA; Chairman, Creative Industries Advisory Group; Deputy Chairman, Business in the Community; VP, Royal Television Society; Director, International Council; Non Executive Director, Tesco.
Interests: Boating.
Contact details: London TV Centre, Upper Ground, London SE1 9LT (tel: 0209 261 3002, fax: 0207 620 2866, email: callen@granada.co.uk).

ALLEN, Professor John Charles, PhD, BSc, FRSC, CChem, FIFST

Positions: Chairman, Manchester Science Park; Chairman, Manchester Technopark; Visiting Professor, Manchester Business School; Director, Pythia Consulting Ltd; Chairman, NW Innovation Network; Governor, Royal Northern College of Music; Member, UK Enterprise Panel.
Areas of Influence: Commerce, Education, Arts.
Profile: *b.* June 18th, 1938; *m.* Sue; 2 sons.
Educated at City of London School (1949-57) and King's College, London (1957-63). A university teacher of biochemistry for twenty years, John Allen spent the first twelve at St Bartholomew's Hospital Medical College, London before becoming Dean of Research at the North E Wales Institute. John then changed career to become CEO of the Newtech Science Park in North Wales (1983), which assisted the foundation of 300 SME and 1800 new jobs between 1984 and 1993. He then became CEO of Manchester Science Parks and expanded it from 2 buildings to 11 between 1993 and 2000. Retiring as CEO to become Chairman (2000) John now has his own company, Pythia Consulting, which provides advice on technology exploitation, science parks, and innovation in general. He has undertaken consultancy work on science parks and innovation in 25 countries in all parts of the world. John has published over 100 papers, principally in food and cell biochemistry, and several books on both scientific and business topics. He received the Distillers Co. Research Award (1960). Clubs and Societies: Fellow, Royal Society of Chemistry; Fellow, Institute of Food Science and Technology; Companion of the UK Science Park Association; Member, St James Club; Chairman, UK Science Park Association (1990-92, 1995-97), the only person to have held this office twice.

Interests: Music, trying to play the piano and organ, reading, travelling, badminton.
Contact details: Castle View, The Underway, Halton Village, Cheshire WA7 2AJ (tel: 01928 566 247, email: allen@pythia.u-net.com); (email: allen@mspl.co.uk).

ALLEN, John Philip

Positions: Regional Corporate Director, Barclays North West Larger Business Team (2001 - present); North West Regional Councillor, CBI.
Areas of Influence: Finance, Commerce.
Profile: *b.* June 3rd, 1953; *m.* Judith Ann; 2 sons.
Educated at High Arcle Grammar School, Dudley, West Midlands. Since joining Barclays Bank PLC (1971 - present), John Allen has held a number of roles in both the Corporate and Private Banking Divisions: Assistant General Manager, Barclays Private Bank Suisse, Geneva (1991-94); Area Manager Rugby and Davenport (1994-96); Corporate Director, Birmingham and Coventry Region (1996-98); Corporate Director, Manchester Larger Business (1998-01).
Interests: Playing golf and watching sport, football in particular, lifetime supporter of Wolverhampton FC.
Contact details: Barclays Bank PLC, North West Larger Business Team, PO Box 228, 51 Mosley Street, Manchester M60 3DQ (tel: 0161 251 2127, fax: 0161 251 2421, email: john.p.allen@barclayscorporate.com).

ALLWEIS, Martin Peter, BA (Hons) (1969)

Positions: Designated Family Judge, Greater Manchester (1996 - present); Recorder (1990); Circuit Judge (1994); Governor, King David Infant School.
Areas of Influence: Law.
Profile: *b.* December 22nd, 1947; *m.* Tracy Barr; 1 son, Steven; 1 daughter, Sophie.
Education: King David Infant and Junior School; Manchester Grammar School; Sidney Sussex College, Cambridge; Barrister practising in Manchester (1970 - 1994); Appointed Circuit Judge (1994); Designated Family Judge for Greater Manchester (1996 - present). Martin Allweis is a regular contributor to conferences on family law, with specialist interest in contact and domestic violence, adoption, neglect and abuse of children.
Interests: Football (Manchester City FC), squash, family.
Contact details: C/O Manchester County Court, Crown Square, Manchester M60 9DJ (tel: 0161 954 1800).

ALMOND, George Haylock, MBE (1993), CBE (2000), SBStJ (2000), DL(1999), FIFireE, FCIPD,

Positions: Commander, St John Ambulance, Greater Manchester (2002 - present); President, The Rotary Club of Manchester.
Areas of Influence: Voluntary Sector, Public Sector, Health.
Profile: *b.* January 19th, 1944; *m.* Elizabeth Ann; 1 son, Mark; 1 daughter, Ruth.
Educated at Portsmouth Technical High School and Eastleigh Technical College, Southampton. Career profile: Fireman and Junior Officer, Hampshire Fire Service (1962-70); Station Officer to Divisional Officer, Cheshire Fire Service (1970-82); Assistant County Fire Officer to County Fire Officer and Chief Executive, Greater Manchester County Fire Service (1982-00). George Almond has published several books on fire engineering and has delivered numerous papers on fire related subjects at conferences around the world. He was made a Freeman of the City of London (1999), awarded an Honorary Fellowship by Bolton Institute (2000), and appointed Chairman of the Fire Services National Benevolent Fund (2000).
Interests: Rotary, music, walking, reading.
Contact details: 4 Stonehouse, Chapeltown Road, Bromley Cross, Bolton, Lancs. BL7 9NB (tel: 01204 309 630, email: georgeh@almond44661.freeserve.co.uk).

ANDERSON, Farida Sharon, MBE (2000)

Positions: Director and original founder, Partners of Prisoners (POPS) Families Support Group; Chief Executive; Board Member of National Probation Service, Common Purpose Programme; National Black Caucus (1997 - present); Greater Manchester Immigration Aid Unit (1991 - present); Campaign Against Double Punishment (1991 - present); Anti Deportation Campaigns and Moss Side Initiatives (1991 - present); Representative on various national Committees including the HMP Headquarters Race Advisory Group, Chair of National Body of Black Prisoner Support Group, and member of the Common Purpose Group.
Areas of Influence: Voluntary Sector.
Profile: *b.* December 23rd, 1962; *m.* Basil; 2 sons; 1 daughter.
Educated at Lauriston high School (1973-97), Ducie High School (1990-91), and Manchester University (1991-92). Voluntary work experience: Somali Association (1980-89); Samaritans (1988-89); ESOL Teacher, Ducie High School (1989-91). POPS provides a service to prisoners' families and Black prisoners. These services cover a wide area, primarily urban-based inner city areas of Greater Manchester where there is high unemployment and other difficult socio-economic factors. They are unique to the North of England, and Farida Anderson has been a forerunner in influencing national policy to positively affect the experience of the Criminal Justice System for both prisoners and their families. Farida has led the growth of POPS from a self-help initiative to a nationally recognised organisation.

Interests: Proprietor of Caribbean Restaurant, member of health club, public speaker. **Contact details:** POPS Ltd, Suite 4b, Wilsons Park, Monsall Road, Manchester M40 8WN (tel: 0161 277 9066, fax: 0161 277 9066, email farida@ partnersofprisoners.co.uk); 148 St Anns Road, Prestwich, Manchester M25 9GJ.

ANDERTON, Sir James (Cyril), Kt (1991), QPM (1977), OStJ (1978), CBE (1982), KStJ (1989), DL (1989), KLMJ (1998), KHS (1999), Cross Pro Ecclesia et Pontifice (1982), Hon. RNCM (1984), Hon. FBCA (1976).

Positions: Although retired, Sir James Anderton is very active within the Voluntary Sector acting in prominent roles for numerous well known local charities and organisations.
Profile: *b.* May 24th, 1932; *m.* Joan Baron; 1 daughter.
Areas of Influence: Voluntary Sector, Youth Work, Community Relations.
Education: St Matthews Church School, Wigan; Wigan Grammar School; Manchester University, Certificate in Criminology 91960); Police Staff College (1962, 1967). Career profile: Corps of Royal Military Police (1950-53); Constable to Chief Inspector, Manchester City Police (1953-67); Chief Superintendent, Cheshire Constabulary (1967-68); Assistant Chief Constable, Leicester & Rutland (1968-72); Assistant to HM Chief Inspector of Constabulary, Home Office, London (1972-75); Deputy Chief Constable, Leicestershire (1975); Greater Manchester (1975-76); Chief Constable, Greater Manchester Police (1976-91) President, Association of Chief Police Officers (1986-87); Interpol Conference, Paris (1973); Foreign & Commonwealth Office Lecture Tour of Far East & SE Asia (1973); UK Delegate, UN Congress on Prevention of Crime, Budapest (1974); President, Christian Police Association (1979-81); County Director, St John Ambulance in Greater Manchester (1976-89);, Commander (1989-96); President, Manchester Branch BIM (1984-93); Chairman, NW Regional Board BIM (1986-90); Trustee, Manchester Olympic Bid Committee (1985-93). Sir James has given many lectures and published various articles in professional journals and newspapers.
Interests: Music, theatre, books, gardening, DIY, the countryside, rugby league football.
Contact details: 9 The Avenue, Sale, Cheshire M33 4PB (tel: 0161 969 8140).

ANDREWS, Anthony John David, MA, Bed

Position: Principal, Xaverian College, Manchester (1996 - present).
Areas of Influence: Education, Faith Groups.
Profile: *b.* September 1946; *m.* Barbara; 1 son; 2 daughters.
Educated at Stoneyhurst College, Manchester University and Reading University. Career profile: Assistant teacher, West Park Grammar School (1969-72); Part time Lecturer, Further Education (1970-72); Head of Department, Oaklands Road High

School, Waterlooville (1972-81); Deputy Headmaster, St Nicholas RC High School, Northwich (1981-95). Clubs and societies: President, Catenian Association (1993-94); Member, High Legh Golf Club; Member, Manchester Chamber of Commerce. **Interests:** Golf, photography, travel.
Contact details: Xaverian College, Lower Park Road, Manchester M14 5RB (tel: 0161 224 1781, fax: 0161 248 9039, email: a.andrews@xavarian.ac.uk); Merrywood, 2 Pevensey Drive, Knutsford, Cheshire WA16 9BX (tel: 01565 632 823, email: ajandrews@tircali.co.uk).

ANGLESEY, Natalie Ann, ALAM

Positions: Managing Director, Natalie Anglesey Associates; National Union of Journalists; Manchester Evening News Drama Panel.
Areas of Influence: Arts, Media, Education.
Profile: 2 sons.
Education: Caledonian School, Perth, Scotland; Perth Academy; Allerton High School for Girls, Leeds; City of Leeds College; Manchester University; Manchester School of Music; London Academy of Music and Dramatic Art. Career profile: Teacher of English and Drama; Newsreader, Turkish Radio Television; Presenter, World Service; Presenter, British Forces Network; Founding Member, Royal Exchange Theatre; Public Relations Officer, Royal Exchange Theatre; Artistic Director of International Theatre Festival, Royal Exchange Theatre; Presenter and Producer, BBC1 Television, BBC2 Television, BBC GMR Radio, BBC Radio 2, BBC Radio 4.
Interests: Theatre, dance, arts, travel.

ANGUS, Thomas

Position: Head of Corporate Banking, North of England, Bank of Scotland.
Areas of Influence: Finance, Commerce.
Profiles: *b.* November 19th, 1960; *m.* Julie; 3 daughters.
Educated at Falkirk High School and University of Glasgow (1978-81). Career profile: Qualified as a Chartered Accountant, TMcL (1981-85); Bank of Scotland (1985); Manager/Senior Manager, Head Office (1988-94); Seconded to IKB Deutsche Industrie Bank (1994-95); Regional Manager, Newcastle Upon Tyne (1995-97); Regional Director, Acquisition Finance, English Regions (1997-99). Clubs and societies: Scarcroft Golf Club; Lord Taverners Regional Committee.
Interests: Playing golf, watching football, travel, food, drink, genealogy, Scottish history, astronomy.
Contact details: Bank of Scotland, 19/21 Spring Gardens, Manchester M2 1FB (tel: 0161 251 6356, fax: 0161 251 6374, email: tom_angus@bankofscotland.co.uk, thomasagangus@aol.com).

APPLEBY, Professor Louis, BSc (Hons), MB, ChB, FRCP, MD FRCPsych.

Positions: National Director for Mental Health, Dept. of Health, England (2000 - present); Professor of Psychiatry, University of Manchester (1996 - present); Director, National Confidential Inquiry into Suicide and Homicide by people with mental illness (1996 - present).
Areas of Influence: Health.
Profile: *b.* February 27th, 1955; *m.* Juliet (nee Haselden); 2 sons; 2 daughters.
Educated at Bathgate Academy, West Lothian (1967-73) and University of Edinburgh (1973-80). Senior Lecturer in Psychiatry, University of Manchester (1991-96). Publications include A *Medical Tour through the whole island of Great Britain*, 2nd ed. Faber and Faber (1995), and numerous research papers on suicide and postnatal mental disorders.
Interests: Family, clarinet, Manchester United.
Contact details: Centre for Suicide Prevention, Williamson Building, University of Manchester M13 9PL (tel;0161 275 0714, fax: 0161 275 0716, email: louis.appleby @man.ac.uk); Richmond House, Whitehall, London SW1A 2NS.

APPLEGATE, The Venerable Dr John, BSc (Hons), DipHE, PhD

Positions: Archdeacon of Bolton; Honorary Research Fellow, Dept. of Religions and Theology, University of Manchester.
Areas of Influence: Faith Groups, Voluntary Sector, Education.
Profile: b. 1956; Publications: *The Heavenly City: The Quality of Life of Clergy Families in UPAs; The Fate of Zedekiah; Peace, Peace when there is no Peace; Jeremiah and the Seventy Years; Narrative Patterns for the Communication of Commissioned Speech in the Prophets.*
Contact details: Church House, 90 Deansgate, Manchester M3 2GU (tel: 0161 761 6117).

ARDITTI, Samuel Jack Victor, MA, DL (1987), MBE (1984),

Positions: Trustee / Director, Environmental Campaigns; Director, ERCU; Trustee, Executive Council, Broughton House for Ex-Service Personnel; Member, Greater Manchester Police Advisory Committee on Racial Issues; Trustee, Greater Manchester Police Community Charity; Trustee, Greater Manchester Shrievalty Police Trust; Member of court, University of Manchester.
Areas of Influence: Voluntary Sector.
Profile: *b.* December 13th, 1927; *m.* Carol; 1 son; 2 daughters.
Education: Rydal School, Colwyn Bay; MA (Hons) Natural Sciences, Jesus College, Cambridge. Samuel Arditti always worked in the family business of Victor S Arditti & Son which was founded in Manchester in 1885. In 1988 he sold his business to William Baird plc, for whom he continues to work until the end of 1991 when he

retired from full-time employment and became a Non-executive Director until 1995. National Service: Lieutenant 7th Royal Tank Regiment (1947-48). Previous Public Offices: High Sheriff of greater Manchester (1992-93); Chairman, Trafford Healthcare NHS Trust (1994-97); General Commissioner for Income Tax (1991-98); Secretary of Manchester Consular Association (1979-91), President (1990); Honorary Consul for Mexico (1984-00); Honorary Consul for Spain (1973-84); Cheshire Special Constabulary (1956-91), Chief Commandant (1996); Chairman, China Technology Link (1991-94); Chairman, Greater Manchester Regional Appeal, The Prince's Trust (1993-94); Director of Manchester Chamber of Commerce and Industry (1987-94). Clubs and societies: Rotary Club of Manchester; Manchester Literary and Philosophical Society; Commanderie Bordeaux de Manchester; International Police Association. Prizes and awards: Special Long Service Medal and two bars (1975,1985); Officer of the Order of Civil Merit (1981); Knight of the Order of Isabel la Catolica.

ARKLE, Richard

Positions: Partner, KPMG LLP and Head of Transaction Services, Northern Business Unit.
Areas of Influence: Finance, Commerce.
Profile: *b*. April 12th, 1949; *m*. Julie; 3 daughters.
Educated at Clifton College, Bristol and Britannia Royal Naval College. Career profile: Qualified as a Chartered Accountant, Peat Marwick Mitchell and Co (1974); Partner, Peat Marwick Mitchell and Co (1982). Member of Trearddur Bay Sailing Club.
Interests: Tennis, skiing, sailing.
Contact details: KPMG LLP, St James Square, Manchester M2 6AS (tel: 0161 838 4000, fax: richard.arkle@kpmg.co.uk).

ARNOLD, Professor John Andre, FCA, MSc (London), MA (Manchester), CCMI

Positions: Director and Dean, Manchester Business School and KPMG Professor of Accounting and Financial Management (1994 - present).
Areas of Influence: Education, Finance.
Profile: *b*. April, 30th, 1944; *m*. Sylvia; 2 daughters.
Educated at Haberdashers' Aske's (1955-62) and London School of Economics (1967-69). Career profile: Articled Clerk then Chartered Accountant, DF Webster & Co, London (1962-67); Teaching Fellow, London School of Economics (1967-69); Lecturer in Accounting, University of Kent (1969-71); Lecturer, Senior Lecturer, KPMG Professor of Accounting, University of Manchester (1971-94); Visiting Professor, Graduate School of Business, University of Washington, USA (1981-82); Pro-Vice-Chancellor, University of Manchester (1990-94); President, Manchester Society of

Chartered Accountants (1991-92); Author of 20 books and monographs, and numerous articles in learned journals.

Interests: Squash, tennis, opera, watching Stockport County FC.

Contact details: Director's office, Manchester Business School, Booth Street West, Manchester M15 6PB (tel: 0161 275 7149, fax: 0161 275 6585, email: John.Arnold@mbs.ac.uk).

ARORA, Ashi

Positions: Legal Executive, Davis Blank Furniss, Manchester.

Areas of Influence: Law, Personal Development, Commerce.

Profile: *b.* March 31st, 1968.

Education: After A levels in Birmingham, Ashi Arora attended College in Rugby to undertake a Diploma in Legal Administration before returning to Birmingham in 1988 to commence the Institute of Legal Executives examinations, qualifying in 1995. Career profile: Trainee Legal Executive, Mander and Sharma, Walsall (1988); Trainee Legal Executive, Berry and Berry, Cocker, Smith and Co, Manchester (1990); Trainee Legal Executive, Fox Brooks Marshall, Manchester (1992), Legal Executive, Manchester City Council (1996); President of Manchester Junior Chamber of Commerce; Treasurer of the Institute of Legal Executives, Manchester, being the first Asian female President of Manchester Junior Chamber of Commerce in its 54 year history; Asian Achievers Award (2002).

Interests: Travelling, reading, community projects.

Contact details: Davis Blank Furniss, 90 Deansgate, Manchester M3 2QJ (tel: 0161 832 3304, fax: 0161 834 3568, email: ashi.arora@ dbf-law.co.uk).

ASANTE-MENSAH, Evelyn Justina

Position: Chief Executive, Black Health Agency

Areas of Influence: Health, Voluntary Sector, Public Sector

Profile: *b.* October 11th, 1965; *m.* Yoni; 1 son, Leon; 2 daughters, Sade and Esi.

Education: Nicholls Ardwick High School, Ardwick Green, Manchester (1976-1981); Sheena Simon Sixth Form College (1981-82); St. Johns College, Manchester (1988-89); South Manchester College, Fielden Park Centre (1989-90); Manchester Metropolitan University (1995-97); University College, Salford (1996). Career profile: Greater Manchester Councils for Voluntary Organisations (1998); HAZ Fellowship (2000); Clerical Assistant, Credit Control Company (1984); Buyer' s Clerk, Lewis's Department Store; School Administrator, Loreto Sixth Form College (1987-90); Clerical Receptionist, Homeless Families Unit, Manchester City Council; Rehousing Clerk, Manchester City Council; Young Person's Support Worker, Single Homeless Team (1991-93); Outreach Worker for Young Black people, Shades City Centre Project; Co-ordinator, Black HIV/AIDS Forum; External assessor, National Lotteries

Charities Board; Board, Manchester Health Authority; Chair, Central Manchester Primary Care Trust; Member of: Association of Chief Executives of Voluntary Organisation; Whalley Range Methodist Church, Manchester. Publications: *Study into the Experiences of African Women, Their Lived Experiences of Education and Employment*, Dissertation Thesis (1997); *Commissioning and the Third Sector*, HAZ Fellowship (2000). **Interests:** Gardening, reading, going to the gym, Methodist Church.
Contact details: Black Health Agency, 339 Stretford Road, Hulme, Manchester M15 4ZY (tel: 0161 226 9145, fax: 0161 226 9380, email: evelyn@blackhealthagency.org.uk).

ASHBROOK, Viscount Michael Llowarch Warburton Flower, BA (1959)

Positions: Landowner; Historic House Owner; Vice Lord Lieutenant for Cheshire (1990 - present);
Areas of Influence: Heritage, Rural Land, Voluntary Sector.
Profile: *b.* December 9th, 1935; *m.* Zoe Mary; 2 sons; 1 daughter.
Educated at Eton College (1949-54) and Worcester College, Oxford (1956-59). Career profile: 2nd Lieutenant, Grenedier Guards (1955-56); Solicitor, Padier Farrer & Co, London (1966-76); Solicitor, Pannone & Partners (1985-94); Magistrate, Vale Royal (1983-2000).
Interests: Gardening, countryside, shooting.
Contact details: Arley Estate Office, Northwich, Cheshire, CW9 6NA (tel: 01565 777 353, fax: 01565 777 465, email: enquiries@arleyestate. zuumet.co.uk); The Old Parsonage, Arley Green, Northwich, Cheshire CW9 6LZ (tel: 01565 777 277).

ASHTON, Dr John Richard, CBE (2000), MBBS (1970), MSc (1978)

Positions: North West Regional Director of Public Health and Regional Medical Officer.
Areas of Influence: Health, Media, Politics.
Profile: *b.* May 27th, 1947, Liverpool; *m.* Pamela Scott (1968, *div.* 2001); Catherine Benedicte Morris (partner); 3 sons, Keir, Matthew and Nick.
Education: Mosspits CP, Liverpool; Quarry Bank High School, Liverpool; University of Newcastle upon Tyne Medical School; London School of Hygiene and Tropical Medicine. Career profile: Medical Doctor, Newcastle; Psychiatrist Specialist Training, Newcastle; Family Doctor, Newcastle and Southampton; Public Health, London School of Hygiene and Tropical Medicine, Liverpool University; North West of England, World Health Organisation. Publications on planned parenthood, family planning, abortion, urban health, futures, suicide, epidemiology. Prizes and awards: Charlton Prize Medicine (1975); Social Medicine Medallist (LSHTM) (1978); Alwyn Smith Medal, Public Health (2002). Member of the Duncan Society.

Interests: Liverpool FC, walking, cycling, spaniels, poultry, politics.
Contact details: 15 Church road, Much Woolton, Liverpool L25 5JE; 24 Avon Road, Hale, Cheshire WA1 50CB.

ASHTON, Michael, BSc (Hons), Med

Position: Chief Executive, Wigan Borough Chamber of Commerce.
Areas of Influence: Commerce, Education, Public Sector.
Profile: *b.* October, 1955; *m.* Diane; 1 son; 1 daughter.
Educated at Ellesmere Port Grammar School, Liverpool Polytechnic, Leeds University, and Liverpool University. Career profile: Director, St Helen's Education Business Partnership (1990-94); Head of Enterprise Development, Liverpool John Moores University (1994-01). Member of Northop Golf Club and Hooton Tennis Club.
Interests: Golf, tennis, badminton, family.
Contact details: Wigan Investment Centre, Waterside Drive, Wigan WN3 5BA (tel: 01942 705 308, fax: 01942 705 453, email: mashton@wbp.org.uk, web: www.wbp.org.uk).

ATHERTON, Revd Canon Dr John R, BA (Hons), Mphil, PhD

Positions: Canon Theologian, Manchester Cathedral; Honorary Lecturer, Department of Religion and Theology, University of Manchester.
Areas of Influence: Faith Groups, Education, Voluntary Sector.
Profile: *b.* April 3rd, 1939; *m.* Vannie; 1 son; 1 daughter.
Education: Chalfont St County Primary School; Bolton County Grammar School; University College, London; College of the Resurrection, Mayfield; University of Manchester. Career profile: Curate in Inneraty, Aberdeen, Glasgow (Gorbals), Bury and Manchester. Director, William Temple Foundation; Industrial Chaplain; Cathedral Canon; Vice Chair, Manchester Diocesan Board for Ministry in Society. Publications: *The Scandal of Poverty; Faith in the Nation; Christianity and the Market; Social Christianity: a reader; Public Theology for Trying Times.* Clubs and societies: Theological Society; Lancashire and Cheshire Antiques Society.
Interests: Hillwalking.
Contact details: The Cathedral, Manchester M3 1SX; 3 Booth-Clibborn Court, Salford M7 4EJ.

ATHERTON, Robert Kenneth

Position: Circuit Judge.
Areas of Influence: Law.
Profile: *b.* June 22nd, 1947.
Educated at Boteler Grammar School, Warrington and Liverpool University.
Interests: Gardening, music, travel.
Contact details: Courts of Justice, Crown Square, Manchester M60 9DJ (tel: 0161 954 1800).

AUSTIN, Jason Richard Alexander

Position: Partner and Head of Information Technology, Eversheds.
Areas of Influence: Law.
Profile: *b.* March 26th, 1968; *m.* Andrea.
Education: Northgate High School, Ipswich; BA Hons, Christ Church, Oxford. Career profile: Qualified Solicitor (1993); Head of Technology Department, Anderson Legal, Garretts, Manchester. Clubs and societies: Northern Lawn Tennis Club.
Contact details: Eversheds, Eversheds House, 70 Great Bridgewater Street, Manchester, M1 5ES (tel: 0161 831 8000).

AVARI, Burjor, MBE (1987), BA (Hons), MA, Dip.Ed

Positions: Co-ordinator for Continuing Education in Multicultural Studies at the Manchester Metropolitan University (1988 - present); Member of Greater Manchester Police Advisory Committee on Race and Community Affairs; Chairperson, North West Zoroastrian Community.
Areas of Influence: Education, Faith groups, Public Sector.
Profile: *b.* November 9th, 1938; *m.* Zarin; 2 daughters.
Education: East Africa (1943-54); Portsmouth College of Technology (1955-57); Manchester University (1957-61); Oxford University Institute of Education (1961-62); Manchester University (1967-70). Career profile: Teacher of History in Secondary Schools, Kenya and Britain (1962-74); Head of History, Central High School, Manchester (1974-82); Head of Faculty of Humanities, Brookway High School, Manchester (1982-84); Team Leader, Multicultural Support Service, Borough of Tameside Education Department (1984-87). Burjor Avari has authored a book with Yung-Yung Wah and Simon Buckley, about the Chinese in Britain. He has also written articles on Indian and South Asian History in *Asian Voice* and on Multicultural Education, and is a life member of the Indian Association, Manchester. Burjor organises and promotes a variety of lecture programmes in the field of Multicultural Studies, which aim to help people to appreciate difference, to understand the past and the present and to learn to respect all people.

Interests: Light walking, cooking, visiting museums, watching British 'soaps'.
Contact details: Academic Division, Manchester Metropolitan University, All Saints, Manchester M15 6BH (tel: 0161 247 1023, fax: 0161 247 6311, email: b.avari@mmu.ac.uk).

AXFORD, Colonel Arthur, DL (1977), MBE (1958), OBE (1964), TD (1964)

Profile: *b.* August 10th, 1921, Ashton-under-Lyne; *m.* Flora Isabel Hampson, 1941; 2 sons, 1 daughter.
Areas of Influence: Public Sector.
Educated at Ashton-under-Lyne Grammar School. Career profile: The Manchester Regiment (1939-96); Royal Ulster Rifles, Korean War (1950-52); 9th Bn., The Manchester Regiment (1952-64), Commanding Officer (1960-64); Deputy Commander, 127 Brigade, TA (1964-70); ADC to HM The Queen (1965-70); Commander, East Lancs. ACF (1970-74); Hon. Colonel, East Lancs. ACF (1980-85); High Sheriff of Greater Manchester (1987-88); Honorary Fellow, Institute of Quality Assurance. Societies: Buxton and High Peak Golf Club, Captain (1970), President (2000-02); English Golf Union.
Contact details: 18 Temple Court, Temple Road, Buxton SK17 9BA (tel: 01298 73468).

BAILEY, Richard Charles, ACA

Positions: Executive Chairman, N M Rothschild & Sons, UK Regions; Non-executive Directorship, Hallé Orchestra; Cheshire Building Society; Governor, Chethams School.
Profile: *b.* December 26th, 1951; *m.* Hilary; 2 sons; 2 daughters.
Education: King's School Pontefract; BA (Hons) English and American Literature Manchester University (1974). Career profile: Commercial Manager, Marks and Spencer (1974-76); Chartered Accountant, PWC (1976-81); Investment Banker, NM Rothschild (1999); Partner, NM Rothschild.
Interests: Drama, music, tennis, golf, skiing.
Contact details: NM Rothschild & Sons Limited, 82 King Street, Manchester M2 4WQ (tel: 0161 827 3800, fax: 0161 832 2554, email: Richard.bailey@rothschild.co.uk).

BAKER, Stephen Roy, FCA, BSC

Positions: Senior Partner, Grant Thornton Corporate Finance North (2000 - present); Governor, Terra Nova School; Member, London Stock Exchange Regional Advisory Group.
Areas of Influence: Finance, Education.
Profile: *b.* August 16th, 1955; *m.* Marite; 1 son; 1 daughter.
Educated at Erith Grammar School, Kent and Manchester University. Career profile: Grant Thornton UK (1976-83); Grant Thornton US (1983-85); Grant Thornton UK (1985 - present), Appointed Partner (1987), UK Head of Corporate Finance (1993-99). Member, Hale Golf Club.

Interests: Golf, family, wine, art.
Contact details: Grant Thornton, Heron House, Albert Square, Manchester M60 8GT (tel: 0161 834 5414, fax: 0161 953 0212, email: stephen.baker@gtuk.com).

BALDWIN, Jonathan Francis (Jon), BA, MBA, FCIS, MIMGT, FRSA

Positions: Secretary and Registrar, UMIST (2000 - present); Governor, Hopwood Hall College; Council Member, ICSA; Institutional Reviewer, Quality Assurance Agency for Higher Education.
Areas of Influence: Education, Public Sector, Commerce.
Profile: *b.* November 9th, 1959; *m.* Tracy Patricia; 3 daughters.
Education: ONC Public Administration (1979); HNC, Business Studies (1981); ICSA Qualified, Wigan (1985); BA (Hons), business Studies, Lancashire Polytechnic; MBA, Open University (1992). Career profile: Admin roles, Lancashire County Council Education Department (1976-83); Admin role, Humanities / Combined Studies, Lancashire Polytechnic (1983-84); Combined Studies Programme Administrator, Lancashire Polytechnic (1984-89); Academic registrar / Deputy Secretary, Queen Margaret College, Edinburgh (1989-92); Director, Modular & Access Programmes, Queen Margaret College, Edinburgh (1992-95); Registrar, University of Wolverhampton (1995-00). Jonathan Baldwin has also taught at the Open University and in Further Education and has travelled extensively including a period of secondment in North America. He is a Fellow of the Institute of Chartered Secretaries and Administrators, a member of the Institute of Management, a Fellow of the Royal Society of Arts, Manufacture, and Commerce, and holds Company Directorships via UMIST. Jonathan has published over 35 papers and over 20 publications.
Interests: Manchester United, family, all sports, reading.
Contact details: PO Box 88, Sackville Street, Manchester M60 1QD (tel: 0161 200 3990, fax: 0161 200 4008, email: jon.f.baldwin@umist.ac.uk).

BALL, Michael, D.Mus (Lond.), ARCM

Position: Composer.
Areas of Influence: Arts.
Profile: *b.* November 10th, 1946 (Manchester, England).
Educated at the Royal College of Music, London. Michael Ball studied principally with Herbert Howells, also with Humphrey Searle and John Lambert and later in Italy with Franco Donatoni. Compositions include orchestral, wind & brass band, chamber, choral and educational works. Clubs and societies: British Academy of Composers & Songwriters; Incorporated Society of Musicians; Society for Promotion of New Music.
Contact details: c/o Novello & Company Limited, 8/9 Frith Street, London W1D 3JB.

BALLARD, The Venerable Andrew Edgar

Position: The Archdeacon of Rochdale.
Areas of Influence: Faith Groups.
Profile: *b.* January 14th, 1944; *m.* Marian Caroline; 1 Son; 2 Daughters.
Educated at Rossall School, University of Durham, and Westcott House Cambridge.
Career profile: Ordained Deacon (1968); Ordained Priest (1969); Assistant Curate, St
Mary Bryanston Square and Assistant chaplain, Middlesex Hospital, London (1968-
72); Senior Assistant Curate, St Mary Portsea (1972-76); Vicar, St James Haslingden
with St Stephen Haslingden Grane (1976-82); Vicar, St Paul Walkden Moor with St
John The Baptist, Little Hulton(1993-98); Area Dean, Farnworth (1990-98); Priest in
Charge, St Chad, Rochdale (1998-00); Team Rector, Rochdale Team Ministry (2000);
Honorary Canon, Manchester Cathedral (1998-00); Archdeacon of Rochdale (2000).
Awarded the Pilkington Prize, Diocese of London (1968).
Interests: Church music, church architecture, playing the organ.
Contact details: 57 Melling Road, Oldham OL4 1PN (tel: 0161 678 1454, fax: 0161 678
1455 email: andrew.ballard@virgin.net).

BANISTER, Christopher Edward, BSc (1971), MSc (1973), MCIT, MRTPI

Positions: Senior Lecturer in School Planning and Landscape, Dean for
Undergraduate Studies, Faculty of Arts, University of Manchester; Member,
University Senate (1983 - present); Member, University Court (1984); Member,
University Council (1986-87, 1991-96, 2000 - present).
Areas of Influence: Education, Transport.
Profile: *b.* July 9th, 1950; *m.* Cecily Maria; 2 daughters.
Education: Godalming County Grammar School, Surrey; BSc (Hons) class 2i
Warwick University (1968-71); Leeds University (1971-75). Christopher Banister has
worked as an academic member of staff at the University of Manchester since 1975.
He has held various posts including Head of Department and current position as
Dean for Undergraduate Studies in Faculty in the Arts. He has had an active
involvement with the Association of University Teachers including being the
National President of the Association (1998-99). Christopher was also involved with
Community Transport (1981-91), chairing Manchester Community Transport's
Management Committee for a period. During this time, he was involved with the
establishment Manchester Ring and Ride through Chairing its Steering Committee.
Some recent publications: with Gallent, N (1998) *Trends in Commuting in England and
Wales: becoming less sustainable,* Area Vol. 30 No. 3 (p. 331-341); with Gallent, N (1999)
Sustainable Commuting: A Contradiction in Terms? Regional Studies Vol. 33 No. 3 (274-
280); with Richardson, T and Turner, J (2000) *Untangling the web: delivering the new
transport realism in a complex policy Environment,* Landor London.
Interests: My family, hill walking, transport, gardening, computers.

Contact details: University of Manchester, Manchester, M13 9PL (tel: 0161 275 6883, fax: 0161 275 6893, email: c.banister@man.ac.uk).

BARKWORTH, Glen Leigh

Position: General Manager, Manchester Arndale Centre (2000 - present).
Areas of Influence: Property Management, Media, Commerce
Profile: *b.* November 14th, 1947; *m.* Linda; 3 daughters.
Educated at City Grammar School, Lincoln. Career profile: Member of Rotary Club and Manchester Chamber of Commerce; Chair, British Council for Shopping Centres (Northern Region); Board Member, Manchester City Centre Management Company; Chair, Manchester City Centre Large Stores Group; Currently overseeing the £12m refurbishment of the southern part of the Manchester Arndale Centre.
Interests: Golf, sport in general, church, cinema, gardening, family.
Contact details: Manchester Arndale Centre, 1st Floor, Arndale House, Manchester M4 3AQ (tel: 0161 833 9851, fax: 0161 833 6768, email: glen.barkworth@propim.com); 1 Marford House, Kingsmead, Cheshire CW9 8WW (tel/fax: 01606 40739, email: g.barkworth@aol.com).

BARNETT, Joel, PC, JP, FCCA

Positions: Member, House of Lords (1983 - present); Trustee, Open University (1998 - present).
Areas of Influence: Finance, Media, Arts.
Profile: *b.* October 14th, 1923; *m.* Lilian; 1 daughter.
Educated at Manchester Jewish Primary, Manchester Central High and British College of Accountancy. Career profile: Member, Prestwich Borough Council (1956-59); Elected MP, Heywood and Royton (1964-83); Elevated House of Lords (1983); Chief Secretary to the Treasury (1974-79); Member of the Cabinet (1977-79); Front Bench, House of Lords (Fin./Econ) (1983-86); Vice Chairman, BBC (1986-93); Trustee, Victoria & Albert Museum (1986-99). Publication: Inside the Treasury (1982). Clubs and societies: Fabien Society; Hansard Society.
Interests: Walking in Derbyshire Peak District, watching Manchester United.
Contact details: House of Lords, London, SW1 (tel: 0207 219 5440, fax: 0207 219 5979, email: barnettj@parliament.uk); 7 Hillingden Road, Whitefield, Manchester M45 7QQ (tel: 0161 766 3634).

BARRETT, Professor Peter Stephen, MSc PhD FRICS

Positions: Pro Vice Chancellor for research and graduate studies.
Areas of Influence: Education, Commerce.
Profile: *b.* November 16th, 1957; *m.* Lucinda; 1 son; 3 daughters.

Education: Wood Green Comprehensive School, Witney, Oxon (1969-76); MSc Construction Management, Brunel University (1984-83); PhD, South Bank Polytechnic (1986-89). Career profile: Trainee and qualified Building Surveyor, King and Chasemore, Chartered Surveyors, Oxford (1976-82); Practising Building Surveyor, Buckell and Ballard, Chartered Surveyors, Oxford (1982-84); Building Surveyor, Hunter and Partners, London (1984-85); Lecturer, South Bank Polytechnic, London (1985-88); Lecturer, Senior Lecturer, Professor of Management in property and construction, Chairman of Dept. of Surveying, Director of Research Centre for the Built Environment, Dean of Business and Informatics, University of Salford (1988 - present); has written or edited four books and around 100 Academic papers; Clubs and Societies: Conseil International du Batiment; Coordinator of Working Group 65, a group concerned with the organisation and management of construction.
Interests: Badminton, walking, dancing.

BASHIR, Mazamil

Position: Special Appeals Manager, National Post.
Areas of Influence: Commerce, Media, Voluntary Sector.
Profile: Managed Imran Khan Cancer Appeal; European Arm. Prizes and awards: Achievements Award from the House of Lords. Clubs and societies: Member, Commonwealth Business Club; Committee member, Asian-e-Foundation.
Interests: Music, reading, swimming, keen on encouraging and motivating the younger generation.
Contact details: (tel: 07900 607 850).

BASHIR, Mumtaz, JP, BSC (Hons)

Positions: Volunteer Programme Manager, Manchester 2002 Commonwealth Games Management Team (1999 – present).
Profile: Educated at Manchester Metropolitan University. Career profile: General Manager (1997-99), Branch Manager (1995-97) Manchester Business Link; Branch Manager, East Manchester Business Link (1994); Business Information Officer , Manchester TEC (1993); Business Advisor, Manchester Chamber of Commerce (1993); Self-employed, Overseas Trading Company, Manchester (1985-93). Clubs and societies: Court Member, The University of Manchester; Diversity Sub Group to the Cabinet Office; Manchester Council for Community Relations; Forward Northwest; Founder & Organiser, Manchester Annual Asian Business Dinner.
Interests: Swimming, dress designing, needlepoint.

BATTERS, Royce

Positions: Non-Executive Director, Trafford Healthcare NHS Trust; Pro- Chancellor, Member of Court and Council, and Chairman of the Finance Comm. University of Salford.
Areas of Influence: Health, Education, Voluntary Sector.
Profile: *b.* June 12th, 1938; *m.* Susan; 1 son; 1 stepson; 1 daughter.
Educated at Stockport School (1949-54). Career profile: Taxation Accountant, Turner and Newell plc (1963-67); Partner, Appleby & Wood, Appleby English & Partners (1967-75); Partner, Ernst & Young 1975-93; Director of Finance, Christie Hospital NHS Trust (1994-00); Freeman of City Of London; Member of Heaton Moor Golf Club (Captain 1996) and Old Stopfordians Association (president 1989-90); Hon. Secretary, East Lancashire Masonic Benevolent Association
Interests: Golf, freemasons, church.
Contact details: Longbourne, 19 Tanyard Drive, Hale Barns, Cheshire (tel: 0161 980 2969, fax: 0161 980 0765, email: roycebatters@uk2.net).

BATTON, Carol Joyce

Position: Poet
Areas of Influence: Poetry, Performance Poetry.
Positions: *b.* March 1st, 1951.
Carol Batton has held a variety of posts in shops, assembly, the catering department at Aytoun Street Unemployment Agency, selling nuts at Lewis's department store, folding and packing work etc. She later became a poet and has produced many poems, and has published work in her book *Page Fright.* She is Poet National to Hearing Voices Network and is considered Resident Poet all over Manchester, especially in the Northern Quarter. Carol is Jewish, but has attended Quaker a lot in the past, and also follows TAO where it occurs for her to do so. Her aim is to fight prejudice and talk to a lot of people.
Interests: My poetry and my friends.

BAUME, Carole Diane

Position: Regional Director, The Open University, North West.
Areas of Influence: Education.
Profile: *b.* August 20th, 1949; *m.* David; 2 sons; 1 daughter.
Education: Kesteven and Sleaford High School for Girls; UMIST; Oxford Brookes University; BSc Hons, MA, FSEDA. Career profile: Administrator to Senior Lecturer, North East London Polytechnic (1972-93); Staff and Educational Developer, Oxford Brookes University (1993-97); Higher Educational Funding Council for England (1997-02); Publications: Articles on staff and educational development in higher

education; a book on project management. Clubs and societies: Staff and Educational Development Association; Institute for Learning and Teaching.

Interests: Travel, theatre, cinema, trying to keep fit.

Contact details: The Open University in the North West, 351 Altrincham Road, Manchester M22 4UN (tel: 0161 998 7272, fax: 0161 945 3356, email: c.baume@open.ac.uk).

BEALE, James Robert, M.A, PhD

Positions: Journalist; Music Critic.

Areas of Influence: Media, Arts, Faith Groups.

Profile: *b.* July 5th, 1948; *m.* Patricia; 2 sons; 1 daughter.

Educated at King Edward VII School Sheffield, The Queen's College Oxford and City University London. Publications: *Say Something Simple: The Local Church's Communications Handbook* (1981); *The Hallé: A British Orchestra in the 20th Century* (2001).

Contact details: Manchester Evening News, 164 Deansgate, Manchester M3 3RN (tel: 0161 211 2495, fax: 0161 839 0968, email: robert.beale@men-news.co.uk); 37 Eddisbury Avenue, Flixton, Manchester M41 8GE (tel: 0161 748 9999, email: robert.beale@btinternet.com).

BEAUMONT, Martin Dudley, MA, FCA

Positions: Chief Executive, The Cooperative Group (2002 - present); Deputy Chairman, The Cooperative Bank (2000 - present)

Areas of Influence: Commerce, Finance, Co-operative Sector.

Profile: *b.* August 6th, 1949; *m.* Andrea; 3 daughters.

Education: Stowe School, Buckingham; Magdelene College, Cambridge University; The Institute of Chartered Accountants. Career profile: Trainee to Partner, KPMG (1971-87); Group Financial Director, Egmont (1987-90); Chief Financial Officer to Chief Executive, United Co-operatives (1990-2002)

Interests: Family, fishing, tennis, reading.

Contact details: The Cooperative Group, PO Box 53, New Century House, Manchester M60 4ES (tel: 0161 834 1212, fax: 0161 832 6388).

BECKETT, Roy George

Positions: Managing Partner, DLA Manchester Office (1998 - present); Trustee, Bridgewater Hall Educational Trust.

Areas of Influence: Law.

Profile: *b.* 6th December, 1958; *m.* Suzanne; 1 son; 1 daughter.

Educated at Malet Lambert Senior High School, LLB (Hons), Manchester University

(1977-1980); College of Law (1980-81); Admitted as a Solicitor (1983); Graham & Rosen (1981-84); Bullivant Jones & Co (1984-85); Chafie Street (1985-87); DLA (1987 - present); Partner, DLA (1989 - present); Head of Real Estate, DLA Manchester Office (1992-99). Has published various legal articles. Member: Law Society; Bowdon Lawn Tennis Club; Bowdon Cricket, Hockey, & Squash Club; Interact.
Interests: Tennis, skiing, reading.

BECKETT-HUGHES, Melinda Jane, BA, MA, MCIPD, MBAC, MBPS

Positions: Managing Director, Portland International Consulting Group; Director and Trustee, Community Foundation of Greater Manchester; Chair, Portland International Charitable Trust.
Areas of Influence: Commerce, Voluntary Sector.
Profile: *b.* June 23rd, 1957; *m.* John Beckett; 1 son (3); 1 daughter (1).
Educated at West Kirby County Grammar School for Girls, Bath University, and Manchester University. Melinda Beckett-Hughes graduated in languages and spent the first 3 years of her career in marketing / operations developing a commercial base for the subsequent 20 years in the consultancy sector. Melinda floated one small consultancy (1998) before being headhunted to join a large consulting group as Business Development Director of H R Consulting Subsidiary, She then bought out this business, Portland International (1991), and has developed this in different stages to now offer a broad range of change management consulting and coaching services. Melinda now spends the majority of her time as an Executive Coach working with corporate directors. Clubs and Societies: CIPD, BPS, BAC, IOD, RSA, International Who's Who.
Interests: Personal development, self and others. Distance swimming, cooking and entertaining, family.
Contact details: Portland International, Portland Tower, Portland Street, Manchester M1 3LF (tel; 07000 226 224, fax: 07000 226 225, email: melinda@portland international.com); Ringley House, Ringley Park, Whitefield, Manchester M45 7NT (tel: 0161 796 2707, fax: 0161 796 0609, email: melinda@becketthughes.com).

BECKHAM, David Robert Joseph

Position: Professional Footballer.
Areas of Influence: Sport.
Profile: *b.* May 2nd, 1975; *m.* Victoria; 2 sons, Brooklyn and Romeo.
Educated at Leytonstone School. Born in London, David Beckham's childhood dream was to play football and that dream came true when he signed for Manchester United as an apprentice in 1989. Since then he has become arguably Manchester United and England's most valuable player, and one of the world's most recognisable sports stars. Appearances: England U21, 7; Manchester United, over 289; England,

over 37. Prizes and awards: Manchester United Player of the Year (1996-97); Young PFA Player of the Year (1997); Runner up Player of the Year (1997); SKY Football Personality of the Year (1997); Runner up World Player of the Year (1999-00); Runner up European Player of the Year (1999-00); Runner up BBC Sports Personality of the Year (1999-00); Captain England v Italy (2000-01). Honours: 4 Premiership Winner Medals; 2 FA Cup Winner Medals; 1 European Champions League Winner Medal; 2 Charity Shield Winner Medals.
Interests: Golf
Contact: details: Manchester United FC, Sir Matt Busby Way, Old Trafford, Manchester M16 0RA (tel: 0161 868 8000, fax: 0161 876 5502).

BEER, Professor Janet Patricia

Positions: Dean of Faculty of Humanities and Social Science; Pro Vice Chancellor, Manchester Metropolitan University; Special Advisor, House of Commons Education and Skills Select Committee; Parent Governor, Marple Hall School, Stockport; Member, AHRB Peer Assessment Panel for English.
Areas of Influence: Education, Arts, Media
Profile: *b.* August 1st, 1956; *m.* David Woodman; 1 son; 1 daughter.
Education: City of Bath Girls School (1967-74); BA English Language and Literature, University of Reading (1975-78); MA American Literature, University Warwick (1978-80); Yale Fellowship, Yale University (1980-81); PhD in Literature, University of Warwick (1981-83). Career profile: Education Officer, ILEA, County Hall, London (1983-89); Senior / Principal Lecturer, University of Surrey, Roehampton (1989-97); Head of Dept. of English, MMU (1998-02). Publications include: *Edith Wharton: Traveller in the Land of Letters* (1990); *Kate Chopin, Edith Wharton and Charlotte Perkins Gilman: Studies in Short Fiction* (1997); *Edith Wharton* (2002). Clubs and societies: Vice Chair, British Association for American Studies; Modern Language Association of America; British Association for Canadian Studies; Edith Wharton Society.
Interests: Theatre, music, film, swimming, dancing, reading.
Contact details: Faculty of Humanities and Social Science, Geoffrey Manton Building, Rosamond Street West, Manchester, M15 6LL (tel: 0161 247 1749, fax: 0161 247 6590, email: J.Beer @ mmu.ac.uk).

BENSON, Stephen John

Position: Partner, Head of Property, Cobbetts Solicitors.
Areas of Influence: Arts, Law.
Profile: *b.* November 5th, 1955; *m.* Gillian; 1 son; 2 daughters.
Educated at Bishop Vesey's Grammar School, Sutton Coldfield, Manchester University and Chester College of Law. Career profile: qualified as a Solicitor of the Supreme Court; joined Cobbetts Solicitors (1981), became Partner (1985). Clubs and

societies: American Bar Association; International Bar Association.

Interests: Fine arts, motor cars, photography.

Contact details: Cobbetts, Ship Canal House, King Street, Manchester M2 4WB (tel: 0161 833 5232, fax: 0161 830 2704, email: stephen.benson@cobbetts.co.uk).

BENZIE, Alan Athol Emslie, FCE

Positions: Chairman, Northern Business Area, Partner (1977 - present), Member UK Board (1998 - present), KPMG; Member, Business in the Community National Education Leadership Team; Director, Manchester Pool 50 New Sports and Leisure Trust.

Areas of Influence: Commerce, Finance.

Profile: *b.* may 5th, 1947; *m.* Penny; 2 sons; 1 daughter.

Educated at Lindisfarn College, North Wales. Career profile: Articled to Grant Thornton (1964-69); Peat Marwick Mitchell, now KPMG (1969 - present), seconded to South Africa (1970-74), seconded to London (1974-75), Office Managing Partner (1989-95), KPMG; Ex-Chairman of the Christie Hospital £25m Appeal - Corporate Sector. Clubs and Societies: Wilmslow Golf Club, Birdsgrove Fly Fishing Club.

Interests: Golf, fishing, shooting, gardening, watching sport.

Contact details: KPMG, St James Square, Manchester M2 6DS (tel: 0161 838 4000, fax: 0161 246 4163, email: alan.benzie@kpmg.co.uk).

BERG, Alan

Position: District Judge, Magistrates Court (2001 - present).

Areas of Influence: Law.

Profile: *b.* February 17th, 1943; *m.* Lorna Berg; 2 sons.

Educated at King George V Grammar School, Southport and Liverpool Law School. Career profile: Solicitor, private practice, Cantor Levin & Berg of Liverpool (1967-94); appointed Stipendiary Magistrate, Manchester (1994).

Interests: Swimming, reading.

Contact details: Manchester City Magistrates Court, Crown Square, Manchester M60 1PR (tel: 0161 832 7272, fax: 0161 832 5421).

BERGIER, Jerzy Witold J (George)

Positions: Food and Beverage Services Manager, Crowne Plaza Manchester - The Midland (1998 - present); Chairman, The Guild of Sommeliers, Manchester (1986 - present)

Areas of Influence: Food and Wines, Sport.

Profile: *b.* July 23rd, 1946; 1 daughter, Natalia Louisa Alexandra.

Education: Warsaw Primary School; Warsaw Secondary School, Henryka Modzelewskigo; Diploma in Hotel and Catering Management, Warsaw, Poland (1967). Career profile: General Manager, The St James's Club, Manchester (1984-96); Restaurant Manager, The Four Seasons Hotel, Hale (1996-98). Prizes and awards: The Academy of Food & Wine Service, The Dom Perignon Award for Excellence (1999); 3 times National Semi Finalist in Ruinart Champagne and the Academy of Food & Wine Service Sommelier of the Year Competition, London; Former member of Trafford AC; Polish Army Junior Long Jump Champion (1965); Northern Counties Long Jump Champion (1973).

Interests: Sport, athletics.

Contact details: Crowne Plaza Manchester - The Midland, Peter Street, Manchester M60 2DS (tel: 0161 236 3333, fax: 0161 932 4100, email: george.bergier@6c.com); 51 Hillingdon Road, Stretford, Manchester M32 8PH (tel: 0161 865 9315, fax: 0161 865 9315).

BERKELEY, Leslie David JP

Positions: Chairman, Bury Greater Manchester Magistrates Bench and Justice of the Peace.

Areas of Influence: Law, Voluntary Sector, Public Sector.

Profile: *b.* November 4th, 1934; *m.* Valerie Sanora; 1 son; 3 daughters.

Educated at Stand Grammar School. Career profile: Managing Director, Clothing Manufacturer Co; Borough Councillor (1958-63); Governor of Stand Grammar School (1958-63); Post Executive member of Manchester Chamber of Commerce; Magistrate (1982 - present). Member, The Disability Living Appeals Service, The Child Support Appeals Tribunal and The Manchester North Valuation Tribunal.

Interests: Local charities.

BERKLEY, David QC (1999), LLB (Hons)

Positions: Head of Chambers, Merchant Chambers, Manchester; Recorder (Civil) (2001); Secretary, Northern Circuit Commercial Bar Association.

Areas of Influence: Law, Commerce.

Profile: *b.* December 3rd, 1955; *m.* Debby (nee Hather); 1 son; 4 daughters.

Educated at Manchester Jewish Grammar School, Gateshead Talmudical College, and Manchester University College of Law, Chancery Lane. Career profile: called to the Bar, Middle Temple, (1979); Litigation Assistant, pupil of FMS Hudson, Halliwell Landau Solicitors, Manchester (1978-79); Founding Head, Merchent Chambers (1996); Deputy District Judge (1999-01).

Interests: Early printed books, music.

Contact details: Merchant Chambers, 1 North Parade, Parsonage Gardens, Manchester M3 2NH (tel: 0161 839 7070, fax: 0161 839 7111)

BERNSTEIN, David Alan, FCA

Positions: Chairman, Manchester City FC; Non-Executive Chairman, Blacks Leisure Group plc and Adams Childrenswear; Chairman, Skills Show, Supervisors Board.
Areas of Influence: Sport, Finance, Commerce.
Profile: *b.* May 22nd, 1943; *m.* Gillian; 4 sons.
Educated at Christies College, Finchley. Career profile: Partner, Bright Grahams Murry, Chartered Accountants; Managing Director, Pentland Group plc; Non-Executive Chairman, French Connection Group plc.
Contact details: 48 Fitzalan Road, Finchley, London N33 PE2 (tel: 0208 346 2345, fax: 0208 343 0625).

BERNSTEIN, Howard

Positions: Chief Executive, Manchester City Council (1998); Clerk, Greater Manchester Passenger Transport Authority; Various Directorships including Bridgewater Hall, URBIS, GMPTE, and Manchester Airport Developments Ltd; RIBA Client of the Year (2001); Property Personality of the Year (2000); Construction Client of the Year (2002).
Areas of Influence: Public Sector, Commerce, Finance.
Profile: *b.* April 9th, 1953; 1 son, Jonathon; 1 daughter, Natalie.
Educated at Ducie High School (1971) and External Student at London University. Career profile: Manchester City Council (1971); Deputy Chief Executive (1990 - 1998); appointed Chief Executive of the Task Force to oversee renewal of the City Centre following the terrorist bomb in 1996.
Interests: Walking, cinema, football.
Contact details: Chief Executive, Manchester City Council, Town Hall, Albert Square, Manchester M60 2LA (Tel. 0161 234 3006, Fax. 0161 234 3098).

BERRY, Grant, BA (Hons), ACA

Position: Investment Director, Lloyds TSB Development Capital Ltd, Manchester.
Areas of Influence: Finance
Profile: October 19th, 1966; *m.* Joanne; 1 daughter.
Educated at Wrekin College, Shropshire, Loomis Chaffee School, Connecticut, USA and UCW Aberystwyth. Grant Berry has been with PricewaterhouseCoopers for 10years.
Interests: Rugby, golf, cricket, guitar.
Contact details: email: gberry@ldc.co.uk

BERRY, Paul Karfoot

Positions: President, Manchester Statistical Society Committee and Manchester Midday Concerts Society.
Areas of Influence: Voluntary Sector.
Profile: *b.* May 31st, 1943.
Educated at Calday Grange Grammar School (1953-61) and St Peters College, Oxford (1961-64). Career profile: Co-operative Insurance Society (1964-2001). Clubs and societies: Lancashire County Cricket Club; Talyllyn Railway Preservation Society; Manchester Statistical Society; Manchester Literary and Philosophical Society; Buxton Festival Society; Hallé Concert Society; Friends of RNCM; Friends of Royal Exchange Theatre; Friends of Opera North; Hauergal Brian Society.
Interests: Cricket, rugby, opera, music, theatre, railway preservation, fell walking.
Contact details: 36 Chepstow House, Chepstow Street, Manchester M1 5JF (tel: 0161 236 0182, email: paulkberry@supanet.com).

BESTERMAN, Tristram Paul, MA (Cantab), AMA, FMA, FGS, FRSA

Positions: Director, The Manchester Museum, University of Manchester (1994 - present); Member, Ministerial Group on Human Remains (2000)
Areas of Influence: Museums, Cultural Sector, Public Sector.
Profile: *b.* September 19th, 1949; *m.* Perry; 2 sons; 1 daughter.
Educated at Stowe School, music scholarship and prizes (1963-67) and University of Cambridge (1968-71). Career profile: Studio Manager, BBC, London (1971-73); Preparators Assistant, Geological Survey, Geological and Mining Museum, Sydney, NSW (1974); Education Officer, Sheffield City Museums, Sheffield City Council (1974-1977); Deputy Curator and Keeper of Geology, Warwickshire Museums, Warwickshire County Council (1977-85); City Curator, Plymouth City Museums and Art Gallery, Plymouth City Council (1985-94); Convenor, Museums Association Ethics Committee (1994-01); Board member of other museums and national and regional museum bodies. Tristram Bersterman has produced or contributed to 13 publications on museum issues.
Interests: Music ('cellist), tennis, gardening, viticulture.
Contact details: The Manchester Museum, The University of Manchester, Oxford Road M13 9PL (tel: 0161 275 2649, fax: 0161 275 2676, email: tristram.besterman@man.ac.uk).

BESWICK, Allan

Position: Broadcaster.
Areas of Influence: Media.
Profile: *b*. 8th October, 1948.
Had an 'ordinary' education and pursued previous careers as a Soldier, Driving Instructor, Psychiatric Nurse, Bus Driver, and Citizens Advice Bureau Manager.
Interests: Theatre, rugby.
Contact details: BBC, Oxford Road, Manchester M60 1SD (tel: 0161 244 3052, email: allan.beswick@bbc.co.uk).

BIANCHI, Adrian, MOM (1995)

Positions: Specialist Paediatric and Neonatal Surgeon; Consultant Specialist Paediatric and Neonatal Surgeon to the North West Region.
Areas of Influence: Health, Education.
Profile: *b*. January 19th, 1948, Malta; *m*. Claire; 2 sons; 1 daughter.
Education: MD, Royal University of Malta, Medical School (1969); FRCS, Royal College of Surgeons of Edinburgh (1975); FRCS, Royal College of Surgeons of England (1975). Adrian Bianchi has dual Maltese - English Nationality. He specialised in Paediatric and Neonatal Surgery through surgical programmes in Liverpool and Manchester. Since 1984 he has been consultant specialist paediatric and neonatal surgeon with a strong background in plastic surgery. He was Director of Neonatal Surgery from 1987 to 2002 and since 1984 he has participated in hospital management for the Children's Hospitals and at St Mary's Hospital, Manchester. He has produced 58 publications in various medical journals, 8 chapters in paediatric surgical operatives and general surgical textbooks in England and Italy. He has also developed original surgical techniques and new surgical approaches. It has been his long term intention to critically review surgical procedures for the reconstruction of congenital anomalies and to develop teamworking with parents, assisting parents in the care of their children. He has made particular contributions to the surgical management of children with 'Short Bowel', developing innovative approaches and surgical techniques such as bowel lengthening, and has disseminated surgical concepts through active participation at local, national, and international meetings.
Interests: Reproduction of antique furniture, ancient civilisations, swimming, gardening, bonsai.
Contact details: Royal Manchester Children's Hospitals (tel: 0161 727 2193, email: adrian.bianchi@cmmc.nhs.uk).

BIRD, Nicholas Charlton Penrhys, KStJ (2001), DL (2001)

Position: Partner, Finlay Robertson Chartered Accountants, Manchester and Liverpool, Chairman: Council, St John Ambulance - The Priory Of England and the Islands, Greater Manchester (1999).
Areas of Influence: Finance, Voluntary Sector.
Profile: *b.* 28th September 1952.
Educated at Tre-Arddur House School, and Malvern College. Career profile: Financial Advisor to numerous private companies and individuals; Fellow, Institute of Chartered Accountants in England and Wales (1980). Publications: several papers on the taxation consequences of divorce and separation.
Contact details: Finlay Robertson, Fifth Floor, Brook House, 77 Fountain Street, Manchester M2 2EE (tel: 0161 228 3924, fax: 0161 236 1108, email: fr@finrob.co.uk); The Mews, The Cedars, Woodbrook Road, Alderley Edge, Cheshire SK9 7DB (tel: 01625 585169, fax.01625 585169, email: ncpbird@aol.com).

BIRKETT, Peter Vidler, QC (1989), LLB (Hons)

Positions: Barrister at Law; Recorder of the Crown Court (1989).
Areas of Influence: Law.
Profile: *b.* July 13th, 1948; *m.* Jane; 2 sons.
Educated at Sedbergh School, Yorkshire, Leicester University and The Honourable Society of the Inner Temple. Peter Birkett was called to the Bar in 1972. He practised at the Bar in London until 1977, when he came to Manchester, since which time he has practised from 18 St John Street. Other roles include Master of the Bench of the Inner Temple (1996), Acting Deemster of the High Court, Isle of Man and Leader of the Northern Circuit (1999-01). Peter is also a member of Wilmslow Golf Club.
Interests: Golf, music, keyboard player for 'The Prestons', travel, old films.
Contact details: 18 St John St, Manchester, M3 4EA (tel: 0161 278 1800); Gable End, Nursery Lane, Nether Alderley, nr. Macclesfield SK10 4TX (tel: 01625 861354).

BISHOP, Sir Michael David, CBE, KBE

Positions: Chairman, British Midland PLC (1978 - present); Chairman, D'Oyly Carte Opera Trust.
Areas of Influence: Arts, Commerce, Media.
Profile: *b.* February 10th, 1942, Bowdon, Greater Manchester;
Educated at Mill Hill School. Career profile: Joined Mercury Airlines, Manchester Airport (1963); Area Manager (1964-69), General Manager and Director (1969-72), Managing Director (1972-78), British Midland, Manchester; Deputy Chairman (1991-

93), Chairman (1993-97), Channel 4 Television; Director (1987-96), Deputy Chairman (1996-01), Airtours plc. Sir Michael is a member of Brooks's and St James's Club, Manchester.
Contact details: Donington Hall, Castle Donington, Derby DE74 2SB (tel: 01332 854201, fax: 01332 850301).

BLACK, Michael, QC

Positions: Barrister in practice as Advocate, Arbitrator and Mediator, 2 Temple Gardens and Byrom Street Chambers; Recorder; Deputy Judge of Technology and Construction Court; Member, Civil Procedure Rule Committee; Member, Court of Appeal Panel of Mediators.
Areas of Influence: Law, Construction Industry.
Profile: *b.* March 31st, 1954.
Education: Stand Grammar School; Bachelor of Law University College, London; Inns of Court School of Law, Barrister. Career profile: Slater Heels Solicitors (1977-78); Deans Court Chambers (1978-95); Byrom Street Chambers (1995-00); Fellow, Chartered Institute of Arbitrators and Institution of Civil Engineering; Visiting Fellow, UMIST. Michael Black has published numerous articles and lectures, most recently contributing to chapters on construction and arbitration in *The Law and practice of Compromise*, 5th ed. Clubs and societies: Liveryman of the Worshipful Company of Arbitrators; Northern Commercial Bar Association; Association of Northern Mediators; American Bar Association; Technology and Construction Bar Association.
Contact details: 12 Byrom Street, Manchester M3 4PP (tel: 0161 829 2100, fax: 0161 829 2101, email: mbqc@2tg.co.uk).

BLACKMORE, John Ashurst, BSc (1964)

Position: Executive Director, Octagon Theatre, Bolton.
Areas of Influence: Arts, Education.
Profile: *b.* January 20th, 1941; *m.* Stella Christine; 2 daughters.
Education: Whitgift School (1951-69); BSc Psychology (Hons), University of Hull (1964); Diploma in Drama, University of Manchester (1966). John Blackmore started his career as a Director of plays and has directed over 100 professional theatre productions in the West End, the Regions, and on tour. He has been Chief Executive of five major regional theatres, Library Theatre, Manchester Dukes Playhouse, Lancaster, the Tynewear Theatre Company (now Northern Stage) and the Haymarket Theatre, Leicester. He has founded a new regional theatre, Tynewear, two Theatre in Education Companies, Lancaster and Newcastle, and a community theatre company, Birmingham. He has also run The Midland Arts Centre, Birmingham, Warwick Arts Centre, been Executive Director of the English

Shakespeare Company and worked as Executive Director for one of the largest West End producers, Bill Kenwright. He was a member of the Labour Party Arts Study Group chaired by the late Renne Short MP, a member of the Arts Council of England Touring Board and was a Board member and Chair of the English Shakespeare Company. He is currently Chair of Out of Joint Theatre Company. Recently he successfully raised funding and drew up plans for the new producing theatre company in Liverpool running the Playhouse and Everyman Theatres.
Interests: Visiting art galleries, cooking, sport.
Contact details: 33 Acacia Road, Leamington Spa, Warwickshire CV32 6EF (tel: 01926 452 343 / 01204 536 509, mob: 07774 246 216, email: jab@jbarts90.freeserve.co.uk).

BLASKEY, Roger Waldo, BSc (Hons), FCA

Position: Partner, Kay Johnson Gee (1991 - present)
Areas of Influence: Commerce, Finance.
Profile: *b.* April 28th, 1951; *m.* Elizabeth; 1 son; 1 daughter.
Educated at Westbourne prep School (1956-64), Rugby School (1964-68), and UMIST (1969-72). Roger Blaskey was articled with Spicer & Pegler where he qualified before moving to J Allen & Co as Partner till 1981. He spent 10 years in Industry as a Financial Director before his current position. Member of Dunham Forest Golf Club.
Interests: Charity work, Masonic work, golf, supports Sheffield Wednesday!!
Contact details: Kay Johnson Gee, Griffin Court, 201 Chapel Street, Salford, M3 5EQ (tel; 0161 832 6221, email: roger.blaskey@kayjohnsongee.com).

BLOOM, His Honour Judge Charles, QC, LLB (Hons)

Positions: Circuit Judge (1997 - present); Deputy High Court Judge (1992).
Areas of Influence: Law.
Profile: *b.* November 6th, 1940; *m.* Janice Rochelle; 1 son; 1 daughter.
Educated at Manchester Central Grammar School, Manchester University and Inns of Court School of Law. Career profile: Barrister, Northern Circuit (1963-87); Deputy Circuit Judge (1978-83); Crown Court Recorder (1983-97); Head of Chambers, aged 28, St John Street, Manchester (1985-97); Queen's Counsel (1985-97). Since being appointed Queen's Counsel in 1987, Charles Bloom practised from chambers in Manchester and London, and specialises in Family Law. He is also an editor for Butterworth Family Law Service. Clubs and Societies: Friedland Postmusa Tennis Club, Larner Vinifloral Society.
Interests: Tennis, gardening, theatre, wine.
Contact details: Court Service, Manchester Inner Group, Group Managers Office, 15 Quay Street, Manchester M60 9FD.

BLOXHAM, Thomas Paul Richard, MBE (Hons) (1999), FRIBA (1999), FRSA, PJMU (2000)

Positions: Chairman, Urban Splash; Chair, North West Arts Board, Galaxy 102 and Baa Bar Limited; Board Member, Government Property Advisory Group and Urban Sounding Board; Trustee, The Big Issue in the North.
Areas of Influence: Arts, Commerce.
Profile: *b.* December 20th, 1963; *m.* Jo; 2 sons.
Education: BA (Hons) Politics and Modern History, Manchester University. Tom Bloxham moved to Manchester from South London when he was 19 to attend University. To supplement his student grant, he began selling second hand records and posters on market stalls in the city. Tom's next venture was to set up Urban Splash (Properties) and take under-utilised buildings and transform them into specialist shopping centres and managed workspace. Tom then focused on a gap in the residential property market - city centre loft living. Tom and Co-Director Jonathan Falkingham set up Urban Splash Limited (1993), and have developed over £15 million projects, which have won over 50 awards including 6 RIBA awards for architecture and 5 Housing Design Awards. Tom has also won the Ernst & Young National Young Entrepreneur of the Year Award, 4 other Business of the Year awards, and has received an Honorary Fellowship from the Royal Institute of British Architecture, from John Moores University, Liverpool and the John Owens Award from Manchester University.
Interests: Avid Manchester United Football fan.
Contact details: Urban Splash Head Office, Timber Wharf, 16-22 Worsley Street, Castlefield, Manchester M15 4LD (tel: 0161 839 2999, 0161 839 8999, tombloxham@urbansplash.co.uk).

BODMER, Sir Walter (Fred), Kt (1986), FRCPath (1984), FRS (1974), FiBiol (1990)

Positions: Principal, Hertford College Oxford (1996 - present); NRPB (1998 - present); Chairman, British Association for Cancer Research (1998-02); Vice-President, Research Defence Society (1990 - present); Sir John Soane's Mus. (1992 - present); Chancellor, Salford University (1995 - present); Chairman, Laban Centre, London (1999 – present).
Areas of Influence: Health, Education
Profile: *b.* January 10th, 1936; *m.* Julia Gwyneth Pilkington (*d.* 2001); 2 sons; 1daughter.
Educated at Manchester Grammar School and Clare College, Cambridge (BA 1956; MA, PhD 1959). Career profile: Research Fellow (1958-61), Official Fellow (1961), Hon. Fellow (1989), Clare College Cambridge; Demonstrator in Genetics, University of Cambridge (1960-61); Assistant Professor, (1962-66), Associate Professor (1966-68), Department of Genetics, Stanford University; Professor of Genetics, University of

Oxford (1970-79); Director of Research (1979-91), Director General (1991-96), ICRF; Non-executive Director, Fisons, plc (1990-96). BBC Sci. Consultative Group (1981-87); Member, BBC General. Advisory Council (1981-91); Council, International Union Against Cancer (1982-90); Advisory Board for Res. Councils (1983-88); Chairman, COPUS (1990-93); Organisation of European Cancer Institutions (1990-93); President (1984-85), Vice-president (1983-84, Honorary Fellow (1997), Royal Statistical Society; BAAS (1987-88); ASE (1989-90); Vice-president, BAAS (1989-01); Human Genome Organisation. (1990-92); British Society for Histocompatibility and Immunogenetics (1990-91), Honorary Member (1992); EACR (1994-96); first President, International Federation of Associations for Advancement of Science and Technology (1992-94); Chairman (1988-93). Trustee, BM (Natural History) (1983-93). Many publications, awards, and research papers in genetical, statistical and mathematical journals.
Interests: Playing the piano, riding, swimming, scuba diving.
Contact details: Hertford College, Oxford OX1 3BW (tel: 01865 279407).

BOLTON, M Clare, BA, FCA, ATII

Positions: Partner, PricewaterhouseCoopers (1985 - present)
Areas of Influence: Finance.
Profile: *m.* Andrew; 2 sons.
Educated at Combe Bank, Sevenoaks, Kent and Liverpool University. Clare Bolton originally joined Harwood Barber in Liverpool which merged with Deloitte & Co which became Deloitte Hoskins & Sell which merged with Coopers & Lybrand which then merged with Price Waterhouse. Non-Executive Director, North West Water (1988-95).
Interests: Family, opera, theatre, music generally, Manchester United, Liverpool FC.
Contact details: PricewaterhouseCoopers, 101 Barbirolli Square, Lower Mosely Street, Manchester M2 3PW (tel: 0161 247 4032, fax; 0161 247 4251, email: clare.bolton@uk.pwcglobal.com).

BOOKBINDER, Alan Peter, BA, MA

Position: Head of Department, BBC Religion and Ethics (2001 - present).
Areas of Influence: Media, Faith Groups, Public Sector.
Profile: *b.* March 16th, 1956; Vicki Ambery-Smith (partner); 1 son; 1 daughter.
Educated at Manchester Grammar School, Oxford University, and Harvard University; BBC Television (1980 - present); Producer (1986); Executive Producer (1992). Publications: *Comrades*, BBC Books (1986), contributor to *The Spectator, The Tablet, The Listener*.
Interests: Football, travel, asking questions.

Contact details: BBC Manchester, Oxford Road, Manchester M60 1SJ (tel: 0161 244 3252, email: alan.bookbinder@bbc.co.uk).

BOOTH, Arthur Thomas, CBE (1991), FCA

Position: Chairman of Governors, Manchester Metropolitan University.
Areas of Influence: Finance, Education.
Profile: *b.* September 22nd, 1935; *m.* Patricia Alys; 1 son; 1 daughter.
Educated at St Peter's School, York. Tom Booth qualified as a Chartered Accountant in 1958. He joined Refuge Assurance in 1961 and became Managing Director in 1979 and then Chairman of Refuge Group plc (1987-96). He was appointed Accountant Laureate by Funding Societies of Chartered Accountants in 1989. Clubs and societies: Disley Golf Club, St James Club, Manchester Luncheon Club.
Interests: Golf, gardening, walking.
Contact details: Lee Wood, Reservoir Road, Whaley Bridge, High Peak, SK23 7BW (tel: 01663 732927, email: tom.booth@tesco.net).

BOOTH, Michael John, QC

Positions: Queen's Counsel (1999 - present); Chairman, Northern Chancery Bar Association.
Areas of Influence: Law.
Profile: *b.* May 24th, 1958; Salford; *m.* Sarah; 2 sons; 1 daughter.
Educated at Partington Central Infants, Stamford Park Junior, Manchester Grammar School (Foundation Scholarship), and Trinity College Cambridge to read Law having won an Open Scholarship; President, Cambridge Union Society (1979); Called to the Bar, Lincolns Inn (1981); Member of Denning Society and St James's Club.
Contact details: 40 King Street, Manchester M2 6BA (tel: 0161 832 9082, fax: 0161 835 2139, email: clerks@40kingstreet.co.uk; michael.j.booth@yconnect.com).

BOULTON, Francis Ann

Position: Director, Dizzy Heights Fundraising Consultancy.
Areas of Influence: Voluntary Sector.
Profile: *b.* October 11th, 1938; *m.* Roger Boulton (1960, diss. 1971); 1 son; 1 daughter.
Educated at Maude Allan School, Littlehampton, West Sussex, and Preston Technical College, Brighton. Career profile: Northern Fundraiser and Communications, Turning Point - best job of all; Sales Manager, Carcanet Press; Admin Secretary, Manchester Literary and Philosophical Society; Hon. Secretary, Manchester Luncheon Club (1984-96); Medical Secretary, King Khalid Hospital, Jeddah; Daily Mail; own guest house; PA to Lord Bowden, UMIST; PA to Lord Selkirk, Foreign Office; Senior Stenographer to Lord Mountbatten, Women's Royal Naval Service;

Chairman, Hayfield Parish Council (1989-90, 1995). Clubs and societies: Manchester Literary and Philosophical Society; Manchester Luncheon Club; Manchester Statistical Society.

Interests: Archaeology, gardening, living life to the full.

Contact details: Dizzy Heights Fundraising Consultancy, 157 Kinder Road, Hayfield, High Peak, Derbyshire SK22 2LE (tel: 01663 743372, fax: 01663 746705).

BOWDUR, Helen, BA (Hons)

Position: Executive Producer at Granada Television for Channels Business (1995 - present).

Areas of Influence: Media

Profile: *b.* August 18th, 1959.

Education: North Manchester High School for Girls; BA (Hons) Politics, Nottingham University; Post Graduate Radio Journalism Certificate, London College of Printing. Career profile: Reporter / Producer, BBC Radio and TV (1982-87); News Editor, Granada Television (1988-93); Producer, Ray Walter Associates (1993-95).

Contact details: Granada Television, Quay Street, Manchester, M60 9EA (tel: 0161 835 6345, email: helen.bowdur@granadamedia.com).

BOWKER, Professor Peter

Positions: Pro-Vice-Chancellor and Professor of Prosthetics and Orthotics, University of Salford; Fellow of the Institute of Physics & Engineering in Medicine.

Areas of Influence: Education, Health.

Profile: *b.* July 15th, 1946. *m.* Patricia; 1 son.

Educated at Lancaster Royal Grammar School (1957-63) and The University of Salford (1963-70). Career profile: Senior Research Associate, University of Newcastle upon Tyne (1970-73); Lecturer, University of Aberdeen (1973-81); Lecturer, Senior Lecturer, and Professor, University of Salford (1981 - present). 71 publications in learned journals.

Interests: Gardening, photography.

Contact details: University of Salford, Salford M5 4WT (tel:0161 295 5050, fax:0161 295 5040, email: p.bowker@salford.ac.uk).

BOYD, Douglas Gavin, FRAM (1986), ARAM (1990).

Positions: Principal Conductor, Music Director of Manchester Camarata; Associate Conductor, City of London Sinfonia; Principal Guest Conductor, Royal Northern College of Music Sinfonia; Professor, Royal Northern College of Music.

Areas of Influence: Arts, Education.

Profile: *b.* March 1st, 1959; *m.* Sally Pendlebury; 1 son, Sam; 1 daughter, Iona.

Educated at The High School of Glasgow (1976), Royal Academy of Music (1976-80) and private study, Paris (1980-82). Career profile: Principal Oboe and Founding Member, Chamber Orchestra of Europe (1981-02); Soloist at major international venues including Vienna, Salzburg Festival, Berlin, Edinburgh Festivals, New York Carnegie Hall; Soloist with major orchestras including Cincinnati Symphony, Academy of St Martins in the Fields, Vienna Symphony, Chamber Orchestra of Europe; Hong Kong Philharmonic; Conductor (1996 - present); Co-director, Gardner Chamber Orchestra, Boston; guest appearances with Scottish Chamber Orchestra, Hong Kong Philharmonic, Royal Scottish National Orchestra; Conductor in Residence, World Youth Orchestra. Prizes and awards: Young Concert Artists Winner, New York (1984); Leila Bull Oboe Prize, Royal Academy of Music (1977).
Interests: Gardening, soccer, tennis with my son, reading, politics.
Contact details: c/o Ingpen & Williams, 26 Wadham Road, London SW15 2LR (tel: 0208 8874 3222, fax: 0208 8877 3113, email: ds@ingpen.co.uk); dougieboyd @dial.pipex.com.

BOYD, James Michael, FCMA

Positions: Finance Director, Cobbetts Solicitors; Business Mentor, Princes Trust.
Areas of Influence: Finance, Law.
Profile: *b.* May 2nd, 1966; *m.* Erika; 1 son; 1 daughter.
Educated at Knutsford High School, Macclesfield College, and Manchester University. James Boyd has previously worked at Ricksons, Thorn Emi, BP, and Ingersoll Rand, and has published various articles in the legal press as well as achieving the RNR TS Royalist Award.
Interests: Badminton, Manchester City supporter, music.
Contact details: Cobbetts Solicitors, Ship Canal House, King Street, Manchester M2 4WB (tel: 0161 833 5213, fax: 0161 833 3030, email: james.boyd@cobbetts.co.uk).

BOYERS, Jonathan Mark, BA, FCA

Positions: Corporate Finance Partner, KPMG Corporate Finance.
Areas of Influence: Finance, Commerce.
Profile: *b.* February 9th, 1967; *m.* Cathy; 2 sons.
Educated at Upholland High School, Wigan, Winstanley College, Wigan and the University of Lancaster. Jonathan Boyers trained as a Chartered Accountant with KPMG and worked for two years in Corporate Recovery. He specialised in Corporate Finance (1992) and currently advises on Acquisitions, Disposals, Management Buy Outs, and Private Equity. He was awarded the Brooke Prize for Academic Achievement, Bowland College, University of Lancaster, and the Reuters

Prize for Investment Analysis, Securities Institute.
Contact details: KPMG Corporate Finance, St James Square, Manchester (tel: 0161 246 4136, fax: 0161 246 4095, email: Jonathan.Boyers@KPMG.co.uk).

BRACEGIRDLE, Cyril

Position: Author.
Areas of Influence: Arts, Media, Journalism.
Profile: *b.* December 23rd, 1930.
Cyril Bracegirdle had a private education. He has been the author of hundreds of magazine articles in the UK and abroad on subjects such as travel, antiques, and natural health, and has also published 5 non-fiction books: *The Dark River, Zoos are News, Beginners Guide to Antiques, Collecting Railway Antiques* and *Dr William Price.* Cyril is a member of the Society of Authors and the Fellowship of European Medical Union.
Interests: Theatre, travel, music, literary study.
Contact details: 7 Langdale Road, Sale, Cheshire M33 4EN (tel: 0161 973 6215, fax: 0161 973 6215).

BRADFORD, Professor Michael Graham

Position: Pro-Vice Chancellor, University of Manchester.
Areas of Influence: Education, Public Sector.
Profile: *b.* December 6th 1944; *m.* Sheila.
Education: St Catharine's College, Cambridge (1964-1967); University of Wisconsin, Madison, USA (1967-1968); Cambridge (1968-1971). Career profile: Lecturer, School of Geography, University of Manchester (1971-1989), Senior Lecturer (1989-1997); Undergraduate Dean (1992-96); Head of School (1996-2000). Publications: *Human Geography: Theories and Their Applications*, Oxford University Press (1977); *Understanding Human Geography: People and their Environment*, Oxford University Press, (1993). Clubs and societies: Grove Park Squash Club; Bramall Park Golf Club; President of the Geographical Association (2000).
Contact details: School of Geography, University of Manchester M13 9PL (tel. 0161 275 3650; fax. 0161 275 7878).

BRADLEY, Keith, PC (2001)

Position: MP, Withington, Manchester.
Areas of Influence: Health, Public Sector.
Profile: *b.* 17th May, 1950.
Educated at Bishop Vesey's Grammar School, Sutton Coldfield; BA (Hons) Social Science, Manchester Polytechnic; M.Phil, Social Administration, York University.

Career profile: Articled Clerk, Chartered Accountants; Research Officer, Manchester City Council; Chief Officer, Stockport Community Health Council; MP, Manchester Withington (1987 - present); Part Under Secretary of State, Social Security (1997-98); Deputy Chief Whip, Treasurer Queen's Household (1998-2001); Minister of State, Home Office (2001-02).
Contact details: Investment House, 425 Wilmslow Road, Withington M20 9AF (tel: 0161 446 2047, fax: 0161 445 5543, email: KeithBradley@parliament.uk).

BRADY Graham Stuart, BA (Law).

Positions: Member of Parliament for Altrincham and Sale West (1997 - present); Shadow Minister for Schools (2001 - present).
Areas of Influence: Education, Health.
Profile: *b.* May 20th 1967; *m.* Victoria; 1 son; 1 daughter.
Educated at Heyes Lane Infants and Junior School, Timperley (1972-78), Altrincham Grammar School (1978-85) and University of Durham (1986-89). Career profile: Graduate Trainee in Public Relations, Shandwick Plc; Centre for Policy Studies (1990-92); Public Affairs Director, The Waterfront partnership (1992-97).
Interests: Family, garden.
Contact details: House of Commons, London SW1A 0AA (tel: 0207 7219 1260, fax: 0207 7219 1647, email: bradyg@parliament.uk).

BRADY, Mark David, LLB (Hons), ACA, MSI

Position: Director of Corporate Finance, Brewin Dolphin Securities Ltd.
Areas of Influence: Finance.
Profile: *b.* September 23rd, 1961; *m.* Susan; 1 son; 1 daughter.
Educated at Chislehurst and Sidcup Grammar School and the University of Leeds. Career profile: KPMG (1983-88); Thomas Coombs / Stoy Hayward (1988); Charlton Seal / Wise Speke Ltd (1988-90); Manchester Exchange & Investment Bank (1990-91); Wise Speke / Brewin Dolphin Securities Ltd (1991 - present).
Contact details: Brewin Dolphin Securities Ltd, PO Box 512, National House, 36 St Ann Street, Manchester M60 2EP (tel: 0161 214 5552, fax: 0161 832 1672, email: mark.brady@brewin.co.uk).

BRAGARD, Dr Jean Claude, BA (Hons), Dphil

Position: Executive producer, BBC Religion & Ethics (2000 - present)
Areas of Influence: Faith Groups, Media.
Profile: *b.* May 2nd, 1952; *m.* Debbie; 1 son; 1 daughter.
Education: St George's College, Buenos Aires; Oakham School, Rutland; BA (Hons) class 1 Sociology, Warwick University; DPhil Politics, Balliol College, Oxford

University. Career profile: Lecturer, Warwick University (1978); Researcher / Producer, London Weekend Television (1980-93); Senior Producer, BBC (1993-99). Publications: *The Shattered Dream: Unemployment in the 1980's* 1981); *Evil* (1996). Jean Bragard received the Sandford St Martin Premier Award for Religious Broadcasting (1987).
Contact details: BBC North, PO Box 27, Manchester M60 1SJ (tel: 0161 244 3329, email: jean.claude.bragard@bbc.co.uk)

BRAILSFORD, David, MSc, CEng, MRAeS

Positions: Mayor of Stockport (2002-03); Retired Aeronautical Engineer; Justice of the Peace; Governor, Ridge Danyers College.
Areas of Influence: Public Sector, Education, Voluntary Sector.
Profile: *b.* October 20th, 1933; *m.* Margaret; 2 Sons; 1 Daughter;
Educated at Queen Elizabeth Grammar School, Gainsborough; Royal Technical College, Salford; College of Aeronautics, Cranfield. Career profile: Aeronautical Engineer Apprenticeship, A.V.Roe, Manchester; Aerodynamicist and Aircraft Performance Engineer, A.V.Roe; Aircraft Performance Engineer, Rolls Royce, Derby; Manager, Systems Engineer, Hawker Siddeley Dynamics, Manchester; Engineering and Group Manager, Ferranti, Manchester; Quality Assurance Manager, Ferranti, Manager. Prizes and awards: AVRO 504 Trophy, Best all round Apprentice. Clubs and societies: AVRO 504 Club; Hallé Concerts Society; National Trust; Royal Society for Protection of Birds; Magistrates Association; Greater Manchester Passenger Transport Authority.
Interests: Gardening, nature, environment.
Contact details: 61 Andrew Lane, High Lane, Stockport SK6 8HY (tel: 0161 221 2969, fax: 0161 221 2969, email: cur.david.brailsford@stockport.gov.uk).

BRAIN, The Right Rev Terence

Position: Bishop of Salford.
Areas of Influence: Faith Groups.
Profile: *b.* December 19th, 1938.
Educated at Cotton College (1952-58) and Oscott College, Birmingham (1958-64). Career profile: Ordained Priest (February 22nd, 1964); Assistant Priest, St Gregory, Longton, Stoke on Trent (1964-65); Staff of Cotton College (1965-69); Hospital Chaplain (1969-71); Secretary to Archbishop of Birmingham (1971-82); Appointed Monsignor (December 1978); Parish Priest, Stoke on Trent (1982-88); Prison Chaplain (1982-88); Parish Priest in St.Austin, Stafford (1988-91); Ordained Auxiliary Bishop, Birmingham (April 1991), Appointed Bishop, Salford (August 1997).

Interests: Painting, crosswords.
Contact details: Wardley Hall, Manchester M28 2ND (tel: 0161 794 2825, fax: 0161 727 8592, email: bishop@wardleyhall.org.uk).

BRASLAVSKY, Nicholas Justin, QC (1999), LLB(Hons), PhD(Birm)

Positions: Barrister: Queen's Counsel; Recorder of the Crown Court (2000 - present).
Areas of Influence: Law, Health.
Profile: *b.* February 9th, 1959; *m.* Jane; 2 sons; 1 daughter.
Education: Blackpool Grammar School, Blackpool, Lancs; High Pavement Grammar School, Nottingham, University of Birmingham; Inns of Court School of Law. Nicholas Braslavsky has practised as a Barrister since 1983. He has produced many legal publications in addition to winning various legal and educational sponsorships. Clubs and Societies: Northern Circuit of the Bar; Personal Injuries Bar Association; Professional Negligence Bar Association.
Interests: Golf, music, sport.
Contact details: 40 King Street, Manchester M2 6BA (tel: 0161 832 9082, fax: 0161 835 2139, email: nbraslavsky@40kingstreet.co.uk).

BRAZIER, Professor Margot Rosetta, OBE (1998), LLB (1971)

Positions: Professor of Law, University of Manchester (1989 - present); Chairman, NHS Retained Organs Commission (2001 - present).
Areas of Influence: Law, Health, Education.
Profile: *b.* November 2nd, 1950; *m.* Rodney; 1 daughter.
Educated at Roedean School (1962-68), Queen Mary School, Lytham (1965-68) and University of Manchester (1968-71). Career profile: Lecturer in Law (1971-83, Senior Lecturer in Law (1983-88), Reader in Law (1988-89), University of Manchester; Chairman, Animal Procedures Committee (1994-98); Chairman, Surrogacy review (1998); Margot Brazier is a member of the Society of Legal Scholars and has produced various professional publications.
Interests: Theatre, family.
Contact details: School of Law, Williamson Building, University of Manchester, Manchester M13 0PL (tel:0161 275 8593, fax: 0161 275 3579, email: shirley.tiffany@man.ac.uk).

BREEDON, Paul Heath, LLB (1973)

Position: Partner, Breedon Taylor Solicitors.
Areas of Influence: Law, Sport.
Profile: *b.* November 11th, 1951; *m.* Carol Ann; 2 sons.
Educated at King Edward VII Grammar School, Lytham and Liverpool University.

Paul Breedon was articled to a commercial practice in 1986. He developed a strong commercial niche property practice together with a portfolio of quality private client work. He has taken part in the London and New York marathons where he raised over £8000 for Whizz-kids. Clubs and societies: Royal Lytham St Anne's Golf Club; Greenmount Golf Club; LA Fitness.

Interests: All sport (participation and watching), performing arts, theatre, concerts, playing the piano and guitar, animals, especially my golden retriever 'Tara'.

Contact details: Cough & Willis Solicitors, 2 Manchester Road, Bury BL9 0DT (tel: 0161 764 5266, fax: 0161 797 6157, email: info@clough-willis.co.uk).

BRINNAND, John, BA (Hons)

Position: Superintendent, Sub-divisional Commander, Longsight.
Areas of Influence: Law, Public Sector, Media.
Profile: *b.* April 1st, 1954; 1 son; 1 daughter.
Education: Sale Grammar School; BA (Hons), Dunhelm. Career profile: Joined Police (1976; Sergeant (1980); Inspector (1989); CI (1992); Superintendent (1997); has had roles in Crime prevention, planning, development and inspectorate, operational policing.
Interests: Tennis.
Contact details: Longsight Police Station, 2 Grindlow Street, Longsight, Manchester M13 0LC (tel: 0161 856 4201, fax: 0161 856 4126).

BRODIE, Rabbi Jeffrey, BA (Hons)

Positions: Chief Executive, Manchester Kastrus Authority; Registrar, Manchester Beth Din.
Areas of Influence: Faith Groups, Law, Voluntary Sector.
Profile: *b.* October 3rd, 1950; *m.* Anny; 4 sons; 2 daughters.
Educated at Broughton Primary School, Bury Grammar School, Manchester Metropolitan University, and Manchester Talmudial College. Jeffrey Brodie has a Law degree in addition to his Rabbinical Diploma (2002).
Interests: Charitable work, educational sector.
Contact details: 435 Cheetham Hill Road, Manchester (tel: 0161 240 9711, fax: 0161 721 4349, email: mbethdin@aol.com).

BROMLEY-DAVENPORT, John, QC (2002)

Position: Queen's Counsel Recorder of the Crown Court (1989); Barrister, Dean's Court Chambers, Manchester.
Areas of Influence: Arts, Law, Voluntary Sector.
Profile: *b.* March 13th, 1947; *m.* Judy; 1 son; 2 daughters.

Education: Tanglin School, Singapore; Abberley Hall, Worcestershire; Eton College; London Academy of Music and Dramatic Art; College of Law; BAR Exams, Inns of Court School of Law. John Bromley-Davenport has practiced on the Northern Circuit since 1972. During this period he has built up a major criminal practice and become a leading member of the criminal Bar. John has written *Sober in the Morning*, an anthology of the literature of drink and drinking which is to be published next year. He and his wife acted for many years at Capesthorne Theatre where he produced plays and two one man shows: *A Christmas Carol*, by Charles Dickens, and *Three men in a Boat*, by Jerome K Jerome. He has also toured with these shows in Britain, and America including London and New York. Clubs and societies: Criminal Bar Association; Grays Inn; Tarporley Hunt Club; The Ancient & Loyal Corporation of Ardwick; Manchester Tennis & Racquets Club; Delamere Forest Golf Club.
Interests: Literature, theatre, music, food and wine, hunting, shooting, fishing, stalking, golf, tennis.
Contact details: Dean's Court Chambers, 24 St John Street, Manchester M3 4DF (tel: 0161 214 6000, fax; 0161 214 6001, email: bromley@deanscourt.co.uk).

BROWN, Donald James, BA (Hons), PGCE

Position: Chief Superintendent, Greater Manchester Police, Bolton Division.
Areas of Influence: Law, Public Sector, Voluntary Sector.
Profile: *b.* July 21st, 1953, Dumfries, Scotland.
Education: Wilbraham Junior School. Manchester; Wythenshawe Technical High School for Boys; Brookway High School; Manchester Polytechnic; Warrington Polytechnic. Career profile: Constable, Manchester and Salford Police (1972); Sergeant, Greater Manchester Police (1980); Inspector (1990); Detective Chief Inspector (1992); Detective Superintendent (2002). Donald Brown has been awarded the Queen's Commendation for Bravery and several Chief Officer Commendations. He has also achieved the Protection of Life from Fire Certificate, Royal Humane Society. Clubs and Societies: Superintendent Association: Committee Member, Manchester Youth Theatre (1976); Ryecroft Sports Club (1990); New Cumnock & District Anglers Association.
Interests: Watersports, wild trout fishing, hiking, reading, theatre, athletics, classic vehicles and vintage tractors, travel, a sense of humour.
Contact details: Greater Manchester Police, K Division, Howell Croft North, Bolton (tel: 0161 872 5050, email: Donald Brown@GMP.ukpolice).

BROWN, Robert Alexander Lindsay, BA DipCAM

Position: Public Relations Director, McCann-Erickson, Manchester.
Areas of Influence: Media, Commerce.
Profile: *b.* December 17th, 1962; *m.* Keri Lewis; 1 son, 2 daughters.

Educated at Manchester Grammar School (1974-81) and University of York (1981-84). Leaving the University with a degree in Economics and Politics, Rob Brown spent a year at Key 103 as broadcast assistant and occasional presenter. Moving into public relations he led the PR team for the launch of Granada Studios Tour attraction in the late eighties. He set up his own media PR business in 1991 with Granada Television, Channel Four and Simply Red's management company as clients. In 1995 he sold the business to Leedex Public Relations and became Managing Director of Leedex, a position held until January 2001, when he joined McCann Erickson as PR Director. He is responsible for National and International PR Programmes for clients such as Durex, Scholl, and Magnet. The agency with over 350 staff is the largest advertising agency outside London. Rob has previously held the post of Chairman, Institute of Public Relations, North West (1995-98), is a member of the Institute of Public Relations and was awarded Best UK Consumer PR Campaign (1990). He is also a visiting Lecturer in Public Relations at Manchester Metropolitan University.

Interests: Long distance walking, body boarding, music.

Contact details: McCann Erickson, Bonis Hall, Prestbury, Cheshire SK10 4EF (tel: 01625 822 200, fax: 01625 820100, email: rob_brown@europe.mccann.com).

BROWNSON, Susan Ann, OBE (1998)

Positions: Chief Executive, Blue Bell BMW Group; Fellow, Institute of the Motor Industry (1994); Main Board Director, Retail Motor Industry Federation (1996); Director, Retail Motor Industry Training (1997); Member, Small Business Council (2002).

Areas of Influence: Education, Finance, Commerce

Profile: June 1st, 1941, Wales; *m.* Christopher; 1 son; 2 daughters.

Educated at Hamden House and London University. Sue Brownson joined Blue Bell (1973) having previously had her own exhibitions company. In 1975 she became Finance Director and Blue Bell Wilmslow took on the BMW Franchise. Blue Bell BMW opened its second site in Crewe in 1989 on a green field site of which she is also Managing Director. In 1989 Sue was made BMW Regional Dealer Council Chairman for 2 years and in 1992 was asked to become a BMW National Dealer Council Chairman. She was made a Liveryman of the Worshipful Company of Coach Makers and Harness Makers (1996) and in 1997 was admitted to the Freedom of the City of London. Also in 1997, she became a member of the Institute of Directors. During 1999 Susan was appointed to the Board of the MITC, the South & East Cheshire Tec and the Institute of the Motor Industry. She was elected President of the National Franchised Dealers Association and became President of Ben, the Motor Trade Charity. In 2000 Mrs Brownson became Chair of RMI Franchised Dealer Division, and during 2001 she became Director of Total People Training in Cheshire.

Interests: Sewing, interior design, cookery, reading.

Contact details: Blue Bell, Manchester Road, Wilmslow, Cheshire SK9 2LE (tel: 01625 529 955, fax: 01625 446 644, email: suebrownson@hotmail.com, web: www.bluebell. co.uk).

BRYANT, Professor Christopher Gordon Alistair, BA, MA (1966), PhD (1974)

Positions: Professor of Sociology, University of Salford (1982 - present); Dean of Faculty of Arts, Media and Social Sciences (1999 – present); Member of Advisory Board, Central European University, Warsaw (1998 – present).
Areas of Influence: Education, Public Sector.
Profile: *b.* April 14th, 1944; *m.* Elizabeth Mary; 2 daughters.
Education: Kingston Grammar School (1955-62); BA 1st class (Hons) Social Sciences, University of Leicester (1965); MA Sociology, University of Leicester (1966); PhD, University of Southampton (1974). Career profile: Lecturer in Sociology, University of Southampton (1966-76); Senior Lecturer in Sociology, University of Salford (1976-82); Member of Executive Committee, British Sociological Association (1987-91); Member of Editorial Board, British Journal of Sociology (1990-00). Publications: *Sociology in Action*, Allen and Unwin (1976); *Positivism in Social Theory and Research*, Macmillan (1985); *What has Sociology Achieved*, co-editor with H Becker, Macmillan (1990); *Giddens Theory of Structuration*, co-editor with D Jary, Routledge (1991); *The New Great Transformation?* co-editor with E Mokrzycki, Routledge (1994); *Practical Sociology*, Polity (1995); *Democracy, Civil Society and Pluralism*, co-editor with E Mokrzycki, IFIS (1996); *Anthony Giddens: critical assessments*, 4 vols, co-editor with D Jary, Routledge (1997); *The Contemporary Giddens*, co-editor D Jary, Palgrave (2001). Christopher Bryant has held visiting research and teaching appointments in Frankfurt, Colombus Ohio, Utrecht, and Warsaw.
Interests: Watching football, 'gym and swim', walking, the arts, fuchsias.
Contact details: Dean's Office, Faculty of Arts, Media, and Social Services, University of Salford, Salford M5 4QT (tel: 0161 295 3366, fax: 0161 295 4128, email; c.g.a.bryant@salford.ac.uk).

BUCKLEY, John Spencer

Positions: Managing Director, The Pda Partnership Ltd; Director, Manchester Chamber of Commerce and Industry; Director, C.B.E; Member, Court of UMIST; Deputy Chairman, The East Manchester Partnership.
Areas of Influence: Commerce.
Profile: *b.* June 28th 1943; *m.* Susan Janet Maslin; 2 daughters.
Education: Heywood Grammar School (1954-1961); Wigan and District Mining and Technical College (1961-1965); Liverpool College of Building (1965-1969). Career profile: Architectural appointments, Eric Levy and Partners; Oldham and Rochdale Borough Councils; The Ardin and Partnership. Projects: The Bae Centre, Colwyn

Bay; White City Retail Park; Merchants House, Chester; 80 stores in North West for Aldi Stores Ltd. Clubs and societies: The St. James's Club; Lancashire County Cricket Club; Bury Football Club; The Manchester Literary and Philosophical Society. **Interests:** Sport, theatre, reading, travel, walking. **Contact details:** The Pda Partnership Ltd., St. Andrews House, 62 Bridge Street, Manchester M33BW (tel. 0161 832 2393; fax. 0161 832 1862, e-mail, pda@clara.co.uk); 12 Rozel Square, St. Johns Gardens, Manchester M34FQ (tel. 0161 839 2393; fax. 0161 833 0992, E-mail, SJbuckley@ukonline.co.uk).

BUCKLEY, Liam Joseph

Position: Managing Partner, Hammond Suddards, Manchester.
Areas of Influence: Law, Commerce.
Profile: *b.* November 1st, 1961; *m.* Corin; 2 sons.
Educated at St. Bedes Grammar School, Bradford (1975-1980) and Manchester University (1980-1983). Career profile: Trained as a solicitor, Last Suddards, Bradford and Leeds (1985-1987); Commercial Property Lawyer, Leeds (1987-1993); Head of Commercial Property Team, Hammond Suddards, Manchester (1993). Articles published in the Legal and Property Press. Clubs and societies: Lancashire County Cricket Club; Northcliffe Golf Club.
Interests: Sport, theatre, art.
Contact details: Hammond Suddards Edge, Trinity Court, 16 John Dalton St, Manchester M60 8HS (tel. 0161 830 5000, fax. 0161 830 5001).

BULLOCK, Alan David

Position: Managing Director, 999 Design.
Areas of Influence: Arts.
Profile: *b.* March 26th, 1961. *m.* Rosalind Cuschieri.
Educated at Eccles Grammar School/ Ellesmere Park High School (1972-77); Eccles Sixth Form College (1977-1979); Salford Tech (1979-80); North Staffordshire Polytechnic, BA (Hons) (1980-83). Career profile: Bowden Dyble Heyes and Partners, Junior Art Director, Bowden (1985-87); Nigel Warren Design, Designer (1987-88); Flying Colours, Senior Designer (1988-91); Studio Bryant (Rotterdam), Senior Designer (1991-93); Protocol, Group Head (1993-96); Protocol (Edinburgh), Design Manager (1996-98); 999 Design, Creative Director (1999); 999 Creative Design, Managing Director (2001-present); Salford Arts Council Award (1982).
Interests: Music, film, travel, restaurants.
Contact details: 999 Design, Eastgate, Castle Street, Castlefield, Manchester M3 4LZ (tel: 0161 828 5900, fax: 0161 828 5901, email: alan@999design.com).

BURGESS, Tim

Position: Director of Training, GMP.
Areas of Influence: Education, Law.
Profile: *b.* January 27th, 1956; m. Michele; 1 son, Mike; 1 daughter, Liz.
Educated at St. Ambrose College, Halebarns; Manchester Metropolitan University, BA (Hons); Warwick Business School, MBA; Career profile: Tozer Gallagher and Partners, Quantity Surveyors (1974-75); Lancashire Constabulary (1975-78); Greater Manchester Police (1978-present); Seconded to Home Office Central Planning and Training Unit (1987-92); First Trust Administrator for Greater Manchester Shrievalty Police Trust (1994-96); Subdivisional Commander, Manchester Airport and Chair of UK Airport, Police Commanders Group (1997-2002); Publications: *Service Breakdown and Service Recovery* in The Police Journal (July 1994); *Disruptive Passengers at Manchester Airport, a Problem Oriented Approach* in The Police Journal, (July 2002). Prizes and awards: Ernst and Young Police Foundation Award, Highly commended 'Service Recovery' (1994). Clubs and societies: National Trust; English Nature.
Interests: Rugby union, Sale Sharks, gardening, English Nature Volunteer.
Contact details: The Greater Manchester Police, Chester House, Boyer Street, Old Trafford, Manchester M16 0RE (tel: 0161 856 0400, fax: 0161 856 1406, email: tim.burgess@gmp.police.uk).

BURKE, John Kenneth

Position: Circuit Judge.
Areas of Influence: Law.
Profile: *b.* August 4th, 1939; *m.* Margaret Anne; 3 daughters.
Educated at Stockport Grammar School. Career profile: Cheshire Regt, UK and Far East (1958-60); 12/13 Parachute Regt T.A (1962-67); Called to the Bar (1965); Recorder of the Crown Court (1980); Queen's Counsel (1985); Bencher, Middle Temple (1992).
Interests: Painting, drawing, gardening, walking, skiing.
Contact details: Manchester Crown Court, Minshull Street, Manchester M3 3FL (tel: 0161 954 7500).

BURNETT, Paul J

Position: Area Director, Manchester South Medium Business Team, Barclays Bank plc.
Areas of Influence: Finance.
Profile: *b.* October 16th, 1954; *m.* Triona; 2 Daughters.
Educated at Ilkley Grammar School Paul Burnett has spent 28 years with Barclays Bank PLC, starting in Yorkshire, in London and then Manchester in 1992. Clubs and societies: Bramhall Lane Tennis Club and Total Fitness Health Club.

Interests: Tennis, rugby league.

Contact details: Barclays Bank PLC, Corporate Banking Centre, PO Box 216, Southmark Building, Barrington Road, Altrincham, Cheshire WA14 1FF (tel: 0161 251 3014, fax: 0161 251 3060).

BURNHAM, Andrew (Andy), MA (Hons)

Positions: MP for Leigh (2001 - present); Member, Health Select Committee (2001 - present); Chair, Supporters Direct, a government scheme to promote supporter and community ownership of football clubs (2002 - present).

Areas of Influence: Health, Education, Sport.

Profile: January 7th, 1970; *m.* Marie France van Heel; 1 son; 1 daughter.

Educated at St Aelred's RC High School, Newton-le-Willows (1981-88) and Fitzwilliam College, Cambridge University (1988-91). Career profile: Researcher for Tessa Jowell MP (1994-97); Parliamentary Officer, NHS Confederation (1997); Advisor to Football Task Force (1997-98); Special Advisor to Rt. Hon Chris Smith (1998-01). Clubs and societies: Lowton Labour Club; Hindley Labour Club; Leigh Catholic Society.

Interests: Everton Football Club.

Contact details: House of Commons, London SW1A 0AA (tel: 0207 219 8250, fax: 0207 219 4381, email: burnhama@parliament.uk); 10 Market St, Leigh WN7 1DS (tel: 01942 682 353, fax: 01942 682 354).

BURNS, Professor Alistair, MBChB, FRCPsych, MD, MPhil, FRCP, DHMSA

Positions: Professor of Old Age Psychiatry, University of Manchester; Consultant Psychiatrist, Manchester Mental Health and Social Care Trust; Non-Executive Director, South Manchester University Hospitals NHS Trust.

Areas of Influence: Health.

Profile: *b.* July 4th, 1958; *m.* Alison; 2 daughters.

Educated at Hutcheson's Boy's Grammar School, Glasgow (1970-75) and University of Glasgow (1975-80). Career profile: Graduated in Medicine (1980); Pre-Registration House Jobs, Glasgow and Dumfries; trained in psychiatry, Maudsley Hospital, London; Foundation Chair in Old Age Psychiatry in Manchester (1992). Alistair Burns has produced 180 publications on mental health problems in older people, particularly Alzheimers Disease including writing and editing 12 books. Clubs and societies: Tytherington Club; Manchester Medical Society.

Interests: Gardening, cars, dogs.

Contact details: Wythenshawe Hospital, Education and Research Centre, Manchester M23 9LT (tel: 0161 291 5887, fax: 0161 291 5882, email: A_BURNS@man.ac.uk).

BURNS, Josephine, BA Hons

Positions: Partner, Burns Owens Partnership; Chair, FOCI; Governor, Royal Northern College of Music
Areas of Influence: Arts, Media, Public Sector.
Profile: *b.* March 27th, 1951; 1 Son.
Education: University of Ulster, BA Hons; University of Manchester, PGCE. Jo Burns has been an independent consultant in the cultural and creative industries sectors since 1991. She has worked extensively in the north west and beyond specialising in strategy development work for local authorities, action based research projects, and the use of culture in regenerative initatives. The rise of the regional agenda is of particular interest and Jo has worked on a range of cultural planning issues with NWDA and the regional cultural consortium for the north west. She has also worked with One North East and on the development of the region's cultural strategy for Culture North East. BOP is now recognised as a leading consultancy in the field of regional and sub-regional cultural planning. Jo regularly chairs events and presents at conferences including to the EU Ministers of Culture during the UK presidency in 1998. She is board member of several voluntary organisations. Consultant, Manchester Evening News Hornarian Award for City of Drama (1994).
Contact details: Burns Owens Partnership, 14 Chequers Road, Manchester M21 9DY (tel/fax: 0161 860 0046, email: jo@bop.co.uk).

BURNS, Stephen Mark, FNAEA (1990), CertREA (1992)

Positions: Managing Director, Burns Corporation Ltd, Stephen Burns & Co, Stephen Burns Mortgages Ltd, Reds Developments Ltd.
Areas of Influence: Media, Law, Property.
Profile: *b.* July 1st, 1966; *m.* Jacqueline; 1 son; 1 daughter.
Education: Secondary School; Fellow of the National Association of Estate Agents; Certificate in Residential Estate Agency. Stephen Burns joined the Armed forces at 16 (1982-87) before becoming a Junior in an Estate Agency (1987) and progressing through the ranks to Area Manager. He left to commence his own business (1996) and now has 3 offices dealing with Real Estate and other property businesses. His company features regularly in local, regional, and national press winning 'Best Independent Estate Agency - National UK Winners' (1997). Member of Hammond Golf Club.
Interests: Golf, motorcycling.
Contact details: 18 Bolton Street, Bury, BL9 0LQ (tel: 0161 763 4141, fax: 0161 763 4140, email: sales@stephenburns.co.uk).

BURSLEM, Alexandra Vivien, OBE (1993), JP (1981), FRSA (1986)

Positions: Vice Chancellor, Manchester Metropolitan University (1997 - present); National Learning and Skills Council (2001-present); General Teaching Council (2000-02); Board member, Chethams School of Music (2000 - present); Board of Universities, UK (1997 - present); Member, Council of Association of Commonwealth Universities (2001-present); Chair, UK Council for Overseas Student Association (2002-present); Director e-University Holdco (2001-present).
Areas of Influence: Education, Public Sector, Media.
Profile: *b.* May 6th, 1940; *m.* R.W. Burslem (*dec.*); 2 sons; 1 daughter.
Education: Arnold High School for Girls, Blackpool (1951-58); Newnham College, Cambridge (1959-60); BA (Hons) class I, Politics and Modern History, Manchester University (1971); Dip BA, Manchester Business School (1986); LLD (Hons) Manchester University (2001). Career profile: Lecturer to Principal Lecturer, Politics, Manchester Polytechnic (1973-82); Head of Department, Applied Communication Studies (1982-86); Dean, Faculty of Communication Studies and Education (1986-88); Academic Director (1988-92); Deputy Vice Chancellor (1992-97); Companion of the Institute of Management (2001); Chair, BBC NW Regional Advisory Council (1983-92); Member, BBC General Advisory Council (1983-92); Member, Manchester Family Practitioner Committee (1974-89); Chair, Medial Services Committee; Member, Anchor Housing Association Board and Chair, Manchester and Cheshire Region (1995-97);Board Member, Eccles College (1995-97); Member, Further Education Funding Council (2000-01). Clubs and societies: Royal Overseas League; Manchester Lit & Phil.
Interests: Opera, theatre, family, reading.
Contact details: Manchester Metropolitan University, All Saints, Manchester M15 6BH (tel: 0161 247 1559, fax: 0161 247 6358, email: a.v.burslem@mmu.ac.uk); Lone Oak, Mereside Road, Mere, Knutsford, Cheshire WA16 5QR.

BURTON, Khumi Tonsing

Positions: General Commissioner of Taxes for Manchester Central and South (1994 - present); Appointed Member, Air Transport Users Council, London (1995 - present); Magistrate, Manchester Bench (1998 - present).
Areas of Influence: Voluntary Sector.
Profile: *b.* September 21st, 1948, Manipur State, India; *m.* Sidney.
Educated at boarding school in North India and then University in Bombay. Career profile: Air Hostess posted in Beirut, Hong Kong, New York, and London, Air India (1969-76); Board of Visitors, Styal Women's Prison (1996-2000); Governor, Lacey Green Primary School, Wilmslow, Cheshire. Khumi Burton speaks English and Hindi as well as understanding Gujerati, Bengali, and Punjabi etc, and is involved with BBC-GMR History Alive exhibitions. Khumi has recently raised over £3400 for

families affected by the earthquake in Gujarat State, India. She has also been involved in local events organising a Street Party in Wilmslow for the Golden Jubilee, and was a Team Attaché for Turks and Caicos Islands during the Commonwealth Games. Clubs and societies: Army and Navy Club, London; Nitework UK North; Soroptimist International of Wilmslow and District; Women of the North Luncheon; Portico Library; Royal Society of St George.

Interests: Meeting people, organising events, having lively dinner parties, travelling, cinema, theatre, I also like challenge!

Contact details: Cliff Cottage, Lacey Green, Wilmslow, Cheshire Sk9 4BA (tel: 01625 548 664, fax: 01625 532 002, email: khumi.burton@virgin.net).

BUTLER, Stella Vera Frances, JP, BSc, PhD, PGCE, AMA

Position: Head of Special Collections, The John Rylands University Library, University of Manchester (2000 - present).

Areas of Influence: Education, Arts.

Profiles: *b.* May 8th, 1956; *m.* Andrew Taylor; 1 son; 1 daughter.

Educated at the University of Manchester and UMIST. Career profile: Keeper of Curatorial Services, Museum of Science and Industry, Manchester (1982-90); Freelance Consultant to Museums and Libraries (1990-00). Publications: *Science and Technology Museums*, Leicester University Press (1992); *Centre and Peripheries, The development of British Physiology 1870-1914*, in Journal of the History of biology (1988) p. 473-500; *The Universal Agent of Power: James Prescott Joule Electricity and the Equivalent of Heat*, in John Stock and Mary Orna (eds), Electrochemistry past and present, American Chemical Society, Washington (1989). Achieved the Gulbenkian prize for best museum children's publication (1995). Clubs and societies: British Society for the History of Science; Cheadle Civic Society; Royal Society of Chemistry Historical Group.

Interests: Family and friends.

Contact details: John Rylands Library, 150 Deansgate, Manchester M3 3EH (tel: 0161 834 5343, fax: 0161 834 5574, email: stella.butler@man.ac.uk); 3 Brooklyn Crescent, Cheadle, Cheshire SK8 1DY.

BUTTERS, Andrew Martin

Position: Chief Executive, Manchester Mental Health Social Care Trust.

Areas of Influence: Health, Public Sector.

Profile: *b.* July 18th, 1954; m. Dorothy Carolyn; 1 son; 1 daughter.

Educated at Sweyne Grammar School; Rayleigh, Essex; Emmanuel College, Cambridge; Touche, Ross and Company, qualified as a chartered accountant. Career profile: Lucas Industries PLC; Balfour Beatty; Seafield Holdings Limited; NHS, Broadgreen Hospital, Liverpool (1993); Manchester Health Authority (1995);

Director, Mental Health Services (1998); Chief Executive, Manchester Mental Health Partnership.
Interests: History, music, squash, swimming.
Contact details: Chorlton House, 70 Manchester Road, Chorlton, Manchester M21 9UN (tel: 0161 882 1057, fax: 0161 882 1101, email: andrew.butters@mhsc.manchester.nhs.uk).

BUTTERWORTH, Arthur Eckersley, MBE (1995), ARCM

Positions: Composer and Conductor (1962 - present).
Areas of Influence: Music.
Profile: *b.* August 4th, 1923; *m.* Diana; 2 daughters.
Educated at North Manchester High School for Boys (1934-39) and Royal Manchester College of Music (1947-49). Career profile: Royal Engineers (1942-47); Orchestral Player, Scottish National Orchestra (1949-55); Hallé Orchestra (1955-62); Music Staff of former West Riding Education Authority (1962-70); Lecturer in Musical Composition, Huddersfield University (1971-80); Conductor, Huddersfield Philharmonic Orchestra (1962-93); Guest Conductor, BBC Regional Orchestras; Music Director, National Youth Brass Band of Great Britain (1975-83). Arthur Butterworth has contributed to many articles in a variety of musical journals and was awarded the Alexander Owen memorial prize in 1939. He was commissioned to compose *Mancunians op. 96* for the Hallé Society to mark the final season in the Free Trade Hall (1995), which was inspired by Adolphe Valette's paintings of Manchester in City Art Gallery. He is a member of the RSPCA.
Interests: Oil and water colour painting, all aspects of care for animals, British archaeology, industrial archaeology, railway history.
Contact details: Pohjola, 11 Dales Avenue, Embsay, Skipton BD23 6PE (tel: 01756 792 968).

BUTTERWORTH, Michael George

Position: Managing Director, The Trafford Centre LTD.
Areas of Influence: Commerce.
Profile: *b.* June 6th, 1953.
Education: Diploma in Valuations and Estate Management. Clubs and societies: Royal Institution of Chartered Surveyors.
Contact details: The Trafford Centre, Manchester M17 8AA.

CADMAN, Major James Rodney, TD, JP, DL, FCIOB

Positions: Company Director, Construction Industry; Justice of the Peace; Deputy Lieutenant of Greater Manchester.
Areas of Influence: Commerce, Voluntary Sector.
Profile: *b.* April 21st 1933; *m.* Birgit; 1 daughter; 1 son.
Educated at Manchester Grammar School (1943-1949) and Manchester College of Technology (1949-1954). Career profile: Apprenticeship Family Business - James Cadman and Sons Ltd (1949-1954); Manchester College of Technology (1949-1954); National Service Royal Engineers (1954-1956); Rejoined family business (1956-1997). Clubs and societies: Member, Army and Navy Club, Pall Mall, London; Rotary Club of Swinton and Pendlebury; Lancashire County Cricket Club; Territorial Army (1956-1970). Prizes and awards: Territorial Decoration (1970).
Contact details: Brambles, 6 Bramley Close, Swinton M27 0DR (tel: 0161 794 3730).

CALTON, Patsy, MP, BSC, PGCE

Positions: Liberal Democrat MP for Cheadle, Northern Ireland Team (2001 - present); School Governor (1984 - present).
Areas of Influence: Public Sector, Health, Education.
Profile: *b.* September 9th, 1948; *m.* Clive; 1 son; 2 daughters; 1 granddaughter.
Education: Wymondham College, Norfolk; BSc Biochemistry, UMIST; PGCE, University of Manchester. Career profile: Teacher of chemistry (1971-79); Full time parent, Night School Teacher, Book Sale supervisor (1979-87); Part time teacher (1987-88); Head of Chemistry, Poynton High School (1989-01); Councillor for West Bramhall Ward, Stockport MBC (1994-2002); Deputy Leader Council (1996-98, 1999-01). Patsy Calton has published various newspaper articles. Clubs and societies:

Stockport Cerebral Palsy Society, Amnesty International, UNA. Member of All Party Groups in Parliament: Secretary, Epilepsy; Vice Chair, British Council; Breast Cancer; Cancer; America; Gender Balance; Cycling; Poverty; Race and Community; Markets; Children and Young People in Care; Regeneration; Scouts; Sewers; Smoking and Health; Warm Homes; Pharmacy; Parliamentary Reform; Non Profit Making Clubs; Maternity; Men's Health; Electoral Reform.
Interests: Gardening, reading, running, 3 London Marathons completed in 1999, 2001 and 2002.
Contact details: House of Commons, London SW1A OAA (tel: 0207 219 8471, fax: 0207 219 1958, email: caltonp@parliament.uk); Hillson House, 3 Gill Bent Road, Cheadle Hulme, Cheadle SK8 7LE (tel: 0161 435 6560, fax: 0161 486 9005).

CAMPBELL, Bill

Positions: Director, Matta; Director/owner, Islington Mill; Founder, Chapel St Open Group.
Areas of Influence: Arts, Design, Property.
Educated at Central St Martins, Bill Campbell has a BA (Hons) in Fashion Design. Career profile: Established Matta (1999); Founded Chapel St Open Group (2000); Formed Islington Mill Development Company(2002). Publication: (Contributor) *The Mancunian Way*, Clinamen Press.
Interests: Art, collection and promotion.
Contact details: Islington Mill, St James St, Manchester M3 5HW (tel: 0161 661 6358, fax: 0161 950 2353, email: bill.campbell@islington.com)

CAMPBELL, Colin JP

Position: Chairman, Stockport Magistrates Court.
Areas of Influence: Law, Public Sector, Education.
Profile: *b.* August 11th 1936; 2 sons.
Educated at Stockport Grammar School (1947-54); University of Manchester (1954-58); Royal Army Educational Corps (1958-1969); Russian Teacher Canon Slade School, Bolton; Ofsted School Inspector (1993-2000). Member of Ryecroft Park Tennis Club.
Interests: Sport, reading, classical music, cinema, theatre.
Contact details: Flat F, Grove House, Station Rd, Heaton Mersey, Stockport, Cheshire SK4 3EY (tel. 0161 442 4950).

CAMPBELL, Darren Andrew

Position: Athlete.
Areas of Influence: Sport, Media.
Profile: *b.* September 12th, 1973; *m.* Clair Jacobs; 1 son.
Educated at Cherry Manor Junior School and Ashton-on-Mersey County High School. Darren Campbell runs for England and Great Britain in the 100m, 200m, and 4x100m relay events and trains with Sale Harriers: European Junior Champs, 100m and 200m (1991); World Junior 2nd, 100m and 200m (1992); World Junior 1st, 4x100m (1992); World Champs 3rd, 4x100m (1997); European Champs 1st, 100m and 4x100m (1998); Commonwealth Games 1st, 4x100m (1998); World Champs 2nd, 4x100m (1999); Olympic Games 2nd, 200m (2000); European Champs 3rd, 100m (2002); European Champs 1st, 4x100m (2002); Commonwealth Games 3rd, 200m (2002); Commonwealth Games 1st, 4x100m (2002).
Interests: Watching Manchester United play, spending my spare time with my son.
Contact details: Nuff Respect, 107 Sherland Road, Twickenham, London (tel: 0208 891 4145, fax: 0208 891 4140, email: nuf_respect@msn.com, web: www.nuff-respect.co.uk).

CARLISLE, Lord Mark of Bucklow, PC (1979), QC (1971), DL, LLB

Positions: Trustee, Campaign for Children with Leukaemia; Chairman, Drugwatch Trust; Chairman, Friends of St Wilfrids Church, Mobberley.
Areas of Influence: Public Sector, Law, Education.
Profile: *b.* July 7th, 1929; Sandra Joyce; 1 daughter.
Educated at Radley College and Manchester University. Public Offices: MP (C) Runcorn (1964-83), Warrington South (1983-87); Minister of State, Home Office (1972-74); Secretary of State for Education (1979-81); Chairman, Parole Review Committee (1988). Career profile: Called to the Bar, Gray's Inn (1953); Bencher (1980); Judge of the Court of Appeal of Jersey & Guernsey. Clubs and societies: Garrick; St James Club, Manchester.
Interests: Golf, travelling.
Contact details: 3 Holt Gardens, Mobberley, Cheshire WA16 7CH (tel: 01565 872275, fax: 01565 872775).

CARTER, B V JP

Position: Chairperson, Rochdale Magistrates Court; Chairperson, Rochdale Connections Trust.
Areas of Influence: Law, Education.
Profile: *b.* April 4th 1946; 2 daughters.
Educated at Rivington and Blackrod Grammar School, College of All Saints, and

London University. Career profile: Teacher, British Gas; Teacher, British Coal; Chairperson, Old Canal Smithy. Member of Ribble Link Trust.
Interests: Boating, travel, language studies, cookery.
Contact details: Old Canal Smithy Ltd, Nanholme Mill, Shaw Wood Road, Todmorden OL14 6DA (tel. 01706 819659, fax. 01706 819071, E-Mail ocsgen@btopenworld.com).

CARTER, Rev Joseph

Positions: Industrial Chaplain, Trafford Park; Area Dean, North Trafford R.C.
Areas of Influence: Voluntary Sector, Social Justice, Faith Groups.
Education: St. Bede's College, Manchester; English College, Lisbon; Ushan College, Durham. Career profile: Assistant Priest, St. Patrick's, Collyhurst; Assistant Priest, St. Alphonsus, Old Trafford; Parish Priest, St. Anthony's, Trafford Park; Chaplain, St. Anthony's Centre for Church and Industry; Regional Chaplain, Young Christian Workers Movement; Chaplain, National Council of Lay Associations (R.C.); Past Chairman, National Council of Priests; Present Chairman Diocesan Council of Priests.
Interests: Walking, theatre, music, golf.
Contact details: St. Anthony's Presbytery, Eleventh Street, Trafford Park, Manchester M17 1JF (tel. 0161 872 0311, fax. 0161 872 2764, email jelge@ukonline.co.uk).

CASE, Professor Richard Maynard, BSc, PhD

Position: Brackenbury Professor of Physiology (1979 - present), Dean (2001 - present), School of Biological Sciences, University of Manchester.
Areas of Influence: Science, Education, Faith Groups.
Profile: *b.* July 23rd, 1943; *m.* Miriam Diane, nee Shaftoe.
Education: BSc Physiology class II div.1, King's College University of Durham; MRC Scholar, PhD, Department of Physiology, University of Newcastle Upon Tyne (1967). Career profile: Lecturer, Senior Lecturer, Reader in Physiology, University of Newcastle (1967-79); Lecturer in Physiology, Aarhus University, Denmark (1970-71); Lecturer in Physiology, Sydney University, Australia (1976-77); Member, Animal Science and Psychology Subcommittee, SERC Biological Science Committee (1981-84); Member, Grants Committee A, MRC Cell Board (1983-87); Member, UGC/UFC Biological Science Subcommittee (1985-89); Member, Biological Sciences and Medicine Panel, UFC Research Assessment Exercises (1986,89,92); Dean of Biological Sciences, University of Manchester (1990-94); Wellcome Trust Research Leave Fellow, University of Manchester (1994-97); Member, Biochemistry and Cell Biology Committee, BBSRC (1994-96). Maynard Case has published many papers and articles within the professional journals, and has received research grants from Cystic Fibrosis Trust, BBSRC, European Commission, Wellcome Trust, and MRC.

60

Interests: Gardening, Italy.
Contact details: G38, Stopford Building, University of Manchester, Oxford Road, Manchester M13 9PT (tel: 0161 275 5406, fax: 0161 275 5600, email: rmcase@man.ac.uk).

CASEY, Ben

Positions: Chairman and Creative Director, The Chase Creative Consultants, Manchester; Professor of Visual Communication, University of Central Lancashire.
Areas of Influence: Arts, Education.
Profile: *b.* October 19th, 1949; *m.* Fiona Candy.
Education: St. Ignatious School, Preston; Blackpool College of Technology and Design (1969). Career profile: Typographer, Horniblow Cox-Freeman, London; Graphic Designer, Berkoff Associates, London; Graphic Designer, Conways, London; Graphic Designer, Gask and Hawley, Manchester; Lecturer in Design, Preston Polytechnic; Head of School of Design, Preston Polytechnic; Co-founder, The School of Communication Arts, London; Director, British Design and Art Directors Association (D&AD); Chairman of D&AD Education Group; Designer, Deepdale Stadium, Preston North End; Graphic Designer, The Faith Zone, Millenium Dome; Graphic Designer, National Football Museum; Corporate Identity Designer, UK's first internet bank. Clubs and societies: Chartered Society of Designers; D&AD.
Interests: Football.
Contact details: 1 North Parade, Parsonage Gardens, Manchester M3 2NH (tel. 0161 832 5575, fax. 0161 832 5576, email ben.casey@thechase.co.uk).

CASH, David Charles

Positions: Director, Architecture, Building Design Partnership; Chairman, BDP North; Chairman, Pro-Manchester (2001-2002).
Areas of Influence: Arts, Commerce.
Profile: *b.* November 20th 1952; *m.* Carys; 1 son; 1 daughter.
Educated at Bristol Grammar School and University of Sheffield. Career profile: Joined BDP (1980), became Director (1989), Chairman (1993); Design projects include: The Lanes Redevelopment Carlisle (1984); Sconbuhl Centre Lucerne (1989); Lancaster Common Garden Centre (1996); Vasco Da Gamma Centre, Lisbon (1999); The Lanes Extension Carlisle (2000); Piccadilly Station Refurbishment (2002); Gloucester Blackfriars (2002). Clubs and Societies: Pro-Manchester; RIBA; ARCUK.
Interests: Running, badminton, theatre, cycling, travel, gardening.
Contact details: Sunlight House, PO Box 85, Quay Street, Manchester M60 3JA (tel: 0161 834 8441, fax: 0161 832 4280, email: dc-cash@bdp.co.uk).

CASKEN, Professor John, FRNCM (1996), BMus, MA, Dmus

Positions: Professor of Music and Head, School of Music and Drama, University of Manchester (1992 - present).
Areas of Influence: Arts, Education.
Educated at University of Birmingham (1967-71) and Academy of Music, Warsaw, Poland (1971-72). Career profile: Lecturer in Music, University of Birmingham (1973-79); Research Fellow in Composition, Huddersfield Polytechnic (1980-81); Lecturer in Music, University of Durham (1981-92). John Casken has produced numerous compositions published by Schott Music Publishers, including works for orchestra, chamber and instrumental works and opera. Prizes and awards: First Britten Award for Composition for Chamber Opera; GOLEM (1990, 1991); Gramophone Award for best contemporary recording; Prix Musicale de Fondation Prince Pierre de Monaco (1993).
Interests: The visual arts, painting, creativity and the imagination, photography, cooking, gardening.
Contact details: Department of Music, University of Manchester (tel: 0161 275 4987, fax: 0161 275 4994, email: John.Casken@man.ac.uk).

CATLOW, Richard

Position: Editor in Chief, Greater Manchester Weekly Newspapers (North).
Areas of Influence: Media, Local History.
Profile: *b.* October 13th, 1949; *m.* Helen; 4 daughters.
Education: Bacup and Rawtenstall Grammar School; Salford University. Career profile: Editor, *Pennine Magazine* (1979-1989); Editor, *Nelson Leader/Colne Times* (1986-1988); Editor, *Burnley Express* (1988-1992); Editor, *West Lancashire Evening Gazette* (Blackpool) (1992-1994); Founder, Richard Catlow Public Relations (1994-1995); Group Editor, Rochdale Observer series (1995-2000). Prizes and awards: United Newspapers Prize For Innovation. Publications: *The Pendle Witches; Over The Setts; Lakeland Looking Glass; Exploring Historic Lancashire; Burnley in Old Picture Postcards; Ribble Valley Rendezvous; A Closer Look at Lakeland; Memory Lane Rochdale; Images of Rochdale.* Clubs and Societies: Kimberley Club; John Muir Trust; Mountain Bothies Association.
Interests: Hill walking, running, orienteering, caving.
Contact details: Rochdale Observer, Drake Street, Rochdale, Lancashire OL16 1PH (tel.01706 35432, fax. 01706 526314, email richard.catlow@gmwn.co.uk).

CATLOW, Ronald Eric, Bed, MA, PhD, DipManEd, FRGS

Positions: Ofsted Team Inspector of Schools; Teacher, Ducie High School, Manchester.
Areas of Influence: Education; Public Sector.
Profile: *b.* June 3rd, 1941.
Education: Greenfield County Secondary School (1952-1956); Ashton College of Further Education (1957-1961); Derby Training College (1961-1964); North East Wales Institute of Higher Education (1973-76); Manchester Polytechnic (1975-1977); University of York (1977-1979); University of Hull (1982-1991). Career profile: Two Trees Secondary School, Denton, Manchester (1964-1979); Breeze Hill School, Oldham (1979-1994); Member of Court, The University of Manchester. Clubs and Societies: Vice-President, The Manchester Literary and Philosophical Society; Royal Geographical Society; National Association of Headteachers; National Union of Teachers; National Association of Educational Inspectors, Advisors and Consultants; General Teaching Council for England and English Heritage.
Interests: Theatre, Hallé, walking in the Peak District, travelling, football.
Contact details: Ducie High School, Lloyd Street North, Manchester M14 4GA (tel. 0161 232 1639, fax. 0161 232 1640, email rca@duciehigh.manchetser.sch.uk); 2 Lychwood, Station Road, Marple, Stockport, Cheshire SK6 6AL (tel. 0161 427 5771, email: ronaldcatlow@talk21.com).

CAWSON, (Peter) Mark, LLB, QC (2001)

Position: Recorder (2000).
Areas of Influence: Law.
Profile: *b.* June 4th, 1959; *m.* Julia Louise; 2 sons; 1 daughter.
Educated at Wrekin College and Liverpool University. Peter Cawson was born and brought up in the North West and has now been practising as a Barrister in Manchester since 1983. His practice covers most areas of Chancery and Commercial work, with emphasis on Commercial Litigation and Professional Negligence work. Clubs and societies: Royal Birkdale Golf Club; Church Society.
Interests: Church affairs, Church Warden of St John's Knutsford, sport - purely a spectator following Sale Sharks, an armchair politician.
Contact details: Exchange Chambers, 4 Ralli Courts, West Riverside, Manchester M3 5FT (tel: 0161 833 2722, fax: 0161 833 2789, email: cawsonqc@exchangechambers.co.uk).

CEBERTOWICZ, Janina Dorota, BA, PGCE

Position: Head of Art and Design, Bury Grammar School (Girls).
Areas of Influence: Arts, Education.

Profile: *b.* April 30th, 1953.
Education: Werneth Convent, Oldham, (1972-75);Loreto College, Manchester; Manchester Polytechnic (1971-1972); Bath Academy of Art; Manchester Polytechnic (1977-1978). Career profile: Resident Artist at the Royal Northern College of Music; Major One Person Shows: Bluecoat Gallery, Liverpool; Bede Gallery, Jarrow; Blackburn Art Gallery; Bury Art Gallery; Ashton Art Gallery; Royal Northern College of Music; Tib Lane Gallery, Manchester; Portico Gallery, Manchester; Mixed Shows: Manchester Academy of Fine Art Annual Open Exhibition; Tib Lane Annual Exhibitions; Lectures and Demonstrations to North West Arts Societies; M.A.F.A. Prizewinner (1981 & 1982); Edward Oldham Trust Bursary (M.A.F.A.) (1997). Clubs and Societies: Manchester Academy of Fine Art; Salford Choral Society; RNCM Friends; Manchester Literary and Philosophical Society; Friends of Whitworth Gallery.
Interests: Art, music, vocal studies, modern greek; gardening, travel and educational visits abroad, web design.
Contact details: Slipper Factory Studio, Union Mill, Bacup Rd, Rawtenstall, Rossendale, Lancashire BB4 7JN (tel. 01706 219211, email: mail@cyberceb-art.com).

CHAMBERLAIN, Dr Leslie Neville, CBE (1990), BSc, MSc, FInstP, CCIM, FinstEn, FRSA,

Positions: Chairman, Urenco Ltd; Chairman, The Manufacturing Institute; Chairman, Envirolink NWP; Chairman, International Nuclear Energy Agency; Board Member, NW Development Agency (2001 - present); Member, Council of Salford University, Board Member, Manchester 2002 Ltd (1999-02); Director, ESCL (1999 - present).
Areas of Influence: Commerce, Education, Public Sector.
Profile: *b.* October, 3rd, 1939; *m.* Joy Rachel; 1 son; 3 daughters.
Educated at King James I Grammar School, Bishop Auckland and King's College, University of Durham. Career profile: Nuclear Industry, including 10 years as Chief Executive of BNFL, retiring as deputy chairman (1999); Chairman, British Energy Association (1998-01); Chairman, TEC National Council (1999-01); Board Member, New East Manchester Ltd (1999-02). Neville Chamberlain has published various international papers on nuclear energy. He was also chairman of the NW Business Leadership Team (1995-99) and Chairman of the North West Partnership, the forerunner of the NW Regional Assembly, of which he was a founding member and first leader of the Economic Activity Group and Assembly Deputy Chairman. Prizes and awards: Melchett Medal, Inst. of Energy (1989); Hon. Fellow, European Nuclear Society; Hon. Fellow, Institute of Nuclear Engineers; Hon. DSc, University of Salford.
Interests: Regional affairs, swimming, fell-walking, light classical music, opera.

Contact details: NW Development Agency, Renaissance House, Centre Park, Warrington; Oaklands, 2 The Paddock, Hinderton Road, Neston, Cheshire (tel: 0151 353 1980, fax: 0151 353 1981, email: nchamberlain@msn.com).

CHAMPION, Sarah

Position: CEO, Chinese Arts Centre.
Areas of Influence: Arts.
Profile: *b.* July 10, 1969.
Educated at Prince William School. Career profile: Freelance Community Artist (1991-95); Arts Manager, Rotherham Arts Centre (1992-94); Arts Development Officer, Ashfield District Council (1994-96); Part-time Lecturer, Huddersfield F.E. College; Course Leader, Counselling Skills.
Interests: Horse riding, animal welfare, gardening.
Contact details: Chinese Arts Centre, 39-43 Edge Street, Manchester M4 1HW (tel: 0161 832 7513, fax: 0161 832 7513, email: info@cac39.freeserve.co.uk).

CHAN, Charles

Positions: Chairman, Federation of the Chinese Associations (Manchester); Chairman, NG Yip (U.K.) Association.
Areas of Influence: Law.
Profile: *b.* November 26th, 1930; *m.* Janet; 2 sons; 3 daughters.
Contact details: 125a Manley Road, Manchester M16 8WE (tel. 0161 881 9713, fax. 0161 881 9929).

CHAPLIN, Graeme Edgar

Position: Deputy Agent, Bank of England North West Agency; Board Member, Young Enterprise North West Educational Charity.
Areas of Influence: Public Sector, Commerce, Finance.
Profile: *b.* December 12th, 1968; 2 Daughters.
Education: The Haberdashers' Aske's School, Elstree (1980-1987); Trinity Hall Cambridge (1987-1990); London School of Economics (1993-1995); University College, London (1995-1996). Career profile: Bank of England (1992-date).
Contact details: Bank of England, North West Agency, PO Box 301, 82 King St, Manchester M60 2HP (tel: 0161 834 6199, fax: 0161 8391131, email: northwest@bankofengland.co.uk)

CHAPMAN, Brian, BA (1974)

Positions: Director, Lime.
Areas of Influence: Arts, Health, Public Sector.
Profile: *b.* September 14th, 1954; *m.* Angela; 1 son; 2 daughters.
Educated at: Riley High School, Hull and Manchester Metropolitan University, Degree in Fine Art. Brian Chapman has been the Director of Lime, formerly Hospital Arts for 28 years. He lists his previous occupations as Artist, Project Manager, Consultant, and Advocate of Arts and Health Work and has had numerous articles published in Arts / Health Journals e.g. *Hospital Development*, vol. 32 (1). Won BBC 'It's my City' Award jointly with sister organisation START.
Interests: Angling, walking, life the universe and everything, my family.
Contact details: LIME, Saint Mary's Hospital, Hathersage Road, Manchester M13 0JH (tel: 0161 256 4389, fax: 0161 256 4390, email: Lime@ic24.net).

CHAUDHRY, Bashir Ahmed, MBE (1998), BSc (1957)

Positions: Interpreter / Translator for various voluntary and statutory bodies; Committee Member of: Age Concern Trafford, Trafford Community Representatives Group; Trafford Ethnic Community Health Forum; Greater Manchester Police Policy Advisory Committee on Racial Issues, Ethnic Minorities Police Consultative Group, Whalley Range High School for Girls, Manley Park Infants & Junior School and Manchester Council for Community Relations.
Areas of Influence: Education, Faith Groups, Voluntary Sector.
Profile: *b.* September 9th, 1937; *m.* Mrs R Chaudhry; 3 sons; 1 daughter.
Education: BSc Textile Chemistry, Blackburn (1957); Diploma in Public Service Interpretation, Manchester (1995). Career profile: Since coming to the UK (1954) Bashir Chaudhry has sought to promote the British Asian community by positive contribution. Training in welfare rights has enabled him to support and develop his own community whilst at the same time building bridges for tolerance, understanding and harmony between all sections of the communities that make up the North West. Bashir's skill as an interpreter, coupled with his passionate concern for effective community relations and caring for the elderly is at the heart of his career. He is extremely active within the community with hospital visiting and taking older people out for shopping. He has also worked with Trafford Borough Council and Family Housing Association providing advice on housing for elderly Asians. Bashir was the first British Pakistani in the North of England to be honoured with an MBE, and lists his greatest achievement as preventing Whalley Range High School for Girls from becoming co-educational (1996). He is a member of the Whalley Range Council of Faiths.
Interests: Current affairs, debating, socialising, travelling, squash, badminton, walking, raising awareness of each other's cultures, customs and religion.

CHAYTOR David Michael,

Positions: Labour MP, Bury North (1997 - present); Member, Education and Employment, Trade and Industry, Environment, Transport and Regions, Labour Party Departmental Committee (1997 - present); Secretary, Warm Homes Group (1998 - present), Adult Education Group (1999 - present), Globe Group UK (2000 - present), All Party Groups; Chair, Further Education Group (1999 - present), Associate Environment Group (2001 - present).
Areas of Influence: Public Sector.
Profile: *b.* August 3rd, 1949, Bury; 1 son; 1 daughter.
Education: East Ward Primary School, Bury; Bury Grammar School; BA (1970), Mphil (1979), London University; PGCE (1976), Leeds University. Career profile: Various lecturing posts (1973-82); Councillor, Calderdale Council (1982-97); Senior Staff Tutor, Manchester College of Adult Education (1983-90); Contested Calder Valley, General Elections (1987, 1992); Head of Department of Continuing Education, Manchester College of Arts and Technology (1990-97); Member, Environmental Audit Select Committee (2000-01). Clubs and societies: Member, T&GWU; Rochdale Labour; All Party Groups. Member, Education and Skills Select Committee (2000-01). David Chaytor's political interests are environment, education, foreign policy, international development, transport, France, Albania, USA and Kazakhstan. He has presented the following Bills to Parliament: Recycled Content of Newsprint Bill; Lifelong Learning, Participation and Entitlement; Schools and Colleges funding formula; Selective Schools, Transitional Arrangements Bill.
Interests: Walking, cycling, restoration of old buildings.
Contact details: House of Commons, London SW1A 0AA (tel: 0207 219 6625, fax: 0207 219 0952, email: chaytord@parliament.uk); Janet Turner, 14a Market Street, Bury BL9 0AJ (tel: 0161 764 2023, fax: 0161 763 2410, email: turnerj@parliament.uk).

CHEETHAM, Andrew

Positions: Creative Director, Cheetham Bell JWT; Regional Chairman and Full Council Member, Institute Practitioners in Advertising.
Areas of Influence: Media, Arts.
Profile: *b.* April 18th 1966; *m.* Barbara; 2 sons.
Educated at St David's College, Llandudno (1978-82) and Wrexham College of Art (1982-86); Career profile: Bowden Byble Hayes (1986-89); Charles Barber Advertising (1989-91); Broadbent Cheetham Veasey (1991-92); Cheetham Bell (1992-01); Cheetham Bell JWT (2001 - present); Has been responsible for various well known TV campaigns including Purple Ronnie for Vimto; has received over 200 local, national, and international industry awards in the last 14 years.
Interests: Sailing, rugby, art.

Contact details: Cheetham Bell JWT, Astley House, Quay Street, Manchester M3 4AS (tel: 0161 832 8884, fax: 0161 832 2198, email: andy.cheethamjwt.com, home tel: 07768 977648).

CHISWICK, Professor Malcolm Leon, MBBS Manchester (1965), MB BS Newcastle (1965), MD Newcastle (1974), FRCP London (1980), FRCPCH (1997)

Positions: Medical Director, Central Manchester and Manchester Children's University Hospitals NHS Trust; Professor of Child Health and Paediatrics, University of Manchester (2002). President, British Association of Perinatal Medicine (2002).
Areas of Influence: Health, Public Sector.
Profile: *b.* July 26th 1940; *m.* Claire. 1 son; 1 daughter.
Education: Preston Manor County Grammar School, Wembley Middlesex (1951-58); School of Medicine, University of Newcastle upon Tyne (1960-65). Career profile: Trained in clinical paediatrics in London, Southampton, and Manchester; Appointed Research Fellow in the Department of Health, University of Manchester (1971) and studied lung development in relation to respiratory distress in the newborn; appointed Consultant Paediatrician to the Neonatal Medical Unit at St Mary's Hospital, Manchester (1975). Publications: Has published extensively on care of the newborn and causes and prevention of disability in childhood; editor and contributor to books on perinatal care and birth asphyxia. Clubs and societies: Neonatal Society, European Association of Science Editors, and Manchester Medico-Legal Society; Patron, Alcohol and Drug Abstinence Service; Medical Committee member, BLISS.
Interests: Coronation Street, collecting old photographs, dead heading roses.
Contact details: Room 217, Cobbett House, Manchester Royal Infirmary, Oxford Road, Manchester M13 9WL (tel: 0161 276 4840, fax: 0161 276 8033, email: m.chiswick@man.ac.uk); Highclere, Parkfield Road, Altrincham, Cheshire WA14 2BT (tel: 0161 928 8579, fax: 0161 929 5564, email: *m.*chiswick@btinternet.com).

CHUI, Peter Chee Keung, MBE (2001), BA (Econ) (Hons), FCA, ATII, MIMgt, FHKSA, MILPA

Positions: Chartered Accountant; JP, Manchester City Bench (1985 - present); Founder and Chairman, Tung Sing Housing Association; Board Member, Northern Counties Housing Association; Founding Member, EU Migrant Forum (1991 - present).
Areas of Influence: Finance, Law, Voluntary Sector.
Profile: *b.* February 8th, 1936; *m.* Rosalie; 2 sons; 1 daughter.
Education: Pui Ching Middle School, Hong Kong; Manchester College of Commerce; Manchester University (1959-62). Career profile: Trustee and Board Member,

Manchester Care; Trustee and Treasurer, Central Manchester Victims Support Scheme; Founder and Chair, Chinese Information Centre; Founder and Chair, Chinese Arch, Manchester; Member, GMR Manchester Advisory Committee; Chairman, Council of Chinese Organisations, NW; Chairman, Manchester Chinatown Neighbourhood Association; Member, Manchester Family Practitioner Committee; Member, Manchester TEC; Judge Panel, CRE Race in the Media awards. Clubs and societies: Manchester Lit & Phil Society; Manchester Luncheon Club.
Interests: Reading, photography.
Contact details: 2 Waterloo Street, Manchester M1 6HY.

CLAVELL-BATE, Michael Frederick

Positions: Partner, Eversheds; Head of Commercial Litigation Team, Eversheds Manchester; President, Manchester Law Society (2001-02).
Areas of Influence: Law, Commerce.
Profile: *b.* March 25th, 1966; *m.* Judith; 2 daughters.
Educated at Newcastle University and Chester College of Law; Trained with Manchester Law Firm Alexander Tatham; qualified as a Solicitor (1990) and became a Partner (1997).
Interests: Spending as much time as possible with my young daughters, A.C. Cobras, most sport.
Contact details: Eversheds, Eversheds House, 70 Great Bridgewater Street, Manchester M1 5ES (tel: 0161 831 8000, fax: 0161 832 5337).

CLAYTON, Judith Margaret

Position: Director of Personnel, UMIST (1992 - present).
Areas of Influence: Education.
Profile: *b.* 9th August, 1952; *m.* Steve.
Educated at Rochdale Grammar School for Girls and Greenhill Senior High (1963-1970), The University of Sussex (1970- 1971) and The Open University (1978-1980). Initally employed as an assistant and subsequently Area Manager for the British Market Research Bureau (1972-1974); Administration Assistant, UMIST (1974-80); Senior Administrative Officer, UMIST (1981-92); Member, Board of Educational Competence Consortium Limited.
Interests: Music, foreign travel, theatre and film.
Contact details: UMIST, Po Box 88, Manchester M60 1QD (tel: 0161 200 4053, fax: 0161 200 2037, email: judith.clayton@umist.ac.uk).

CLEMENT, Roger

Position: Director, Ricket Mitchell & Partners Ltd.
Areas of Influence: Finance, Commerce.
Profile: *b.* October 13th, 1962; *m.* Charlotte; 1 son; 2 daughters.
Education: Trent College, Derbyshire; Bedford College; University of London. Career profile: EXCO Group (1984-1985); Kleinwort Benson (1985-1988). Clubs and Societies: Manchester Tennis and Racquets Club; Savile Club.
Contact details: Rickitt Mitchell & Partners, Clarence House, Clarence Street, Manchester M2 4DW (tel. 0161 455 5252, fax. 0161 834 0452, email roger@rickittmitchell.com).

CLIFFORD, Chris

Positions: Regional Director, CBI North West; Governor, Warrington Collegiate Institute; Chair, Standards & Curriculum Committee; Member, Warrington Arts Trust; Member, North of England Zoological Society Advisory Council; Advisory Board Member, a2e Venture Catalysts.
Areas of Influence: Commerce, Education, Media.
Profile: *b.* November 19th, 1945; *m.* Vera; 2 sons; 2 daughters.
Education: Loughborough University of Technology (1964-68), B.Tech (Hons), Chemical Engineering. Spent 18 years in the manufacturing sector covering production, production planning, sales and marketing. Joined CBI in East Midlands in 1986 before moving to North West in 1993 as Regional Director.
Interests: Sport, cooking, DIY, gardening.
Contact details: CBI North West, Emerson House, Albert Street, Eccles, Manchester 30 0BG (tel: 0161 707 2190, fax: 0161 787 7571, email: chris.clifford@cbi.org.uk).

COCKSHAW, Sir Alan, Kt (1992), Hon DEng (1997), Hon DSc (1998)
BSc, FREng, FICE, FIHT.

Positions: Chairman, The Roxboro Group PLC, Capitaland UK Holdings Ltd, British Airways Regional Ltd; Director, Capitaland Ltd, Singapore; Chairman, Manchester Millennium Ltd (1996 - present); Chairman, PCS International; Chairman, New East Manchester Ltd (2000 - present)
Areas of Influence: Built Environment, Commerce.
Profile: *b.* July 14th, 1937; *m.* Brenda; 1 son; 3 daughters.
Educated at Farnworth Grammar School and Leeds University. Career profile: Sir Alan's early career spanned engineering design and construction in both public and private sectors before joining Fairclough Civil Engineering in 1973. He was appointed Chief Executive in 1978 and Board Member of Fairclough Construction Group in 1981, becoming Group Chief Executive of AMEC plc in 1984 and Chairman

in 1988 until retirement in 1997. He became President of the Institution of Civil Engineers (1997-98) and maintained a strong interest in regeneration. Sir Alan was appointed by UK Government Chairman of English Partnerships (1998-01), its national regeneration agency, and the Commission for New Towns, which were merged in early 1999. He is a Life-president of the North West Business Leadership Team, and has been both Member of the British Overseas Trade Board (1992-95) and Chairman of the Overseas Projects Board (1992-95).

Interests: Cricket, walking, rugby (both codes)

Contact details: PCS International Ltd, 1st Floor, 81 Fountain Street, Manchester M2 2EE (tel: 0161 228 0558, fax: 0161 228 1520).

COGLEY, Stephen William

Position: Barrister.
Areas of Influence: Law.
Profile: *b*. April 13th, 1961; *m*. Sally Jane; 2 sons; 2 daughters.
Education: Spalding Grammar School; Ripon Grammar School; Newcastle University; Inns of Court School of Law. Stephen is a member of the Manchester Tennis and Racquets Club.
Interests: Climbing, shooting, stalking.
Contact details: Merchant Chambers, 1 North Parade, Parsonage Gardens, Manchester M3 2NH (tel: 0161 839 7070, fax: 0161 839 7111, email: joe@merchantcharter.com).

COLLIER, Professor Christopher George

Positions: Dean, Faculty of Science, Engineering, and Enviroment; Professor, Enviromental Remote Sensing; Vice President, Royal Meteorological Society (2000-02).
Areas of Influence: Public Sector, Commerce, Education.
Profile: *b*. September 10th, 1946; *m*. Cynthia; 2 sons.
Educated at Hyde Grammar School for Boys, and Imperial College, University of London, BSc (Hons) Physics; University of Salford, PhD Hydrometeorology. Career profile: Assistant Director, Meteorological Office, Bracknell (1968-95); Met. Office Radar Research Laboratory, Royal Signals and Radar Establishment, Malvern (1976-84); Chairman of the European Union, COST-73 Project, International Weather Radar Networking (1986-91); Director, Talford Research Institute, University of Salford (1996-98); Dean of Faculty, University of Salford (1999 - present). Publications include: over 100 Science Papers and Reports; *Applications of Weather Radar Systems*, John Wiley & Sons, Wiley-Praxis, Chichester (1996). Awards include: Royal Meteorological Society Hugh Roberts Mill Medal and Prize (1982); L.G Groves Memorial Prize for Meteorology, Met Office (1984); World Meteorological

Organization Vaisala Award (1986). Member of: Royal Meteorological Society, American Meteorological Society, British Hydrological Society, Chartered Institute of Water and Enviromental Managers
Interests: Swimming, gardening, reading, Church of England.
Contact details: University of Salford, Peel Building, Salford, Greater Manchester M5 4WT (tel: 0161 295 5465 fax: 0161 295 4382 email: c.g.collier@Salford.ac.uk).

COLLINS, Nicholas Frank

Position: Managing Director, ALSTOM T&D Ltd, Distribution Switchgear.
Areas of Influence: Commerce.
Profile: *b.* July 26th, 1949.
Educated at Leicester Polytechnic. Career profile: Started at ALSTOM in 1973. Member of The Manchester Literary and Philosophical Society.
Interests: Walking.
Contact details: ALSTOM T&D Ltd Distribution Switchgear, Edge Lane, Higher Openshaw, Manchester 11 1FL (tel: 01613712200, email: nick.collins@tde.alstom.com).

COLLINSON, Leonard, DL (2002), FCIPD, FCMC, CCMI, FRSA

Positions: Deputy Lieutenant, County of Merseyside (2002); Chair, Central Plastics; Chair, Industry North West; Chair, The Campaign Company; Director, Collinson Grant Group; Director, Universities Superannuation Scheme; Chair, The Forum of Private Business; Chair, Small Business Research Trust; Member, CBI's North West Regional Council; Trustee, People's History Museum; Trustee, Mission in the Economy; Director, Salford Foundation; Member of Court, University of Manchester; Chair, Assembly of Economic Partners.
Areas of Influence: Commerce, Finance, Media.
Profile: *b.* March 30th, 1934; *m.* Shirley Grace; 2 sons.
Educated at Humberstone Foundation School Cleethorpes, Co-operative College; Founded Collinson Grant, Management Consultants (1971); National Provincial Bank; Education Officer, Trades Union Congress; Personnel Officer, Bristol Co-operative Society; Deputy National Manager, Baking Group of Co-operative Wholesale Society; Director of Manpower, Plessey Telecommunications and Office Systems (1965); Publications: with CM Hodkinson *Employment Law Keynotes'*(1985), *The Line Managers Employment Law* (1975, 16 editions); Awarded the 25th Anniversary Cup (1992), and the Award for Meritorious Service, Chartered Institute of Personnel and Development (1995); Member of the Royal Automobile Club, The Portico Library, and Devonshire House Management Club.
Interests: Wales, collecting picture postcards, Liverpool Football Club.
Contact details: Colgran House, 20 Worsley Road, Swinton, Manchester M27 5WW (tel: 0161 793 9028, fax: 0161 794 0012, email: lcollinson@collinsongrant.com).

CONDON, Allyn

Profile: Athlete.
Areas of Influence: Sport.
Profile: *b.* August 24th, 1974.
Career profile: 2 Gold medals, European Junior Champs (1993); Gold, World Junior Champs 4x100m relay (1992); Bronze, European Indoors 200m (1998); Gold, European Cup, European Championships and World Cup 4x100m (1998); Silver, World Champs 4x100m (1999); AAA Indoor Champion 400m (1999); Bronze, World Indoor 4x400m (1999); Sydney Olympics 4x100 Team (2000); AAA Indoor Champ 200m (2001); Gold, Commonwealth Games 4x100m, Manchester (2002). Allyn Condon is ranked 4th on UK all time list, 200m indoors and 5th in World indoor 200m.

CONN, Edith, OBE (2000), JP, DL, BA (Hons)

Positions: President, Greater Manchester Red Cross; Deputy Lieutenant, Greater Manchester (2001 - present); JP Bolton Bench (1995 - present); National Humanity Award Chairman (1995 - present); Manchester Gala Ball Organiser (1990 - present).
Areas of Influence: Voluntary Sector.
Profile: *b.* October 7th, 1948; *m.* Stephen Leonard (1970); 1 son; 1 daughter.
Education: BA (Hons) Humanities, Manchester Metropolitan University (1987-91). Career profile: Fundraiser, British Red Cross (1978 - present); Treasurer (1983), NSPCC (1979-85); Chairman (1988-00), Bolton Day Care Centre Project (1984-00); CAB Counsellor (1983-85); Branch Member (1988), Branch Trustee (1988), Vice President (1988); Member Finance Committee (1988-89), Member, Awards Panel (1989), Chairman of Awards Panel (1967 - present), Deputy President (1990), Hon, Chief Executive (1991), Northern Regional Council Member (1994 - present), British Red Cross; Member and Visitor, Greater Manchester and Macclesfield War Pensions (1991-00); Chairman, Greater Manchester International Festival of Expression (1991-92); Landmines Appeal North West Chairman (1995); Chairman, Heart Research, Greater Manchester (1998-00); Director, British Red Cross Events Ltd (2000); International Red Cross Gala Committee (2000). Prizes and awards: Badge of Honour for Devoted Service and Honorary Life Membership (1989); Badge of Honour for Distinguished Service (1993). Clubs and societies: Magistrates Association; The Arts Guild; Markland Hill Lawn Tennis Club.
Interests: Art, music, football, tennis, travel, good food and wine.
Contact details: 17 Oakley Park, Heaton, Bolton BL1 5XL (tel / fax: 01204 846 248, email: eydieconn@hotmail.com).

CONNOR, Bill

Positions: General Secretary, USDAW (1997 - present); Member, Government Partnership Fund Assessment Panel; Member, Central Arbitration Committee; Member, General Council and Executive Committee, TUC (1997 - present).
Areas of Influence: Commerce, Industrial Relations.
Profile: *b.* May 21st, 1941; *m.* Carol; 1 son; 1 daughter.
Educated at Secondary Modern School. Career profile: Production Planner, Alcan Aluminium (1965-68); Production Planner, Pharmaceutical (1968-71); Area Organiser (1971-78), National Officer (1978-89), Deputy General and Secretary (1989-97), USDAW; Member, Labour Party NEC (1990-97).
Interests: Reading, computers, psychology, hypnotherapy, psychotherapy.
Contact details: 188 Wilmslow Road, Fallowfield, Manchester M14 6LJ (tel: 0161 249 2401, fax: 0161 257 2566, email: bill.connor@usdaw.org.uk).

CONRAD, Alan David QC (1999), BA (Hons) (Oxon)

Positions: Barrister; Recorder (1997 - present).
Areas of Influence: Law
Profile: *b.* December 10th, 1953; 1 son; 1 daughter.
Educated at Bury Grammar School and Brasenose College, Oxford. Career profile: Called to the Bar (1976); Assistant Recorder (1993).
Interests: Travel, food and drink, classic cars, cricket.
Contact details: Lincoln House Chambers, Brazenose Street, Manchester M2 5EL (tel: 0161 832 5201, fax: 0161 832 0839, email: info@lincolnhouse.co.uk).

COOK, Ben

Positions: Artist; Research Fellow and Lecturer in Fine Art, M.I.R.I.A.D, Manchester Metropolitan University.
Areas of Influence: Arts, Education.
Profile: *b.* June 15th, 1967; *m.* Julie Attwell-Cook; 1 son.
Education: Queen Elizabeth Grammar School Wakefield; Sunderland Polytechnic, BA (Hons) Fine Art (Painting); Manchester Metropolitan University, PGCE Art & Design, MA Fine Art. Group Exhibitions: EAST, Norwich Gallery, Norfolk (1993); John Moores Exhibition 18, Liverpool (1993); 'In Transit', New York City (1998); 'New Contemporaries', Liverpool Bieniale/ London (1999). Solo Exhibitions: The Castlefield Gallery, Manchester (1994); The Dean Clough Galleries, Halifax (1995); The Whitworth Art Gallery, Manchester, (2000); The Mappin Art Gallery, Sheffield (2000); West Park Museum, Macclesfied (2001); The Lowry, Salford (2002); Publications: *Ben Cook Found Paintings*, Trice Publications (1999). Prizes and awards: The Ernest Cassel Educational Trust Award (R.O.S.L) (1993); Pebeo International Art

Competition, Marseilles (1998); Arts Council of England National Touring Exhibition Award (2001). Member of: Manchester Artists Studio Association; Manchester Independents.
Interests: Extreme Sports.
Contact details: Ben Cook Found Paintings, M.A.S.A. Ferguson House, 11 Blackfriars Road, Salford, Manchester M3 7AG (tel: 07973 337 357, email: bencookfoundpaintings@hotmail.com).

COOKE, Darryl John, LLB, LLM

Positions: Member of Board, Addleshaw Booth; Head of Private Equity, Addleshaw Booth; Director, Bex Ltd.
Areas of Influence: Law, Commerce.
Profile: *m.* Pamela; 2 sons.
Educated at Hulme Grammar School, Oldham, Leeds University and Inns of Court School of Law. Career profile: Practising Barrister, 11 Old Square, London; Hoechst UK; DLA; SJ Berwin. Publications: *Management buy-outs, Venture capital: Law and practice, Due diligence: a practical guide,* Sweet & Maxwell. Clubs and societies: Tytherington Golf Club; Prestbury Tennis Club; IOD; TEC.
Interests: Golf, tennis, running, football, arts, reading.
Contact details: Addleshaw Booth, 100 Barbirolli Square, Manchester M2 3AB (tel: 0161 934 6416, fax: 0161 934 6060, email: darryl.cooke@addleshawbooth.com).

COOMBS, Professor Roderick Wilson, BSc, MSc, PhD

Positions: Professor of Technology Management, Manchester School of Management, UMIST; Pro-Vice Chancellor, External Relations, UMIST; Chairman, Wilmslow Running Club.
Areas of Influence: Education, Commerce, Government Science Policy.
Profile: *b.* October 16th, 1950; *m.* Professor Karen Luker; 2 daughters.
Education: BSc Physics, Kent (1969-72); MSc Science and Technology Policy, Manchester (1975); PhD, Economics of Innovation, Manchester (1982). Roderick Coombs spent a short period as a natural scientist in Oxford before converting into a social scientist via a Manchester PhD. Since then his career has been spent researching, teaching, and consulting on the development and application of technology by large companies. He is advisor and consultant to several large plcs and to Government, and has written more than 10 books and more than 60 other articles and publications in academic journals.
Interests: Running, music.
Contact details: Manchester School of Management, UMIST, Manchester M60 1QD (tel: 0161 200 3435, fax: 0161 200 8787, email: rod.coombs@umist.ac.uk); 8 Grange Park Avenue, Wilmslow, Cheshire SK9 4AH (tel: 01625 522 763, fax: 01625 549 497).

COOPER, Professor Cary Lynn, CBE (2001), Hon MSc (1979), Hon DLitt (1998), Hon DBus (1999), CIMgt (1997), FRSA, FBPsS, FRSM, FRSH, FBAM, Hon DSc (2002)

Positions: Professor of Organisational Psychology (1979 - present), Pro-Vice Chancellor (1995 - present) UMIST; Professor of Organizational Psychology, UMIST (1980 – present); Member, Board of Trustees, American Institute of Stress (1984 - present); President, British Academy of Management (1999 – present); President, Institute of Welfare Officers (1999 – present); Vice-President, Br. Association of Counselling (2000 - present); Ambassador, The Samaritans (2000 - present); Academician, Acad. Soc. for Social Science (2000).
Areas of Influence: Education.
Profile: *b.* April 28th, 1940; *m.* (Edna) June Taylor (1970, *dis.* 1984); 1 son, Hamish Scott (1972); 1 daughter, Natasha Beth (1974); *m.* Rachel Faith Davies (1984); 2 daughters, Laura Anne (1982) and Sarah Kate (1985).
Education: Fairfax School, Los Angeles; BS, MBS, University of California; PhD, University of Leeds. Career profile: Lecturer in Psychology, University of Southampton (1967-73); Professor of Management Education Methods, UMIST (1975-79); Pro-Vice and Deputy Vice Chamcellor, UMIST (1995-02); Temp. Advisor, WHO and ILO (1982-84), Home Office (1982-84); Pres. Br. Academy of Management (1986-90, 1990 - present); Treas. Int. Federation of Scholarly Association of Management (1990-92); Editor, Journal of Organisational Behaviour (1980-98), co-editor, Stress Medicine (1992 - present). Over 100 books and 200 scholarly publications.
Interests: Raising children, trying to learn the piano, swimming, watching in anticipation Manchester City FC, following politics.
Contact details: 25 Lostock Hall Road, Poynton, Cheshire (01625 871 450); Manchester School of Management, UMIST, PO Box 88, Manchester M60 1QD (tel: 0161 200 3440, fax: 0161 200 3518, email: cary.cooper@umist.ac.uk).

COX, Edward Rawson

Positions: Research and Liaison Officer Community Pride Initiative, Member of the Neighbourhood Renewal Unit Community Forum (2002); Governor, Northern College, Manchester; Director, Community Technical Aid Centre; Chair, Greater Manchester Jubilee 2000 Network (1997-00).
Areas of Influence: Voluntary Sector, Faith Groups.
Profile: *b.* September 22nd, 1969; *m.* Ruth; 1 son; 1 daughter.
Educated at King Edwards School, Birmingham (1981-88) School Captain (1987-88); JCR President, Mansfield College, Oxford (1989-92); Partnership for Theological Education, Manchester (1995-99); Periods of time in South Africa, Jamaica and India involved in church-based Community Development work; Minister of Religion in the United Reformed Church, Ordained (2000); Research and Liaison Officer,

Community Pride Initiative (1999 - present). Publications: Contributed to various prayer anthologies; Contributed to *Faithworks – Vol III.*
Contact details: 491 Mill Street, Openshaw, Manchester M11 2AD (tel: 0161 231 4111, fax: 0161 231 4555, email: edcox@communitypride.org.uk).

COX, Sophie

Positions: Judo Coach and Competitor.
Areas of Influence: Sport, Coaching.
Profile: *b.* December 23rd, 1981.
Education: St Mary's RC Primary School, Littleborough; Crossley Heath Grammar School, Halifax; Leeds University; National Judo Academy, University of Buckingham and Chilterns. Sophie was the first female to play rugby league at Wembley (1993) and since the age of 12 she has represented Great Britain in Judo at Cadet, Junior and now Senior levels. Winning over 30 medals, she has been under 20 champion twice, national age-banded Champion twice, 5th in Junior Worlds, Bronze in Junior European, Silver in World Schools and Team Silver, World Student Games (2001). She is now a British Judo Association 1st Dan, reigning Senior GB Champion at under 57k, Gold medal winner at the Austrian Open (2002) and England Judo Team member for the Commonwealth Games competing in the Under 57k Group. Sophie has written many articles on Judo and her own career and has been a member of the Women's Sports Foundation since the age of 11. Sophie has trained at Bacup Judo Club since the age of 8. Still an outstanding rugby player, she captained Leeds University Women's RFL to the National Students Sevens Title in 2001. Sophie has given numerous talks and demonstrations to various organisations and made the speech of Welcome when the Jubilee Baton entered Rochdale. Prizes and awards: three times N W Junior Player of the Year; N W Senior Player of the Year (2001); Halifax Plc / Crossley Heath Sports Achievement Award; Runner up, Iceland Champion's Children Award; Winner, Team and Individual, WSF / Tampax awards.
Interests: Cinema, reading, music, plays piano and clarinet.
Contact details: National Judo Academy, Bispham Abbey, nr. Marlowe, Bucks SL7 1RT; 40 Halifax Road, Littleborough OL15 0HB (tel: 01706 378 361).

CRAIG, Ian Alexander, BA (1982)

Positions: Solicitor of the Supreme Court; Senior Partner, Halliwell Landau; Secretary, British Ski & Snowboard Federation.
Areas of Influence: Law, Sport, Finance.
Profile: *b.* September, 28th, 1957; *m.* Sally; 3 sons.
Educated at Wellfield High School, Leyland, Sheffield University (1979-82) and College of Law, London (1983). Career profile: Partner (1990), Senior Partner (1999), Halliwell Landau (1986 - present); Non-Executive Director of several public and

private companies. Clubs and societies: RSC Club, Lancashire County Cricket Club.
Interests: Sport.
Contact details: St James's Court, Brown Street, Manchester, M2 2JF (tel: 0161 831 2691, fax: 0161 831 2641, email: lacraig@halliwells.co.uk); The Quinta, Beechfield Road, Alderley Edge, Cheshire SK9 7AU (tel: 01625 585 241, fax: 01625 585 351).

CRAIG, Susan

Position: Chairman of The Bench, Trafford Metropolitan Magistrates' Court; Justice of The Peace.
Areas of Influence: Law, Public Sector, Voluntary Sector.
Profile: *b.* May 7th, 1948; *m.* Mike; 1 son; 2 daughters.
Educated at Secretarial College; secretary till the age of 20, worked in sales and marketing till age 24, then as a Stewardess with BOAC, "to see the world before I married!". From a working class family, Susan left school at the age of 16 despite wanting to continue in education. She became a single parent with 3 young children before meeting her present husband. Susan has been employed for the last 10 years as a secretary to her husband, a retired BBC producer, comedy scriptwriter and broadcaster at GMR who now lectures about comedy on cruise ships all over the world. Clubs and societies: Grand Order of Lady Ratlings.
Interests: Travel, interior design, art, communicating with people from all walks of life, nationalities and backgrounds.
Contact details: 29 Park Road, Timperley, Altrincham, Cheshire WA14 5AS (tel: 0161 962 9555, fax: 0161 969 6789, email: craigsusan29@hotmail.com).

CREED, Professor Francis, MA, MD, FRCP, FRCPsych, FMedSci

Positions: Professor of Psychological Medicine, University of Manchester (1997 - present); Honorary Consultant Psychiatrist, Manchester Royal Infirmary (1981 - present).
Areas of Influence: Health, Public Sector.
Profile: *b.* February 22nd, 1947.
Educated at Kingswood School, Cambridge University, and St Thomas' Hospital, London. Career profile: Mental Health Leverhulme Research Fellow, London (1978-80). Professor of Community Psychiatry, University of Manchester (1992-97); Research Dean, Faculty of Medicine, Dentistry, Nursing and Pharmacy, University of Manchester (1997-2001); Professor Francis Creed has conducted research into links between stress, depression and bodily symptoms, in addition to stress in ethnic minority populations.
Contact details: Rawnsley Building, Manchester Royal Infirmary, Oxford Road, Manchester M13 9WL (tel: 0161 276 5331, fax: 0161 273 2135, email: francis.creed@man.ac.uk).

78

CREWDSON, James, BSc, CENG

Position: Principal, Wigan & Leigh College
Areas of Influence: Education.
Profile: *b.* May 5th, 1949; *m.* Brenda; 1 daughter.
Educated at Cardinal Allen Secondary Modern, Fleetwood, Blackpool, Fylde College and Lancashire Polytechnic. Career profile: Apprentice toolmaker, General Motors / Ford; Programmer, General Motors / Ford; Lecturer, Blackpool and Fylde College; Principal Lecturer, Blackburn College; Dean of Faculty, Blackburn College; Vice Principal, South Kent College; Principal, South Kent College.
Interests: Reading, walking, travel.
Contact details: Wigan & Leigh College, 53 Parsons Walk, Wigan WN1 1RS (tel: 01942 761801, email: j.crewdson@wigan-leigh.ac.uk).

CUMBES, Jim

Position: Chief Executive, Lancashire County Cricket Club (1997 - present).
Areas of Influence: Sport, Media.
Profile: *b.* May 4th, 1944; *m.* Elizabeth Anne; 1 son; 1 daughter.
Educated at Didsbury C/E Junior School and Didsbury Technical High School. Professional Cricketer: Lancashire (1962-67); Surrey (1968-71); Worcestershire (1972-81); Warwickshire (1982). Professional Footballer: Tranmere Rovers (1964-68); West Bromwich Albion (1968-70); Aston Villa (1970-76); Portland Timbers (1976). Salesman, Martin Price Bolts & Nuts (1977-82); Commercial Manager, Warwickshire County Cricket Club (1982-87); Sales & Marketing Manager, Lancashire County Cricket Club (1987-97). Awards: Benson & Hedges Losing Finalist, Worcestershire (1973); County Championship Medal, Worcestershire (1974); League Cup Winners Medal, Aston Villa 1 - Norwich 0
(1975). Member of Lancashire County Cricket Club, MCC, and the Institute of Directors. Jim Cumbes is the only person to win a County Championship Medal and a League Cup Final Medal for 2 different sports in a 12 month period.
Interests: Sport, reading, gardening, family, moderate DIY!!, keeping fit.
Contact details: Lancashire County Cricket Club, Old Trafford, Manchester M16 0PX (tel: 0161 282 4011, fax: 0161 282 4151).

CURT, John Reginald Newstead OBE (1990), RD (1977), DL, RNR (RTD), BAR to RD (1987), MBChM, FRCS, FRCSE

Position: Deputy Lieutenant, Greater Manchester.
Areas of Influence: Health, Voluntary Sector.
Profile: *b.* June 29th, 1932; *m.* Margaret; 2 sons; 1 daughter.
Education: Spring Grove Grammar School, Isleworth, Middlesex (1945-47); Haris

Academy, Dundee (1947-51); St Andrew University (1951-57). Career profile: Surgeon Lieutenant (1958-61), Royal Naval Reserve (1965-92), Surgeon Commander, Royal Navy; Surgical Training, Dundee Royal Infirmary (1961-73); Research Fellow, University of Florida (1968-69); Consultant Surgeon, Salford Royal Hospital and Hope Hospital, Salford. Publication: *The Enigma of Gastric Antrum*, ChM Thesis. Clubs and societies: Chairman, Manchester Navel Officers Association; Chairman, Broughton House, Home for Disabled ex-Serviceman; President T S Ilex - Seacadets and Salford Old Souls, Manchester Medical Society.
Interests: Rugby and cricket as a spectator, photography.
Contact details: Moss Cottage, 1 Kenilworth Road, Sale, Cheshire M33 5DU (tel: 0161 973 9313).

CURTIN, Liam

Positions: Director, The Art Department; Director, The Department Store.
Areas of Influence: Arts.
Profile: *b.* June 8th, 1951; 2 daughters.
Career profile: Teacher, Ceramics (1970-74); Potter, (1974-80); Teacher, Ceramics (1980-84); Making Ceramics (1984-02); Manchester Renaissance Award, Civic Society (2002).
Interests: Piano playing.
Contact details: The Art Department, 46 Edge St., Manchester M4 1HN (tel:0161 835 3345, fax: as above, email: liam@the-art-dept.co.uk).

Da-COCODIA, Louisa Adassa BEM (1992), JP (1990), MA (hc) (1992), DL (1999), RGN, SCM, QN, NDN, H/Vcerts

Positions: Project Consultant; Assessor, County Court UK, Advisory Committee of the Duchy of Lancaster.
Areas of Influence: Health, Voluntary Sector.
Profile: November, 9th, 1934; *m.* Edward (*dec.*); 1 son, Richard; 1 daughter, Sarah.
Education: Attained School Certificate STD, Jamaica, West Indies. Louisa Da-Cocodia has 26 years of Nursing experience in the NHS, has held a range of Senior Nursing Management posts and has been involved in the training and practical instruction of trainees and Degree Nursing Students. Career profile: District Nurse, Midwife, Health Visitor, Berkshire County Council (1960-66); Asst. Super, District Nurses, Manchester Corporation (1967-71); Nursing Officer, Health Visitor and Fieldwork Instructor, Cheshire County Council (1971-75); Nursing Officer, Acting Senior Director of Acute Services, Tameside Area Health Authority (1975-88); Counsellor / Advisor (Haemoglobinopathics), Sickle Cell & Thalassaemia Central Manchester Health Authority (1990-91); Associate Consultant, Training Dept., Regional Health Authority, North West (1991); Project Consultant / Advisor, Government Moss Side & Hulme Task Force, DOE (1991-95). Prizes and awards: National Anti-racist Award, Manchester, for promoting good race relations. Louisa is a Member of the Court, Manchester University, a Board member for MMU and the Corporation of the City College Manchester and serves on the Executive Board for Christian Aid. She also holds a number of Directorships and Committee positions in Voluntary Sector organisations including Cariocca Enterprises Manchester Lt, Arawak Walton Housing Assoc., and Moss Side & Hulme Women's Action Forum.

Interests: Music, dancing, reading, voluntary community activities.
Contact details: 9 Arliss Avenue, Levenshulme, Manchester M19 2PD (tel: 0161 224 0209).

DALE, Nigel Andrew, LLB (1983)

Positions: Partner and Head of Banking, Eversheds Solicitors
Areas of Influence: Law
Profile: *b.* August 16th, 1962; *m.* Gillian; 2 sons.
Educated at Nottingham University and College of Law, Chester. Career profile: Admitted as a Solicitor (1986); Solicitor, Eversheds Heyworth & Chadwick (1986); Solicitor, Hammond Suddards (1990); Partner, Hammond Suddards (1993); Partner, Eversheds (1996).
Contact details: Eversheds House, 70 Great Bridgwater Street, Manchester M1 5ES (tel: 0161 831 8000, email: nigeldale@eversheds.com).

DARROCH, Lieutenant Colonel Peter Lyle Keith, DL (2001)

Positions: Chairman, Greater Manchester Army Benevolent Fund Committee; President, Tameside (1st UK) Branch, 8th Army Veterans Association; Trustee and Secretary, Broughton House Home for Ex-Service Personnel; Council Member, Order of St John in Greater Manchester.
Areas of Influence: Ex-Service Community, Voluntary Sector, Health.
Profile: *b.* June 27th, 1937; *m.* Anita Florence; 1 son.
Educated at Gordon's School, Woking, Army Apprentices College, Chepstow and Royal Army Medical College, London. Career profile: Enlisted RAMC (1952); Service in Kenya (1959-62), Malaya (1966), Hong Kong (1966-68), Germany (1971, 1977-80), Australia (1982-84), USA (1988), Commissioned (1972), Retired (1991); British Defence Liaison Staff, Australia (1982-84); Staff Officer Grade 1, Surgeon Generals Dept. MOD (1984-85); Technical Training Officer RAMC (1985-89); Commander Medical HQ Eastern District (1989-91); Army Careers Service (1997-02); Regional Welfare Officer, Ex Service Mental Welfare Society (1997-02); Army Careers Officer, Grade 1 (1991-97). Peter Darroch has published a History of the Royal Chapel, Royal Victoria Hospital, Netley, and a report on all Army medical training for non-RAMC personnel in the British Army. Clubs and societies: Conseil, Commanderie de Bordeaux, Manchester; Chevalier of 3 French Wine Orders; 1820 Club; RAMC Association; RAMC non-medical Officers Dinner Club; Movement Control Officers Club, London.
Interests: Good food and wine, travel, countryside pursuits, cricket, golf, ex-service organisations.
Contact details: 19 Woolley Avenue, Poynton, Cheshire SK12 1XU (tel / fax: 01625 859 923, email: peter@darrochp.freeserve.co.uk).

DAS, Dr Bhagabat Charan, MBE (1998), LMP, MBBS, MRCP, DTM&H

Position: President, Indian Senior Citizens Centre, Manchester.
Areas of Influence: Health, Voluntary Sector.
Profile: *b.* August 3rd, 1920. *m.* Adaramoni; 2 sons.
Education: LMP; MBBS (Honours), Orissa, India (1954); MRCP, Edinburgh (1962); DTM&H, London (1961). Career profile: Licentiase in Medical Practice (1938-42); Orissa Government Medical Service (1942-44, 1947-54, 1954-59); Emergency Commission Medical Officer, World War II (1944-47); Senior House Officer, General Medicine (1962); Registrar, Geriatric Medicine, Warrington General Hospital (1962-68); Geriatric Specialist, Hope Hospital, Salford Health Authority (1968-90). Prizes and awards: Honours and First Prize in every year of Medical Career; Best Graduate Gold medal / standing 1st in University, Utkal (1954); MBE (1966); Gold Medal for standing 1st in DTM&H, London (1961) National Whitbread Annual Volunteer Award (1994); Order of Mercy, London (2002); Nava Rattan, India Government (2001). Publications: *Drug taking in Elderly* (1964); *Induction for Junior Doctors in NHS* (1965); *Statistics of Indian Pensioners* (1987). Clubs and societies: Indian Association, Manchester; Indian Religious & Charitable Trust; Voluntary Action Manchester; Age Concern Manchester; Manchester Race and Health Forum; GMCVO; Salford Link Project; BCCCF; Focus BME; Community Network; Old Peoples Reference Group, London; National Council of Voluntary Organisation London.
Interests: Football, tennis, cricket, reading.
Contact details: 16-18 Whalley Road, Whalley Range, Manchester M16 8AB (tel: 0161 232 7994, fax: 0161 232 7272, email: iscc@talk21.com); 67 Half Edge Lane, Eccles, Manchester M30 9AZ (tel: 0161 789 6642).

DAUBNEY, Stephen Gordon

Position: Managing Director, Woodford Group (1993 - present)
Areas of Influence: Commerce.
Profile: *b.* January 31st, 1961; 1 son; 2 daughters.
Educated at Smithhills Moor Grammar, Bolton and London University. Owner and sole shareholder, Woodford Group, one of the country's leading land reclamation companies. The company has regenerated many major derilict brownfield sites throughout the country.
Interests: Painting, music, football.
Contact details: 55 Chorley New Road, Bolton BL1 4QR (tel: 01204 521144, fax: 01204 521214, email: stephen.daubney@woodfordgroup.com).

DAVENPORT, Colin, FCIB

Positions: Managing Director, Davenham Group Plc (1991 - present); Chairman, Peoples History Museum Trading Co. Ltd; Member, Manchester Cathedral Investment Committee; Member, Wigan Hospice Council.
Areas of Influence: Finance, Commerce, Voluntary Sector.
Profile: *b.* April 4th, 1943; *m.* Constance; 2 sons.
Educated at Wigan Grammar School. Career profile: Early career with Royal Bank of Scotland in UK and overseas; Manager International Division, RBS (1982-85); Regional Manager, ABN AMBRO (1985-89); Managing Director, Burns Anderson Finance Ltd (1989-91); Member, Deposit Protection Board (1992-96); Chairman, Manchester Merchant International Bankers (1993-96); Chairman, Pro-Manchester (1998). Colin Davenport lectures extensively in the UK and overseas on Credit and Banking related topics. He is also a visiting Lecturer at Manchester Business School. Clubs and societies: Wigan Golf Club, Army and Navy Club, Pall Mall.
Interests: Walking, cycling, golf, theatre, history, music.
Contact details: Davenham Group Plc, 8 St John Street, Manchester M3 4DU (tel: 0161 834 8484, fax: 0161 852 9164, email: cd@davenham.co.uk).

DAVID, Professor Ann Rosalie, BA (Hons), PHD, FRSA.

Positions: Professor of Egyptology, University of Manchester.
Areas of Influence: Education, Arts, Health.
Profile: *b.* May 30th, 1946; *m.* Antony E.
Education: Howell's School, Llandaff, Cardiff; BA (Hons) Ancient History with Egyptology, University College, London (1967); PhD Egyptology, University of Liverpool (1971). Rosalie David began her career as an Egyptologist at Manchester in 1972. Her main aim has been to establish a new university specialisation - Biomedical Research in Egyptology. She inaugurated the internationally renowned Manchester Mummy Project in 1973 which has pioneered a multidisciplinary approach to the scientific study of Egyptian mummies. Rosalie was awarded a Personal Chair by the University of Manchester in 2001, becoming Britain's first woman Professor of Egyptology. Rosalie has appeared regularly on radio and TV programmes, is the author of over 20 books and many academic articles and is consultant and presenter for several television films about Egyptology. She has lectured widely in Britain, and in many other countries including USA, Canada, Colombia, Chile, Greenland, Europe, and lectures regularly on Nile Cruises in Egypt. Prizes and awards: The Osler Medal, University of London (1996); The British Council Medal, Anglo-French Medical Society (1999). Clubs and societies: The Egypt Exploration Society; Bowdon District Decorative and Fine Art Society; International Congress of Egyptologists.

Interests: Travel, reading, painting, photography.
Contact details: University of Manchester, Manchester M13 9PL (tel:0161 275 2647, email: rosalie.david@man.ac.uk).

DAVID, Professor Timothy J, MBchB, PLD, MD, FRCP, FRCPCH, DCH

Positions: Professor of Child Health and Paediatrics, University of Manchester.
Areas of Influence: Health, Education.
Profile: January 13th, 1948.
Educated at Clifton College and the University of Bristol.
Interests: Baseball, cricket.
Contact details: Booth Hall Children's Hospital, Charlestown Road, Blackley, Manchester M9 7AA (tel: 0161 795 7000, fax: 0161 220 5387).

DAVIES, Chris, MEP, MA (Cantab)

Positions: Liberal Democrat Member of the European Parliament, North West (1999 - present).
Areas of Influence: Public Sector, Environmental Issues.
Profile: *b.* July, 7th 1954; *m.* Carol; 1 daughter.
Educated at Cheadle Hulme School, Stockport (1965-72) and Cambridge University (Gonville & Caine College) (1972-75). Career profile: Chairman, Housing Committee, Liverpool City Council (1981-83); Public Relations and Marketing Consultant (1983-95); Member of Parliament, Littleborough and Saddleworth (1995-97). Clubs and societies: Saddleworth Runners; Vice President, Altrincham Electric Railway Preservation Society.
Interests: Fell running, ultra distance running.
Contact details: 87a Castle Street, Stockport SK3 9AR (tel: 0161 477 7070; fax: 0161 477 7007, email: chrisdaviesmep@cix.co.uk); 4 Higher Kinders, Greenfield, Oldham OL3 7BH.

DAVIES, Jane, MA (Oxon)

Position: Chief Executive, Manchester Science Park Limited
Areas of Influence: Commerce.
Profile: *b.*June 3rd, 1952; *m.* Wyn.
Educated at Launswood High School, Leeds and St Anne's College, Oxford. Jane Davies spent 18 years with BP including oil trading in New York, a two year secondment to the FCO's 'think tank' and Regional Manager of AirBP, BP's international aviation fuel business. She spent some years as General Manager of the Buxton Festival and joined Manchester Science Park in 2000. Clubs and societies: Fellow, RSA; Friend of Buxton Festival; BBC Philharmonic; Northern Chamber

Orchestra; Member of the Art Fund; Manchester Chamber Concerts Society.
Interests: Theatre, opera, music, all things Italian.
Contact details: Kilburn House, Manchester Science Park, Lloyd Street North, Manchester M15 6SE (tel: 0161 226 1000, fax; 0161 226 1001, email: jane.davies@mspl.co.uk).

DAVIES, His Honour Judge Sir Rhys, KB (2000), LLB (Hons) (1961), QC (1981)

Positions: Honorary Recorder of Manchester (1990 - present); Chairman, Greater Manchester Criminal Justice Strategy Committee; Member, Sentencing Advisory Panel.
Areas of Influence: Law, Education, Arts.
Profile: *b.* January 13th, 1941; *m.* Katharine Lady Davies; 1 son; 1 daughter.
Educated at Cowbridge and Neath Grammar Schools, University of Manchester and Grays Inn. Career profile: Called to the Bar (1964); Practised on Northern Circuit (1964-90); Recorder of the Crown Court (1980); Queen's Counsel (1981); Former Head of Chambers, 18 St Johns Street, Manchester; Bencher of Gray's Inn; Former Chairman, Manchester Camerata; Member of Court and Deputy Chairman of Council, University of Manchester; Chairman of various committees including Whitworth Art Gallery Committee; President, Manchester and District Medico-Legal Society.
Interests: Music, walking, travel, the arts.
Contact details: Manchester Crown Court, Crown Square, Manchester M3 3FL (tel: 0161 954 1800).

DAVIES, Stephen, MA (Cantab)

Position: Member, 8 King St Chambers; Barrister (1985 - present)
Areas of Influence: Law.
Profile: *b.* February 2nd, 1963; *m.* April Marland; 2 daughters.
Educated at Baines School, Poulton-le-Fylde and Downing College, Cambridge.
Contact details: 8 King Street Chambers, 8 King Street, Manchester M2 6AQ (tel: 0161 834 9560).

DAVIS, Gregory Barrie

Positions: Development Manager, United Estates of Wythenshawe (1990 - present).
Areas of Influence: Voluntary Sector.
Profile: *b.* January 1st, 1968; *m.* Sharon Marie; 2 daughters.
Educated at Crossacres Junior School, South Manchester High School, West Wythenshawe College, Openshaw Technical College, and Manchester Polytechnic. Career profile: Door Supervisor, Manchester (1990); Opened Diplomat, Doorstaff

Agency (1992); Assited A Division Police and Local Authority in devising 'Door Safe' Training Scheme (1994); Established 'Christmas Food Distribution' (1994); Manager, Copperdale Hostel (1997-98); Established United Estates of Wythenshawe (1997); Head, Outreach, Copperdale Trust (1998); opened 'Fareshare', Manchester (1998-99). Publications: *Social and Physical Regeneration in Wythenshaw; Why Regeneration isn't working.* Member of Community Action Network.
Interests: Wide range of sporting activities, boxing, weight lifting, ex-competitive body builder.
Contact details: United Estates of Wythenshawe, The Gym, Broadoak Road, Wythenshawe, Manchester (tel: 0161 945 8238, fax: 0161 437 1363, email: copperdale_trust@hotmail.com); 60 Holliney Road, Peel Hall, Wythenshawe, Manchester M22 (tel: 0161 437 1363).

DAVIS, Susan Elizabeth, FIMgt

Positions: Executive Director, Learning and Skills Council, Greater Manchester (2000 - present); Advisor, Connexions Service Greater Manchester, Chamber Business Enterprises; Non-Executive Director, CAR NW Ltd.
Areas of Influence: Education, Public Sector.
Profile: *m.* Steven; 1 daughter.
Educated at Altrincham County Grammar School for Girls. Prior to her present post Susan Davis was Chief Executive of South and East Cheshire Training and Enterprise Council. Prior to that she worked for the Employment Service as Job Centre Manager and for Professional and Executive Recruitment. She is a Fellow of the Institute of Management and a member of the Institute of Directors.
Contact details: (tel: 0845 -19 4142, fax: 0161 261 0370, email: info@isc.gov.uk).

DAWBER, Graham Derek

Positions: Partner, PricewaterhouseCoopers; Deputy President, Manchester Society of Chartered Accountants; Member of the Manchester Metropolitan University Business School Advisory Board; Fellow of the Institute of Chartered Accountants in England and Wales.
Areas of Influence: Finance, Education.
Profile: *b.* July 23rd, 1948; *m.* Alison Mae; 1 Son.
Educated at Manchester Grammar School (1959-65); Coopers & Lybrand, Manchester (1965-78). Coopers & Lybrand, Lagos, Nigeria (1978-80); Admitted to Partnership, Coopers & Lybrand UK (1980); Partner, Coopers & Lybrand (1980-98); Partner, PricewaterhouseCoopers, Manchester (1998 - present).
Interests: Family, aviation, Jaguars (member of the Jaguar Drivers Club), gardening,

sport, travel, wine.

Contact details: PricewaterhouseCoopers, 101 Barbirolli Square, Lower Mosley Street, Manchester M2 3PW (tel: 0161 247 4118 / 245 2000, fax: 0161 247 4101, email: graham.d.dawber@uk.pwcglobal.com).

DAWSON, Peter

Position: Greater Manchester Police Sub-Divisional Command, Middleton.
Areas of Influence: Law, Personnel Development.
Profile: *b.* January 1st, 1948; *m.* Wendy Patricia; 1 son, 1 daughter.
Education: Secondary Modern. Career profile: Constable (1975); Sergeant (1980); Inspector (1990); Chief Inspector (1997); Superintendent (2001). Peter Dawson is a member of the Chartered Institute of Personnel and Development, Superintendents Association.
Interests: Ancient History; Reading; Music; Theatre.
Contact details: Greater Manchester Police, Middleton Sub-Division, Oldham Road, Middleton M24 1AY (tel: 0161 856 8701, fax: 0161 856 8709, email: p.dawson@GMP.co.uk).

DAY, Michael Philip

Positions: University Librarian, UMIST; Hon. Treasurer, Society of College, National & University Libraries.
Areas of Influence: Education.
Profile: *b.* April 14th, 1947; *m.* Diane; 2 sons.
Education: Queen Elizabeth's Grammar School, Barnet; University College, Cardiff; University of Sheffield. Career profile: Information Officer, Head of Technical Services, Hatfield Polytechnic Library (1968-1974); Sub-Librarian, Deputy Librarian, Preston Polytechnic (1975-1979); Deputy Librarian, University Librarian, UMIST (1980-).
Interests: Walking; music.
Contact details: UMIST Library & Information Service, PO Box 88, Manchester M60 1QD (tel. 0161 200 4920, fax. 0161 200 4939, email m.day@UMIST.ac.uk).

de COVERLEY-WILKINS, Colonel John Alfred ERD (1966), DL (1989) Order of Arts and Letters (1990)

Positions: Vice President, SSAFA Forces Help (1999 - present); Committee member, Cheshire Monarchy Association (1999 - present).
Areas of Influence: Voluntary Sector, Public Sector.
Profile: *b.* June 28th, 1931; *m.* Patricia; 1 daughter.
Education: Purbrook, Hants (1939-45); Portsmouth S. Grammar (1945-49); Diploma,

RADA (1949, 1953). Career profile: Senior Studio Manager, Alpha TV, Birmingham (1958-68); Facilities manager, Yorkshire TV (1968-70); Senior Floor Manager, Granada TV (1970-79); Public relations officer, Granada TV (1979-89); Past Chairman, Army Benevolent Fund, Manchester (1988-98); Hon. Colonel, 75 Engineer Rgt. (v) (1990-96). Awarded Commandeur Emérite, Commanderie de Bordeaux, France (2001). Clubs and societies: Movement Control Officers Club; Royal Commonwealth Society; Manchester Franco / British Club; Manchester Naval Officers Association; Former Maitre of Commanderie de Bordeaux, Manchester. John de Coverley-Wilkins served his National Service in the Royal Engineers in Trieste (1949-51), then went into the TA before finally retiring in 1970. He was the founding Maitre of Greater Manchester Commanderie de Bordeaux which is acknowledged as one of the most successful organisations open to everyone with wine interests.

Interests: Motoring abroad, theatre, TV, wines of France, member of 10 french wine orders, good food, helping others.

Contact details: Flaundon, 114 Altrincham Road, Wilmslow, Cheshire SK(5NQ (tel: 01625 526606).

de VALDA, Michael Anthony Frederick

Position: Chairperson, Hearing Voices Network; Director, Voluntary Action Manchester.

Areas of Influence: Health, Voluntary Sector.

Profile: *b.* August 2nd, 1947; *m.* Helen Sharon; 1 son; 1 daughter.

Educated at Secondary School in Manchester and passed 2 Counselling Courses. After passing an extremely deviant life earlier, Michael deValda has, in the past 10 years, turned that around to become "mildly influential" in mental health circles. He has moved from being considered mentally ill to having an input into the education of workers in Mental Health. Michael also works for the Hearing Voices Network and speaks at conferences. He has published *Asylum* in Magazine for Democratic Psychiatry. In addition to monitoring his wife's mental health, he facilitates Self Help groups both in the community and in Manchester Prison where he will shortly be working as a Counsellor.

Contact details: The Heaaring Voices Network, 91 Oldham Street, manchester M4 1LW (tel: 0161 834 5768, fax: 0161 834 5768, email: hearingvoices@care4free.net).

DEIRANIYA, Abdulilah Kheiro, MBChB (1962), FRCS, FESC, FETCS.

Positions: Consultant Cardiothoracic Surgeon, South Manchester University Hospitals NHS Trust (SMUHT) (1978 - present), Clinical Director of Transplantation, SMUHT (1997 - present);

Areas of Influence: Health.

Profile: *b.* October 5th, 1939; *m.* Brenda; 2 sons; 1 daughter.

Educated at Sheffield University Medical School (1957-62). Career profile: Registrar Cardiothoracic Surgery, Sheffield (1968-70); Senior Registrar, Harefield Hospital (1970-73); Senior Registrar, Queen Elizabeth Hospital, Birmingham (1973-78). Abdulilah Deiraniya has published over 70 peer reviewed papers. He contributed to the development and safety of cardiac surgery and to the establishment of heart and lung transplantation in the North West. Clubs and societies: Fellow, European Society of Cardiology; Member, Society of Thoracic Surgeons, USA; Member, International Society of Heart and Lung Transplantation.
Interests: Classical music, history.
Contact details: Department of Cardiothoracic Surgery, Wythenshawe Hospital, Southmoor Road, Manchester M23 9LT (tel: 0161 291 2565, fax: 0161 946 0454, email: ADeiraniya@aol.com); 2 Allandale, Bradgate Road, Altrincham WA14 4PQ (tel: 0161 929 1479, fax: 0161 928 1038).

DERBY, Edward Richard William Stanley, 19th Earl of, 12 Bt, DL (1999)

Positions: Baron Stanley of Bickerstaffe; Baron Stanley of Preston. Director, Robert Fleming Int Ltd (1998 - 2001), Haydock Park Racecourse Co Ltd (1994 - present); President, Liverpool C of C (1995 - present), Royal Liverpool Philharmonic Society (1995 - present), Royal Lytham & St Anne's Golf Club (1995 - present); Formby Golf Club (1995 - present); Royal Botanical and Horticultural Society of Manchester and the Northern Counties (1995 - present); Henshaw's Society of the Blind (1996 - present); Sefton C of C (1998 - present); Knowsley C of C (1995 - present), Vice-president PGA (2001 - present); Hon. President, Liverpool Cncl. of Social Services, Boys Brigade Liverpool Battalion (1995 - present); Trustee, National Museums and Galleries on Merseyside (1995 - present); Aintree Racecourse Charitable Appeal Trust (1995 - present); Patron, Friends of Liverpool Cathedral (1995 - present); Liverpool branch RNLI (1995 - present); Life President, Rugby Football League (1996 - present).
Areas of Influence: Commerce, Arts, Voluntary Sector.
Profile: *b.* October 1st, 1962; *m.* Hon Caroline Emma Neville (1995); 2 sons, Edward John Robin, Lord Stanley (1998); The Hon Oliver Hugh Henry Stanley (2002); 1 daughter, Lady Henrietta Mary Rose (1997). Educated at Eton and RAC Cirencester. Career profile: Commander, Grenadier Guards (1982-85); Director, Fleming Private Asset Management Ltd (1992-00), Robert Fleming & Co Ltd (1996-98); Member of Council, University of Liverpool (1998); Patron, Liverpool Area Princes Trust and numerous other charities. Clubs and societies: White's, Jockey Club Rooms.
Contact details: Knowsley, Prescot, Merseyside L34 4AF (tel: 0151 489 6148, fax: 0151 482 1988, email: private.office@knowsley.com, web: www.knowsley.com).

DEVITT, Paul, LLB (Hons)

Positions: Partner, Addleshaw Booth & Co (1993 - present).; Trustee, The Lowry Centre Trust.
Areas of Influence: Law
Profile: *b.* August 19th, 1964; 1 son; 1 daughter.
Educated at Barrow Grammar School for Boys and the University of Bristol. Career profile: Turner Kenneth Brown, Solicitors, London (1986-91); Freshfields, Solicitors, London (1991-93);
Interests: Family, sport and wine.
Contact details: Addleshaw Booth & Co, 100 Barbirolli Square, Manchester M2 3AB (tel: 0161 934 6000, fax: 0161 934 6060, email: paul.devitt@addleshawbooth.com).

DEVONSHIRE, The Duke of, KG (1996), MC, PC (1964), Hon LLD, Hon Dr Law

Position: Director.
Areas of Influence: Commerce.
Profile: *b.* January 2nd, 1920; *m.* Hon Deborah Freeman-Mitford (1941); 1 son, The Marquess of Hartington; 2 daughters, The Lady Emma Tennant and The Lady Sophia Topley.
Educated at Eton and Trinity College Cambridge. Career profile: Served with Coldstream Guards (1939-45); Contested Chesterfield by-elections, Conservative (1945, 1950); Parliamentary Under-Secretary of State for Commonwealth Relations (1960-62); Minister of State, Commonwealth Relations Office (1962-64), and for Colonial Affairs (1963-64); Executive Steward, The Jockey Club (1966-69); Member, Horserace Totalisator Board (1977-86); Chancellor, Manchester University (1965-86). President or former President: Royal Hospital & Home, Putney; Lawn Tennis Association; RNIB; National Deaf Children's Society; Barnardos Year of the Volunteer; East Midlands MENCAP; Contact the Elderly; Derbyshire Boy Scouts Association. Chairman, Grand Council of British Empire Cancer Campaign (1956-81) and Thoroughbred Breeders Association (1978-81). Mayor of Buxton (1952-54). Publication: *Top Park*, a romance of the turf (1976, rep. 2000). The Duke of Devonshire has many associations with a wide variety of charitable organisations and campaigns both in Derbyshire and nationwide, is Director of several Chatsworth companies and President of Chesterfield Football Club.
Interests: Owns 7 racehorses and is a very keen supporter of a wide range of sports including football and golf.
Contact details: Chatsworth, Bakewell, Derbyshire DE45 1PP (tel: 01246 582204, fax: 01246 582937).

DIXON, Barry

Positions: County Fire Officer; Chief Executive, Greater Manchester Fire Service.
Areas of Influence: Public Sector.
Profile: *b.* January 5th, 1951; *m.* Jill; 1 son (Jack), 1 daughter (Hannah).
Education: Stand Grammar School (1962-1967). Career profile: Greater Manchester Fire Service (1967).
Interests: Clay pigeon shooting, fishing, the countryside.
Contact details: Greater Manchester Fire Service, 146 Bolton Road, Swinton, M25 3DQ (tel. 0161 608 4001, fax. 0161 608 4006).

DIXON, Paul, MA (Oxon), MIBiol, Cbiol

Positions: Headmaster, Cheadle Hulme School (2001 - present).
Areas of Influence: Education, Sport.
Profile: *b.* July 8th, 1951; *m.* Pat; 1 son; 2 daughters
Educated at Bexhill Grammar School and St Edmund Hall, University of Oxford. Career profile: Assistant Master, Winchester College (1973-76_); Assistant Master, Brighton College (1976-80); Head of Biology, St Dunstan's College (1980-90); Deputy Head, Stockport Grammar School (1990-96); Headmaster, Reigate Grammar School (1996-01). Paul Dixon has published various Biology teaching papers. He was awarded a distinction for his Diploma of Education course, and an Oxford Blue for basketball. Clubs and societies: Institute of Biology, Vincent's Club, East India Club and is Chairman, Northern Schools Crosscountry Association.
Interests: Music, theatre, fishing, breeding and training pedigree Labradors.
Contact details: Cheadle Hulme School, Claremont Road, Cheadle Hulme SK8 6EF.

DJANG, Alex Emmanuel

Positions: Senior Manager, Electronic and Biomedical Engineering Department, The Pennine Acute Hospitals; Justice of the Peace; Chair, Broad African Representative Council; Patron, Ghana Union, Manchester; Patron, Millennium Youth Club, Ghana; Member, Greater Manchester Police Advisory Committee on Racial Issues.
Areas of Influence: Health, Voluntary Sector.
Profile: *b.* January 15th, 1942; *m.* Patience; 2 Sons; 2 Daughters.
Educated at Secondary Technical School, School of Marine Navigation, Bolton Institute, and Manchester Metropolitan University (B. Eng, I. Eng); Second Officer, Merchant Navy gaining Second Officers Ticket in Marine Navigation; Experimental Officer; Medical Engineer; Senior Manager;
Interests: Sports and music.
Contact details: Pennine Acute Hospitals, Royal Oldham Hospital, EBME Department, Rochdale Road, Oldham 0L1 2JH (tel: 0161 627 8677, fax: 0161 627 8795

email: alex.djang@oldham-tr.nwest.nhs.uk); 127 Leicester Road, Broughton Park, Salford M7 4HJ (tel: 0161 720 7448, email: alexdjang@hotmail.com).

DOBBIN, Jim

Positions: Fellow, Institute of Biological Sciences; Member of Parliament for Heywood and Middleton (1997 - date).
Areas of Influence: Health, Public Sector.
Profile: *b.* May 26th; *m.* Patricia; 2 sons; 2 daughters.
Educated at St Columba's High, Cowden Beath, St Andrew's High, Kirkaldy and Napier College, Edinburgh. Career profile: Microbiologist, NHS, for 33 years; Victoria Infirmary, Kirkaldy; Public Health Laboratory, Glasgow; Royal Oldham Hospital, Oldham; Rochdale Labour Councillor (1983-97); Leader, Rochdale Council (1996-97); Member, European Select Committee. Various scientific papers published. Clubs and societies: Rochdale Catholic Club; Heywood Cricket Club, Middleton Cricket Club.
Interests: Football, walking, gardening.
Contact details: 45 York Street, Heywood, Lancs OL10 4NN (tel: 01706 361135, fax: 01706 361137); 43 Stonehill Drive, Rochdale, Lancs OL12 7JN (tel: 01706 342632).

DOHERTY, Ellie

Positions: Managing Director.
Areas of Influence: Commerce, Media, Voluntary Sector
Profile: *b.* August 10th, 1947; 1 son; 1 daughter.
Educated at St Annes Secondary Modern and Moston College of FE. Ellie Doherty left college in 1963 confused as to where her future career lay. She was briefly employed as a junior secretary before moving into the travel industry in the late 70's. She found this to be a challenging career, and went on to be employed as Operations Manager for Sunset Holidays (1980) before moving on to open her first branch of Miss Ellies Travel (1986). Ellie opened further branches in Urmston, Warrington, Chorlton, and Stockport to compliment her busy Head Office in Manchester. Miss Ellies Travel is the largest Independant Travel Agency in the North West, and includes a tour department. Ellie finds charity work just as rewarding and raised £20,000 for the Dianne Campbell Trust and she has an affiliation with children's charity work and gives her time rewardingly. She now feels privileged to be trustee of Dianne's appeal.
Interests: Writing poetry and prose, swimming, cooking, and reading if time allows.
Contact details: 72-86 Oldham Road, New Cross, Manchester M45 4EB (tel: 0161 228 7363, fax: 0161 228 7453, email: edoherty@traveleye.net).

DONE, Frances Winifred, BA (econ), FCA

Positions: Chief Executive, Manchester 2002 Ltd (2000 - present).
Areas of Influence: Public Sector, Finance.
Profile: *b.* May 6th, 1950; *m.* Jim Hancock; 2 sons.
Educated at Colston's Girls School, Bristol and Manchester University. Career profile: KPMG (1971-78); Regional Finance Manager, Housing Corporation, Manchester (1978-84); Chair, Finance Committee, Manchester City Council (1984-88); Senior Manager, Public Sector Dept., KPMG (1988-91); Treasurer, Rochdale Metropolitan Borough Council (1991-97); Chief Executive and Treasurer, Rochdale MBC (1997-00).
Interests: Walking, swimming, canals and inland waterways.

DONNACHIE, Professor Alexander, BSc, PhD (Glasgow), FInstP, CPhys

Positions: Emeritus Professor, University of Manchester (2001 - present); Chairman, Standing Committee of Physics Professors (1993 - present); Chairman, Scientific Advisory Committee to NIKHEF-H, The Netherlands (1992 - present); Member, Programme Advisory Committee, Jefferson Laboratory, USA (2002); Hon. Sec., Manchester Literary and Philosophical Society (2001 - present).
Areas of Influence: Education
Profile: *b.* May 25th, 1936 Kilmarnock; *m.* Dorothy Paterson; 2 daughters.
Educated at Kilmarnock Academy (1948-54); Glasgow University, BSc Hons (1958), PhD (1961). Career profile: DSIR Research Fellow, University College, London (1961-63); Lecturer, UCL (1963-65); Research Associate, CERN Geneva (1965-67); Senior Lecturer, University of Glasgow (1967-69); Professor of Physics, University of Manchester (1969-97); Research Professor (1997-01). Member, SRC Theory Sub-Committee (1975-77); Nuclear Physics Board Member, Particle Physics Committee (1977-81); Postgraduate Training Committee (1978-81); Chairman, SERC Nuclear Physics Board (1989-93); Vice-chairman, Particle Space and Astronomy Board (1993-94); Member, SERC Council (1989-94); Member, Commission on Particles and Fields, IUPAP (1984-92); Chairman, SPS and LEAR Committee, CERN (1988-93); Member, Scientific Policy Committee, CERN (1988-93); Research Board, CERN (1988-93); UK Scientific Delegate to CERN Council (1988-94); Member, Dutch Universities Review Committee for Physics (1996); Chairman, Department of Physics and Astronomy, University of Manchester (1988-94); Dean, Faculty of Science and Engineering, University of Manchester (1986-87, 1994-97); Chairman, Standing Committee of Physics Professors (1993-97); Chairman, Scientific Advisory Committee to NIKHEF-H, the Netherlands (1992-96). Published 160 articles in scientific journals. Societies: Manchester Lit and Phil, President (1995-97).
Interests: Golf, sailing, walking, history.
Contact details: Dept. of Physics & Astronomy, University of Manchester, Manchester M13 9PL.

DRIVER, Betty Mary, MBE (1999)

Position: Life-time Actress, Coronation Street, Granada TV, Manchester.
Areas of Influence: Arts, Media.
Profile: *b.* May 20th, 1920.
Educated at: Private school. Career profile: Works on stage, radio, screen, and television. Publications: Autobiography.
Contact details: Granada TV, Quay Street, Manchester M60 9EA (tel: 0161 832 7211).

DUNN, Dennis, BA (Hons) MA

Positions: Pro-Vice Chancellor and Dean of Faculty, Manchester Metropolitan University. Chairman, BITWorld. Chairman, Japan Centre North West. JP (1988). Former Chairman, Leigh Magistrates Court.
Areas of Influence: Education, Law.
Profile: *b.* September 23rd, 1951; *m.* Denise Taylor-Dunn; 1 son, Marc; 1 daughter, Natalie.
Education: BA (Hons) Business Studies, Manchester Polytechnic; MA Management Learning, Lancaster University. Career profile: 16 years commercial experience in the retail sector. Joined Higher Education in 1985 and was influential in developing Business Information Technology as a major subject discipline in the UK and internationally. Currently holds a Senior Academic role as Pro-Vice Chancellor and Dean of Faculty at MMU, and as Chairman of Business Information Technology World International Conference Series. Is also a visiting academic in a number of overseas universities and a Senior Magistrate. Has published *Business Information Technology Managment: Alternative and Adaptive Futures*, Hackney and Dunn (2000). Clubs and societies: Leigh Cricket Club and Magistrates Association.
Interests: Keeping fit, travel, cultural studies, walking on the Lake District Fells, Bolton Wanderers.
Contact details: Manchester Metropolitan University, Crewe & Alsager Faculty, Crewe Green Road, Crewe, Cheshire CW1 5DU (tel: 0161 247 5812; fax: 0161 247 6371; email: D.Dunn@mmu.ac.uk).

DWEK, Joseph Claude (Joe), CBE, BSc, BA, AMCT, FTI Hon DSC UMIST.

Position: Executive Chairman, Worthington Group (1999 - present)
Areas of Influence: Commerce.
Profile: *b.* May 1st, 1940; *m.;* 2 children.
Educated at Carmel College and University of Manchester. Career profile: Chairman, Mersey Basin Campaign (DETR); Chairman, Bodycote International Plc (1972-98); Chairman, Penmarric plc and j4b/zameta; Director, Jerome Group plc; City Invoice

Finanace Group; Mercury Recycling Ltd; Manchester Federal School of Business and Management; Chairman, Healthy Waterways Trust; Member ct., UMIST; Past Chairman (1994-96), Vice Chairman (1994, 1997), CBI NW; President of UMIST Association (1992-94); Director, NWIDB, DTI (1980-90); Past Director, Royal Exchange Theatre, NORWIDA/INWARD, North West Broadcasting Limited.
Interests: Golf
Contact details: Penmarric plc, Suite One, Courthill House, 66 Water Lane, Wilmslow SK9 5AP (tel: 01625 549081/2, fax: 01625 530 791, email: penjcdwek@AOL.com).

DYBLE, Michael, FCIM

Positions: Chairman, Piccadilly Radio (2002); Trustee, Museum of Science and Industry in Manchester.
Areas of Influence: Commerce, Media.
Profile *b*. July 21st, 1936; *m*. Pauline; 2 sons; 2 daughters.
Educated at Liverpool College; Director of Osborne-Peacock, advertising agency (1963); Founder Partner and Chairman, Bowden Dyble Hayes & Partners, advertising agency (1964-91); Marketing Director of Manchester's 2000 Olympic Bid and 2002 Commonwealth games Bid (1991-95).
Interests: Tennis, skiing.
Contact details: Brooklands, Maltmans Road, Lymm, Cheshire WA13 0QP (tel/fax: 01925 753420, email: mike@dyble.fsnet.co.uk).

DYER, Philip Arthur, BSc, PhD, FRCPath, SRCS

Positions: Consultant Clinical Scientist; Honorary Reader in Transplantation Science; President, British Transplantation Society (2002-05); Director of Transplantation Laboratory, Manchester Royal Infirmary (1981 - present)
Areas of Influence: Health, Public Sector.
Educated at University of Nottingham (1974) and University of Birmingham (1978). Career profile: Post-Doctoral Research (1978-87); Founding Chair, British Society for Histocompatability and Immunogenetics (1990-93). Philip Dyer has published over 150 articles in peer reviewed scientific and medical journals. He is a member of various scientific and medical societies in immunology and transplantation. His aim is to support effective organ and tissue donation in the North West and nationally.
Interests: Walking, gardening, angling.
Contact details: Transplantation Laboratory, Manchester Royal Infirmary, Oxford Road, Manchester M13 9WL (tel: 0161 276 6397, fax: 0161 276 6148, email: pdyer@mint.cmht.mwest.nhs.uk); email: philipdyer@bigfoot.com).

DYSON, Richard George, MA (Cantab), FCA

Positions: Head of Forensic Services, North Region, Ernst & Young LLP; National Risk Management Partner, Ernst & Young LLP; Council Member, Institute of Chartered Accountants in England and Wales (2001 - present).
Areas of Influence: Commerce.
Profile: c. April 6th, 1949, Huddersfield; *m.* Valerie (1986) (div. 1997); 2 daughters; *m.* Jane Kay (1998); 1 son; 1 daughter.
Educated at Clifton College, and Queens' College, Cambridge. Career profile: Articled with Whinney Murray & Co, London, qualified (1974); transferred to Manchester (1982); Partner, Ernst & Whinney (1983); President, Manchester Society of Chartered Accountants (1995-96). Clubs and societies: Hawks Club, Cambridge; St James' Club, Manchester; Stockport Golf Club; Formby Golf Club, Denham Golf Club.
Interests: Golf, music.
Contact details: Ernst & Young LLP, 100 Barbirolli Square, Manchester, M2 3EY (tel:0161 333 3000, fax: 0161 333 3010).

DYSON, Robert William

Positions: Executive Chairman, Dunlop Heywood Lorenz.
Areas of Influence: Commercial Property, Development, Finance.
Profile: *b.* January 10th, 1949; *m.* Judith, 2 daughters.
Education: Wellacre, Manchester; MSc, City of London University. Career profile: British Road Services (1966-68); Manchester Corporation Waterworks (1968-70); Stockport Council (1970-72); Dunlop Heywood Lorenz (1972 - present); Fellow, Royal Institution of Chartered Surveyors. Clubs and societies: Royal Institution of Chartered Surveyors; The 1913 Wilderness Club; The Chartered Surveyors 1938 Club; The 1984 Club; The Company of Chartered Surveyors.
Interests: Skiing, sailing, walking, Manchester United.
Contact details: Dunlop Heywood Lorenz, Abbey house, Booth Street, Manchester M2 (tel: 0161 237 7777, fax: 0161 237 7778, email: rwd@dhlproperty.co.uk).

EAGELSTONE, Diana Barbara H.H.J.

Position: Circuit Judge.
Areas of Influence: Law.
Profile: May 24th, 1949; *m.* Michael Redfern QC; 3 Daughters.
Educated at Manchester University, LLB; Law Degree (1970); Barrister (1971); Judge (1995); Member of Gray's Inn.
Interests: Family, tennis.

EAGLETON, Professor Terry, MA (Cantab), MA (Oxon), PhD (Cantab)

Positions: Professor of Cultural Theory and John Rylands Fellow, University of Manchester (2001 - present).
Areas of Influence: Arts, Education.
Profile: *b.* February 22nd, 1943; *m.* Willa Murphy; 3 sons.
Educated at De La Salle College, Salford (1954-60), Trinity College, Cambridge (1961-64) and Jesus College, Cambridge (1964-69). Career profile: Fellow of Jesus College, Cambridge (1964-69); Fellow and Tutor in English, Wadham College, Oxford (1969-89); Lecturer in Critical Theory, Oxford University (1989-92); Thomas Warton Professor of English Literature, University of Oxford (1992-00); Honorary D.Litt, Salford (1988), Dalien China (1989), Galway (1995), Santiago (1999). Publications: *Crazy John and the bishop, Saints and scholars, Marxism and literary criticism, Saint Oscar; Literary theory: an introduction; Heathcliffe and the great hunger; Criticism and ideology.* Terry Eagleton has received the Isaac Deutscher Prize (1987) and the Sunday Tribune Award (1989). He is a member of the Irish Club, London.
Interests: Irish music.

Contact details: Department of English and American Studies, University of Manchester, Oxford Road, Manchester M13 9PL (tel: 0161 275 3160, fax: 0161 275 3186).

EAKIN, Michael George

Position: Regional Executive Director, North West Arts Board.
Areas of Influence: Arts, Public Sector.
Profile: b. August 16th, 1957; m. Kim; 2 daughters.
Educated at Calday Grange Grammar School, West Kirby (1972-76); St Catharine's College, University of Cambridge (1976-79). Career profile: Assistant Manager, Beck Theatre, Hayes, Middlesex (1979-84); Operations Manager, Hexagon Theatre, Reading (1984-88); Director, Hexagon, Reading (1988-92); Head of Arts and Museums, Reading Borough Council (1992-97); Corporate Director, Arts and Leisure, Reading Borough Council (1997-01); Executive Director, North West Arts Board (2001 - present).
Interests: Literature, theatre, walking, cycling, watching football, popular music.
Contact details: North West Arts Board, Manchester House, 22 Bridge Street, Manchester M3 3AB (tel: 0161 834 6644, email: meakin@nwarts.co.uk).

ECCLES, Frances Mary (Fran)

Position: Executive Director, Manchester Law Society (1988 - present).
Areas of Influence: Law.
Profile: b. July 8th, 1963; m. Christopher Searles; 1 son.
Educated at Bishop Bright R.C High School, Longton, Stoke-on-Trent; St Dominics Convent School 6th Form, Hartshill, Stoke-on-Trent.
Interests: My son Jack and husband Chris, cooking, dieting and eating (in no particular order), reading and running.
Contact details: Manchester Law Society, Rational House, 64 Bridge Street, Manchester M3 3BN; (tel: 0161 831 7337, fax: 0161 839 2631, email: fran@manchester lawsociety.org.uk).

EDWARDS

Positions: Youth and Community Worker West Indian Centre and Community Activist (1977-present)
Areas of Influence: Voluntary Sector.
Profile: b. June 26th, 1930; m. Elouise Edwards; 4 sons.
Education: Elementary Industrial Administration (1964); Certificate in Youth and Community Work (1977); Psychology of Self, Manchester University. Career profile: Shop Steward, SOGAT (1965-67); Secretary, Guyana Association 1969-77); Secretary,

PNC Guyana (1970-77); Secretary, Campaign Against Racial Discrimination (1966-68); Secretary, West Indian Organisations Co-ordinating Committee (1975-770; Treasurer, Moss Side people's Association. Received Manchester Evening News Award for Work in the Community. Mr Edwards has also been involved in the following projects: Saturday Schools for children that lack confidence and who are culturally deprived; summer and Easter play schools; youth clubs; organisation of conferences, seminars, and lectures; job creation for youths; cultural activities to create good community relations.

Interests: Community work, black organisations, drama, sports, athletics, world politics, working with people.

Contact details: West indian Centre, Carmoor Road, Chorlton-on-Medlock, Manchester M13 0FB (tel / fax: 0161 257 2092).

EGAN, Brigit Colleen

Positions: Director, CMC Ltd (2002 - present); Non Executive Director, Business in the Arts; Chair, Advisory Panel for Common Purpose; Chair, Institute of Directors, Manchester Branch.

Areas of Influence: Commerce, Education.

Profile: *b.* February 6th, 1964.

Education: Matriculation Certificate; Certified Institute of Marketing; INLPTA Certified Practitioner in Neuro Linguistic Programming; Diploma in Business Coaching. Career profile: Managing Director, The Chief Ezecutives Office (2001-02); Head of Marketing, Barclay's Bank Plc, South Africa/UK (1982-88); Account director, Whitehead & Partners (1988-90); Marketing Director, B&R Design & Marketing Consultancy (1990-93); Principal Consultant/ Marketing Executive, Drake Beam Morin Inc (1993-94); Business Development Manager (1994-96), Regional Manager Yorkshire (1996-98); Director (1998-01), Coutts Consulting Group (1994-01). Awarded Network UK National Women of Achievement (2000); Managing Director, The Chief Executive's Office. Clubs and societies: Business in the Arts; Institute of Directors; Network UK; International Association of Career Management Professionals; Common Purpose; Founder Member of The Rainmaker Charity.

Interests: Horse riding, travel, food and wine, books.

Contact details: 25 Farnborough Avenue, Richmond Park, Lees OL4 3HG (tel: 0161 633 8875, fax: 0161 633 8204, email: brigit.egan@virgin.net).

EINOLLAHI, Maghsoud, BSc (1975), MSc (1976)

Positions: Partner, Head of UK Corporate Finance excluding London, Deloitte & Touche.

Areas of Influence: Finance, Commerce.

Profile: *b.* April 22nd, 1953; *m.* Patricia; 2 sons; 1 daughter.

Education: London School of Economics; Fellow, Institute of Chartered Accountants; Fellow, Society of Turnround Professionals. Career profile: Financial Director, and then Managing Director of Subel, a small venture capital buiness (1986-88) investing in start up technology businesses; Partner, Audit Practice, Spicer & Oppenheim (1989); Partner, Corporate Finance for the north of England (1992) following merger with Touche Ross.
Interests: Wine, walking, work.
Contact details: Deloitte & Touche, PO Box 500, 201 Deansgate, Manchester M60 2AT (tel: 0161 455 6307, fax: 829 3811, email: meinollahi@deloitte.co.uk).

EJOH, Sonya, BA (Hons)

Positions: Employment Officer.
Areas of Influence: Health, Voluntary Sector, Education
Profile: 1 son; twin daughters.
Education: St Albans School, Oldham; Tameside College of Technology; Hollins Polytechnic, Manchester; BA (Hons) Degree in Humanities & Social Service, Manchester Metropolitan University; PGCE in Adult Education, Bolton Higher Institute of Higher Education. Sonya Ejoh worked as a practice manager for 6 years and delivered lectures in cultural studies, and health and social care. As a community Support Worker she provided practical and emotional support to service users mental illness. The main focus of Sonya's work has been within disadvantaged communities and currently her role as Employment Link Officer includes supporting individuals with mental illness to access education, training and employment. Sonya is a member of the Bernie Grant Community Leadership Programme, and her ultimate goal is to work towords connecting regeneration initiatives with the community at a grass roots level, influencing policies and decisions in health and social care; addressing the issues of equality in the care and treatment for black and ethnic communities. Until 1998 Sonya acted as a personal assistant to the exiled Ethiopian Royal Family and assisted with the establishment of the Ethiopian Peace Foundation
Interests: Travelling, swimming, reading, overseas development with particular reference to Third World Countries.
Contact details: African & Carribean Mental Health Services, Zion Community Resource Centre, 339 Stretford Road, Manchester M15 4ZY (tel: 0161 226 9562, fax: 0161 226 7947).

ELDER, Mark, CBE (1989), MA, BA

Position: Music Director, Hallé Orchestra
Areas of Influence: Arts.
Profile: *b.* June 2nd, 1947; *m.* Mandy; 1 daughter.

Education: Canterbury Cathedral Choir School (1957-61); Bryanston School, Dorset (1961-66); Corpus Christi College, University of Cambridge (1966-69). Career profile: Music Director, English National Opera (1979-93); Music Director, Rochester Philharmonic, USA (1989-94); Principal Guest Conductor, City of Birmingham Symphony Orchestra (1992-95); Regular appearances with Royal Opera House, Covent Garden; Metropolitan Opera, New York, Opéra National de Paris; Glyndebourne Festival Opera; Bavarian State Opera. Symphonic engagements with London Philharmonic Orchestra; Orchestra of the Age of Enlightenment; Chicago Symphony Orchestra; Royal Concertgebouw Orchestra; Los Angeles Philharmonic. Prizes and awards; Olivier Award (1991); Evening Standard Award. Honorary Fellow, Royal Academy of Music.
Interests: Cinema, theatre.
Contact details: Hallé Concerts Society, The Bridgewater Hall, Manchester M1 5HA (tel: 0161 237 7000, fax: 0161 237 7029, web: halle.co.uk).

ELLERAY, Anthony, John, MA (Cantab), QC (1993)

Positions: Recorder; Deputy High Court Judge, Barrister (1979 - present).
Areas of Influence: Law.
Profile: *b.* August 19th, 1954; *m.* Alison (nee Potter); 1 son; 1 daughter.
Educated at Bishop's Stortford College and Trinity College Cambridge; called to Bar (1977); Inner Temple Major Award (1976); Member of Manchester Tennis and Racquets Club and Oxford and Cambridge Club.
Interests: Art, tennis, garden.
Contact details: Exchange Chambers, 4 Ralli Courts, West Riverside, Manchester M3 5FT; (tel: 0161 8332722; fax: 0161 8332789; email: ellerayqc@exchangechambers.co.uk).

ELLIOTT, Marianne Pheobe

Position: Artistic Director, Royal Exchange Theatre (2000 - present)
Areas of Influence: Arts. Education.
Profile: *b.* December 27th, 1966; *m.* Nick Sidi.
Educated at St Hilarys School, Alderley Edge, Stockport Grammar School and Hull University. Marianne Elliott worked as an independent television and film casting assistant on various productions including Terence Davies' *The long day closes* and *Prime suspect* I, II, and III. She then worked part-time with Granada Television's drama department while directing for her new writing company, the award-winning Small Talk Theatre, funded by London Arts Board. She has directed shows at Hull University, Hull Truck Theatre Company and on the London Fringe. Credits include *Sexual Perversity in Chicago, Zoo Story,* and *Can't Stand Up for Falling Down.* She was an assistant Director at the Open Air Theatre, Regents Park with Ian Talbot and Brian

Cox. Marianne was also Assistant Director for the Royal Exchange Theatre's productions of *An Experienced Woman Gives Advice*, *The Rivals*, and *Misfits*. She also directed a late night show *Coyote Ugly*. Marianne became an Associate Director of the Royal Exchange in 1996 and has since directed *I have Been Here Before*, *Poor Super Man* which won Manchester Evening News Award for Best Production (1997), *Mad For It*, *The Deep Blue Sea*, *Martin Yesterday*, *Fast Food*, Noel Coward's *Nude with a Violin* and most recently, *A Woman of no Importance*, *As You Like It*, and *Les Blancs*. Recently she has directed at Birmingham Rep, Hampstead Theatre, the Royal Court Theatre and *The Little Foxes* at the Donmar Warehouse.
Contact details: Royal Exchange Theatre, St Anns Square, Manchester M2 7DH (0161 833 9333)

ELLIS, David, FRNCM, ARNCM.

Position: Chairman, North West Composers Association (2002-03).
Areas of Influence: Arts.
Profile: *b*. March 10th, 1933, Liverpool; *m*. Patricia.
Educated at Liverpool Institute (1944-51) and Royal Manchester College of Music (1953-57). David Ellis' compositions gained recognition not only through performances, but also in the form of commissions and awards: The Royal Philharmonic Prize, the Royal College of Music Patrons' Award, the Theodore Holland Award, the Royal Manchester Institution Silver Medal, the Ricordi Prize and a Gulbenkian Award. From 1964 he worked at the BBC, initially having responsibility for BBC Philharmonic Orchestra programmes and subsequently as Head of Music, BBC North, until 1986 when he became Artistic Director and Composer in Residence for the Northern Chamber Orchestra. In 1994 David left the NCO to assist with the setting up of the Orchestra Sinfonica Portuguesa based in Lisbon, eventually returning to the UK in order to concentrate exclusively on composition. His works have also been played with considerable success in Canada, the USA, Israel, Portugal, Denmark, Australia and throughout Europe in more recent years. Clubs and societies: British Academy of Composers and Songwriters; Performing Right Society.
Contact details: 14 Patch Lane, Bramhall, Cheshire SK7 1JB (tel/fax: 0161 440 9007, email: delliscomposer@aol.com).

ELLIS, Roger Martin, LLB (Hons)

Position: Chief Executive, Rochdale Metropolitan Borough Council.
Areas of Influence: Public Sector.
Profile: *b*. September 26th, 1954; *m*. Tracey; 1 son; 4 daughters.
Educated at Lawrence Sheriff School, Rugby (1966-70); Clee Humberstone Foundation School, Cleethorpes (1970-72); Nottingham University (1972-75); College

of Law (1976). Career profile: Norwich City Council (1976-78); Preston Borough Council (1978-83); Oxford City Council (1983-87); Lancaster City Council (1987-93); Chief Executive, Burnley Borough Council (1993-2000). Clubs and societies: RSPB; Lancashire Health and Racquets Club.
Interests: Walking, travel, photography, Coventry City F.C.
Contact details: Rochdale MBC, Municipal Offices, Smith Street, Rochdale OL16 1LQ (tel: 01706 865 401, fax: 01706 865 450, email: roger.ellis@rochdale.gov.uk).

ELSTEIN, Professor Max, MB, ChB (1955), MRCOG (1964), MD (1969) MSc (1978), FRCOG (1980), Hon FFFP (1995)

Positions: Emeritus Professor of Obstetrics, Gynaecology and Reproductive Health Care, University of Manchester; Chairman of the Council of the Institute of Medicine, Law and Bioethics.
Areas of Influence: Health, Education, Healthcare Law & Bioethics.
Profile: *b.* June 25th, 1932; *m.* Cecile Hoberman; 1 son (dec.); 1 daughter, Maureen. Education: Matriculated with distinction in Mathematics, Latin and Physical Science from Wynberg Boys' High School, Cape Town (1949); Qualified in Medicine at the University of Cape Town (1950-55). Career profile: Demonstrator in Anatomy; Resident posts, Professorial Units, Groote Schuur Hospital; Teaching Hospital Posts in Infectious Disease, Cape Town; Senior Resident Post, Obstetrics and Gynaecology, Group General Practice, Stellenbosch (1958-61). Specialist training, Queen Charlotte's Hospital, Hammersmith Hospital and Charing Cross Hospital; Lecturer, Obstetrics and Gynaecology, Charing Cross Hospital Medical School; Research Fellow, Royal College of Obstetricians and Gynaecologists (1967-69); Visiting Consultant and Senior Lecturer, University of Cape Town (1969); Senior Lecturer, Human Reproduction and Obststrics, University of Southampton (1970-77); Professor, Obstetrics and Gynaecology, University Hospital of South Manchester (1977); Head of Department, Obstetrics and Gynaecology and Reproductive Healthcare, University of Manchester; St Mary's Hospital (1993); Executive Director, Institute of Medicine, Law and Bioethics, IMLAB, Universities of Manchester and Liverpool (1995-00). Over 150 publications within Obstetrics and Gynaecology and Reproductive Healthcare.
Interests: Music, art, literature, sailing, rambling.
Contact details: 25 Spath Road, Didsbury, Manchester M20 2QT (tel: 0161 445 1723, fax: 0161 445 7680, email: max.elstein@man.ac.uk).

ELTON, Dr Peter Joseph, MB, ChB, MSc, FFPHM

Positions: Director, Public Health, Bury, North West; Regional Prison Health Lead; Chairman, Outreach Care Services; Member, North West Action on Smoking and Health Council.

Areas of Influence: Health, Public Sector, Voluntary Sector.
Profile: March 2nd, 1952. *m.* Mavis. 2 Sons.
Educated at Carmel College, Wallingford (1959-70) and Manchester University (1970-75 and 1977-79). Career profile: Clinical Medicine (1975-77); Public Health (1977-82); Consultant, Public Health, North Manchester (1983-93); Consultant, Public Health, Tameside/West Pennine (1993-95); Director, Community Services, North Manchester (1986-93); Director, Public Health, Health Authority, Wigan and Bolton (1995-2002). Member of Whitefield Golf Club.
Interests: Piano (badly), golf (worse).
Contact details: Bury PCT, Silver Street, Bury (0161 762 3138, email: Peter.Elton@burypct.nhs.uk) (tel: 0161 720 7169).

ENSOR, His Honour George Anthony, LLB

Positions: Circuit Judge, Manchester Crown Court; Trustee, Empire Theatre Liverpool Trust (1986 - present); Governor, Malvern College (1993 - present)
Areas of Influence: Law.
Profile: *b.* December 4th, 1936, Portmadoc; *m.* Jennifer Caile (1968); 2 daughters.
Educated at Malvern College (1950-55) and Liverpool University (1955-58). Career profile: Partner (1962-95), Senior Partner (1992-95), Weightman Rutherfords Solicitors; Director, Liverpool FC (1985-93); HM Deputy Coroner, Liverpool (1965-95); Part time Chairman, Industrial Tribunals (1975-95); Deputy Circuit Judge (1978-83); Recorder of the Crown Court (1983-95). Prizes and awards: Atkinson Conveyancing Medal, Law Society (1961); Timpron Martin Medal (1961). Clubs and societies: Artists Club, Liverpool; Liverpool Law Society; Formby Golf Club; Waterloo Football Club.
Interests: Golf, music, theatre.

ENTWISTLE, Tim

Positions: Northern Region Managing Partner, PKF; Fellow of the Institute of Chartered Accountants in England and Wales.
Areas of Influence: Finance.
Contact details: PKF, Sovereign House, Queen Street, Manchester M20 2RU (tel: 0161 8325481, fax: 0161 832 3849, email: tim.entwistle@uk.PKF.com).

ESTEBANEZ, Dr Salvador, BEd (1974), MEd (1982), MA (1984), DrPhil (1997)

Positions: Director, Instituto Cervantes, Manchester; Spanish Ministry of Education And Culture.
Areas of Influence: Linguistics, Arts, Education.
Profile: *b.* September 28th, 1954; *m.* Jill; 1 son.

Education: BEd, Pamploma, Spain (1974); MEd, Madrid (1982); MA, Applied Linguistics, London University; DrPhil, Linguistics, University of Wales. Career profile: Language Teacher (1974-79); Headteacher, Spanish School, London (1979-84); Head of Department of Spanish, Marymount School, Kingston-Upon-Thames (1984-88); Teacher of English, Pamploma, Spain (1988-91); Language Adviser, Spanish Embassy, London (1991-97). Clubs and societies: Association of Language Learning; National Association of Language Advisers.
Interests: Literature, music, sports.
Contact details: Instituto Cervantes, 326 Deansgate, Manchester M3 4FN (tel: 0161 661 4200, fax: 0161 661 4203, email: dirman@cervantes.es) 1 Woodgate Close, Horsham, West Sussex RH13 5RS (tel: 01403 259 563).

EVANS, Gareth Antony, BA

Positions: Deputy Secretary to Council and Senate, University of Manchester; Member of the Court, University of Keele.
Areas of Influence: Education.
Profile: *b.* October 20th, 1961; 1 son; 1 daughter.
Educated at Priory School, Lewes (1973-80); University of York (1980-83). Career profile: Administrative Assistant, Academic Office, University College of North Wales, Bangor (1984-87); Assistant to the Registrar and Principal, University College of North Wales (1987-88); Several posts at the University of Manchester including: Graduate Administrator, Faculty of Medicine (1989-92); Executive Assistant to the Vice-Chancellor (1992-94); Secretary to the Faculty of Education (1994-97); Secretary to the Faculty of Medicine, Dentistry, Nursing and Pharmacy (1997-02). Clubs and societies: Association of University Administrators; UK Medical School and Faculty Secretaries Conference; Association of Football Statisticians.
Interests: Cinema, popular music, literature, travel, speaking Welsh, various sports, running competitively, North West Counties League squash player, Stockport County F.C.
Contact details: University of Manchester, Oxford Road, Manchester M13 9PL (tel: 0161 275 2086, fax: 0161 275 5697, email: gareth.a.evans@man.ac.uk).

EVANS, Michael Norman Gwynne, B.Sc, FCA

Position: Chairman, Wood Street Mission.
Areas of Influence: Voluntary Sector, Education.
Profile: *b.* December 12th, 1939; *m.* Janet; 3 sons.
Educated at Kings School, Macclesfield; Bristol University; Chartered Accountant; Senior Partner, North West, PricewaterhouseCoopers (1966-99); Member of the Board of Manchester Metropolitan University and City College, Manchester; Chairman, Multimedia Marketing. Clubs and societies: St. James's Club; Hon Treasurer,

Manchester Literary and Philosophical Society; Committee Member, Stockport Cerebral Palsy Society.
Interests: Walking, gardening, D.I.Y.
Contact details: Lime Cottage, 144 Grove Lane, Cheadle Hulme, Cheshire Sk8 7NH (tel: 0161 439 2088, fax: 0161 439 2649).

EVANS, Richard David, BA (Hons), ACA, MSI

Position: Director Corporate Finance, Brewin Dolphin Securities Ltd.
Areas of Influence: Finance
Profile: *b.* June 19th, 1959; *m.* Elizabeth; 1son, 2 daughters.
Education: Westcliff High School for Boys, Southend-on-Sea, Essex; Manchester Victoria University. Career profile: Barnes Roffe, Chartered Accountants, London; BDO Stoy Hayward, London; London Stock Exchange; Wise Speke Limited, Manchester.
Interests: Family, football, films.
Contact details: Brewin Dolphin Securities Ltd, Po Box 512, National House, 36 St Anne Street, Manchester M60 2EP (tel: 0161 214 5553, fax: 0161 832 1672, email: richard.evans@brewin.co.uk).

FAIRWEATHER, Eric, FCIB

Positions: Head of Asset Finance, The Co-operative Bank PLC; Deputy Chairman, Bolton Wide.
Areas of Influence: Finance, Commerce.
Profile: *b.* November 9th, 1942; *m.* Deb; 2 sons; 2 daughters.
Educated at Carlisle Grammar School. Career profile: Midland Bank, Carlisle (1961); Manager, Corporate Finance Division (1978-81); Senior Assistant Manager, Poultry and Princes Street (1981-84); Director, Industrial Development Unit, Department of Trade and industry (1984-86); Manager, Central Management and Planning (1986-87); Area Manager, Corporate Banking, Manchester (1987-93); Area Manager, Manchester (1993-94); Area Manager, South Yorkshire (1994-95); Regional General Manager, Co-operative Bank, North West (1995-98); Director, Wigan Borough Partnership (1996-2002). Deputy Chairman, Bolton Wide; Council Member, Pro.Manchester (1997-2002) Prizes and awards: University of London Gilbart Examinations on Banking: Certificate of Honour Class II (1965); Certificate of Honour Class I (1966); Prizewinner (1967).
Interests: Association football, Bolton Wanderers, golf, classical music.
Contact details: Asset Finance Dept, The Co-operative Bank PLC, 1 Balloon Street, Manchester M60 4EP (tel: 0161 829 5318, fax: 0161 839 2387, email: eric.fairweather@co-operativebank.co.uk) 5 The Hamlet, Lostock, Bolton BL6 4QT (tel: 01204 493505, fax: eric.fairweather@aol.com)

FALLOWS, David (Nicholas), BA, MMus, PhD, Chevalier de l'Ordre des Arts et des Lettres

Positions: Professor of Musicology, University of Manchester; President, International Musicological Society; Vice-President, Royal Musical Association; Co-editor, Manchester Sounds; Editorial Board of Musica Britannica; Early English Church Music; Early Music History; Musiek en Wetenschap.
Areas of Influence: Arts, Education.
Profile: *b.* December 20th, 1945; *m.* Pauléne (sep. 1996); 1 son; 1 daughter.
Educated at Shrewsbury School, Jesus College Cambridge, King's College London and the University of California, Berkeley. Career profile: Reviews Editor, Early Music (1976-95, 1999-00); General Editor, Royal Musical Association Monographs (1982-95); Chair of Programme Commitee for Quinquennial International Congress of the International Musicological Society (1993-97). Prizes and awards: Dent Medal, International Musicological Society and Royal Musical Association (1982); Ordinary Fellow of the British Academy (1997). Clubs and societies: Corresponding Member of the American Musicological Society (1999). Vincent Duckles Award (2001); C.B Oldham Award for *A catalogue of Polyphonic Songs* (2001).
Contact details: Department of Music, University of Manchester (fax: 0161 275 4994, email: david.fallows@man.ac.uk); 10 Chatham Road, Old Trafford, Manchester M16 0DR (tel: 0161 881 1188).

FAWCETT, Julia

Positions: Group Chief Executive, The Lowry, Arts Venue; Non - Executive Director, Portsmouth Harbour Trust; Committee Member of Trends in Leisure and Entertainment Conference and Exhibition.
Areas of Influence: Arts, Media, Commerce.
Profile: *b.* March 6th, 1965; *m.* Neil; 1 son,
Education: B.A (Hons) Drama, Film, Television, Bristol University. Career profile: Granada Leisure (1988-97); Chief Executive, Dynamic Earth, Edinburgh (1997-02); Scottish Thistle Award for Business Tourism (2001).
Interests: Reading, travel, chess.
Contact details: The Lowry, Pier 8, Salford Quays M50 3 AZ (tel: 0161 876 2023, fax: 0161 876 2021, email: julia.fawcett@thelowry.com).

FAWCUS, Simon James David, M.A CANTAB

Position: Circuit Judge.
Area of Influence: Law, Education.
Profile: *b.* July 12th, 1938. *m.* Joan Mary. 1 Son. 4 Daughters.
Educated at Aldenham School; Trinity Hall, Cambridge; Practice, Northern Circuit

(1962-85); Governor of Mount Carmel School for Girls, Alderley Edge (1976-2001), Chairman (1995-98 and 2000-01); Called to the Bar, Gray's Inn (1961); Member of: Manchester Tennis and Racquet Club; John Shaw's Club; M.C.C.; Wilmslow Golf Club; Manchester Chamber Concert Society.
Interests: Real tennis, golf, gardening, listening to music, travel.
Contact details: Courts of Justice, Crown Square, Manchester.

FELL, Brian Stephen, BA (Hons) Fine Art, MA Fine Art

Position: Self employed Artist.
Areas of Influence: Arts.
Profile: *b.* August 31st, 1952; *m.* Virginia; 1 son.
Educated at Waterloo Grammar School, Liverpool (1963-70); Manchester Polytechnic (1975-79). Career profile: Various part time lecturing posts in Art Colleges in the North West (1980-84); Gallery Technician, Cornerhouse Arts College; Gallery Technician, Yorkshire Sculpture Park (1985-90); Cheltenham College of Art Sculpture Fellowship (1979-80); Yorkshire Arts Association, Artist in Industry Fellowship (1982); Henry Moore Fellowship, Yorkshire Sculpture Park (1990-92). Prizes and awards: The Lord Mayors Civic Award for Design, Merchant Seamens Memorial, Cardiff (1997); Major commissions for Southport, Morecambe, Lancaster, Plymouth, Cardiff, Liverpool, Manchester. Member of Glossop Labour Club.
Interests: Fish, guitars, armchair sailing, cranes.
Contact details: 4 Bank Street, Glossop, Derbyshire (tel: 07961 061 214).

FERGUSON, Professor Mark William James, CBE (1999)

Positions: Professor of Basic Dental Sciences, School of Biological Sciences, University of Manchester; Co-founder, Director and Chief Executive Officer, Renovo Ltd.
Areas of Influence: Health, Commerce, Education.
Profile: *b.* October 11th, 1955; *m.* Dr Sharon O'Kane; 3 daughters.
Educated at Ballykelly Primary School (1956-66), Coleraine Academical Institution (1966-73) and The Queen's University of Belfast (1973-82). Renovo is a biotechnology company spinout of the University of Manchester, which is developing novel pharmaceutical therapies to prevent scarring or accelerate healing following wounding. Professor Ferguson is also a member of the UK Governments Genome Valley Steering Group, the Committee of Safety of Medicines Biological Subcommittee, the HEFCE Preclinical Foresight Panel on Health and Life Sciences. His research interests focus on developmental mechanisms in normal and cleft palate formation, wound healing, paticularly prevention of scarring and stimulation of chronic wound healing and temperature dependent sex determination in alligators and chickens. He is the recipient of a number of international awards and honours

for this research work and the author of over 300 research papers, patents and books including 38th Edition of Grays Anatomy. Clubs and societies: President, European Tissue Repair Society; Member of Anatomical Society of Great Britain and Ireland; British Society for Cell Biology; British Society for Developmental Biology; Zoological Society of London.

Interests: Scientific investigation, travel, antique collecting, philately.

Contact details: Immunology, Microbiology & Developmental Division, School of Biological Sciences, University of Manchester, 3.239 Stopford Building, Oxford Road, Manchester, M13 9PT (tel: 0161 275 6775, fax: 0161 275 5945, email: mark.ferguson@man.ac.uk).

FIELD, Patrick John, QC

Position: Barrister, Deans Court Chambers.
Areas of Influence: Law.
Education: Wilmslow County Grammar School; Kings College, London. Patrick Field was called to the Bar by the Honourable Society of Gray's Inn in 1981 and has practised at Dean Court Chambers since 1982, a Member of the Northern Circuit, Junior of the Northern Circuit in 1985.
Interests: Fishing; Shooting; Travel.
Contact details: Deans Court Chambers, 24 St John Street, Manchester M3 4DG (tel: 0161 214 6000, fax: 0161 214 6001, email: field@deanscourt.co.uk).

FIELDEN, John Anthony Haigh, MA

Positions: Trustee of the Manchester Guardian Charitable Trust; Solicitor.
Areas of Influence: Law, Voluntary Sector.
Profile: *b.* March 3rd, 1937; *m.* Deryl Anne; 1 son; 1 daughter.
Education: Heronwater (1945-50); Rossall (1950-55); Keble College, Oxford (1955-58). Career profile: Solicitor (1961); Partner Emerson & Fielden (1962-68); Merged with Whitworths (1968); Partner, Leak, Almond & Parkinson (1970); Senior Partner, Leak, Almond & Parkinson (1985); Senior Partner, Cobbett Leak Almond (1987); Consultant, Cobbetts (2000-2002). Clubs and societies: M.C.C.; Manchester Tennis and Racquet Club; numerous other cricket clubs.
Interests: Cricket, real tennis, travel.
Contact details: Wardfall, Ribchester Road, Dinkley, Blackburn BB6 8AH.

FINCH, David Francis

Position: Chairperson, Victim Support and Witness Service, Greater Manchester; Volunteer, The Wildlife Trust (Lancashire, Manchester and North Merseyside).
Areas of Influence: Public Sector, Voluntary Sector.

Profile: *b.* February 12th, 1933; *m.* Avril; 2 sons.
Education: The Masonic School for Boys; University of Nottingham; Keele University; Bolton Institute of Higher Education. Career profile: National Service; Assistant Farm Manager, Brazil; Deputy Chief Probation Officer, Greater Manchester. David Finch is a member of The Hallé Concert Society.
Interests: Wildelife conservation, walking, gardening, music.

FINDON, The Rev Dr John Charles

Positions: Rector of Bury; Chaplain, Royal Regiment of Fusileers (Lancashire); Chaplain, Bury ATC; Executive Member, Bury Local Strategic Partnership.
Areas of Influence: Education, Voluntary Sector.
Profile: *b.* June 20th, 1950; *m.* Christa; 1 son; 2 daughters.
Education: King Edward VI Grammar School, Stratford-upon-Avon; Keble College, Oxford; Cuddesdon Theological College. Career profile: Tutor, Keble College and Christ Church, Oxford (1972-77); Curate, Middleton Parish Church (1977-80); Lecturer, Bolton Parish Church (1980-83); Vicar, St Stephen's, Astley (1983-91); Vicar, St John the Divine, Sale (1991-98). John Findon has published various articles relating to church History and in new dictionary of National Biography.
Interests: Music, walking, cricket, criticizing other peoples Sermons.
Contact details: The Rectory, Tithe Barn Street, Bury BL9 OJR (tel: 0161 764 2452, fax: 0161 764 2452).

FINESTEIN, Jonathon Eli

Positions: District Judge, Salford; Recorder of the Crown Court.
Areas of Influence: Law.
Profile: *b.* April 9th, 1950; *m.* Elaine; 1 daughter.
Education: Hull Grammar School; Leeds University. Career profile: Called to the Bar (1973); Barrister, Hull (1974-92); Recorder (1992); District Judge (1992); Moved to Salford (2001); Recorder, Manchester Crown Court.
Interests: Walking.
Contact details: Salford Magistrates' Court, Bexley Square, Salford M3 6DJ (tel: 0161 834 9457).

FINLAY, Ian, DipArch, DA (Manc), RIBA

Position: Principle, Ian Finlay Architects (1991 - present).
Areas of Influence: Arts, Media, Voluntary Sector.
Profile: *b.* February 26th, 1951; Marilyn (partner); 1 daughter, Sophie.
Educated at Bournville Technical Grammar School, Birmingham and Manchester Polytechnic School of Architecture. Career profile: Project Architect with Rod

Hackney Associates on the UK's second Black Road Self Help Housing Scheme in Macclesfield (1975-80); Founder member of Design Cooperative, amongst the first architectural cooperatives in the country and Manchester's first Community Architecture Practice (1980-85); Director of DC Architects and Principal Partner behind the Paradise Wharf regeneration project (1985-91); Chair, RIBA Community Architecture Group and founder of the Community Projects Fund (1981-93); Co-founder of the Ancoats Buildings Preservation Trust and former Chair (1996); Co-founder of the Manchester Civic Society and Manchester Forum Newspaper (1996); Designer of the Northmoor Homezone, Britains first Homezone (2000); Designer, Wing Yip Manchester Project (2001). Publications: Co-author with Lesley Klein of the *RIBA Architect's Appointment: Community Architecture Services* (1988); Co-author of *Draft Planning and Design Guide for the Ancoats Urban Village* (1997). Prizes and awards: ICE Award (2002); BURA Best Practice Award (2001) Clubs and societies: Member, RIBA; The Community Projects Fund established by Ian to support community based building schemes at the crucial feasibility stage raised and expended £1.5m of feasibility grants and generated over £250m of capital building works and community schemes over a 10 year period.

Interests: Following Birmingham City FC, improving the environment, travel.

Contact details: The Stables, Paradise Wharf, Ducie Street, Manchester (tel: 0161 272 8475, fax: 0161 273 1550, email: architecture@ianfinlay.com).

FINNEY, Barbara Gill, JP

Positions: Chairman of the Leigh Bench; Govenor of Canon Slade School.
Areas of Influence: Law, Education.
Profile: *b.* March 19th, 1941; *m.* John; 2 sons.
Education: King Edward VI High School for Girls, Birmingham (1952-60); Girton College, Cambridge (1960-64); Victoria University of Manchester (1975-77). Career profile: Teacher, Bolton School for Girls (1964-65); Adult Literacy Advisor, Wigan (1978-80); Head of Department, Canon Slade School, Bolton (1980-97). Clubs and Societies: Branches Secretary, The Classical Association; Magistrates' Association; Mothers' Union.
Interests: Reading; Theatre; Cinema; Icon Painting; Travel; Crosswords; National Trust Properties.
Contact details: 36 Station Road, Blackrod, Bolton BL6 5BW (tel: 01204 698 010, email: barbara@finney41.fsnet.co.uk).

FIRTH, Mary Flora Mackinnon, OBE, JP, DL

Position: Deputy Lieutenant of the City of Manchester; Chairman, Oldham Health Authority (1987 – present).
Areas of Influence: Voluntary Sector, Health.

Profile: *b.* October 13th, 1929; *m.* Lee; 1 son; 2 daughters.
Educated at Oldham Hume Grammar School. Career profile: Justice of the Peace (1971); Chairman, Oldham Health Authority (1986-91); Chairman, Oldham NHS Trust (1991-2002); President, British Red Cross Society, Greater Manchester (1988-94), High Sheriff of Greater Manchester (1996-97). Clubs and societies: Saddleworth Bridge Club; High Sheriffs Association.
Interests: Bridge, reading, tennis, theatre, golf.
Contact details: The Orchards, Westfield Drive, Grasscroft, Oldham OL4 4HT (tel: 01457 872 186, fax: 01457 872 186).

FISH, David Thomas, QC

Positions: Barrister; Recorder.
Areas of Influence: Law, Finance.
Profile: *b.* July 7th, 1949; *m.* Angelina; 1 son; 1 daughter.
Education: Ashton-under-Lyne Grammar School; London School of Economics. Career profile: Called to the Bar (1973); Assistant Recorder (1989); Recorder (1994); Q.C. (1997). Clubs and societies: Aston-under-Lyne Golf Club; Racehorse Owners Association.
Interests: horse racing, golf.
Contact details: Deans Court Chambers, 24 St John Street, Manchester M3 4DG (tel: 0161 214 6000, fax: 0161 214 6001).

FISHER, Catherine Jane, LLB (Hons), BCL.

Position: Barrister, Merchant Chambers.
Areas of Influence: Law.
Profile: *b.* October 20th, 1966.
Education: Halstead School, Woking, Surrey; Guildford High School, Guildford, Surrey; London University (LSE); Oxford University (Hertford College). Catherine Fisher was called to the Bar in 1990 and appointed to a one year post as a research assistant at the Law Commission, London (1990-1991). She was then admitted to the New York State Bar as a US Attorney-at-Law and undertook pupillage at Blackstone Chambers, Middle Temple and at 8 New Square, Lincoln's Inn (1991-1992). Following this, she then practised from Ropewalk Chambers (1992-97) before joining Merchant Chambers in 1997. Catherine is instructed frequently in partnership disputes, acts in insolvency matters and is also instructed in finance leasing work. Prizes and awards: Gray's Inn Entrance Scholarship; Gray's Inn Stuart Cunningham Macaskie KC Scholarship; Gray' Inn Lord Justice Holker Award.
Interests: Sculpture, antiques.

Contact details: Merchant Chambers, No 1 North Parade, Parsonage Gardens, Manchester, M3 2NH (tel: 0161 839 7070, fax: 0161 839 7111, email: cjfisher@cjfisher.demon.co.uk).

FISHWICK, Avril, OBE (1997), DL (1982), MA (1996), LLM (1948), LLB (1948)

Positions: Deputy Lieutenant, Greater Manchester (1982 - present).
Areas of Influence: Law, Public Sector.
Profile: *b.* March 30th, 1924; *m.* Tom (d. 1999); 2 daughters.
Educated at Woodfield Private School, High School for Girls, Wigan and Liverpool University. Career profile: Foreign Office, Bletchley Park (1942-45); Admitted as a solicitor (1949); Partner, Frank Platt & Fishwick Solicitors (1958-94); High Sherriff, Greater Manchester (1983-84); Member, Wigan & Leigh, Hospital Management Committee (1960-73); Chairman, Wigan Area Health Authority (1973-83); Member, NW Regional Health Authority (1984-88); Vice Lord- Lieutenant, Greater Manchester, (1988-98); Director, Nat West Bank, North (1984-92). Instrumental in raising £1.25m for a CT Scammer at Wigan Infirmary. Prizes and awards: Scholarship, Columbia University, New York; Law Society Prize for Conveyancing; HM Queen Mothers Birthday Award, Environmental Improvement; Bronze Medal and Certificate, Meritorious Service, RSPCA, Paul Harris Fellow, Rotary International; Freedom, Metropolitan Borough of Wigan. Clubs and societies: Hon. Member, Soroptimist International; President, Wigan RSPCA (1988-01), Wigan Little Theatre (2001), Friends of Drumcroon Arts Centre, D. Day and Normandy Veterans Association; Director, Environment and Research Consultancy of Tidy Britain; Vice President, Greater Manchester West Scout Council; Trustee, Skelton Bounty, Friends of Rosie, The Law Society.
Contact details: 6 Southfields, Richmond Road, Bowdon, Nr Altrincham WA14 2TY (tel: 0161 941 6660).

FITZSIMONS, Lorna, BA (Hons) (1988)

Position: Member of Parliament for Rochdale.
Areas of Influence: Politics.
Profile: *b.* August 8th, 1967; *m.* S. Cooney; 1 son; 1 daughter.
Educated at Wardle High School, Rochdale College of Art & Design and Loughborough College of Art & Design.
Contact details: 81 Durham Street, Rochdale, Lancs. OL11 1LR (tel: 01706 644911, fax: 01706 759826, email: fitzsimons@parliament.uk).

FITZWALTER, Raymond Alan

Positions: Director, Ray Fitzwalter Associates (1993 – present); Visiting Professor, Salford University (1993 – present).
Areas of Influence: Media, Law, Commerce.
Profile: *b*. Feburary 21st, 1944; *m*. Luise; 2 sons; 1 daughter.
Education: The Derby School; London School of Economics. Career profile: Trainee Reporter, Telegraph & Argus, Bradford (1965); Feature Writer, Telegraph & Argus, Bradford (1966); Deputy News Editor, Telegraph & Argus, Bradford (1968); Researcher (1970), Producer (1975), Editor (1976), Executive Producer (1987-93), *World in Action*, Granada Television; Executive Producer, *What the Papers Say* (1988-93); Executive Producer, Drama Documentaries (1988-93); Head of Current Affairs, Granada Television (1987-93); Chairman, Salford Conference (1995 -); Northern Representative, Pact (1993-01); Chairman, Campaign for Quality Television (1995 -); Visiting Professor, International Media School, Salford University (2002 -); Commonwealth Press Union Scholar (1969); Young Journalist of the Year (1969); 35 National and International Awards under Ray Fitzwalter's Editorship; BAFTA (1986); BAFTA (1990). Publications: *Web of Corruption* (with David Taylor) (1981); *The Purposes of Broadcasting* (with others) (1998). Ray Fitzwalter is also a Fellow of the Royal Television Society.
Interests: Naval history; chess; garden.
Contact details: Ray Fitzwalter Associates, Tower View, Lumb Carr Road, Holcombe, Near Bury, Lancs, BL8 4NN (tel: 01706 825 222, fax: 01706 821 833, email: fitzwalter@btconnect.com).

FLYNN, Barry, BSc, MBA, FCA

Positions: Partner (1994 - present) and Head of Audit (2001 - present), North of England, Ernst & Young.
Areas of Influence: Finance.
Profile: May 24th, 1958; *m*. Julie; 2 sons; 1 daughter.
Educated at Blydon Grammar, Tyne & Wear, and Liverpool University achieving a First in Chemistry. After joining Arthur Young (1980), Barry Flynn spent 2 years in corporate finance and corporate recovery before spending a year on secondment to an enterprise agency helping SMEs (1985). After a spell in the Midlands (1988-93) he returned to the North West becoming Managing Partner of Liverpool (1998). Although he is based in Liverpool, Ernst & Young has a client base that covers the North West and he is frequently in the Manchester Office.
Interests: Holidays, socialising, theatre, cinema.
Contact details: Ernst & Young, Silkhouse Street, Tithebarne Street, Liverpool, L2 2LE (tel: 0151 210 4200, fax: 0151 210 4202, mob: 0777 197 4959).

FOLKMAN, Peter John

Positions: Managing Director, North of England Ventures Ltd; Member, Council and Court, University of Manchester; Chairman, Manchester Federal School of Business and Management; Chairman, Manchester Technology Fund; Director Royal Exchange Theatre.
Areas of Influence: Finance, Education, Arts.
Profile: *b.* August 30th, 1945; *m.* Judy; 3 sons.
Education: BA, Oxford University; MBA, Wharton School, University of Pennsylvania. Career profile: Director, 3i plc, Manchester; Founder, North of England Ventures (1989); Council of the British Venture Capital Association (1993-95).
Interests: Skiing, tennis.
Contact details: Director, Granville Baird Capital Partners Ltd, 3rd Floor, Brazennose House, Brazennose Street, Manchester M2 5BP (tel: 0161 236 6600, fax: 0161 236 6650, email: pfolkman@gbcp.com); 6 Oakfield Road, Manchester M20 6XA (tel: 0161 434 9489, fax: 0161 448 1018, email: peterfolkman@hotmail.com).

FORD, Anna

Positions: Broadcaster/Journalist, BBC TV News; Chancellor, University of Manchester; Trustee, Royal Botanic Gardens, Kew.
Areas of Influence: Arts, Education, Media.
Profile: *b.* October 10th, 1943; *m.* Mark Boxer (deceased 1988); 2 daughters.
Education: White House Grammar School, Brampton, Cumbria; Manchester University; Christies Fine Art Department. Career profile: Lecturer, Belfast (1970-72); Staff Tutor, Open University (1972-74); Reporter/Presenter Granada TV (1974-76); Presenter, BBC (1976-78); ITN News (1978-81); Freelance TV & Radio work and Breakfast TV AM (1981-88); BBC News (1988-02); Men - A Documentary (1985).
Interests: Reading; gardening; walking; environmental matters.
Contact details: The Chancellor of The University of Manchester, University of Manchester, Oxford Road, Manchester M13 9PL (tel. 0161 275 2000).

FORRESTER, Jim

Position: Director, Imperial War Museum North.
Areas of Influence: Arts, Education, Public Sector.
Profile: *b.* February 25th, 1952; *m.* Caroline; 1 son; 1 daughter.
Education: Clifton College, Bristol; University of Durham; David Jones Boatbuilders, Chester. Career profile: Truck Driving & Stunt Driving Crew (1974); Apprentice Boatbuilder (1975); Journeyman Boatbuilder (1978); Museum Conservator, Merseyside County Museum (1984); Museum Public Programmes Officer & Project

Officer, National Museums & Galleries, Merseyside (1989); General Manager, Museum Trading Company, National Museums & Galleries, Merseyside (1998). Clubs and societies: Museums Association; RSPB; National Trust.
Interests: Social history, industrial archaeology, arts, boats, food, wild places, family life.
Contact details: Imperial War Museum North, Trafford Wharf Road, Trafford Park, Manchester M17 1TZ (tel:0161 836 4010, fax: 0161 836 4012, email: jforrester@iwm.org.uk).

FOSS, The Rev Dr David Blair

Positions: Vicar, St Chads; Team Rector, Rochdale.
Areas of Influence: Faith Groups, Voluntary Sector.
Profile: *b.* July 18th, 1944; *m.* Valerie; 2 daughters.
Education: Bristol University; Cambridge University; Durham University; London University. Career profile: Curate, Barnard Castle (1969-72); Lecturer, University of Sierra Leone (1972-74); Chaplain and Lecturer, St. John's College, York (1974-75); Chaplain and Senior Lecturer, Christ Church College, Canterbury (1975-80); Chaplain and Head of Divinity, Elmslie Girls School, Blackpool (1980-83); Tutor and Lecturer in Doctrine, College of the Resurrection, Mirfield (1983-88); Vicar, Battyeford, Mirfield (1988-99); Vicar, All Saints, Ryde, Isle of Wight (1999-01). Clubs and Societies: Canterbury and York Society; Ecclesiastical History Society.
Interests: Church history, walking, theatre, railways, cricket.
Contact details: The Vicarage, Sparrow Hill, Rochdale OL16 1QT (tel. 01706 645 014).

FOSTER, Jonathan QC

Positions: Head of Chambers; Deputy High Court Judge; Recorder.
Areas of Influence: Law.
Profile: *b.* July 20th, 1947; *m.* Sarah; 4 sons.
Clubs and societies: St. James Club.
Interests: Outdoor activities, bridge.
Contact details: 18 St John Street, Manchester M3 4EA.

FOUNTAIN, Neil Taylor, BA

Positions: Chief Executive, MIDAS (1997 - present); Director of Economic Development and Deputy Chief Executive, Manchester Enterprises (2001 - present)
Areas of Influence: Commerce, Public Sector.
Profile: *b.* May 8th, 1946; *m.* Carolyn; 1 son.
Education: Oldham Hulme Grammar School (1957-58); Baines Grammar School,

Poulton-le-Fylde (1958-63); Colne Grammar School (1963-64); BA Economics and Geography, Leeds University (1964-67); Diploma in Industrial Administration, Bradford University (1971-72). Career profile: Cost Controller and Systems Analyst, Plessey Telecommunications Ltd, Chorley and Liverpool (1967-71); Corporate Planner / Senior Corporate Planner, Sunderland MBC (1972-79); Various positions culminating in Head of Economic Initiatives, Manchester City Council (1979-97).
Interests: Theatre, music, opera, walking, gardening.
Contact details: MIDAS, Midas House, Trafford Wharf Road, Wharfside, Trafford, Manchester M17 1EX (tel: 0161 877 3000, fax: 0161 848 8638, email: neil.fountain@midas.org.uk).

FOX, David John

Positions: Consul for Chile; Secretary General, International Congress of Americanists; Honorary Secretary, Manchester Consular Association.
Areas of Influence: Education, Public Sector.
Profile: *b.* July 15th, 1931.
Education: Chipping Campden Grammar School; Woking County School for Boys; University College, University of London; McGill University, Montreal; University of California, Berkeley. Career profile: RAF National Service; Research Assistant, McGill University Sub-arctic Research Laboratory; Teaching Assistant, University of California, Berkeley; Visiting Professor, Southern Illinois University; Warden, Woolton Hall, University of Manchester; Senior Lecturer, School of Geography, University of Manchester; Consul for Chile. Clubs and societies: Manchester Consular Association; Society for Latin American Studies; Quaker Bolivia Link.
Interests: Travel, writing, exploring, reading.
Contact details: Consulate of Chile, 22 Bollin Hill, Wilmslow, Cheshire SK9 4AW (tel: 01625 528 000, email: david.fox@ man.ac.uk).

FOX, Harry

Position: Managing Director, Housing Units LTD.
Areas of Influence: Commerce.
Contact details: Housing Units LTD, Failsworth, Manchester M35 9BA (tel: 0161 681 5678).

FRASER, Ian Robert, MA (Hons), MBA

Position: Chief Executive, Brammer plc (1998 - present).
Areas of Influence: Commerce.
Profile: *b.* May 20th, 1955; *m.* Penny; 1 son; 2 daughters.
Education: Dynevnor Grammar School, Swansea (1966-73); Jesus College, Oxford (1973-77); Harvard Business School, USA (1981-83). Career profile: Raychem (1983-91); Reliance Security Group plc (1991-98).
Interests: Rugby, squash, fine wine, antiques.
Contact details: Brammer plc, Station House, Stamford New Road, Altrincham WA14 1EP (tel: 0161 925 2503, fax: 0161 929 6546, email: cm@brammer.plc.uk).

FRASER, Vincent, QC (2001), MA

Position: Recorder (2002).
Areas of Influence: Law.
Profile: *b.* October 18th 1958; *m.* Mary Elizabeth; 1 son; 2 daughters.
Educated at St Mary's College, Crosby and University College, Oxford. Called to Bar (1981). Publication: *Planning decisions digest*, Sweet and Maxwell, (1992).
Interests: Music, literature, sport.
Contact details: 40 King Street, Manchester M2 6BA (tel: 0161 832 9082, fax: 0161 835 2139).

FRISBY, Norman, JP (1973-94), DL (1992)

Positions: Deputy Lieutenant, Greater Manchester (1992 - present); Trustee, Springhill Hospice, Rochdale (1998 - present)
Areas of Influence: Faith Groups, Media, Voluntary Sector.
Profile: *b.* January 9th, 1928; *m.* Iris; 1 son; 2 daughters.
Educated at King Edward VII Grammar School, East Retford, Notts. (1939-46). Career profile: Military Service, Sixth Airborne Division (1946-49); Journalist, Newark Advertiser, Lincolnshire Echo, Liverpool Evening Express, Daily Express and TV Times (1949-59); Television Publicist (1959-88); Chief Press and PR Officer, Granada Television, Manchester (1974-88); Retired (1988). Manchester City Justice of the Peace (1973-94); Chairman of Courts Training Committee; Founder, *Manchester Justice* Magazine and Consultant to *The Magistrate*; Involved in Hospice Movement with St Ann's Hospice, Manchester (1968-98); Chairman, Rochdale Parish Church Communications Committee .Publications: *What is a TV Centre?* (1968-74); *Television in the University*, edited (1964); *The Granada Years* (1981-87).
Interests: Community affairs, media studies, the hospice movement.
Contact details: 6 Lowerfold Way, Healey, Rochdale OL12 7HX (tel: 01706 644224).

FROST, Ronald, BMus (Dunelm), FRCO, Articts

Positions: Director of Music, Organist and Choir Master, St Ann's Church, Manchester.
Areas of Influence: Arts, Education, Faith Groups.
Profile: *b.* March 30th, 1933; *m.* Barbara.
Educated at Bury Grammar School and Royal Manchester College of Music. Career profile: Kirtland Organ Scholarship to RNCM, studied with Harold M Dawber (1951); Meadowcroft Organ Scholarship (1953); Lancashire County major Scholarship (1954); ARMCM, Performers Diploma with Distinction (1954); Royal Manchester Institution medal for Organ Playing with Perry Heywood Certificate (1954) ARCO, Limpus Prize (1953); FRCO, Limpus Prize (1955); BMus, Dunelm (1966); Tutor, RMCM and RNCM (1955-01); Director of Studies, RMCM (1968-71) Principal lecturer, RNCM (1971-2001); Organist and Choirmaster, Stretford Parish Church (1958-69); Accompanist, Hallé Choir (1956-72); Choral Master, Hallé Choir (1972-92); Principal Organist to the Hallé Orchestra (1974-96); Hon. President, ORTOA. Ronald Frost has composed many works for organ, voices and choral groups as well as having published articles within various musical journals. At St Ann's Church, he has given nearly 750 recitals, made many recordings, and done much work for radio and television. Clubs and societies: Oldham, Rochdale and Tameside Organists Association; Manchester Organists Association; Manchester Luncheon Club; Royal Society of Arts.
Interests: Dog walking, crosswords, football, as a spectator!
Contact details: St Ann's Church, St Ann Street, Manchester M2 7LF (tel: 0161 834 0239); The Clefs, 510 Holcombe Road, Greenmount, Bury, Lancs BL8 4EJ (tel: 01204 883 338, email: ronaldfrost@ukgateway.net).

FURBER, Professor Stephen Byram, BA (1974), PhD (1980)

Positions: ICL Professor of Computer Engineering (1990 - present) and Head of Computer Science, University of Manchester (2001- present).
Areas of Influence: Education.
Profile: *b.* March 21st, 1953; *m.* Valerie Margaret; 2 daughters.
Education: Manchester Grammar School (1963-70), Cambridge University (1971-78); BA Maths, class I, Cambridge (1974); PhD Aerodynamics (1980); Fellow, Royal Society (2002); Fellow, Royal Academy of Engineering (1999). Career profile: Rolls Royce Research Fellow, Emmanuel College, Cambridge (1978-81); Acorn Computers Ltd, Cambridge, Design Engineer and Design Manager (1981-90). Publications: *VLSI RISC Architecture and Organisation* (1989); *ARM System Architecture* (1996); *ARM System-on-chip Architecture* (2000). Clubs and societies: PCC Member, St Chad's, Handforth.
Interests: 6 string and bass guitar, church music group.

Contact details: Department of Computer Science, The University of Manchester, Oxford Road, Manchester M13 9PL (tel: 0161 275 6129, fax; 0161 275 6236, email: sfurber@cs.man.ac.uk); 1A Gorsey Road, Wilmslow, Cheshire SK9 5DU (tel: 01625 522 370).

GACESA, Professor Peter, BSc, PhD, CBiol, FIBiol

Position: Pro-Vice Chancellor; Dean of Science and Engineering, Manchester Metropolitan University.
Areas of Influence: Education.
Profile: *b.* May 10th, 1951; *m.* Karen; 2 sons.
Educated at Reading School; University of Bath; Postdoctoral Scientist, Cardiff University (1976-79). Career profile: Lecturer/Senior Lecturer, Cardiff University (1979-95); Professor and Head of Applied Biology, University of Central Lancashire (1995-97). Publications: 120, including 3 books. Non Executive Directorships: National Centre for Business and Sustainability; The Incubation Partnership; Microarray; Sustainability North West.
Contact details: John Dalton Building, Manchester Metropolitan University, Chester Street, Manchester M1 5GD (tel: 0161 247 1783, fax: 0161 247 6315, email: p.gacesa@mmu.ac.uk).

GALASKO, Professor Charles Samuel Bernard, MBBCh (1962), FRCS (1966), ChM (1970), MSc (1980), FMedSci (2002)

Positions: Professor of Orthopaedic Surgery, University of Manchester and Honorary Consultant Orthopaedic Surgeon, Salford Royal Hospitals NHS Trust (1976 - present). Honorary Consultant Orthopaedic Surgeon, Royal Manchester Children's Hospital (1976-02); Member of Council, Royal College of Surgeons of England (1991-03); Member, Medical Committee, British Olympic Association (1988 - present).
Areas of Influence: Health, Sport.

Profile: *b.* June 29th, 1939; *m.* Carol; 1 son; 1 daughter. Educated at King Edward VII School, Johannesburg and University. of Witwatersrand. Career profile: Johannesburg General Hospital. (1963-66); University. of Witwatersrand (1964-65); Hammersmith Hospital and Royal Postgrad. Medical School (1966-69); Nuffield Orthopaedic Centre and Radcliffe Infirmary, Oxford (1970-73); Dir. of Orthopaedic Centre, Hammersmith Hospital and Royal Postgrad. Medical School (1973-76); Clinical Dir., Salford General Hospitals (1989-92); Medical Dir., Salford Royal Hospitals (1993-96). President, British Orthopaedic Association (2000-01), Vice President (1999-00); Vice President, Royal College of Surgeons of England (1999-01); Sir Arthur Sims Commonwealth Professor (1998). Publications: over 300 articles in learned journals; 8 books on Orthopaedic topics. Prizes and awards: Moynihan Prize (1969); Hunterian Professor (1971); AO International Award (1981); Australian Commonwealth Fellowship (1982); Air Arthur Sims Commonwealth Professor (1998). Lectureships: Annandale Lecturer, RCS, Edinburgh, and many others in USA, Switzerland, Israel, India, Singapore, Japan, Netherlands, South Africa, Egypt, UK, Canada, South America, China, Italy, Greece, Norway, Germany, Belgium and Australia.
Interests: Sport, music.
Contact details: Department of Orthopaedic Surgery, Clinical Science Building, Hope Hospital, Eccles Old Road, Salford, M6 8HD (tel: 0161 787 4291, fax: 0161 787 4706, email: djones@fs1.ho.man.ac.uk); 72 Gatley Road, Gatley, Cheadle, Cheshire SK8 4AA (tel: 0161 428 3582, fax: 0161 428 4588, email: cgalasko@fs1.ho.man.ac.uk).

GALE, Susie

Position: PR and Marketing Consultant.
Areas of Influence: Media, Training and Development.
Profile: *b.* October 10th, 1955; *m.* Blythe; 1 daughter.
Susie Gale has worked within PR and Media sectors for over 20 years both nationally and internationally. She has lived and worked in the Caribbean, USA, Middle East, Portugal and Spain as a fundraiser, a journalist, a presenter and in PR. For the past 3 years she has provided a PR and Marketing Consultancy within the retail and fashion industry. She is also a visiting Lecturer at the University of Central Lancs in Fashion Promotion. Clubs and societies: Vice Chairman, Training and Development Council, Institute of Public Relations; Chairman, Professional Advisory Committee, Manchester Metropolitan University.
Interests: Travel, yoga, pilates, theatre, reading, sailing.
Contact details: 46 Macclesfield Road, Presbury, Cheshire SK10 4BH (tel: 01625 820 432, fax: 01625 827 694)

GARNER, Alan, ESQ, OBE (2001)

Position: Writer.
Areas of Influence: Arts, Archaeology, Education.
Profile: *b*. October 17th, 1934; *m*. Griselda; 2 sons; 3 daughters.
Educated at Alderley Edge Council School; Manchester Grammar School; Magdalen College, Oxford. Publications: 8 Novels; 3 Libretti; Television Plays; Essays; Lectures. Prizes and awards: The Carnegie Medal; The Guardian Award; The Phoenix Award of America; First Prize Chicago International Film Festival; The Lewis Carrol Shelf Award; Member of the Portico Library.
Interests: Work.
Contact details: Blackden, Holmes Chapel, Cheshire CW4 8BY.

GARNER, The Reverend Keith Vincent, MTh (Oxon)

Positions: Chairman of Methodist District, Bolton and Rochdale (2001 - present); President of Churches Together, Greater Manchester.
Areas of Influence: Faith Groups, Voluntary Sector.
Profile: *b*. January 4th, 1955; *m*. Carol; 2 sons; 1 daughter.
Educated at Wardley Grammar School, Cliff College, Wesley College, Bristol and Westminster College, Oxford. Career profile: Layworker, Victoria Hall, Bolton (1976); Plymouth Central Hall, Devon (1980-83); Elm Ridge, Darlington (1983-92); St John's, Llandudno (1992-2001). Publications: *Growing with Christ Book, Sermons, Prayers* (1984); *In Fellowship Book* (1990).
Interests: Bolton Wanderers, Lancashire County Cricket Club, travel.
Contact details: District Office, 5 Hillside, Heaton, Bolton (tel: 01204 843 302, email: keithvgarner@btinternet.com).

GARRITY, Michael, OBE (2000) MA, MSc, Bed

Positions: Dean, Faculty of Health and Social Care, University of Salford; Governor, Salford College; Trustee, Bury Hospice.
Areas of Influence: Education, Health.
Profile: *b*. August 25th, 1946; *m*. Erica Maria; 2 sons; 2 daughters.
Interests: Walking, keeping fit, reading.
Contact details: University of Salford, Allerton Building, Frederick Road, Salford M6 6PU (tel: 0161 295 2363, fax: 0161 295 2368, email: m.garrity@salford.ac.uk) 66 Higher Ainsworth Road, Radcliffe, Mnchester M26 4JF (0161 764 5014).

GARSIDE, Professor John, BSc (Eng), PhD, DSc (Eng), FREng, FIChemE

Position: Principal and Vice-Chancellor, UMIST.
Areas of Influence: Education, Science, Engineering.
Profile: *b.* October 9th, 1941; *m.* Patricia Louise; 1 son; 1 daughter.
Educated at Christ's College, Finchley (1953-60); University College, London (1960-66). Career profile: Chemical Engineer, ICI, Billingham (1966-69); Lecturer, Chemical Engineering, University College, London (1969-81); Fulbright Senior Scholar and Visiting Professor, Iowa State University, USA (1976-77); Professor, Chemical Engineering, UMIST (1982-2000); President, Institution of Chemical Engineering (1994-95). Publications: Co-author of 2 books; Co-editor of 5 books. Prizes and awards: State Scholarship (1960); Elected Fellow of Royal Academy of Engineering (1988); Elected Fellow of University College, London (1994).
Interests: walking, sailing, gardening, music, playing the piano.
Contact details: UMIST, PO Box 88, Manchester M1 5JF (tel: 0161 200 4011, fax: 0161 236 7219, email: j.garside@umist.ac.uk).

GARSTON, Clive Richard, LLB(Hons)

Position: Partner, Halliwell Landau.
Areas of Influence: Law, Finance.
Profile: *b.* April 25th, 1945; *m.* Racheline; 1 son; 1 daughter.
Educated at Manchester Grammar School (1955-62) and University of Leeds (1962-65). Career profile: Articled Clerk (1966-68), Assistant Solicitor (1968-71), Partner (1971-78), Hall Brydon Ltd, Manchester; Chairman, Sports & Leisure Group plc and Ultimate Finance plc. Clubs and societies: Member, International Bar Association, Corporate Law Committee of CBI, American Bar Association; RAC, Lancashire County Cricket Club.
Interests: Keep fit, watching Manchester United.
Contact details: St James's Court, Brown Street, Manchester M2 2JF (tel: 0161 831 2668, fax: 0161 831 2641, email: cng@halliwells.co.uk); Sandy Ridge, Bollinway, Hale, Cheshire WA15 0NZ (tel: 0161 904 9822, fax: 0161 980 4412, email: clive.garston1@btinternet.com).

GARTSIDE, Major Edmund Travis, TD, DL (1990), MA

Positions: Chairman, Shiloh plc; General Commissioner of Taxes, Rochdale Division (1966 - present)
Areas of Influence: Commerce, Finance, Health.
Profile: *b.* November 11th, 1933, Rochdale; *m.* Margaret Claire Nicholls (1959) (diss. 1982); 1 son; 1 daughter; *m.* Valerie Cox (1983); 1 steps; 2 stepd.
Educated at Winchester College (1947-52) and Trinity College Cambridge (1954-57).

Career profile: National Service (1952-54) Royal Engineers and Lancashire Fusiliers; Lancashire Fusiliers; Territorial Army Service (1954-68); Management Trainee (1957), Director (1960), Deputy Chairman (19663), Chairman (1966-), Managing Director (1965-00), Shiloh plc; Proprietor, Portico Library, Manchester; High Sheriff of Greater Manchester (1995-96); Governor, Manchester Grammar School (1984-98); President / Representative on Various National, European and International Textile Associations. Clubs and societies: Army & Navy Club, London.
Interests: Travel, skiing, tennis, reading.
Contact details: Shiloh plc, Holden Fold, Royton, Oldham OL2 5ET (tel: 0161 624 8161, fax: 0161 627 3840).

GARVIE, Wayne, BA (Hons), PhD

Positions: Head of Entertainment Group, BBC; Trustee, National Museum of Labour History.
Areas of Influence: Media.
Profile: *b*. September 9th, 1963; *m*. Tracey Stephenson; 2 daughters.
Career profile: Producer Factual, Entertainment and Sport, Granada Television; Director of Broadcasting, Granada Television (1997-98); Head of Entertainment and Features, Manchester, BBC (1998-2000); Head of Entertainment and Features, Head of Music and Centre, Manchester (2000-2001); Member of: BAFTA; RTS; Electric Club; Notting Hill.
Interests: Football, travel, history, pop music, politics.
Contact details: BBC Manchester, Oxford Road, Manchester M60 1SJ (tel: 0161 244 3523, fax: 0161 244 3603, email: wayne.garvie@bbc.co.uk).

GELDART, William

Positions: Artist, Illustrator and Gallery Owner.
Areas of Influence: Arts, Media.
Profile: *b*. March 21st, 1936; *m*. Anne Mary; 1 son; 1 daughter.
Educated at All Saints Primary School, Marple and Hyde Grammar School; Cine Photographer, 14 Fighter Squadron, Germany (1954-56); College of Art, Manchester (1956). Career profile: A small advertising agency in Manchester (1957); Assistant, Art Department, Whitethorn Press (1958); Art Editor, Whitethorn Press (1961); Freelance Artist and Illustrator (1972); Geldart Gallery, Henbury (1975 - present); *Geldarts Cheshire*, Limited Edition signed book; has illustrated numerous books for leading publishers in England and France. Exhibited at the Royal Academy and Chris Beetles in St James, London. Commissons for leading Companies include AstraZeneca, Rolls Royce, Hallé Orchestra, CIS, Pilkingtons and many others.
Interests: Reading, music, opera, theatre, films, sketching (mainly in Majorca).
Contact details: Geldart Gallery, Chelford Road, Henbury, Nr Macclesfield, Cheshire

SK11 9PG (tel: 01625 425 392, fax: 01625 503 237, email: william.geldart@virgin.net, web-site: www.geldartgallery.com); Spinks Farm, Chelford Road, Henbury, Cheshire SK11 9PG.

GIBBS, Colonel Donald Edwin, TD (1960), JP (1969), CBE (1970) ADC (1973), DL (1974)

Positions: Chief Executive, Broughton House Home for Ex-Service Personnel; President, BLESMA Salford Branch (1988 - present); President, Middleton Royal Brittish Legion (1995- present); Chairman, Old Elizabethans Association (1997 - present); Chairman, Manchester Regimental Chapel Committee (1997- present).
Areas of Influence: Military, Voluntary Sector.
Profile: *b.* March 13th, 1926; *m.* Heather (deceased 1993); 1 son; 1 daughter.
Educated at Queen Elizabeth Grammar School, Middleton. War Service: RAC, Indian Army (1942-47); Territorial Army (1947-76). Career Profile: Sales Executive, National Food Company (1953-77); Chairman, Army Benevolent Fund Greater Manchester Committee (1969-88); Hon. Colonel, 156 Regiment RCT(V) (1974-88); Chairman, Broughton House (1976-77); Chairman, Juvenile Bench (1977-83); High Sheriff of Greater Manchester (1981-82). Clubs and societies: Member of Army and Navy Club London; Joint University Defence; Dining Club; Commanderie de Bordeaux; Chante Flute; Manchester Regiment Officer Association. Publication: *Collects of the Services.*
Interests: Football, cricket, wine.
Contact details: Broughton House, Home for Ex-Service Personnel, Park Lane, Salford M7 4JD (tel: 0161 740 2737, fax: 0161 720 7640 email: deg@broughtonhouse.com); 228 Manchester New Road, Alkrington, Middleton, Manchester M24 4BX (tel: 0161 643 2794).

GIBSON, Alan David

Positions: Pro-Chancellor and Chair of Council, University of Salford; Board Member, Universities and Colleges Employers' Association; Member, Advisory Group on Human Resource Management for Higher Education Funding Council for England; Parochial Church Council Member and Chair of Finance, St George's Church, Chorley, Lancashire; Governor and Chair of Staffing, St George's Church of England Primary School, Chorley, Lancashire; Chair, Steering Group on Skills for Work, St Michael's Church of England High School, Chorley, Lancashire.
Areas of Influence: Human Resource Management, Education, Faith Groups.
Profile: *b.* March 1st, 1946; *m.* Christine Frances; 1 daughter, Victoria (27).
Alan Gibson has worked in both the public and private sectors. He started his career in the finance, personnel and policy areas of the MOD. After attending the year long Army Staff Course, as a civilian, he became the finance and personnel advisor to the British Ambassador at NATO in Brussels. Alan next oversaw the transfer of Royal

Ordnance to the private sector. He then concentrated on human resource management holding a range of senior appointments in the private sector, initially in Royal Ordnance plc and later in British Aerospace plc. Alan took early retirement in 1996 at the age of 50. Clubs and societies: Deputy Chairman, Chorley Tennis Club. **Interests:** Playing tennis.
Contact details: University of Salford, Greater Manchester M5 4WT (tel: 0161 295 5050, web: www.salford.ac.uk).

GILBART, Andrew James, QC (1991), MA (Cantab)

Positions: Head of Chambers, 40 King Street (2001 - present); Bencher, Middle Temple; Recorder of the Crown Court; Mental Health Review Tribunal; Member, Northern Circuit of the Bar (1973 - present).
Areas of Influence: Law.
Profile: *b.* February 13th, 1950; 1 son; 1 daughter.
Education: Vinehall School, Robertsbridge, East Sussex; Westminster School, London, SW1; Trinity Hall, Cambridge. Andrew Gilbart has practised from Chambers in Manchester since 1973 and has a specialist practice in Planning, Environment, and Public Law. He has also appeared for promoter of Manchester Airport Second Runway and has published various articles in Local Government Chronicle and Journal of Planning Law. Clubs and associations: Planning and Environment Bar Association; Administrative Law Bar Association; UK Environmental Law Association; American Bar Association; European Circuit of The Bar.
Interests: Theatre, history, walking, computing.
Contact details: 40 King Street, Manchester M2 6BA (tel: 0161 832 9082, fax: 0161 835 2139, email: agilbart@40kingstreet.co.uk).

GILBERT, Dr Anthony John, FRNCM (1981), MA, Dmus

Positions: Composer; Tutor in Composition, Royal Northern College of Music.
Areas of Influence: Arts, Education, Environment.
Profile: July 26th, 1934; 2 sons; 1 daughter.
Educated at Gunnersbury Grammar School, Institut Francais de Londres (Universites de Paris et Lille), Morley College, London and Leeds University. Career profile: Translator of French, Spanish and Russian (1954-59); Warehouseman, Copyist, Music Editor, Scott & Co Ltd (1959-70); Granada Arts Fellow, Composer in Residence, Visiting Lecturer, University of Lancaster (1970-73); Tutor in Composition, Royal Northern College of Music (1973-78); Senior Lecturer, Composition, New South Wales Conservatorium (1978-79); Senior Tutor, Director of Composition Studies, Head of School of Composition and Contemporary Music, Royal Northern College of Music (1979-99). Anthony Gilbert has produced over 90 compositions including 2

symphonies, 2 operas, 4 string quartets, 3 piano sonatas, 6 song cycles, piano concerto, violin concerto, 3 works for wind orchestras, 4 works for chamber orchestra, numerous works for chamber ensemble, duos and solo players, 12 educational compositions, much recorder music and 7 cds. Clubs and societies: Society for the promotion of new music; British Academy of Composers and songwriters; Performing Rights Society; Mechanical Copyright Protection Society.
Interests: Visual Arts, walking, reading, poetry, visual arts, wildlife photography, cross country running, birdwatching.
Contact details: Royal Northern College of Music, 124 Oxford Road, Manchester M13 9RD (tel: 0161 907 5276, fax: 0161 273 7611); 4 Oak Brow Cottages, Altrincham Road, Styal, Wilmslow, Cheshire Sk9 4JE (tel: 01625 536 462).

GILLESPIE, Colin Stephen

Positions: Corporate Finance Partner and Head of NW Corporate Finance, PricewaterhouseCoopers, Manchester (1998 - present).
Areas of Influence: Finance.
Profile: *b.* December 23rd, 1954; *m.* Carole; 2 daughters (Suzi 18, Laura 14).
Educated at Brooklands County Primary School, Sale Grammar School and Nottingham University, Mathematics Degree 1st class, ACA 1st Time Passes (National 1st Place at PEI in ASDP); from Graduate Trainee to Senior Manager, Manchester Accounting and Audit Division, Arthur Andersen & Co (1976-88); from Senior Manager to Director, Corporate Finance Division, Barclays De Zoete Wedd Limited, Manchester, (1988-97); Corporate Finance Director, Credit Suisse First Boston, Manchester (1998). Publications: various miscellaneous articles in regional press and business magazines; Member of ICAEW (FCA).
Interests: Family, cricket (MCC member), football (Manchester United season ticket holder), rugby union (Sale), golf (Bramall Park Golf Club), holidays, food, wine.
Contact details: PricewaterhouseCoopers, 101 Barbirolli Square, Lower Mosely Street, Manchester M2 3PW (tel: 0161 245 2404, fax: 0161 245 2912 email: colin.gillespie@uk.pwcglobal.com).

GILLESPIE, Professor Iain Erskine MBChB (1953), MD (1963), MSc (1974), FRCS (1959, 1970, 1963)

Positions: Professor Emeritus, University of Manchester; Member, Appeals Tribunal Service.
Areas of Influence: Health, Education.
Profile: *b.* September 9th, 1931; *m.* Mary Muriel, nee McIntyre; 1 son; 1 daughter.
Educated at Hillhead High School, Glasgow and University of Glasgow. Career profile: Royal Army Medical Corps, National Service (1954-56); Professor of Surgery,

University of Manchester; Hon Consultant Surgeon, Manchester Royal Infirmary (1970-92); Presenter of Hon Graduates, University of Manchester (1980-92); series of progressive appointments, University of Sheffield and Glasgow (1953-70); USPHS Post-Doctoral Research Fellow, Los Angeles (1961); Dean Medical School, Manchester University (1983-86); Member, University Grants Com., Medical Sub-Com. (1975-86); Member, University and Polytechnic Grants Committee, Hong Kong (1984-89); Past President, Royal Scottish Country Dance Society, Manchester Branch; Founder Chair, Stockport Grammar School Parents Association; Ex-Governor, Stockport Grammar School. Publications: Joint Editor and Author of several books, chapters and articles, mainly on gastroenterological topics in UK, Europe and USA. Prizes and awards: Rorer Prize for Gastroenterology Research (1961). Clubs and societies: Surgical Research Society of GB & Ireland; Association of Surgeons of GB & Ireland; British Society of Gastroenterology; President (1993-94), Manchester Medical Society; Association of Professors of Surgery; 1942 Club of Clinical Professors; Hon Member of Gastroenterology Societies of Australia, Belgium, Argentina; Manchester Luncheon Club; President (1999-01), Manchester Lit & Phil Society.
Interests: Music, reading, golf - Bramall Park Golf Club.
Contact details: 27 Athol Rd, Bramhall, Cheshire SK7 1BR (tel: 0161 439 2811, email: iandmgillespie@aol.com).

GILLETT, The Rt. Revd. David Keith

Positions: Bishop of Bolton (1999 - present); Member, C of E Working Party on Women Bishops; Chair, Diocesan Board for Ministry and Society; Chair, Governing Body of the Manchester Ordained Local Ministry Scheme.
Areas of Influence: Faith Groups, Education, Media.
Profile: *b.* January 25, 1945; *m.* Valerie Susan.
Education: Leeds University, BA 1st class in Theology (1965); Leeds University, M.Phil on Biblical understandings of sexual ethics (1968); Career profile: Lecturer, Old Testament and Mission, St Johns College, Nottingham (1974-79); Co-leader, The Christian Renewal Centre, Rostrevor, N Ireland (1979-82); Vicar, St Hugh's Luton (1982-88); Principal, Trinity College Bristol (1988-99). Publications: *The occult*, Falcon Booklets (1974), *How do congregations learn?* Grove Booklets (1979), *A place in the family?* Grove Booklets (1981), *The Darkness where God is* Kingsway (1982), *Whose Hand is on the Tiller?* Grove Booklets (1983), *Trust and Obey* Darton Longman and Todd (1993), *Treasure in the Field* Harper and Collins (1993).
Interests: Fell walking, photography, gardening, the relationship between Christianity and other faith communities, issues of racial justice, the development of the ministry of lay and ordained ministers of the church, the development of personal and corporate spirituality, often leading quiet days and retreats.
Contact details: Bishop's Lodge, Bolton Road, Hawkshaw, Bury BL8 4JN (tel: 01204 882 955, fax: 01204 882 988, email: David.Gillett@ukgateway.net).

GILLIES, Brian, FInstD, FCMI, FSCTE, MILT

Positions: Director North, Institute of Directors; Non-Executive Director, Business Growth Partners Ltd; Director, Young Enterprise UK Ltd; Director, Partnership Investment Fund Ltd; Chairman, Young Enterprise Yorkshire and Humber Ltd.
Areas of Influence: Commerce, Finance.
Profile: *b.* July 14th, 1961; *m.* Julie; 1 son; 1 daughter.
Brian Gillies was Operations Director of a £32m company for ten years, before starting a telecommunications company. He then became Chief Executive and worked on behalf of a Venture Capital Bank in Switzerland before taking up his current role with the Institute of Directors. Brian is Editor of IOD North West and Yorkshire, and is a regular press Columnist. Member, Chartered Institute of Purchasing and Supply.
Interests: Family takes first place with work second. Fitness is next and the gym is a must on three days a week.
Contact details: Institute of Directors, Lancashire CCC, Old Trafford, Manchester M16 0PX (tel: 0161 282 4152, fax: 0161 282 5533, email: Brian.gillies@iod.com).

GILLILAND, His Honour Judge James Andrew David, QC (1984)

Positions: Judge of the Technology and Construction Court, Manchester.
Areas of Influence: Law, Finance.
Profile: *b.* December 29th, 1937; *m.* Elsie; 2 sons.
Educated at Campbell College and Queens University, Belfast; Lecturer, Manchester University; Qualifications: LLB (1960) and Barrister at Law (1964). Member of Athenaevy, Liverpool.
Interests: Skiing, windsurfing, walking, opera, stamp collecting.
Contact details: Prince William House, Peel Cross Road, Salford M5 2RR (tel: 0161 745 7511, fax: 0161 745 7202).

GLEAVE, Bill, MBE (1999)

Positions: Chief Executive, Lamont Holdings Plc (2001 - present); Chairman, Northern Textiles Plc (2001 - present); Chairman, Gleave Investments Ltd.
Areas of Influence: Commerce, Public sector.
Profile: *b.* July 7th, 1966; *m.* Victoria; 2 daughters.
Educated at Sale Moor Secondary School. Career profile: Founded Northern Textiles Plc (1989); Chairman, Gleave Investments Ltd (1997); CEO, French Plc (1998) Prizes and awards: Hanson Award (1996); Lancashire Businessman of the Year Award (1997).

Interests: Opera, 20th century fiction, cooking, mountain climbing.
Contact details: Northern Textiles Plc, Sycamore Ave, Burnley, Lancs (tel: 01282 416 277, fax: 01282 433 700, email: b.gleave@drew.co.uk).

GODDARD, Paul Frederick, MVO (1990), Pro Ecclesia et Pontifice Cross (1982)

Positions: Clerk to the Greater Manchester Lieutenancy; Member of Court, University of Manchester; Trustee, Manchester Guardian Society Charitable Trust; FEOFFEE, Chethams Hospital and Library; Trustee, Big Issue in the North Trust; Deputy Chairman, Cotton Districts Convalescent Fund / Barnes Samaritan Charity; Committee Member, Emmaus Association of Greater Manchester.
Areas of Influence: Public Sector, Voluntary Sector.
Profile: *b.* May 5th, 1942; *m.* Frances; 1 son; 1 daughter.
Educated at Chetham's School, Manchester. Career profile: Administrative posts with Manchester City Council, Salford City Council and Greater Manchester Council. Clubs and societies: Chair, Friends of Chethams; Member of Friends of RNCM; Manchester Civic Society; Manchester Luncheon Cluband Royal Society of St George.
Interests: Cycling, current affairs, cinema, music.
Contact details: Greater Manchester Lieutenancy Office, Byrom House, Quay Street, Manchester M3 3JD (tel: 0161 834 0490, fax: 0161 835 1536, email: gmlo@btopenworld.com); 7 Stretton Avenue, Sale, Cheshire M33 5EG (tel: 0161 973 2532, email: goddardpf@aol.com).

GODLEE, Richard Crosfield, DL

Positions: President, Manchester Chamber Concerts Society.
Areas of Influence: Arts.
Profile: *b.* June 14th, 1931, Alderley Edge; *m.* Alison Haworth (1958); 2 daughters.
Educated at Ryleys School, Bedales School, and Royal Manchester College of Music. Career profile: Member of Court, RNCM; Hon. Member RNCM; Director, Manchester Mid-day Concerts Society; Deputy Chairman, Hallé Concerts Society; Chairman, Philip Godlee Lodge; Committee Member; Family Welfare Association. Richard Godlee has also been involved with many other welfare associations.
Interests: Music, sailing.
Contact details: The Grange, Clay Lane, Handforth, Cheshire.

GOGGINS, Paul, CQSW

Positions: Member of Parliament for Wythenshawe and Sale East (1997 - present); Parliamentary Private Secretary to Home Secretary, Rt Hon David Blunkett MP.
Areas of Influence: Public Sector
Profile: *b.* June 16th, 1953; *m.* Wyn; 2 sons; 1 daughter.

Educated at St Dunstan's Primary School, St Bede's, and Manchester Polytechnic. Career profile: Social Worker (1974-89); Director of Church Action on Poverty (1989-97); Prior to election to Parliament was a Councillor in Salford (1990-98); Board Member, CAFOD and Campus Ventures.
Interests: Walking, reading, supporting Manchester City.
Contact details: House of Commons, London SW1A 0AA (tel: 0161 499 7900, fax: 0161 499 7911, email: gogginsp@parliament.uk).

GOKAL, Professor Ramanlal, MB, ChB, MD, FRCP

Positions: Consultant Nephrologist (1981); Hon Professor of Medicine, University of Manchester.
Areas of Influence: Health, Faith Groups, Public Sector.
Profile: *b.* January 7th, 1945; Div.; 1 son; 1 daughter.
Education: Morgan High School, Harare, Zimbabwe; University College of Rhodesia (1964-67); Balliol College, University of Oxford (1967-70). Ramanlal Gokal qualified as a physician in 1970 and after prestigious training posts in Oxford and London, took up Renal Medicine including a Medical Research Council Funded Research Project leading to an MD. He is now internationally recognised for research and advances in dialysis for renal failure and related disorders. President, International Society for Peritoneal Dialysis (1998-01); Member, External Reference Group - Renal National Service Framework, Unrelated Live Transplant Regulatory Authority and Ministerial Advisory Board - Purchasing and Supply Agency, Department of Health. Publications: 250 peer-reviewed scientific articles in journals, 30 chapters in textbooks of renal diseases, edited 3 textbooks on Peritoneal Dialysis; Research has led to novel dialysis solutions, which has led to improvements in dialysis. Prizes and awards: Rhodes Scholarship; Hon. Awards at South African, Polish, Italian and USA societies of nephrology in recognition of work. Clubs and societies: Renal Association; Royal College of Physicians; Int. Soc of Nephrology. Ramanlal has a deep interest in spirituality and the wider aspects of religion and lectures regularly within the Community on these aspects. He is President of Bitartiya Vidya Bhavan, a charitable cultural organisation promoting Indian culture.
Interests: Yoga, meditation, music.
Contact details: Manchester Royal Infirmary, Oxford Road, Manchester M13 9WL (tel: 0161 276 4540, fax: 0161 276 8022, e-mail ram.gokal@cmmc.nhs.uk

GOLD, Antony

Positions: Partner and Head of Intellectual Property, Leeds and Manchester, Eversheds (2000 - present); Head of Commercial Department, Manchester, Eversheds (2001 - present).
Areas of Influence: Law.

Profile: *b.*August 26th, 1958; *m.* Sally; 1 son; 2 daughters.
Educated at Birkenhead School (1969-76), Manchester University (1976-79) and Chester College of Law (1979-80). Career profile: Admitted as a Solicitor of the High Court (1983); Head of Eversheds National Litigation Group (1993-98); Head of Litigation Department, Eversheds (1995-00). Member, International Trade Marks Association; Member, London Court of International Arbitration and International Arbitration Club. Interested in areas of intellectual property, particularly internet-related disputes, trade marks, passing off, copyright, and confidential information; has substantial experience in relation to domain name disputes, including High Court proceedings ICANN'S Uniform Dispute Resolution Procedure and Nominet's current dispute resolution procedure. Submissions under the UDRP include Littlewoods -v- Gregg Moores (withdrawn following settlement); CMG Worldwide Inc -v- Bonnie Masterson (successfully defended complaint); Skipton Building Society -v- Peter Colman (successfully pursued complaint); Manchester Airport.com and caledonianmotors.com (successfully acted for claimant). Other recent cases include acting for a successful party in Court of Appeal case of Arrow Nominees -v- Blackledge which has become a major decision relating to courts powers to strike out under the Civil Procedure Rules. Also acted for successful defendants in case reported in Ghee Injunctions; J Siddall & Co -v- P Simmons. Ranked as leading individual in Chambers and The Legal 500.
Interests: Climbing, motorbikes, mountaineering.
Contact details: Eversheds House, 70 Great Bridgewater Street, Manchester M1 SES (tel: 0161 831 8204, fax: 0161 832 5337, email: antonygold@eversheds.com).

GOLDSMITH, Professor Michael James, AcSS (2000), MA (1963), MA (1960)

Positions: Director, Campus and Professor of Government and Politics, University of Salford; Sciences PO, Paris (2001-03).
Areas of Influence: Public Sector, Education, Commerce.
Profile: *b.* June 20th, 1939; *m.* Anne; 1 son; 2 daughters.
Educated at Trinity School, Croydon, Reading University and Manchester University. Career profile: Professor (1984), Pro-Vice Chancellor (1986-00), University of Salford (1963 - present); Visiting Professor, Queen's University, Kingston University (1970-72); Odense University; Denmark (1997, 2002); University of Rennes (1997); Research Coordinator, ESRC Research Initatives, (1979-86); Chair, University of Salford Enterprises Ltd (1999-2002); Governing Board, Wigan & Leigh College (1993-2001). Publications: Author / Editor of seven books and of several chapters on Comparative Local Government. Elected member, Academy of Social Sciences (2000). Clubs and societies: UK Political Studies Association; National Trust.
Interests: Jazz, cricket, photography and walking.
Contact details: Campus, 3rd Floor, Faraday, University of Salford (tel: 0161 743

1727, fax: 0161 275 5109, email: M.J.F.Goldsmith@salford.ac.uk); 51 Park Road, Leyland, Lancs PR25 3AP (tel: 01772 431052).

GOLDSTONE, Anthony Stewart, MBE (1984), OBE (1998), DL (1984), BA (Com), ACA (1962)

Positions: President, Manchester Chamber of Commerce (1996-97), Nat President, British Chamber of Commerce (2000-2002); Chair NW Tourist Board (1982-); Life Vice President, Greater Manchester Museum of Science, Chair, (1981-91); Chair, Lancashire Tourism Partnership (1997-); Councillor in Greater Manchester (1970-86); Greater Manchester Learning and Skills Council and Skills Festival; Life President, Lancashire Tourism Partnership; Former Chair of OFWAT Water Regulatory Body (1990-97); Former Chair, NW & Greater Manchester Youth Association.
Areas of Influence: Education, Commerce, Public Sector.
Profile: *b.* October 6th, 1938, Salford; *m.* Marilyn; 1 son; 3 daughters.
Educated at Manchester Grammar School (1950-56), Manchester University (1956-59) and Institute of Chartered Accountants. Honorary Fellowships: UMIST and Bolton Institute. Anthony Goldstone has lived and worked in Greater Manchester all his life. After graduating and qualifying as a Chartered Accountant, he became Chief Executive and subsequently Chairman of the family clothing company prior to his current position. Chair of NW Chamber of Commerce, Greater Manchester Youth Association, Regional Tourist Board, Greater Manchester Museum of Science and Industry; Former Director, Bolton Octagon and Royal Exchange Theatres. Member of Salford University Court and Dunham Forest Golf Club.
Interests: Golf, bridge, supporter of Manchester City Football Club since 1947.
Contact details: 14 Hollywood, Stamford Road, Bowden, Altrincham, Cheshire WA14 2LL (tel: 07866 732463, email: anthony.goldstone@btopenworld.com).

GOLDSTONE L Clement, BA (Cantab) (1970), QC (1993),

Positions: Circuit Judge (2002); President, Mental Health Review Tribunal, restricted cases (1999 - present).
Areas of Influence: Law.
Profile: *b.* April 20th, 1949; *m.* Vanessa (nee Forster); 3 sons.
Educated at Manchester Grammar School (1960-67) and Churchill College, Cambridge (1967-70). Career profile: Called to the Bar, Middle Temple (1971); Assistant Recorder (1988); Recorder (1992); Treasurer of the Northern Circuit (1997-00); Head of Chambers, 28 St John St (1999-02). President of Withington Congregation of Spanish and Portuguese Jews (1994-97). Clubs and societies: Dunham Forest Golf and Country Club.
Interests: Golf, bridge, theatre, music, travel.
Contact details: Crown Court, Crown Square, Manchester (tel: 0161 954 1800).

GOODDIE, Howard Rowsley, MA (1956), DipTP (1957), FRICS

Positions: Chairman and Managing Director, Longden & Cook (Management) Ltd (2000 - present); Chartered Surveyor and Freelance Property Auctioneer; Director, Unilateral Property Company Ltd; Member of Council and Chairman of Estates and Services Committee, The Victoria University of Manchester (1999 - present).
Areas of Influence: Real Estate, Higher Education, Commerce
Profile: *b.* July 2nd, 1932; *m.* Ruth Edwina (nee Fingerhut); 1 son; 1 daughter.
Educated at William Hulme School, and Cambridge and Manchester Universities. Career profile: Proprietor, BP Lancashire & Co (1956-72); Managing Director, Greensquare Properties Ltd (1972-75); Senior Partner, Longden & Look (1975-85); Chairman, Regional Committee, Anchor Housing Association (1982-96); Proprietor, Longden & Cook Commercial (1985-00); Board Member, Anchor Housing Association (1989-98); Founder Chairman, Manchester Heritage Trust Ltd; PR Officer, Rotary District 1050 (1989-92); Past Chairman, GM Branch, Royal Institute of Chartered Surveyors; Past Member, Listed Buildings Advisory Committee to City of Manchester (1979-81); Founder Chairman, Groyt Housing Association Ltd (1970-75); Chairman, Executive Committee, Guardian Housing (1994-95); Committee Member, Manchester Care & Repair Ltd (1999-02). Publications: *Buying Bargains at Auctions* (2001); *Auction Essentials* (2002). Prizes and awards: Paul Harris Fellow (1997); Heywood Silver Medal; Special Diploma in Town Planning, Victoria University (1957). Clubs and societies: Cambridge University Land Society; Past President, Rotary Club of Manchester.
Interests: Tropical marine reef fish keeping, classical music, kite flying, photography, good food and wine in convivial company, furniture restoration.
Contact details: Longden & Cook (Management) Ltd, 4 Crossgate Avenue, Manchester M22 8AW (tel: 0161 945 1111, fax: 0161 945 4444, email: landcmanagement@ricsonline.org) Foxglove, 25 Delahays Drive, Hale, Cheshire WA15 8DW (email: howgood@man.ac.uk).

GOODEY, Felicity, CBE (2001), DL (1998), BA (Hons) (Oxon) (1971), D.Litt (2000)

Positions: Deputy Chairman, Precise Communications; Chairman, The Lowry Trust and companies; Non Executive Director, Nord Anglia PLC.
Areas of Influence: Commerce, Media, Regeneration.
Profile: *b.* July 25th, 1949; *m.* John; 2 sons.
Educated at St Austell Grammar School, Cornwall and St Hugh's College, Oxford University. Felicity Goodey joined the BBC as a graduate trainee in Journalism. In a broadcasting career spanning 28 years she worked for most major BBC network news and current affairs programmes as a senior correspondent and presenter specialising in Industry and Politics. In 1985 she went freelance, and while continuing to

broadcast, developed a successful media production and communication training company. In 1994 Felicity was asked by Salford City Council to lead a major Millenium bid which secured £64m of lottery funds towards The Lowry Centre. She then chaired the company which built and opened The Lowry which attracts over 1 million visitors a year. In 1998 she gave up her role as regular presenter of BBC political programmes in order to accept a government appointment as Director of the new North West Development Agency and to broaden her business activities. She then merged her own company with Precise Communications and took on the role of part-time executive director. The following year she was also appointed Chair of the Cultural Consortium for the region by the Sec. of State for DCMS. Honorary Fellowship, Bolton Institute (2002). Prizes and awards: Blue Circle Award for Industrial Journalism and the Mayor's Citizen Award, Salford City Council.

Interests: My family, the North West.

Contact details: Precise Communications, Laser House, Waterfront Quay, Salford Quays,
Manchester M5 2XW (tel: 0161 874 5700, fax: 0161 888 2242).

GOODHAND, FLt Lt Brian, JP (1977), RAF VR(T) (Retd.)

Positions: Company Director, H2O Ltd (1997 - present); Freelance Manufacturers' Agent (1992 - present); Chairman, Tameside Magistrates Bench (2002); Deputy Chair, Youth Panel (1987 - present).

Areas of Influence: Law, Commerce.

Profile: *b.* August 24th, 1951.
Educated at Old Hall Drive Primary School, Gorton, Manchester; Didsbury Technical High School, Manchester; Bradford Technical College, West Yorks. Career profile: Contact Lens Technician, Kelvin Lenses Ltd (1968-74); Dispensing Optician, Watson's Opticians (1974-77); Technical Consultant (1977-78) and Quality Control Manager (1978-83), Kelvin Lenses Ltd; Award Administrator, Unilever Port Sunlight (1984-92). Published articles: *The Day a Lion Danced for us* (1976); *Kenya and The Seychelles* (1979). Prizes and awards: Bronze, Silver and Gold, Duke of Edinburgh's Award Scheme; Outward Bound Course, Eskdale Cumbria; Cadet Forces Medal (1985); Best New Business, Shamrock Awards, sponsored by Aer Lingus (2002), with business partner / co-director Rizwan Rashid.

Interests: Travel, health and fitness, literature, community and people.

Contact details: Tameside Magistrates Court, Henry Square, Ashton-u-Lyne, Lancs. LO6 7TP (tel: 07887 776677, fax: 0161 337 9855).

GOODWIN, Dr Neil, MBA, PhD

Positions: Chief Executive, Greater Manchester Strategic Health Authority; Non-Executive Director, UK Transplant Authority.
Areas of Influence: Health, Public Sector.
Profile: *b.* March 1st, 1951; Divorced, 2 sons.
Educated at North Salford County Secondary School, London Business School, and Manchester Business School. Career profile: Chief Executive, Manchester Health Authority (1994-02); Chief Executive, St Mary's NHS Trust (1988-94); Numerous NHS Appointments (1970-88); Honorary Research Fellow, UMIST; Editorial Advisor, British Journal of Healthcare Management and Journal of Management in Medicine; Cabinet Office Review of Public Sector Leadership (2000); Leadership Group, NHS Leadership Centre; Scientific Committee, European Health Management Association. Publications: Academic papers on NHS Leadership and articles in Professional Journals on NHS Management. Clubs and societies: Friends of the David Lloyd George Museum.
Interests: Coronation Street, exercise.
Contact details: Gateway House, Piccadilly Square, Manchester M60 7LP (tel: 0161 237 2011, fax: 0161 237 2264, email: neil.goodwin@GMHA.nhs.uk).

GORB, Adam John Gideon, ARAM (1998), BA (Cantab) (1980), MA (1984); MMus (1992), DipRAM (1993)

Positions: Professional Composer; Head of School of Composition and Contemporary Music, Royal Northern College of Music, Oxford Road, Manchester (2000 - present); Concerts Committee Member, British Academy of Composers and Songwriters.
Areas of Influence: Arts.
Profile: *b.* March 12th, 1958; *m.* Elizabeth; 1 son; 1 daughter.
Education: William Ellis School (1969-76); BA (Hons) Music (1977-80), MA (1984) Peterhouse, Cambridge; Postgraduate study in Composition, Royal Academy of Music (1991-93). Adam Gorb spent several years working as a musical director and repetiteur in the theatre, opera and ballet before graduating from the Royal Academy of Music and becoming a freelance composer. His commissions include works for the Rambert Dance Company (1995), Evelyn Glennie (1998), The Royal Liverpool Philharmonic Orchestra (1999), The Maggini String Quartet (2001) and the Tonyo Kosei Wind Orchestra (2002). He has also been a lecturer in music and teacher of composition at London College of Music and Media (1994-99) and Junior Royal Academy of Music (1992-99). Most of his compositions have been published, are performed all over the world and have been released on CD. Member, Marylebone Cricket Club.
Interests: Walking, watching cricket, theatre, cinema, art galleries, travelling, good

food and good wine in good company.
Contact details: Royal Northern College of Music, 124 Oxford Road, Manchester M13 9RD (tel: 0161 907 5276, fax: 0161 273 7611, email: adam.gorb@rncm.ac.uk).

GORDON, Professor David, BA (1967), MA (1971), MB BChir (1970), MRCP (1972), FRCP (1989)

Positions: Dean of the Faculty of Medicine, Nursing and Pharmacy, and Professor of Medicine, University of Manchester; Honorary Consultant Physician, Central Manchester, Salford Royal and South Manchester Hospital Trusts; Member, Executive Committees of Council of Heads of Medical Schoold (2001 - present) and Association of Medical Schools in Europe (2002).
Areas of Influence: Education, Health, Public Sector.
Profile: *b.* February 23rd, 1947; *m.* C Louise Jones; 3 sons; 1 daughter.
Education: Whitgift School; Magdalene College, Cambridge; Westminster Medical School. Clinical Appointments: Leicester and Cambridge (1970-72); St Mary's Hospital Medical School: Research Fellow (1972-74); Lecturer in Medicine (1974-80); Senior Lecturer in Medicine (1980-83); Honorary Senior Lecturer in Medicine (1983-94); Honorary Consultant Physician, St Mary's Hospital, London (1980-94); Wellcome Trust: Assistant Director (1983-89); Programme Director (1989-98); Director of Special Initiatives (1998-99). Member: Research Sub-Group, Task Force on Support of R&D in the NHS (1994); Academic Working Group, HEFCE-CVCP-SCOP Committee on Postgraduate Education (1995); Independent Task Force in Clinical Academic Careers, CVCP (1996-97); Research Committee, HEFCE (1998-99); Chief Scientist Committee, Scottish Office DoH (1997-99). Fellow of the Academy of Medical Sciences (1999). Publications: Papers, reviews etc. on biomedical research, scientific policy and other subjects in learned journals.
Interests: Music (cello), books, food.
Contact details: Faculty of Medicine, Dentistry, Nursing and Pharmacy, Stopford Building, University of Manchester, Oxford Road, Manchester M13 9PT (tel: 0161 275 5028, fax: 0161 275 5784, email: dean.mdn.gordon@man.ac.uk).

GOULD, John Roger Beresford, MA (Oxon), FCA, CCMI

Positions: Non-Executive Director: Shiloh Plc, Emerson Developments (Holdings) Limited; Governor, Manchester Metropolitan University; Vice President, Manchester Branch, Chartered Management Institute; Honorary Life Member, Manchester Society of Chartered Accountants; Treasurer, Churches National Housing Coalition.
Areas of Influence: Commerce, Faith Groups.
Profile: *b.* January 1st 1940; *m.* Catherine; 1 son; 1 daughter.
Educated at Bolton School and Merton College, Oxford. Career profile: Director, Seton Healthcare Group plc (1974-98); National Vice Chairman (1990-96) and

Manchester Branch Chairman (1984-86, 1999-01), Institute of Management; National Council Member (1995-01) and Manchester Society President (1994-95), Institute of Chartered Accountants. Clubs and societies: Oxford and Cambridge Club and Saddleworth Golf Club.
Interests: Methodist local preacher, charities, golf, theatre.
Contact details: 4 The Park, Grasscroft, Oldham, OL4 4ES (tel: 01457 876 422, fax: 0161 627 3840, email: rogerg@shiloh.co.uk).

GOULTY, Ian Oliphant, MA

Position: Partner, Addleshaw Booth and Co.
Areas of Influence: Law.
Profile: *b.* September 10th, 1954; *m.* Susan; 1 daughter.
Educated at Bootham School, York; Corpus Christ College, Oxford; Qualified Solicitor (1980); Member of: Hale Golf Club; Manchester Tennis and Racquet Club; St. James's Club; Bowdon Cricket, Hockey and Squash Club; Hale Lawn Tennis Club; Bowdon Lawn Tennis Club; Oxford University Sportsman of the Year (1976).
Interests: Golf, real tennis, lawn tennis, hockey.
Contact details: Addleshaw Booth and Co, 100 Barbirolli Square, Manchester M2 3AB (tel: 0161 934 6000, fax: 0161 934 6060).

GOURLAY, James, MMUS, FLCM

Positions: Head of Wind and Percussion, Royal Northern College of Music.
Areas of Influence: Education, Arts.
Profile: *b.* May 21st, 1956, Scotland; *m.* Lea Havas.
Educated at Buckhaven High School, Fife Scotland, the Royal College of Music and Leeds University. James Gourlay learned to play the tuba at an early age becoming Scottish National Solo Champion at the age of 11. He entered the Royal College of Music at 17, but left after a year to become principal tubist of City of Birmingham Symphony Orchestra. In 1979 he joined the BBC Symphony and Philip Jones Brass Ensemble and in 1989 joined the orchestra of the Zurich Opera. He has made numerous solo appearances including the Proms. In 1998 he returned to the UK to be Director of Brass Studies at RNCM and was later promoted to his current position. James has also been conductor of Williams Fairey Band and Grimethorpe Colliery. Compositions include: *The Eagle; Thunders; Amazonia!; Matto-Grosso-Forest Song; Concerto Piccolo*. CD recordings: *Gourlay Play Tuba; East meets West*. Fellow of the London College of Music.
Interests: Languages, Harley-Davidson motorcycles.

GRADWELL, Lorraine, MA

Position: Chief Executive, Breakthrough UK Ltd (1998 - present).
Areas of Influence: Commerce, Public Sector, Voluntary Sector.
Profile: *b.* July 24th, 1953; Tony Baldwinson (partner); 1 son; 1 daughter.
Education: O levels and A Levels, Associateship of Clothing Institute, and an M.A in Disability Studies. Career profile: Production assistant in a clothing factory; civil servant, Jobcentres; Team leader, Greater Manchester Coalition of Disabled People; Co-ordinator, Healthy Manchester. Has published numerous articles and reviews in a variety of publications including *Coalition*, *Community Care* and *Health Matters*. Lorraine Gradwell is very active in the disability community, locally and also at a national level. She is involved in Local Strategic Partnership work and North West Regional Assembly work.
Interest: Swimming, scuba diving, old films, 60's music!
Contact details: Breakthrough UK Ltd, BEVC, Aked Close, Ardwick, Manchester M12 4AN (tel: 0161 273 5412, fax: 0161 274 4053, email: chief.exec@breakthrough-uk.co.uk).

GRAHAM, Ronald Henry Joseph, MA

Positions: Partner, Eversheds Solicitors.
Areas of Influence: Law, Finance.
Profile: *b.* November 14th, 1951.
Education: Kendal Grammar School; MA Merton College, Oxford; Jurisprudence Diploma in Criminology, Corpus Christi College. Ronald Graham spent 6 years post-university working in conservation at the Wildfowl Trust, Slimbridge, Gloucestershire. He joined Alexander Tatham & Co Solicitors, St Ann St, Manchester as an articled clerk in 1983 and qualified as a Solicitor in 1985, becoming Partner in 1990. Alexander Tatham became the Manchester Office of Eversheds. Ronald now leads the 12 strong team of pensions lawyers in Eversheds Leeds and Manchester Offices. He was awarded a Churchill Fellowship in 1979. Clubs and societies: National Association of Pension Funds, Manchester region; Association of Pension Lawyers.
Interests: Wildlife, theatre, travel, music.
Contact details: Eversheds House, 70 Great Bridgewater Street, Manchester M1 5ES (tel: 0161 831 8000, fax: 0161 832 5337, email: ronaldgraham@eversheds.com).

GRANGE, Professor Philip Roy, BA (1979), PhD (1984)

Position: Professor of Composition, Manchester University Music Department (2001 - present).
Areas of Influence: Arts, Music Composition; Education.
Profile: *b.* November 17th, 1956; *m.* Elizabeth Caroline; 1 son; 1 daughter.
Education: Cavendish Grammar School, Hemel Hempstead (1968-75); Dartington Summer School of Music (1975-81); Private Study with Peter Maxwell Davies (1977-78); York University (1976-1984). Career profile: Fellow Commoner in the Creative Arts, Trinity College, Cambridge (1985-87); Northern Arts Composer Fellow, Durham University (1988-89); Lecturer (1989-95), Reader (1995-99), Professor (1999-00), Exeter University, founding Entire Composition Course. Performance debuts: First foreign performance, Freiburg Hochschule fur Neue Musik, Germany (1980); First London performance: Cimmerian Nocturne, Queen Elizabeth Hall (1981); BBC Proms (1983); first USA, Boston, New England. Compositions promoted by British Council in Taiwan (1997, 2000). Compositions featured at the Music Factory Festival, Bergen, Norway. Publications: c. 34 compositions published, recorded onto CD or broadcast nationally and internationally. Clubs and societies: Associate Member, Performing Right Society; Member, Society for the Promotion of New Music. Philip Grange lecturers throughout the world on contemporary music in general and on his own music in particular. His compositions have been performed and broadcast throughout the UK and Europe as well as in the USA and Far East.
Interests: European and American literature, languages - French, German, Russian, Mandarin Chinese.
Contact details: Music Department, University of Manchester, Denmark Road, Manchester M15 6HY (tel: 0161 275 4990, fax: 0161 275 4994, email: philip.r.grange@man.ac.uk).

GRANT, Lawrence Coleman, FCMA, MBA

Positions: Financial Director, Manchester Metropolitan University (1997 - present); Member, Audit Committee, OGE Buying Solutions.
Areas of Influence: Education, Finance, Public Sector.
Profile: *m.* November 23rd, 1953; 1 daughter.
Educated at Manchester Metropolitan University, Manchester Business School, and the Univerity of Wales. Career profile: Management Accountant (1989-91), Financial Controller (1991-97), Acting Financial Director (1997), Manchester Metropolitan University; Head of Finance and Adminstration, Greater Manchester Waste Disposal Authority (1986-89); Chief Accountant, Greater Manchester County Council, County Engineers Dept. (1979-1986); Finance Manager, Salford / Blackburn Health Authorities (1976-79); Callaghan & Co (1974-76).
Interests: Golf, member of Worsley Golf Club.

143

Contact details: Manchester Metropolitan University, All Saints, Oxford road, Manchester M15 6BH (tel: 0161 247 1868, fax: 0161 247 6355, email: l.grant@mmu.ac.uk).

GRANT, Len

Position: Freelance Photographer.
Areas of Influence: Arts.
Profile: *b.* February 22nd, 1960.
Educated at Xavarian College, Manchester (1971-78) and Trent Polytechnic (1978-82). Len Grant became a freelance photographer in 1990 after a brief career in sales and marketing. He has documented much of the reinvention of Manchester in the past decade: The building of the MEN Arena (1991-94); The Bridgewater Hall (1992-95); The Lowry (1997-00) and The Imperial War Museum North (2000-02). He has also documented the regeneration of Hulme (1992-97), the building of Manchester Airport's second runway (1997-01), and the rebuilding of the city centre after the 1996 IRA bomb. In 2002 he began photographing the innovative rejuvenation of the Cardroom Estate in Ancoats and in 1999 became the Founder Chair of Redeye, the Manchester Photography Network, later becoming the North West Photography Network. Publications: *Arena! The Building of the Nynex Arena, Manchester* (1995); *Built to Music: the Making of the Bridgewater Hall* (1996); *A Way of Life: Portraits from the Funeral Trade* (1999); *Making the Lowry* (2000); *The Mancunian Way* (2002).
Contact details: (email: len@lengrant.co.uk).

GRAY, Bryan Mark, MBE (2001), DL (2002), FRSA, FIMgt

Positions: Chairman, North West Development Agency (2002 - present); Deputy Chairman, Baxi Group Limited (2000 - present); Chairman, CBI NW Region (2000-02); Immediate Past President, Society of British Gas Industries; Chairman, Central Heating Information Council.
Areas of Influence: Commerce, Public Sector.
Profile: *b.* June 23rd, 1953; *m.* Lydia; 3 sons.
Education: Wath-upon-Dearne Grammar School, Yorkshire; BA Chemistry, University of York (1971-74). Career profile: Chief Executive (1993-00), Baxi Group Limited (1993 - present); Chairman, Preston North end plc (1994-01); ICI (1974-93); Board Member, University of Central Lancaster; Founder Chairman of Trustees, National Football Museum.
Interests: Reader, Church of England.
Contact details: North West Development Agency, Renaissance House, PO Box 37, Centre park, Warrington, Cheshire WA1 1XB.

GRAY, David

Positions: Regional Managing Partner, Eversheds.
Areas of Influence: Law.
Profile: *b.* January 9th, 1955; *m.* Julie.
Educated at Leeds Grammar School and Magdalene College Cambridge. Held following positions at Eversheds: Qualified Solicitor (1979); Partner (1982); Head of Corporate, Leeds (1992); Head of Corporate, Leeds and Manchester (1995); Head of Coporate, National (1999); Deputy Regional Managing Partner, Leeds and Manchester (1998); Regional Managing Partner, Leeds and Manchester (2000). Member of Alwoodley Golf Club and Wetherby Steeplechase Club.
Interests: Golf, horse racing, travel, all sports.
Contact details: Eversheds, Cloth Hall Court, Infimary Street, Leeds (tel: 0113 200 4555, fax: 0113 200 4409, email: davidgray@eversheds.com).

GREEN, Charles, BSc, MRTPI

Position: Director of Strategy and Regeneration, Salford City Council.
Areas of Influence: Public Sector, Regeneration, Economic Employment.
Profile: *b.* July 20th, 1953.
Educated at Preston Lodge High School, East Lothian and Dundee University. Charles Green is a chartered town planner with some 25 years experience covering public policy, regeneration, economic development and planning. For the last 8 years he has been heavily involved in driving the strategic agenda at Salford City Council in the Chief Executive's Department.
Interests: Tennis, drums, percussion, walking, travel, all aspects of the environment.
Contact details: Director of Strategy and Regeneration, Chief Executive's Department, Salford Civic Centre, Chorley Road, Swinton, Salford M27 5FJ (tel: 0161 793 3406, fax: 0161 793 3931, email: charles.green@salford.gov.uk).

GREEN, Lorna, BA (Hons), Mphil, FRBS

Positions: Sculptor, Environmental Artist, Visiting Lecturer throughout UK and Abroad.
Areas of Influence: Arts, Public Sector, Education
Profile: *m.* David Rose; 2 daughters.
Education: Stand Grammar School for Girls; Stockport College of Technology; BA (Hons) Fine Art, Manchester Polytechnic (1982); MPhil Fine Art, Leeds University (1991). Lorna Green's main interest over the last few years has been Art in Public Places. Lorna has worked throughout the UK as well as overseas in both urban and rural landscapes, indoors and outdoors and has made sculptures which have been both permanant and temporary. Her sculpture is site specific taking into

consideration the architecture, landscape, history, economy or mythology of the area and many projects are functional. Lorna uses a wide variety of materials, and enjoys working on both large and small scale. She has produced over 50 sculpture projects since 1984. Awards: various travel burseries and Architecture 2000, Commendations by Leeds City Council (2000). Clubs and societies: Landscape and Arts Network; Manchester Academy of Fine Art; Art and Architecture; Women Artists Library; Artists in Nature International Network; Fellow, Royal Society of British Sculptors. **Contact details:** Mount Pleasant Farm, 105 Moss Lane, Bramhall, Cheshire SK7 1EG (tel: 0161 439 7459, email: lg@lornagreen.com, web: www.lornagreen.com).

GREENWOOD, Michael John, BSc, MSc, CPFA

Position: Chief Executive, Tameside Metropolitan Borough Council.
Areas of Influence: Public Sector, Arts, Finance.
Profile: *b.* September 8th, 1947; *m.* Rita Clarke; 2 daughters.
Educated at Fleetwood Grammar School; Leeds University; Management Centre, Bradford University; Cadbury Schweppes Foods (1968-71); IBM (UK) LTD (1974); Leeds City Council (1974-84); Chief Executive, Powys County Council (1984-90); Director, Hallé Concerts Society.
Interests: Literature, food and wine, urban and country walking, music.
Contact details: Tameside MBC, Council Offices, Wellington Road, Ashton-Under-Lyne OL6 6DL (tel: 0161 342 3502, fax: 0161 342 3543).

GREGSON, Professor Edward, BMus (Hons), GRSM, LRAM, Hon DMus (1996), FRAM (1990), Hon FLCM (1999), FRNCM (2000), FRCM (2001),

Positions: Composer; Principal, Royal Northern College of Music, Manchester (1996 - present); fellow, Dartington College of Arts (1997).
Areas of Influence: Arts
Profile: *b.* July 23rd, 1945; *m.* Susan Carole Smith (1967); 2 sons.
Educated at Manchester Central Grammar School, Royal Academy of Music and Goldsmiths College, University of London. Career profile: Lecturer in Music, Rachel McMillan College, London (1970-76); Senior Lecturer (1976-89), Reader (1989-94), Professor of Music (1994-96), Goldsmiths College, University of London. Hon Professor of Music, University of Manchester (1996). Member, Music Industry Forum, DCMS (1998 - present). Vice-Chairman, Composers Guild (1976-78); Chairman, Association of Professional Composers (1989-91); Director: PRS (1995 - present); Associated Board of Royal Schools for Music (1996 - present); Hallé Orchestra (1998 - present). Governor, Chethams's School for Music (1996 - present). Trustee: National Foundation for Youth Music (1999 - present). As a Composer, he has worked only to commission since 1970 producing a series of commissions including *Blazon*, Bournemouth Symphony Orchestra (1992); *Clarinet Concerto*, BBC

Philharmonic (1994); *Violin Concerto*, Hallé Orchestra (2000). He has also written music for the theatre (Royal Television Company), television and film. Other works include: RSC History Play Cycles: *Plantagenets Trilogy* (1988-89); *Henry IV parts 1 and 2* (1990-91). Fellow, Dartington College of Arts (1997). Edward Gregson has produced numerous compositions and has published many music articles in professional journals.

Interests: Walking, wine, watching sport.

Contact details: Royal Northern College of Music, 124 Oxford Road, Manchester M13 9RD (tel: 0161 907 5273, fax: 0161 273 8188).

GRIFFITHS, Elaine Christine, BSc, MHCIMA, PGCE

Positions: Project Leader, The Monastery of St Francis & Gorton Trust; Chief Executive, The Angels, Manchester; Board Member, The Princes Trust (Business), Cheshire.

Areas of Influence: Voluntary Sector, Education.

Profile: *b.* 11th December, 1955; *m.* Paul; 1 son; 2 daughters.
Educated at Stockport High School for Girls (Head Girl) (1966-73); Huddersfield Polytechnic (1973-77). Career profile: Kitchens of Sara Lee (UK) (1977-79); ESS Food (UK) Ltd (1979-82); Country House Products (1983-86); Consultancy Roles (1986-99) included Roberts and Smith, ASDA Manufacturing and Sooty International. Chair, Gorton Monastery Trust (1996-99). Elaine Griffiths became Co-founder of the Monastery Project Trust in 1996, giving up a successful career in Sales & Marketing, and personally investing over 5 years of voluntary effort and dedication in the project. 20 years experience in the Food, Retail, & Leisure Sectors, launching products, managing people, and developing new projects provided a useful platform of experience for this demanding and challenging project. Elaine has an understanding of fundraising and commercial projects, which includes being a former consultant team member for a Millenium Project raising £18.6m. Involvment in Community and Charitable Projects ranges from a 2 year consultancy for BBC Children in Need, to 5 years as a Cheshire Board Member of the Princes Trust. Clubs and societies: Member, Community Action Network; Graduate of Common Purpose; Member of The Pugin Society; Manchester Civic Society.

Interests: Heritage, travel, children, Springer Spaniels, walking, Reiki, good food & wine.

Contact details: The Angels and Gorton Monastery Trust, 3 Assisi Gardens, Gorton, Manchester M12 5AS (tel: 0161 223 3211, fax: 0161 230 8741); (tel: 01565723838, fax: 01565 723845, email: elaine@theangelsmanchester.com).

GRIME, Mark Stephen Eastbourne (Stephen), QC (1987), MA (Oxon), FCIArb

Positions: Barrister (1970 - present); Recorder, Technology and Construction Court (1990 - present).
Areas of Influence: Law.
Profile: *b.* March 16th, 1948; *m.* Christine; 2 daughters.
Educated at Terra Nova School, Wrekin College and Trinity College, Oxford. Career profile: Bencher of Middle Temple (1997); Head of Deans Court Chambers (2000); Past Chairman, Northern Arbitration Association and Northern Circuit Medical Law Association.
Interests: Gardening, viticulture, sailing, antiquarian horology.
Contact details: Dean's Court Chambers, 24 St John Street, Manchester M3 4DF (tel: 0161 214 6037, fax: 0161 214 6054, email: grime@deanscourt.co.uk); Homestead Farm, Jackson's Edge, Disley, Cheshire SK12 2JR (tel: 01663 966 976).

GUILLEMAIN Virginia, BA (Hons)

Position: Honorary Consul, Czech Republic.
Areas of Influence: Public Sector.
Profile: January 15th, 1952; *m.* Alain M.J; 2 sons; 1 daughter.
Educated at Altrincham Grammar School for Girls (1966-71); Middlesex Polytechnic (1971-75); Sorbonne, Paris (1976-77); Sciences Pô, Paris (1976). Clubs and societies: Manchester Consular Association; Manchester Literary and Philosophical Society; Portico Library.
Contact details: Honorary Consulate for the Czech Republic, 26 Church St, Altrincham, Cheshire WA14 4DW (tel: 0161 928 9988, fax: 0161 926 8726, email: manchester@honorary.mzv.cz).

GUTERMAN, Henry, MBE (2000), AMCT, MLIA (dip)

Position: Training and Competence Coach.
Areas of Influence: Faith Group, Voluntary Sector.
Profile: *b.* January 22nd, 1926; separated; 2 sons; 1 daughter.
Educated at Didsbury Central School, and Manchester College of Technology. Career profile: Manufacturing and Life Insurance; Board Member, Heathlands Village for the Elderly; Executive Member, Outreach; Executive member, The Project for North Manchester Jewish Youth; Past President, the Jewish Representative Council of Greater Manchester Region. Clubs and societies: Manchester Council Community Relations; Vice President, Disabled Living; Vice Chairman, Council of Christians and Jews; Co-chairman, Indian-Jewish Association.
Interests: Watching football, voluntary organisation work.
Contact details: Inter Alliance Plc, 73 Mosley Station, Manchester M2 3JN (tel: 0161

228 2321, fax: 0161 236 5976, email: henry-guterman@inter-alliance.com); 42 Lidgate Grove, Didsbury, Manchester (tel: 0161 434 4019, email: henryg@lidgate42.freeserve.co.uk).

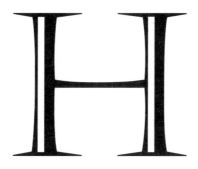

HACKETT, Cllr Mark, BA (1970)

Positions: Deputy Executive Member, Culture and Leisure, Manchester City Council; Council Member, Manchester University; Governor, City College, Manchester; Governor, King David High School and Pike Fold Primary School; Member, Manchester City Council, representing Charlestown Ward; Trustee, Creative Partnership in Education, CADE UK Ltd; Director, Contact Theatre; Management Committee, Heaton Park.
Areas of Influence: Public Sector, Education.
Profile: *b.* April 26th, 1949.
Educated at: Kenton School, Newcastle upon Tyne (1960-97); University of York, BA Biochemistry (1967-70); Manchester Polytechnic, Diploma in Careers Guidance (1974-75). Career profile: Unemployment Specialist Careers Officer, Bury MBC (1981); Senior Careers Officer, Bury MBC (1985); Acting Assistant Principal Careers Officer, Bury MBC (1991); Senior Careers Officer, MBC; Lifetime Careers, Rochdale Careers Advisor (1996); Rochdale Chamber of Commerce, Careers Advisor, Adults (2000). Clubs and societies: RSPB; Friends of the Earth; SERA; Wildfowl & Wetland Trust; The National Trust; The Woodland Trust; Member, Institute of Career Guidance; Member of Unison; Member of The Labour Party. Mark Hackett has been a member of Manchester City Council (1996-90 and (1991 - present); Deputy Chair, Economic Development (1987-90); Chair, Education (1995-99).
Interests: Travel, classical music, food and wine, sport especially Rugby Union, Cricket, and Football. science, literature, industrial archeology, theatre, inland waterways, nature, international affairs and politics, ancient and modern history.
Contact details: Chamber Pathways, The Old Post Office, The Esplanade, Rochdale

OL16 1AE (tel: 01706 644 664, fax: 01706 649 979, email: m.hackett@rochdale chamber.co.uk); 73 Greetland Drive, Blackley, Manchester M9 6DP (tel: 0161 795 8533, email: cllr.m.hackett@notes.manchester.gov.uk).

HADFIELD, Charles Alexander, FRICS

Position: Sole Principal, Charles Hadfield & Co, Chartered Commercial Property Surveyors.
Areas of Influence: Commerce, Voluntary Sector.
Profile: *b.* July 13th, 1944; *m.* Bonnie Mary (1972); 2 daughters.
Educated at Magdelen College School, Brackley, Northants. Career profile: Previously Partner, WH Robinson & Co. Chairman, Manchester Salford and District Branch, NSPCC; Director of Management Company, Wood Street Mission. Clubs and societies: Vice President, The St James's Club; Trustee, Hale Conservative Club; Hon Secretary, 1925 Club; Manchester Society of Land Agents and Surveyors; Railway and Council Historical Society.
Interests: Industrial archeology, walking, travelling.
Contact details: Charles Hadfield & Co, 2/4 Oxford Road, Manchester M1 5QA (tel: 0161 237 5969, fax: 0161 238 8700, email: charles.hadfield@btinternet.com); 11 Gilbert Road, Hale, Altrincham, Cheshire WA15 9NR (tel: 0161 941 3530).

HAGUE, Gillian, BSocSci

Position: Group Manager, The Court Service (2001 - present).
Areas of Influence: Public Sector.
Profile: *b.* August 12th, 1962.
Educated at Sale Girls Grammar School (1974-80) and Birmingham University (1980-83). Gillian Hague commenced work at Bolton Combined Court Centre in 1983. Thereafter she worked in Crown and County Courts throughout Greater Manchester including a post as Deputy Court Manager of Stockport County Court and Manchester County Court and Manager of Salford County Court. In 1996 she was transferred on promotion to Liverpool Combined Court before returning, again on promotion, to the Greater Manchester Group as Group Manager in 2001.
Interests: Reading, swimming, historical buildings, gardening.
Contact details: Manchester's Group Manager's Office, The Court Service, 15 Quay Street, Manchester M60 9FD (tel: 0161 833 1005, fax: 0161 835 1725, email: gill.hague@courtservice.gsi.gov.uk).

HAIG, The Reverend Christopher Duncan

Positions: Regional Minister (Pastoral), North Western Baptist Association; President, Greater Manchester Churches.
Areas of Influence: Faith Groups, Public Sector, Voluntary Sector.
Profile: *b.* 25th Jannuary, 1939; *m.* Jacqueline Helen; 3 daughters.
Education: Preston Grammar School; BD, London Bible College (1962). Career profile: Minister, Dumfries Baptist Church (1962-67); Minister, Larbert Baptist Church (1967-74); Lecturer in Theology, WEC Bible College, Glasgow (1969 - 1974; Lecturer in Theology, Bible Training Institute, Glasgow (1970 - 74); Minister, St Annes on Sea Baptist Church (1974-86); Minister, Friar Lane Braunstone Baptist Church (1986-89); General Secretary, Lancashire and Cheshire Association of Baptist Churches (1989-2001); Regional Minister (Pastoral), North Western Baptist Association (2001 - present); President, Greater Manchester Churches Together (2001 - present).
Interests: Golf
Contact details: (bus. tel: 01925 633 929, bus. fax: 01925 418 796, home tel: 01925 652 659, email: BAPTNW@AOL.com).

HALDER, Dr Ajit Kumar, MSc, PhD

Positions: Project Manager, UKonline ICT Learning Centre, ISCC, Whalley Range, Manchester; Member, Steering group of the Manchester Local Strategic Partnership; Member, Independent Remuneration Panel, Manchester City Council; Executive Committee Member, Indian Association, Manchester; Executive Committee Member, Manchester Interfaith Forum; Member, Steering Group, Manchester Community Network.
Areas of Influence: Arts, Voluntary Sector, Faith Groups.
Profile: *b.* January 4th, 1935; *m.* Tripti; 1 son; 1 daughter.
Education: Postgraduate study and research, Calcutta University; PhD Electrical Engineering, Liverpool University. Career profile: Lecturer, Salford University (1964-97); Senior Research Scholar, Liverpool University (1963-64); Research Student, Liverpool University (1960-63); J C Bose Research Student, Bose Institute, Calcutta (1958-59). Publications: 30 articles in learned Electrical Engineering and Technology Journals; 40 articles on popular science, logic, culture and scriptural literature. Ajit Halder contributes regularly to UK and Indian Magazines and is very much involved in interfaith dialogue and contributing to social harmony among faith communities through understanding beliefs and spirituality. Received literary Award, Manchester Libraries (2001).
Interests: Travel, reading world literature, internet surfing to access resources of learning, writing narratives on rational interpretation of faith literatures.
Contact details: Project Manager, UKonline ICT Learning Centre, ISCC, 16-18

Whalley Road, Whalley Range, Manchester M45 6TY (tel: 0161 727 8704 / 0161 232 7994 / 0161 232 0999, fax: 0161 232 7272, email: iscc@talk21.com); 28 Barnard Avenue, Whitefield, Manchester M45 6TY (tel: 0161 773 5635, email: ajit.halder@freezone.co.uk).

HALHEAD, Robert

Position: General Manager, Granada Learning LTD.
Areas of Influence: Education, Media.
Contact details: Granada Learning LTD, Quay Street, MAnchester M60 9EA (tel: 0161 827 2927, fax: 0161 827 2966, email: robert.halhead@granadamedia.com).

HALL, Daniel Charles Joseph

Positions: Head of Corporate, Eversheds; Chairman of Trustees, Charles Hallé Foundation; Commitee, North West Advisory Board London Stock Exchange.
Areas of Influence: Law, Arts.
Profile: *m.* Melanie Jane; 1 son Benjamin Charles Joseph; 1 daughter Isabel Kate.
Education: Repton Prep School; Repton School; Bristol University; London College of Law. Career profile: Trainee Solicitor, Eversheds (1985-87); Solicitor, Clifford Chance (1987-92); Partner, Eversheds (1992-99); Head of Corporate, Eversheds. Clubs and societies: Prestbury Golf Club; St. James Club; Law Society.
Interests: Golf; Shooting; Fishing.
Contact details: Head of Corporate, Eversheds, Eversheds House, 70 Great Bridgewater Street, Manchester M1 5ES (tel: 0161 831 8080, fax: 0161 832 5337); Pendle House, 10 Styal Rd, Wilmslow, Cheshire SK9 4AE (tel. 01625 251 803).

HALL, Sir Iain Robert, Bsc

Positions: Headteacher; Consultant to DFES; Member, Bristol Partnership Board.
Areas of Influence: Education
Profile: *b.* February 13th, 1943; Kristy Sheldon (partner); 3 sons to former marriage.
Educated at Liverpool Collegiate School and Liverpool University. Iain Hall has been a teacher since 1965. He has worked for five schools as a Physicist, Head of Physics, Head of Science, Deputy Headteacher and Headteacher of 2 schools. He was appointed to his first headship at 37 in a Liverpool inner city school, Breckfield, before being appointed Head of Parrs Wood in 1990. He was knighted for services to Education in 2002. Member of Court, Manchester University. Publications: *Nuffield Physics Book*; Contributor to Educational Journals.

Interests: Education, Education, Education! But in any spare time, cooking, fellwalking, supporting Liverpool FC.
Contact details: Parrs Wood Technology College, Wilmslow Road, East Didsbury, Manchester M20 5PC (tel: 0161 445 8786, fax: 0161 445 5974, email: irh@parrswood. manchester.sch.uk).

HALL, Nigel Mark

Position: Deputy Controller of Entertainment, Granada TV.
Areas of Influence: Arts, Education, Media.
Profile: *b.* February 9th, 1960; Siobhan; 2 sons.
Educated at Poynton County High School. Career profile: Graduate Trainee, BBC Newsroom. Creative work: BAFTA Awards; *This morning*; *Stars in their eyes*; *Ant & Dec's Saturday Night Takeaway*; *You've Been Framed*; *Popstars: the Rivals*. Prizes and awards: BAFTA; 3 National TV Awards; 1 Golden Rose of Montreux.
Contact details: Granada TV, Quay Street, Manchester M60 9EA.

HALLAM, Ian William

Positions: Director of Personnel, Manchester Metropolitan University; Vice Chair, Board of Govenors, Ridge Danyers Sixth Form College, Stockport.
Areas of Influence: Education, Public Sector.
Profile: *b.* August 8th, 1949; *m.* Jane; 1 daughter.
Education: University of Manchester; University of Nottingham; University of Salford. Career profile: Lecturer, Manchester Polytechnic; Senior Lecturer, Manchester Polytechnic; Principle Lecturer, Manchester Polytechnic; Head of Department, Manchester Polytechnic (1986-92); Director of Personnel, Manchester Polytechnic (1992 -). Clubs and Societies: Universities Personnel Association; Mellor and Towncliffe Golf Club.
Interests: Golf, theatre, cinema.
Contact details: Personnel Director, Manchester Metropolitan University, All Saints Manchester M15 6BH (tel: 0161 247 3315, fax: 0161 247 06338).

HAMILTON, His Honour Judge Iain McCormick

Positions: Circuit Judge (2000 - present); Patron, Child Concern; Vice-Chair, Northern Circuit Domestic Violence Group.
Areas of Influence: Law.
Profile: *b.* November 11th, 1948; *m.* Marilyn; 1 son; 2 daughters.
Educated at Heversham Grammar School and Manchester Polytechnic, BA (Lan). Career profile: Qualified as Solicitor (1974); Partner, Walls Johnston & Co, Stockport

(1976); Partner, Jones Maidment Wilson, Manchester (1994).
Interests: Music, reading, cooking, sport.
Contact details: Manchester County Court, The Courts of Justice, Crown Square, Manchester M60 9DJ (tel: 0161 954 1800 email: imhamilton@lix.compulink.co.uk).

HAMMOND Robert Michael

Positions: Consul, Norway; Consultant, Hammond Raggett & Co Ltd; Magistrate, City of Manchester Bench; Greater Manchester Police Authority; Magistrate Member.
Areas of Influence: Law, Public Sector.
Educated at Stockport Grammar School (1942-52). National Service: Royal Air Force; RAFVR. Career profile: Yarn Dyer, Bleacher, R.P. Lawson & sons Ltd; Insurance Broker and Independent Financial Advisor, Hammond Raggett & Partners Ltd. Clubs and Societies: St. James Club; Portico Library; Army and Navy Club; Manchester Consular Association.
Interests: Reading, travel, gardening, walking.
Contact details: Royal Norwegian Consulate, Elizabeth House, St. Peters Square, Manchester M2 3DF (tel: 0161 236 8198); Merrymans Cottage, Merrymans Lane, Great Warford, Alderley Edge, Cheshire SK9 7TP (tel: 01565 872 002, fax: 01565 873 540).

HANCOCK, Jim, Queens Silver Jubilee Medal (1977)

Positions: Political Editor, BBC (North West) (1998 - present); Member, Council of Manchester University; Governor, Lymm High School.
Areas of Influence: Media, Regional Devolution.
Profile: *b.* 10th October 1948; *m.* Frances Done; 2 sons.
Education: Shebbear College, North Devon (1962-67); BA, Manchester University (1970). Career profile: President, Student Union (1972-73); Current Affairs Reporter, Piccadilly Radio (1973-78); TV Reporter, BBC North West (1979-80); Lobby Correspondent, IRN (1980 - 82); Deputy Head, Current Affairs, Piccadilly Radio (1982-87); Political Correspondent, Granada TV (1982-94); National Political Correspondent, BBC TV (1994); Presenter, Breakfast Programme, GMR (1995-97). Prizes and awards: Sony Radio Silver Award (1997). Clubs and societies: National Union of Journalists.
Interests: Plymouth Argyle, politics, media, gardening.
Contact details: Political Unit, BBC N.W., Oxford Road, Manchester M60 1SJ (tel: 0161 244 3119 email: jim.hancock@bbc.co.uk).

HANKINS, Harold Charles Arthur

Position: Chairman, Military Education Commitee, Greater Manchester Universities; President, Cheadle Hulme School.
Areas of Influence: Education, Military History.
Profile: *b.* October 18th, 1930; *m.* Kathleen; 3 sons; 1 daughter.
Education: Crewe Grammar School; UMIST, BSc Tech (1955); UMIST, PhD (1971). Career profile: Assistant Chief Engineer, MVE Co Ltd (1955-66); Professor, UMIST; Principal & Vice Chancellor, UMIST; Retired Principal and Vice Chancellor, UMIST (1983-85); Past Chairman, Trafford Park Manufacturing Institute (1995-01); Non-executive Director, Thorn EMI Lighting Ltd; Bodycote International PLC; Board Member, Trafford Park Development Corporation; Board Member & Chairman, Trafford Park Manufacturing Institute; Consultant to many national and overseas companies and colleges. Clubs and societies: Hon Life Member, Manchester Literary and Philosophical Society; Western Front Association.
Interests: Military history, walking, music.
Contact details: Rosebank, Kidd Road, Glossop, Derbyshire SK13 9PN (tel: 01457 853 895, fax:01457 854 377, email: HHan700698@aol.com).

HARFORD, Ian

Position: District Secretary, Workers' Educational Association.
Areas of Influence: Education, Voluntary Sector.
Profile: *b.* June 17th, 1943; *m.* Lindsay; 1 son; 1 daughter.
Educated at Bristol University. Career profile: Community Relations Officer, Bexley, London; Director, Benwel Community Development Project, Tyneside. Ian Harford is a member of Ski Club of Manchester and is the Initiator and coordinator of the Greater Manchester Community Grid for Learning.
Interests: Walking, Reading, Jazz, New Technologies.
Contact details: District Secretary, Workers' Educational Association, NW District, 4th Floor, Crawford House, Oxford Road, Manchester M13 9GH (tel: 0161 277 5400, fax: 0161 274 4948, email: iharford@wea.org.uk); 42 Kingston Road, Manchester M20 2SB (tel: 0161 445 3642).

HARLOE, Professor Michael Howard, MA (oxon), PhD (Essex), AcSS, FRSA.

Positions: Vice-Chancellor, The University of Salford (1997 - present); Chair, Chapel Street Partnership Regeneration Group; Chair and Member, North West Universities Association; Trustee, Foundation for Urban Regional Studies Ltd; Director & Chair, SITEC Ltd.
Areas of Influence: Education, Public Sector, Commerce.
Profile: *b.* October 11th, 1943; *m.* Judy; 1 son, 2 daughters.

Educated at Watford Boys GS and Worcester College, Oxford. Career profile: Research Officer, Dept. of Social Science & Administration, London School of Economics and Political Science (1969-72); Principal Scientific Officer, Centre for Environmental Studies, London (1972-80); Professor (1990-97), Dean of School of Sciences (1988-91), Pro-Vice Chancellor, Research and Development (1992-97), Department of Sociology, University of Essex. Clubs and societies: Royal Society of Arts, Oxford and Cambridge Club. Author of numerous books and articles on housing and urban development including: *Working Capital: Life and Labour in Contemporary London*, co-author, Routledge, London and New York 2002, *Cities after Socialism: Urban and Regional Change and Conflict in Post-Socialist Societies*, co-editor with G. Andrusz and I. Szelenyi and contributor Basil Blackwell, Oxford and Cambridge MA, (1996); *The People's Home: Social Rented Housing in Europe and America*, Basil Blackwell, Oxford and Cambridge MA (1995); *Divided Cities: New York and London in the Contemporary World*, co-editor with S.Fainstein and I. Gordon and contributor, Basil Blackwell, Oxford and Cambridge MA (1992); *Place, Policy and Politics*, contributor and editor with C. Pickvance and J.Urry, Unwin Hyman, London (1990); *Private Rented Housing in the United States and Europe*, Croome Helm, London and St Martins Press, New York (1985).
Interests: Cycling, gardening, travel, reading.
Contact details: The University of Salford, Salford M5 4WT (tel: 0161 295 5050, fax: 0161 295 5040, email: m.harloe@salford.ac.uk).

HARNDEN, Professor David Gilbert, FRSE, BSc (1954), PhD (1957), FIBiol, FRCPath, Hon MRCP

Positions: Chairman, South Manchester University Hospitals NHS Trust (1997 - present); Emeritus Professor, University of Manchester (1997 - present); Chairman of Trustees of Friends of Rosie (1998 - present); Trustee, New Heart / New Start Transplant Charity (1998 - present) and Gray Laboratory Cancer Research Trust (2000 - present).
Areas of Influence: Health, Education, Biomedical Research.
Profile: *b.* June, 22nd, 1932; *m.* Thora Margaret (nee Seatter); 3 sons.
Educated at George Heriot's School, Edinburgh and University of Edinburgh. Career profile: Scientific Member, Medical Research Council (1957-69); Research Fellow in Oncology, University of Wisconsin (1963-64); Professor of Cancer Studies, University of Birmingham (1969-83); Director of the Paterson Institute for Cancer Research, Christie Hospital Manchester (1983-97); Hon. Professor of Experimental Oncology, University of Manchester (1983-87). Chairman, British Association of Cancer Research (1984-87); Member, MRC Cell Board (1956-90); Member, CRC Scientific Committee (1984-92); Executive Director, Christie Hospital NHS Trust (1991-97); Chairman, Editorial Board, British Journal of Cancer (1985-97); Member, National Radiological Protection Board (1995-99); Chairman of Scientific Advisors to Kay

Kendall Leukaemia Fund (1986-98); Emeritus Fellow of the Cancer Research Campaign (1997). Over 100 publications in learned journals in Genetics and Cancer Research. Member, The Heriot Club.
Interests: Gardening, sketching.
Contact details: Trust Headquarters, South Manchester University Hopitals NHS Trust, Wythenshawe Hospital, Southmoor Road, Wythenshawe, Manchester M23 9LT (tel: 0161 2912021, fax: 01612912037, email: david.harnden@smuht.nwest.nhs.uk); Tanglewood, Ladybrook Road, Bramhall, Stockport SK7 3NE (tel: 0262 485 3214, email: d.harnden@globalnet.co.uk).

HARNEY, Marie

Position: Mayor of Trafford.
Areas of Influence: Public Sector.
Profile: Marie Harney was born in Liverpool and moved to Eccles as a small child. She spent two years as an evacuee in Morecombe. She attended Adelphi Grammar School and Sedgely Park Training College and went on to Manchester Training College where she became a student teacher for Special Needs Children and taught in Eccles and Stretford. She met her husband in 1962, married and they had four children which added to the three children of her husband, making the total seven! She was elected to Trafford Council in 1989 and became Chairman of Social Services and Housing. More recently she has served on Pivotal Overview and Scrutiny, Altrincham Area Board and the Adoption Panel. She is currently the Chairman and Foundation Governor at Blessed Thomas Holford High School. Marie is a member of the Club Theatre and Action Aid.
Interests: Roman history, reading, sport including football, animals.
Contact details: Mayor's Office, Trafford Town Hall, Talbot Road, Stretford, Manchester M32 0YT (tel: 0161 912 4106, fax: 0161 912 1251).

HARRIS, Professor Sir Martin Best, CBE, DL

Positions: Vice-Chancellor, University of Manchester; Member, North West Development Agency Board; Director, Universities Superannuation Scheme Ltd.
Areas of Influence: Education, Public Sector.
Profile: *b.* June 28th, 1944.
Education: Devonport High School for Boys, Plymouth; Queens College, Cambridge; School of Oriental and African Studies, London. Career profile: Lecturer, Leicester University (1967-72); Senior Lecturer, Salford University (1972-76); Professor, Salford University (1976-87); Pro-Vice-Chancellor, Salford University (1981-87); Vice-Chancellor, Essex University (1987-92); Vice-Chancellor, University of Manchester (1992 -); Chairman, Commitee of Vice-Chancellors and Principals (1997-99); Chairman, North West Universities Association (1999-01). Publications: *The Evolution*

of French Syntax (1978); *The Romance Languages* with Nigel Vincent (1988); numerous articles in Journals and Anthologies.
Interests: Gardening, travel, wine.
Contact details: Vice-Chancellor, University of Manchester, Oxford Road, Manchester M13 9PL (tel: 0161 275 7399, fax: 0161 275 6313, email: martin.harris@man.ac.uk); Broomcroft Hall, Ford Lane, Didsbury, Manchester M20 2RU (fax: 0161 448 9436)

HARRIS, Paul

Positions: Editor (1979 - present) and Managing Director (1982 - present) , Jewish Telegraph Group of Newspapers.
Areas of Influence: Media.
Profile: *b.* 2nd June, 1951; *m.* Lauren; 2 sons.
Educated at Manchester Grammer School. Career profile: Trainee, Rochdale Observer Series, Reporter, Jewish Telegraph (1970); Deputy Editor, Jewish Telegraph (1974); Member, Institute of Directors. Publications: *Israel at 40; The Manchester Connection*, Archive Publications (1988).
Interests: Travel, dining out, football
Contact details: Jewish Telegraph, Telegraph House, 11 Park Hill, Bury Old Road, Prestwich, Manchester M25 0HH (tel: 0161 740 9321, fax: 0161 740 5555, email: pharris@jewishtelegraph.com).

HARRISON, Jane Elinor, JP, DL, BSc

Positions: Magistrate, Bolton; Chairman, Bolton Carers Support; Chairman, Mrs Lum Housing Association; Vice-Chairman, Age Concern, Bolton; Vice-Chairman, Asian Elders Initiative.
Areas of Influence: Voluntary Sector, Health, Community.
Profile: *m.* George Anthony (*dec.* 1992); 2 sons; 1 daughter.
Education: Pwllheli Grammar School; Howell's School, Denbigh; University of London. Career profile: Social Worker, Wolverhampton MBC; Training officer, Social Services, City of Salford; Student Supervisor, Various Voluntary Agencies; Bolton Woman of the Year (2000). Clubs and Societies: Magistrates Association; Royal Horticulural Society; Bolton Ladies Speakers Club; Bolton Community Health Council; Better Government for Older People; Action for Sick Children; Horwich Citizens Health Group; Health and Care Forum.
Interests: Community work, gardening, photography.
Contact details: 20 Crompton Road, Lostock, Bolton BL6 4LP (tel: 01204 693 920).

HAWES, Roger

Positions: Partner and Corporate Division Manager, Cobbetts.
Areas of Influence: Law.
Profile: *b.* October 30th, 1949.
Qualifications: LLB, Sheffield.
Contact details: Cobbetts, Ship Canal House, King Street, Manchester M2 4WB.

HAWORTH, Ian James

Position: Director of External Relations and Communications, UMIST.
Areas of Influence: Education, Public Sector.
Profile: *b.* November 7th, 1960.
Education: St. Josephs Secondary School, Heywood, Lancashire; Cardinal Langley Secondary School, Middleton. Career profile: Executive Officer, Inland Revenue (1982-84); Finance Officer, Labour Party (1984-90); North West Regional Officer, Labour Party (1990-92); National Youth and Student Officer, Labour Party (1992-94); Campaigns Officer, Parliamentary Labour Party (1994-98); Assistant Secretary, then Secretary, Labour Party Conference Arrangements Commitee (1993-96,1996-98); Head of the Key Campaigns Unit, General Election Campaign, Labour Party (1997). Ian Haworth has been a member of the Labour party since 1975.
Interests: Manchester City Football Club, cinema, music, reading, walking.
Contact details: Director of External Relations and Communications, UMIST, PO Box 88, Manchester M60 1QD (tel: 0161 200 3526, fax: 0161 955 8066, email: ian.haworth@umist.ac.uk); 126 Ederton Street, Heywood, Lancashire OL10 1HL (tel: 01706 364 633).

HAYDEN, Anthony, QC

Position: Recorder, Queens Counsel.
Areas of Influence: Law.
Profile: *b.* June 24th, 1961.
Education: Manchester University (1979-83); City University, London (1983-84). Anthony Hayden is a Member of the Society of The Middle Temple.
Interests: Reading, gardening, opera.
Contact details: 28 St John Street, Manchester M3 4DJ (tel: 0161 834 8418).

HAZELWOOD, Colette, BA (1999)

Positions: Owner of Colette Hazelwood, Contemporary Jeweller; Chairperson, Manchester Craft & Design Centre Management Committee.
Areas of Influence: Arts, Education.

Profile: *b.* February 17th, 1971; *m.* John Crossfield.

Education: St Judes Primary School, Ancoats; Moston Brook High School, Moston; Tameside College, Ashton; BA Hons Class I 3D Design, Manchester Metropolitan University, Manchester. Career profile: Princes Trust Volunteer, Manchester (1996); Silversmith Assistant, Chris Knight, Sheffield (1998); Started own business (1999); Lecturer, Tameside College, Ashton (2001); Lecturer, de Monfort University, Leicester (2002); Workshop Leader, North West (2000-02). Steering Committee Member, Association for Contemporary Jewellry. Colette Hazelwood is a working class girl brought up in Ancoats. She likes to give back to children from deprived communities by providing jewellery making workshops thereby inspiring them to follow their dreams. Collette's work has appeared in Manchester Evening News (2001, 2002) and various fashion shoots for magazines. Prizes and awards: Regional Winner, Shell Livewire Young Entrepreneur Award (2002); North West Arts Board (2000, 2001).

Interests: Gardening, cycling, design led fashion and crafts, a VW Camper Van and travel with my Boxer Dog, Kafka.

Contact details: Manchester Craft & Design Centre, 17 Oak Street, Manchester M4 5JD (tel: 0161 819 1108, fax: 0161 832 3416, email: john-col@ukonline.co.uk).

HEAGERTY, Professor Anthony Michael

Positions: Professor of Medicine, University of Manchester (1991 - present); Consultant Physician, MRI; Head of Cardiovascular Research Group, University of Manchester; Director Designate of Wellcome Trust Clinical Research Facility, Manchester.

Areas of Influence: Health.

Profile: *b.* September 11th, 1952; *m.* Beverley Carol; 3 sons; 1 daughter.

Education: St Joseph's College Preparatory School, London (1960-65); St Joseph's College, London (1965-1972); The Middlesex Hospital Medical School, University of London (1972-77). Career profile: Lecturer in Medicine, University of Leicester (1982-87); Senior Research Fellow, British Heart Foundation (1987-91). Anthony Heagerty has more than 200 papers published in peer review journals dealing with his research interests into cardiovascular diseases, such as hypertension and hypercholesteremia. Most recently, work on gene therapy for coronary artery restenosis following balloon angioplasty has been published in *Circulation*. Prizes and awards: Sir Ernest Finch Prize for Clinical Research, Trent Regional Health Authority (1983); International Society of Hypertension, Smithkline & French Outstanding Investigator Award (1988); Royal College of Physicians Goulstonian Lecturer (1990). Clubs and societies: Manchester Medical Society; Associations of Physicians; Academy of Medical Sciences, American Heart Association; British Hypertension Society; The 1942 Club; The Athenaeum Club.

Interests: I like to keep fit, read avidly and travel as much and as far as possible.

Contact details: Department of Medicine, Manchester Royal Infirmary, Oxford Road, Manchester M13 9WL (tel: 0161 276 4575, fax: 0161 274 4833, email: tony.heagerty@man.ac.uk); 39 Parkway, Wilmslow, Cheshire SK9 1LS (tel: 01625 528 019).

HEALEY, Eric J G, FCA

Positions: Senior Partner, Grant Thornton.
Areas of Influence: Finance, Commerce.
Profile: *b.* March 29th, 1948; *m.* Gillian; 2 sons; 2 daughters.
Educated at Boteler Grammar School, Warrington (1959-66). Career profile: Qualified as a Chartered Accountant (1971); Partner, Grant Thornton, Manchester (1984). Eric Healey specialises in advice to commercial enterprises. Clubs and societies: The Royal Birkdale Golf Club; Hale Golf Club; The Bowdon Lawn Tennis Club; Bowdon Cricket, Hockey and Tennis Club.
Interests: Playing sports, golf, tennis, skiing, watching Manchester United.
Contact details: Grant Thornton, Heron House, Albert Square, Manchester M60 8GT (tel: 0161 834 5414, fax: 0161 832 6042, email: eric.healey@gtuk.com); Woodlea, 11 The Firs, Bowdon, Atrincham, Cheshire WA14 2TG (tel/fax: 0161 929 8251, email: ericjhealey@aol.com).

HEALEY, Professor Nigel Martin, BA, MA, MBA, FCMI, ILTM

Positions: Dean and Pro-Vice- Chancellor, MMUBS; Executive Board Member, Association of Business Schools; Management Development Committee, Chartered Management Committee; External Examiner, Various Universities.
Areas of Influence: Education, Public Sector, Commerce.
Profile: *b.* October 21st, 1957; *m.* Emma; 4 sons; 2 daughters.
Education: Peter Symonds College, Winchester; Nottingham Universiity; Leeds University; Warwick University. Career profile: Research Assistant, Loughborough University (1980-83); Lecturer, University College, Northampton (1983-85); Senior Lecturer, Leeds Metropolitan University (1985-88); Jean Monnet Chair of European Economics, Leicester University (1988-96); Professor and Head of Business Studies, Manchester Metropolitan University (1996-00); Professor and Dean, Manchester Metropolitan University Business School (MMUBS). Professor Healey has published over one hundred articles in various journals and has co-written ten books and is a member of the Royal Economic Society.
Interests: Running, motorcycling, traveling, reading.
Contact details: Dean & Pro-Vice-Chancellor, Manchester Metropolitan University Business School, Aytoun Street, Manchester M1 3GH (tel: 0161 247 3701, fax: 0161 247 6350, email: n.healey@mmu.ac.uk).

HEATHCOTE, Paul

Position: Managing Director, Heathcotes Restaurants.
Area of Influence: Arts, Education, Media.
Profile: *b.* October 3rd, 1960; *m.* Georgia Sam; 1 son; 1 daughter.
Educated at Turton High, Bolton and Bolton Catering College. Career profile: Sharrow Hotel, Ullswater; Connaught Hotel, Mayfair; Le Manoir Aux Quat' Saisons, Oxford; Opened Paul Heathcote's Restaurant (1990); Simply Heathcote's Preston (1995), Manchester (1996), Liverpool (2000), Leeds (2001); Paul Heathcote School of Excellence (1997); Caterers of Preston North End FC, Liverpool FC and Sale Sharks. Publication: *Rhubarb and Black Pudding*. Paul Heathcote is also a weekly columnist for the Manchester Evening News and the Liverpool Post. Prizes and awards: First holder of 2 Michelin Stars in the North West; Egon Ronay Chef of the Year (1995); Restaurateur of the Year Catey Award (1998); Honorary Fellow, University of Lancashire and Bolton Institute.
Interests: Sport, football, golf, skiing.
Contact details: 106 Higher Road, Longridge, Preston PR3 3SY (tel; 01772 784969, fax: 01772 785713, email: paulh@heathcotes.co.uk).

HEATON, Stephen John

Positions: University Secretary and Clerk to the Board of Governors, The Manchester Metropolitan University; Governor, Myerscough College; Chairman, North West Fine Food Ltd (2001 - present).
Areas of Influence: Education, Law, Sport.
Profile: *b.* September, 27th 1956; *m.* Fiona.
Educated at Preston Catholic College (1968-75), University of Lancaster (1975-78) gaining a BSc Hons (2.i) in Psychology, and University of Central Lancashire (1987-92) gaining an LLB Hons (first) in Law and awarded the Sweet and Maxwell Law Prize. Career profile: Ministry of Agriculture, Fisheries and Food (1979-84); Regional Director for the North West, National Farmers Union (1995-02). Clubs and societies: Life Member, Lancashire County Cricket Club; Member, Sherlock Holmes Society of London.
Interests: Cricket, photography, music, cinema, food, wine and foreign travel.
Contact details: The Manchester Metropolitan University, Secretary's Department, Ormond Building, Lower Ormond Street, Manchester M15 6BX (tel: 0161 247 3400, fax: 0161 247 6868, email: S.Heaton@mmu.ac.uk).

HEGARTY (Thomas) Brendan, QC (1992), MA, LLB

Position: Mercantile Judge.
Areas of Influence: Law
Profile: *b.* June 6th, 1943; *m.* Irene Letitia; 1 son; 1 daughter.
Education: St Joseph's College, Dumfries (1953-61); St John's College, Cambridge 1961-65). Career profile: Assistant Lecturer, University of Manchester (1965-68); Lecturer, University of Manchester (1968-74); Elected Member of Senate, University of Manchester (1971-74); Elected Member of Council and Court, University of Manchester (1972-74); Called to the Bar, Middle Temple (1970); Practised at the Bar, Northern Circuit (1973-96); Circuit Judge (1996); Mercantile Judge (1997). Clubs and societies: Manchester Tennis and Racquet Club; Queen's Club; Racquet Club of Philadelphia.
Contact details: The Court Service, 15 Quay Street, Manchester M60 9FD.

HEGINBOTHAM, Peter LLB

Positions: Senior Partner, Davis Blank Furniss (1994 - present); Councillor andDirector, Manchester Chamber of Commerce & Industry (1989 - present); Deputy Chairman, Manchester Enterprises Ltd (1999 - present); Chairman, Employment and Regeneration Ltd (2000 - present); Member, Regional Steering Group, Skill City (2002). Trustee, Lord Mayor's Emergency Appeal Fund (1996 - present).
Areas of Influence: Law, Commerce, Public Sector.
Profile: *b.* February 25th, 1946; *m.* Jean; 2 sons.
Educated at Oldham Grammar School (1956-64) and Leeds University (1964-67). Career profile: Solicitor, Davis Blank Furniss (1968 - present), Managing Partner (1989-94); President, Manchester Chamber of Commerce & Industry (1995-96); Member of North West Regional Assembly (2002); Director of Marketing Manchester (1996-00); Chairman, Glossop North End AFC (1991-96). Publications: the Lawlines articles, MC2 journal of Manchester Chamber. Clubs and societies: Manchester Chamber of Commerce and Industry.
Interests: Writing, watching sports, particularly football.
Contact details: Davis Blank Furniss, 90 Deansgate, Manchester M3 2QJ (tel: 0161 832 3304, fax: 0161 834 3568, email: peter.heginbotham@dbf-law.co.uk).

HENFIELD, Martin Owen, BSc (Econ) (Hons)

Position: Presenter, BBC TV.
Areas of Influence: Media.
Profile: *b.* January 10th, 1944. *m.* Maggie.
Educated at Queen Elizabeth's Grammar School, Hartlebury, Worcestershire; Oxford College of Technology. Career profile: Reporter, Worcester Evening News (1966-68);

Reporter, Sunday Mercury, Birmingham (1968-70); News Editor, BBC Radio, Birmingham (1970-75); Deputy Manager, BBC Radio, Manchester (1975-79); TV Reporter, North West Tonight (1979-88); Manager, BBC GMR (1988-92). Clubs and societies: Pleasington Golf Club; Manchester Literary and Philosophical Society.
Interests: Golf, telling stories, building and flying radio controlled model aeroplanes.
Contact details: BBC TV North West, Oxford Road, Manchester M60 1SJ (tel: 0161 200 2020, email: martin.henfield@bbc.co.uk); (email: martinhenf@aol.com).

HENNESSEY, Jan

Positions: Owner and Managing Director, Anne Shaw Consultants, Human Resources Management Services; Deputy Chairman, Council of University of Manchester; Chairman Elect, Hulme Hall Council; General Committee Member, Gaddum Centre.
Areas of Influence: HR Management Consultancy, Education, Media.
Profile: *b.* May 10th, 1940; *m.* Terry (dec.); 2 sons.
Education: BA Open University; Chartered Institutes of Personnel and Development and Management Consultants; SRN. Following her nurse training and degree Jan Hennessey pursued a career in training and development. She gained a position with the company founded by Anne Shaw (1978), now called Anne Shaw Consultants. In addition to her commercial business interests, she has a keen interest in the furtherance of lifelong learning and has been able to develop this through involvement with the University of Manchester. Jan was elected to the University Court in 1992 and to Council in 2000, and has served on a range of committees spanning audit, student counselling, residential conference facilities and contributed to formulating strategy for management of change. Recently appointed Deputy Chairman of Court, Jan will also be taking over the Chairmanship of a student's residence, Hulme Hall, in 2003. Jan is actively involved in supporting a trust in memory of her husband that was established through the generosity of family, friends, and colleagues called the Terry Hennessey Microbiology Fellowship. It awards grants to young research scientists working in the field of infectious disease.
Interests: Nurturing friendships, theatre, music, cinema, reading, walking and fitness activity.
Contact details: Anne Shaw Consultants Ltd, Adelphi Mill, Bollington, Macclesfield, Cheshire Sk10 5JB (tel: 01625 576225, fax: 01625 576262, email: consult@anneshaw.com); Ravens Oak, Davey Lane, Alderley Edge, Cheshire SK9 7NZ (tel: 01625 582148).

HENSHALL, Nicholas Guy, MA, PGCE,

Positions: Lecturer in History, University of Manchester (1998 - present).
Areas of Influence: Education, Arts, Media.
Profile: *b.* October 3rd, 1944.
Educated at Stockport Grammar School (1952-64), Emmanual College Cambridge (1964-67) and Manchester University (1968-71). Career profile: Assistant Master (1971-74), Head of History Dept (1974-93), Head of Upper School (1990-93), Stockport Grammar School; Schoolmaster Fellowships at New College Oxford (1977) and St John's College Cambridge (1990); Editor of *History Review* Magazine (1995-98); Writer for Sky TV's History Channel, Web Site (1996-01); Commission to write *The Zenith of Absolute Monarchy* for 2003. Publications: *The Myth of Absolutism* (1992); Contributor, *Der Absolutismus: Ein Mythos?*; Regular contributor to *History Today* Magazine. Clubs and societies: Oxford and Cambridge Club, Pall Mall, London; Georgian Group; National Trust. Nicholas Henshall is interested in the concept of 'Heritage' and its application to Urban Regeneration in Manchester and Stockport. He is involved in the restoration of Stockport's ancient marketplace and the design and planning of the 'Stockport Story' interactive museum.
Interests: Lakeland and Alpine walking; 18th century painting, architecture, music, British films of the 1930s and 40s.
Contact details: 64 Bridge Lane, Bramhall, Cheshire SK7 3AW (tel: 0161 439 1048, email: nickhenshall@btinternet.com).

HERSOV, Gregory Adam, BA

Position: Artistic Director, Royal Exchange Theatre.
Areas of Influence: Arts
Profile: *b.* May 4th, 1956;
Educated at Bryanstone School, Mansfield College, Oxford. Greg Hersov has produced and directed over 35 productions at the Royal Exchange Theatre. His most recent include *Les Blancs*, co-directed with Marianne Elliott, *Uncle Vanya*, *The Homecoming* and *American Buffalo*.
Contact details: Royal Exchange Theatre, St Anns Square, Manchester M2 7DH (tel: 0161 833 9333, fax: 0161 832 0881, email: greg.hersov@royalexchange.co.uk).

HERWALD, Basil M J, MA (Cantab)

Positions: Solicitor and Partner, Herwald Law; Chair, Special Educational Needs Tribunal; President, Mental Health Review Tribunal; Immigration Adjudicator.
Areas of Influence: Law, Media.
Profile: *b.* July 27th, 1953.
Educated at Salford Grammar School (1964-71); Queen's College Cambridge (1972-

75); College of Law (1975-76). After training in London and Brussels, Basil Herwald returned to Manchester to pursue a career as a Criminal Law Advocate. For the last 20 years he has run his own law firm specialising in the law relating to mental health and to children. He also lectures in these areas. In addition to this, he produces edits and presents BBC GMR's weekly magazine programme for and about the Jewish community *It's Kosher,* which will celebrate its 10th anniversary this year. Basil is also a sometime chair of governors of local schools, college, victim support and CAB. Clubs and societies: Jewish Historical Society of England, Friend of Manchester Jewish Museum; Member, Chester Zoo Society, Jersey Zoo and many others.

Interests: Walking Lancashire's hills with Douglas the deaf dog, watercolours, avoiding courtroom dramas on the TV.

Contact details: Herwald Law Solicitors, 306 Great Cheetham Street East, Salford M7 4US (tel: 0161 792 2770, fax: 0161 792 3771).

HEWISON, John E, LLB

Positions: Senior Partner, George Davies Solicitors; President; Fifa Football Arbitration Tribunal Chamber of Presidents.

Areas of Influence: Law, Sport.

Profile: *b.* November 16th, 1948. *m.* Lesley. 1 Son. 1 Daughter.

Educated at Manchester Grammar School; Nottingham University; College of Law, Guildford. Career profile: Qualified as a solicitor, George Davies Solicitors; Managing Partner, George Davies Solicitors. Publications: articles for Law journals, Sports Law. Clubs and societies: British Association for Sport and the Law; Legal Adviser, Professional Footballers Association; Chairman, Fifa's Football Arbitration Tribunal.

Interests: Golf (playing and watching), football, rugby, cricket.

HEYES, David Alan

Positions: M.P, Ashton-Under-Lyne; Councillor, Oldham Metropolitan Borough Council.

Areas of Influence: Public Sector, Voluntary Sector.

Profile: *b.* April 2nd, 1946; *m.* Judith Egerton Gallagher; 1 son; 1 daughter.

Educated at Blackley Technical High School, Manchester (1956-62) and Open University (1980-86). Career profile: Manchester City Council (1962-74); Greater Manchester Council (1974-86); NALGO, Trade Union (1986-87); Oldham Metropolitan Borough Council (1987-90); Self Employed, Computer Graphics (1990-95); Deputy District Manager, Citizens Advice Bureaux Service, Manchester (1995-2001).

Contact details: St. Michaels Court, St. Michaels Square, Stamford Street, Ashton-under-Lyne OL6 6XN (tel: 0161 331 9307, fax: 0161 330 9420, email: heyesd@parliament.uk).

HICKMAN, James Paul

Positions: Swimmer.
Areas of Influence: Sport, Media.
Profile: *b.* February 2nd, 1976, Stockport.
Educated at: William Hulme Grammar School (1987-94) and Manchester University (1994-95). Swimming has been the love of James Hickman's life and he has been taking part in international competitions for Great Britain since 1992. He has been 4 times World Champion Short Course in the 200m Butterfly (1997,1999,2000,2002) and has swam in the 1996 Olympics, the 2000 Olympics, and also the Commonwealth Games of 1994, 1998, and in his home town of Manchester in 2002 where, at the opening ceromony, he took the oath on behalf of all the athletes. In addition to the many TV appearances made throughout his career, James has recently developed an interest in journalism and has his own column published in the Manchester Evening News. He intends to pursue both avenues at a later stage.
Interests: Travelling, meeting people.
Contact details: c/o ASA, Harold Fern House, Derby Square, Loughborough LE11 5AL (web: www.jameshickman.com).

HIGGINS, Joan Margaret, BA(Hons), DipSocAdmin, PhD

Positions: Professor, Health Policy and Director, Manchester Centre for Healthcare Management at the University of Manchester; Chair, Christie NHS Hospital Trust; Chair, Patient Information Advisory Group.
Areas of Influence: Health, Education, Public Sector.
Profile: *b.* June 15th, 1948; *m.* Professor John Martin (died 1997); 3 stepsons.
Education: Mirfield Grammar School (1959-66); Rutherford College of Advanced Technology (1966-69); University of York (1970-71); PhD, University of Southampton (1979). Career profile: Research Assistant and Lecturer, Portsmouth Polytechnic (1971-74); Lecturer, Senior Lecturer, Professor of Social Policy, University of Southampton (1974-92); Chair, Manchester FHSA (1992-96); Chair, Manchester Health Authority (1996-99); Regional Chair, North West Region of the NHS (1999-2001). Publications: 4 Books; 50 Articles on Social Policy and Health Policy. Prizes and awards: American Council of Learned Societies Visiting Fellow (1978); Elected Fellow of the Royal Society of Arts (1993); Honorary Fellow, Faculty of Public Health Medicine (1997); Honorary Fellow, Institute of Health Record Information and Management (2000).
Interests: Travel, gardening, walking, classical music (especially Hallé), reading,

theatre, food and drink, sailing.

Contact details: The Manchester Centre for Healthcare Management, University of Manchester, Oxford Road, Manchester M13 9PL (tel: 0161 275 2910, fax: 0161 273 5245, email: joan.higgins@man.ac.uk).

HIGGINS, Geoffrey Paul, MA, MPhil, PGCE, FRSA, ACP

Positions: Principal, Ashton-under-Lyne Sixth Form College (1985 - present); Justice of the Peace; President, Ashton-under-Lyne Rotary Club (2002-03); Chair, Greater Manchester Principals Group (2002); School Governor.
Areas of Influence: Education, Public Sector.
Profile: *b*. May 26th, 1947; *m*. Jennifer Anne; 1 son; 2 daughters.
Educated at St Brendan's College, Bristol (1958-65), University of Liverpool (1965-70), and University of London (1971-72). Career profile: Teaching in Grammar and Comprehensive Schools in Cheshire and the Wirral (1970-82); Vice Principal, Yale College, Wrexham (1982-85); Board Member, NU Joint Matriculation Board; Council Member, Sixth Form Colleges Employers Forum (1992-97). Publications: Articles and reviews in local learned journals; Contribution to Austin and Flint ed. *Going Further* (1994). Clubs and societies: Fellow, Royal Society of Arts; Magistrates Association; Romiley Golf Club; Historic Society of Lancs and Cheshire; Chetham Society; Lancs and Cheshire Antiquarian Society; Lancs and Cheshire Historical Record Society.
Interests: Theatre, opera, county and local history, concert going, sport, especially cricket and golf.
Contact details: Ashton Sixth Form College, Darnton Road, Ashton-under-Lyne, Lancs OL6 9RL (tel: 0161 330 2330, fax: 0161 612 6725, email: gph@asfc.ac.uk).

HILL, The Reverend Canon (Roger) Anthony John, BA (1967), MA (1979)

Positions: Rector, St Ann's, Manchester (2002 -); Hon Canon, Manchester Cathedral (2002 -); Chaplain to the Queen (2001 - present)
Areas of Influence: Faith Groups, Voluntary Sector.
Profile: *b*. March 23rd, 1945; *m*. Joanna; 3 sons.
Education: Moseley Grammar School, Birmingham (1956-63); University of Liverpool (1964-67); Ripon Hall, Oxford (1967-70). Career profile: Ordained Deacon (1970); Ordained Priest (1971); Curate, St Peter, St Helier (1970-74); Curate (1974-76), Team Vicar (1976-80), Team Rector (1980 88), Telford Team, Diocese of Lichfield; Rector of Newark (1988-02); Rural Dean of Newark (1990-95); Canon of Southwell Minster (1997-02).
Interests: Travel, reading, walking, listening to music, watching rugby.
Contact details: St Ann's Church, St Ann's Street, Manchester M2 7LF; St Ann's Rectory, 296 Wilbraham Road, Chorlton-cum-Hardy, Manchester M21 0UU (tel: 0161 881 229).

HINCHLIFFE, Professor Tom Alan, BSc Tech (Hons), CEng, FIEE, FBCS, FEICL

Positions: Chairman of Council, UMIST; Pro Chancellor, UMIST; Governor, The Manchester Grammar School; Chairman, The BCS Computer Conservation Society (NW); Visiting Professor, Computation; Visiting Professor, Electrical Engineering.
Areas of Influence: Computer Science, Education.
Profile: *b.* June 28th, 1938; *m.* Eva; 3 sons.
Education: Audenshaw Grammar School (1949-56); 1st Class Honours Electrical Engineering, Graduate of the Year, Manchester University Faculty of Technology (1960). Tom Hinchliffe has spent the whole of his professional career with one company in Manchester, whose name changed from Ferranti Ltd to ICT and finally ICL as the British computer industry consolidated through various mergers and acquisitions. Career profile: Design Engineer, Computer Department (1960-63); Senior Design Engineer, Mainframe Systems (1963-68); Design Manager, Large Computer Systems and Director of Systems Engineering (1968-88); Director, Mainframe Systems (1988-92); Managing Director (1992-96); Board Member, Fujitsu Systems Europe (1994-01). Prizes and awards: Three Queen's Awards for Technological Achievement (1985,1988,1993); North West Business & Industry Award (1988); United Kingdom Quality Award for Business Excellence (1995); Naruto Medal, Japan, for outstanding engineering achievement (1998). Clubs and societies: Fellow, British Computer Society; Rotary Club.
Interests: Photography, digital imaging, travel, reading, electronics.
Contact details: Chairman and Pro-Chancellor, UMIST, PO Box 88, Sackville Street, Manchester M60 1QD (tel: 0161 200 3990); email: tom.hpt@dial.pipex.com

HINDSHAW, Jennifer Mary, TD (1982), JP (1991), DL (1999)

Positions: Self-Employed Management Consultant (1992 - present); President, Soroptimist International of Salford (2002-03); Secretary / Treasurer, GMACF Sports and Welfare Committee (1991 - present); Greater Manchester Committee Army Benevolent Fund (1973 - present), Treasurer (1984 - present).
Areas of Influence: Finance, Voluntary Sector.
Profile: *b.* September 27th, 1938.
Educated at Leeds Girls' High School (1948-55) and Yorkshire Secretarial Training School (1956); Career profile: Secretary, Theodore B. Jones and Co, Leeds (1957); Articled Clerk / Accountant, Haworth & Wheatley Jones, Chartered Accountants, Manchester (1958-64); Chartered Accountant, ICI Pharmaceuticals and ICI Specialties (1964-1991); Major (Rtd), Territorial Army (1969-88); Greater Manchester Army Cadet Force (1988-1994); Member of Inland Waterways Association, Boat Museum Society, Ellesmere Port and Rolls Royce Enthusiasts Club, owns a 1960 Bentley S2; Member Hallé Concerts Society (1973 - present); Took part in Granada TV's 'The Krypton Factor' and was the first female finalist, though came last in final! (1979).

Interests: Classical music, Gilbert & Sullivan operas.
Contact details: 78 Worsley Road, Worsley, Manchester M28 2SN (tel / fax: 0161 727 8044, email: jennifer@hindshaw.fsnet.co.uk).

HODGKISS, Susan Katrina DL

Positions: Company chairman, William Hare Limited; Vice President, Millgate Project Appeal, Chetham's School (2001 - present); Member, Remunerations Committee, Bolton Metro (2001 - present); President, Bradshaw Cricket, Tennis and Bowling Club (2000 - present); Member, Standards Committee, Bolton Metro; Deputy Lieutenant of the County of Greater Manchester (1999 - present); Appeals Director, Octagon Theatres Rescue Package (1999 - present); Committee Member, Association of Emmaus in Greater Manchester (1999 - present); Patron of Emmaus Bolton (1999 - present). Governor and Bursary Appeals Director, Bolton School (1998 - present); Director, Bolton Training Group (1995 - present).
Areas of Influence: Arts, Education, Voluntary Sector.
Profile: *b.* June 23rd, 1950; 1 daughter, Sally.
Educated privately.
Interests: Theatre, music, tennis, salmon fishing, game and clay pigeon shooting, sailing.
Contact details: William Hare Ltd, Brandlesholme House, Brandleshome Road, Bury BL8 1JJ (tel. 0161 609 0000, fax: 0161 609 0415, email: susan.hodgkiss@hare.co.uk).

HODGKISS, Frank Lewis, FCA

Positions: Chair, Oldham Chamber of Commerce; Member, Oldham Local Strategic Partnership Board; Director, Business Link North Manchester; Senior Partner, Davenport Hodgkiss Chartered Accountants.
Areas of Influence: Commerce.
Profile: *b.* April 18th, 1947; *m.* Lynda; 1 son; 1 daughter.
Educated at St Philips CE Primary School, Atherton (1951-57) and Bolton School. Frank Hodgkiss has spent his career in Accountancy, public practise, at various firms in Greater Manchester. He has been a partner in Davenport Hodgkiss since 1991. Clubs and societies: Deane Golf Club; Lancashire and Yorkshire Railway Preservation Society; CAMRA.
Interests: Playing golf, watching cricket and football, steam railways.
Contact details: The Old Bank, 1A Wilton Street, Manchester Road, Oldham, OL9 7NZ (tel: 0161 624 9314, fax: 0161 627 2791).

HOLLAND, Stephanie Annice

Positions: Managing Partner, Rapport; Trustee and Founder, Speakeasy; Co-founder, Positive Vision.
Areas of Influence: Training, Spirituality.
Profile: *b.* July 7th, 1949; David Morton (partner); 1 son; 1 daughter.
Education: Bury Grammar School; Qualifications in Counselling, Gestalt psychotherapy, transactional analysis, neurolinguistic programming and Reiki healing. Career profile: ran family business; Speech Therapist (1977); Training and Management Consultancy; Chateau du Ludaix. Stephanie Holland spends half the year in the centre of France, at a beautiful Chateau which she uses as a retreat for clients, friends, and family. She runs courses, mainly for women, which help them enjoy the positive aspects of their life. Publications: *Assertiveness: a practical Approach; Living Positively.*
Interests: cooking puddings, travelling, talking, going on courses, having massages.
Contact details: Rapport, Market Chambers, Market Place, Ramsbottom BL0 9AJ (tel: 01706 82 7299, fax: 01706 82 1799, email: partners@rapport-online.com).

HOLLOWOOD, Philip John

Positions: Divisional Commander, Bury Division, Greater Manchester Police; Joint Chair, Bury Community Safety Partnership.
Areas of Influence: Public Sector.
Profile: *b.* March 22nd, 1957. *m.* Tracy (1989).
Educated at Brooklands County Primary School, Manchester Grammar School and Warwick University. Career profile: Constable (1979); Sergeant (1984); Inspector (1985); Chief Inspector (1989); Superintendent (1994); Chief Superintendent (1998). Prizes and awards: Police Long Service and Good Conduct Medal (2002). Clubs and societies: Brooklands Squash Club; Season ticket holder, Manchester United; Superintendents Association.
Interests: Squash, cinema, Ireland, Manchester United, rambling.
Contact details: Divisional Police HQ, Irwell Street, Bury, Lancashire (tel: 0161 856 8005).

HOLMAN, Richard Christopher, MA (CANTAB)

Positions: Circuit Judge; Designated Civil Judge, Manchester; Member of the Civil Procedure Rule Commitee (1997-2002).
Areas of Influence: Law.
Profile: *b.* June 16th, 1946. *m.* Susan Holman, MBE; 2 sons.
Educated at Watford Grammar School for Boys (1957-59); Eton College (1959-64); Gonville and Caius College, Cambridge (1965-68). Career profile: Admitted as a

solicitor (1971); Partner Foysters (Davies Wallis Foyster) (1973-94); Appointed Circuit Judge (Sept 1994); Appointed Designated Civil Judge (July 1998); Fleming Bursary to Eton (1959); Member of: The Wilmslow Golf Club; The Manchester and District Medico Legal Society; The Manchester Law Society.

Interests: Golf, gardening, theatre, music.

Contact details: Courts of Justice, Crown Square, Manchester M60 9DJ (tel: 0161 954 1800).

HONER, Chris, BA (Hons)

Positions: Artistic Director, Library Theatre Company; Deputy Chair, Acting Accreditation Board, National Council for Drama Training.

Areas of Influence: Arts.

Profile: *b.* June 8th, 1948. *m.* Marian Blaikley (divorced 1997); 2 sons.

Educated at Whitgift School, Croydon; Lincoln College, Oxford; Artistic Director, Derby Playhouse (1980-87); Artistic Director, Gateway Theatre, Chester (1976-80); Associate Director, Birmingham Rep (1973-76); Productions: *Pygmalion* (2002); *Amy's View* (2001); *Death of a Salesman* (2001); *Measure for Measure* (2000); *Arcadia* (1999); *A Doll's House* (1998); *The Life of Galileo* (1996).

Interests: Reading, walking, bird watching.

Contact details: Library Theatre Company, St. Peters Square, Manchester M2 5PD (tel: 0161 234 1913, fax: 0161228 6481, email: ltc@libraries.manchester.gov.uk).

HOPKINS, Reverend Tim

Positions: Parish Priest, RC Parish of St. Brigid and St. Vincent; Chair, East Manchester Education Action Zone; Chair, East Manchester E-Learning Foundation.

Areas of Influence: Faith Groups, Education, Voluntary Sector.

Profile: *b.* 7th March, 1967.

Educated at St Dunstan's RC Primary, Moston (1972-1978); St Bede's RC Grammar School, Manchester (1978-1985); Christ's College, Cambridge (1985-1988); Venerable English College and Pontifical Gregorian University, Rome (1988-1994). Career profile: Ordained RC Priest (1994); Assistant Priest, St. Willibrord's RC Church, Clayton (1994-1995); Parish Priest, St Brigid's, Beswick, and St Vincent's, Openshaw (1995 - present); Chaplain, St Gregory's RC High School, Openshaw (1994-1999; Chair, East Manchester Education Action Zone (1999 - present); Vice-Chair, Manchester University Settlement (1999 - present); Chair, East Manchester E-Learning Foundation (2001 - present); Secretary, Salford RC Diocese Council of Priests (1998 - present), Chaplain, Lord Mayor of Manchester (2001-2002); Chaplaincy Team Leader, Athletes Village, Commonwealth Games (2002); School Governor, St Brigid's (Chair), St Bede's, Corpus Christi with St Anne (Chair).

Interests: Cookery, ICT, pedagogy, travel, Italy.

Contact details: St Vincent's RC Church, 25 Craydon Street, Openshaw, Manchester M11 2FW (tel: 0161 223 1010, fax: 0161 223 1010, email: tim@vincents.fslife.co.uk).

HORLOCK Timothy John QC, MA (CANTAB)

Positions: Queen's Counsel; Recorder.
Areas of Influence: Law.
Profile: *b.* January 4th, 1958; *m.* Kate; 4 sons.
Educated at Manchester Grammar School; St. John's College, Cambridge. Career profile: Barrister.
Interests: Football, tennis, golf.
Contact details: 9 St. John Street, Manchester M3 4DN (tel: 0161 955 9000, fax: 0161 955 9001, email: minesjs@gconnect.com).

HORROCKS, Paul John

Positions: Editor, Manchester Evening News; Press Complaints Commission.
Areas of Influence: Media.
Profile: *b.* December 19th, 1953; *m.* Linda; 2 sons; 1 daughter.
Educated at Bolton School. Career profile: Reporter, News Editor, Deputy Editor, Editor, MEN (1997 - present). Prior to Joining MEN in 1976, Paul Horrocks worked on Daily Mail, Manchester. He began his career in journalism at Joe Horrocks Press Agency, Bury, which was his father's freelance press agency after leaving school at the age of 16. Member, Society of Editors. Patron, Francis House Appeal.
Interests: Golf, rugby, football, sailing.
Contact details: Manchester Evening News, 164 Deansgate, Manchester M3 3RN (tel: 0161 832 7200, fax: 0161 839 9115, email: paul.horrocks@ men-news.co.uk).

HOUGH, Robert Eric, DL, LLB (1967), DBA (1996), DLitt (1996)

Positions: Deputy Chairman, Peel Holdings plc; Chairman, Manchester Ship Canal Company; Chairman, Liverpool John Lennon Airport Plc.
Areas of Influence: Commerce, Sport, Transport.
Profile: *b.* July 18th, 1945, Urmston, Manchester; *m.* Pauline Elizabeth (1975); 2 sons.
Educated at William Hulme's Grammar School, Manchester (1956-64) and Bristol University (1964-67). Career profile: Articled with Slater Heelis Solicitors, Manchester (1968-70); admitted as Solicitor, (1970); Partner, Slater Heelis, specialising in corporate, commercial and banking law (1974-89); Non-executive Director, Peel Holdings plc (1986); Non-executive Chairman, Manchester Ship Canal Company (1987); Executive Chairman, Manchester Ship Canal Company and Executive Deputy Chairman, Peel Holdings plc (1989); Non-executive Chairman, Brammer plc (1993); Non-executive Deputy Chairman, QA plc (2000); Non-executive Chairman, Opal

Telecom plc (2000); Non-executive Chairman, Century Radio 105 Limited. Vice President and former Chairman of Organising Committee, Manchester 2002 Commonwealth Games; Chairman, North West Business Leadership Team; Member, North West Regional Assembly; Past President, Manchester Chamber of Commerce & Industry.
Interests: Sport, gardening, golf.
Contact details: Peel Holdings plc, Peel Dome, The Trafford Centre, Manchester M17 8PL (tel: 0161 629 8200, fax: 0161 629 8333, email: rhough@peel.co.uk); 10 Theobald Road, Bowdon, Cheshire WA14 3HG (tel/fax: 0161 941 6198, email:roberthough99@yahoo.co.uk).

HOUGH, Stephen Andrew Gill, MMUS, FRNCM

Position: British Pianist
Areas of Influence: Arts
Profile: *b.* November 22nd, 1961, Heswall, Cheshire.
Educated at Chetham's School of Music, Royal Northern College of Music and Julliard School, New York. Career profile: Regular guest performer with London Symphony, Philharmonia, Royal Philharmonic and London Philharmonic Orchestras; visiting Professor RAM; Regular appearances with Major Orchestras in USA, Europe, Australia, Far East and at international music festivals; MacArthur Foundation Fellowship 2001; Dayas Gold Medal (Royal Northern College of Music), Terence Judd Award (1982), Naumberg Int. Piano Competition (1988); Gramophone Record of the Year (1996). Recordings include: Complete Beethovan violin sonatas, Hummel piano concertos, recitals of Liszt and Schumann, Brahms concerto nos 1 and 2, The Piano Album Vols. I, II, Britten Music for One and Two Pianos, Scharwenka and Sauer concertos, Grieg, Liszt, Rubinstein cello sonatas, Brahms violin sonatas, York Bowen piano music, Franck piano music, Mompou piano music, Liebermann piano concertos, Mendelsohn piano and orchestral works, Schubert sonatas and New York Variations, Brahms Clarinet Trio, The New PianoAlbum, Liszt Sonata, Mozart Piano and Wind Quintet, Brahms F minor Sonata, Saint-Saens Complete Music for Piano and Orchestra.
Interests: Reading
Contact details: c/o Harrison Parrott Ltd, 12 Penzance Place, London W11 4PA (web: www.stephenhough.com).

HOWARTH, Nigel John Graham, LLB (1957), LLM (1959)

Position: Circuit Judge (1992).
Areas of Influence: Law.
Profile: *b.* December 12th, 1936; *m.* Janice Mary; 2 sons; 1 daughter.
Educated at Manchester Grammar School (1949-54); Manchester University (1954-57,

1957-59); Council of Legal Education (1959-60); Chancery Bar, Manchester (1961-92); Assistant Recorder (1983-89); Recorder (1989-92); Acting Deemster, Isle of Man (1985 and 1989); Gray's Inn, Macaskie Scholar (1960); Atkin Scholar (1961); Council of Legal Education, Certifcate of Honour (1960); Chairman, Northern Chancery Bar Association (1990-92); President, Manchester Incorporated Law Library Society (1986-89); Vice President, Disabled Living.

Interests: Music, theatre, fell walking, Altrincham FC.

Contact details: Courts of Justice, Crown Square, Manchester M60 9DJ (tel: 0161 954 1729, email: nhowarth@lix.compulink,co.uk).

HOWARTH, Councillor Robert Lever (Bob)

Position: Executive, Management and Finance Group, Bolton Metropolitan Borough Council (1973 - present).

Areas of Influence: Public Sector.

Profile: *b.* July 31st, 1927; *m.* Josephine Mary Doyle (1952); 1 son; 1 daughter.

Educated at Bolton County Grammar School and Bolton Technical College. On leaving College, Bob Howarth became a draughtsman with Hawker Siddeley Dynamics. In 1964 he was elected as MP for Bolton East Constituency and served until 1970 becoming Chairman of the Aviation Committee and Vice-Chairman of the Defence Committee in the House of Commons. He was Parliamentary Private Secretary at the Foreign and Commonwealth Office for a period of two years. He was a lecturer in Liberal Studies at Leigh Technical College from 1970 to 1976 and was appointed Senior Lecturer in General Studies at Wigan College of Technology from 1977 until his retirment in 1987. He served on the Bolton County Borough Council from 1958 to 1960, 1963 to 1966, and again from 1972-1974. He was elected Leader of the (Opposition) Labour Group on the Council in 1975, a position which he maintained until 1980 when control passed to the Labour Group. He was then elected Leader of the Council and Chairman of the Management and Finance Committee. In his many years of service to the Council, he has served as it's representative on a great number of bodies. He currently represents the council on: Local Government Association; Local Government International Bureau; Association of Greater Manchester Authorities; North West Regional Assembly; Manchester Airport Group; Midland Hotel and Conference Centre Limited; Modesole Limited; Federation of Economic Development Authorities; Bolton Business Centre Limited; Bolton Strategic Economic Partnership; Bolton Town Centre Company Limited.

Interests: Gardening, reading, walking, films.

HOWELL, Professor Anthony, BSc (1965), MBBS (1968), MRCP (1971) MSc (1974); FRCP (1986)

Positions: Professor of Medical Oncology, CRC Department of Medical Oncology, University of Manchester (1997 - present).
Areas of Influence: Health.
Profile: *b.* August 20th, 1942; *m.* Shelagh; 1 son; 1 daughter.
Education: Plymouth College, Devon (1953-60); Charing Cross Hospital Medical School, London (1961-68); University of London Intercollegiate (1963-65); Research Fellow, University of Saskatchewan, Canada (1965). Career profile: Teacher, Northwest River High School and Radiographer, Northwest River Hospital, Central Labrador, Canada (1960-61); House Physician (1969), House Surgeon (1969), Charing Cross Hospital; Post-registration House Physician, Whittingdon Hospital (1970); SHO, Northwick Park Hospital (1970-71); MRC Research Fellow and Honorary Medical Registrar, Clinical Research Centre, Harrow (1971-74); Medical Research Council (1974-75); Lecturer in Medicine, University of Birmingham (1975-79); Senior Lecturer in Clinical Oncology, University of Birmingham (1979-80); Senior Lecturer in Medical Oncology, CRC Dept. of Medical Oncology, University of Manchester (1980-97). Professional societies: Association of Cancer Physicians; British Association for Cancer Research; British Breast Group; Endocrine Society; American Society for Clinical Oncology; International Association for Cancer Research; American Association for Cancer Research; European Society for Medical Oncology. Professor Howell serves on over 30 Hosptial, Regional, National, and International Committees. Publications: Over 300 papers in scientific and medical journals.
Interests: Hill walking, travel, science.
Contact details: CRC Department of Medical Oncology, Christie CRC Research Trust, Christie Hospital NHS Trust, Wilmslow Road Manchester M20 4BX (tel: 0161 446 8037, fax: 0161 446 8000, email: maria.parker@christie-tr.nwest.nhs.uk).

HOWITT, Basil William, MA, ARCM, PGCE

Positions: Author and Journalist
Areas of Influence: Arts.
Profile: *b.* October 23rd, 1940; *m.* Dr Clare Gallaway.
Educated at Chetham's (1951-59) and Trinity College Cambridge (1959-63). Publications: *Life in a Penguin Suit* (1993); *Love Lives of the Great Composers* (1995); *Grand Passions and Broken Hearts: Love Lives and lusts of the Great Composers* (1998); *More Love Lives of the Great Composers* (2002). In Press: *Walter and his Daughters: The Story of The Carroll Family of Manchester.*
Interests: Living in French Pyrenees, walking, wine, food.
Contact details: 21 Mauldeth Road West, Manchester M20 3EQ (tel: 0161 445 6650, email: basil_howitt@compuserve.com).

HOYLE, John Roger Horrocks, BSc, FCA

Positions: Managing Director, Ashley Hoyle Ltd.
Areas of Influence: Commerce.
Profile: *b.* May 25th, 1947; *m.* Elizabeth; 2 sons; 2 daughters.
Educated at Wrekin College (1960-65) and Bradford University Business School (1965-68). Career profile: T & HP Box, Chartered Accountants, Preston (1968-71); Arthur Young McClelland Moores (1971-73); County Bank (1973-78); N M Rothschild & Sons (1978-89); Managing Director, Mynshull Group (1989-91); Director, Goddard Kay Rogers Northern (1991-95); Speirhead (1995-99). Clubs and societies: RHS; NACF; National Trust; St James's Club.
Interests: Sport, gardening, horology.
Contact details: The Grafton, Stamford New Road, Altrincham, Cheshire WA14 1DQ (tel: 0161 928 5777, fax: 0161 926 8843, email: roger.hoyle@ashleyhoyle.co.uk).

HUGHES, Eric

Positions: Chairman, Associated Home Fabrics Ltd (1955 - present); Team Coach, Sale Harriers, Manchester.
Areas of Influence: Sport, Commerce.
Profile: *b.* February 4th, 1929; *m.* Doris Helena; 1 son; 1 daughter.
Educated at Central School and Technical College. Eric Hughes has enjoyed a 25 year soccer career playing as a non-professional for Manchester City and other clubs, and concluding as a player/coach in the amateur leagues. He entered athletics in 1970 joining Sale Harriers and developed their women's team from scratch to what is today one of the top European clubs. Received Matt Busby Lifetime Achievement Award (1996).
Interests: Athletics, soccer.

HUGHES, Richard Ian

Position: Managing Director, Altium Capital Limited (1997-02).
Areas of Influence: Finance, Commerce.
Profile: *b.* May 27th, 1968; *m.* Clare; 2 sons.
Educated at Castlebrook High School and Mid Cheshire College of Further Education; Career profile: Wise Speke Limited (1987-92); BWD Rentley Limited (1992-93); Peel Hunt & Company Limited (1993-97); Apex Partners & Co Corporate Finance Limited.
Interests: Running, football.
Contact details: Altium Capital Ltd, 5 Ralli Court, Manchester M3 5FT (tel: 0161 831 9133, fax: 0161 831 9144, email: richard.hughes@altiumcapital-m.co.uk).

HUGHES, Stephen

Positions: Editor in Chief, Bolton Evening News and Bury Times group of newspapers; Member of Bolton Metropolitan Borough Council's Racial Harrassment Forum.
Areas of Influence: Media, Commerce.
Profile: *b.* February 25th, 1956; *m.* Joanna; 3 daughters.
26 years in a variety of roles in the Regional Press.
Interests: Watching Bolton Wanderers, sometimes running.
Contact details: Bolton Evening News, Churchgate, Bolton BL1 1AN (tel: 01204 537 257, fax: 01204 365 068 email: steve.hughes@boltoneveningnews.co.uk).

HUGHES, Chief Superintendent William, MPhil, LLB (Hons)

Positions: Divisional Commander, Stockport Division, Greater Manchester Police (1994 - present); Chair, Stockport Drugs Action Team.
Areas of Influence: Law, Public Sector.
Profile: *b.* May 1st, 1946; Patricia Clarke (partner); 1 son; 1 daughter.
Education: Victoria University of Manchester (1976-79); Brunel University (1985-87). William Hughes joined Salford City Police in 1965 and worked up through ranks in various Greater Manchester Divisions. He was Head of Force Inspectorate (1988-90) and of Research and Development Inspectorate (1991-92). Publication: *The Principle of Retribution versus the Utilitarianism of Deterrence, Justice of the Peace* (1985).
Interests: Live entertainment.

HUGHES-LUNDY, Jacqueline Ann, B.A (Hons), Dip.C.G, ALIA (DIP), FRSA

Positions: Director of Financial Planning, Cobbetts Solicitors; Chair, Independent Television Commission, Viewers Consultative Council, Granada Region; Founder and Organiser of Winning Women Awards (2000 - present); Member, Weekly Business Commentory Team, BBC GMR.
Areas of Influence: Finance, Voluntary Sector, Community.
Profile: *b.* August 21st, 1956; 1 son; 1 daughter.
Educated at Grove Park Grammar School for Girls, Manchester University (1976-79) and Manchester Polytechnic (1979-80). Career profile: Trainee Careers Officer, Tameside MBC (1979-86); Manager, Careers Officer (1981); Trainee Broker, Financial Services (1986); Promoted to various management levels through to Director; Director, Community Foundation for Greater Manchester; Founder, The Rainmakers Foundation; Founder and Organiser, North West Women of Achievements Awards (1992-2000); Patron, Tommys Birth of Hope Appeal. Publications: Was a regular writer for *Woman* magazine on financial planning issues; Runner up in Norwich Union's Virtual Investment Competition (2000) Clubs and societies: Westminster

Dining Club; WIG, Womens IFA Group.
Interests: Art, theatre, media, charities.
Contact details: Cobbetts Solicitors, Ship Canal House, King Street, Manchester M2 4WB (tel: 0161833 5294, fax: 0161 830 2760, email: jacqueline.hughes-lundy@cobbetts.co.uk).

HUMPHRIES, Gerard William, LLB.B (Hons), KCHS, KHS

Positions: Circuit Judge (1980-); Foundation Governor, St. Bede's College, Manchester (1978-)
Areas of Influence: Law, Education.
Profile: *b.* December 13th, 1928; *m.* Margaret Valerie (died 1999); 4 sons; 1 daughter; 13 grandchildren.
Educated at St Mary's Elementary School, Barrow (1933-40), St. Bede's College, Manchester (1940-47) and Manchester University (1947-50). Career profile: Council of Legal Education (1950-51); Flying Officer, RAF (1951-53); Called to Bar, Middle Temple (1952); Admitted N.Circuit (1954); Barrister, N.Circuit (1954-80); Assistant Recorder, Salford (1969-71); Recorder, Crown Court (1974-80); Chairman, Medical Appeals Tribunals (1976-80); Chairman, Vaccine Damage Tribunals (1979-80).
Lectures: *Trials of Christ; Trials of St Paul; Trial of J.H Newman; Vocation to priesthood and religious life.* Clubs and societies: Serra International, North Cheshire (1963-); Northern Lawn Tennis Club; Northenden Golf Club; Cheadle Golf Club.
Interests: Tennis, golf (bad), fell-walking, caravanning, holidays abroad (especially France), gardening, church choir, piano playing, computer, wining and dining with family and friends.
Contact details: Crown Court, Crown Square, Manchester M3 3FL.

HUNTER, Mark James

Positions: Leader, Stockport Metropolitan Borough Council; Leader, Liberal Democrat Group; Member, AGMA Executive; Non-Executive Director, Manchester Airport Board.
Areas of Influence: Public Sector, Media, Commerce.
Profile: *b.* July 25th, 1957; *m.* Lesley Graham; 1 son Robert; 1 daughter, Francesca.
Educated at Audenshaw Grammar School. Mark Hunter spent most of his life in media related industries before becoming full time Leader in 2002. He was previously employed by Guardian Media Group. He was first elected to SMBC in 1996 representing Marple North Ward, having previously been the youngest ever councillor elected to Tameside MBC aged 22 (1980), where he led the (then) Liberal Group and served for 9 years. Clubs and societies: National Trust, Amnesty International, Marple Civic Society.

Interests: Keen long time supporter of Manchester City FC, travel, theatre, reading, the outdoors.
Contact details: Town Hall, Stockport SK1 3XE (tel: 0161 474 3282, fax: 0161 474 3308, email: cllr.mark.hunter@stockport.gov.uk); 34 Cote Green Road, Marple Bridge, Stockport SK6 5EW (tel: 0161 427 8836).

HURST, Malcolm, BA (Hons), FCA

Positions: Senior Partner, Hurst Chartered Accountants (1982 - present); President, Stockport Chamber of Commerce.
Areas of Influence: Commerce, Finance.
Profile: *b.* February 26th, 1950; *m.* Gill; 2 daughters; 2 stepdaughters.
Educated at Bablake School, Coventry, Manchester Polytechnic and Institute of Chartered Accountants. Career profile: Trainee to Senior Tax Manager, Price Waterhouse, Manchester (1973-81); Founder Member and Director, Association of British Independent Accounting Firms; Chair of UK Firms, International Group of Accounting Firms. Clubs and societies: Stockport Chamber of Commerce; Bramall Park Golf Club.
Interests: Travel, golf, theatre, arts, food and wine, cars, history.
Contact details: Hurst, Chartered Accountants, Lancashire Gate, 21 Tiviot Dale, Stockport SK1 1TD (tel; 0161 477 2474, fax: 0161 476 4423, email: malcolm.hurst@hurst.ac.uk); Hurst Corporate Transactions Office, 82 King Street, Manchester M2 4WQ (tel: 0161 935 8266, fax: 0161 935 8166); Hurst Merseyside Office, Orleans House, Edmund Street, Liverpool L3 9NG (tel: 0151 237 5900, fax: 0151 237 5901).

HURST, Jonathon Paul Fenton, BSc (1980), ACA (1983), FCA (1993)

Position: Head of Assurance, KPMG, North of England (2002).
Areas of Influence: Finance.
Profile: *b.* August 21st, 1959; *m.* Judith; 2 sons.
Education: Cheadle Hulme School, Cheshire (1970-1977); BSc Geography, Bristol University (1977-80). Career profile: Qualified, KPMG, Bristol (1983); KPMG, London (1986); Secondment to MOD (1987); Financial Director, Family Business (1988-89); Set up KPMG, Swindon (1989-92); moved to Manchester (1993); Partner (1995); Head of Consumer Market, KPMG (1998). Member of Bramhall Golf Club.
Interests: Golf handicap of 7; ex-Captain, Bristol University Football Club.
Contact details: KPMG, St James' Square, Manchester M2 6DS (tel: 0161 246 4080 / 0161 485 2782, fax: 0161 246 4094, email: jonathan.hurst@kpmg.co.uk).

HUSBAND, Tony

Profile: Freelance Cartoonist and writer.
Areas of Influence: Arts, Media, Sport.
Profile: b. August 28th, 1950; m. Carole; 1 son, Paul.
Educated at Holy Trinity Primary School Gee Cross, Hyde and Greenfield Street
Secondary School, Hyde. Tony Husband turned full time cartoonist in 1984. He
started working for Private Eye, Punch etc. and devised, co-wrote and edited *Oink*
comic for IPC. He then co-wrote and devised *Round the Bend*, a kids TV series for
Yorkshire TV and Hatrick. He co-wrote a play, *Save the Human*, which toured the
country and became a book. He also co-wrote a screenplay with Rory McGrath for
Hatrick. He has had 20 cartoon books published in UK and Germany, and has
illustrated many more. He has had several ranges of greetings cards published for
Carlton and Hallmark. He works daily for the Times (Sport), Sunday Express (Sport),
Private Eye, Spectator, Harpers, The Sun, Playboy and many others. He won
Cartoonist of the Year 6 times in gag section, twice in strip section and twice in sports
section and was Times Cartoonist of the Year in 1989. He is currently Cartoonist of
the Year, and is doing Poetry/Cartoon live stand up shows with Ian McMillan, *The
Bard of Barnsley*. In addition, he is currently working on a sitcom with Griff Rhys
Jones, and has recently had an exhibition at the Lowry Centre where his cartoons
were used as lead-ins to LS Lowry's works. Clubs and societies: Werneth Low Golf
Club, Groucho Club (London).
Interests: Music, golf, football (Manchester United), the environment.
Contact details: tel: 0161 366 0262, fax: 0161 368 8479, email:
toonyhusband@hotmail.com. Web: www.tonyhusband.co.uk).

HUSH, Gillian, MBE, MA

Positions: Chairman of Governors, Manchester High School for Girls; Member of
Manchester University Court; Board member, Manchester University Press; Member
of Management Commitee, Arvon Foundation, Lumb Bank; Cartwheel Community
Arts.
Areas of Influence: Education, Arts, Media.
Profile: b. September 17th, 1935.
Educated at Middlesbrough High School for Girls; Manchester University; Career
profile: Journalist, Evening Gazette, Middlesbrough (1957-62); News Assistant, BBC,
Newcastle Upon Tyne (1962); Radio talks and features (1963); Radio producer (1970).
Interests: Music (particularly opera), theatre.

HUTCHINGS, Alan, BA (Hons), MA, Cert.Ed

Position: Chief Superintendent, Divisional Commander of Trafford.
Areas of Influence: Public Sector.
Profile: *b.* August 16th, 1951; *m.* Susan; 2 Sons.
Educated at Manchester Polytechnic; Exeter University and Manchester University. Career profile: Constable, Lancashire Constabulary (1970); Greater Manchester Police, Constable (1974); Sergeant (1977); Inspector (1984); Chief Inspector (1988); Superintendent (1990); F.B.I, National Academy, Quantico, USA (1992); TNT/Cabinet Office Modernising Government Prizes and awards: Partnership Award (2002). Clubs and societies: Secretary, Silverdale First Responders Association.
Interests: Walking, paintings, local history.
Contact details: Divisional Police HQ, PO Box 6, Talbot Road, Stretford, Manchester M32 0XB (tel: 0161 8567700, fax: 0161 8567714, email: alan.hutchings@gmp.police.uk).

HYTNER, Benet Alan, MA (Cantab), QC (1970)

Positions: Head of Chambers, 12 Byrom Street, Manchester and 22 Old Buildings, Lincoln's Inn, London; Senior Bencher, Middle Temple (1997 - present).
Areas of Influence: Law.
Profile: *b.* December 29th, 1927; *m.* Joyce; 3 sons; 1 daughter.
Educated at Kings Road Council School, Prestwich, Manchester Grammar School and Trinity Hall, Cambridge. Career profile: Called to Bar (1952); Crown Court Recorder (1971-96); Deputy High Court Judge (1976-97); Judge of Appeal, Isle of Man (1980-97); Leader, Northern Circuit, elected (1984-88); Reader (1995), Middle Temple; Bencher, Middle Temple (1977-97). Clubs and societies: MCC, Labour Party.
Interests: Reading, fell walking, theatre, music, travel.
Contact details: 12 Byrom Street, Manchester M3 4PP (tel: 0161 829 2100, fax: 0161 829 2101).

IDDON Brian, BSc, PhD, DSc, CChem, FRSC

Positions: Member of Parliament, Bolton SE; Visiting Professor, Department of Chemistry, The University of Liverpool (2002 -)
Areas of Influence: Public Sector.
Profile: *b.* July 5th, 1940, Tarleton.
Education: Tarleton Church of England CP School; Christ Church Boys' School, Southport; Southport Technical College; BSc (Hons) Chemistry, University of Hull (1961). Career profile: From 1964 to 1966, Dr Brian Iddon was on the staff at Durham University. In 1966 he joined the department of Chemistry and Applied Chemistry at the emerging University of Salford. At monthly intervals for 29 years, Brian presented a popular lecture *The Magic of Chemistry* at venues throughout Britain and across Europe. From 1977 to 1998, Brian served as Councillor on Bolton Metropolitan Borough Council. He was Vice-Chairman of the Housing Committee from 1980-82 and Chairman of that Committee from 1986 to 1996. Bolton elected him an Honorary Alderman for his services to the town in 1998. Brian's interests in Parliament cover a wide variety of topics in the Education, Health and Social Security and Science and Technology areas, such as the policy on illicit drugs, euthanasia, legislation surrounding the use of herbal substances, the Middle East Peace Process and the politics of Kashmir. He is Chairman of the All-Party Parliamentary Misuse of Drugs Group, Treasurer to the Warm Homes Group, Secretary to the Britain-Palestine Group and a Vice-President of the Parliamentary and Scientific Committee. He was a Founder member of the Environmental Audit Select Committee, but is now a Member of the Science and Technology Select Committee.
Interests: Gardening, philately, cricket (as a spectator).
Contact details: House of Commons, London, SW1A 0AA (tel: 0207 219 2096/4064, fax: 0207 219 2653, email: iddon@parliament.uk, web: www.brianiddonmp.org.uk).

INCARICO, Marcella

Position: Managing Director, Out There Events Ltd.
Areas of Influence: Commerce, Media.
Profile: *b.* November 14th, 1970; *m.* Martin Morgan.
Educated at St Richard Gwyn High School, Flint, Flintshire (1981-89); University Central England, Birmingham (1989-93); Following graduation spent 12 months travelling around the world, returned to work with Emap Radio and spent 6 years in stations including Metro FM, Newcastle, Hallam FM Sheffield, Aire FM Leeds and Key 103 Manchester. Positions ranged from Promotions Assistant to Sponsorship and Promotions Manager for the Northern Region. Set up own business in November 2001 organising conferences, corporate hospitality, and promotional events for a cross section of industry clients.
Interests: Travel, food and drink, gym, golf.
Contact details: Out There Events, Wilmott Street, Manchester M15 6BQ (tel: 0161 244 5825, fax: 0161 244 5823, e-mail, marcie@outthereevents.com).

INHELDER, Max

Positions: Consul General of Switzerland in Manchester (1998 - present); President, Manchester Consular Association (2002).
Areas of Influence: Public Sector.
Profile: *m.* Silvia; 1 son.
Max Inhelder has held previous postings in Europe, North and South America and the Far East (1992-98), Consul General in Vancouver (1988-92), and Chargé d'affaires of Switzerland in Bolivia (la Paz) (1992-98). Honorary Member of the Swiss Club Manchester.
Interests: Development politics, photography, golf, skiing.
Contact details: Consulate General of Switzerland, Portland Tower, Manchester M1 3LD (tel: 0161 236 2933, email: Max.Inhelder@mch.rep.admin.ch); (minheld @yahoo.co.uk).

ISHERWOOD, Professor Ian, CBE (1996), MBchB (1954), MD, FRCR, FRCP, FFR, RSCI, FACR

Positions: Hon. Medical Librarian, Manchester Medical Society; Chairman, UK Radiology History & Heritage Charitable Trust; Vice President, The Royal Institution of Great Britain.
Areas of Influence: Health, Education.
Profile: *b.* March 30th, 1931; *m.* Jean, nee Pennington) 1son; 2 daughters.
Education: Eccles Grammar School (1941-48); University of Manchester (1948-54);

Post Graduate Training in Manchester, Sweden and Norway. Career profile: Consultant Neuroradiologist, Derby Royal Infirmary (1961-63); Consultant Neuroradiologist, Manchester Royal Infirmary (1963-93); Emeritus Professor of Diagnostic Radiology, University of Manchester (1975-93); President: North of England Neurological Association (1984-85); Manchester Medical Society (1985-86); European Association of Radiology (1989-91); Radiology Section, Royal Society of Medicine (1992-93); UK Röntgen Centenary Congress (1995); British Society of Neuroradiologists (1994-96). Dean, European College of Radiological Education (1992-96); Commissioner, International Commission on Radiological Units. Publications: over 250 scientific papers, books, and chapters in the field of Diagnostic Imaging with particular reference to Computed Tomography and Magnetic Resonance Imaging. Prizes and awards: Hon Doctorate of Medicine, University of Zaragoza; Gold Medal, Royal College of Radiologists; Rajewski Medal, European Association of Radiology; Barclay Prize, British Institute of Radiology; Jephcott Medal, Royal Society of Medicine.
Interests: Egyptology, history of medicine, cricket.
Contact details: Woodend House, Strines Road, Disley, Cheshire SK6 7GY (tel: 01663 764 980, fax: 01663 766 498, email: ian.isherwood@man.ac.uk).

JACKSON, Kenneth

Positions: Non-Executive Director, Kelda Group PLC; Non-executive Chairman, PM Group PLC.
Areas of Influence: Commerce, Finance.
Profile: *b.* September 23rd, 1939; *m.* Joyce; 1 son.
Education: Wheelwright Grammar School (1952-56); Bailey Technical College (1956-62); Harvard Business School, Senior Managers Programme (1975). Career profile: Student Apprentice, Spencer and Halstead Ltd; Research and Development Engineer Training Officer; Personal Director to General Manager, Spencer and Halstead Ltd; V.P. Europe, Africa and M.E. Carborundum Co. in Manchester (1978-83); MD of Management buy-out of Carbo Plc (1983-90); Director, Hopkinsons Group Plc (1990-93); Chief Executive, Hopkinsons Group Plc (renamed Carbo Plc) (1993-02); Members of Companion of Institute of Management; Non Executive Director, Motorworld Group Plc; Non-Executive Director, Nightfreight Plc, Chairman, Ring Plc.
Interests: Gardening, travel.
Contact details: Carbo Plc, Lakeside, Trafford Park Road, Trafford Park, Manchester M17 1HP (tel: 0161 872 8291, fax: 0161 872 1471, email: confide@carbo.plc.uk); Savile Ings Farm, Broadcarr, Holywell Green, Halifax HX4 9BS (tel: 01422 372 608, fax: 01422 378 730).

JANSKI, Stefan, FRNCM; LRAM, LUD, DipNCSD, CertEd

Position: Director of Opera Studies, Royal Northern College of Music (1993 - present).
Areas of Influence: Education, Arts, Media.
Profile: *b.* September 23rd, 1951;

Educated at Tottenham County Grammar (1963-70), New College of Speech and Drama (1970-73), London University and Royal Academy of Music (1975). Career profile: Director of Workshops, Sadlers Wells / English National Opera (1972-86); Speech and Drama Teacher, ILEA Primary and Secondary Schools (1973-78); Training Officer, South London Theatre Centre and Actor / Teacher, Theatre in Education, Curtain Theatre, London (1978-79); Staff Producer, English National Opera (1978-82); Associate Producer, Glyndebourne Festival Opera (1979-85); Director, Glyndebourne Touring Opera (1981-83); Drama Tutor / Director, Mountview Theatre and Middlesex Polytechnic (1984-85); Guest Director, National Opera Studio (1985-86); Senior Lecturer, Theatre and Opera Studies, RNCM (1986-92); Assistant Director of Opera Studies, RNCM (1992-93); Freelance theatre, opera, musicals, orchestral concerts in UK, Ireland, USA, Europe, Australia. Publication: *The Snowman of Kashmir* (1973). Prizes and awards: Manchester Evening News Best Opera Awards for *Don Carlo* (1990); Michelob City Life Best Opera Award for *The Maid of Orleans* (1994), *the Rape of Lucretia* (1996) and *Falstaff* (2001); City Life Best Opera Award for *Albert Herring* (1997). Clubs and societies: Equity, NATFHE.
Interests: Theatre, concerts, travel, gardening, food and wine.
Contact details: RNCM, 124 Oxford Road, Manchester M13 9RD (tel: 0161 907 5209, fax: 0161 273, 7611, email: paula.redway@rncm.ac.uk); 5 Hanlith Mews, Manchester M19 2JS (tel: 0161 248 7391, email: tillijan@aol.com).

JARMAN, Professor Douglas, FRNCM, BA, PhD

Position: Principal Lecturer, School of Academic Studies, Royal Northern College of Music, Manchester.
Areas of Influence: Arts, Education.
Profile: *b.* November 21st, 1942; *m.* Angela; 2 daughters. Educated at University of Hull, University of Durham and University of Liverpool. Career profile: Temporary Lecturer, University of Leeds (1970-71); Lecturer, Leeds College of Music (1972-73); Lecturer/Senior Lecturer, Royal Northern College of Music (1973-86). Publications: *The Music of Alban Berg* (Faber and Faber, University of Calif, 1979); *Alban Berg, Wozzeck* (C.U.P 1989); *Alban Berg, Lulu* (C.U.P 1991); *Kurt Weill* (University of Indiana 1981); *A Berg Companion* (McMillan 1989); *Berg, Violinkonzert* (Universal,Vienna 1996): Chairman, Psappha New Music Ensemble; Artistic Director, Young Musicians Festival.
Contact details: Royal Northern College of Music, 124 Oxford Road, Manchester.

JEANES, Clive Frederick, OBE (1986), MA

Positions: Chairman, Excellence North West; Board Member, North West Development Agency; Chairman, Wigan Borough Partnership.
Areas of Influence: Commerce, Education, Business Excellence.

Profile: *b.* May 7th, 1933. *m.* Alison. 1 son. 1 daughter.
Educated at Wallington County Grammar School and Christ Church, Oxford. Career profile: Managing Director, Milliken European Division (1972-95); Publications: Numerous articles on Business Excellence.
Contact details: (email: clives@jeanes1.freeserve.co.uk).

JELLICOE, Colin

Positions: Painter; Gallery Director.
Areas of Influence: Arts.
Profile: *b.* November 1st, 1942.
Educated at Heald Place School, Manchester and Regional College of Art, Manchester (1959). Colin Jellicoe opened his gallery in Rusholme in 1963 and has been painting for over 40 years. Following a business partnership formed with Alan Behar, the gallery was moved to the city centre in 1968. Colin has shown many group, oneman, open and mixed exhibitions at his gallery since it opened its door. His own works exist in many private collections both in this country and abroad, including Granada Television , Abbey National, and Withington Hospital. Publications: *Who's Who in Art; Handbook of modern British Paintings 1900-1980; Dictionary of Artists in Britain since 1945.* Clubs and societies: B-Western Film Association; Eagle Society.
Interests: History of the American West, history of the American western film including artists and illustrators.
Contact details: 82 Portland Street, Manchester M1 4QX (tel: 0161 236 2716).

JESS, Dr Digby Charles BSc(Hons), LLM, PhD, FCIArb (1992), FRSA,

Positions: Barrister; Chartered Arbitrator; Treasury Counsel, Northern Region (1990 - present); Barrister; Chartered Arbitrator; Legal Assessor, General Medical Council Fitness to Practise Committee (2002 - present)
Areas of Influence: Law.
Profile: *b.* November 14th, 1953; *m.* Bridie; 1 son; 1 daughter.
Educated at Plymouth College, Aston University, Manchester University, and Inns of Court School of Law. Digby Jess has been in practice at the Bar in Manchester from 1981 specialising in Commercial Litigation, especially insurance disputes, and Building Litigation / Arbitration. Career profile: Committee member (1984-94), Chairman (1992-93), NW Branch of CIArb; CIArb Panel of Arbitrators and Chartered Arbitrator (1999); Part time Lecturer in Law, Manchester University (1985-86); Chairman, NW BIIBA Liability Society (1995-99). Publications: *The Insurance of Commercial Risks: Law and Practice* (2001); *The Insurance of Professional Negligence risks: Law & Practise* (1989); *Insurance in The Encyclopaedia of Forms and Precedents* (1988).

Clubs and societies: Northern Circuit Commercial Bar Association; Technology and Construction Court Bar Association.
Interests: Fencing, cars, holidays with family.
Contact details: 8 King Street, Manchester M2 6AQ (tel: 0161 836 9560, fax: 0161 834 2733, email: djess@eightkingstreet.co.uk).

JOHNS, Peter Andrew, BSc (Econ) (1973), ACIB (1975)

Position: Managing Director, NM Rothschild and Sons Ltd.
Areas of Influence: Finance.
Profile: *b.* December 31st, 1947. *m.* Rosanne; 3 sons; 1 daughter.
Educated at Bridgend Grammar School and University College, London. Career profile: Chairman, Five Arrows Commercial Finance (1996-). Clubs and societies: Mottram Hall Golf Club; Royal Automobile Club.
Interests: Golf, music, history, current affairs.
Contact details: NM Rothschild and Sons LTD, 82 King Street, Manchester M2 4WQ (tel: 0161 827 3840, fax: 0161 834 0245, email: peter.johns@rothschild.co.uk).

JOHNSON, Philip Michael, BSc, ACA, MSI

Position: Director, Corporate Finance, Brown Shipley & Co Ltd.
Areas of Influence: Finance.
Profile: *b.* March 12, 1957; *m.* Kathryn.
Education: Manchester Grammar School (1968-75); University of Manchester, Institute of Science and Technology (1975-78). Career profile: Corporate Recovery Accountant, Thornton Baker (1978-84); Corporate Recovery Accountant, Arthur Young (1984-85); Accountant, Henry Cooke Corporate Finance (1985-96); Managing Director, Henry Cooke Corporate Finance (1996- 99).
Interests: Theatre, ballet, opera, football, cricket, tennis, travel, walking, photography.
Contact details: Director, Brown Shipley, One King Street, Manchester M2 6AW (tel: 0161 214 6540, fax: 0161 214 6541, email: philip.johnson@brownshipley.co.uk).

JOHNSON, Robert William Greenwood, MB, BS, MS, FRCS, FRCS, Ed

Positions: Medical Director, Central Manchester and Manchester Childrens University Hospitals NHS Trust; Consultant Surgeon, Manchester Royal Infirmary; President, Association of Surgeons, Great Britain & Ireland.
Areas of Influence: Education, Health.
Profile: *b.* March 15th, 1942; *m.* Carolyn; 1 son; 1 daughter.
Education: Licensed Victuallers School, Ascot, Berkshire; College of Medicine, University of Durham (1960-65). Career profile: HO, RVI, Newcastle upon Tyne

(1965-66); Surgical training, Newcastle upon Tyne (1966-72); Assistant Professor of Surgery, UC San Francisco (1972-74); Senior Lecturer/ Reader in Surgery, Manchester University (1974); Director of Transplantation, North West Region (1979), Consultant Surgeon, MRI (1987); President, British Transplantation Society (1996-99). Publications: Papers on Renal & Pancreatic Transplantation. Awards: Goyder Scholarship; Fullbright Scholar; Hunterian Professor of Surgery RCS Eng (1981); Hunterian Medal; Pybus Medal N.Eng, Surgical Society; Honorary Fellow RCS Edinburgh (1994). Clubs and Societies: Athenaeum, Royal Birkdale Golf Club; British Transplantation Society; European Transplant Society; American Transplant Society. **Interests:** Skiing, golf, theatre, travel.
Contact details: Consultant Surgeon, Manchester Postgraduate Centre for Health Sciences, Manchester Royal Infirmary, Oxford Rd, Manchester M13 9WL (tel: 0161 276 3560, fax: 0161 2768924, email: rwgj@bigfoot.com);41 Chapel Lane, Evergreen, Halebarns, Altrincham WA15 0AJ (tel: 0161 980 8840, fax: 0161 276 8924, email: rwgj@bigfoot.com).

JOHNSON, Trevor

Positions: Creative Director and Proprietor, VIA Design and Communications, and Object 57 Artboutique (2000 - present).
Areas of Influence: Graphic Design, Arts.
Profile: *b.* June 6th, 1957; *m.* Michelle Lamon Johnson.
Educated at Blackfriars Road Primary School (1961-68) and Broughton Modern (1968-73). Career profile: Junior Artist, ICA Publicity (1973-75); Design Associate, Fox Transfers (1975-77); Senior Designer, Drawing Board (1977-84); Partner, Johnson / Panas (1984-93); Sole Trader, Johnson Design (1993-95); Senior Partner, Via Design (1995-98); Creative Director, Via Communications (1998-02). Publications: *Hacienda must be built; The Art of the Club Flyer; Terence Conran on Design*; Articles in *Design Week* and *City Life*. Exhibitions: *A Different Kitchen*, Manchester University; *MCR*, Locomotive, Paris; *Sublime*, Cornerhouse, Manchester; *MDC Design*, Granada, Manchester; *Johnson*, Boarowalk, Manchester; *Flyers*, V&A, London; *80's Design*, Hotel of the Rising Star New York, Barbican London, and Tokyo; *Square City*, Holden Gallery, Manchester; *Music*, Annual Programme, Manchester. Member of MUFC.
Areas of Influence: Art, football.
Contact details: VIA Design and Communications, 57 Thomas Street, Northern Quarter, Manchester M4 1NA (tel: 0161 832 0856, fax: 0161 835 2856, email: trevor@viamcr.co.uk).

JOHNSTON, Commander David Riley OBE DSC DL RN (Rtd)

Position: Life Vice President, Brougton House Home for Ex-service Personnel;
Areas of Influence: Service Charities.
Profile: *b.* April 3rd, 1922; 3 daughters.
Education: Down House Preparatory School, Esher; Royal Naval College, Dartmouth (King's Dirk 1939); Royal Naval Staff College, Dartmouth. Career profile: Regular Naval Officer (1936-75); Submarine Officer (1942-48); Submarine Commander (1948-55); served in various surface ships (1955-70); Captained HMS Rooke (Gibraltar) (1970-72); Queens Harbour Master, Milford Haven (1972-75); Regional Naval Officer, North West (1975-87). Clubs and Societies: Army and Navy Club; Association of Retired Naval Officers; Vice Chairman, Manchester Naval Officers Association; Submarine Officers Association.
Interests: Fishing, music.
Contact details: 24 Winton Road, Bowden, Cheshire WA14 2PB (tel: 0161 928 9125).

JOHNSTON, T Keith, LLB (Hons) (1973)

Positions: Partner (1981 - present) and Board Member (1990 - present) Addleshaw, Booth& Co; Company Secretary, API Group plc (1995 - present); Governor, The Grange School, Hartford, Cheshire; Chairman, North West Company Secretaries Forum; Solicitor and member of the Law Society.
Areas of Influence: Commerce, Education, Law.
Profile: *b.* July 3rd, 1952; *m.* Alison Eleanor; 2 daughters.
Educated at Bootle Grammar School for Boys, London University (External) LLB (Hons), and Liverpool Polytechnic; Articled Clerk, Alexander, Tathom & Co (1974-76); Solicitor, Addleshaw Sons & Lathom (1976-81).
Interests: Chess, skiing, badminton, Liverpool F.C., travel, Member of the Wine Society.
Contact details: Addleshaw Booth & Co, 100 Barbirolli Square, Manchester M2 3AB (tel: 0161 934 6303, fax: 0161 934 6060, email: keith.johnston@addleshawbooth.com).

JONES, Bill

Positions: Controller, Documentary, History and Science, Granada Manchester; Controller, Granada Bristol (2002 - present).
Areas of Influence: Media.
Profile: *b.* July 14th, 1954; *m.* Kay; 2 sons.
Education: Bridlington Grammar School (1965-72); BA (Hons) Political and Religious Thought, University of Lancaster (1972-75); Diploma in Journalism Studies, University College, Cardiff (1975-76). Bill Jones was a feature writer for the Yorkshire Evening Post (1976-79) and a reporter for the Bolton Evening News (1979-

82), before joining Granada Reports where he quickly became News Editor. He worked in current affairs, entertainment, and documentaries, becoming a producer of the long running series *This England* (1984). As producer, his credits include *Planet Ustinov, Savage Earth, The Trial of Lord Lucan, Crime Story, The Forgotten Front*. He became an executive producer in 1995 working on *7-Up 2000, Secrets of the Stone Age, Eye of the Storm, The Real Spartacus, Savage Planet, Football's Fight Club*, and then others for C4, C5, BBC, and ITV. Publications: *Homo Northwestus* (1982); The book of the Roy Gosling documentary series. Prizes and awards: San Francisco Film Festival Award for *Warship*; New York Film Festival and Atlantic Film Festival Awards for *Savage Seas*. Member of MUFC.

Interests: Skiing, sailing, Isle of Skye.
Contact details: Granada Television, Quay Street, Manchester M60 9EA (tel:0161 827 2282, email: Bill.Jones@granadamedia.com); (email: BJ@lefkimi.freeserve.co.uk).

JONES, Donald Saunders, NCTJ

Positions: Head of Sport, Granada Television (1997 - present).
Areas of Influence: Sport, Media.
Profile: *b.* July 10th, 1955; *m.* Cynthia; 3 sons.
Educated at Fulwood High School Preston, Preston Sixth Form College, and Preston Polytechnic. Donald Jones joined the Lancashire Evening post as junior reporter aged 18. He became sports reporter aged 21 covering Blackburn Rovers, and then joined Granada Television aged 24 as a sports researcher. Leaving GTV to go freelance, he became producer of daytime programmes at BBC (1988), producing various LE and Sports programmes before rejoining Granada in 1994. He produced Granada Reports for two years prior to his current position. Prizes and awards: 2 Royal Television Society awards for Best TV Programme for a Regional Audience for Granada Reports coverage of the Manchester bomb; Best Regional Documentary for Chester City - An American Dream. Clubs and societies: Prince Albert Angling Society; Anglers Cooperative Association; Bowdon Cricket, Hockey and Squash Club.
Interests: Angling, cricket, football.
Contact details: Sports Department, Granada Television, Quay Street, Manchester, M6 9EA (tel: 0161 832, 7211, fax: 0161 953 0270, email: don.jones@granadamedia.com).

JONES, Peter Emerson

Positions: Chairman, Emerson Group of Companies; Member of the Board of Governors, Manchester Metropolitan University; Estates Committee Vice President of Elected Council of the East Cheshire Hospice.
Areas of Influence: Education, Commerce, Health.
Profile: *b.* March 18th, 1935; *m.* Audrey Jones; 2 Sons.

Educated at Mount Carmel, Manchester, Manchester School of Building and Manchester School of Technology; Commenced work as Carpenter and Joiner, gained City and Guild Certificates and took technical classes in building, construction and engineering. Commenced house building and formed P.E. Jones Contractors Ltd. (1959). Formed Emerson Developments Ltd 26 Years ago, and Orbit Developments Ltd building high rise offices, shopping centres, sports, leisure and industrial projects. Emerson International has been developing in Portugal since 1970 and Florida, USA since 1980; Member of Manchester Wheelers, St James's Club, Living Well, Penina Golf Club, Boavista Golf Club; Former Non-executive Member of Southern Manchester Health Authority; Former Chairman of Single Site Working Group for Southern Manchester Health Authority, instigating PFI for a £40m new hospital; Former President, Manchester YMCA.

Interests: Family, walking, cycling, swimming, keep fit, snooker, golf, regularly attends R.C. Church,

Contact details: Emerson House, Heyes Lane, Alderley Edge, Cheshire SK9 7LF.

JONES, Sheila Margaret, MA (Hons), MSc

Positions: Northern Correspondent, Financial Times; Chair, National Union of Journalists, Manchester Branch.

Areas of Influence: Commerce, Finance, Economics.

Profile: *b*. October 23rd, 1955.

Educated at Maris Stella High School, Essex University, BA, Birbeck College, and London University. Career profile: Trainee Reporter, Birkenhead News (1974-79); Sub-editor, East Kent Newspaper Group (1982-83); Sub-editor, Financial Times (1983-84); Economics Reporter, IRN/LBC Radio (1984-85); Freelance Reporter, Germany (1985-87); News Editor, Northern Correspondent and Technology Editor, Financial Times (1997 - present). Clubs and societies: Labour Party, National Union of Journalists.

Interests: Politics, economics, literature, eating and drinking out, swimming.

Contact details: Financial Times, Alexandra Buildings, Queen Street, Manchester M2 5LF (tel: 0161 834 9381, fax: 0161 832 9248, email: sheila.jones@ft.com); Canal Street, Manchester M1 3EZ (fax: 0161 236 2654).

JONES, Stephen Morris

Positions: Chief Executive, Wigan Council; Clerk, Greater Manchester Fire Authority; Secretary, Association of Greater Manchester Authorities.

Areas of Influence: Public Sector, Performance Management.

Profile: *b*. March 12th, 1948; *m*. Rosemary; 1 son; 2 daughters.

Education: Buckhurst Hill County High School; Manchester University. Career profile: Project Manager, Private and Public Sectors (1970-78); Assistant Chief

Executive, Bolton Council (1978-85); Chief Executive, Blackburn Council (1985-90); Directorship of a number of private companies and public boards. Stephen received the Heyward Medal for Town Planning and Development. He is a member of the New Hall Tavern Monday Society and the Society of Local Authority Chief Executives.
Interests: Walking, golf, soccer, wine, South Africa.
Contact details: Chief Executive, Wigan Metropolitan Borough Council, New Town Hall, Library Street Wigan, WN1 1YN (tel: 01942 827 001, fax: 01942 828 174, email: cexec@wiganmbc.gov.uk).

JONES, Susan

Position: Arts Sponsorship Manager, Manchester Airport.
Areas of Influence: Arts.
Profile: 1 son; 1 daughter.
Susan Jones has worked for the past ten years at Manchester Airport, being responsible for the development and implementation of the Arts Sponsorship Strategy. She won the Garrett Award in 1996.
Interests: Arts, opera, music, theatre, dance.
Contact details: Head of Sponsorship, Manchester Airport, 5th Floor Olympic House, Manchester M90 1QX (tel: 0161 489 3602, fax: 0161 489 2702, email: sue.jones@manairport.co.uk).

JONES, Wendy Ann

Position: Director, The Art Department; Director, The Department Store.
Areas of Influence: Arts.
Career profile: Teaching ceramics and illustrating as well as Art Curating.
Interests: Work, music, arts.
Contact details: The Art Department, 46 Edge Street, Northern Quarter, Manchester M4 1HN (tel: 0161 835 3343, fax: 0161 835 3343, email: wendy@the-art-dept.co.uk).

JOSEPH, Rachel Jacqueline

Position: Director of Sales and Marketing (North), Granada TV.
Areas of Influence: Commerce, Media.
Profile: *b*. August 21st, 1968.
Education: Sarum Hall School, London; The Arts Educational School, Tring Park, Hertfordshire. Career profile: Studio Manager, London Studios LWT (1996 -). Rachel Joseph is a member of The Landsdown Club, Mayfair.
Interests: Horseracing, golf, reading, films.
Contact details: Director of Sales & Marketing (North), Granada TV, Quay St,

Manchester M60 9EA (tel: 0161 827 2052, fax: 0161 832 8809, email: rachel.joseph@granadamedia.com); Flat 9, Hanover House, 6 Olive Shapley Ave, Didsbury, Manchetser M60 9EA (tel: 0161 445 1648).

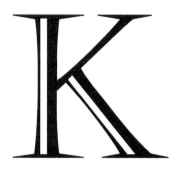

KANARIS, Dr Andreas Demitri

Positions: Non-executive Chairman, Delta Travel; Honorary Commissioner for the Republic of Cyprus, Manchester; Honorary Chairman, Hellenic Brotherhood, Manchester; Treasurer, Greek Orthodox Community, Manchester.
Areas of Influence: Education, Commerce, Community Affairs.
Profile: *b.* May 23rd, 1928; *m.* Vivi Gouda; 2 sons; 3 daughters.
Education: Pancyprian Gymnassium, Nicosia (1941-47); Manchester University (1955-61). Career profile: Employee, Bank of Cyprus (1947-54); Instructor of Physics, Columbia University, NY (1961-64); Lecturer, Manchester University (1964-80); Managing Director, Delta Travel (1980-96). Dr Kanaris has published several articles in Physics journals and received Samuel Bright Research Scolarship (1958) and J.R. Ashworth Research Scholarship (1958,1959,1960).
Interests: Philosophy, reading, walking, community affairs.
Contact details: Commission of Cyprus, University Precinct, Oxford Road, Manchester M13 9RN (tel: 0161 274 4444, fax: 0161 274 3555, email: adkanaris@deltatravel.co.uk); Fallibroome House, 68 Macclesfield Road, Prestbury, Cheshire SK10 4BH (tel: 01625 828 144).

KAPADIA, Babubhai, MBE (1999), BCom

Positions: Chairman, Mercer Ltd and Indo-African Exports Ltd.
Areas of Influence: Faith Groups, Commerce, Voluntary Sector
Profile: *b.* March 13th, 1919; *m.* Saroj; 3 sons.
Educated at Bombay University, Babubhai Kapadia arrived in UK from India in 1945. Career profile: Vice President, India League, Manchester; Chairman, Grey Cloth Merchants Association; Treasurer, Manchester Council for Community Relations;

President, Jain Sarney, Manchester; Chairman, National Council of Varnik Associations. Clubs and societies: Dunham Forest Golf and Charity Club; Hazel Grove Golf Club.
Interests: Golf.
Contact details: IndoAfrican Exports, Failsworth Mill, Ashton Rd West, Manchester M35 0FR (tel: 0161 934 4004, fax: 0161 683 4280, email: indo@fabric.co.uk); tel: 0161 428 7349.

KAUFMAN, The Right Hon. Gerald Bernard, MA (Oxon)

Positions: Member of Parliament, Manchester Gorton; Chairman, House of Commons Culture, Media and Sport Select Committee (1997 - present)
Areas of Influence: Public Sector, Media, Arts.
Profile: *b.* June 21st, 1930.
Educated at Leeds Council Schools, Leeds Grammar School, and The Queen's College, Oxford. Career profile: Assistant General Secretary, Fabian Society (1954-55); Political Staff, Daily Mirror (1955-64); Political Correspondent, New Statesman (1964-65); Prime Minister's Political Staff (1965-70); MP Manchester Ardwick (1970-83); Parliamentary Under-Secretary, Department of the Environment (1974-75); Parliamentary Under-Secretary, Department of Industry (1975); Minister of State for Industry (1975-79); Opposition Spokesman, Housing (1979-80); Member of Shadow Cabinet: Environment (1980-83); Home Affairs (1983-87); Foreign Affairs (1987-92). Member, Labour Party National Executive Committee (1991-92); Chairman, National Heritage Select Committee (1992-97). Publications: *To Build the Promised Land; How to Live Under Labour; Renewal; How to be a Minister; My Life in the Silver Screen; Inside the Promised Land; Meet me in St Louis.* Clubs and societies: Belle Vue British Legion Club; Gorton labour Club.
Interests: Cinema, opera, travel.
Contact details: House of Commons, London SW1A 0AA (tel; 0207 219 5145, fax: 0207 219 6825).

KEARY, Ged, AUB

Position: Managing Director, Commercial Banking North, The Royal Bank of Scotland.
Areas of Influence: Finance, Commerce.
Profile: *b.* June 16th, 1958; *m.* Julie; 1 son; 2 daughters.
Educated at St Frances RC and St Marks RC. Career profile: Joined Royal Bank of Scotland (1976); Head of North of England, Inspection Department (1980-88); Corporate Finance, Manchester (1989-96); Regional Director North West, Corporate Banking (1997); Regional Director, North West and Merseyside (1999); Managing Director North West, Corporate and Commercial Banking (2000).

Interests: Gardening, golf, football, family.
Contact details: 100 Barbirolli Square, Manchester M60 3NA (tel: 0161 242 1100, fax: 0161 242 1155, email: GED.KEARY@rbs.co.uk).

KEATON, Dr James

Position: Chairman, Campus Ventures Group Ltd; Chairman, Magna Colours Ltd; Deputy Chairman, Manchester Science Enterprise Centre; Chairman, MGP Investment Management Ltd; Member, North West Science and Daresbury Development Group; Member, North West Regional Assembly (2002).
Areas of Influence: Commerce, Finance, Education.
Profile: *b.* October 29th, 1934; *m.* Angela; 1 son; 1 daughter.
Education: St. Edwards College, Liverpool; The University of Liverpool; Harvard University USA. Career profile: Researcher, CIBA; A.G.; Basle; Researcher, John Heathcoat & Co; ICI Ltd (1969); Divisional Board, ICI (1979). Dr Keaton has published many papers in journals relating to dyes and colouring. He has also been awarded Gold and Silver Medals of the Society of Dyers and Colourists. Clubs and societies: Society of Dyers and Colourists; Liveryman of the Worshipful Company of Dyers; St. James Club, Manchester; Regional Commitee Member, National Trust; Trustee, Quarry Bank Mill Trust Ltd; Trustee, RC Diocese of Shrewsbury; Chairman, Finance and Planning Commitee, RC Diocese of Shrewsbury; Governor, St Edwards Junior School, Liverpool.
Interests: Sport, reading.
Contact details: Chairman, Campus Ventures Ltd, The University of Manchester, Oxford Road, Manchester M13 9PL (tel: 0161 273 5110, fax: 0161 273 5111); Torpenhow, Montgomery Hill, Caldy, Wirral CH48 1NF.

KELLY, Ruth

Position: Financial Secretary to the Treasury.
Areas of Influence: Politics, Finance.
Profile: *b.* May 9th, 1968. *m.* Derek Gadd; 1 son; 2 daughters.
Education: Queens College, Oxford; London School of Economics. Career profile: Economics Writer, The Guardian (1990-94); Deputy Head of Inflation Report Division, Bank of England (1994-97); PPS to Nick Brown (1998-01); Economic Secretary to the Treasury (2002).
Interests: Walking, swimming, Bolton Wanderers FC.
Contact details: House of Commons, London SW1A 0AA (tel: 0207 219 3496, fax: 0207 219 2211, email: kellyr@parliament .uk).

KENNEDY, John Thomas, DL, FIHT, CIGE

Positions: Company Director and Deputy Lieutenant of the County of Greater Manchester (1997); Honorary Companion, Member of the Court and Founder Member of the Board of the Foundation, Manchester Victoria University.

Areas of Influence: Commerce, Voluntary Sector, Education.

Profile: *b.* June 17th, 1938; *m.* Vera; 2 sons; 2 daughters.

Educated largely in Ireland; completed courses with the Institution of Gas Engineers. After working in the construction industry, Mr Kennedy founded John Kennedy (Civil Engineering) Ltd (1961). From then until his retirement (1997) he was the Chairman and Chief Executive of the company carrying out contracts throughout the UK from its Manchester Headquarters. Awards: Business Man of the Year, Allied Irish Bank in association with The Irish Post (1997); Honorary Fellow, Liverpool John Moores University (2002); Formerly Chairman, Trafford Advisory Committee to the Chancellor to the Duchy of Lancaster. Member of: St James's Club, Manchester; Northenden Golf Club; Hale Barns Cricket Club; United Services Club, Dublin. Honorary Life Member, Enniscrone Golf Club, County Sligo, Ireland. John Kennedy is involved in a wide range of charitable and other interests especially those that are concerned with the health and well-being of young people, those that foster understanding between the peoples of Ireland and Britain, and those that assist the economic regeneration of the North West.

Interests: Music, swimming, golf.

Contact details: June Corner, Hawley Drive, Halebarns, Cheshire WA15 0DP (tel: 0161 904 9977, fax: 0161 980 7565).

KENNEDY, Michael, CBE (1997); OBE (1981)

Position: Chief Music Critic, Sunday Telegraph (1989 - present)

Areas of Influence: Arts, Media

Profile: *b.* February 19th, 1926; *m.* Eslyn (d. 1999); *m.* Joyce; 1 stepson; 2 stepdaughters.

Educated at Berkhamsted School. Career profile: joined Staff at Daily Telegraph, Manchester (1941); Served in Royal Navy (1943-46); Sub-editor (1947-58), Staff Music Critic (1950 -), Assistant Northern Editor (1958-60), Northern Editor (1960-86), joint Chief Music Critic (1986-89), Daily Telegraph, Manchester. Hon. MA, Manchester University (1975). Publications: *The Hallé Tradition* (1960); *The Works of Ralph Vaughan Williams* (1964); *Portrait of Elgar* (1963); *History of Royal Manchester College of Music* (1971); *Barbirolli, Conductor Laureate* (1971); *Mahler* (1974); *Richard Strauss* (1976); *Oxford Dictionary of Music* (1980, 1985); *Britten* (1981); *Adrien Boult* (1987); *Portrait of Walton* (1989); *History of Royal Northern College of Music* (1997); *Richard Strauss: man, musician, enigma* (1999). Clubs and societies: The Athenaeum, London; Lancashire

County Cricket Club; Elgar Society; Barbirolli Society; RVW Society.
Interests: Cricket, music.
Contact details: Longbridge Road, Trafford Park, Manchester, M17 1SL (tel: 0161 848 7899); 62 Edilom Road, Manchester M8 4HZ (tel: 0161 740 4528, email: majkennedy@bungalow62.fsnet.co.uk).

KENT, The Rev Graham Richard, MAFA (2001), FRSA (2002), MA

Position: Ecumenical Development Officer for Greater Manchester Awareness Together (2001 - present)
Areas of Influence: Faith Groups, Arts.
Profile: *b.* October 22nd, 1953; *m.* Lynne.
Education: Tadcaster Grammar School; Bachelor of Divinity (Hons), King's College, London University; MA Art History, Leeds Metropolitan University; PGCE, University of Bristol. Graham Kent has been a Methodist Minister since 1976 serving in Brixton, South London, Keighley and Huddersfield Circuits. He was Superintendent Minister in Calder Valley until 2001 and has held a variety of other posts over the years. Article: *Theology and Painting* (1995). Prizes and awards: Methodist Preachers Doctrine prize (1972); Sabbatical Guides on Arts in Theological Education. Clubs and societies: National Art Collections Fund; Manchester Academy of Fine Arts.
Interests: Britain's political issues, history of architecture, foreign food, walking the dog.
Contact details: Ecumenical Office, St Peter's House, Oxford Road, Manchester, M13 9GH (tel: 0161 273 5508, fax: 0161 272 7172).

KENYON, Christopher George

Positions: Chairman, William Kenyon & sons Ltd; Chairman, Quality Assurance Agency for Higher Education (1997 - present); Member of Court, University of Manchester (1983 - present); Governor, Manchester Grammar School (1980 - present); Chairman of Governors, Manchester Grammar School (1998 - present); Foffee, Chetham's Hospital and Library (1982 - present); Chairman of Foffees, Chetham's Hospital and Library (1992 - present)
Areas of Influence: Education, Arts.
Profile: *b.* August 19th, 1939; *m.* Margaret; 2 sons.
Education: Stowe School; Christ Church, Oxford. Career profile: Member of Council, University of Manchester (1986-00); Chairman of Council, University of Manchester (1990-00); Governor, RNCM (1988-00).
Contact details: Chairman, William Kenyon & Sons Limited, PO Box 33, Dukinfield SK14 4RP (tel: 0161 308 6001, fax: 0161 308 6060, email: cgk@williamkenyon.co.uk)

KENYON, Sir George Henry, JP, DL, BSc, LLD

Position: Chairman of Trustees of Hyde Lads Club
Areas of Influence: Commerce, Education, Voluntary sector.
Profile: *b.* July 10th, 1912. *m.* Christine Brenthall; 2 sons; 1 daughter.
Education: Fulneck School, Pudsey (1919-22); Mustyn House, Parkgate, Wirral (1923-26); Radley College (1926-29); Manchester University (1929-32). Career profile: Chairman, William Kenyon & Sons Ltd (1961-82); Chairman, Tootal Ltd (1976-80); Chairman, Williams & Glyns Bank (1978-83); Director, Williams & Glyns Bank (1972-83); Director, Royal Bank of Scotland (1978-83); Chairman, Council, Manchester University (1972-80); Treasurer, Manchester University (1980-82).
Interests: Various youth charities.
Contact details: 11 Brook View, Brook Lane, Alderley Edge SK9 7QG (tel:01625 584 850).

KENYON, Margaret, DL, MA

Positions: Trustee, Museum of Science and Industry in Manchester (1998 – present); Member of Advisory Council, Granada Foundation (1986 - present); Member of Court, University of Manchester (1991 - present); Governor, Bolton School (2001 - present); Governor, Cheadle Hulme School (2001 - present); Governor, Haberdashers' Aske's Schools, Elstree (2002 - present).
Areas of Influence: Education, Arts.
Profile: *b.* June 19th, 1940; *m.* Christopher George; 2 sons.
Education: Merchant Taylors' School for Girls, Crosby; Somerville College, Oxford. Career profile: Assistant French Mistress, Cheadle Hulme School (1962-63 and 1974-83); Head of French, Withington Girls' School (1983-85); Headmistress, Withington Girls' School (1986-00); President, Girls Schools Association (1993-94).
Contact details: Westow Lodge, Macclesfield Road, Alderley Edge, Cheshire SK9 7BW (tel: 01625 583 924, fax: 01625 583 405, email: mk@westow99.freeserve.co.uk).

KERSHAW, Walter, BA (Hons) (1962)

Position: Artist of independent mind and means.
Areas of Influence: Arts, Commerce.
Profile: *b.* December, 7th, 1940; *m.* Gillian Halliwell; 1 son; 1 daughter.
Educated at De la Salle College, Salford (1951-57) and Durham University (1958-62). Walter Kershaw is a painter of large external and internal murals, in oil and watercolour, at home and abroad. His murals can be seen at Trafford Park, British Aerospace, Wensum Lodge Norwich, Airtours, Manchester United, University of São Paulo and Metro Recife Brazil, Sarajevo International Arts Festival and in Bosnia. He has exhibited paintings and photographs at the V & A, Tate Gallery, National

Portrait Gallery and abroad at the British Council in Berlin and São Paulo. Prizes and awards: Salisbury Heywood Prize, Manchester Academy; Gulbenkian Foundation, Lisbon, for external mural painting. Clubs and societies: Littleborough Cricket Club. **Interests:** Travel, cricket, photography.
Contact details: The Studio, Todmorden Road, Littleborough, Lancashire OL15 9EG (tel: 01706 379653).

KEY, Geoffrey George Bamford

Position: Painter and Sculptor.
Areas of Influence: Arts.
Profile: *b.* May 13th, 1941.
Education: High School of Art, Manchester; Manchester College of Art. Geoffrey Key has been an artist for forty years and has pieces of his work displayed throughout the art galleries of the world. His pulications include: *G. Key Drawings*, Margin Press, *Handbook of Modern British Painting*, Scholar Press, *Dictionary of British Art*, Antique & Collectors Club, *European Painters*, Clio Press and *Who's Who in art*, Art Trade Press. He was also awarded 1st prize at both the Manchester Academy and Leek arts festival.
Interests: Asian art & antiques.
Contact details: 59 Acresfield Road, Pendleton, Salford M6 7GE (tel: 0161 736 6014, email Enquiries@geoffkey.com).

KILBURN Andrew, MBA, BA (Hons)

Position: Chief Executive, Oldham MBC.
Areas of Influence: Public Sector.
Profile: *b.* February 9th, 1953.
Education: BA (Hons), Political Studies; MBA. Career profile: Birmingham Social Services (1975-76); Research and Development, Leicestershire Social Services (1976-79); Town Clerk's and Chief Executive's Dept, Manchester City Council (1979-90); Head of Policy Unit, Oldham MBC (1994); Assistant Chief Executive, Oldham MBC (1994-95); Chief Executive, Redcar and Cleveland Borough Council (1995-99).
Contact details: Chief Executive, P.O Box 160, Civic Centre, West Street, Oldham OL1 1UG (tel: 0161 911 3000, fax: 0161 911 4045, email: ce.a.kilburn@oldham.gov.uk).

KINGSLEY, Joy

Positions: Managing Partner, Pannone and Partners; Governor, Manchester Grammar School.
Areas of Influence: Law.
Profile: *b.* January 16th, 1956. *m.* Michael Blackburn. 2 sons.

Educated at Manchester High School for Girls (1967-1974) and Nottingham University, LLB (1) (1977-1980). Career profile: Solicitor of Supreme Court of Justice; has spent 24years in various positions, from trainee to Managing Partner.
Interests: Travel, reading, family, cinema, theatre.
Contact details: Pannone and Partners, 123 Deansgate, Manchester M3 2BU (tel: 0161 909 3000, fax: 0161 909 4444, email: joy.kingsley@pannone.co.uk)

KIRKWOOD, Colonel David, DL (1999), FCIS, FCMgt, MCIPD

Positions: Director, Jarvis Projects Ltd; President, Parachute Regiment Association, Tameside; Chairman, Greater Manchester Sabre Committee; Trustee, Broughton House.
Areas of Influence: Commerce, Finance, Voluntary Sector.
Profile: *b.* March 26th, 1945; *m.* Sandra; 3 sons; 1 daughter.
Educated Bearsden Academy. Commissioned into Royal Artillery; Garrison Commander of Greater Manchester (1967-97). Clubs and societies: Glossop Golf Club and Manchester Luncheon Club.
Interests: Skiing, golf, gardening.
Contact details: Jarvis Projects Ltd, Atlantic St, Altrincham, Cheshire WA14 5DD (tel: 0161 927 2924, fax: 0161 929 4603, email: davidkirkwood@Jarvis-uk-com).

KITCHENER, Professor Henry, MD, FRCS, FRCOG

Positions: Professor of Gynaecological Oncology, University of Manchester (1996 - present); Member, Advisory Committee on Cervicle Screening (1997 - present); President, British Society of Colposcopy and Cervical Pathology (2000-03).
Areas of Influence: Health.
Profile: *b.* July 1st, 1951; *m.* Valerie; 1 daughter, Sophie.
Educated at Eastwood High School, Renfrewshire and University of Glasgow. Career profile: Florence and William Blair-Bell Research Fellow (1980-82); Lecturer, Dept. of Obstetrics and Gynaecology, University of Singapore (1983-84); Consultant / Senior Lecturer, Dept of Obstetrics and Gynaecology, University of Aberdeen (1988-96). Publications: Numerous publications in research into cervical cancer and its causes, cervical screening, colposcopy and related clinical trials. Visiting Professor, McGill University, Montreal (2002). Clubs and societies: Royal Dornoch Golf Club; Prestbury Golf Club.
Interests: Golf, hillwalking, performing arts, red wine, travelling, the Guardian.
Contact details: Academic Dept. of Obstetrics and Gynaecology, St Mary's Hospital, Whitworth Park M13 0JH (tel: 0161 276 6461, fax: 0161 276 6134, email: hkitchener@central.cmht.nwest.nhs.uk).

KNIGHT, Brigid Agnes

Position: District Judge, Oldham Magistrates Court (2002).
Areas of Influence: Law.
Profile: *m.* 1 son; 2 daughters.
Education: Liverpool University, LLB (Hons); Solicitor in Private Practice (1975-02).
Interests: Family, theatre, ballet, contemporary dance.
Contact details: Oldham Magistrates' Court, St Domingo Place, West Street, Oldham OL1 1QE (tel: 0161 620 2331, fax: 0161 652 0172).

KNOPF, Elliot Michael

Position: Circuit Judge, Northern Circuit.
Areas of Influence: Law.
Profile: *b.* December 23rd, 1950; *m.* Elizabeth; 1 son; 1 daughter.
Education: Bury Grammar School; University College, London. Career profile: Solicitor (1976-91); District Judge (1991-02); Assistant Recorder, Crown Court (1996-00); Recorder, Crowncourt (2000-02).
Interests: Entertaining, reading, travel, family.
Contact details: Bolton Combined Court Centre, Blackhorse St, Bolton BL1 1SH.

KNOWLES, Janet Susan

Positions: Partner, Eversheds; Board Member, Manchester Science Enterprise Centre.
Areas of Influence: Law, Education.
Profile: *b.* August 7th, 1959; *m.* Selman Uzturk.
Education: Penwortham Girls Grammar School; University of Manchester; College of Law, Chester; Open University. Career profile: Eversheds (1981 -); Partner, Eversheds (1989). Janet Knowles is a member of the English Lacrosse Association and Network North.
Interests: Lacrosse, badminton, cinema.
Contact details: Eversheds, Eversheds House, 70 Great Bridgewater Street, Manchester M1 5ES (tel: 0161 832 8000, fax: 0161 832 5337, email: janetknowles@eversheds.com).

KUSHNICK, Professor Louis, AB (Colombia), MA (Yale), PhD (Man)

Positions: Director, Ahmed Iqbal Ullah Race Relation Archive (1999 - present); Professor of Race Relations, University of Manchester (2001 - present); Editor, Safe Race Relations Abstracts (1980 - present).
Areas of Influence: Education, Race Relations.
Profile: *b.* December 12th, 1938; *m.* Patricia; 1 son; 1 daughter.

Educated at Columbia College, New York (1955-59) and Yale University, New Haven (1959-63). Career profile: Leverhulme Fellow (1963-64); Assistant Lecturer, Department of American Studies, University of Manchester (1964-67); Lecturer (1967-90), Senior Lecturer (1990-96), Department of American Studies; Senior Lecturer, Department of Sociology (1996-01). Publications: *Race Class and Struggle* (1997); *A New Introduction to Poverty* (1999); *Against the Odds* (2002). Member of the Council of Institute of Race Relations.

Interests: Wine, travel, cooking, reading.

Contact details: Ahmed Iqbal Ullah Race Relations Archive, Ground Floor, Devonshire House, Oxford Road, Manchester M13 9PL (tel: 0161 275 2920, fax: 275 0916, email: rrarchive@man.ac.uk).

LANCASTER, Roger, LLB

Position: Head of Planning and Environmental Law, Halliwell Landau
Areas of Influence: Law.
Profile: *b.* February 4th, 1951; *m.* Margaret; 2 sons; 1 daughter.
Educated at University of Leicester. Career profile: Admitted as a Solicitor (1975).
Interests: Cricket, golf, squash.
Contact details: Halliwell Landau, St James's Court, Brown Street, Manchester M2
7JF (tel: 0161 831743, fax: 0161 831 2836, email: rlancaster@halliwell.co.uk).

LANE-SMITH, Roger

Positions: Senior Partner, DLA Solicitors (1998 - present); Council Member, CBI;
Audit Committee, UMIST
Areas of Influence: Law, Finance.
Profile: *b.* October 19th, 1945; *m.* Pamela; 1 son; 1 daughter.
Educated at Stockport Grammar School and Guildford College of Law.
Career profile: Articled Clerk, Barlow Parkin (1965-69); Admitted as a Solicitor,
England and Wales (1969); Dunn Cox & Orrett, Kingston, Jamaica (1970); Bailey &
Bailey (1970-72); Founding Partner, David Blank & Co (1973-77); Started own firm,
Lee Lane-Smith (1977); merged to become Alsop Stevens (1984); merged to become
Alsop Wilkinson and was admitted to practice in Hong Kong (1988); Founder
Director, Legal Resources Group (1990); Chairman, Alsop Wilkinson (1993); Deputy
Senior Partner, DLA (1996). Prizes and awards: Robert Ellis Memorial Prize,
Manchester Law Society (1967). Clubs and societies: St James Club.
Interests: Golf, tennis, shooting.

Contact details: DLA, 3 Noble Street, London EC2V 7EC (tel: 0207 796 6096, fax: 0207 796 6595, email: roger.lane-smith@dla.com).

LARNER, Gerald, Officer de L'Ordre des Arts et des Lettres (2001)

Position: Freelance Writer.
Areas of Influence: Arts, Media.
Profile: *b.* 9th March, 1936; *m.* Lynne Walker; 2 daughters by former marriage. Education: Leeds Modern School (1947-54); BA, College Oxford (Senior Scholar) (1956-59). Career profile: National Service, RAF (1954-56); Assistant Lecturer, University of Manchester (1961-62); Music Critic, Guardian (1962-93); Music Critic, The Times, (1993-2002); Director, Bowdon Festival (1993), Wooburn Festival (1998), and Mananan Festival (1999); Panel Member, Royal Philharmonic Society Awards. Though specialising in French music and culture, Gerald Larner has written on most aspects of the classical music repertoire, including the complete piano music of Chopin and Schumann; *The Glasgow Style,* Paul Harris Publishing (1979); *Maurice Ravel,* Phaidon Press (1996); Opera Libretti and Translations; numerous scholarly articles. Devised and Directed: *A Chabrier Caberet,* Edinburgh Festival (1994); *Peter and the Women,* Royal Exchange Theatre (1993); *Ravel Unravelled.*
Interests: Walking, ornithology, theatre, cinema, wine.
Contact details: 38 Heyes Lane, Alderley Edge, Cheshire SK9 7JY (tel: 01625 585378 fax: 01625 590175).

LASH, Very Rev. Archmandrite Christopher John Alleyne (Ephrem), MA(Oxon), STB

Positions: Archmandrite of the Greek Orthodox Archdiocese of Thyateira and Great Britain; Speaker and Translator; Hon Research Fellow, Department of Middle Eastern Studies, University of Manchester (1998 - present).
Areas of Influence: Faith Groups.
Profile: *b.* December 3rd, 1930, India.
Education: Downside School (1944-48); St John's College, Oxford (1950-54); Seminaire Saint Sulpice, Paris (1965-69); Diploma de l'Ecole Pratique des Hautes Etudes, Sorbonne (1969-72); Diplomas in Greek, Hebrew, Syriac and Ge'ez, Institut Catholique, Paris (1968-71). Career profile: Schoolmaster, Classics and English (1956-62); Lecturer, Institut Catholique, Paris (1970-74); Chaplain, Lycée Michelet, Paris (1969-74); Assistant Editor, Oxford Hebrew Dictionary (1974-78); Lecturer, Biblical and Patristic Studies, University of Newcastle (1978-84); Priest (1978); Monk, Mt Athos (1984-87), Normanby (1987-96), Manchester (1996 - present). Father Ephrem has produced many articles and publications. Clubs and societies: Society of Old Testament Studies; British Association of Jewish Studies; Joint Liturgical Group of Great Britain. Father Ephrem has been and still is involved in eccumenial work in a

number of ways. As secretary to the Anglican Orthodox Theological Dialogue, as a member of the Keivan Study Group, as a member of the Enabling Group of CTE, as a church representative on CTBI, as an Orthodox representative on the C of E General Synod and as Church Leader for the Orthodox Churches on Greater Manchester Churches Together.

Interests: Translating, music, maintaining webpage www.anastasis.org.uk.

Contact details: Monastery of St Andrew, 217 Clarendon Road, Whalley Range, Manchester M16 0AY (tel: 0161 881 5774, fax: 0161 860 4752, email: ephrem@chorlton.com).

LATHAM, Glenys, DipAD, CIE, PPMAFA.

Positions: Vice President, Trustee (1993 - present), Manchester Academy of Fine Arts; Practicing and Exhibiting Artist (1979 - present).
Areas of Influence: Arts, Education.
Profile: *b*. March 2nd, 1946; *m*. Robert (Bob).
Educated at Bolton Secondary Art School, Bolton College of Art, Wolverhampton College of Art, and Manchester Regional College of Art. Career profile: Self employed Artist, Teacher and Lecturer, Winton County Secondary School (1968-71); Leigh Girls Grammar School (1971-76); Head of Art, Leigh College (1976-92); Head of Creative Arts, Wigan & Leigh College (1995-96); Artist-in-Residence, Drumcroon Art Centre, Wigan (1981082); Manchester City Art Gallery, Artist's at Work (1988); Leigh Turnpike Gallery, Leigh Arts Festival (1994); Glenys Latham's most recent solo exhibition was at St Georges Chapel, Windsor Castle (2001). There are examples of her sculptures and drawings in numerous private and public collections in North America, Far East and the UK. President, Manchester Academy of Fine Arts (1990-93); North West Chair, NSEAD (1984-85). Commissioned to make a Millennium font for Chowbent Unitarian Chapel, Atherton, Lancashire (2000).
Interests: Travel, wildlife, the arts in general.
Contact details: Longridge, 30 Bank Side, Westhoughton, Bolton Bl5 2QP (tel: 01942 811 691, email: glenys-lathamn@lineone.net).

LAWLEY, Janet M, BA (1959)

Positions: Lecturer and ISI Inspector; Fellow of the 21st Century Learning Initiative.
Areas of Influence: Education
Profile: *b*. May 20th, 1938.
Education: The Friary School, Lichfield, Staffs. (1948-56); BA Geography, University of Bristol (1956-59); Diploma in Education with Distinction in Theory and Practice, University of Oxford (1959-60). Career profile: Teacher, City of Bath Girls School (1960-64); Head of Dept. and Senior Mistress, Merchant Taylors Girls School, Crosby, Liverpool (1964-78); Vice Principal, King George V Sixth Form College, Southport,

Merseyside (1978-87); Headmistress, Bury Grammar School for Girls, Bury, Lancs. (1987-98). Clubs and societies: Geographical Association; Hon. Member, Girls School Association. Janet Lawley's passion is to understand how humans learn. The implications of that knowledge for education and the development of communities worldwide leads her to read widely from Neuro-biology to cognitive science, modern economics to sociology and anthropology to the evolutionary sciences. Janet is a governor for two outstanding schools, Withington Girls School and Dame Alice Harpur School, Bedford, and acts as consultant and lecturer.

Interests: Embroidery, knitting, driving interesting cars, travel, enjoying the company of my cats.

Contact details: Greenmount, Bury, Lancs (tel: 01204 884540).

LAWRENCE, Margaret Gillian, DL (1995), MCSP

Positions: Vice President, Henshaws Society for Blind People; Company Secretary, Dennemeyer & Co Ltd (1972 - present).
Areas of Influence: Voluntary Sector, Health.
Profile: *b.* August 15th, 1938; *m.* John Gordon; 2 daughters.
Educated at Queen Ethelburga's School, Harrogate, Brillantmont College, Lausanne Switzerland and St Thomas's Hospital London. Career profile: Physiotherapist, Booth Hall Children's Hospital, North Manchester General; Manchester South Community Health Council; Chairman of the Board, (1983-02), Henshaws Society for Blind People(1975 - 2002). Clubs and societies: Past Captain (1995), Wilmslow Ladies Golf Club.
Interests: Golf, travel, gardening, theatre.
Contact details: The Barn, Hollies Lane, Wilmslow, Cheshire Sk9 2BW (tel: 01625 522454, fax: 01625 525 750); (email: lawrence@cix.co.uk).

LAWSON, Andrew Stuart, FCA

Positions: Managing Director, Lawson Alexander Bank Ltd; Director, Willan group Ltd.
Areas of Influence: Commerce, Finance.
Profile: *b.* April 27th, 1950; 2 sons; 2 daughters.
Educated at Brentwood School, Essex and London Guildhall University. Career profile: Arthur Anderson, London and Manchester, (1970-82); J Bibby and Sons Plc (1982-87); Finance Director, Industrial Operations; Chief Executive of US Operations. Clubs and societies: member, East India Club; Sale FC.
Contact details: Lawson Alexander Bank Plc, Camellia House, 76 Water Lane, Wilmslow SK9 5BB (tel: 01625 547 100, fax: 01625 547 109, email: andrew.Lawson @lab.co.uk).

LAWTON, Lawrence Duncan, OBE (1987), DL (1987), BA, FRSA

Positions: Chairman, LDL Leisure Ltd; President, Lord Rhodes Foundation Scholarship Trust; Governor, Oldham 6th Form College; Chairman, Saddleworth Festival of the Arts.
Areas of Influence: Public Sector, Education.
Profile: *b.* January 27th, 1928; *m.* Pamela; 1 daughter.
Educated at Altrincham Grammar School and Indian Army Academy, Bangalore. Career profile: Indian Army; Junior Aide, Lord Louis Mountbatten; Viceroy, India; MD, Luxan Ltd; Director and Deputy Chairman, British VITA, Plc; Vice Lord Lieutenant, Greater Manchester (1993-94); Past National President, Round Table (1965-66); Founder Chairman, Rochdale Training and Enterprise Council. Clubs and societies: Army and Navy, London.
Interests: Shooting, gardening.
Contact details: LDL Leisure Ltd, La Pergola Hotel, Rochdale Road, Denshaw, Oldham (tel: 01457 875750, email: reception@lapergola.freeserve.co.uk); Tunstead House, Tunstead Lane, Greenfield, Oldham OL3 7NT.

LAYZELL, Paul John, B.A (Econ), M.Sc, PhD, FBCS, CEng, MILT

Positions: Pro Vice-Chancellor, UMIST.
Areas of Influence: Education.
Profile: *b.* July 23rd, 1957. *m.* Pamela.
Educated at Ernest Bevin Secondary School, London (1968-75), University of Manchester (1975-78) and UMIST (1978-82). Career profile: Research Assistant, UMIST (1979-82); Lecturer, UMIST (1982-90); Senior Lecturer, UMIST (1990-95); Professor of Software Management (1995-); University Halls of Residence Warden (1984-2001); Publications: Over 70 books. Fellow, British Computer Society.
Interests: Gardening, walking.
Contact details: UMIST, PO Box 88, Manchester M60 1QD (tel: 0161 200 3338, fax: 0161 200 3745, email: paul.layzell@umist.ac.uk).

LEATHER, David William BA

Positions: Deputy Chief Executive and Finance Director, Manchester 2002 Limited (2000 - present).
Areas of Influence: Sport, Finance, Commerce.
Profile: *b.* August 24th, 1964; *m.* Kate; 1 son; 2 daughters.
Educated at Bolton School (1975-82) and Sheffield University (1982-85). Career profile: KPMG, Manchester (1985); qualified as a Chartered Accountant (1989); Senior Manager, Retail and Distribution Department, KPMG, Manchester (1989-97); Finance Director, Commonwealth Games (1998); Director in Charge of Commonwealth

Games (1998).
Interests: Keen swimmer and golfer (when time is available!)
Contact details: Manchester 2002 Limited, Commonwealth House, 22-30 Great Ancoats Street, Manchester M4 5AZ (tel: 0161 220 2010, fax: 0161 2202090, email: david.leather@manchester2002.co.uk); (tel: 0161 929 0083).

LEE, Adrian, BPhil (1978), LLB (1985), MPhil (1993), MA (1998)

Position: Divisional Commander, South Manchester Division.
Areas of Influence: Law, Public Sector.
Profile: *m.* Agnes; 2 daughters.
Education: St Ambrose Grammar School (1970-77); Gregorian University, Rome (1977-79); Manchester University, LLB (1982-85), Mphil (1991-93); Masters Degree in Management (1997-98). Career profile: Police Constable (1988); Patrol Sergeant (1988); Detective Sergeant (1989); Relief Inspector (1990); Economic Development Officer (1992); Relief Inspector (1995); Chief Inspector (1996); Operational Chief Inspector (1997); Superintendent (1998). Publication: *Do We Need a Code of Ethics?* in Policing vol. 8 (1992). Clubs and societies: North Cheshire Serra; Trustee, Serra (UK) Foundation; Committee member of the National Office of Vocation; Governor, St Hugh's Primary School; Northenden Golf Club.
Interests: Golf, squash, DIY, cooking.
Contact details: South Manchester Divisional Headquarters, Elizabeth Singer Road, West Didsbury, Manchester M20 2ES (tel; 0161 872 5050).

LEE, John Robert Louis, DL, FCA

Positions: Chairman, Association of Leading Visitor Attractions; Chairman of Trustees, Withington Girls School; Vice President, Museum of Science and Industry in Manchester; Non-executive Director, Emerson Developments (Holdings) Ltd; Manchester and London Investment Trust.
Areas of Influence: Finance, Tourism, Politics.
Profile: *b.* June 21st, 1942; *m.* Monique; 2 sons.
Educated at William Hulme's Grammar School. Career profile: Fellow, Institute of Chartered Accountants; Stockbroker, Investment Banking; Member of Parliament (1979-92); MP Under Secretary of State, Defence Procurement (1983-86); MP Under Secretary of State, Department of Employment and Minister of Tourism (1986-89); Member, English Tourist Board (1990); Chairman of Trustees, Museum of Science and Industry in Manchester; Chairman, Christie Hospital NHS Trust; High Sheriff of Greater Manchester (1998-99); Chairman, Steering Group, NW. Britain in Europe. Financial Journalist. Member of Hale Golf Club.

Interests: Investment, politics, golf, fishing, antiques.
Contact details: Bowdon Old Hall, 49 Langham Lane, Bowdon, Altrincham, Cheshire WA14 3NS (tel: 0161 928 0696, fax: 0161 929 5096).

LEE, K H

Positions: Company Director; Chairman, North West Chinese Council; Chairman, Lee Kai Hung Foundation.
Areas of Influence: Education, Voluntary Sector, Commerce.
Profile: *b.* July 16th, 1935; *m.* Chan Koon Woon; 1 daughter.
Mr Lee describes himself as an Industrialist. He has also published a booklet of western etiquette in Chinese cartoon illustrations. These booklets are distributed freely to Chinese students studying in the UK. Mr Lee founded the Lee Kai Foundation which supports Chinese students studying in the UK. He is a member of the St James Club, Manchester Cruising Association, Cheshire polo Club, Dunham Forest Golf Club, and the Royal Hong Kong Yacht Club.
Interests: Sailing, riding, walking, skiing, reading.
Contact details: Leepark House, 44 Chester Road, Manchester M16 9HA (tel: 0161 873 7788, fax: 0161 873 7799, email: www.cshelpling.org).

LEE, Paul Anthony, DL, MA, LLB

Positions: Senior Partner, Addleshaw Booth and Co; Deputy Lieutenant, Greater Manchester.
Areas of Influence: Law, Arts, Education.
Profile: *b.* January 26th, 1946. *m.* Elisabeth. 2 sons. 1 daughter.
Educated at Manchester Central Grammar School and Clare College, Cambridge. Career profile: Qualified Solicitor, Addleshaw Sons and Latham (1970); Appointed Partner (1973); Appointed Managing Partner (1991); Chairman, Royal Exchange Theatre, Manchester; Chairman, Board of Governors, Cheetham's School of Music; Governor, Royal Northern College of Music; Board member, Northern Ballet Theatre. Clubs and societies: Saville Club, London; Real Tennis and Racquets Club, Manchester.
Interests: The arts, travel, tennis, wine.
Contact details: 100 Barbirolli Square, Manchester M2 3Ab (tel: 0161 934 6000, fax: 0161 934 6060) Riverbank Cottage, 2 Stanton Avenue, Didsbury, Manchester M20 2PG.

LEECH, Emma Jane, BA

Position: Managing Partner, Leech & Co, specialist personal injury solicitors.
Areas of Influence: Law.
Profile: *b.* April 10th, 1958; *m.* James Gleave.
Educated at Harrow County Grammar School and Keele University. Emma set up Leech & Co approximately 15 years ago. The firm is now one of the largest firms of solicitors in the North West, specialising in personal injury work. The firm now has 7 partners. Emma is a council member of the Manchester Law Society, and a main committee member of the Portico Library. She is also on the committee of the Association for Women Solicitors, Manchester branch.
Interests: Theatre, reading.
Contact details: Leech & Co, Heron House, Albert Square, Manchester M2 5HD (tel: 0161 279 0279, fax: 0161 279 1300, email: emma.leech@leech.co.uk); Swingate Cottage, Hole House Lane, Whitely Green, Macclesfield SK10 5SJ.

LEE-JONES, Christine, M.A, M.I Mgt, F.R.S.A

Positions: Head Mistress, Manchester High School for Girls; Member of Court, University of Manchester; Vice Chair of Professional Development Commitee, Girls School Association.
Areas of Influence: Education.
Profile: *b.* June 13th, 1948. *m.* Denys; 1 daughter.
Education: Lawnswood High School, Leeds (1959-66); St. Mary's College, Bangor, North Wales (1966-69); University College, North Wales (1969-70); University of London, Institute of Education (1979-82); Open University (1989-90). Career profile: Primary Teacher, Bethnal Green (1970-71); Head of Religious Education, Archbishop Temple School, London (1971-74); Teacher/Tutor, University of London, Institute of Education (1978-79); Head of Religious Education, Archbishop Michael Ramsey School, London (1974-82); Senior Lecturer, Woolwich College of F.E, London (1983-86); Vice-Principal, Leyton Sixth Form College, London (1986-91); Principal of Eccles Sixth Form College, Salford (1991-98). Clubs and societies: University Women's Club; Network; The Wine Society; Friends of the Royal Exchange Theatre; Royal Shakespeare Company; Hale Barns Tennis Club.
Interests: Theatre, travel, literature, tennis.
Contact details: Manchester High School for Girls, Grange Thorpe Road, Manchester M14 6HS (tel: 0161 224 0447, fax: 0161 224 6192, email: admin@manchester high.co.uk).

LEEMING, Marie Jennifer Jacqueline

Positions: HM Coroner for Manchester West District; Council Member of the Law Society of England and Wales; Non Executive Director, East Cheshire NHS Trust.
Areas of Influence: Law, Health.
Profile: *b.* 20th June 1949; *m.* James David (decd. 1988); 1 son, David.
Educated at Loreto College, Manchester and The University of Sheffield; First female Coroner for Greater Manchester.
Interests: Cricket, theatre, travel, good food, good wine and good friends.
Contact details: H M Coroner, Greater Manchester (West), Paderborn House, Civic Centre, Howell Croft North, Bolton BL1 1JW (tel: 01204 527 322, fax: 01204 387 674).

LEESE, Richard Charles, CBE (2001), BSc (Hons)

Positions: Leader, Manchester City Council (1996 - present); Board Member, North West Development Agency; Board Member, New East Manchester Ltd; Vice Chair, Local Government Associations Society; Inclusion Executive and Chair of its Community Safety Panel; Chair, Manchester Airport Committee; Executive Member, Eurocities; Chair, Warwick University Local Government Research Consortium Steering Group.
Areas of Influence: Public Sector.
Profile: *b.* April 21st, 1951; 1 son; 1 daughter.
Education: Brants Grammar School, Mansfield; BSc (Hons) Pure Mathematics, Warwick University (1969-72). Career profile: Teacher, Sidney Stringer School and Community College, Coventry, including one year as an exchange teacher in Duluth, Minnesota, USA (1974-78); Youth Worker, Abraham Moss College, Manchester (1979-82); Various research, youth work and community work posts (1982-88); Elected to Manchester City Council (1984); Chair, Education Committee (1969-90); Chair, Finance Committee (1990-95); Deputy Leader (1990-96). Past positions include being a board member for Hulme Regeneration Ltd and Millenium Manchester Ltd, the vehicles which respectively regenerated Hulme and rebuilt the City Centre after the 1996 bomb. Clubs and societies: Crumpsall Labour Club; Irish World Heritage Centre, Cheetham Hill, AMICUS, The Labour Party.
Interests: Cinema, music, travel, sport, walking, test cricket, Manchester City FC, politics, Manchester, swimming.
Contact details: Town Hall, Manchester M60 2LA (tel: 0161 234 3004, fax: 0161 234 3356, email: r.leese@notes.manchester.gov.uk).

LEES-JONES, Christopher Peter, FRICS

Positions: Vice Chairman and Joint Managing Director, J.W Lees & Co. (Brewers) Ltd.; Vice Chairman and Trustee, Royal Schools for the Deaf, Manchester; Chairman and Trustee, Rycroft Children's Fund; Trustee, Bowdon Lawn Tennis Club.

Areas of Influence: Education, Law, Voluntary Sector.

Profile: *b.* March 4th, 1937; *m.* Anne; 1 son; 1 daughter.

Educated at Rugby School (1944-54) and College of Estate Management. Career profile: W.H Robinson and Co., Chartered Surveyors, Manchester; Member of the Council, British Beer and Pub Association; Chairman, North West British Beer and Pub Association; Renter Warden, Worshipful Company of Brewers. Member of St. James' Club,
Manchester Tennis and Racquet Club and Knutsford Golf Club.

Interests: Shooting, fishing, golf, lawn tennis.

Contact details: J.W. Lees and Co. (Brewers) Ltd., Greengate Brewery, Middleton Junction, Manchester M24 2AX. (tel: 0161 643 2487, Fax: 0161 655 3731, email: mail@jwlees.co.uk); Hermitage Farm, Holmes Chapel, Cheshire CW4 8DP (tel: 01477 532875).

LEES-JONES, Simon Christopher, MRICS, BSc (Hons)

Position: Property Director, J W Lees & Co (Brewers) Ltd, independent family brewery since 1928.

Areas of Influence: Commerce.

Profile: *b.* April 30th, 1966; *m.* Christine.

Educated at Rostherne, Knutsford; Packwood Haugh, Shropshire; Rugby School; Royal Agricultural College, Cirencester. Simon Lees-Jones has worked as a Land Agent and a Chartered Surveyor. Clubs and societies: Manchester Tennis & Raquets Club; Royal Geographical Society; the Farmers Club.

Interests: Pubs, family, sport.

Contact details: J W Lees & Co, Greengate Brewery, Middleton Junction, Manchester M24 2AX (tel: 0161 643 2487, fax: 0161 655 3721).

LEES-JONES, William George Richard, BA (Hons) London.

Positions: Managing Director, J W Lees & Co (1994 - present); Director, Manchester Grammar School Trust.

Areas of Influence: Commerce.

Profile: October 16th, 1964; *m.* Ariel; 1 son; 2 daughters.

Educated at Rugby School (1978-1982) and London University (1984-87); Held various jobs in Advertising (1987-94).

Contact details: J W Lees, Greengate Brewery, Middleton Junction, Manchester M2 2AX (tel: 0161 643 2487, fax: 0161 655 3731).

LEITCH, Dr Diana Mary, BSc (Hons), PhD

Positions: Assistant Director and Deputy University Librarian, John Rylands University Library of Manchester (1973 - present); Chair of Trustees, Parrs Wood Rural Trust (1991 - present); Governor, Didsbury C of E Primary School; Chair of Governors Buildings Committee, Didsbury C of E; Member of Court and Council, University of Manchester.
Areas of Influence: Education, Voluntary Sector.
Profile: *b.* January 10th, 1946. David Shaw Leitch; 1 son; 1 daughter.
Educated at The Queen's School, Chester (1954-65) and University of Edinburgh (1965-71). Career profile: Abstractor, Indexer and Translator for World Textile Abstracts, Shirley Institute (1971-72); Scientific and Technical Information Officer, CPC International, Trafford Park (1972-73). Publications: Various publications in Library, Information and Pharmaceutical Journals; *Dalton Tradition* with Alfred Williamson; Histories of St James Church, Didsbury and Didsbury Church School. Prizes and awards: Class Medals for Geology and Meterology, University of Edinburgh (1966, 1967); Rotary Club of Didsbury and District Charles Austin Award for Service to the Community (2000). Clubs and societies: Didsbury Civic Society; Chemical Structure Association; Edinburgh University Club of Manchester; Queen's School Association; Manchester Literary and Philosophical Society.
Interests: Gardening, family and local history, fund raising, history of science, photography, family, pets.
Contact details: John Rylands Library, University of Manchester, Oxford Road, Manchester M13 9PP (tel; 0161 275 3737 / 3770, fax: 0161 273 7488, email: diana.leitch@man.ac.uk); 11 Wingate Drive, Didsbury, Manchester, M20 2RT (tel/fax; 0161 445 9461, email: diana@leitch.u-net.com).

LEON, Anthony Jack, DL (2001), FCA

Positions: Non-executive Chairman, Rowe Cohen, Solicitors; Chairman, Bright Futures Plc; Non-exec Director, Mercury Re-cycling plc; Treasurer, UMIST; Director, Central Manchester and Manchester Children's University NHS Trust.
Areas of Influence: Education, Health, Finance.
Profile: *b.* May 3rd, 1938; *m.* Sula Leon JP; 2 sons; 2 daughters.
Educated at Mill Hill School. Practising Chartered Accountant (1960-96).
Contact details: 2 Elm Road, Didsbury, Manchester M20 6XB (tel: 07801 232 768, fax; 0161 448 8842, email: anthonysula@hotmail.com).

LEVER, Lady Ray Rosalia

Areas of Influence: Education, Arts.
Profile: *b.* 23rd September, 1916; *m.* Leslie Lever, Lord of Ardwick; 1 son; 1 daughter.

Educated at Granville School Leicester, Mansfield College Hove, Cheltenham Ladies College and Leicester School of Art. Magistrate (1951-85); Lady Mayoress of Manchester (1957).
Interests: Current affairs, reading, family.

LEVER, Judge Bernard Lewis, MA (Oxon)

Positions: Circuit Judge (2001 - present).
Areas of Influence: Law
Profile: *b.* February 1st, 1951; Anne (nee Ballingall); 2 daughters.
Educated at Clifton and Queens, Oxford; Neale Exhibitioner. Career profile: Called to the Bar, Middle Temple (1975); Co-founder of SDP in the North West (1981); Contested Manchester Withington (1983); Recorder (1995-01); Standing Counsel to the Inland Revenue (1997-01). Member of Vincents.
Interests: Walking, music, fishing, picking up litter.
Contact details: Manchester Crown Court, Minshull Street, Manchester M1 3FS (tel: 0161 954 7500).

LEVY, Robert Adrian, LLB (Hons) (1981)

Positions: Executive Partner (2000) and Head of Corporate at Kuit Steinart Levy.
Areas of Influence: Law, Commerce.
Profile: *b.* October 13th, 1959; *m.* Sally; 2 sons; 1 daughter.
Educated at Manchester Grammar School (1971-78) and University College, London (1979-81). Career profile: Articled with Kuit Steinart Levy (1982); Qualified (1984); Made Partner (1988). Robert Levy is a member of the Royal Exchange Theatre Special Events Committee and is actively involved in the Starlight Foundation.
Interests: Tennis, theatre, amateur dramatics, golf, public speaking.
Contact details: Kuit Steinart Levy, 3 St Mary's Parsonage, Manchester M3 2RD (tel: 0161 832 3434, fax: 0161 832 6650 email: robertlevy@kuits.com).

LEWIS, The Right Reverend Michael Augustine Owen, MA(Oxon)

Positions: Bishop of Middleton (1999 - present); Chair of Manchester Diocesan Board of Education (2000 - present); Warden of Readers and Lay Assistants, Diocese of Manchester (2001 - present).
Areas of Influence: Faith Groups, Education, Voluntary Sector.
Educated at King Edward VI School Southampton, Merton College Oxford and Cuddeson Theological College. Career profile: Ordained Deacon (1978); Ordained Priest (1979); Curate, Christ the King, Salfords Diocese of Southwark (1978-80); Chaplain, Thames Polytechnic, Woolwich (1980-84); Vicar, St Mary the Virgin, Welling, Diocese of Southwark (1984-91); Team Rector, Worcester South East,

Diocese of Worcester (1991-99); Rural Dean of Worcester (1993-99); Canon of Worcester Cathedral (1998-99); Chair of Worcester Diocesan House of Clergy (1998-99). Awarded Pusey and Ellerton Junior and Senior Hebrew Prizes, Oxford (1974, 1975).

Interests: The Caucasus and the Middle East, travel, study.

Contact details: The Hollies, Manchester Road, Rochdale OL11 3QY (tel: 01706 358 550, fax: 01706 354 851, email: maolewis_2000@yahoo.com).

LEWIS, His Honour Judge Jeffrey Allan, BA, LLB

Positions: Circuit Judge (2002)

Areas of Influence: Law.

Profile: *b.* May 25th, 1949; *m.* Elizabeth Ann (nee Swarbrick); 1 son; 1 daughter.

Education: BA, University of the Witwatersrand (1969-71); PGCE, University College, Cardiff (1972-73); LLB, University of Leeds (1975-77). Career profile: Teacher (1973-75); Called to the Bar, Middle Temple (1978); Practised on North Eastern Circuit (1978-02); Part time Chairman, Industrial Tribunals (1991-95); Assistant Recorder (1993-97); Recorder (1997-02).

Interests: Music, reading, skiing, gardening.

Contacts: Manchester Crown Court, Minshull Street, Manchester M1 3FS (tel: 0161 954 7500).

LI, Tyze Kai Tai, BA (Hons), C Eng., MIEE

Positions: Specialist Advisor, Highways Agency of the Department of Transport; Governor and Chairman of the Chinese School of the Manchester Chinese Education Cultural Community Centre.

Areas of Influence: Education, Public Sector, Voluntary Sector.

Profile: *b.* September 24th, 1944; m. Moi Mai; 2 sons; 1 daughters.

Tyze Kai Tai Li finished his Hong Kong secondary education in 1963 to become a semi professional musician. He left Hong Kong in 1964 to enter the restaurant business in England. Tyze had saved enough money to part own a restaurant, which he had managed since 1966 until he had sold his share in 1972. On top of his restaurant business, he was a full time technical officer in local education authorities form 1966 to 1969. On winning a university scholarship in 1969 he graduated with honours in Electronics and followed with a Teacher Certificate. Tyze then went on to head the research department of a scientific instruments company (1973) before joining the West Yorkshire Metropolitan County Council to set up an Urban Traffic Control Unit (1975). In 1896 he joined the Department of Transport to be responsible for the electrical and motorway communications schemes in the North West of England. Through reorganisations of the DTP, Tyze is now a specialist advisor of the Highways Agency of the DTP. Inventor of a Passive Bus Detector System. Prizes and

awards: Innovation Award of the Design Council (1975). Clubs and societies: Education Committee Member of IERE.
Interests: Music, photography, cooking, sport, gardening.
Contact details: Room 617, Sunley Tower, Piccadilly Plaza, Manchester M1 4BE (tel: 0161 930 5745, fax: 0161 930 5658, email: tyzeli.lo@highways.gsi.gov.uk).

LIBESKIND, Daniel, BArch, MA, BDA

Positions: Architect of Imperial War Museum North; Principal of Studio Daniel Libeskind, Berlin; Professor at the Hochshule für Gestaltung, Karlsruhe; Cret Chair, University of Pennsylvania.
Areas of Influence: Arts.
Profile: *b.* May 12th, 1946; *m.* Nina; 2 sons; 1 daughter.
Education: American-Israel Cultural Foundation Scholarship of Music (1959); Architecture, Cooper Union School of Architecture, New York (1965-70); Postgraduate degree, History and Theory of Architecture, Essex University (1970-71). Daniel Libeskind is an international figure in architectural practice and urban design and is well known for introducing a new critical discourse into architecture and for his multidisciplinary approach. Publications: *Between Zero and Infinity* (1981); *Chamberworks* (1983); *Theatrum Mundi* (1985); *Line of Fire* (1988); *Marking the City Boundaries* (1990); *Countersign* (1992); *Kein ort an seiner Stelle* (1995); *El Croquis: Daniel Libeskind* (1996); *Unfolding* (1997); *Fishing from the Pavement* (1997); *Radix: Matrix: Works and Writings of Daniel Libeskind* (1997); *The Space of Encounter* (2001). Prizes and awards: Berlin Cultural Prize (1996); American Academy of Arts and Letters Award for Architecture (1996); Deutscher Architektur Preis (1999); Goethe Medaillon (2000); Hiroshima Art Prize (2002). Clubs and societies: Member of European Academy of Arts and Letters and the Akademie der Kunst. Among many architectural, urban and landscape projects: The Jewish Museum, Berlin (1999); Felix Nussbaum Hause, Osnabruck (1998). Projects in London, Denver, Tel Aviv, Bern, Toronto, San Francisco and Copenhagen are due for completion between 2003 and 2006.
Contact details: Studio Daniel Libeskind, Windscheidstr 18, 10627 Berlin, Germany (tel: 49 30 32 77 820, fax: 49 30 32 77 82 99, email: info@daniel-libeskind.com).

LIEBERMAN, Dr Brian Abraham, MBBCH (1965), MRCOG (1970), FRCOG (1980)

Positions: Director, Department of Reproductive Medicine, St Mary's Hospital, Manchester; Consultant, Obstetrics and Gynaecology, St Mary's Hospital, Manchester (1978 - present); Director, Manchester Fertility Service, Russell House, Manchester; Director, Regional IVF and DI unit, St Mary's Hospital (1981 - present)
Areas of Influence: Health, Education.
Profile: *b.* February 28th, 1942; *m.* Bernice; 2 sons; 1 daughter.
Education: Grey College, Bloemfontein, South Africa (1955-59); University of

Witwatersrand, Johannesburg, South Africa (1960-65). Career profile: Initial post graduate training, Groote Schuer Hospital, Cape Town (1968-69); subsequent post graduate training, St Mary's Hospital, London (1970-78); Founder of Regional IVF and DI unit which was the first to be established within the NHS. Dr Leiberman has had over 80 peer reviewed publications in medical journals. Clubs and societies: Member of Royal College of Obstetricians and Gynaecologists, by exam, Gynaecological Travellers, by invitation, and Dunham Forest Golf Club.
Interests: Golf, jazz, walking.
Contact details: Manchester Fertility Services, Russell House, Russell Road, Whalley Range M16 8AJ (tel: 0161 232 2635, fax: 0161 860 6120, email: mfs@bupa.u-net.com).

LINDSAY, Sally, BA (Hons)

Position: Actress.
Areas of Influence: Media.
Profile: *b.* July 8th, 1973.
Sally Lindsay is best known as barmaid and manageress of The Rovers Return, Weatherfield.

LIU YIN, Professor John Ahman, BSc, MBChB, FRCP, FRCPath

Position: Consultant Haematologist, Manchester Royal Infirmary (1985 - present).
Areas of Influence: Health, Haematology.
Profile: *b.* May 24th, 1949; *m.* Jackie; 2 sons.
Educated at Manchester University (1969-75). Career profile: Senior Registrar, Royal Postgraduate Medical School, Hammersmith Hospital, London (1982-85); Honorary Professor of Haematology, University of Manchester (2001). John Liu Yin has published over 100 scientific and medical papers in peer-reviewed journals and has received substantial grant income from UK Leukaemia Research Fund, for whom he also fundraises, to support his research in the Infirmary. He is a member of Manchester Medical Society and the British and American Societies of Haematology.
Interests: Walking, reading, supporting Manchester United.
Contact details: Department of Haematology, Manchester Royal Infirmary, Manchester M13 9WL (tel: 0161 276 4984, fax: 0161 276 4814, email; jyin@labmed.cmht.nwest.nhs.uk).

LIVESEY, Philip Grimshaw FCA

Positions: Chartered Accountant; Honorary Life Governor, Royal Shakespeare Company; Director, Corpfin Worldwide Ltd.
Areas of Influence: Arts, Finance.
Profile: *b.* January 13th, 1925; *m.* Joan; 1 son; 3 daughters.

Career profile: 47 Royal Marine Commander (1943-44); Partner in Charge, Coopers & Lybrand North West (1980-87); various directorships (1987 - present). Treasurer & Hon Life Member, Manchester Academy of Fine Arts; Clubs and societies: St James's Manchester; Royal Overseas, London.
Contact details: 15 Leycester Road, Knutsford WA16 8QR (tel: 01565 653 345).

LIVINGSTONE, Jack

Positions: President, London Scottish Bank plc; Chairman, Record Printing Ltd; Chairman, Manchester City Art Gallery Development Trust; Trustee, Jerusalem Foundation Committee; Christie for Cancer Appeal.
Areas of Influence: Arts, Finance, Voluntary Sector
Profile: *b.* April 27th, 1934; *m.* Janice; 1 son; 1 daughter.
Educated at King George V School, Southport (1944-48), Ackworth School, Yorks (1948-53) and Kings College, London University (1953-55). Career profile: Jack Livingstone joined the family firm after leaving the RAF in 1958. The Firm became London Scottish Bank in 1971 and Jack was Managing Director until 1988 and then Chairman till 1995. He remained a Director until 2000 but has now retired with Honorary title of President. Member of the Bank of England Deposit Protection Board (1990).
Interests: IT, walking, sailing, reading.
Contact details: Westholme, The Springs, Bowdon, Altrincham, Cheshire WA14 3JH (email: jackandjan@btinternet.com).

LLOYD, Anthony Joseph (Tony), BSc (Hons), DipBA

Positions: Member of Parliament for Manchester Central (1997 - present); Leader, UK Parliamentary delegation to Council of Europe (2002 - present).
Areas of Influence: Public Sector, Government, Legislation.
Profile: *b.* February 25th, 1950; *m.* Judith; 1 son; 3 daughters.
Education: Moss Park Primary; Seymour Park Primary; Stretford Grammar for Boys; University of Nottingham; Manchester Business School. Career profile: Lecturer in Business Studies, Salford University; Councillor, Trafford Metropolitan Borough Council; Deputy Leader, Labour Group, Trafford Council; Member of Parliament for Stretford (1983-97); Front bench opposition Spokesman (1987-97); Minister of State, Foreign and Commonwealth Office (1997-99); Chair, Trade Union Group of Labour MP's, 'Lets Get Serious' a not for profit company and North West Drug Treatment Commission (2002). Publication: *Offering a new tomorrow: Report of the NW Drug Treatment Commission,* Joint authorship (2002). Clubs and societies: Stanley Road Working Men's Club, Higher Openshaw.
Contact details: House of Commons, London SW1A 0AA (tel: 0161 819 2828, fax: 0161 839 6875, email: tonylloyd@hotmail.com).

LLOYD, David

Position: Sky Sports Cricket Commentator.
Areas of Influence: Sport.
Profile: Lancashire County Cricket Club (1965-83), Captain (1973-77); 9 England caps, highest score 214 not out v India; England cricket Coach (1997-99); Daily Telegraph Cricket Columnist; Member of Test Match Special Commentary Team; Author of 3 books on Cricket. Member of Bramall Park Golf Club.
Interests: Golf, horse racing, football.

LONDON MORRIS, Hope, JD, MFA, BA

Positions: Consultant Director, Castlefield Gallery, Manchester; Executive Director, Commissions in the Environment.
Areas of Influence: Arts, Commerce, Higher Education, Artist Training.
Profile: *b.* September 9th, 1951.
Education: Juris Doctor, New York University School of Law; Master of Fine Art, Brooklyn College, City University of New York; BA (Hons) (Phi Beta Kappa, summa cum laude), Queens College, City University of New York. Creating opportunities for artists has been a constant theme throughout an eclectic career, starting as a painter in New York during the burgeoning co-operative galleries movement of the 1970's, leading to a degree in Law in order to understand the relationship of art and commerce. Hope London Morris worked in the animation industry in Los Angeles prior to relocation to the UK where she has been instrumental in artists' professional development including work as a lecturer at Liverpool Institute for the Performing Arts (1996-02). Her most recent achievement has been redevelopment of Manchester's Castlefield Gallery. Publications: *Marketing for Artists and Crafts People* (1994); *Jumping Hurdles* in Arts Professional, Issue 23, April 2002. Prizes and awards: Walter J Derenburg Fellow in Copyright Law, New York University School of Law (1978) and ASCAP Writing Award, American Society of Composers, Authors, and Publishers. Member of Engage, Gallery Education. Hope considers herself as an adopted Mancunian since 1987, and is committed to making a positive difference here through the arts.
Interests: The countryside, city life, cooking, all forms of visual art including film, photography, multimedia and music.
Contact details: (tel: 07702 421720, email: hopelondonmorris@aol.com).

LOVELL, Alfred Charles Bernard, Kt (1961), OBE (1946), FRS (1955), PhD, LLD, DSc, Hon FIEE, Hon FINT PHYS, Duniv

Positions: Emeritus Professor of Radio Astronomy, University of Manchester
Areas of Influence: Science, Education.

Profile: *b.* August 13th, 1913; *m.* Mary Joyce Chesterman (d. 1993); 2 sons; 3 daughters.
Education: Kingswood Grammar School, Bristol; BSc, PhD, University of Bristol (1936). Career profile: Assistant Lecturer, University of Manchester (1936-39); Telecommunication Research Establishment (1939-45); Founder and Director, Jodrell Bank 2000 (1951-81); President, Guild of Church Musicians (1976-89); Master, Musicians Company (1986-87); President, Lancashire County Cricket Club; Church Organist (rtd. 2000). Prizes and awards: Hon. Freeman, Manchester (1977); Order of Merit, Poland (1975). Publications: Many papers and books on Physics and Astronomy. Clubs and societies: Athenaeum; MCC.
Interests: Music, cricket, gardening.
Contact details: The Quinta, Swettenham, Cheshire CW12 2LD (tel: 01477 571 254).

LOWCOCK, His Honour Judge Andrew Charles, M.A (oxon).

Positions: Circuit Judge; Governor, The Ryleys School (1996 - present).
Areas of Influence: Law.
Profile: *b.* November 22, 1949; *m.* Sarah; 2 sons.
Educated at Malvern College and New College, Oxford; Barrister, 28 St John Street Chambers, Manchester (1973-01); Assistant Recorder (1993-97); Recorder (1997-01); Member of Lancashire County Cricket Club.
Interests: Music, theatre, watching cricket, football.
Contact details: Minshull Street Crown Court, Minshull Street, Manchester M1 3FS.

LOWE, The Right Reverend Bishop of Hulme, Stephen Richard, BSc (1966)

Position: Bishop of Hulme (1998 - present)
Areas of Influence: Faith Groups, Urban Regeneration, Voluntary Sector
Profile: *b.* March, 1944; *m.* Pauline; 1 son; 1 daughter.
Education: Leeds Grammar School; BSc Econ., London University, Birmingham; Ripon Hall, Oxford. Career profile: Ordained as a curate of St Michael's Anglican Methodist Church in Gospel Lane, Birmingham (1968-72); Minister-in-Charge of Woodgate Valley Anglican Methodist Church (1972-75); Team Rector of East Ham (1975) where he served for 13 years; Chairman, Newham Council for Voluntary Service, and member, Council Social Service Committee; Honorary Canon of Chelmsford (1985-88); Chelmsford Diocesan Urban Officer (1986-88); Archdeacon of Sheffield and Canon residentiary (1988-99); Member of the Duke of Edinburgh's Commonwealth Study Conference (1989); Chairman, Sheffield Somalia Refugees Trust (1990-94); Chairman of the Diocesan Faith in the City Committee (1988-99), Yorkshire / Humberside Regional Advisory Council of the BBC (1992-96), and of the Diocesan Social Responsibility Committee (1988-99); He served on the Commission into Church Institutions and was trustee of the Church Urban Fund and Chair of its

Grants Committee (1993-96). Stephen Lowe is a keen supporter of the ordination of women, ecumenical partnerships and has developed a passionate interest in and knowledge of, Urban Ministry and Regeneration. He was asked to continue on the Bishoprics and Cathedrals Committee of the Church Commissioners, and was elected on to the House of

Bishops in 2001 and became Deputy Chairman in 2002. He was elected back on to the Board of Governors in 2002

Interests: Manchester City FC.

Contact details: 14 Moorgate Avenue, Withington, Manchester M20 1HE (tel: 0161 445 5922, fax: 0161 448 9687, email: lowehulme@btinternet.com).

LOWRY, John Christopher, MB, CHB, FDSRCS (Eng and Ed), FRCS (Eng and Ed), MHSM

Positions: Consultant Oral and Maxillofacial Surgeon, Royal Bolton Hospital, Blackburn Royal Infirmary (1976 - present); Chairman, Standing Dental Advisory Committee to Secretary of State for Health (2000 - present); Dean, Faculty of Dental Surgery, Royal College of Surgeons of England (2001-04); Secretary General, European Association for Cranio Maxillofacial Surgery (1998 - present); Chairman, Senate of Dental Specialities (2001 - present); Chairman, Joint meeting of Dental Faculties of the Surgical Colleges of UK and Ireland (2001 - present).

Areas of Influence: Health, Education, Public Sector.

Profile: *b.* June 6th, 1942; *m.* Valerie (nee Smethurst); 1 son, Jonathon (1974); 1 daughter, Michelle (1970).

Education: Wadham House School; Altrincham Grammar School; University of Manchester. Career profile: House Officer, Senior House Officer, Senior Registrar, Oral and Maxillofacial Surgical Rotation Programme; Consultant (1976); Lecturer, University of Manchester (1976-01). Publications on General Maxillo-Facial Surgery, Trauma, Reconstruction and Saliviary Disease. Prizes and awards: Leverhulme Travelling Fellowships; Honorary Fellowship American Association of Oral and Maxillofacial Surgeons (1999). Clubs and societies: Fellow British Association Oral and Maxillofacial Surgeons; Fellow, Royal Society of Medicine; Fellow, Manchester Medical Society; British Medical Association; British Dental Association.

Interests: Music, jazz - traditional and modern, athletics, motor sport.

Contact details: Department of Oral and Maxillofacial Surgery, Royal Bolton Hospital, Farmworth, Bolton BL4 0JR (tel: 01204 390 0521, fax: 01204 390937, email: jlowry@rcsemg.ac.uk); 50 Ravens Wood, Bolton, BL1 5TL (tel: 01204 848815, fax: 01204845821, email: johnlowry@btinternet.com).

LUNNISS, Vivien

Positions: Calligrapher and Bookbinder.
Areas of Influence: Arts, Education.
Profile: *b.* January 12th, 1949; 2 sons; 1 daughter.
 Education: Calligraphy and Lettering Arts Society Intermediate; Diploma with Distinction, Accredited Tutor; Society of Scribes and Illuminators Training Scheme; book repair and restoration at Scriveners Books, Buxton. Vivien Lunniss has studied formal lettering since 1982 and now teaches a variety of courses to calligraphy and book enthusiasts throughout the North West, undertaking varied commissions for private and corporate clients. Publication: *Celtic Calligraphy*, Search Press. Exhibitions: Calligraphy & Lettering Arts Society; Society of Scribes & Illuminators; Stockport Art Gallery.
Interests: My Hobby is my work and my work is my hobby, this enables me to experiment in other fields such as mixed media and textile arts, and to see how they can be incorporated with lettering and book design.
Contact details: 12 Heathfield Avenue, Gatley, Cheshire SK8 4PJ (tel: 0161 283 7221, email: LUNNISS@cwctv.net).

LUPTON, Paul Nigel Carus, FCA, ICAEW, MSI

Positions: Corporate Finance Partner, Deloitte & Touche (2002 - present); Member of The NWOA Biotech Steering Committee.
Areas of Influence: Finance, Commerce.
Profile: *b.* February 14th, 1965; m Jean; 1 son; 1 daughter.
Education: Hutton Grammar School Preston (1976-1983); Bsc (Hons), Management and Chemical Sciences, UMIST (1983-86). Career profile: Audit Senior, Arthur Anderson, Manchester (1986-89); Corporate Finance Executive (1989-91); Corporate Finance Manager (1991-94); Corporate Finance Director (1994-97); Corporate Finance Partner (1997-02); UK Leadership Team, Andersen Corporate Finance (2000-02). Rainmaker (2001), Sunday Times and Initiative Europe (UK Buyouts 1998-2000); Rainmaker (2002) Initative Europe (UK Buyouts 1999-2001 £50-150 Million, 1st Place).
Interests: Running and weight training, contempary art, rugby (watching), football (playing).
Contact details: Deloitte & Touche, Deansgate, Manchester (tel: 0161 200 0361, e-mail plupton@deloitte.co.uk).

LYON, Judge Adrian Pirrie, LLB (Hons)

Position: Circuit Judge.
Areas of Influence: Law.
Profile: *b.* October 18th, 1952; *m.* Christina Margaret; 1 son; 1 daughter.
Educated at Leeds Grammar School, Hampton Grammar School and University College, London. Career profile: Barrister, Liverpool (1975-00); Elected member of Bar Council (1995-98); Head of Chambers, 14 Castle Street, Liverpool (1997-2000).
Interests: Theatre, music, travel.
Contact details: c/o Northern Circuit Admin, 15 Quay Street, Manchester M60 9FD (tel: 0161 833 1005, fax: 0161 832 8596).

MACDONALD, James William Ian, BA (Hons)

Positions: Chairman of the Bench, City of Salford Magistrates.
Areas of Influence: Law, Public Sector, Voluntary Sector
Profile: *b.* March 12th, 1937; *m.* Eileen Anne; 2 sons.
Educated at Stockport Grammar School (1949-53) and Salford University. Career profile: Former Managing Director, Meredith Ray & Littler Ltd, Law Stationers.
Interests: Fell walking, historical reading, politics, chess, crossword compiling, crossword solving.
Contact details: 24 Worsley Road, Worsley, Manchester M28 2GQ (tel: 0161 794 2079, email: macdonaldjwimac@aol.com).

MACHELL, Raymond Donatus, QC (1988), MA, LLB (Cantab)

Positions: Recorder of Crown Court; Deputy High Court Judge; Barrister, Byrom Street Chambers (2001 - present).
Areas of Influence: Law, Education.
Profile: *b.* April 8th, 1949; *m.* Elke (dec. 2000); 2 daughters.
Educated at St Patricks, Collyhurst, St Bedes, Whalley Range, and Christ's College, Cambridge. Raymond Machell works in private practice, specialising in personal injury and professional negligence. Career profile: Junior Counsel (1973-88); Dean's Court Chambers (1973-01). Clubs and societies: Personal Injuries Bar Association; Professional Negligence Bar Association; Reform Club, Pall Mall. Governor, St Vincent's Infant School, Altrincham and St Bede's, Whalley Range.
Interests: Reading, hiking, cycling, watching sport.
Contact details: Byrom Street Chambers, 12 Byrom Street, Manchester M3 4PP (0161 829 2100, fax: 0161 829 2101, email: RDM@byromstreet.com).

MADDOCKS, His Honour Judge Bertram Catterall, MA

Positions: Circuit Judge, Chancery Division (1990 - present).
Areas of Influence: Law
Profile: *b.* July 7th, 1932; *m.* Angela; 2 sons; 1 daughter.
Educated at Malsis Hall Yorkshire, Rugby School and Trinity Hall Cambridge.
Career profile: Called to the Bar, Middle Temple (1956); Member, Lincoln's Inn;
Chairman, VAT Tribunals (1977-90); Recorder, (1983-90). Clubs and societies:
Manchester Tennis and Racquet; Northern Counties, Newcastel upon Tyne; The
Queen's Club, London.
Interests: Bridge, real tennis, lawn tennis.
Contact details: Court of justice, Crown Court, Manchester M60 9DS (tel: 0161 954
1800); Moor Hall Farm, Prescot Road, Aughton, Lancashire L39 6RT (tel: 01695 421
601).

MAHER, Christina Rose OBE (1994); MA (Hons) (1995); DUNIV Open (1997).

Position: Founder Director, Plain English Campaign (1979).
Areas of Influence: Voluntary Sector, Education.
Profile: *b.* April 21st, 1938. *m.* George; 3 sons; 1 daughter.
Educated at St. Cecilia's School, Liverpool. Career profile: Community worker (1969-
98); Founder, Tuebrook Bugle, first community newspaper (1971); Liverpool News,
first newspaper for people with learning disabilities (1974); Chairman, Impact
Printers Foundation (1974-98); Founder, Salford Forum Market (1975); Publications:
*The Plain English Story; Utter drivel; Language on trial; How to write letters in plain
English; How to write reports in plain English.*
Interests: Swimming, dance, theatre.
Contact details: Plain English Campaign, PO Box 3, New Mills, High Peak SK22 4QP
(tel: 01663 744 409, fax: 01663 747 038, email: info@plainenglish.co.uk).

MAHMUD, Talat, MBE (2000)

Positions: Manager, Route Network Development, Manchester Airport PLC (1995 -
present).
Areas of Influence: Commerce, Voluntary Sector, Aviation.
Profile: *b.* August 20th, 1950; *m.* Tahira; 3 sons; 1 daughter.
Talat Mahmud's strong committments not only to the company, but also to the
community at large have resulted in significant achievements, corporately, politically
and in the field of human relations. He has over 24 years experience at Manchester
Airport spanning various disciplines of airport operations and the aviation industry,
and has been directly involved in operational issues and strategic planning to meet
the specific observations and needs of the diverse communities passing through the

airport, such as: creating facilities for ablution (wudu), securing the availability of Halal food, and Diversity Awareness in conjunction with Human Resources. He was responsible for changing the perception, understanding and awareness of colleagues at the airport in the principles of other cultures, particularly the Muslim culture by producing a book about the Haji (pilgrimage) for staff, which resulted in a huge direct impact on customer service. He is fluent in a number of Asian Languages, has a basic knowledge of Arabic, and has acted as the official interpreter / translator for the Police Forces, HM Prison / Immigration / Customs and Crown Prosecution Service. He also provides freelance service to various other organisations. Liaises with Local Government bodies, giving information and advice on Islamic Laws.

Interests: Playing and watching cricket and football, formula 1 racing, meeting and socialising with people.

Contact details: Manchester Airport PLC, Manchester M90 1QX (tel:0161 489 5872, fax: 0161 489 3549, email: talat.mahmud:manairport.co.uk); 50 Edge Lane, Stretford, Manchester M32 8JP (tel: 0161 865 7224).

MAKEPEACE, Christopher Edmund

Positions: Local Historian and part time Tutor in local history for Manchester University; Dept. of Continuing Education, WEA and Manchester Education Dept. Adult Services; Fellow Society of Antiquaries of London.

Areas of Influence: Local History, Education, Public Sector.

Profile: *b.* March 6th, 1944; *m.* Hilary Clare; 1 son; 1 daughter.

Educated at King Henry VIII Grammar School, Coventry, Manchester University, and Manchester Library School; Senior Planning Officer and Local Historian, Greater Manchester Council; Secretary, North West Buildings Preservation Trust. Publications include: *Two hundred years of science and technology in Manchester; Manchester as it was; Lost villages of Manchester; Manchester in old postcards; Britain in old photographs; Manchester a century ago; Manchester past and present; History of Prestwich; Manchester Ship Canal.* Won the Dorothy McCulla Memorial Prize for services to local studies librarianship.

Interests: Industrial archaeology, music, local history, travel.

Contact details: 5 Hilton Road, Disley, Cheshire SK12 2JU (tel / fax: 01663 764 910, email: chris.makepeace@talk21.com, tel: 01663 763 346).

MALLICK, Professor Sir Netar Prakash, DL   (1999) KB (1998) BSc, ChB, FRCP, FRCPI, MB, CLB, FRCP, FRCPI

Positions: Professor Emeritus, Renal Medicine in Manchester; Medical Director, Advisory Committee on Distinction Awards; High Sheriff of Greater Manchester (2002-03); Deputy Lieutenant of Greater Manchester.

Areas of Influence: Health, Education, Public Sector.

Profile: *b.* August 3rd, 1935; *m.* Mary; 3 daughters.

While in the University Department of Medicine in Cardiff, where he planned the Renal Unit, Sir Netar Mallick was a member of the Minister of Health's Working Party on Treatment for Renal Failure (1965-67). From 1967 he worked in the University Department of Medicine in Manchester as Lecturer then Senior Lecturer in Medicine and was Associate Director of the Renal Transplantation Unit from its inception in 1968. From 1973, as Consultant Renal Physician, he developed an internationally recognised Department of Renal Medicine integrated with the Transplantation Service. He has been President of the Renal Association of Great Britain and Ireland and Adviser to Her Majesty's Government on renal disease. President, Nephrology Board, Union European des Medicins Specialistes, Chairman of the European Dialysis and Transplantation Assocation Registry and as such a Council Member of the European Renal Replacement Therapy. Until 2000 he was Medical Director of Central Manchester Trust. Sir Netar is a past President of the Lit and Phil, Maitre of the Commanderie de Bordeaux, Manchester, and a member of the Catenian Association.

Interests: Sport (cricket and swimming), theatre, music, books, travel.

Contact details: 43 Porchfield Square, St John's Gardens, Manchester M3 4FG (tel: 0161 279 1621).

MALONE, Kevin, BMus, MMus, PhD

Positions: Lecturer and Composer; Undergraduate Admissions Tutor and Director of Electronic Music Studies, Music Department, University of Manchester (1999 - present).

Areas of Influence: Arts, Education.

Profile: *b.* August 1st 1958; *m.* Pamela Nash; 1 daughter.

Education: Eastman School of Music, University of Rochester, New York (1976-78); New England Conservatory, Boston (1978-80); Conservatoire Nationale Superieure, Paris (1980-81); University of Michigan, Ann Arbor (1982-85); Goldsmiths College, University of London (1985-90). Kevin Malone has been a composer since 1980 and a writer and European correspondent since 1980 for *Winds Quarterly*, *Flute Journal* and *Saxophone Journal* and other publications including *Contemporary Music Review* and *Harpsichord & Fortepiano Magazine*. Prior to his current position at the University of Manchester Kevin was a Lecturer at Manchester Metropolitan University. He has had works published by Dorn inc., Forsyth Music and Recital Music.

Interests: Postmodern art & theory, film studies.

Contact details: Department of Music, University of Manchester, Denmark Road, Manchester M15 6HY (tel: 0161 275 3289, fax: 0161 275 4994, email: khmalone@aol.com).

MANSFIELD, Dr Nicholas Andrew, BA (Hons) (1973), BPhil (1976), AMA (1986), PhD (1997)

Positions: Director, People's History Museum (1989 - present); Governor, Roundwood School, Northenden.
Areas of Influence: Arts, Education, Voluntary Sector
Profile: *b.* August 3rd, 1952; *m.* Julia; 2 sons; 1 daughter.
Education: Honours Degree, Politics and Modern History, Manchester University (1973); BPhil Social Admin, Exeter University (1977); Diploma of the Museums Associations (1986); Doctor of Philosophy, Wolverhampton University (1997). Nicholas Mansfield has had a career in local government and then various types of service since 1977. He is also active in adult education and social history research. Honorary Research Fellow, Department of History, University of Manchester. Publications: Many academic journal articles and book titles on social history; *English Farmworkers and Local Patriotism 1900 to 1930* (2001); *Radical Rhymes and Union Jacks* (2000). Prizes and awards: Simon Industrial and Professional Fellow, Dept. of History, University of Manchester (1999-00).
Interests: Walking in the Welsh Marches, old churches, military history.
Contact details: People's History Museum, 103 Princess Street, Manchester M1 6DD (tel: 0161 228 7212, fax; 0161 237 5965).

MANDUELL, Sir John, CBE (1982), DMus

Positions: Composer;
Areas of Influence: Arts, Media, Education.
Profile: *b.* March 2nd, 1928; *m.* Renna (nee Kellaway); 3 sons; 1 daughter.
Educated at Haileybury, University of Strasbourg, Jesus College, Cambridge and Royal Academy of Music. Career profile: BBC (1956-68): Music Producer (1956-59); Producer to BBC Symphony Orchestra (1959-61); Head of Music, Midlands and East Anglia (1961-64); Head of Music Programme (Radio 3) (1964-68). First Director of Music, University of Lancaster (1968-71); Founder Principal, RNCM (1971-96). Publications: Various music compositions and writings on music. Prizes and awards: CBE (1982), Knighthood (1989); Chevalier des Arts et Lettres (1990); Honorary Degrees: Lancaster, Manchester, RSAMD; Honorary Fellowships: RAM, RCM, RNCM, RWCMD, TCM, GSMD, and Manchester Poloytechnic; Honorary Freeman, Cheltenham; other British and Overseas Awards inc. France and Poland. Clubs and societies: MCC, Royal Overseas; President, British Arts Festivals Association; Chairman, National Association of Youth Orchestras; Past President, Incorporated Society of Musicians; Chairman, Music, National Curriculum Review; Chairman, Music and Touring, Arts Council of Great Britain; Chairman, Music, British Council;

Royal Opera House Board.
Interests: Cricket, travel.
Contact details: Chesha, High Bentahm, via Lancaster LA2 7JY.

MARIGLIANO, Emma

Positions: Librarian, The Portico Library and Gallery. Membership Secretary, Association of Independent Libraries.
Areas of Influence: Arts.
Profile: *b.* February 22nd, 1951; 2 sons.
Education: St Chad's, Cheetham Hill; St Anthony's, Blackley; Open University, Manchester Metropolitan University. Before the Portico Library Emma Marigliano built up a wealth of experience from insurance, to property management and each step taught her a new skill. "I came into the Library as a part-time admin assistant and 15 years later I'm still here, and moved up to Librarian where I've probably used every skill I ever learned!" Currently researching for a Ph.D. (Illustrations to Danté's 'Divine Comedy').
Interests: Reading, drawing, walking, driving, cooking, living.
Contact details: The Portico Library, 57 Mosley Street, Manchester M2 3HY (tel: 0161 236 6785, Fax: 0161 236 6803, email: emma.marigliano@theportico.org.uk); (emma_marigliano@hotmail.com).

MARKS, Richard Leon, QC (1999)

Positions: QC (1999 - present); Recorder (1994 - present); President, Mental Health (Restricted Patients) Review Tribunal (2000 - present).
Areas of Influence: Law.
Profile: *b.* November 20th, 1953; *m.* Jane; 1 son; 1 daughter.
Educated at Beech Hall, Macclesfield, Clifton College, Bristol, and The University of Manchester (LLB). Career profile: Called to the Bar (1975); Assistant Recorder (1991-94).
Interests: Cinema, travel, modern art, Clarice Cliff, cooking, visiting the Theatre of Dreams.
Contact details: Peel Court Chambers, 45 Hardman Street, Manchester M3 3PL (tel: 0161 832 3791, fax: 0161 835 3054, email: rm@peelcourt.co.uk).

MARSH, John, BA (Hons) (Oxon)

Positions: Senior Consultant, Robinson Keane Search & Selection; Advisory Committee, Trafford Magistrates.
Areas of Influence: Industry, Commerce, Public Sector.
Profile: *b.* June 26th, 1948; *m.* Felicity; 2 sons.

Educated at Merchant Taylors School, Northwood and Wadham College, Oxford. On graduating from Oxford, John Marsh joined ICI in Runcorn as a graduate trainee and had a career in international sales and marketing, which included 2 years living in Milan as Commercial Director of ICI Italy. In 1996 he changed careers, becoming a Headhunter specialising in executive and non-executive board appointments, a role he has enjoyed for the last 6 years. Clubs and societies: Bowdon Cricket, Hockey & Squash Club.

Interests: Flyfishing, shooting, walking, squash, opera, theatre, making bread.

Contact details: Robinson Keane, Denzell House, Dunham Road, Bowdon, Cheshire, WA14 4QE (tel: 0161 929 9105, fax: 0161 929 1142).

MARSH, Rosemary Caroline, BA, PGCE

Positions: Vice Chairman, Friends of the Whitworth Art Gallery; (2001 - present); Vice President, British Association of Friends of Museums (BAFM) (1996 - present); Vice President, Europe, World Federation of Friends of Museums (WFFM) (1998 - present).

Areas of Influence: Arts, Museums and International Development, Voluntary Sector.

Profile: *b.* February 24th, 1936; *m.* Dr R D Marsh; 2 sons.

Education: BA Hons Fine Art, Kings College, University of Durham; PGCE, University of London. Career profile: Teacher of Art: King Edwards School for Girls, Handsworth, Birmingham; Wilmslow County High School, Cheshire; The Birtles Education Centre, Wythenshawe. Honorary Secretary; Chairman, BAFM (1989-94). Publications: *Margaret Pilkington*, a leaflet to accompany an exhibition at the Whitworth Art Gallery (1999); *Margaret Pilkington and her Circle,* text of a lecture given to the Lancashire & Cheshire Antiquarian Society (2000); Member of steering committees which oversaw publication of *Volunteers in Museums and Heritage Organisations* (1991) and *Museums among friends - the wider museum community* (1992). Clubs and societies: Friends of the Whitworth; Manchester Lit & Phil; Royal Lancastrian Pottery Society; Hexham Historical Society.

Interests: Traditional jazz, reading and research, looking at pictures and occasionally attempting to draw and paint.

Contact details: Friends of the Whitworth, Whitworth Art Gallery, University of Manchester, Oxford Road M15 6ER (tel: 0161 275 7496, fax: 0161 275 7451, email: fow@man.ac.uk); 66 The Downs, Altrincham, Cheshire WA14 2QJ (tel: 0161 928 4340, email: rosemary@wffm.u-net.com).

MARSHALL, Wayne

Position: Organist in residence, Bridgewater Hall, Manchester.
Areas of Influence: Arts.
Profile: *b.* January 13th 1961.
Educated at Chetham's School of Music, Manchester, Royal College of Music, London and Hochschule fur Musik, Vienna.

MARTIN, F A Peter CEng FIEE FIMgt FMS

Positions: Owner, Peter Martin Associates; Chair, Tame Valley Regeneration Consortium.
Areas of Influence: Commerce, Finance, Public Sector.
Profile: *b.* November 4th, 1936; *m.* Enid Dorothy; 2 daughters.
Educated at Southampton Technical College. Career profile: Unilever Senior Professional Manager across a number of industries, particularly in food and chemicals; Speciality in Manufacturing Management and Logistics; Director and Treasurer, Manchester Chamber of Commerce and Industry; Past Captain, Mere Golf and Country Club.
Interests: Golf, DIY, gardening.
Contact details: High Croft, 23 Park Road, Bowdon, Cheshire WA14 3JJ (tel: 0161 928 9390, fax: 0161 928 9390, email: peter@highcroft.nwnet.co.uk).

MARTIN, James, FCCA

Positions: Deputy Chairman, Brown Group Plc (1984-); Court of University of Manchester; Chairman, Ethel Austin.
Areas of Influence: Education, Finance.
Profile: *b.* December 9th, 1942; *m.* Jean; 2 sons.
Educated at John Marley School, Newcastle Upon Tyne. Career profile: Joined Dunlop as a University Leaver; Number of Accountant positions; Joined Brown Group Plc (1973); Non Executive Director, Redrow Plc; Member of Hale Golf Club.
Interests: Golf, sport, shooting.
Contact details: N Brown Group Plc, 53 Dale Street, Manchester M60 6ES (tel: 0161 238 2202, fax: 0161 238 2662, email: jim.martin@nbrowngroup.co.uk).

MARTIN, William (Scott), FCA, FBRP, FIPA, LLP

Position: Ernst & Young LLP.
Areas of Influence: Finance, Law, Commerce.
Profile: *b.* March 11th, 1953; *m.* Judith; 1 son; 1 daughter.
Educated at Mosley Hall Grammar School, Cheadle. Scott Martin joined the

predecessor firm of Ernst & Young as a chartered accountant in 1971. He qualified in 1975 and transferred to corporate restructuring work. He became Partner in 1986 and continued to work on various restructuring situations including Laker Airways, Scraggs of Macclesfield, Warrington plc, Chester Business Park, Arrows Limited and in 2001 was appointed one of the four special railway administrators of Railtrack plc. Clubs and societies: St James Club, Manchester; St Andrew's Society.
Interests: Motor racing, horse racing, football, Manchester United.
Contact details: Ernst & Young, 100 Barbirolli Square, Manchester, M2 3AW (tel: 0161 333 2950, fax: 333 3008, email: smartin3:uk.ey.com); (tel: 01565 751200, fax: 01565 632 198).

MARTIN-SMITH, Nigel

Positions: Managing Director, Nemesis Modal Agency, Lime Actors Agency, Essential Night Club Limited and Nemesis Casting.
Areas of Influence: Media.
Profile: *b.* June 20th, 1958; Daniel Firkin-Flood (partner).
Educated at Chorlton High School, Manchester (1969-74); Nigel Martin-Smith launched Nidges Model and Casting Agency (1981), later merging with another agency to form Boss Agency (1989). He resigned from that company (1992) to create and manage Boy Band *Take That*. He then launched Nemesis Agency (1993) which is now the largest model and casting agency outside London having offices in Manchester, Birmingham and Leeds. He recently opened Manchester's biggest gay club and venue, 'Essential', in the Gay Village. Nigel also occasionally appears as a TV Pundit on shows like *Star for a Night, The Millionaire Show, This Morning,* and others.
Contact details: Nemesis, 4th Floor, 54 Princess Street, Manchester M1 6HS (tel: 0161 237 9237, fax: 0161 236 1771, email: nigel@nmsmanagement.co.uk).

MASSEY, Nick

Position: Chief Executive, Community Foundation, Greater Manchester.
Areas of Influence: Voluntary Sector, Corporate and Social Responsibility.
Profile: *b.* May 5th, 1960; *m.* Deborah; 2 daughters.
Educated at The Manchester Grammar School (1971-78). Career profile: The Co-operative Bank Plc (1978-97); Head of Corporate Marketing (1994-97); Marketing and Business Consultant (1997-99); Trustee, Manchester Carers Centre; 2 SWOT Awards for Marketing Excellence, Chartered Institute of Marketing (1994and 1996).
Interests: Cycling, Manchester United, 2 daughters.
Contact details: Community Foundation for Greater Manchester, Beswick House,

Beswick Row, Manchester M4 4LE (tel: 0161 214 0940, fax: 0161 214 0941, email: nick@communityfoundation.co.uk) 'Ivy Dene', 42 Queens Road, Urmston, Manchester M41 9HA (tel: 0161 7479239, email: massey@easy.com).

MASTERS, Roger William, BA, ACIB

Position: Head of Customer Services, HSBC Bank Plc, Trade Services.
Areas of Influence: Finance.
Profile: *b.* September 8th, 1949; 5 sons.
Educated at Wembley County Grammar School (1961-66); Harrow College of Higher Education; Open University. Career profile: 12 years with Standard Chartered Bank, UK, West Africa, USA; 22 years with HSBC Group, Credit Audit Manager, London; Manager, HSBC Trade Services, Manchester (1994); Divisional Manager (2000). Clubs and societies: Poynton Motorcycle Club; Landrover Series III Owners Club; Chartered Institute of Bankers.
Interests: Off road driving, motorcycling, QPR supporter.
Contact details: HSBC Bank PLC, Trade Services, Westminster House, 11 Portland Street, Manchester M60 1PX (tel: 0161 253 4418, fax: 0161 253 4490, email: rogermasters@hsbc.com)

MATHER, Elaine Grace, SRN

Positions: Proprietor of The Gallery, Manchester's Art House.
Areas of Influence: Arts, Commerce, Voluntary Sector.
Profile: *b.* December 19th, 1945; 3 sons;
After training as a state registered nurse and working as publisher of *The Connoisseur* (1979-82), Elaine opened The Gallery on Portland Street in 1993 and it is now the largest fine art Gallery outside London. The Gallery exhibits British Contemporary Art and particularly helps to raise the profile of young artists. It maintains a unique educational programme giving commercial gallery experience to under- and post-graduates. Publications: *The Graphic of Roger Hampson: Lancashire People and Places* (2000). Clubs and societies: Chairman, Manchester Appeals Committee for Children in Need in Greater Manchester; Rhosneigr Boat Owner's Association.
Interests: Gym, tennis, sailing, music, gardening, publishing.
Contact details: The Gallery, Manchester's Art House, 131 Portland Street, Manchester M1 4PY (tel: 0161 237 3551, fax; 0161 228 3621, email: elaine@manchestersarthouse.com).

MATTISON, Mark Robert, LLB, MCIARB

Positions: Partner and Head of Construction team, Leeds / Manchester, Eversheds; Chairman, North West Branch, Chartered Institute of Arbitrators.

Areas of Influence: Law, Construction.
Profile: *b.* April 26th, 1951; *m.* Charmaine; 1 son; 1 daughter.
Education: Liverpool College; Studied Law in Liverpool; CEDR Mediation Accreditation (1998). Career profile: Articled with Alexander Tatham (1972-74); Partner (1978); President, Manchester Law Society and Head of Litigation, Eversheds (1991-92). Clubs and societies: Manchester Law Society; Society of Construction Law; Chartered Institute of Arbitrators.
Interests: Travel, cycling, swimming.
Contact details: Eversheds, Eversheds House, 70 Great Bridgewater Street, Manchester M1 2ES (tel: 0161 831 8000, fax: 0161 832 5337, email: markmattison@eversheds.com).

MAXWELL, Melinda Sara, Hon ARAM (1995), BA, ARCM, LTCL

Position: Director of Woodwind Studies, RNCM.
Areas of Influence: Arts, Media, Education.
Profile: *b.* October 23rd, 1953; *m.* David Purser.
Education: York University (1972-75); Royal College of Music (1975-76); DAADScholarship to Helmut Winschermann at Kedetmold Musikakadamie, Germany (1977-79).
Melinda Maxwell has been a soloist at Edinburgh, Warwick, Cheltenham, Aldeburgh andHuddersfield Festivals, and on tours in Japan, Mexico and Europ. She is Principle Oboewith Sinfonia 21 and Endymisn Ensemble and a regular player with London Sintonietta. Inthe world of commercial music, she has played on Inspector Morse as well as majorfilms. She is a composer and teacher, and does creative education work with LondonSinfonietta and the National Youth Orchestra. She was Professor of Oboe at Royal Academy of Music (1995-00) and Trinity College of Music (1999-00). She also holdsmasterclasses and Dartington Summer School. Compositions: three for Oboe (1981, 1992,1997); five for chamber ensemble (1990, 1995, 1998, 1999); one for solo clarinet (1990). Clubs and societies: Society for the promotion of new music; Royal Society of Musicians.
Interests: Painting, drawing, reading, cooking.
Contact details: RNCM, 124 Oxford Road, Manchester M13 9RD (tel: 0161 907 5266, email: melinda.maxwell@rncm.ac.uk).

MAYER, Christine Alexander

Positions: Circuit Administrator, Northern Circuit, The Court Service.
Areas of Influence: Law, Public Sector.
Profile: *b.* January 6th, 1955; *m.* David James; 1 daughter.
Career profile: Lord Chancellor's Department (1976); Probate Division (1976-79); Manchester Crown Court (1979-83); Northen Circuit Administrator's Office (1983-85);

Court Manager, Bolton Combined Court (1985-90); Court manager, Manchester Crown Court Square (1990-94); Courts Administrator, Lancashire & Cumbria Group (1994-96); Group Manager, Manchester Central Group (1996-01). Member of Lancashire Health and Racquets Club.
Interests: Sports, reading, politics, walking, music.
Contact details: 15 Quay Street, Manchester M60 9FD (tel: 0161 833 1005, fax: 0161 832 8596, email: chris.mayer@courtservice.gsi.gov.uk).

McCABE, Terence

Positions: Chairman, Pennine Care NHS Trust (2002); Member, Employment Tribunals.
Areas of Influence: Education, Health.
Profile: *b.* November 23rd, 1942; *m.* Lesley Ann; 2 sons; 1 daughter.
Educated at Ashton-u-Lyne Secondary Technical School. Terence McCabe joined the Police Service from school where he served in various posts and ranks in the Greater Manchester Area. During a 32 year career he rose to the rank of Chief Superintendent occupying such posts as Commandant of the District Police Training School and Director of Training for Greater Manchester Police. In 1994 he retired from GMP and was appointed as a Non-executive Director with Greater Manchester Ambulance Service. He was appointed Vice Chairman in 1997 and then in 2000 took the position of Chairman of West Pennine Health Authority. Chairman of Governors, Saddleworth School. Fellow of Chartered Institute of Personnel and Development. Member of Stamford Golf Club.
Interests: Caravan and boating holidays, reading, motor sports, golf.
Contact details: Pennine Care NHS Trust, Trust HQS, Tameside General Hospital, Fountain Street, Ashton-u-Lyne Ol6 9RW (tel: 0161 331 5001, fax: 0161 331 5007, email: terry.mccabe@penninecare.nhs.uk).

McCARTNEY, Ian

Positions: MP, Minister of State for Pensions.
Areas of Influence: Public Sector.
Profile: *b.* 1951; *m.*; 1 son (dec. 1999); 2 daughters; 7 grandchildren.
After leaving School Ian McCartney had a number of jobs including working as a seaman and a local government manual worker. He was a Councillor for Wigan Borough from 1982 to 1987 and elected member of Parliament for Makerfield in 1987. Before joining the Cabinet Office, Ian was Minister of State at the Department of Trade and Industry. During this time he succeeded in steering through legislation creating a national minimum wage, the fairness at work legislation and the Competition Act. Prior to this he held a number of positions in Opposition, spokesperson on Health, Employment, Education and Employment, and Social

Services. In addition to his current role, Ian is also involved in the Better Government for Older People Initiative. He was previously Minister of State for the Cabinet Office responsible for modernising Government and E-Government, and for the co-ordination of the 2002 Commonwealth Games. He also supported Mo Mowlem in her co-ordination of drugs policy.
Interests: Wigan Rugby League.
Contact details: House of Commons, London SW1A 0AA.

McCOLLUM, Professor Charles Nevin, MBChB (1972), FRCS (London) (1976), FRCS (Edin.) (1976), MD (1981).

Positions: Professor of Surgery, University of Manchester; Honorary Consultant Surgeon, South Manchester University Hospitals.
Areas of Influence: Health
Profile: *b.* April 17th, 1950; Margie (*div.*); 2 daughters.
Education: Tettenhall College, Worcestershire (1959-64); Millfield School, Street, Somerset (1964-67); The Medical School, University of Birmingham (1967-72). Following basic surgical training in Leeds, he was Lecturer in Surgery to Sir Geoffrey Slaney in Birmingham until 1983. He then moved to London as Senior Lecturer / Reader and Consultant Surgeon at Charing Cross Hospital. In 1989 he was appointed to the Chair in Surgery in Manchester based at South Manchester University Hospitals. His main areas of interest are arterial and venous disease, thrombosis, setting up a minimally invasive vascular laboratory, major community leg ulcer service and autologous blood transfusion services. His special interests include carotid surgery in the prevention of stroke conditions, aortic aneurysm surgery and leg ulceration and chronic wounds. Prizes and Awards: Moynihan Prize (1979); Patey Prize (1983); Geoffrey Holt Award (1983); Huntarian Professor (1985); Hahn Prize (1988; Major Grant Award (1988); Patey Prize (1995). Clubs and societies: Scientific Committee, International Society on Thrombosis and Haemostasis; Treasurer and Committee Member, Surgical Research Society of Great Britain and Ireland.
Interests: Tennis, travel, skiing, sailing, country pursuits.
Contact details: Department of Academic Surgery, Education and Research Centre Wythenshawe Hospital, Southmoor Road, Wythenshawe, Manchester M23 9LT (tel: 0161 291 5853, fax: 0161 291 5854, email: cnmcc@man.ac.uk); Birtles Old Hall, Birtles, Nr Macclesfield, Cheshire SK10 4RS.

McCOMBS John, NDD, ROI, RBA, FRSA, MAFA

Positions: Professional Artist; Art Teacher.
Areas of Influence: Arts, Education.
Profile: *b.* December 28th, 1943, Manchester.
Educated at Manchester High School of Art (1957-62) and St Martins School of Art,

London (1962-67). John McCombs has dedicated his career as a professional landscape and figure painter to making a complete visual record, in terms of paint, of the Pennine Village of Delph and the surrounding landscape. He has painted every vista and has recorded every nook and cranny before development spoils the character of the area. John now enjoys a national reputation as 'the painter of Delph'. He has work in private collections all over the world and in public collections in the North West including Manchester City Art Gallery, Oldham Art Gallery and Saddleworth Museum. He exhibits mostly in London and Manchester and has his own studio and gallery in Delph. Publications: works published in numerous art books and shown on television. Prizes and awards: College Prize, St Martins (1966); David Murray Scholarship (1966); Stanley Grimm Prize (1990); The Peoples Prize, Manchester Academy of Fine Arts (1991); Alan Gourlay Memorial Award, ROI (2001).
Interests: Walking, theatre, listening to serious music, watching cricket.
Contact details: John McCombs Gallery, 12 King Street, Delph, Nr Oldham OL3 5DQ (tel: 01457 874705); 12 Berry Street, Greenfield, Nr Oldham, Lancs OL3 7EF (tel: 01457 874755).

McCULLOCH, Right Reverend Nigel Simeon, M.A

Positions: Lord Bishop Designate of Manchester; Lord High Almoner to H.M The Queen; Member of the House of Lords; National Chaplain, The Royal British Legion.
Areas of Influence: Faith Groups.
Profile: *b.* January 17th, 1942; *m.* Celia; 2 daughters.
 Educated at Liverpool College, Selwyn College Cambridge and Cuddesdon College, Oxford. Career profile: Ordained, Chester Cathedral (1966); Curate, Ellesmere Port (1966-70); Chaplain, Christ's College, Cambridge (1970-73); Director of Studies in Theology, Christ's College, Cambridge (1970-75); Diocesan Missioner, Norwich (1973-78); Rector, St Thomas's, Salisbury (1978-86); Archdeacon of Sarum (1979-86); Suffragan Bishop of Taunton (1986-92); Diocesan Bishop of Wakefield (1992-02). Publications: *A Gospel to Proclaim*, Darten, Longman, Todd; *Barriers to Belief*, Darten, Longman, Todd. Clubs and societies: The Anthenaeum, Pall Mall.
Interests: Music, the Lake District, brass bands.
Contact details: Bishopscourt, Bury New Road, Manchester M7 4LE (tel: 0161 792 2096, fax: 0161 792 6826, email: bishop@bishopscourt.manchester.anglican.org).

McCURDY, Cleveland

Positions: Chair, Positive Action Coriocca Training (PACT).
Areas of Influence: Education, Finance, Voluntary Sector.
Profile: *b.* June 2nd, 1948; *m.* Victoria; 2 sons.
Education: Electrical and Electronic Engineer; Business Studies; Various Financial

Advisor Qualifications. Career profile: Junior Manager, Ultra Electronics, Greenford/Loudwater, Bucks; Supervisor, Instron Electronics, High Wycombe; Headhunter, Siemons, London and Manchester; Self Employed Financial Advisor, Allied Dunbar/ Zurich. Oversaw the transition and growth of South Manchester College from LEA control to City College Manchester. Past Chair, City College, Manchester; Past President, Wythenshawe Rotary Club.
Interests: Qi Gong.
Contact details: Zurich Advice Network, 8th Floor, Oakland House, Talbot Road, Manchester M16 0PQ (tel: 0161 254 4226, fax: 0161 872 0071, email: cleve.mccurdy@zurichadvice.co.uk); 9 High Elm Drive, Halebarns, Altrincham, Cheshire WA15 0JD (tel/fax: 0161 980 3832, mob: 07774 414424, email: cleveland.mccurdy@virgin.net).

McDERMOTT, Gerard Francis, QC (1999), LLB (Hons) (1977)

Positions: Barrister and Head of Chambers, 8 King Street, Manchester (1979 - present); Recorder (1999).
Areas of Influence: Law.
Profile: *b.* April 21st, 1956; *m.* Fiona Johnson.
Education: De La Salle College, Salford (1967-74); Manchester University (1974-77); College of law (1977-78). Career profile: Barrister at Law (1978); Attorney at Law (1990). President-Elect, American Counsel Association; Member, International Association of Defence Counsel, USA.
Interests: Theatre, opera, travel.
Contact details: 8 King Street Chambers, 2nd floor, 8 King Street, Manchester M2 6AU (tel: 0161 834 9560, fax: 0161 834 2733, email: gerard.mcdermott@8ks.co.uk).

McDONALD, James William Ian, BA

Positions: Chairman of the Bench, City of Salford Magistrates.
Areas of Influence: Law, Public Sector.
Profile: *b.* March 12th, 1937; *m.* Eileen Anne; 2 sons.
Educated at Stockport Grammar (1949-53). Career profile: Former Managing Director, Meredith Ray & Littler Ltd.
Interests: Fell walking, historical reading, politics, chess, crossword compiling and solving.
Contact details: 24 Worsley Road, Worsley, Manchester, M28 2GQ (tel: 0161 794 2079, email: macdonaldjwimac@aol.com).

McGRATH, Eamonn John, BA(Hons), FCA

Position: Regional Managing Partner, North West, Ernst & Young.
Areas of Influence: Finance.
Profile: *b.* May 10th, 1956; *m.* Moira; 2 sons.
Education: St Edwards College, Liverpool (1967-74); Accounting and Finance, Lancaster University (1974-77). Career profile: Arthur Young McClelland Moore (1977-83); Toronto Office, Ernst & Young (1984-85); London Office, Ernst & Young (1985-95), Partner (1987); Manchester Office, Ernst & Young (1995 - present); Member, North West Regional Council CBI. Clubs and societies: Alderley Edge Cricket Club and Tytherington Golf Club.
Interests: Cricket, golf.
Contact details: Ernst & Young LLP, 100 Barbirolli Square, Manchester M2 3EY (tel: 0161 333 2648, fax: 0161 333 3013, email: emcgrath@uk.ey.com).

McGUIRE, John Charles

Positions: Managing Director, Royal Bank of Scotland, Corporate Banking; Immediate Past President, Manchester Chamber of Commerce; Chairman, Marketing Manchester; Chairman, Chamber Business Enterprises; Trustee, Hallé Concerts Society.
Areas of Influence: Finance, Commerce.
Profile: *b.* July 30th, 1948; *m.* Pamela; 1 son; 1 daughter.
Educated at North Manchester Grammar School. Career profile: Williams Deacon's Bank, Manchester (1966); Williams Glyn's Bank, London (1977); Royal Bank of Scotland, Zurich, Switzerland (1983); Royal Bank of Scotland, Manchester (1987). Clubs and societies: St. James Club; Northenden Golf Club; Royal Birkdale Golf Club.
Interests: Golf, music, photography, reading.
Contact details: Royal Bank of Scotland, Corporate Banking, 100 BArbirolli Square, Manchester M60 3DU (tel: 0161 242 1296, fax: 0161 242 1301, email: john.mcguire@rbs.co.uk)

McHUGH, Ian David, BA, MA, Dip Soc Admin, DMS

Positions: Director, Voluntary Action Manchester; member of steering group, Manchester Local Strategic Partnership (2002-03).
Areas of Influence: Voluntary Sector.
Profile: *b.* November 3rd, 1955 (Crumpsall); *m.* Helen; 2 sons.
Education: Bazeley Road Primary School, Northenden; Manchester Grammar School, Christ's College, Cambridge; York University; Warwick University; Open University; Bolton Institute. Career profile: Voluntary work with Manchester Youth and Community Service (1970-73); International Social Projects Organiser, Quaker Social

Responsibility and Education Dept. (1977-80); Assistant Industrial Relations Officer, Chartered Society of Physiotherapy (1981-82); Development Officer, Nottingham Council for Voluntary Service (1982-3); Senior Community Development Worker, Forest Fields Neighbourhood Centre, Nottingham (1984-90); General Secretary, Bolton District Council for Voluntary Service (1990-98); Principal Policy and Review Officer, Blackburn Borough Council (1998-99); Area Co-ordinator, Bury West, Chief Executives Department, Bury Metropolitan Borough Council (1999-01). Publications: *Health & safety at work handbook for physiontherapists* (1981); *Without a roof in Bolton: support for homeless people* (1991); *Bury West Local Community Plan* (2001). Clubs and Societies: Religious Society of Friends (Quakers); East Lancs. Railway Preservation Society; Bolton Wanderers Supporters Association; World Development Movement; Campaign against Arms Trade. Ian McHugh is a founder member of the Bolton Interfaith Forum, Bolton Cycling forum, and Friends of Queens Park, Bolton.

Interests: Cycling, country walks, railways, music, ecology, France, football, social and political history, literature, bird watching, real ale, visiting art galleries, pub quizzes.

Contact details: Voluntary Action Manchester, North Square, 11-13 Spear Street, Manchester M1 1JU (tel: 0161 236 3206, fax: 0161 228 0464, email: ian@vamanchester. org.uk).

McKEITH, David William, MA (Oxon), FCA

Positions: North West Senior Partner of PricewaterhouseCoopers (2001 - present); Associate Councillor, Manchester Chamber of Commerce and Industry.

Areas of Influence: Finance, Commerce.

Profile: *b.* December 18th, 1951; *m.* Mary; 1 son; 1 daughter.

Educated at Cheadle Hulme School (1963-65), Crewe Grammar School (1965-70); Pure Mathematics at St Catherine's College, Oxford (1970-73). After University, David McKeith worked in the Textile Industry for two years before becoming an Inspector of Taxes. In 1979 he moved into Accountancy, qualifying as a chartered accountant in 1982 and joined Price Waterhouse as a partner in 1989, becoming senior tax partner for Manchester and then for the Regions. On the merger to form PWC in 1998, he joined the firm's UK and European Leadership Teams, managing the specialist tax networks returning to Manchester in 2001. Clubs and societies: Bramall Park Golf Club; Institute of Chartered Accountants in England and Wales.

Interests: Golf (enthusiastic and improving), football (Man U), sailing (occasional), theatre, film, opera, food and wine.

Contact details: PricewaterhouseCoopers, 101 Barbirolli Square, Lower Moseley Street, Manchester M2 3PW (tel: 0161 245 2231, fax: 0161 245 2913, email: david.mckeith@uk.pwcglobal.com).

McKERNAN, Vincent, BA (Hons), MArAd.

Position: County Archivist, GMCRO.
Areas of Influence: Public Sector.
Profile: *b.* April 17th, 1963.
Educated at Liverpool University (1981-84; 1985-86); Archivist, Greater Manchester
County Record Office (1987-88); Deputy County Archivist, GMCRO (1988-99).
Contact details: GMCRO, 56 Marshall Street, New Cross, Manchester M4 5FU (tel:
0161 819 4704, fax: 0161 839 3808, email: vm@gmcro.co.uk).

McKIE, James Murray (Jim), BA, CA, ATII

Position: Senior Tax Partner, PricewaterhouseCoopers.
Areas of Influence: Finance.
Profile: *b.* March 17th, 1958. *m.* Margaret; 2 sons; 1 daughter.
Educated at Dumfries Academy and Heriot-Watt University. Career profile: Joined
PricewaterhouseCoopers after University (1979), Moved from Edinburgh to
Manchester (1988) and became a Partner (1989). Prizes and awards: 2nd prize part 2
of Scottish Institute of Chartered Accountants Exams (CA) (1981). Clubs and
societies: St Andrews Society.
Interests: Walking, theatre, watching sporting exploits of my children.
Contact details: PricewaterhouseCoopers, 101 Barbirolli Square, Lower Mosley
Street, Manchester M2 3PW; (tel: 0161 247 4036, fax: 0161 247 4251, email:
jim.m.mckie@uk.pwcglobal.com).

McKINLAY, Donald Norval, NDD, MAFA

Positions: Painter; Sculptor; Printmaker.
Areas of Influence: Arts, Education.
Profile: *b.* October 4th, 1929.
Educated at Liverpool Art School (1947-50). Career profile: Scenic Painter, Liverpool
Playhouse (1953-58); Assistant Designer Liverpool Playhouse (1958-60); Teacher of
Art, Warwick Bolam High School (1960-63); Lecturer in Visual Art, Manchester
Polytechnic (1963-96). Selected One Person Shows: 7 shows at the Bluecoat Gallery,
Liverpool (1973-88); Bede Gallery (1989); Liverpool Academy (1991); Merkmal
Gallery (1992); Salford Art Gallery (1995); Storey Institute, Lancaster (1996); Tib Lane
Gallery (1997); Rawtenstall Market (2000). Selected Group Shows: Cartwright Hall,
Bradford (1984); Williamson Art Gallery (1992); Two Man with Adrian Henri,
Liverpool Academy (1998). Creative works: *Tagore Theatre Mural*, Ahmedabad, India;
Holcombe Moor Rossendale, *Ellen Strange Memorial*; St Margaret's, Anfield;
Christopher Gray Memorial, Pieta; Lancaster Priory, *Madonna*; Liverpool Anglican
Cathedral, *Christ Child for Della Robbia Madonna*. Prizes and awards: 8 Manchester

Academy of Fine Arts Awards; Year of the Artist, Rawtenstall Market Project. Clubs and societies: Manchester Academy of Fine Arts; Victory Club, London; Patron, Salford Choral Society.
Interests: Art, music, reading, travel.
Contact details: 9 Hareholme Lane, Cloughfold, Rossendale, Lancs BB4 7JZ.

McLACHLAN, Murray Alexander Chree, KStJ, KSS, FRSA, MA (Cantab),CRAM

Positions: Head of Keyboard, Chetham's School of Music (1997 - present); Tutor, Royal Northern College of Music (2001 - present).
Areas of Influence: Arts, Education, Media.
Profile: *b.* January 6th, 1965; Kathryn Louise Page; 1 son; 1 daughter.
Education: Chetham's School (1979-83); Magdalene College, Cambridge (1983-86); Private study with Ryszard Balkst, Peter Katin, Norma Fisher and Ronald Stevenson. Career profile: Concert Pianist and Recording Artist for labels including Olympia, Linn, Divenart, Somm, Dunelm etc.; Visiting Professor of Piano, St Andrews University (1993-01); Pianist in Residence, Strathclyde University (1993-97); Tutor in Piano, Royal Scottish Academy of Music and Drama (1995-97). Publications: Articles and reviews for International Piano Quarterly, Piano Magazine, BBC Music Magazine etc.; 35 commercial recordings made to date. Prizes and awards: Rosette for Penguin Guide to CD's; Finalist and Prize wimmer in various competitions. Clubs and societies:
Incorporated Society of Musicians; European Piano Teachers Association; Ronald Stevenson Society; Royal Society of the Arts; British Federation of Festivals.
Interests: Writing, walking, reading, theatre.
Contact details: Chetham's School of Music, Long Millgate, Manchester M3 1SB (tel: 0161 834 9644, fax: 0161 839 3609, email: murraymclachlan@chetham's.com).

McLEOD, Professor David, BSc, MBChB (1969), FRCophth

Positions: Professor of Ophthalmology, School of Medicine, University of Manchester (1988 - present); Honorary Consultant Ophthalmologist, Manchester Royal Eye Hospital (1988 - present); Civilian Consultant in Ophthalmology to Royal Air Force (1984 - present).
Areas of Influence: Health, Education.
Profile: *b.* January 16th, 1946; *m.* Jeanette; 1 son; 1 daughter.
Education: Rosehill Junior School, Burnley, Lancs (1951-57); Burnley Grammar School (1957-63); BSc (Hons) Class I Physiology, Edinburgh University (1966). Career profile: House Officer, Edinburgh Royal Infirmary (1969-71); Resident Surgical Officer (1972-77), Consultant Ophthalmic Surgeon (1978-88), Moorfields Eye Hospital, London. Vice-president, Royal College of Ophthalmologists, London (1997-00). Over 200 Publications in scientific literature on various aspects of eye diseases

and their management, especially vascular occlusions, diabetic retinopathy and retinal detachment. Prizes and awards: Ettles Scholar and Medallist (most distinguished medical graduate), University of Edinburgh (1969); Lang Medallist, Royal Society of Medicine (1989); Duke-Elder Medallist, Royal College of Ophthalmologists (1993).
Interests: Golf, ballroom dancing, walking.
Contact details: Academic Department of Ophthalmology, Manchester Royal Eye Hospital, Oxford Road, Manchester M13 9WH (tel: 0161 276 5620, fax: 0161 273 6354, email: d.mcleod@man.ac.uk); Langdale, 370 Chester Road, Woodford SK7 1QG (tel: 0161 440 0737).

McMANUS, Catherine Mary, BA (Hons)

Positions: SRB programme manager, Progress Trust.
Areas of Influence: Voluntary Sector, Black and Ethnic minorities.
Profile: *b.* February 26th, 1963; *m.* Julian Haigh; 1 daughter; Catherine McManus has worked at the Progress Trust since 1997. Prior to that she had a wide variety of different jobs.
Contact details: Progress Trust, Barclay House, 35 Whitworth St West, Manchester M1 5NG (tel: 0161 906 1121, fax: 0161 906 1121, email: catherine.mcmanus@ progresstrust.com).

MEACHER, Rt Hon MP, Micheal

Positions: Minister of State for the Environment and Privy Councillor (1997 - present); Labour Member for Oldham West & Royton (1970).
Areas of Influence: Environment, Sustainable Development, Public Sector.
Profile: *b.* November 4th, 1939; *m.* Lucianne; 2 sons; 2 daughters.
Educated at Berkhamstead School, New College Oxford and London School of Economics. Career profile: Joined the Labour Party (1962); Parliamentary representative of UNISON; Under Secretary of Health and Social Security (1975-79); Member of the Select Committee on the Treasury and Civil Service; Candidate for Labour Party Leadership (1983); Member of Labour Party National Executive Committee (1983-89); Member of Shadow Cabinet (1983-97). Labour Party Chief Opposition Spokesman on Health and Social Security (1983-87); on Employment (1987-89); on Social Security (1989-92); on Overseas Development and Co-operation (1992-93); on Public Service and Citizens' Rights (1993-94); on Transport (1994-95); on Employment (1995-96); on Environmental Protection (1996-97). Special political interests: Environmental Protection and Sustainable Development; Economic Policy; Industry and Trade Policy; Reform of the machine of Government; Reford of the Media; Housing; Education; Social Services. Publication: *Diffusing the Power: The Key to Socialist Revival* (1992). Clubs and societies: The Fabian Society; SERA; The Child

Action Group.
Interests: Sport, reading.
Contact details: House of Commons, London SW1A 0AA (tel: 0207 219 6461 / 4532, fax: 0207 219 5945, email: massonm@parliament.uk).

MEACOCK, Lucy

Positions: TV Presenter/Journalist, Granada TV; Patron Hospice of the Good Shepherd, Chester.
Areas of Influence: Arts, Media, Voluntary Sector.
Profile: Educated at Ursuline Convent, Chester; Morongo Girls College, Geelong, Victoria, Australia; Upper Chine School, Shanklin, Isle of Wight. Career profile: Chester Chronicle; Evening Leader; BBC Radio, Newcastle; Tyne Tees Television, Newcastle; BBC Television, Lime Grove, London; Anglia TV. Royal Television Society Award, *Manchester Bomb Programme*; Royal Television Society Award, *Organ Retention Scandal Late Debate* (2001).
Interests: Football, golf, classical music.
Contact details: Granada TV, Quay Street, Manchester, M60 9EA (tel: 0161 832 7211, email: lucymeacock@granadamedia.com).

MEASOR, Duncan Harty

Positions: Author; Hon. Secretary, Manchester Naval Officers' Association; Trustee, Broughton House for Disabled ex-Service Personnel; Pat Seed Fund Central Committee.
Areas of Influence: Ex-Service Associations.
Profile: *b.* July 25th, 1924, Sunderland; *m.* Marjorie Douglas (1952); 2 daughters. Educated at Bede Collegiate, Sunderland; College of the Sea. Career profile: Royal Navy (1942-46); Staithmaster Sunderland South Docks; Reporter, Sunderland Echo, Northern Daily Mail; Chief Sub-editor, Manchester Evening News, 'Mr Manchester' columnist for 22 years. Publications include *Twin Cities, 75 Years under Sail, Unholy Terror*.
Contact details: Damian Place, Brook Lane, Alderley Edge, Cheshire SK9 7QL (tel: 01625 582 426).

MEEUSS, John Francois Ferdinand, MRICS BSc

Positions: Self-Practitioner, Surveying and Construction; Hon. Consul, Belgium.
Areas of Influence: Commerce, Voluntary Sector.
Profile: *m.* Mary; 1 son.
Educated at Emanuel School, London. John Meeus has followed a career in Building and Civil Engineering and as a Quantity Surveyor; Founder President, Rotary Club

of Bramhall and Woodford; Committee member, RICS; Past President, Cons. faculty, Manchester; Member, Consular Association, Manchester and Liverpool. Member, Bramall Park Golf Club.

Interests: Golf, walking, theatre, music.

Contact details: John F Meeus, Chartered Surveyor, 76 Moss Lane, Bramhall, Stockport SK7 1EJ (tel: 0161 439 9864); (tel/fax: 0161 439 5999).

MELLOR, Ian, MA, Dip Ed

Position: Headmaster, Stockport Grammar School (1996-)
Areas of Influence: Education.
Profile: *b.* June 30th, 1946. *m.* Margery. 3 sons.
Educated at Alexandra Park County Primary School, Oldham (1950-57), Manchester Grammar School (1957-64) and Sidney Sussex College, Cambridge (1964-68). Career profile: Assistant Modern Languages Teacher, King's School, Chester (1968-73); Head of Modern Languages, Kirkham Grammar School, Lancs (1974-76); Head of Modern Languages, Bristol Grammar School (1976-83); Deputy Headmaster, Sale Boys' Grammar School, Trafford (1984-90); Headmaster, Sir Roger Manwood's School, Sandwich, Kent (1991-96).
Interests: All forms of sport, reading, bridge.
Contact details: Stockport Grammar School, Buxton Road, Stockport SK2 7AF (tel: 0161 456 9000, fax: 0161 419 2407, email: sgs@stockportgrammar.co.uk).

MELLOR, Katharine Margaret, MA Hons

Positions: Senior Partner, Elliotts; Non Executive Director, South Manchester University Hospitals NHS Trust.
Areas of Influence: Law, Health.
Profile: *b.* May 26th, 1949; *m.* Lawrence Manners Hass.
Education: Fairfield Grammar School, Bristol (1960-67); St. Andrews University (1967-71); Manchester Polytechnic (1971-72); College of Law, Chester (1974-75). Career profile: Articled, Rowleys and Blewitts, Manchester (1972-74); Assistant, Rowleys and Blewitts (1975-76); Assistant, Philip Conn and Co (1976-79); Assistant, Elliott and Company (now Elliotts) (1979-80); Partner, Elliotts (1980). Clubs and societies: President, The Manchester Law Society (1989-90); Manchester Business Network; Manchester Luncheon Club; National Trust; The Wine Society.
Interests: Gardening, cookery, wine, classical music.
Contact details: Elliotts, Centurion House, Deansgate, Manchester M3 3WT (tel: 0161 214 6239, fax: 0161 214 6339, email: katharine.mellor@elliott-law.co.uk) Heughfield, 5 Chesham Place, Bowdon, Altrincham, Cheshire WA14 2JL.

MELMOTH, Sir Graham John, FCIS, FIGD, CiMgt

Positions: Chief Executive, Co-operative Group (CWS) Ltd (1996-02); Chairman, Manchester Enterprises Group (1999-02); Director, The Co-operative Insurance Society Ltd.
Areas of Influence: Commerce
Profile: *b.* March 18th, 1938; *m.* Jennifer Mary; 2 sons.
Educated at City of London School (1948-57) and Lycée Henri IV (1954). Career profile: Assistant Secretary, Chartered Institute of Patent Agents (1961-65); Secretary, Chemical Plant Division, BOC Limited (1966-69); Deputy Secretary, Fisons plc (1969-72); Secretary, Letraset plc (1972-75); Secretary, Co-operative Society Limited (CWS) (1975-95). Clubs and societies: Reform Club.
Interests: Co-operative history, prison reform, opera, theatre.
Contact details: Co-operative Group (CWS) Ltd, PO Box 53, Newcentury House, Manchester M60 4ES (tel: 0161 827 5181, fax: 0161 832 6388, email: grahammelmoth@hotmail.com).

MENZIES, Walter Stuart, B.Arch (Hons), MA, DipUD, RegArch, FRSA

Positions: Chief Executive, Mersey Basin Campaign; Commissioner, UK Sustainable Development Commission.
Areas of Influence: Public Sector, Voluntary Sector.
Profile: June 1st, 1949; *m.* Jacquetta; 1 son; 1 daughter.
Education: George Watsons College, Edinburgh; Perth Academy, Perth; Edinburgh College of Art, School of Architecture; Oxford Brookes University. Career profile: Architect and Urban designer, private practice, London (1973-77); Special Projects Manager, Riverside Housing Association, Liverpool (1977-83); Regional Director, Groundwork, North West England (1983-97); Chief Executive, Sustainability North West (1997-2001); Non Executive Directorship, Healthy Waterways Trust and Sustainability North West. Clubs and societies: Fellow, Royal Society of Arts; Member, Bollington Arts Centre.
Interests: Cities, architecture, visual arts, literature, creative photography.
Contact details: Mersey Basin Campaign, 28th Floor, Sunley Tower, Piccadilly Plaza, Manchester M1 4BT (tel: 0161 242 8200, fax: 0161 242 8201, email: w.menzies@merseybasin.org.uk) 13 Irwell Rise, Bollington Cheshire SK10 5YE (tel: 01625 572 197, fax: 01625 572 197, email: wmenzies@beeb.net).

MERRICK, Linda, MMus, GRSM (Hons), ARAM, FLCM, FRSA, ILTM, Hon VCM

Positions: Head of Performance Studies and Senior Tutor in Clarinet, RNCM.
Areas of Influence: Arts, Education.
Profile: *b.* May 11th, 1963; *m.* Martin Ellerby.

Educated at Royal Academy of Music and Reading University. Career profile: International Clarinet, Soloist & Recording Artist; Head of Music, London College of Music and Media. Recordings: *Concerti for Clarinet & Concert Band* (2000); *Wilfred Josephs Clarinet Quintet & Clarinet Sonatas* (1999); *The Hemlock Stone* (1999); *New York Counterpoint* (1996-98); *The Music of John Lambert: Sounds Positive* (1993); *Collage* (1992-99); *Martin Ellerby Chamber Music* (1990) Clubs and societies: ICA, CASS, SPNM, BASBWE.

Contact details: RNCM, 124 Oxford Road, Manchester M13 9RD (tel: 0161 907 5382, email: linda.merrick@rncm.ac.uk).

MEUDELL, Professor P R

Positions: Pro-Vice-Chancellor, External Affairs (2001 – present) and Professor of Neuropsychology, University of Manchester (1993 – present).
Profile: *b.* November 11th, 1944; *m.* Lesley; 1 son; 1 daughter.
Educated at Rotherham Grammar School, University of Hull and University of Manchester. Career profile: Lecturer, University of Manchester (1967-81); Senior Lecturer, University of Manchester (1982-93); Dean of Science and Engineering, University of Manchester (1997-00). Clubs and societies: Manchester Literary and Philosophical Society; British Neuropsychology Society; Experimental Psychology Society.
Interests: Cooking, wine, reading, computers.

MICHAEL, Richard, BSc

Positions: Director, Manchester Poetry Festival (1994 - present); Director, North West Arts Board (2000-02); Arts and Regeneration Officer, Manchester Arts Council (2002 -)
Areas of Influence: Arts, Media.
Profile: *b.* April 16th, 1967; *m.* Elizabeth.
Educated at Cheadle Hulme School and Hull University. Career profile: Manager, International One; Co-Owner, Roadhouse; Proprietor, RGM Events. TV: Mrs Merton Show (1996-98); Red Velvet (1999). Radio: Signal Radio, KFM, Radio Space, Radio Regan. Co-ordinator, *Literatures of the Commonwealth Festival* (2002). Publications: *Poetry Slam* (1996) Richard Michael constituted the Manchester Poetry Festival and wrote the Lottery winning bid which has ensured the festival is a year round event over the next two years. He has made various Radio appearances, acted in Red Velvet (Channel 4), and played drums in Las Vegas on the Mrs Merton Show. Clubs and societies: Chelsea FC; Poetry Society.
Interests: Live events, football, cooking, writing, seeing the countryside with my

dog, Olive.
Contact details: 114 Fog Lane, Didsbury, Manchester M20 6SP (tel: 0161 438 0550, email: ric@rgevents.co.uk).

MIDGLEY, The Reverend John (A)ndrew, BA (1964), BD (1966), MA (1970), MEd (1986)

Positions: Minister, Cross Street Chapel, (Unitarian) Manchester (1997 - present); President, General Assembly of Unitarian and Free Christian Churches UK (2001-02).
Areas of Influence: Faith Groups.
Profile: *b.* November 13th, 1939; *m.* Celia; 2 sons.
Education: Yardley Grammar School, Birmingham (1950-55); Unitarian College, Manchester (1960-66); Manchester University (1961-66, 1984-86). Career profile: Minister, Nazareth Unitarian Chapel, Padiham, Lancs (1966-68); Minister, Dunham Road Unitarian Chapel, Altrincham and Queen's Road Unitarian Free Church, Urmston (1968-89); Tutor, Unitarian College, Manchester (1969-89); Development Officer, Unitarian and Free Christian Churches (1989-95). Publications: *The Growing Edge* (1996); *One and Universal* (2002).
Interests: Classical music, jazz, has promoted Cross Street Chapel as a music venue.
Contact details: Cross Street Chapel, Cross Street, Manchester, M2 1NL (tel: 0161 833 1176, fax: 834 0019); The Parsonage, Sylvan Grove, Altrincham, Cheshire WA14 4NN (tel: 0161 928 0246).

MILLAR, Professor Thomas Joseph, BSc, PhD, DSc, FRAS

Positions: Professor of Astrophysics, Department of Physics, UMIST; Pro-Vice Chancellor, UMIST.
Areas of Influence: Education.
Profile: *b.* February 23rd, 1952; *m.* Susan. 2 sons; 1 daughter.
Educucation: St. Mary's Grammar School, Belfast; UMIST, BSc Mathematics (1970-73); UMIST, PhD Astrophysics (1973-76). Career profile: Research Fellow, York University, Toronto (1976-78); Oxford University (1978-81); UMIST (1981-83); Lecturer, UMIST (1983-89); Senior Lecturer (1989-92); Reader (1992-95). Publications: Over 170 scientific research papers; Co-editor of 5 books on astrophysics.
Interests: Music, theatre, reading, watching Manchester United win!
Contact details: Department of Physics, UMIST, PO Box 88, Manchester M60 1QD (tel: 0161 200 3677, fax: 0161 200 4303, email: tom.millar@umist.ac.uk)

MILLER, John, MA (Cantab) (1974); FGSM (1993)

Positions: Director of Brass Studies, RNCM (1999 - present).
Areas of Influence: Education.
Profile: *b.* December 26th, 1951; June Wilkinson (Partner).
Educated at King's College, Cambridge. Career profile: Member, Philip Jones Brass Ensemble (1972-80); Member, Philharmonia Orchestra, London (1977-94). Publications: *Simple Studies for Beginners Brass; Progressive Studies for Trumpet; The Baroque Trumpet; Trumpet Basics; The Good Brass Guide.*
Interests: Fell walking, food.
Contact details: Royal Northern College of Music, 124 Oxford Road, Manchester M13 9RD (tel: 0161 907 5364, email: john.miller@rncm.ac.uk).

MILLER, Dr John Paul, MA (Oxon), BM, BCh (Oxon), MSc, DPhil, FRCP

Positions: Consultant Gastroenterologist, South Manchester University Hospitals; Chairman of Council, Medical Protection Society; Chairman, Medical Protection Investments; Pension Fund Trustee, Medical Protection Society; Chairman, Board of Faculty of Medicine, Dentistry, Nursing and Pharmacy (1997 - present); Chairman, Clinical Governance Committee, South Manchester University Hospitals (1998 - present); Member of Court, University of Manchester (1999 - present).
Areas of Influence: Health.
Profile: *b.* July 10th, 1940; *m.* Dr Mary Anderson; 2 sons; 2 daughters.
Education: Repton School (Exhibitioner); Open Scholar in Natural Sciences, Keble College, Oxford. Career profile: House Officer posts at Guy's Hospital, Addenbrookes Hospital; Registrar, Hammersmith Hospital, London; Save the Children Fund, Nigerian Civil War (1969-70); Lecturer in Medicine, University of Leeds (1972-75); Senior Lecturer in Medicine, University of Manchester (1975-81); MRC Travelling Fellow and Visiting Professor, Baylor College of Medicine, Houston, Texas (1978-79); Regional Advisor, Royal College of Physicians (1987-93); Treasurer, British Hyperlipidaemia Association (1988-91); Chairman, Speciality Training Committee in Medicine, NW Region (1993-97); Treasurer, British Atherosclerosis Society (1997-02); Chairman of Council, Manchester Medical Society (1997-01). Has published numerous papers on Respiratory Physiology, Peptic Ulceration and Lipoprotein Disorders. Clubs and societies: Association of Physicians of GB and Ireland; Royal Society of Medicine; British Society of Gastroenterology; American Heart Association.
Interests: Walking, cycling, music.
Contact details: South Manchester University Hospitals NHS Trust, Wythenshawe Hospital, Manchester M23 9LT (tel; 0161 291 2400, fax: 0161 291 2635, email: paul.miller@smuht.nwest.nhs.uk); (email: jpmiller@talk21.com).

MILLER, Lucie Kathleen

Positions: Chairman, Manchester Centre National Trust and Middleton RNLI Committee; Public Speaker.
Areas of Influence: Voluntary Sector, Education.
Profile: *m.* Leslie.
Education: St Lukes Primary School, Chadderton, Oldham; Chadderton Grammar School; Qualified Teacher, St Katherines College, Liverpool; National Froebel Foundation Certificate, Long Millgate College, Manchester. Career profile: Teacher, Alkrington CP Infants School, Middleton; Teacher then Deputy Head, Boarshaw CP Infants School, Middleton; Head Teacher, All Saints C of E Infants, Rhodes, Middleton; Head Teacher, Little Heaton C of E Primary; President Rochdale NAHT (1976). Clubs and societies: National Trust English; Heritage; Lancashire Association of Change Ringers; Middleton Civic Association; RSPB; Norden Cricket Club; The Thomas Handy Society; Galapagos Conservation Trust; Woodland Trust; Hawk and Owl Trust.
Interests: Watching cricket, bellringing, travel, wildlife, education, books, walking, needlework, listening to music, theatre visits, ballet, gardening.
Contact details: 27 Scarfield Drive, Rochdale, Lancs Ol11 5SA (tel: 01706 641 405).

MILLS, William Stirling, BSc (Econ)

Position: Principal, City College, Manchester (1999 - present).
Areas of Influence: Education, Public Sector.
Profile: *b.* March 22nd, 1951; 3 sons.
Educated at Falkirk High School (1963-69), Glasgow Caledonian University (1972-76) and Jordan Hill College (1976-77). Career profile: College Lecturer and Senior Lecturer (1977-85); Assistant Principal, Renfrewshire Tertiary College (1986-89); Vice Principal, Grantham College (1989-92); Principal, Northumberland College (1992-99).
Interests: Sports, travel, reading.
Contact details: City College Manchester, City Campus, Whitworth Street, Manchester M1 3HB (tel: 0161 957 1551, email: wmills@ccm.ac.uk).

MITCHELL, Paul

Positions: Managing Director, Rickitt Mitchell & Partners Ltd; Chairman, NCC Group Ltd; Director, Hollins Murray Group Ltd.
Areas of Influence: Finance.
Profile: *b.* May 10th, 1951; *m.* Patricia Ann; 1 son, 1 daughter.
Educated at Knaresborough Grammar School, BSc (Hons) and Manchester University (1969-72). Career profile: Coopers & Lybrand (1972-78); County Bank (1978-81); Rickitt Mitchell & Partners (1981 - Present). Member, Wilmslow Golf Club.

Interests: Golf, tennis, sport, music, reading, theatre.
Contact details: Rickitt Mitchell & Partners Ltd, Clarence House, Clarence Street, Manchester M4 4DW (tel: 0161 834 0600, fax: 0161 834 0452, email: Paul@rickitmitchell.com).

MITCHELL, Lieut-Commander Noel G, DSC (1945), VRD, RNR, DL

Positions: Member and Fundraiser, Parkinson's Disease Association.
Areas of Influence: Voluntary Sector.
Profile: *b.* December 25th, 1920; widowed; 2 daughters.
Education: Wadham House School, Hale; Tudor House, Wrekin College, Wellington, Salop. Career profile: Self employed. Prizes and awards: The Lord Mayor's Special Commendation (2001).

MITHA, Alnoor, BA (1983), MA (1986)

Positions: Director, Shisha, the International Agency for Contemporary South Asian crafts and visual arts.
Areas of Influence: Arts, Education, Public Sector.
Profile: *b.* February 2nd, 1961; *m.* Shanaz; 2 daughters.
Educated at Maharaja Sayajrao University, Baroda, India (1984-86). Career profile: Multicultural Curator and Manager of the Multicultural Service Unit, Huddersfield (1991-97); Exhibition Curator, Oldham Metropolitan Council (1997-01); Seconded to North West Arts Board, developing international research and Shisha (1998-01). Publications: *Tampered Surface: Six artists from Pakistan* (1995*); Lines of Desire* (1998). Prizes and awards: Exchange Scholarship, Ecole de Beaux Arts, Angers, France (1982); Commonwealth Scholarship to study Fine Arts at Baroda University, India (1984). Advisor, The Arts Council of England; AXIS multimedia national artist database
Interests: Swimming, reading, visiting art galleries, travelling.
Contact details: Shisha, The Department Store, 5 Oak Street, Manchester M4 5JD (tel: 0161 838 5250, fax; 0161 838 5255, email: alnoor@shisha.net).

MOAKES, Adrian, BA (Hons)

Position: Professional Sculptor, self employed.
Areas of Influence: Arts, Education.
Profile: *b.* April 6th, 1959; *m.* Siobhain; 2 sons; 1 daughter.
Education: Doncaster Grammar School (1972-76); Doncaster Art College (1976-77); Preston Polytechnic (1977-80). Career profile: Over 150 exhibitions nationwide, including major one man shows at Battersea Arts Centre, London, Aberdeen Art

Gallery, Cornerhouse, South Hill Park Arts Centre and Brewery Arts Centre, Kendal (1979 - present); Helped to establish and run Start Studios, Lancaster (1980); moved to Manchester to join The Arch Artists Studio. Undertook North West Arts Board's first 'Artist in Schools' residency at Woodford Lodge School, Winsford (1983); 13 corporate and gallery commisions, 34 public sculpture commissions, most recently in Watford, Dunstable, Wigan and Rochdale (1985 - present); Associate Lecturer at South Trafford College, Manchester, establishing the sculpture department and teaching on the art foundation course (1986-9); Calouste Gulbekian Award (1990); RSA Art for Architecture Award (1994); Adrian Moakes considers that the most important aspect of his work is to create opportunities for the public to participate in his sculpture commissions, and has always involved the local residential and business community in the development of designs, increasing the sense of ownership and pride. Many of his recent pieces have been sequential or illusory sculptures in which the viewer seeks out or accidentally discovers the formation of recognisable images from different viewpoints.

Contact details: 3 Chelford Road, Old Trafford, Manchester M16 0BE (tel/fax: 0161 881 3184 email: info@adrianmoakes.com website: www.adrianmoakes.com).

MOGHAL, Nasrullah Khan, BSc (Eng), C.Eng

Positions: Chief Executive, Manchester Council for Community Relations (1994 - present).
Areas of Influence: Education, Community Relations.
Profile: *b.* May 4th, 1947.
Education: Primary and Secondary Education, Nairobi, Kenya; BSc (Eng) (Hons) Aeronautical Engineering, University of Manchester (1970); Certificate in Supervisory Studies, Coventry Technical College (1972); Chartered Engineer, Institute of Gas Engineers (1973); Certificate in Quality Assurance Auditing, Bywater Technology (1990); Diploma in Race and Community Relations, University of Liverpool (1996). Career profile: Graduate Trainee West Midlands Gas Board then Engineering Assistant / Technical Assistant (Special Projects), British Gas West Midlands (1970-74); Planning Engineer, Quality Evaluation Engineer, Quality Assurance Engineer and Quality Assurance Consultant, International Computers Ltd (1975-91); Immigration and Nationality Advisor, Rochdale Racial Equality Council (1993-94). Awarded Certificate of Service by community organisations. Clubs and societies: Circle of Literary Friends, Pakistani Community Association, All Pakistan Women's Association.
Contact details: Manchester Council for Community Relations, Suite A4, 3rd Floor, Elisabeth House, St Peters Square Manchester M2 3DF (tel: 0161 228 0710, fax; 0161 228 0745, (Will relocate Dec 2002 to: 141-143 Princess Road, Manchester M14 4RE) email: nkmoghul@mccr.org.uk); 20 Corringham Road, Manchester M19 2RG (tel: 0161 292 1516).

MOHAN, Marie Frances

Position: Regional Director, Common Purpose (1999 - present).
Areas of Influence: Leadership Development, Civil Society.
Profile: *b.* June 21st, 1959; *m.* Mark Watts; 1 son; 2 daughters.
Education: Mount Lourdes Grammar School (1970-77); BA (1980), Dip Information Studies, (1985), Queen's University, Belfast; MA, University of Manchester (1989). Career profile: Regional Information Officer, Sport England (1985-89); Special Projects Officer, Countryside Agency (1989-91); Communications manager, Countryside Agency, Visitor and Convention Bureau (1991-96); Director of Communications, Marketing Manchester (1996-98). Publications: A range of promotional articles and reports; MA Thesis on Speculative Fiction.
Interests: Looking after young family - immensly time consuming and enjoyable! Travel, entertaining, reading, theatre, art galleries.
Contact details: c/o 113 – 115 Portland Street, Manchester M1 6DW (tel: 0161 237 3439, email: marie.mohan@commonpurpose.org.uk).

MONTGOMERY, Lady Joyce, DL (1992)

Positions: Chairman, Harvest Housing Group; Advisor to South Manchester University Hospital Trust; County President, St John Ambulance.
Areas of Influence: Voluntary Sector, Health.
Profile: *b.* June 23rd, 1937; *m.* Sir Fergus Montgomery
Education: Newcastle upon Tyne Church High School; Physical Education Diploma, Lady Mabel College of Physical Education. Career profile: Convent of the Sacred Heart Grammar School, Newcastle upon Tyne (1958-65); St Mary's College of Education, Newcastle upon Tyne (1965-72); Lecturer in Physical Education, Wolverhampton College of Education (1972-74). Board Member, South Manchester University Hospital Trust (1993-99); Housing Corporation Board Member (1987-97). Member of the Garrick Theatre, Altrincham.
Interests: Theatre, swimming, holidays when I have time.
Contact details: Harvest Housing Group, Apex House, 266 Moseley Road, Levenshulme M19 2LH (fax: 0161 248 4524, web: www.harvesthousing.org.uk); 6 Groby Place, Altrincham, WA14 4AL (tel: 0161 928 1983, fax; 0161 929 1983, email: mjoymont@aol.com).

MONTGOMERY, Sir William (Fergus)

Positions: Guest Lecturer.
Areas of Influence: Public Sector.
Profile: *b.* November 25th, 1927; *m.* Joyce.
Educated at Hedburn Methodist, Jarrow Grammar (1939-50 and College of Venerable

Bede, Durham (1948-50). Career profile: National Service, (1946-48); Schoolteacher (1950-59); Hedburn Urban District Councillor (1950-59); Vice Chairman, National Young Conservatives (1954-57); National Chairman Young Conservatives (1957-58); MP, Newcastle upon Tyne East (1959-64); MP Brierley Hill (1967-74); MP Altrincham and Sale (1974-97); Parliamentary Private Secretary to Margaret Thatcher as Secretary of State for Education and Science (1973-74) and as leader of the opposition (1975-76); Chairman of the House of Commons Committee of Selection (1992-97). Sir Fergus has lectured extensively in USA and also on the QEII and Caronia.
Interests: Theatre, politics, bridge.
Contact details: 6 Groby Place, Altrincham, Cheshire WA14 4AL (tel: 0161 928 1983, fax: 0161 929 1983).

MOONEY, Claire

Position: Editor, Tameside and Glossop Advertiser.
Areas of Influence: Media
Contact details: 35-37 Booth Street, Ashton-Under-Lyne OL6 7LB (tel: 0161 339 7611, fax: 0161 343 2997, email: tamesideadvertiser@gmwn.co.uk).

MOORE, Professor Stuart Alfred, BA (Admin) (1964), MA (Econ) (1967), DSoc.Sc (h.c.) (2001)

Position: Chairman, Stockport Primary Care NHS Trust (2001 - present); Justice of the Peace, Manchester City Bench (1996 - present).
Areas of Influence: Health, Education, Law.
Profile: *b.* October 9th, 1936; *m.* Diana Mary (nee Connery); 2 sons; 1 daughter. Educated at Stockport School and the University of Manchester. Career profile: Economic Statistician, University of Manchester (1960-96); Dean, University of Manchester, Economic and Social Studies (1981); Pro-Vice Chancellor, University of Manchester (1985-90); Acting Vice Chancellor (1990-92); Chairman, Central Manchester Healthcare NHS Trust (1992-01); Deputy Vice-Chancellor (1990-96); Professor, University of Manchester (1992); Professor Emeritus (1996); Pro Vice-Chancellor (1996-99). Prizes and awards: Cobden Prize for Political Economy; various publications in scholarly journals.
Contact details: Stockport PCT, Springwood House, Hazel Grove, Stockport SK7 5BY (tel: 0161 419 4706); 2 Carisbrooke Ave, Hazel Grove, Stockport SK7 5PL (tel: 0161 483 8109).

MOORE, Christopher, FCCA

Profile: Chairman, Oldham Athletic AFC Ltd; Chairman, Torex plc.
Areas of Influence: Public Sector, Sport, Voluntary Sector.
Profile: *b.* November 11th, 1954; 3 sons.
Educated at Stockport Tech and and Manchester Polytechnic. Christopher Moore was a certified Accountant for Simon Engineering and Oxford Instruments before becoming a major shareholder and chairman of Oldham Athletic, Torex plc, and The Torex Foundation, which is a charity fundraising for good causes. He was awarded the Oxfordshire Businessman of the Year (2001) and was a City Awards finalist (2000).
Interests: All sports, fundraising for charities, family.
Contact details: OAFC, Boundary Park, Oldham, OL1 2PA (tel: 01608 737612, email: cmoore@torex.co.uk).

MORAN, Andrew Gerard, QC (1994), BA (Oxon)

Positions: QC, Byrom St Chambers; Recorder (1992 - present).
Areas of Influence: Law, Clinical Negligence.
Profile: *b.* October 19th, 1953; *m.* Carole Jane; 6 sons; 1 daughter.
Education: West Park Grammar School, St Helens; Brittania Naval College, Dartmouth; Balliol College, Oxford. Formerly a Royal and Merchant Navy Officer, Andrew Moran commenced practising at the Bar in Liverpool in 1977. On becoming a QC he moved to Chambers in Manchester and London. He now practises general commercial litigation shipping, and clinical negligence, and pollution and environmental law. Member of Vincent's Club, Oxford.
Interests: Family, sport, travel.
Contact details: Byrom Street Chambers, 12 Byrom Street, Manchester M3 4PP (tel: 0161 829 2100, fax: 0161 829 2101, email: agmgc@aol.com);)tel: 01704 567662, fax; 01704 551929).

MORAN, Terence (Terr) Anthony

Position: Director North West, Jobcentre Plus.
Areas of Influence: Public Sector, Education.
Profile: *b.* April 23rd, 1960.

MORELAND, Claire Josephine, BA (Oxon), MA (Oxon), PGCE

Position: Head, Chetham's School of Music (1999 - present).
Areas of Influence: Education, Arts.
Profile: *b.* August 2nd, 1958; 1son.

Education: Devonport High School for Girls (1970-76); Oxford University, St Hugh's College (1976-80); Oxford University, Dept. of Educational Studies (1980-81). Career profile: Teacher of German, French and Spanish, Sevenoaks School (1981-84); Head of German, Croydon High School (1984-88); Housemistress, Rugby School (1992-99); Deputy Head, Rugby School (1997-99). Publications: Co-author of *Schreib mir Bitte*, Thomas Nelson, UK and Intertaal.
Interests: Music, literature, theatre.
Contact details: Chetham's School of Music, Long Millgate, Manchester M3 1SB (tel: 0161 838 7214, fax: 0161 839 3609, email: clairemoreland@chethams.com).

MORGAN, Glyn

Positions: Chief Executive, Victim Support and Witness Service, Greater Manchester (2000 - present)
Areas of Influence: Voluntary Sector, Law.
Profile: *b*. August 31st, 1945; *m*. Irene; 2 sons.
Grammar school education. Career profile: Trainee Chartered Accountant (1961-64); Police Officer, Greater Manchester, retiring as Detective Chief Superintendent (1964-95); Volunteer of Victim Support, Chair of Stockport Scheme, Member of the Executive Committee of Greater Manchester Federation of VSS and the Witness Scheme (1995-97); Development and Training Officer for The Federation (1997-00).
Interests: Golf, reading, music.
Contact details: Victim Support and Witness Service Greater Manchester, 153-157 Chorley Road, Swinton, Manchester M27 (tel: 0161 727 0241, fax: 0161 727 0249, email: morgang@victimsupport-gm.co.uk).

MORLEY, David John, BPharm, MRPharms

Positions: General Manager, Boots the Chemist, Central Manchester (1995-02); Director, Manchester City Centre Management Company.
Areas of Influence: Commerce, Finance, Public Sector.
Profile: *b*. January 8th, 1948; *m*. Linda.
Educated at Palmer's School for Boys, Grays Essex and King's College, University of London. Career profile: Boots Manager, West London (1969-79); Boots Manager, Cannock, West Midlands (1989-90); Project Management, Head Office, Nottingham (1989-90); Manager, Boots, Macclesfield (1990-93), Swansea (1993-95). Clubs and societies: Life Member, National Trust; Member, Royal Pharmaceutical Society.
Interests: Countryside conservation; Voluntary Countryside Conservation Warden.
Contact details: Boots The Chemist, 32 Market Street, Manchester M1 1PL (tel: 0161 832 6533, fax: 0161 839 7981); email: morleysilverfox@aol.com.

MORRIS of Manchester, Baron Alfred PC (1979, QSO (1989), AO (1991), BA, MA, DipEd

Position: Life Peer; Exec. Committee, CPA UK Branch (1999 - present).
Areas of Influence: Public Sector, Disabled People, Co-operative Movement.
Profile: *b.* March 23rd, 1928; *m.* Irene Jones; 2 sons; 2 daughters.
Educated at Oxford (1949-50,1953) and Manchester University (1954). Career profile: Teacher and Lecturer (1954-56); Electricity Industry (1956-64); MP, Manchester Wythenshawe (1964-97); Parliamentary Private Secretary to Minister of Agriculture, Fisheries and Food (1964-67) and to the Leader of the House of Commons (1968-70); General Advisory Council, BBC (1968-74, 1979-97); Minister for Disabled People (1974-79); Promoted 3 acts of parliament: Chronically Sick and Disabled Persons Act (1970); Food and Drugs Act (1970); Police Act (1972). Member of Select Committee on Privileges (1994-97); Chair, Parliamentary and Scientific Committee (1990-93). Commons Opposition Spokesperson for Social Services (1970-74) and on the Rights of Disabled People (1979-92). Party Groups: Labour League of Youth (1950-52); Parliamentary Co-operative Group (1970-71, 1983-85); Co-operative Congress (1995-96). Commons International Bodies: IPU British Group (1968-74); British-American Parliamentary Group (1983-97). US Congressional Committee of Inquiry. International Bodies: UN Advisory Council, International Year of Disabled People; World Planning Group (1978-80) and Charter for the Millenium (1998-00); Rehabilitation International (2001). Lord Morris has produced three publications and received six personal awards and three honorary degrees. He is Trustee of many charities and of the Hallé Orchestra.
Interests: Tennis, gardening, chess, snooker, the problems and needs of disabled people, cooperative movement, regional development, airport policy, science and technology.
Contact details: House of Lords, London SW1A, 0PW (tel: 0207219 5353).

MORRIS, David

Positions: Company Secretary, GUS plc; Member of Court, University of Manchester; Trustee, GUS Charitable Trust.
Areas of Influence: Finance, Commerce.
Profile: *b.* September 3rd, 1944; *m.* Helen; 1 son; 1 daughter.
Educated at Stand Grammar School, Whitefield. Career profile: Trainee Accountant, Hesketh Hirshfield & Co; Audit Manager, Coopers & Lybrand; Company Secretary, Chloride Technical Limited; Finance Director, JR Crompton plc. Fellow of the Institute of Chartered Accountants in England and Wales. Clubs and societies: Bolton Golf Club; Greenmount Golf Club.
Interests: Golf, football, cricket.
Contact details: GUS plc, PO Box 99, Universal House, Devonshire Street,

Manchester M60 1XA (tel: 0161 277 3059, fax: 0161 277 3069, email: morrida@gusco.com); 4 Greenmount Drive, Greenmount, Bury, Lancashire BL8 4 (tel: 01204 88 4404, fax: 01204 88 7105).

MORRIS, Margaret Ann

Positions: Chairman, Salford Royal Hospital NHS Trust; Councillor, City of Salford Eccles; Governor, Barton Moss Primary School, Eccles.
Areas of Influence: Education, Health, Public Sector.
Profile: *b.* October 19th, 1940; *m.* Peter; 1 son; 2 daughters.
Educated at All Saints School Barton, St Mary's School, Eccles and Salford University. Career profile: Student Nurse, QARANC (1960-63); State Enrolled Nurse (1969-92); Chairman, Salford CHC (1997-98); Chairman, Salford and Trafford Health Authority (1998-02). Margaret Morris' overiding interest is in the NHS. She is passionate about improving services to patients and is of the opinion that all staff who work in the NHS are dedicated and deserve to be treated as such. Her other interest is in adult education and improving chances for people to improve their quality of life.
Interests: Adult education, gardening, caravanning, spending time with her three grand children.
Contact details: Salford Royal NHS Hospitals Trust, Eccles Old Road, Salford M6 8HD (tel: 0161 787 5249); 15 Rochford Road, Peel Green, Eccles Manchester M30 7PS (tel/fax: 0161 950 0847).

MORRIS, Peter John, BA (Hons), MBA, DipHSM

Positions: Chief Executive, South Manchester University Hospitals NHS Trust (2002 - present).
Areas of Influence: Health, Public Sector.
Profile: *b.* April 29th, 1958; *m.* Angela; 1 son; 1 daughter.
Educated at Queen Elizabeth Grammar School, Carmarthen and the University of Exeter. Peter Morris joined the NHS in 1979 and held senior management posts in Leicester, Cardiff, Sheffield and Ipswich as Chief Executive (1998-02). Prizes and awards: Fellowship of the Institute of Health and Management. Clubs and societies: Waldringfield Heath Golf Club.
Interests: Golf, squash, sailing.
Contact details: Wythenshawe Hospital, Southmoor Road, Wythenshawe, Manchester M23 9LT (tel: 0161 291 2023, fax: 0161 291 2037, email: peter.morris@smuht.nwest.nhs.uk).

MORT, His Honour Judge Timothy James, MA (Cantab)

Positions: Circuit Judge, Manchester Crown Court (1996 – present).
Areas of Influence: Law
Profile: *b.* March 4th, 1950; *m.* Phillipa; 1 son; 3 daughters.
Education: Clifton College, Bristol; Emmanuel College, Cambridge. Career profile:
Barrister in Practice on Northern Circuit (1972-96).
Interests: Tennis, real tennis, music, gardening.
Contact details: Minshull Street, Crown Court, Manchester M1 3FJ (tel: 0161 954
7500).

MOSCROP, Martin Richard

Positions: Team leader, adult curriculum, the arts, City College Manchester;
performer, songwriter and producer.
Areas of Influence: Arts, Media, Education.
Profile: *b.* September 24th, 1960; 2 sons.
Martin Moscrop was a founder member of the Manchester band *A Certain Ratio* or
ACR as they became to be known. They were recognised as the most influential and
critically acclaimed experimental acts to come out of Post-Punk Manchester and from
the roster of the seminal Factory Records. After leaving Factory Records in 1987,
ACR signed to A&M and then later to Robs Records. They toured extensively
throughout the UK, USA, Japan, and throughout Europe. During ACR's long and
successful career (18 albums and 64 singles) Martin moved into production and
remixing working for various record companies including A&M, Factory,
Phonogram, MCA, Island (USA), Circa, Sony (Japan), Creation and Rob's Records.
Martin is still very active as a producer / remixer and songwriter. He has recently
written and recorded the title music for the BBC TV's *Question of Pop*. In 1994 he
joined CCM as a part time lecturer in Music Production and Sound Recording and
within months became full time as FE co-ordinator for the Music Technology
department. He became HE Co-ordinator in 1998 and in 2000 became team leader for
all music and performance technology provision at the College. He has led many
music and music tech based curriculum development projects at the college and is a
leading link between education and industry. Martin co-authored the open learning
materials for the Government's New Deal for Musicians scheme and has recently
been working as the Music Co-ordinator for Revolution Films on *24 Hour Party People*
the film starring Steve Coogan about the Manchester Music Industry.
Contact details: City College Manchester, Arden Centre, Sale road, Northenden M23
0DD (tel: 0161 957 1729, email: m.moscrop@ccm.ac.uk).

MOUNT, Peter William, BSc, CEng, MiMechE, Ceng

Positions: Chairman, Central Manchester and Manchester Childrens University Hospitals NHS Trust; Chairman, Greater Manchester Workforce Development Confederation; Board Member, Sector Skills Development Agency; Chairman, Audit Committee of the SSDA; Member, Department of Health Audit Committee; Council Member and Regional Representative on the NHS Confederation.
Areas of Influence: Education, Health, Public Sector, National Productivity issues.
Profile: *b.* January 14th 1940; *m.* Margery; 1 son; 2 daughters.
Educated at De La Salle College, University of Manchester UMIST and University of Vienna. Career profile: Manager, Rolls Royce Oil Engines and Car Division (1961-66); Consultant, PricewaterhouseCoopers (1966-72); Project Director and Managing Director, Chloride Battery Group (1973-82); Venture startup software company (1982-84); Managing Director, several Thorn EMI Group Companies (1984-93); Chairman, Salford Royal Hospital NHS Trust (1993-2001). Member, Institute of Mechanical Engineers.
Interests: Woodworking, computers, walking, travel, music, grandchildren.
Contact details: Central Manchester and Manchester Childrens University Hospitals NHS Trust, Cobbett House, Oxford Road, Manchester M13 9WL (tel: 0161 276 4755, email: peter.mount@cmmc.mhs.uk).

MOUTREY, David John

Positions: Director, Cornerhouse since 1998; Joint winner of MEN Theatre Award for services to Theatres in 1994; Member of Institute of Management, Mossley Community Arts, BAFTA and Manchester Millenium Quarter Trust Board; Governor of Mossley Hollins High School.
Areas of Influence: Arts.
Profile: *b.* February 13th, 1958; *m.* Lindsey; 1 son; 1 daughter.
Educated at Billingham Campus School, Stockton on Tees; Bede Sixth Form College, Stockton on Tees; Leeds Polytechnic; Open Business School. Director, Arts about Manchester (1991-98); Director of Marketing, City of Drama 1994 (1993-94); Manager, Abraham Moss Centre Theatre, Manchester (1984-91); Head of Drama, South Chadderton School (1981-84). Producer of over 12 large scale community plays including *Nets* for MSIM (1998), and *Peterloo* for City of Drama (1994).
Interests: All of the Arts, mountain walking, rugby, music, plays percussion and piano, fireworks and outdoor performance.
Contact details: Cornerhouse, 70 Oxford Street, Manchester M1 5NH (tel: 0161 228 7621, fax: 0161 200 1504, email: director@cornerhouse.org).

MUIRHEAD, Geoffrey, FRSA, FICE, FCIT

Positions: Group Chief Executive, Manchester Airport Group (2001 - present); Board Member, Airport Council International; Council Member, UK Airport Operators Association; Vice President, CBI North West Regional Council; Board Member North West Business Leadership Team; Member of the Organising Council, Manchester 2002 Commonwealth Games; Board Director, Marketing Manchester; Associate Member, Chamber Council, MCCI; Board Director, Piccadilly Radio Limited; Chairman, Wythenshawe Education Action Zone.
Areas of Influence: Education, Commerce, Transport.
Profile: *b.* July 14th, 1949; *m.* Clare; 1 daughter.
Education: Graduate of Teeside Polytechnic, Civil and Structural Engineering. Geoffrey Muirhead commenced his career with British Steel (1965) and was subsequently promoted to senior positions with William Press and Simon Carves and Shand, at posts in Saudi-Arabia, Belgium and Eire. Director of Development, Manchester Airport plc (1988); Director of Business Development Manchester Airport plc (1992); Chief Exectuve, Manchester Airport plc (1993). CBI Business Executive of the year (2001); David Goldstone Award for the most outstanding contribution to tourism, North West Tourist Board (1996). Fellow of the Institution of Civil Engineers and of the Chartered Institution of Transport; Honorary Member of the Aviation Club; Member of the institute of Logistics and Transport.
Interests: Rugby Union, golf.
Contact details: Manchester Airport Group, Manchester M90 1QX (tel: 0161 489 5855, fax: 0161 489 2300, email: anna.korotchenko@manairport.co.uk).

MURRAY, Anthony

Positions: Executive Officer, Catholic Welfare Societies, Diocese of Salford; Trustee: The Charity Service, The Blair Charity, Manchester Relief in Need, Manchester Children's Relief in Need Society and St Joseph's Service to Deaf People; Board Member, Arcon Housing Association and Catholic Caring Services (Lancaster Diocese) Ltd.
Areas of Influence: Voluntary Sector, Public Sector.
Profile: *b.* May 25th, 1938; Gertraude; 1 son; 1 daughter.
Education: De la Salles College, Salford (1949-54); Diploma of Politics Philosophy and Economics, Plater College, Oxford (1961-63); Diploma of Advanced Studies in Social Admin. University of Manchester (1964-66). Career profile: Articled Clerk (1954); Chartered Accountant (1961); Student (1961); Child Care Officer (1963); Student (1964); Child Care Officer (1966); Area Children's Officer (1966); Area Director of Social Services (1971); Assistant Director of Social Services (1983); Executive Officer, Catholic Welfare Society (1990). Throughout the 1990's Anthony Murray was a Trustee of Age Concern Manchester, Crossroads Manchester, and

Voluntary Action Manchester.
Interests: Serious cinema, theatre, walking.
Contact details: Catholic Welfare Society, Henesey House, Sudell St, Manchester M4 4JF (tel: 0161 834 8828, fax: 833 3674, email: ccrs@lineone.net); 10 Marlowe Drive, Didsbury Manchester M20 6DE (tel; 0161 445 2157, email: tonyintraud@aol.com).

MURRAY, Braham Sydney, BA (Hons) (1994)

Positions: Artistic Director, Royal Exchange Theater.
Areas of Influence: Arts, Media, Public Sector.
Profile: *b.* February 12th, 1943; *m.* Johanna; 2 sons.
Education: Clifton College; University College, Oxford; BA Hons, Manchester Metropolitan University (1994). In 1964 Braham Murray's early production of *Hang Down Your Head and Die* transferred from Oxford to the West End and Broadway, immediately establishing his reputation. From the Century Theatre, where he was Artistic Director, he was invited to become a Founding Director of the '69 Theatre company where his productions included *Charley's Aunt, Mary Rose, Endgame,* and the musicals *ERB* and *Catch my Soul,* all of which transferred to London. In addition to Broadway, his work abroad has taken him to Milwaukee, and many of his productions have been seen in the West End, He has directed over 50 varied productions for the Royal Exchange Theatre Company and in 1995 directed Tom Courteney and Amanda Donahoe in *Uncle Vanya* at the Circle in The Square Theatre, New York. In 1999 he directed the world premiere of Tod Machover's *Ressurection* based on Tolstoy's novel, at the Houston Grand Opera. His most recent work includes a Royal Exchange commission, the World Premiere of *Snake in Fridge* by Brad Fraser, *Hedda Gabler* with Amanda Donahoe, and *Time and the Conways.* He is also a translator of French plays.
Interests: Football, food, wine.
Contact details: Royal Exchange Theatre, St Ann's Square, Manchester M2 7DH (tel: 0161 615 6702, email: braham.murray@royalexchange.co.uk).

MURRAY, Jenni, OBE (1999), BA, Dlitt

Positions: Presenter, Woman's Hour (1987 - present) and The Message (2001 - present); President, Fawcett Society; Columnist, Eve Magazine (2000 - present).
Areas of Influence: Media, Public Sector, Arts.
Profile: *b.* May 12th, 1950; *m.* David Forgham-Bailey; 2 sons.
Education: Barnsley High School for Girls; BA French and Drama, Hull University. Career profile: Local Radio, Bristol (1973-78); BBC TV South (1978-82); Newsnight (1982-85); Today (1985-87); Columnist, Daily Express (1998-00). Prizes and awards: Hon D Litt, Bradford and The Open University. Publications: Regular contributor to various newspapers and magazines; *The Woman's Hour: A History of British Women*

since WWII; Is it me or is it hot in here?: a Guide to the Menopause. Awards: Broadcaster of the Year (1998); 300 Group Journalist of the Year (1989).
Interests: Reading, riding, theatre, gardens.
Contact details: c/o Woman's hour, BBC BH, Oxford Road, Manchester (tel: 0161 244 4185, email: jenni.murray@bbc.co.uk).

MURRAY, Professor Richard, BSc, PhD, CText ATI, IMI ITIA (2001)

Positions: Pro-Vice Chancellor and Dean of the Faculty of Food, Clothing and Hospitality Management, Manchester Metropolitan University (1996 - present).
Areas of Influence: Education, Technology, Commerce.
Profile: *b.* January 13th, 1946; *m.* Margaret Kay; 2 sons.
Educated at Northallerton Grammar School (1957-64) and University of Leeds (1964-72). Career profile: Research Scholar, International Wool Secretariat (1968-72); Postdoctoral Research Associate, Science Research Council (1972-75); Lecturer and Senior Lecturer, Queen Margaret College, Edinburgh (1975-85); Head of Department and Professor, Queen Margaret College, Edinburgh (1985-96). Vice-chairman and Chairman, Scottish Section, The Textile Institute (1979-85); Member of 6th, 7th, and 8th Councils, General Teaching Council for Scotland. Publications: Research papers on fibre structure for wool, cotton, carbon and Kevlar, and Textile Technology papers and presentations on consumer studies.
Interests: Painting, high performance clothing systems, invention, innovation.
Contact details: Manchester Metropolitan University, Hollings Campus, Old Hall Lane, Manchester M14 6HR (tel: 0161 247 2616, fax: 0161 247 6395, email: r.murray@mmu.ac.uk); 18 Croft Road, Wilmslow, Cheshire SK9 6JJ (tel; 01625 532 851, email: rmurray2000uk@yahoo.co.uk).

MURREY, Martin

Position: Artist (painter) based at MASA Studios.
Areas of Influence: Arts.
Profile: *b.* April 29th, 1962.
Education: Chester College (1981-82); Manchester Polytechnic, BA (Hons) Fine Art (1982-85); In 1998 Martin Murrey was selected by the Art historian Richard Kendall to exhibit 10 paintings at the Discerning Eye exhibition at the Mall Galleries in London. In 1999 he had a successful exhibition at the Castlefield Gallery in Manchester. He has also appeared in a television programme filmed by Canal Plus, France called *Made in Manchester* which was broadcast in March 2000. Martin Murrey has work in private and corporate collections and recently entered the collection of Reader's Digest in New York. He exhibited at the Lowry Centre, Salford in a solo exhibition (2001-02). This year Martin has completed a commission for Lancashire County Council of a series of four paintings, which are on display at Great Harwood

Library.

Interests: Cinema, music, sports, travel, reading.

Contact details: MASA Studios, 2nd Floor, Ferguson House, 11 Blackfriars Road, Salford M3 7AQ (tel: 0161 832 3361, email: martinmurrey@hotmail.com, web: www.martinmurrey.co.uk).

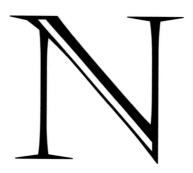

NEWCOMB, Edgar, OBE (2002), BA (1962), Dip Ed (1963)

Position: Registrar and Secretary, University of Manchester (1995- present); Member, Board of the Higher Education Staff Development Agency (1991 - present); Chairman, Association of Heads of University Administration (1998 - present); Member, DFES Student Support Programme Board (1998 - present).
Areas of Influence: Education.
Profile: *b.* October 2nd, 1940; *m.* Barri; 2 sons.
Education: Queen Elizabeths Grammar School, Gainsborough (1952-59); Grey College, University of Durham (1959-63). Career profile: Assistant Secretary, Commitee of Vice-Chancellors and Principals (1976-81); Registrar and Secretary, University of Essex (1981-92); Registrar, University of Leeds (1992-94); Member, The Funding Working Group of the National Commitee of Inquiry into Higher Education (1996-97). Clubs and societies: Lancashire County Cricket Club; Lansdowne Club; Rotary Club.
Interests: Music, literature, wine, cricket.
Contact details: Registrar & Secretary, University of Manchester, Oxford Road, Manchester M13 9PL (tel: 0161 275 7531, fax: 0161 272 6313, email: eddie.newcomb@man.ac.uk); Crantock, 63 Hawthorn Lane, Wilmslow, Cheshire SK9 5DQ (tel: 01625 527 093, email: eddie_newcomb@hotmail.com).

NEWSOME, Dr Roy, PhD, BMus, FRCO, ARCM

Positions: Research Fellow, University of Salford; President, National Association of Brass Band Conductors; Chairman, Association of Brass Band Adjudicators; Conductor Laureate, University of Salford; Music Advisor, Brass in Concert Championships.

Areas of Influence: Arts, Education, Media.
Profile: *b.* July 17th, 1930; *m.* Muriel; 2 sons.
Education: Elland C of E School; Halifax Technical College; Ext. BMus University of Durham; PhD, University of Salford. **Career profile:** Conductor: Black Dyke Mills Band (1966-77); Besses o' th' Barn Band (1978-85); Fairey Engineering Band (1986-89); Sun Life Band (1989-96). Music Director, National Youth Brass Band of Great Britain (1984-00); Presenter, BBC Radio 2 *Listen to the Band* (1986-94). Adjudicator and Guest Conductor throughout British Isles, Holland, Switzerland, Belgium, Sweden, Australia, New Zealand, USA and Japan. Publications: *Beyond the Bandstand* (1992); *Doctor Denis* (1995); *Brass Roots* (1998). c. 100 compositions and arrangements, mainly for Brass bands and many LPs and CDs as a Brass Band Conductor.
Interests: Motoring, reading, good food and wine.
Contact details: 17 Belmont Drive, Bury, Lancs BL8 2HU (tel: 0161 764 2009).

NEWTON, Paul Michael, BA (1985), ICAEW (1988)

Position: Head of Manchester Office, Aberdeen Murray Johnstone Private Equity.
Areas of Influence: Finance, Commerce.
Profile: *b.* April 2nd, 1964; *m.* Susan; 2 sons; 1 daughter.
Career profile: KPMG, Manchester (1985-88); Hill Samuel Commercial Finance (1988-89); Founder Director, Davenham Group Plc; Royal Bank of Scotland (1994-99).
Contact details: Aberdeen Murray Johnstone Limited, 55 Spring Gardens, Manchester M2 2BY (tel: 0161 233 3500, fax: 0161 233 3550, email: paul.newton@aberdeen-asset.com).

NICHOLLS, The Hon Susan Frances Harmar

Position: Actress.
Areas of Influence: Arts, Media.
Profile: *b.* November 23rd, 1943; *m.* Mark Eden.
Education: Woodland Grange School, Wednesbury; St Mary & St Anne, Abbots Bromley, Boarding School; The Royal Academy of Dramatic Art. Sue Nicholls' made her debut in the theatre in 1960. Her appearances have been as varied as weekly repertory theatre, pantomime, cabaret, and a tour of the USA with the Royal Shakespeare Company. However, a major part of her career has been in television, with her first appearance in *Crossroads* in the 1960's. This led to her being a pop star of this era, when her character sang a song which, when released as a record, went on to become a hit in the Top Twenty. She first appeared in *Coronation Street* in 1979 and having made the part of Audrey her own in 1984, she went on to become a regular on the Street's set. Her television roles have been numerous and varied, appearing in *The Duchess of Duke Street, Not on Your Nelly* with Hilda Baker and *Up the Elephant and Round the Castle* with Jim Davidson. One of her favourites was *The*

Rise and Fall of Reginald Perrin with the wonderful Leonard Rossiter, and the much loved character Nadia Popov in the childrens television series *Rentaghost*, for which she still receives fan mail! Sue divides her time between her homes in Manchester and in London.

Contact details: Contact details: c/o Brown & Simcocks, 1 Bridgehouse Court, 109 Blackfriars Road, London SE1 8HW (tel: 0207 928 1229, fax: 0207 928 1909).

NICHOLS, Rupert Henry Conquest, FCIS, FCIT

Positions: Consultant, Fox Brooks Marshall, Solicitors; Chairman, Environmental Polymers Group Plc; Deputy Chairman, Gledhill Water Storage Limited; Honorary Consul for Australia.
Areas of Influence: Commerce, Law, Voluntary Sector.
Profile: *b.* August 11th, 1949; Dianne (partner); 1 son; 2 daughters.
Educated at Wilmslow Grammar School. Career profile: Solicitor, Notary Public and Chartered Secretary, Partner, Vaudrey Osborne and Mellor, Manchester (1974-79); Solicitor, Sydney (1980-82); Senior Counsel, Australian Industry Development Corporation, Sydney (1982-84); Secretary and General Counsel, TNT Limited, Sydney (1984-93); Partner, Alsop Wilkinson, Manchester (1993-95); Solicitor, Director and advisor to SMEs, Director of various companies and Legal Advisor to TNT UK Ltd (1995-02). Member, Chairman (1998-99), Cheshire Police Authority (1994-00); Divisional Officer, Cheshire Special Constabulary (1974-79); Captain, Australian Army (1981-92); Member, CBI Europe Committee (1993-95). Clubs and societies: East India Club; Chairman (1998), St James's Club, Manchester; Royal Sydney Yacht Squadron; Wilmslow Golf Club; Old Boys Park Green Club, Macclesfield.
Interests: Theatre, travel - Spain, Australia, Canada.
Contact details: Little Moss Farm, Red Cat Lane, Crank, St Helen's WA11 8QZ (tel: 07771 974 540, fax: 01744 893 066, email: rupert.nichols@virgin.net).

NIVEN, Alistair Edgar, FLIA

Position: Financial Advisor, Zurich Advice Network.
Areas of Influence: Commerce.
Profile: *b.* June 28th, 1943.
Education: Cranleigh School, Surrey; Institute of Tourraine, University of Poitiers, Tours, France. Career profile: Chairman, Manchester Life and Pension Society (1994-95); Chairman, Manchester and Cheshire Region, Life Insurance Association (1984). Clubs and Societies: Member, Blackpool & Fleetwood Yacht Club; Chairman, St James's Club.
Interests: Sailing, arts.
Contact details: 10 Wood Street, Horwich, Bolton BL6 6BN (tel: 01204 694 222, fax: 01204 435 460, email: aen@aniven.co.uk).

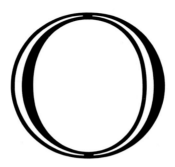

O'BRIEN, Roger William

Positions: Senior Partner, Lawson Coppock and Hart Solicitors; General Commissioner of Income Tax.
Areas of Influence: Law, Commerce.
Profile: *b.* July 3rd 1940; *m.* Barbara; 3 sons-1deceased.
Educated at St Ambrose College, Hale Barns, Altrincham, Cheshire; Member of Hale Golf Club, The St James's Club and Bowdon Cricket, Hockey and Squash Club.
Interests: Golf, gardening.
Contact details: Lawson Coppock and Hart, 18 Tib Lane, Cross Street, Manchester M2 4JA (tel: 0161 832 5944, fax: 0161 834 4409, email: robrien@lawsons-UK.com).

O'BRIEN, Tamsin

Position: Editor, BBC North West Tonight.
Areas of Influence: Media, Education.
Profile: May 11th, 1968; 1 son; 1 daughter.
Education: The Atherley School, Southampton; King Edward VI School, Southampton; Leicester University. Career profile: Journalist, Radio Berkshire (1991); Reporter, BBC Radio WM (1992); Journalist, BBC TV, Midlands Today (1994); Senior Journalists, BBC TV North West Tonight (1995 and 1997); Assistant Editor, BBC North West Tonight (1998); Editor, TV Output, Ceefax, News Online and Manchester *Where I Live* Site (BBC1) (2000).
Interests: Arts, theatre, opera.
Contact details: Editor, North West Tonight, BBC, Oxford Road, Manchester M60 1SJ (tel. 0161 244 3103, fax: 0161 244 3122, email: tasmin.obrien.olwbbc.co.uk).

O'CALLAGHAN, Michael John

Position: Managing Director, Aircraft Services Group, BAe Systems.
Areas of Influence: Finance, Commerce.
Profile: *b.* April 13th, 1952; *m.* Susan; 2 daughters.
Education: St Bonaventures Grammar School, London; Cranfield University, Bedfordshire. Career profile: Various Financial Management Roles, Ford Motor Company (1970-90); Head of Operations, Jetstream Aircraft Ltd, BAe (1990); Director and General Manager, Jetstream Aircraft Ltd, BAe (1992); Managing Director, Jetstream Aircraft Ltd, BAe (1995); Deputy Chief Executive, Airbus Industrie Asia (1996); Managing Director, Regional Aircraft, BAe (1998); Aircraft Services Group Managing Director, BAe Systems.
Interests: Racquet sports, DIY.
Contact details: Managing Director, BAe Systems, Woodford Aerodrome, Woodford, Cheshire SK7 1QR (tel: 0161 955 3245, fax: 0161 955 4176, email: mike.ocallaghan@baesystems.com).

OGLESBY, Professor Katherine Leni, BA, MA, PGCE, FRSA

Positions: Pro-Vice Chancellor & Dean, Manchester Metropolitan University.
Areas of Influence: Education.
Profile: *b.* October 2nd, 1943; *m.* Alan Wellings; 1 son; 1 daughter.
Education: Stretford Grammar School for Girls (1961-63); Keswick School (1955-60). Career profile: Lecturer, University of Leicester (1971-76); Lecturer, University of Sheffield (1976-91); Principal, Higher Education Council for England (1991-93); Associate Dean, Faculty of Education, University of Lancaster (1993-96); Academic Dean & Head of School of Educational Studies, University of Surrey (1996-98).
Interests: Gardening, backgammon.
Contact details: Dean and Pro-Vice Chancellor, Community Studies, Law and Education Didsbury Campus, 799 Wlmslow Road, Didsbury, M20 2RR (tel: 0161 247 2002, fax: 0161 247 6327, email: k.l.oglesby@mmu.ac.uk).

OLDROYD, James Colin, JP (1974), MA

Position: Chairman, Greater Manchester Magistrates Courts Commitee.
Areas of Influence: Law.
Profile: May 28th, 1935; *m.* Susan; 2 sons.
Education: St Peters School, York (1948-53); King's College, Cambridge (1954-57). Career profile: Managing Director, Graham Motor Group Plc (1971-88); Managing Director, HX3 Quick Ltd (1988-91)
Contact details: Chairman of the MCC, GMMCC Secretariat, Manchester City Magistrates' Court, Manchester M60 1PR (tel: 0161 832 7272, fax: 0161 834 2198).

OLSBERG, Rev Leslie Mark, FRSA

Position: Minister, Heaton Park Hebrew Congregation.
Areas of Influence: Education, Faith Groups, Voluntary Sector.
Profile: *b.* May 13th, 1922; *m.* Golda; 3 daughters.
Education: Central School; Manchester Talmudical College. Career profile: President, CCJ Manchester Branch; Chaplain, AJEX Manchester Branch; Chaplain, County & District Scouts; Chaplain, Heathlands; Chaplain, NMGH; Chaplain, Day Centre; Religious Advisor and Admissions Officer King David Schools Campus; Chaplain JNF Manchester Branch.
Interests: Reading, sports, travel.
Contact details: 97 Park Road, Prestwich M25 0DX (tel: 0161 740 2767).

O'NEAL, Eamonn Sean, Cert Ed, BEd, DME

Positions: Executive Producer, Regional Programmes, Granada Television; Board Member, Media Training North West; Committee Member, Royal Television Society North West; Member, NWDA Marketing Forum.
Areas of Influence: Media, Arts, Eduucation.
Profile: *b.* October 5th, 1953; *m.* Sheila; 2 sons; 1 daughter.
Education: St Peter's Primary School, Wythenshawe; St Bede's College, Manchester; Christ's College, Liverpool; Mancheser Metropolitan University. Career profile: Teacher, St Winifred's School, Stockport; Deputy Head Teacher, St Mary's School, Stockport; Deputy Head Teacher, St Winifred's School, Stockport; Producer, BBC Radio Manchester; Presenter BBC GMR; Presenter, Granada TV; Freelance Journalist; Editor, Granada Men and Motors; Executive Producer, Granada Satellite; Executive Producer, *This Morning* ITV; Executive Producer, Regional Programmes Granada TV. Eamonn O'Neal was awarded "Best Regional Presenter" by the Royal Television Society.
Interests: Music, sport, comedy, equal opportunities issues.
Contact details: Executive Producer, Regional Programmes, Granada TV, Quay St, Manchester M60 9EA (tel: 0161 832 7211, email: eamonn.oneal@granadamedia.com).

O'NEILL, C J, BA (Hons)

Positions: Owner / Designer, CJ O'Neill (Lighting Co).
Areas of Influence: Art, Design.
Profile: *b.* October 20th, 1978.
Educated at: Dominican College, Fort William, Belfast, N. Ireland; BTEC Art and Design (1997), 3D Design (2000), Manchester Metropolitan University. CJ O'Neill graduated from MMU and was awarded the 'Next Move' Scheme (2001) and showed at BDC, London (2001) and 100% Design (2001) before producing a large commission

for New Manchester Art Gallery (2002). Currently showing at 100% Design. Publications: *Red, White, and New,* 'World of Interiors Magazine, October 2001; *Light Touch, Kitchen, Bedroom, Bathroom,* March 2002; Sunday Times magazine, Oct 2002; *Translucent Design,* Mitchell Beasley, March 2002.
Contact details: 3d Chatham Building, Cavendish Street, Manchester M15 6BR (tel: 0771 253 7000, email: cj@cjoneill.co.uk, web: www.designation.co.uk); (web: www.cjoneill.co.uk).

O'REILLY, Very Rev Francis John, BSc, LCL

Positions: Episcopal Vicar; Parish Priest, Sacred Heart, Baguley; Judge and Vice-official, Shrewsbury Diocesan Tribunal (1986 - present); Parish Priest, Sacred Heart, Wythenshawe, Manchester (1994 - present); Dean, St Bonaventure's Deanery, Wythenshawe (1995 - present); Episcopal Vicar, Shrewsbury Diocesan Vicariate for Evangelisation, Christian Unity and Inter Faith Dialogue (2000 – present); Member, Greater Manchester Churches Together Presidents (2000 - present).
Areas of Influence: Faith Groups.
Profile: *b.* November 30th, 1945.
Education: St Patricks School, Wellington, Shropshire (1951-56); Adam's Grammar School, Newport, Shropshire (1956-64); North Staffordshire Polytechnic, Stafford (1966-70); St Joseph's College, Upholland, Lancs (Seminary) (1972-75); St Cuthberts College, Ushaw, Durham (Seminary) (1975-76); Saint Paul University, Ottawa, Ontario, Canada (1984-86). Career profile: Sun Alliance Insurance, Horsham, Sussex (1964-66); Imperial Metal Industries, Witton, Birmingham (1970-71); Assistant Priest, Our Lady & the Apostles, Edgeley, Stockport (1976-80); Assistant Priest, St Josephs, Sale, Cheshire (1980-82); Assistant Priest, St Josephs, Seacombe, Wallasey (1982-84); Bishop's Secretary, Bishop Joseph Gray, Shrewsbury (1986-87); Assistant Priest, St Vincents, Altrincham, Cheshire (1987-90); Parish Priest, St Ambrose, Adswood, Stockport (1990-94).
Contact details: Sacred Heart Presbytery, Floatshall Road, Baguley, Wythenshawe M23 1HP (tel: 0161 998 5319).

O'REILLY, Patrick Henry, MD, FRCS, MD, FCBU, URCP, MRCS, MAE

Positions: Consultant Urology Surgeon, Dept. of Urology, Stepping Hill Hospital, Stockport (1981 - present); President Elect, British Association of Urological Surgeons.
Areas of Influence: Health, Fiction writing.
Profile: *b.* April 22nd, 1947.
Educated at Mount St Marys College, Spinkhill, Sheffield and University of Manchester Medical School. Career profile: Rotunda Hospital, Dublin; Norwalk Hospital Connecticut, USA; Albert Einstein Hospital, Bronx, New York, USA; NW

Urology Training Programme. Publications: 5 textbooks, 11 chapters, 70 scientific papers and 4 novels. Prizes and awards: Honorary FRCS, Royal College of Surgeons, Edinburgh; Visiting Professor, Australian Society, Nuclear Medicine; Honoured Guest, Australian Society of Urology; Hon. Member, New York Section, American Urological Society. Clubs and societies: American Urological Association; Irish Society of Urology; Academy of Experts; Society of Authors; Bramhall Golf Club. **Interests:** Fiction writing, music, MUFC, red wine, especially Merlot. Contct details: Dept. of Urology, Stepping Hill Hospital, Stockport, SK2 7JE (tel: 0161 419 5484, fax: 0161 419 5699, email: paddyorlly@aol.com).

O'ROURKE, Aidan

Positions: Photographer; Journalist; New Media Author, Freelance.
Areas of Influence: Media, Arts, Education.
Profile: b. January 9th, 1958; Ann Nazario; 1 daughter Adele (2001).
Education: Our Lady's Primary School, Stockport (1964-1969); Xaverian College Grammar School, Manchester (1969-76); BA / MA Modern Languages German & French (1976-1981) Trinity College, Dublin; PCGE, Avery Hill College, London (1983). Career profile: Lecturer / Teacher in German, French, EFL at South Trafford College (1983-1991) and City College (formerly South Manchester College) (1984-88); English Language Instructor, Saudi Arabian Monetary Agency (1991-1992); Computer Lab English Teacher, United Arab Emirates Armed Forces (1992-1996). Since Jan 1997 author of Eyewitness in Manchester website, part of Manchester Online (Manchester Evening News / Guardian Media Group); Aim: To document and showcase the city and region in photographs and words, with opinion and reader messages. Nominated for Manchester Civic Society Spirit of Manchester Award; Other projects: Books, new media, digital photography seminars.
Interests: Photography, writing, travel, local history, art, design, technology
Contact details: tel/fax: 0161 225 4264, email: aidan@aidan.co.uk, web: www.aidan.co.uk, mob: 07779 290082.

ORRELL, Susan, LLB

Position: City Solicitor, Manchester City Council.
Areas of Influence: Commerce, Law, Public Sector.
Profile: *b.* May 17th, 1948. *m.* Ian. 1 daughter.
Educated at Chatham Grammar School for Girls and University of Manchester.
Contact details: tel: 0161 234 3087, fax: 0161 234 3098.

PANNONE, Rodger John, DL (1998), LLD h.c, D.Litt l.c

Position: Senior Partner, Pannone & Partners.
Areas of Influence: Education, Law, Voluntary Sector.
Profile: *b.* April 20th, 1943; *m.* Patricia; 2 sons; 1 daughter.
Education: St Brendan's College, Bristol; College of Law, London; Manchester Metropolitan University. Career profile: Articled Clerk, Salford (1966-69); Solicitor and Partner, WH Thompson, London and Manchester (1969-73); Partner now Senior Partner, Pannone & Partners, Manchester (1973 - present); Chairman, Council of Manchester University, Governors College of Law and Manchester Concert Hall Ltd; President, Law Society of England and Wales (1993-94); Chairman, Forensic Science Service; Hon. Life Member, Canadian Bar Association; Hon. Fellow, Advanced Legal Education, Birmingham University; Hon Fellow, Manchester University. Member of St James's Club, Manchester.
Interests: Walking, food and wine, the Lake District.
Contact details: Pannone & Partners, 123 Deansgate, Manchester, M3 2BU (tel: 0161 909 4207); 31 Stanton Avenue, West Didsbury, Manchester M20 2PG (tel: 0161 445 4342, fax: 0161 445 9709).

PANTON, Elizabeth Jane

Positions: Headmistress, Bolton School, Girls Division; Liverpool University Council; Sefton FHSA (-1994)
Areas of Influence: Education.
Profile: *b.* June 20th, 1947.
Educated at Clayton Hall Grammar School, Merchant Taylors' School (Jubilee Scholarship), St Hugh's College Oxford (History Hons, Tennis and Hockey Blues);

Taught History, English, and History of Art at Moreton Hall School, Shrewsbury High School for Girls, and Clifton High School for Girls, Bristol; Head of History, Head of Sixth Form Clifton High School for Girls, Bristol; Headmistress, Merchant Taylors' School for Girls, Crosby, Liverpool; Chair, ISIS North Committee; Chair, GSA NW; Member of National Trust and RSPB.

Interests: Fell walking (home and abroad), foreign travel, bird watching, music, art, history, theatre.

Contact details: Bolton School (Girls Division), Chorley New Road, Bolton, Lancashire BL1 4PB (tel: 01204 840 201).

PASS, Anthony John Bradley, MA, BArch, RIBA, MRTPI, FSA

Positions: Head of Properties, Manx National Heritage, The Manx Museum and National Trust (1997 - present).

Areas of Influence: Arts, Architecture and Conservation.

Profile: *b.* May 23rd, 1947.

Education: Stockport School (1958-64); University of Manchester (1964-68, 1969-70). Career profile: Assistant Director of Estates, UMIST (1984-97); Private Practice (1968-73). Publications: *Thomas Worthington: Victorian Architecture and Social Purpose* (1988); Chapter in *Art and Architecture in Victorian Manchester*. Founder member, Association of Conservation Officers; Honorary Architect, Portico Library (1982-90); Member and Chairman, Manchester Conservation Panel (1986-92). Designer of the Peckitt window installed in St Ann's Church, Manchester (1981). Prizes and awards: Civic Trust Award (1981), British Tourist Authority Award (1995); Shortlisted for Portico Library Prize (1988).

Interests: Ships and the sea, Manx history and culture, watercolour paintings, walking, horse riding, motorcycling, restoring old properties.

Contact details: The Properties Division, Manx National Heritage, The Manx Museum, Douglas (tel: 01624 648000, fax: 01624 648001, email: Tony.Pass@mnh.gov.im); Port-E-Chee, Packhorse Lane, Baldrine, Isle of Man IM4 6EA (tel: 01624 861 377, email; tonypass@manx.net).

PATRIARCA, Stephen Richard, B.A Hons (Wales)

Position: Headmaster, William Hulme's Grammar School.

Areas of Influence: Education, Arts.

Profile: *b.* May 3rd, 1953.

Educated at The Sweyne School, Rayleigh (1964-71); University College of Swansea (1972-77); B.A Hons, Wales (1975). Career profile: Assistant English Master, Hulme Grammar School, Oldham (1978); Head of General Studies (1985); Head of Sixth Form (1988); Deputy Headmaster and Director of Studies (1995); Publications: Contributions to *The Gadfly*, review of English Letters; *My Native English*, Ed

Robinson and Maskel. Clubs and societies: Headmasters and Headmistresses Conference; Secondary Heads ASSN; East India and Public Schools Club; The Royal Institute of Philosophy; Director, Independent Schools Information Service (ISIS North).
Interests: Travel, music, literature, philosophy, food and wine.
Contact details: William Hulme's Grammar School, Spring Bridge Road, Manchester M16 8PR (tel: 0161 226 2054, fax: 0161 232 5544, email: hmsec@whgs.co.uk).

PATTERSON, Frances Sylvia, BA, QC(1998)

Positions: Barrister; Recorder.
Areas of Influence: Law
Profile: Educated at Queen's School, Chester and Leicester University.
Contact details: 40 King Street, Manchester M2 6BA (tel: 0161 832 9082, fax: 0161 835 2139).

PEDELTY, Mervyn Kay FCA, FCIB, FRSA

Positions: Chief Executive, Co-operative Financial Services (2002 - present); Chief Executive, The Co-operative Bank (1997 - present); Chair, MIDAS (Manchester Investment and Development Agency Service); Deputy Chair, North West Business Leadership Team; Director, Manchester Enterprises; Vice-President, Community Foundation for Greater Manchester; Chair, FTSE4 Good Advisory Committee.
Areas of Influence: Commerce, Finance, Public Sector.
Profile: *b.* January 16th, 1949.
Educated at Hull and Manchester Primary Schools, Felixstowe Grammar School, and Harvard Business School. Career profile: British Leyland Ltd (1973-76); Phicom PLC/ Gould Inc (1976-83); Abacus Electronics Holdings Plc (1983-87); TSB Group plc, Finance Director, TSB Banking and Insurance, and Chief Executive, Commercial Operations (1987-94); Equity Partner, L.E.K Consulting (1995-97); Chief Executive, The Co-operative Bank plc. Chief Executive, Co-operative Financial Services (2002).
Contact details: The Co-operative Bank plc, Po Box 101, 1 Balloon Street, Manchester M60 4EP (tel: 0161 832 3456).

PENDRY, Baron Thomas, of Stalybridge in the County of Greater Manchester PC (2000)

Positions: Steward, British Boxing Board of Control (1987 - present); President, Music Users Council (1997 - present); Patron, National Federation of Football Supporters (1998 - present).
Areas of Influence: Public Sector.
Profile: *b.* June 10th, 1934; *m.* Moira Anne Smith (sep. 1983); 1 son; 1 daughter.

Educated at St Augustine's Ramsgate and Oxford University. Career profile: RAF (1955-57); Full time Official, National Union of Public Employees (1960-70); Member, Paddington Borough Council (1962-65); Chairman, Derby Labour party (1966); MP, Stalybridge and Hyde (1970-01); An Opposition Whip (1971-74); a Lord Comr of the Treasury and Govt. Whip (1974), resigned (1977); Party Under Secretary of State, NI Office (1978-79); Opposition Spokesman on NI (1979-81), on overseas development (1981-82), on regional affairs and devolution (1982-84), on sport and tourism (1992-97). Member: Select Committee on Environment (1987-92); Select Committee on Members Interests (1987-92). Chairman: All Party Sports Committee (1980-92); PLP Sports Committee (1984-92); All Party Tourism Group; All Party Sports Committee. Member: Speaker's Conference (1973); UK Delegation to WEU and Council of Europe (1973-75); Industrial Law Society Chairman, Football Trust. President, Stalybridge Public Band. Prizes and awards: Freeman, Borough of Tameside and Lordship of Mottram in Longendale (1995). Clubs and societies: Wig and Pen; Lord's Tavernors; Vincent's (Oxford).

Interests: Sport, football, cricket, boxing (sometime Middleweight Champion, Hong Kong, boxed for Oxford University).

Contact details: House of Lords, London SW1A 0PW.

PERRY, Ian Bell, FRICS, MCIArb, MCIoB, MCIH

Positions: Honorary Consul for the Netherlands for Greater Manchester, Lancashire and Cheshire; Chief Executive, Harvest Housing Group.
Areas of Influence: Social Housing.
Profile: *b.* July 11th, 1950; *m.* Julie; 1 son; 2 daughters.
Educated at Archbishop William Temple, Alderman Corgan High School and Kingston-upon-Hull College. A chartered surveyor who previously worked in private practice and local government, Ian Perry has been Chief Executive of Harvest Housing Group for the past 16 years. Harvest is a group of Housing Associations and Companies, owning and managing 15,000 properties in NW England providing a broad range of agency and regeneration services. Ian is involved with the Royal Institute of Chartered Surveyors at both regional and national level. He is a member of the residential faculty board and is the National Housing Spokesman. Ian has been active in the National Housing Holding Federation at national and regional level including past membership of the northern executive committee. He is a Board member of the local Government Task Force and a member of the Housing Forum Steering Group, established to develop the Government's Rethinking Construction Initiative (Egan Report). He chairs the Joint Housing Forum and Local Government Task Force - Repair, Refurbishment and Maintenance Steering Group, and has been appointed North West Champion for the Housing Forum.
Interests: Walking, association football, theatre.
Contact details: Apex House, 266 Moseley Road, Levenshulme, Manchester M19

2LH (tel: 0161 248 2300, fax: 0161 248 2401, email: ian.perry@harvesthousing.co.uk); Wellfield Cottage, 10 Pickhill Lane, Uppermill, Saddleworth OL3 6BN (tel: 01457 875043, fax: 01457 875 041, email: IBP@IBPHHG.freeserve.co.uk).

PETTY, Christopher, R W, (MA) (Cantab)

Positions: Vice President, AstraZeneca
Areas of Influence: Law, Commerce.
Profile: *b.* May 15th, 1953; *m.* Joanna; 3 sons.
Educated at Blundells School, Devon, Selwyn College, Cambridge and College of Law, London. Christopher Petty is an in-house lawyer at ICI / Zeneca / AstraZeneca and is responsible for the legal department, Alderley Park, Cheshire. He is also responsible for AstraZeneca external relations in the North West. Member of Middle Temple and Legal Committee, Association of the British Pharmaceutical Industry. Clubs and societies: North West Business Leadership Team; Governor, Royal Northern College of Music and The King's School, Macclesfield.
Interests: Music, theatre, walking, family.
Contact details: AstraZeneca, Alderley House, Alderley Park, Macclesfield, Cheshire SK10 4TF (tel: 01625 512591, email: chris.petty@astrazeneca.com); Endon Hall North, Kerridge, Macclesfield, Cheshire SK10 5AL.

PHILLIPS, Sheldon, BA, MSc

Position: Regional Director, Sport England (1996 - present).
Areas of Influence: Sport, Public Sector, Voluntary Sector.
Profile: *b.* January 8th, 1953.
Education: Lewis Grammar School, South Wales; University College of North Wales; Loughborough University. Sheldon Philips has 25 years experience in sport and recreation gained through working in Local Authority Sport and Leisure Departments throughout the North West. He has wide knowledge and experience in event management, indoor and outdoor facility managment and sports development.
Contact details: Sport England, Astley House, Quay Street, Manchester M3 4AE (tel: 0161 834 0338, fax: 0161 835 3678).

PICKERING, Janet D, BSc

Position: Headmistress, Withington Girls' School.
Areas of Influence: Education, Voluntary Sector.
Profile: June 21st, 1949. *m.* Dr W Ron Pickering; 2 sons.
Educated at Bridlington High School for Girls (1960-65), Malton Grammar School (1965-67) and University of Sheffield (1967-73). Career profile: Research Biochemist and Immunologist (University of Sheffield, Hallamshire Hospital Protein Reference

Unit); Teaching Fellow, University of Leeds; Proofreader and Editor, Scientific Journals and Textbooks; Text Authority and Editor, ENL. Britannia; Housemistress and Deputy Headmistress, The King's School, Canterbury; Headmistress (St. Bee's School, Cumbria); Publications: Articles in various Scientific Journals (1970's); Co-Author, *Nucleic Acid Biochemistry and Molecular Biology* (1982, Blackwell Scientific Publications); Text Authority, Children's Britannica (1988 Edition). Member, University Women's Club.
Interests: Reading, theatre, cinema, natural history, travel, ornithology, being walked by the dog.
Contact details: Withington Girls' School, Wellington Road, Fallowfield, Manchester M14 6BL (tel: 0161 224 1077, fax: 0161 248 5377, email: head@withington.manchester. sch.uk).

PICKSTONE, Professor John Victor, BA (Cantab) (1965), MSc (1967), MSc (1969), PhD (1974)

Position: Research Professor of History of Science, Technology & Medicine, University of Manchester.
Areas of Influence: Education, Arts, Health.
Profile: *b.* May 29th, 1944; Vivienne Devine; 2 sons.
Education: Burnley Grammar School (1955-62); Natural Sciences, Fitzwilliam College, Cambridge (1962-65); Physiology, Queen's University, Kingston, Ontario (1965-68); History and Philosophy of Science, London University College (1968-69); HPS, London Chelsea College (1969-72). Career profile: Research Fellow, History of Medicine, University of Minnesota (1971-71); Research Fellow (1974-77), Lecturer (1977-85); Senior Lecturer, Department of History of Science, UMIST; Founder and Director, (1986-02), History of Science Technology and Medicine and the Wellcome Unit for the History of Medicine, University of Manchester. Publications: *Medicine and Industrial Society: A History of Hospitals in Manchester and its Regions 1752-1948* (1985); *Medical Innovations in Historical Perspective* (1992); *Medicine in the Twentieth Century* (2000); *Ways of Knowing: a New History of Science, Technology and Medicine* (2001). Clubs and societies: British Society for the History of Science; Society for the Social History of Medicine.
Interests: Walking, natural history, local history, museums, music, Manchester.
Contact details: Centre for the History of Science, Technology and Medicine, Mathematics Building, University of Manchester, Oxford Road, Manchester M13 9PL (tel: 0161 275 5926, fax: 0161 275 5699, email: john.pickstone@man.ac.uk); 12 Fairfax Avenue, Didsbury, Manchester M20 6AJ (tel: 0161 445 3576).

PIDGEON, Brian, BA (Hons)

Position: General Manager, BBC Philharmonic.
Areas of Influence: Arts, Media.
Profile: *b.* July 4th, 1948; *m.* Maureen; 2 sons.
Educated at Stockport Grammar (1959-66); Liverpool University (1966-69). Career profile: General Manager, Royal Liverpool Philharmonic Orchestra (1977-91); Chief Producer, BBC Philharmonic (1991-95); Member of Royal Philharmonic Society; Board Member, RNCM.
Contact details: BBC, New Broadcasting House, Oxford Road, Manchester M60 1SJ (tel: 0161 244 4213, fax: 0161 244 4211, email: brian.pidgeon@bbc.co.uk).

PIKE, Jennifer Elizabeth

Position: Violinist
Area of Influence: Arts.
Profile: *b.* November 9th, 1989.
Education: Violin lessons from age 4; Chetham's School of Music (1998 - present). At age 10 she gave her first full public evening recital, and made her concerto debut performing Haydn's Violin Concerto in G with the Lake District International Summer School. She has also played in the presence of HRH The Prince of Wales in the Associated Board National High Achievers Concert in Covent Garden. She has become the youngest ever recitalist in professional concert series at Salford University, Square Chapel Halifax and the Holywell Music Room, Oxford. In 2001 she appeared with the Hallé Orchestra as a soloist. She has also performed live on BBC Radio 3 and BBC Television. Her solo repertoire ranges from music by Bach, Mozart and Beethoven to contemporary works as well as premiering several new works by her father, Jeremy Pike. Solo Performances: BBC Philharmonic Orchestra in CBBC Proms in the Park, Hyde Park; BBC Concert Orchestra in Royal Festival Hall; London Symphony Orchestra in Gramophone Awards Ceremony, Barbican Hall. Prizes and awards: Musicas Award Winner (2001); Graucob Award Winner (2001); Martin Musical Scholarship (2002); Emanuel Hurwitz Prize for UK violinists; 4th Prize, Yehudi Menuhin International Violin Competition; BBC Young Musician of the Year (2002), youngest ever winner at age 12.
Interests: Art, literature.
Contact details: Young Artists Trust, 23 Garrick Street, London WC2E 9BN (tel: 0207 379 8477, fax: 0207 379 8467, email: info@ycat.co.uk).

PIKE, (Fraser) Jeremy, MA (Cantab), MPhil, PhD, LRAM, HonARAM

Positions: Composer; Head of Composition and Contemporary Music, Chetham's School of Music, Manchester (1994 - present).
Areas of Influence: Arts.
Profile: *b.* November 20th, 1955; *m.* Teresa Pike; 2 daughters.
Education: Abingdon School (1966-73); King's College, Cambridge (1973-76); Royal Academy of Music (1976-77); Katowice Academy of Music, Poland (1978-80); Goldsmith's College, London University (1992-00). Jeremy Pike began composing at the age of 6, studying with many eminent musicians including Gordon Crosse in Cambridge and Henryk Gorecki in Poland. In 1981 he was appointed Director of Contemporary Music at the University of Warwick and in 1987 became Co-ordinator of Electro-Acoustic music at the Royal Academy of Music in London. In 1989 he was appointed to the staff of Chetham's School of Music. He has also held conducting posts in Oxford and Cambridge, as well as conducting the Stamford Chamber Orchestra and the Chetham's Symphony Orchestra. His compositions have been widely performed, and include works for orchestra, chamber ensembles, instumental solo works and vocal music. He is also active as an accompanist, notably with his daughter Jennifer. Principal works include: *A Street Under Siege*, for orchestra; 7 piano sonatas, 6 string quartets, *Missa Brevis*; *Bassoon Concerto*. Prizes and awards: Churchill Composition Prize (1975); Polish Government Scholarship (1978); Honorary Mention, Carl Maria van Weber International Composers' Contest, Dresden (1978); Churchill Fellowship (1998). Clubs and societies: Performing Rights Society, British Academy of Composers and Songwriters; North West Composers Association.
Interests: Literature, art, walking, photography.
Contact details: Chetham's School of Music, Long Millgate, Manchester M3 1SB (tel: 0161 834 9644, fax: 0161 839 3609); email: jeremypike@lineone.net, web: jeremypike.co.uk.

PIKE, Malcolm John, LLB

Positions: Partner, Head of Commercial Division and Member of Management Committee, Addleshaw Booth & Co (1992 - present).
Areas of Influence: Employment Law.
Profile: *b.* August 22nd, 1959; *m.* Rosemary; 2 daughters.
Educated at Leicester University and The College of Law, Chester. Career profile: Articled at Hepworth & Chadwick, Leeds (1982-84); Manager and Asistant Solicitor, Freshfields, London (1984-92). Member of the Advisory Panel of the Rugby Football League. Publications: editor, *The Lawyers Factbook*; legal editor, *Essential Facts Employment*; contributor and advisory editor, *Butterworths Encyclopedia of Forms and Precents*. Clubs and societies: Law Society; International Bar Association;

Employment Lawyers Association; Stockport GC; Ganton GC; Alderley Edge Hockey Club.

Interests: Sport, family.

Contact details: Addleshaw Booth & Co, 100 Barbirolli Square, Manchester M2 3AB (tel: 0161 934 6443, fax: 0161 934 6060, email: malcolm.pike@addleshawbooth.com).

PLUMB, Barry Sidney, CEng (1979), MIEE (1979), FRSA (1992), MSC, IEE (1979)

Position: Deputy Vice Chancellor, Manchester Metropolitan University.
Areas of Influence: Education, Engineering, Training.
Profile: *b.* September 17th, 1944; *m.* Valerie; 1 son; 3 daughters.
Education: Sir Joseph Williamson's Mathematical School, Rochester (1955-60); Medway College of Technology (1960-68); MSc Telecommunications Systems, University of Essex (1968-69); Diploma in Electrical Engineering, Institute of Electrical Engineers. Barry Plumb is a chartered electrical engineer in a career that has spanned more than ten years working, predominantly, in the UK aerpospace industry but also in the USA microelectronics industry together with over 30 years service in senior posts in three UK Universities. Barry acts as a consultant for various UK engineering companies and is author and presenter of over 20 short courses for industry in UK and USA. He has presented at over 20 conferences in UK and overseas, on subjects spanning electronic systems, integrated circuit design, signal processing, communication engineering, avionics, process control, and instrumentation systems. His most recent expertise is related to strategic planning and operational management in higher education.
Interests: DIY, gardening, walking, antique clock restoration.
Contact details: Manchester Metropolitan University, Oxford Road, Manchester, M15 6BH (tel: 0161 247 1020, fax; 0161 247 6311, email: b.s.plumb@mmu.ac.uk); Shawfield House, The Shaw, Dinting, Glossop, Derbyshire, SK13 6DE (tel: 01457 857135).

POLLARD, Professor Brian James, MD, FRCA

Positions: Professor of Anaesthesia, University of Manchester; Honorary Consultant Anaesthesiologist, Central Manchester Hospitals.
Areas of Influence: Health, Education.
Profile: *b.* August 30th, 1949; *m.* Dr Claire Candelier; 1 son; 2 daughters.
Education: Henry Mellish Grammar School, Nottingham; The School of Pharmacy, University of London; University of Sheffield Medical School. Career profile: House Officer, Sheffield and Derby; Senior House Officer, Nottingham; Registrar, Nottingham; Lecturer, University of Nottingham; Senior Registrar, Manchester; Instructor, Michigan, USA; Professor, University of Manchester.
Interests: Bringing up 3 children!

Contact details: Department of Anaesthesia, Manchester Royal Infirmary, Oxford Road, Manchester M13 9WL (tel: 0161 276 8650, fax: 0161 273 5685, email: brian.pollard@man.ac.uk).

POLLARD, John Stanley, LLB (Hons)

Positions: HM Coroner for Greater Manchester South (1995 - present); HM Deputy Coroner for Cheshire (1982 – present); Chairman, Dane Housing Ltd.
Areas of Influence: Law, Health.
Profile: *b.* January 4th, 1952; *m.* Clare Judith Pollard; 3 sons.
Educated at The King's School Macclesfield, Hymer's College Hull and University of Leeds. Career profile: Articled Clerk to firm of solicitors in Congleton and Macclesfield (1974-76); Solicitor in Private Practice (1977-78); Solicitor, Greater Manchester County Council, prosecuting for Trading Standards (1978); Partner in Private Practice specialising in Crime, Family and Children's Law (1979-95); Member of Council of Coroners Society of England and Wales. John Pollard has been a local councillor and a school govenor since 1984. He has additional business interests in that he is chairman of a car sales garage and of a property development company. Most famously (infamously) he was the coroner who ordered the original inquiries into Dr Harold Shipman and who also ordered the subsequent exhumations. Clubs and societies: Fellow, Royal Society of Medicine; Member, Law Society.
Interests: Watching most sport especially football, rugby and cricket. Director of Congleton Town FC.
Contact details: HM Coroners Office, 10 Greek Street, Stockport SK3 8AB (tel: 0161 476 1971, fax: 0161 476 1972, email: john.pollard@stockport.gov.uk).

POOLE, Dr Geoffrey, BA, Bmus, Dmus, LRAM

Positions: Composer, Contemporary Classical; Reader in Composition, University of Bristol.
Areas of Influence: Arts, Education.
Profile: *b.* February 9th, 1949; *m.* Beth Wiseman; 1 son; 2 daughters.
Education: Forest School, Snaresbrook (1960-67); UEA (1967-70); University of Southampton (1970-71); University of Leeds (1973-75). Career profile: Lecturer, University of Leeds (1975-76); Lecturer, University of Manchester (1976-89); Senior Lecturer, University of Kenyatta, Nairobi (1985-87); Senior Lecturer, University of Manchester (1989-2000); Visiting Fellow, Princeton, New Jersey, USA (1997-98); Reader, University of Manchester (2000); Reader, University of Bristol (2001 -).
Interests: Walking, travel, contemporary literature, astrology, koi, environmement, peace issues.

Contact details: Victoria Rooms, University of Bristol, Queens Road, Cliton, Bristol BS8 (tel: 0117 954 5034, email: geoff.poole@ bristol.sc.uk); Old Orchard, 62a Avonfield Avenue, Bradford on Avon, Wiltshire BA15 1JF (tel: 01225 865 383, email: GeoffPooleMusic@aol.com).

POPPLEWELL, Richard Ian, BSc (Hons), M.A

Position: Chief Executive, Stockport Primary Care Trust.
Areas of Influence: Health, Public Sector.
Profile: *b.* March 6th, 1954; *m.* Lynda; 1 daughter.
Educated at Ecclesfield Grammar School (1964-72) and University of Manchester (1972-75). Career profile: Regional Statistician, North West Regional Health Authority (1983-85); Regional Planning Manager, North West Regional Health Authority (1985-87); Director of Planning, North West Regional Health Authority (1987-94); Chief Executive, Manchester Health Authority (1994); Chief Executive, Bury and Rochdale Health Authority (1994-2001); Chairman, Hunshelf Parish Council.
Interests: Walking, bird watching, football, family history.
Contact details: Stockport Primary Care Trust, Springwood House, Poplar Grove, Hazel Grove SK7 5BY (tel: 0161 419 4706, fax: 0161 419 4603, email: richard.popplewell@stockport-pct.nhs.uk) 2 Delph Edge, Green Moor, Sheffield S35 7DW (tel: 0114 288 3838, email: richard@rpopplewell.freeserve.co.uk).

POSTLETHWAITE, Dr Robert Joseph, MB ChB, FRCP, FRCPCM

Positions: Consultant Paediatric Nephrologist (1978 - present) and Clinical Head of Children's Division, Central Manchester and Manchester Children's University NHS Trust; President, British Association for Paediatric Nephrology.
Areas of Influence: Health.
Profile: *b.* December 23rd, 1946; *m.* Catherine; 1 son; 2 daughters.
Educated at Xavarian College, Manchester and Manchester University (1965-70). Publications: Editor, *Clinical Paediatric Nephrology,* 3rd Edition, Oxford University Press; Co-editor, *Munchausen Syndrome by Proxy: a practical approach,* Arnold (2000); 80 other original publications in paediatrics and paediatric nephrology. Member of Royal College of Paediatrics and Child Health, European Society for Paediatric Nephrology, International Nephrology Society, and the Labour Party.
Interests: Classical music, opera, theatre, literature, walking, sport particularly Manchester United.
Contact details: Manchester Children's Hospital, Pendlebury, Manchester M27 4MA, tel: 0161 727 2160, fax: 0161 727 2630, email: robert.postlethwaite@cmmc.nhs.uk).

POWELL, Professor James Alfred, OBE (1996), BSc, MSc, PhD, DSc, AUMIST, FCIM, FIOA, FRSA, FASA, CEng, MIOD

Positions: Pro-Vice Chancellor, Enterprise and Regional Affairs, Salford University (1996 - present); Member of North West Innovation and Technology Board.
Areas of Influence: Education, Media, Public Sector.
Profile: *b.* October 30th, 1945; *m.* Jennifer Elizabeth; 1 son.
Educated at De Burgh School, Tadworth until 1963; UMIST (1964-67); Salford (1968-71). Career profile: ICI Building Development Group (1971-75); Lecturer, Dundee University School of Architecture (1975-80); Reader, then Professor, then Head of School of Architecture, Portsmouth University (1980-92); Deputy Dean, Brunel University (1992-96). Professor Powell's research interests include team building, design, learning for professionals.
Interests: Tai Chi, swimming.
Contact details: Salford University, The Crescent, M5 4WT (tel: 0161 295 5464, fax: 0161 295 3862, email: j.a.powell@salford.ac.uk); 127 Hale Road, Hale WA15 9HQ (tel: 0161 928 2734, fax: 0161 928 2734).

POWNALL, John Harvey

Positions: Pro-Chancellor and Member of Council, Salford University; Chairman, University Estates Commitee.
Areas of Influence: Education, Public Sector.
Profile: *b.* October 24th, 1933; *m.* Pauline; 1 son; 2 daughters.
Educated at Tonbridge School and Imperial College, London, BSc. Eng. Met (1955); Scientific Officer, Atomic Energy Research Establishment, Harwell; Warren Spring Laboratory, DSIR; Board of Trade, Dept. of Economic Affairs; Dept. of Trade and Industry; Director General, Council of Mechanical and Metal Trade Associations; H/d Electricity Division, Dept. of Energy; Advisor to the Executive, CEGB, and Director, Power Plant Contractors Association; Regional Director, DTI North West (1988-93). Member, St James's Club, Manchester.
Interests: Regional economic and higher education issues.
Contact details: The West House, Arley hall, Northwich, Cheshire CW9 6LZ (tel: 01565 777 448).

PRICE, Professor Patricia, M.B, Bchir, M.A, M.D, F.R.C.P, F.R.C.R

Position: Ralston Paterson Professor of Radiation Oncology and Honorary Consultant, Christie Hospital, Manchester University.
Areas of Influence: Research, Health, Education.
Profile: *b.* August 13th, 1957; *m.* Professor Terry Jones; 2 sons; 3 stepchildren.
Education: Stoke Park Girls' Grammar School, Coventry; Newnham College,

Cambridge; King's College Hospital Medical School, London; Oncology Training, Royal Marsden Hospital, London. Career profile: Junior Oncology Posts, Royal Marsden Hospital, London, Cancer Research UK; Research Fellow, Institute of Cancer Research, London; Senior Lecturer and Honorary Consultant, Hammersmith, London; Reader and Head of Cancer Therapeutics Section, Imperial College, London; Professor of Radiation Oncology, Manchester University. Publications: Over 100 scientific articles. Clubs and societies: President, British Oncological Association; National and International Oncology Awards.
Interests: Watching sons play rugby.
Contact details: Academic Department of Radiation Oncology, Christie Hospital, Wilmslow Road, Manchester M20 4BY (tel: 0161 444 8003, fax: 0161 446 8111, email: anne.mason@christie-tr.nwest.nhs.uk).

PRIOR, Michael John, FCA

Positions: Non Executive Director, F.T Morrell and Co Ltd and other companies; Justice of the Peace; Trustee, Museum of Science and Industry, Manchester; Member of Court, University of Manchester.
Areas of Influence: Finance, Public Sector, Education.
Profile: *b.* July 22nd, 1945; *m.* Angela Elizabeth; 2 sons; 2 daughters.
Educated at St, Ambrose College, Altrincham (1953-61). Career profile: Articled Clerk, JOS W Shepherd and Co (1961-66); Qualified (1966); Partner, Heywood Shepherd (1969-89); Partner and Manchester Area Chairman, HLB Kidsons (1989-2000); Non Executive Chairman, Lancashire Dairies LTD (2000-02); Elected member, ICAEW Council (1993-99); Founder Chairman, ICAEW Centre for Business Performance (1998-2002); President, Manchester Society of Chartered Accountants (1988-89); Deputy Chairman of Governors, Stonyhurst College. Clubs and societies: St. James's Club, Manchester; Ringway Golf Club.
Interests: Family, golf, Manchester United.
Contact details: Magnolias, 9 Gaddum Road, Bowdon, Altrincham, Cheshire WA14 3PD (tel: 0161 929 4440, fax: 0161 928 4800, email: mjp@mjprior.co.uk).

PROCTOR, Jean

Positions: Chairman, Age Concern, Salford; Member, Council, University of Salford; Member, Branch Council, Greater Manchester British Red Cross.
Areas of Influence: Health, Voluntary Sector.
Profile: *b.* September 9th, 1938; *m.* Reverend K.N. Proctor; 2 daughters.
Professional qualifications: Registered General and Sick Children's Nurse, Midwife and Health Visitor. Career profile: Extensive Clinical Experience in Nursing, Midwiferey and Health Visiting (1956-78); Nurse Manager, Health Visiting Service, Oldham (1978-84); Director, Community Nursing, Salford (1985-86); Chief Nursing

Officer, Salford (1986-94); General Manager Community Health Services, Salford (1986-94); Chief Executive, Salford Community Health Care NHS Trust (1994-98).
Interests: Church Activities, Voluntary Sector.
Contact details: 4 Banks Croft, Hopwood, Heywood OL10 2NG (tel: 01706 364 197).

PULLAN, Emeritus Professor Brian Sebastian, MA, PhD, FRHistS, FBA

Positions: Emeritus Professor, University of Manchester; Feoffee, Chetham's Hospital and Library.
Areas of Influence: Education.
Profile: *b*. December 10th, 1935; *m*. Janet Elizabeth Maltby; 2 sons.
Education: Epsom College (1949-54); Trinity College, Cambridge (1956-62). Career profile: Research Fellow, Trinity College, Cambridge (1961-63); Fellow, Queens College, Cambridge (1963-72); University Assistant Lecturer, Cambridge (1964-67); University Lecturer, Cambridge (1967-72); Professor of Modern History, University of Manchester (1973-98); Dean, The Faculty of Arts, University of Manchester (1982-84); Presenter of Honorary Graduands (1992-98); Emeritus Professor, University of Manchester (1998). Publications (author or contributor): *Sources for the History of Medieval Europe* (1966); *Crisis and Change in the Venetian Economy* (1968); *Rich and Poor in Renaissance Venice* (1971); *A History of Early Renaissance Italy* (1973); *The Jews of Europe and the Inquisition of Venice 1550-1670* (1983); *Towns and Townspeople in Medieval and Renaissance Europe: Essays in Memory of JK Hyde* (1990); *Venice: A Documentary History, 1450-1630* (1992); *Poverty and Charity: Europe, Italy, Venice 1400-1700* (1994); *A History of the University of Manchester 1951-73* (2000).
Interests: Dogs, theatre.
Contact details: 33 Green Pastures, Heaton Mersey, Stockport SK4 3RB (tel: 0161 442 2858, email: brian@bpullan.freeserve.co.uk).

PURNELL, James Mark Dakin, BA (Hons)

Position: Member of Parliament, Stalybridge and Hyde.
Areas of Influence: Work and Pensions, Education, Media.
Profile: *b*. March 2nd, 1970.
Educated at Royal Grammar School, Guildford, A Levels; Balliol College, Oxford, BA (Hons) Politics, Philosophy and Economics. Career profile: Researcher, RT Hon Tony Blair MP (1989-92); Consultant, Hydra Strategy (1992-94); Research Fellow, PPR (1994-95); Head of Corporate Planning, BBC (1995-97); Special Advisor, Downing Street, Policy Unit on Culture, Media, Sport and Knowledge Economy (1997-2001).
Contact details: House of Commons, London SW1A 0AA (tel: 020 7219 8166, fax: 020 7219 1287, email: basus@parliament.uk).

PYSDEN, Edward Scott, LLB

Positions: Senior Corporate Partner, Eversheds (1974 – present); Chairman, Hallé Concert Society, The Bridgewater Hall (1999 – present).
Areas of Influence: Law, Arts, Commerce.
Profile: *b.* May 6th, 1948; *m.* Maria; 3 daughters.
Education: Dulwich College (1959-60); King's School, Macclesfield (1966-69); Manchester University (1966-69); College of Law, Guildford (1969-70). Career profile: Articled Clerk (1970-72); Assistant Solicitor (1972-74); Past Chairman, Pro-Manchester (1999-00); Director, Marketing Manchester and Hallogen Limited; Lecturer, Manchester Business School, Ashridge and Henley. Publications: Regular articles for regional newspapers and magazines on corporate finance related matters. Prizes and awards: John Peacock Prize. Clubs and societies: Pro-Manchester; Prestbury Golf Club; Institute for Fiscal Studies; Manchester Law Society.
Interests: Classical music, opera, golf, good food and wine.
Contact details: Eversheds, Eversheds House, 70 Great Bridgewater St, Manchester M1 5ES (tel: 0161 831 8000, fax: 832 5337, email: edwardpysden@eversheds.com).

QUAYLE, Robert Samual, MSc, PhD, Ceng, MIEE

Positions: Dean of Undergraduate Studies, Faculty of Science and Engineering, University of Manchester; Senior Lecturer in Electrical Engineering, University of Manchester.
Areas of Influence: Education.
Profile: December 20th, 1948; *m*. Tessa; 1 daughter.
Career profile: Engineer, British Nuclear Fuels; has published research papers in areas of Digital Technology and Radar Signal Processing; Member of Marylebone Cricket Club and the Institute of Electrical Engineers.
Interests: Railways (model and full size), model engineering, classical music.
Contact details: School of Engineering, University of Manchester, Oxford Road, Manchester M13 9PL (email: r.s.quayle@man.ac.uk).

QUEALLY, Jason Paul, BSc Hons, MBE (2001)

Position: Professional Cyclist.
Areas of Influence: Sport.
Profile: *b*. May 11th, 1970; *m*. Vicky.
Educated at Lancaster Royal Grammar School and Lancaster University. Career profile: Commonwealth Games, Silver Medal, 1km Time Trial (1998); World Championships, Silver Medal, Olympic Sprint (1999); Olympic Games, Gold Medal, 1km Time Trial (2000); Olympic Games, Silver Medal, Olympic Sprint (2000); National Championships, Gold Medal, 1km Time Trial (2000); World Championships, Silver Medal, Olympic Sprint (2000); World Championships, Bronze Medal, 1km Time Trial (2000); National Championships, Gold Medal, Olympic Sprint (2001); World Championships, Bronze Medal, Olympic Sprint (2001);

Commonwealth Games, Silver Medal, 1km Time Trial (2002); Commonwealth Games, Silver Medal, Olympic Sprint (2002). Member of Lancaster Cycling Club.
Interests: Food, relaxing.
Contact details: (tel: 07779 305742).

QUINLAN, Rt. Rev. Monsignor Michael, DCL (1969)

Position: Vicar General and Chancellor, Diocese of Salford; Provost of the Cathedral Chapter.
Areas of Influence: Faith Groups, Law.
Profile: *b.* October 14th, 1942.
Education: Primary and Secondary Education at C.B.S. Schools, Tralee, County Kerry, Ireland; Philosophy Theology, All Hallows College, Dublin (1960-66); Post-Graduate Studies, Pontifical University Maynooth (1966-69); Sacred Roman Rota, Rome (1969-70). Career profile: Ordained Priest, 19th June, 1966, and appointed to St Mary's, Mulberry Street Manchester and Matrimonial Tribunal; Judicial Vicar, Diocese of Salford (1973 - 1992); Chancellor of Diocese of Salford (1974); Chaplain of Honour to the Pope (1977); Prelate of Honour (1983); Vicar General of Diocese of Salford (1988); Our Lady's Parish, Haigh, Wigan (1992). Publications: *Marriage and Family*; *Parental Rights and Admission of Children to the Sacraments of Initiation*; *Due Process of Law and Ombudsman*; *The Impediments of Affinity and Consanguinity*.
Interests: Golf, sport, history, archaeology.
Contact details: Cathedral House, 250 Chapel Street, Salford M3 5LL (tel: 0161 834 9052, fax: 0161 839 7027, email: *m*.quinlan@salforddiocese.org).

RABBITT, Professor Patrick Michael Anthony, PhD, MA, MSc, DSc

Positions: Research Chair of Cognitive Psychology and Gerontology; Director, Age and Cognitive Performance Research Centre, University of Manchester (1983 - present).
Areas of Influence: Science, Health, Education.
Profile: *b.* September 23rd, 1934. *m.* Dorothy Bishop; 1 son; 2 daughters.
Education: Sir Joseph Williams Mathematical School, Rochester, Kent; University of Cambridge. Career profile: Medical Research Council, Applied Psychology Research Unit (1962-68); Lecturer, Psychology, University of Oxford (1968-82); Professor and Head of Department, University of Durham (1982-83); Adjunct Professor, University of Western Australia (1990 -). Clubs and Societies: British Psychology Society; Experimental Psychology Society; British Society for Gerontology; British Neuropsychology Society.
Interests: Chess, walking.
Contact details: University of Manchester, Age & Cognitive Performance Research Centre, Oxford Road, Manchester M13 9PL (tel: 0161 275 7335, fax: 0161 275 2873, email: rabbitt@psy.man.ac.uk); 37 Birch Polygon, Manchester M14 5HX (tel: 0161 224 2944, email: prabbitt@btinternet.com).

RACE, Robert Topham, BSc Hons, FSI, ASIP

Positions: Managing Director, Brewin Dolphin Securities, Manchester Office; Chairman, North West Regional Advisory Group, The London Stock Exchange; Member of AIM Advisory Group, The London Stock Exchange, Deputy Chairman of Pro-Manchester, the Manchester Professional Services Association.
Areas of Influence: Finance.

Profile: *b.* June 13th, 1962; *m.* Lorraine; 4 sons.
Educated at Manchester Grammar School and The City University, London. Member of St.James's Club.
Contact details: Brewin Dolphin Securities, National House, 36 St Ann Street, Manchester M60 2EP (tel: 0161 839 4222, fax: 0161 832 9092, email: robert.race@brewin.co.uk).

RADCLIFFE, Mark, BA (Hons) (1979)

Positions: Presenter, Radio One, Radio Two, Five Live and Radio Four (1986 - present).
Areas of Influence: Media
Profile: *b.* June 29th, 1958; *m.* Bella; 3 daughters.
Education: Bolton School; BA English, American Studies and Classical Civilisation, Manchester University. Career profile: Piccadilly Radio (1979-83); Radio One (1983-85); Piccadilly Radio (1985-86). Publications: *Showbusiness: Diary of a Rock and Roll Nobody*. CDs: *Worst Album in the World Ever* (1997), *Our Kid A* (2001), *Songs of the Bach Bar* (1999), *On the Razzle* (2002), all with his band, *The Family Mahore*. Awards: 4 Sony Gold Awards.
Interests: The Family Mahore, Manchester City FC.
Contact details: BBC, Oxford Road, Manchester M60 1SJ (tel: 0161 200 2020, fax: 0161 244 4188, email: mark.radcliffe@bbc.co.uk).

RAFFLE, Tim, MA, ACA

Position: Managing Director, ECI ventures LTD.
Areas of Influence: Finance, Commerce.
Profile: *b.* November 7th, 1962; *m.* Jennifer; 2 sons.
Educated at Manchester Grammar School (1973-80) and Christ's College, Cambridge (1981-84). Career profile: Peat Marwick Mitchell (1984-89); BP Chemicals (1989-90). Clubs and societies: Climbers Club; Leander Club.
Interests: Climbing, skiing.
Contact details: ECI Ventures LTD, St. Andrews Chambers, 20 Albert Square, Manchester M2 5PE (tel: 0161 831 3200, fax: 0161 831 3201, email: tim.raffle@eciv.co.uk); Cramond House, Regent Road, Altrincham WA14 1RR.

RAFFLES, Ralph Leslie Stamford, KStJ, OM (USA), DStJ, TD, JP, DL, FInstPI

Positions: President, United Kingdom Association of Consular Organisations; Consul for Monaco; Bailli Delegue for Great Britian; Chaine des Rotisseurs; Vice-President, Grenadier Guards Association; Member, South Manchester Health Authority; Magistrate, City of Manchester; Chevalier, 11 French Wine Orders; Hon.

Col. Commonwealth of Kentucky USAAF.
Areas of Influence: Commerce, Health, Voluntary Sector.
Profile: *b.* May 5th, 1920, Manchester; *m.* Sally Sieff; 3 sons; 1 daughter.
Educated at Cuckfield House, Sussex, Manchester Grammar School and Manchester
University. War Service: Oxford and Bucks Light Infantry, Service in France, Africa,
India and Burma (1939-46); 5 Bn Kings Own Regt (TA) (1947-54). Career profile: High
Sherrif, Greater Manchester (1979); Deputy Lord Lieutenent; Chairman, North
Manchester HMC (1964); Member, National Whitley Council (1966); Member, Parole
Board Strangeways Prison (1967); President, Manchester Consular Association (1969,
1981); Chairman, Radio Manchester BBC (1975); Chairman, GM Youth Association
(1975); President Cresta Run (1956). Founder of Manchester VSO; Founder of North
West Kidney Research; Co-founder of Les Chasseurs Alpins Sous Marins; Member of
winning GB Bobsleigh Team for European Cup (1956); Member of British Olympic
Bobsleigh Team (1956); Member of British Sandyacht Team attempt on world speed
record. Clubs and societies: International Sportsmen; St Moritz Toboggan; Royal
Ocean Racing; Lyceum.
Interests: Family, fund raising for charity, skin and scuba diving, haute cuisine and
wine drinking, music, ocean racing.
Contact details: Monaco Consulate, Dene Manor, Dene Park, Didsbury, Manchester
M20 2GF (tel: 0161 445 4908, fax: 0161 445 9174).

RAMSDEN, Professor Richard Thomas, MBChB (1968), FRCS (1972)

Positions: Professor of Otolarygology, University of Manchester; Consultant
Otolarygologist, Manchester Royal Infirmary (1977 – present).
Areas of Influence: Health, Education.
Profile: *b.* December 30th, 1944; *m.* Eileen Gillian; 3 sons, 2 daughters.
Education: Madras College, St Andrews (1956-62); University of St Andrews (1962-
68). Career profile: Registrar (1971-73), Senior Registrar (1973-74), Otolarygology,
Royal National Throat, Nose, Ear Hospital, London; Senior Registrar, Otolarygology,
The London Hospital (1974-77); Clinical Director Department of Otolarygology,
Manchester Royal Infirmary. Clubs and Societies: Wilmslow Golf Club; New (Golf)
Club, St Andrews; St Andrews Society of Manchester.
Interests: Survival.

RANDALL, Jill Margaret

Positions: Artist and Sculptor in site-specific work and sited work in public spaces;
Associate Lecturer, B.A.(Hons) Visual Arts Course, University of Salford.
Areas of Influence: Arts, Education.
Profile: *b.* December 14th, 1958.
Education: Falmouth School of Art, B.A Hons Fine Art (sculpture), (1981);

Manchester Polytechnic, M.A Fine Art (sculpture) (1983). Group Exhibitions: *New Contempories*, ICA, London (1980); *Changing Tack*, Castlefield Gallery, Manchester (1990); *Ten*, Cornerhouse, Manchester (1995). Solo Exhibitions: *Barcelona Works* Le Chat Noir Gallery, London (1992); *Last Voyage of the Gilt Dragon*, Perth, Western Australia (1994); *Terra Incognita*, Turnpike Gallery, Leigh (1997). Residencies: Magnesium Electron, Salford (2000-02); Claremont School of Art, Perth, Western Australia (1994); Barcelona, McColl Arts Foundation Travel Scholarship (1991). Commisions: Irwell Sculpture Trail (2001); Tissington and High Peak Trails Interpretation Project (2001); Grizedale Forest Sculpture Residency (1999); Tacchi-Morris Arts Center, Taunton, Somerset (1999); Tay Square, Dundee (1997); Wharfside, Salford Quays, Manchester (1993); George Street Pocket Park, Oldham (1993); Museum of Science and Industry, Manchester (1990). Founder Member, Sculptors in Greater Manchester Association; Director, Mart Network, Organizers of Mart 99 Visual Arts Festival, Manchester. Publications: *Terra Incognita*, Exhibition Catologue (1997); *Pristine*, small artists book (2001). Awards: Oppenheim - John Downes Memorial Award (1990); Royal Society of Arts 'Art for Architecture' Award (1994); Foundation for Sport and the Arts Travel Award (1994); North West Arts Board (1994) (2000). Member, Public Art Forum.
Contact details: S.I.G.M.A, Top Floor, Terres Building, Ellesmere Street, Manchester M15 4LZ (tel: 01706 879 392, fax: 01706 879 392, email: alanbirch@ambirch.freeserve.co.uk).

RAPER, Stuart John

Position: Head Coach, Wigan Warriors.
Areas of Influence: Sport.
Profile: *b.* January 5th, 1965; *m.* Cathy; 1 son, Jake; 1 daughter, Maddison.
Career profile: Professional Rugby League, Australia (1983-93); Coach, Cronulla Sharks lower grades (1994); Assistant 1st Team Coach, Cronulla Sharks (1995-97); NSW Under18's Coach (1996); Head Coach, Castlefield, finished 8th (1997); Head Coach, Castlefield, finished 6th (1998); Head Coach, Castlefield, finished 3rd (1999); Head Coach, Castlefield, finished 5th (2000); Wigan RLFC, Grand Finalists (2001); Wigan RLFC, Challenge Cup Winners (2002)
Interests: Surfing, drummer, golf, obsessive rugby league person.
Contact details: Wigan Warriors, Louvre Drive, Robin Park WN5 0UH (tel: 01942 774 000).

RARITY, Brian Stewart Hall, MA PhD, FRAS.

Positions: CEO, Corpfin Ltd and Corpfin Worldwide Ltd; Director, Financier Worldwide Ltd; Chairman, Portico Library Trust; Hon. Treasurer, Manchester Chamber Concerts Society (1999 - present).

Areas of Influence: Finance, Media, Arts.
Profile: *b.* May 15th, 1938; *m.* Patricia. 4 sons.
Educated at Airdrie Academy, Glasgow University, and Manchester University. Career profile: Mathematician, English Electric Aviation / British Aerospace; Senior Research Fellow, California Institute of Technology; Lecturer / Senior Lecturer, Dept. of Mathematics, University of Manchester; CEO, Applied Financial Information LLP, Los Angeles. Dr Brian Rarity has published various papers in applied mathematics. Clubs and societies: President (1986-88), Vice President (1988-91), Hon Secretary (1982-86), Manchester Literary and Philosophical Society; member of Manchester Chamber Concerts Society.
Interests: Music, photography.
Contact details: Corpfin Worldwide Ltd, Bank Chambers, Faulkner Street, Manchester M1
4EH (tel: 0161 2367754, fax: 01612362672, email: brian.rarity@corpfinworldwide.com); Highstone Wycke, Whitehough, Chinley, High Peak SK23 6BX.

RATCLIFFE, Paul Andrew, BSc Hons

Position: Professional Athlete, Canoeist.
Areas of Influence: Sport.
Profile: *b.* November 12th, 1973.
Education: Fred Longworth High School; Eccles Sixth Form College; Nottingham Trent University, BSc Hons Degree, Maths and Chemistry. Career profile: World Team Champion (1997); World Number 1, World Cup Champion, European Champion (1998); World Number 1, World Cup Champion, World Championships Bronze (1999); Olympic Silver Medal, World Number 1, World Cup Champion (2000); UK Champion (2001); European Champion (2002); Amateur Sports Personality, Nottingham (1998 and 2000); Member of: Llangollen Canoe Club; Vice Patron NSMI.
Interests: Golf, football.

RAYMOND, Peter, BSc, ACST, MBS (1973)

Position: Chairman, Tepnel Life Sciences Plc; Director: Contra Vision; Director, Sheffield University Enterprises Ltd; Chairman, BIONOW; Deputy Chairman, Mersey BIO; Member, Parliamentary Scientific Committee.
Areas of Influence: Education, Commerce.
Profile: *b.* December 10th, 1938; *m.* Dorothy Elisabeth; 3 sons; 1 daughter.
Educated at UMIST. Career profile: Joint Owner, Compounding Ingredients Ltd (1973-83); Director, Corporate Development, Europe (1983-89); Managing Director, UMIST Ventures Ltd (1989-97); Chairman, Tepnel Life Sciences Plc (1997-02); CEO, Tepnel Life Sciences Plc (1998-01); Director, 20 new companies started at UMIST

(1992-97). Clubs and societies: Manchester Football Club; Grove Park Squash Club
Interests: Reading, writing, music, sport, chess, travel, family.
Contact details: Tepnel Life Sciences Plc, Heron House, Crewe Road, Wythenshawe, Manchester M23 9HZ (tel: 0161 946 2205, fax: 0161 946 2211, email: praymond@tepnel.co.uk); 72 Grasmere Road, Gatley, Cheshire SK8 4RS (tel: 0161 428 9102, fax: 0161 428 3686, email: raymo39@attglobal.net).

RAYNOR, Howard Kingsley, BA (Hons), MBA

Position: Chief Executive, Hallogen Group (2098 - present).
Areas of Influence: Arts, Education, Media
Profile: *b.* November 24th, 1960; *m.* Teresa; 2 sons.
Educated at Turton High School, Bromley Cross, Bolton (1973-80); University of Liverpool (1980-83); Cranfield University School of Management (1996-98). House Manager, Derngate, Northampton (1983-87); Deputy House Manager, Barbican, London (1987-89); Deputy Director, Derngate, Northampton (1989-93); General Manager, Derngate, Northampton (1993-98); Chief Executive, Hallogen Ltd (1998-01); Board Member and Director, NW Arts Board. Clubs and societies: Fellow, RSA; Member, National Trust; Associate Member, International Society for the Performing Arts; Company Secretary, Association of British Concert Promoters Ltd; Trustee, Bridgewater Hall Community Education Trust; Honorary life member of Liverpool University Students Union.
Interests: Howard Raynor is a keen advocate of arts and culture in both education and commerce.
Contact details: Bridgewater Hall, Manchester M2 3WS (tel: 0161 950 0000, fax: 0161 950 0001, email: hkr@bridgewater-hall.co.uk); 143 Buxton Road, Hazel Grove, Stockport (email: hkr@lineone.net).

REES, Trevor Merion Emlyn, BSc Hons, F.C.A

Positions: Head, Govenment Services in the North KPMG; Chair of Governors, Ducie High School.
Areas of Influence: Public Sector, Education.
Profile: *b.* November 30th, 1957; *m.* Alison; 3 sons.
Educated at Lancaster Royal Grammar School (1967-75) and Manchester University (1976-79). Career profile: KPMG 1980-present; Qualified Chartered Accountant (1983); Internal Secondments, Corporate Recovery, Corporate Finance; External Secondments, NHS (6 months), Manufacturing Company (6 months); Partner, KPMG, specialising in public sector/government services; Fellow Institute of Chartered Accountants in England and Wales. Member of Tytherington Golf and Leisure Club.
Interests: Golf, swimming, walking, giving something back to the community.

Contact details: KPMG, St. James Square, Manchester M2 6DS (tel: 0161 838 4063, fax: 0161 838 4096, email: trevor.rees@kpmg.co.uk) 6 Weybridge Drive, Macclesfield, Cheshire SK10 2UP (tel: 01625 619 106).

REGAN, Martin Peter

Positions: Director, Excel Publishing (1991 - present); Managing Director, Agency Central; Executive Editor, En, The Magazine for Entrepreneurs; Director, Manchester City Small Shareholders Association; Committee Member, Cheshire and North Wales Chess Association; Delegate, British Chess Federation.
Areas of Influence: Media, Commerce, Arts.
Profile: *b.* August 14th, 1962; *m.* Shirley; 2 sons; 2 daughters.
Educated at Newall Green High School, Wythenshawe; Business Journalist and Author with Wall Street Journal, Financial Times, Sunday Times, North West Times, Daily Telegraph; Editor, North West Insider; Local Government Executive; author of numerous childrens cartoon books and short stories; awarded 'man most likely to start an argument' NGHS (1978). Clubs and societies: Styal Golf Club, Wilmslow Chess Club, and the NWCCA; Captain, North Wales and Cheshire Chess Team.
Interests: Golf, football, chess, philately, avidly collects work by northern artists.
Contact details: EXCEL Publishing Company, Portland Buildings, 127 Portland Street, Manchester (tel / fax: 0161 236 2782, email: Regan@execlpublishing.co.uk).

REID, Professor Steven Robert, FREng (1993), BSc, PhD (Manchester)
MA, ScD (Cambridge), FIMchE, FASME, CMath, FIMA, FRSA

Positions: Conoco Professor of Mechanical Engineering, Dept. of Mech. Aero., and Manufacturing Eng, UMIST (1985 - present); Pro-Vice Chancellor, Research, UMIST (2001 - present); Chairman, UMIST Research Committee; Church Elder, Poynton, Baptist Church.
Areas of Influence: Education.
Profile: *b.* May 13th, 1945; *m.* Susan; 3 sons.
Education: Chorlton Grammar School; The University of Manchester, BSc 1st Class Hons, Maths (1966); The University of Manchester, PhD Mathematics (1969); MA, The University of Cambridge (2001); ScD, The University of Cambridge (1991). Career profile: Research Officer, Engineering Sciences Division, Central Electricity Research Laboratories, Leatherhead, Surrey (1969-70); Lecturer, Department of Mechanical Engineering, UMIST (1970-76); Lecturer, Engineering Department, University of Cambridge (1976-80); Jackson Professor of Engineering Science, University of Aberdeen (1980-84); Pro-Vice Chancellor for Academic Development, UMIST (1992-95); Deputy Principal and Vice Chancellor, UMIST (1994-95); Visiting Professor of Mechanical Engineering, Hong Kong Polytechnic University (1996); President, Institute of Mathematics and its Applications (2000-01). Stephen Reid has

published over 190 papers which reflect his research interests. Broadly they include plastic deformation of metals, dynamic structural plasticity, inelastic deformation of fibre-reinforced composite materials and structures, micromechanics of cellular materials under static and dynamic loading, impact energy absorption, gross deformation of structures and materials, and safety of nuclear plant, pipe-whip in particular; Safety Award in Mechanical Engineering (1982); Best Paper Awards, Composite Materials Division, ASME (1989).
Contact details: Dept. of Mech. Aero. & Manf. Eng., UMIST, PO Box 88, Manchester M60 1QD (tel: 0161 200 3848, fax: 0161 200 3849, email: steve.reid@umist.ac.uk).

RICHENS, Nigel John BA FCA

Positions: Partner, Pricewaterhouse Coopers; Member ICAEW.
Areas of Influence: Finance.
Profile: *b.* December 28th, 1955; *m.* Liz; 1 son; 2 daughters.
Education: King Edward VII School, Lytham; Manchester University. Career pofile: Accountant, PricewaterhouseCoopers (1979); Manager, Pricewaterhouse Coopers (1982); Senior Manager, PricewaterhouseCoopers (1984); Partner, PricewaterhouseCoopers, Manchester (1988).
Interests: Golf, skiing.
Contact details: PricewaterhouseCoopers, 101 Barbirolli Square, Lower Moseley Street, Manchester M2 3PW (tel: 0161 245 2000, fax: 0161 247 4101, email: nigel.richens@uk.pwcglobal.com).

RICKITT, Peter Edward, FCA, NSI

Position: Chairman, Rickitt Mitchell & Partners Ltd (1976 - present); Director, CD Bramall Plc, Mason Williams Ltd and Scott Lang Group Ltd.
Areas of Influence: Finance.
Profile: *b.* January 6th, 1947; *m.* Jill; 4 sons.
Educated at Sedburgh School. Career profile: Corporate Finance Executive, Wm. Brandt's Sons & Co Ltd (1968-71); Director, Henry Ausbacher & Co Ltd. (1972-76). Clubs and societies: Manchester Tennis and Racquets Club; North of England Zoological Society; Aston Martin Owners Club; Lagonda Car Club; BRSCC.
Interests: Motorsport.
Contact details: Rickitt Mitchell & Partners Ltd, Clarance House, Clarence Street, Manchester M2 4DW (tel; 0161 834 0600, fax: 0161 834 0452, email: peter@rickittmitchell.com); Mill House, Cuddington, Cheshire (tel: 01606 301 373).

RILEY, Harold Francis, DL, DLit, DFA, MA

Position: Artist.
Areas of Influence: Arts, Education, Sport.
Profile: *b.* December 21st, 1934; *m.* Ashraf Danesh-Riley; 2 daughters.
Education: Salford Grammar School; Slade School of Fine Art, University College, London (1953-57); Institute of Education, University of London (1958); Courtauld Institute, University of London; Travel Scholarships to Italy and Spain. Harold Riley is a painter from a family of Artisans, Artists and Musicians in Lancashire. After studies he was commissioned into the Army during National Service. He then returned to Salford to complete a scheme with L S Lowry to record Salford and its environs for 100 years. He has painted the portraits of 4 American presidents, 3 Popes, and is court painter to the English Royal Family. He is best known world-wide for his paintings of soccer and golf, and he played for Manchester United as a junior. Harold has been the subject of 8 documentaries made by the BBC and Independent TV Companies (1964-01). An archive of his work is built and being formulated in Salford. Governor, BBC for the North of England; Chairman, National Exhibition of Children's Art; Papal Knight; Chairman, Irish Abroad Charitable Trust; Chairman, Salford Arts and Sports Trust; Director, Riley Archive. Publications include: Various facsimile sketchbooks, *A Swing for Life*; Ryder cup books. Prizes and awards: Young Contempories (1958); British University Art Exhibition, 1ˢᵗ Prize (1958); Slade School Still Life, Composition Prize (1958). Clubs and societies: St James Club; Sam Roane Club, Soto Grande, Spain; Loch Lomond Golf Club; Muirfield Village, Ohio, USA; Omaha Golf Club, Nebraska, USA.
Interests: Cinema, sport.
Contact details: The Riley Archive, Albion Place, The Crescent, Salford, M4 5NL (tel: 0161 736 7654, email: riley.archive@gconnect.com).

RILEY, Very Revd Kenneth Joseph, BA (Univ. of Wales 1961), MA (Oxon, 1968)

Positions: Dean of Manchester
Profile: *b.* June 25ᵗʰ, 1940; *m.* Margaret Denison; 2 daughters.
Education: Holywell Grammar School; University College of Wales, Aberystwyth; Linacre College, Oxford; Wycliffe Hall, Oxford. Career profile: Curate, Fazakerley, Liverpool (1964-66); Chaplain, Brasted Place College (1966-69); Chaplain, Oundle School (1969-75); Chaplain, Liverpool University (1975-83); Vicar, Mossley Hill, Liverpool (1975-83); Diocesan Warden of Readers (1979-93); Rural Dean of Childwall (1982-83); Vice-Dean of Liverpool Cathedral (1983-93); Member of Archbishop's Commission on Cathedrals (1992-94). Public Offices: Hon Chaplain, Greater Manchester Lieutenancy; Member of Court, Manchester University; Governor, Manchester Grammar School; Feoffee, Chetham's Hospital and Library; Governor, Chetham's School of Music; Director, Manchester Cathedral Development Trust;

Booth Centre for the Homeless. Publications: *Liverpool Cathedral*; various hymns. Prizes and awards: Robert Bryan Music Scholar (1958-61). Clubs and societies: St James's Club, Manchester.
Interests: Music, drama.
Contact details: Manchester Cathedral, Manchester M3 1SX (tel: 0161 833 2220, fax: 0161 839 6226).

RINK, Paul J.E, OBE (1985)

Positions: Chairman, Wolstenholme International LTD; Deputy Provincial Grand Master, Masonic Province, East Lancashire.
Areas of Influence: Commerce, Voluntary Sector.
Profile: *b.* December 18th, 1940; *m.* Marlene; 1 son; 1 daughter.
Educated at Sedbergh School, Cumbria. Career profile: Sales Director, Wolstenholme Bronze Powders LTD (1965); Joint Managing Director, Wolstenholme Rink PLC (1972); Managing Director, Wolstenholme Rink PLC (1999); Director, Blackburn Groundwork Trust; Member of: Rugby Football Union; Bolton Golf Club; MCC, Pleasington Golf Club.
Interests: Sports, music, walking.
Contact details: Wolstenholme International LTD (tel: 01254 874 750, fax: 01254 703 430) Anglezarke farm, White Coppice, Chorley, Lancashire PR6 9DF (tel: 01257 274 751).

ROACHE, William Patrick, MBE (2000)

Position: Actor.
Areas of Influence: Arts, Voluntary Sector.
Profile: *b.* April 25th, 1932; Sara McEwen Mottram; 2 sons; 1 daughter.
Educated at Michael House and Rydal School, Colwyn Bay. After leaving school at 19 William Roache joined the Royal Welch Fusiliers for National Service. He then continued as a regular army officer for 5 years serving in Germany, Jamaica and the Bahamas. He was then seconded to the Foreign Office to serve in the Persian Gulf where he kept peace between the Trucial Oman States. After 2 years he returned to England to start his acting career and appeared in several feature films including, *Behind the Mask, Bulldog Breed, His and Hers,* and *The Queens Guards.* This was followed by rep in Clackton-on-sea, Nottingham and Oldham and many TV appearances in *Knight Errant, Skyport, Biggles,* and *Ivanhoe.* In 1959 he was lead actor in the television Play of the Week *Making Time,* and then appeared in *Coronation Street* as Ken Barlow were he has been for the last 43 years. William is also Patron of Crimestoppers, in which he takes a very lively interest. Other charities he supports avidly are The Crocus Trust, Life Education Centres, and The East Cheshire Hospice. Publication: *Ken & Me.* Clubs and societies: Wilmslow Golf Club; Royal St George

Society; SPARKS; the Royal Variety Club.
Interests: Golf, dogs, family.
Contact details: Granada TV, Quay Street, Manchester M60 9EA (tel: 0161 832 7211).

ROBERT-BLUNN, John

Position: Journalist.
Areas of Influence: Arts, Media.
Profile: *b.* May 21st, 1936; 1 son; 1 daughter.
Educated at Burnage High School. Career profile: Student Librarian, Manchester Public Libraries (1952); Reporter, later Editor, Manchester City News (1957-60); The Scotsman, Edinburgh (1960); Music critic, news Sub Editor, Manchester Evening News (1960-93), also Arts Correspondent (1971); Founder chairman and Artistic Director, Forum Music Society (1972-85); Founder Hon Secretary, Friends of Manchester City Art Galleries (1979-83); Member, Manchester Lit & Phil (1974-85). Founded the monthly Manchester Charivari (1956). Publications: *Northern accent, the story of the Northern School of Music* (1972); Reviews and articles for various publications. Clubs and societies: Member, NUJ; National Trust; Cyclists Touring Club; Prayer Book Society; Friends of Manchester City Galleries; Director, The Edgeley Press.
Interests: Pursuing things and people of beauty, walking and cycling (claudication permitting).
Contact details: Molys Hyse, 39 Moscow Road, Edgeley, Stockport, Cheshire (tel / fax: 0161 477 0744, email: john@jr-b.co.uk).

ROBERTS, Professor Carole Alison, MSc, ILTM, RSS, ORS, SRHE

Positions: Dean, Faculty of Business and Informatics, University of Salford (2001 - present); Director, Learning and Teaching Research Centre, University of Salford (2002); Governor, Eccles Sixth Form College.
Areas of Influence: Education, Public Sector.
Profile: *b.* July 12th, 1948; *m.* Robert Burgess; 2 daughters.
Education: Nonsuch County Grammar School for Girls, Surrey (1959-66); University of Southampton (1966-69); University of Birmingham (1975-76). Career profile: Carole Roberts began her teaching career in 1969 at the City of London Polytechnic, now part of London Metropolitan University in the Business Studies Department. Due to marriage, she moved to Wrexham and joined the NE Wales Institue of HE. She joined the University of Salford in 1977 as a lecturer in quantitative business analysis, and in 1996 became the Sub-Dean of the Business Faculty. In 1999 she became Associate Dean of Business and Informatics before taking her current post and establishing the University's Learning and Teaching Research Network and Research Centre. Her research interests have been in the areas of statistics and

systems modelling, and she has published extensively in the area of modeling the epidemiology of HIV and AIDS.

Interests: Church, music, fair weather camping, classical concerts, singing, amateur operatics.

Contact details: Faculty of Business and Informatics, University of Salford, Salford M5 4WT (tel: 0161 295 5969, fax; 0161 295 3173, email: c.a.roberts@salford.ac.uk); Stone Lea, 27 Radcliffe Park Road, Salford M6 7WP (tel: 0161 737 4909).

ROBERTS, Geoffrey

Positions: Mayor of Wigan (2002-03); Auditor, Makerfield Constituency Labout Party.

Areas of Influence: Public Sector, Voluntary Sector.

Profile: *b.* May 5th, 1928 Bradford, Yorkshire; *m.* Betty (1953); 3 sons, David, Stuart and Andrew; 2 daughters, Sheila and Janet.

Educated at St Matthew's C of E Primary School and Carlton High School, Bradford; Civil Service (1944); Royal Navy conscription (1945); Demobilised (1948); Post Office Savings Bank, London (1948-50); Debit Control Officer, Health and Tradings Standards Department, Bradford (1950); Assistant Chief Lettings Officer, Housing Department, Bradford (1966); Senior Assistant, Housing Department Wigan County Borough (1967); Principal Assistant, Wigan (1974-88); A lifelong trade unionist, Geoff was actively associated with the Civil Service Clerical Association and the National and Local Government Officers Association. NALGO Branch Secretary, Bradford and Wigan; Yorkshire, Humberside, and North West / North Wales District and Provincial Councils; North West staff representative, National Joint Council, National Local Government Committee and the Conference Agenda Committee. Winstanley Branch Treasurer, Labour Party (1985-00); Planning and Development, Education, Housing and Public Protection Committees, Wigan Metropolitan Borough Council (1991); Housing Portfolio Holder, Labour Government (2001); Treasurer, Wigan Sea Cadet Corps; Founder member and Officer, Highfield Grange Community Association; He has led a team of Councillors who distributed EC tinned meat across half the borough over a four year period and has been a governor at both the Winstanley County Primary and St Matthew's C of E School for the past 11 years. He attends Wigan Baptist Church on Scarisbrook Street. Both Geoff and Betty raise funds for Barnados, Christian Aid, Salvation Army, and Scope.

Interests: Caravanning, football, supporter and season ticket holder of Leeds United.

Contact details: Mayoral Secretary, Town Hall, Library Street, Wigan WN1 1YN (tel: 01942 827 156, fax: 01942 827 451, email: c.charnock@mbc.gov.uk)

ROBERTS, John Edward

Positions: Chief Executive, United Utilities; Non Executive Director, Volex.
Areas of Influence: Public Sector.
Profile: *b.* March 2nd, 1946; m. Pam; 1 son; 1 daughter.
Educated at Oldershaw Grammar School, Wallasey and Liverpool University. Career profile: Graduate Trainee, MANWEB (1967); Chief Accountant (1984); Finance Director (1990); Managing Director (1991); Chief Executive (1992-95); Chief Executive Swalec, Hyder (1996); Chief Executive, Hyder Utilities (1997-99).
Interests: Scuba diving, watching cricket, listening to opera.
Contact details: United Utilities, Dawson House, Great Sankey, Warrington WA5 3LW (tel: 01925 237 005, fax: 01925 237 020, email: john.roberts@uuplc.co.uk).

ROBERTS, Kieran

Position: Producer, Coronation Street, Granada TV.
Areas of Influence: Media, Arts.
Profile: *b.* June 1st, 1961.
Education: Highcliffe Comprehensive School, Dorset (1972-77); Brockenhurst Sixth Form College, Hampshire (1977-79); University of Bristol. Career profile: Producer's assistant, Catalist Video, London (1983-84); Promotion Scriptwriter, Granada Television, Manchester (1984-86); Researcher, Entertainment and Arts (1986-89); Producer, Entertainment and Children (1989-94); Producer, Childrens Drama (1994-95); Producer, *Childrens Ward* (1995); Producer and Executive Producer, Childrens Drama (1995-98); Producer, *Emmerdale*, Yorkshire TV (1998-01); Producer, *At Home With the Braithwaites*, Yorkshire TV (2001); Producer, *Coronation Street* (2001 -).
Interests: Food, wine, literature, classical music, cinema, mountain sports.
Contact details: Producer, Coronation Street, Granada Content North, Granada TV, Quay St, Manchester M60 9EA (tel: 0161 8272704, email: kieran.Roberts @granadamedia.com).

ROBERTS, Laura Patricia, MSc, BA (Hons), MIHM

Positions: Chief Executive, North Manchester Primary Care Trust (2000 - present).
Areas of Influence: Health
Profile: *b.* October 22nd, 1960; *m.* Michael Connor; 2 sons.
Education: Lady Mary High School, Cardiff; University of Sheffield; University of Manchester, Institute of Science and Technology. Laura Roberts joined an NHS Management Training Scheme in Manchester before completing her MSc and working for ICL (UK) LTD for three years in Business Development and Consultancy. She then returned to the NHS and worked at Trafford Healthcare NHS Trust for almost ten years including a role as Director of Service Development.

Following this she spent a year at Ashworth Hospital as Assistant Chief Executive before commencing her current position.

Interests: Tennis, theatre, cinema.

Contact details: North Manchester Primary Care Trust HQ, 2nd Floor, Newton Silk Mill, Holyoak Street, Newton Heath, Manchester M40 1HA (tel: 0161 219 9404, fax: 0161 219 9430, email: Laura.roberts@northpct.manchester.nwest.nhs.uk).

ROBERTS, Peter Lewis, B.Sc

Positions: Leader, Rochdale Metropolitan Borough Council; North West Regional Assembly; Director, Rochdale Development Agency; Director, Development Board and Services Board, Manchester Airport; Chair, Rochdale Challenge Company; Chair, Rochdale Local Strategic Partnership; Executive Member, Association of Greater Manchester Authorities.

Areas of Influence: Public Sector, Education, Health.

Profile: *b.* June 2nd, 1946; *m.* Gillian Roberts; 1 daughter.

Educated at Gobowen Primary School, Shropshire; Oswsmy Boys High School, Shropshire; Leominster Grammar School, Herefordshire; Liverpool University. Career profile: Technical Support Consultant and Team Leader, ICL Manchester; Leader, Rochdale MBC (1997-); Ex Chair, Social Services (1986-90, 1996-97); Councillor (1982); Former Chair, Manchester Airport Group (2001-02); Member of Rochdale Labour Club.

Interests: Skiing, keep fit, football, classical music, theatre.

Contact details: Town Hall, Rochdale (tel: 01706 864 8000, fax: 01706 864 820) (tel: 01706 632 664).

ROBINS, Michael Raymond, BA (Econ), ACA

Position: Director, Manchester Office, 3i plc (2001 – present).

Areas of Influence: Finance, Commerce.

Profile: *b.* June 18th, 1968; *m.* Lilian; 1 son.

Educated at King Edward's School Birmingham (1979-86) and University of Manchester (1986-89). Career profile: Coopers & Lybrand, Birmingham (1989-93); 3i plc (1993 – present), Birmingham (1993-00), Edinburgh (2000-01).

Interests: Running, cycling, collecting whisky.

Contact details: 3i plc, The Observatory, Chapel Walks, Manchester M2 1HL (tel: 0161 819 4307, fax: 0161 833 9182, email: mike_robins@3i.com).

ROBINSON, Angela Bridie (Angie)

Positions: Chief Executive and Director, Chamber of Commerce and Industry, Manchester.
Areas of Influence: Commerce, Media, Industry.
Profile: *b.* May 10th, 1957; *m.* John Robinson; 1 son; 1 daughter.
Education: Westwood High School, Leek, Staffordshire; Shrewsbury College; Madeley College of Education. Career profile: Manpower Services Commission, Employment Service and Training Division (1977-90); Training and Management Consultant, Training for Advancement, Stoke-On-Trent (1990-91); Deputy Chief Executive, Staffordshire Training and Enterprise Council (1991-97); Chief Executive, Shropshire Chamber of Commerce, Training and Enterprise (1997-2000); Director, Chamber Business Enterprises; Director, Marketing Manchester; Director, Progress Trust; Director, N.W Chambers of Commerce LTD; Director, Mandate; Governor, Salford College; Trustee, GMP Shrievalty Trust; Trustee, MCCI Pension Fund. Publications: Co-Author, *Through the glass ceiling* (1993). Clubs and societies: Institute of Directors.
Interests: Reading, walking, entertaining.
Contact details: Churchgate House, 56 Oxford Street, Manchester M60 (tel: 0161 237 4102, fax: 0161 237 3277, email: angela.robinson@mcci.org.uk).

ROBINSON, Edna J, MA, RGN, RM

Position: Chief Executive, Salford Primary Health Care Trust.
Areas of Influence: Health, Public Sector.
Profile: *b.* January 1st, 1951; *m.* Derek Thomas; 2 daughters.
Educated at Queen Elizabeth Grammar School and Manchester University. Career profile: General Manager, NHS; Professional Midwife and Nurse; Health Care Experience, USA; Inner City Regeneration Initiatives, focuses on health issues. Director, Lets Get Serious Ltd; Chair, Chesham Nature Reserve, Bury.
Interests: Social exclusion and psychological issues relating to young people, green environment sustainability issues.
Contact details: Salford Primary Care Trust, 2nd Floor, St. James's House, Pendleton Way, Salford M6 5FW (tel: 0161 212 4821, fax: 0161 212 4838, email: edna.robinson @salford-pct.nhs.uk).

ROBINSON, Jason

Positions: Fullback, England and Sale Sharks.
Areas of Influence: Media, Sport.
Profile: *b.* July 30th, 1974; *m.* Amanda. 3 sons; 1 daughter.
Education: Secondary; Career profile: Highest profile Rugby player in the Northern

Hemisphere; won every medal available in Rugby League; British Lion.
Interests: Religion, spending time with the family.

ROBSON, Andrew Edward, BA (Hons), BArch, RIBA

Positions: Director, Aedas AHR Architects Ltd; Vice-Chair, Manchester Conservation Area and Historic Buildings Panel.
Areas of Influence: Commerce, Arts.
Profile: *b.* November 24th, 1958; *m.* Jan; 1 stepson.
Educated at Liverpool University, School of Architecture and King Williams College, Isle of Man. Career profile: Partner, Holford Associates; Partner, Abbey Holford Rowe; Manchester Civic Society Victorian City Award for 201 Deansgate (1998). Clubs and societies: Council Member, Manchester Society of Architects; Corporate Member, British Council for Offices.
Interests: Design, sailing, walking, travel.
Contact details: Aedas AHR Architects Ltd, Sunlight House, Quay Street, Manchester M3 3JZ (tel: 0161 828 7900, fax: 0161 828 7930, email: andy.robson@aedas.com).

ROBSON, Brian Turnbull, M.A, PhD, M.A

Positions: Professor, Geography, Manchester University; Director, Centre for Urban Policy Studies.
Areas of Influence: Education, Public Sector.
Profile: *b.* February 23rd, 1939; *m.* Glenna.
Educated at Royal Grammar School, Newcastle-Upon-Tyne and St. Catharine's College, Cambridge. Career profile: Lecturer, UCW, Aberystwyth (1964-67); Harkness Fellow, University of Chicago (1967-68); Lecturer, Cambridge University; Fellow, Fitzwilliam College (1968-77); Professor, Manchester University (1977-); Dean, Arts Faculty, Manchester University (1988-90); Pro-Vice Chancellor, Manchester University (1993-97); President, Institute of British Geographers (1991-93); Member, Urban Task Force (1999-2000); Member, Urban Sounding Board (2001-); President, Manchester Statistical Society (1995-97). Chairman, Manchester Council for Voluntary Services (1986-92); Chairman, Manchester Settlement (1990-97). Publications: 8 books; 100 articles and research reports. Clubs and societies: Royal Geographical Society; Town and Country Planning Association; Manchester Statistical Society; Manchester Literary and Philosophical Society.
Interests: Gardening, water colour painting.
Contact details: School of Geography, Manchester University, Manchester M13 9PL (tel: 0161 275 3639, fax: 0161 275 7878, email: brian.robson@man.ac.uk); 32 Oaker Avenue, Manchester M20 2XH.

RODEN, Angela, BA (Hons), MIF

Positions: Director of Appeals, Christie Hospital (1995 - present); Proprietor, Portico Library; Director, Manchester Camerata; Trustee, Edward Holt Trust.
Areas of Influence: Health, Voluntary Sector, Public Sector.
Profile: *b.* June 22nd, 1949; *m.* Mike; 2 daughters.
Educated at St Philomena's School, Surrey. Career profile: Equal Opportunities Commission (1977-82); Greater Manchester Council for Voluntary Service (1982-86); Director of Field Operations, National Association of Citizen's Advice Bureaux (1986-95).
Interests: Walking, Wordsworth, theatre, Beatles, Bartok, Bob Dylan.
Contact details: Appeals Office, Christie Hospital, Manchester M20 4BX (tel: 0161 446 3988, fax: 0161 446 3991, email: appeal@christies.org).

ROEBUCK, Valerie Jean, MA, PHD (CANTAB)

Position: Writer; Lecturer; Translator; Honorary Research Fellow, University of Manchester.
Areas of Influence: Education, Faith Groups, Arts.
Profile: *b.* February 13th, 1950; *m.* Peter.
Education: Letchworth Grammar School (1961-69); BA Hons (Class 1) Oriental Studies (1973), PhD, Oriental Studies (1979), Newnham College, University of Cambridge (1969-79). Publications: *The Circle of Stars: an Introduction to Indian Astrology* (1992); *The Upanisads* (2000). Publications: Articles on various aspects of Indian arts, culture and religion. Clubs and societies: Hon. Secretary, Manchester Interfaith Forum; British Association for the Study of Religions; Manchester Samatha Association.
Interests: Meditation, inter-faith relations, pottery.
Contact details: 10 Lynwood Avenue, Whalley Range, Manchester M16 8JZ (tel: 0161 860 4716, email: vjroebuck@macunlimited.net).

ROGERS, Michelle Mary, BSc

Position: Sports Person.
Areas of Influence: Sport.
Profile: *b.* June 21st, 1976.
Education: Grosvenor Road Primary School, Swinton (1980-87); Moorside High School, Swinton (1987-92); Eccles College (1992-95); Liverpool John Moores University (1996-01). Career profile: Practising Judo since 1986. Started at St Pauls Judo Club in Monton and then various clubs around the North West. Michelle Rogers has been a member of the British Team since 1991, has had over one hundred caps and has earned more than forty international medals including Gold in The

Commonwealth Games, Manchester 2002 and World Student Champion, Beijing 2001. Member of British Judo Association; British Olympic Association; Urmston Judo Club.
Interests: Cycling, music, travelling, family, friends.
Contact details: Mobile: 07796 235 266.

ROSE, Noah

Position: Professional Self Employed Sculptor.
Areas of Influence: Arts.
Profile: *b*. December 13th, 1965.
Education: Creighton Comprehensive, North London (1977-84); Art & Design Foundation, Middlesex Polytechnic (1984-85); BA (Hons) 3 Dimensional Design, Manchester Polytechnic (1985-88). On graduation, Noah Rose went to London to work as assistant to furniture designer Andre Dubreuil (1988-89). He then became a freelance animation artist (1989-91) before returning to Manchester in 1991. Since then he has developed his freelance sculptural practice, specialising in public art commissions. Creative works include: *Fish Tale* (2002); *Plasma Plasmawr* (2001); *Ribtide* (2000); *Wream* (1999); *Oscillate* (1998); *A Bee Beware* (1998); *Four Corners* (1997); *Tilt 1 & 2* (1997); *Celestial Seats and Broken Arcs* (1996); *Time Untied* (1995); *Station Gates* (1995); *Elephant Seat* (1994). He has also worked as an artist and designer on several event based projects, notably Holocaust Memorial Day in Manchester 2002 and as a freelance arts consultant for North West Arts Board and Trafford MBC Arts Service, amongst others. Member: British Artist Blacksmith Association.
Interests: Visual and performing arts, literature, music, travel, cartography, diving, cheese, whiskey.

ROSS, Hilary Muriel

Positions: Chairman, League of Jewish Women, North West Region; Justice of the Peace, Stockport (1983).
Areas of Influence: Voluntary Sector, Law.
Profile: *b*. February 25th, 1946; 1 son; 1 daughter.
Educated at Broughton High School for Girls (1957-64) and Didsbury College of Education (1964-67). Career profile: Primary School Teacher (1970); Voluntary Worker for League of Jewish Women (1978); Secretary, Chairman of Local Group (1983-91); Roles, Co-ordinator (1991-94); Publicity Officer (1994-99); Vice Chairman (1999-2002); Part time tour guide, Manchester United (1995-99). Prizes and awards: Distinction, Leadership course, League of Jewish Women. Clubs and societies: League of Jewish Women; WIZO; Manchester United.
Interests: Singing, watching football, music, theatre, cinema.

ROTHWELL, Professor Nancy Jane, BSc, DSc, FMedSci, FIBiol, FRSA

Positions: MRC Research Professor of Physiology, University of Manchester; President, British Neuroscience Association; Chairman, UK Life Science Committee.
Areas of Influence: Education.
Profile: *b*. October 2nd, 1955.
Education: Penworthan Girls Grammar School (1981-92); University of London (1973-81). Career profile: Royal Society Research Fellow, St Georges Medical School (1981-92); Reader, School of Biological Sciences.
Contact details: School of Biological Science, University of Manchester, Oxford Road, Manchester. M13 9PT (tel: 0161 275 5357, fax: 0161 275 5948, email: nancy.rothwell@man.ac.uk).

ROWBOTHAM, Sheila, BA (Oxon)

Positions: Reader, Sociology Department, Manchester University (2001-02); Co-ordinator, International Centre for Labour Studies.
Areas of Influence: Arts, Education, Media.
Profile: *b*. February 27th, 1943; 1 son.
Education: Hunmanby Hall Methodist School, nr Filey, Yorkshire; St Hilda's College, Oxford University; Chelsea College London University. Career profile: Lecturer, Liberal Studies, Chelsea College (1964-68); Extra Mural Lecturer, WEA London University (1968-80); Visiting Professor, Women's Studies, University of Amsterdam (1981-83); Research Officer, Economic Policy Unit, Greater Manchester London Council (1983-86); Course Tutor, MA Women's Studies, University of Kent (1987-91); Visiting Professor, University of Paris VIII (1989); Consultant Record Advisor, Women's Studies World Institute for Development Economic Research, UN University (1987-91); Consultant, Institute for New Technology, UN University (1992-93); Senior Research Fellow (Simon) (1993-94); Hon Doctorate in Social Studies, University of North London (1994); Research Fellow (Univ) (1995-00); Senior Lecturer (2000-01). Publications include: *Womens Resistance & Revolution* (1973); *Woman's Conciousness Man's World* (1973); *Hidden from History* (1973); *A Century of Women* (1997); *Promise of a Dream* (2000). Plays: *Friends of Alice Wheeldon; Hindsight*.
Interests: Films, swimming, historical sites.
Contact details: Sociology Department, Manchester University, Roscoe Building, Oxford Road, Manchester M13 9PL (tel: 0161 275 2921, email: sheila.rowbotham@man.ac.uk).

ROWLAND, Dr Christopher Selwyn, MA, ARAM, FRNCM, Dmus

Positions: Director of Chamber of Music, Royal Northern College of Music; Consultant in String Chamber Music, Chetham's School of Music; Trustee and

Member, London International String Quartet Foundation.
Areas of Influence: Education, Arts.
Profile: *b.* December 12, 1946; Lizzy (separated); 2 sons; 1 daughter.
Education: Buckhurst Hill CHS (1958-65); Trinity College, Cambridge (1965-68); Royal Academy of Music (1968-71). Career profile: Leader, Sartori Quartet, Sussex University (1970-71); Leader, Sartori Quartet, Lancaster University (1971-74); Leader, Fitzwilliam Quartet, Warwick University (1974-77); Leader, Fitzwilliam Quartet, York University (1977-84); Leader, Resident Quartet, Bucknell University, USA (1976-84); Professor, Chamber Music Yehudi Menuhin School (1990-98); Teacher, Chethams School of Music (1984 -); Course Director, Lake District Summer Music (1986 -); Director of, Chamber Music, RNCM (1984).
Interests: Christian Faith, sport, art, poetry, outdoors.
Contact details: Director of Chamber Music, Royal Northern College of Music, 124 Oxford Road, Manchester M13 9RD (tel: 0161 273 6283, email: chris.rowland@rncm.ac.uk); 22 Appleby Lodge, Wilmslow Road, Fallowfield, Manchester M14 9RD (tel: 0161 224 9010).

ROWLINSON, (Geoffrey) Mark, MA (Oxon), ARAM

Positions: Self employed Singer (1972 - present); Golf Writer (1991 - present).
Areas of Influence: Arts, Sport.
Profile: *b.* December 15th, 1948; Lavinia (nee Johnston); 2 sons; 1 daughter.
Education: BA (1971), MA (1974), Christ Church Oxford (1967-71); Leverhulme Postgraduate Fellowship, Royal Academy of Music (1972-74). Career profile: Lay Vicar, Westminster Abbey (1975-79); Senior Music Producer, BBC (1979-99). Publications: *The Times Guide to Golf Courses* (2001); *Globetrotter Golfer's Guide* (2001); *The World Atlas of Golf* (2002). Life member, Conwy Golf Club; Vice President, Lindow Cricket Club.
Interests: Golf, food and wine, gardening.
Contact details: 6 Sylvan Avenue, Wilmslow, Cheshire SK9 6LR (tel: 01625 527628, fax: 01625 521709, email: mark_rowlinson@telinco.co.uk).

RUBINSTEIN, Shelly, CPsychol, AFBPsS, BSc (Hons)

Positions: Director, Impact Consulting Business Psychologists Ltd (1994 - present); Chair, North West in Business; Non-Executive Director, Bury Healthcare NHS Trust; Member, BPS Division of Occupational Psychology Training Committee.
Areas of Influence: Commerce, Health, Faith Groups.
Profile: *b.* February 18th, 1959; *m.* Michael.
Education: North Manchester High School for Girls; City University London; Manchester University; UMIST; Postgrad Dip. in Social Admin.; BSc (Hons) Psychology; Dip. In Counselling; Level B, Psychometric testing; Chartered

Occupational Psychologist. Career profile: Personnel and Training Officer, ORT Training Centre (1982-85); Management Training Officer, Manchester City Council (1985-87); Professional Development Manager, NW Regional Health Authority (1987-90); OMD Consultants, NHS Internal Consultancy (1990-93). Shelly Rubinstein has presented at a range of conferences such as BPS and CHI. She has researched into stress in allied health professionals during major organisational change. She has facilitated the opening of a multi-faith centre at Fairfield Hospital, Bury and designed a teachers pack for Holocaust Education. Shelly was involved in voluntary youth work from the age of 15 to age 24. She is interested in change management within the public sector to bring about improved services for consumers. She has been involved in multi faith education and managing diversity since the 1980s as part of various voluntary organisations and charitable groups. She has carried out investigations into workplace bullying and appeared as an expert witness in this areas as well as appearing on TV as a psychologist for the BBC. Clubs and societies: '2nd Generation', children of Holocaust Survivors Group; Associate Fellow of British Psychological Society.
Interests: Bridge, yoga.
Contact details: 205 Bury Old Road, Prestwich, Manchester M25 1JF (tel: 0161 773 3709, fax: 0161 798 5960, email: shelly@impactconsulting.co.uk).

RUMBELOW, His Honour Judge Arthur Anthony, BA, QC

Positions: Circuit Judge (2002 – present); Recorder of the Court; Queens Counsel; Chairman, Mental Health Review Tribunal (2001 - present).
Areas of Influence: Law.
Profile: *b.* September 9th, 1943; 3 daughters.
Education: Salford Grammar School; Queens College, Cambridge (Squire Scholar). Career profile: Called to the Bar, Honorable Society of the Middle Temple (1967); Recorder of the Crown Court (1988); Chairman, Medical Appeal Tribunal (1988-02); Queens Counsel (1990).
Interests: Food, drink, theatre, gardening.
Contact details: The Court Service, 15 Quay Street, Manchester M60 9FD.

RUNDELL, Clark Eugene

Position: Director of Contemporary Music, Royal Northern College of Music; Music Director, University of Manchester Symphony Orchestra; Freelance Conductor.
Areas of Influence: Arts, Education.
Profile: *b.* October 20th, 1961; Katharine; 1 son Christopher; 1 daughter Clara.
Education: Thomas Jefferson High School, Bloomington, Minnesota, USA (1980); Northwestern University, Chicago, Illinois, USA (1984). Career profile: Junior Fellow in Conducting, Royal Northern College of Music (1986). Fellow in Music Education,

Royal Northern College of Music; Director of Jazz Studies and of Contemporary Music, Royal Northern College of Music; Freelance Conducting, Hallé, BBC Philharmonic, Northern Sinfonia, BBC Concert Orchestra, Philharmonic Orchestra; Radio Presenter, BBC Radio 2,3 and 4 and GMR; Director, Daily Telegraph Young Jazz Project; Music Director, University of Manchester Symphony Orchestra; Merseyside Youth Orchestra; Youth Orchestra, RLPO.
Interests: Walking, wine, modern art.
Contact details: Royal Northern College of Music, 124 Oxford Road, Manchester M13 9RD (tel: 0161 907 5268, fax: 0161 273 7611, email: clark.rundell@rncm.ac.uk); Sunningdale, Rivermead Avenue, Hale Barns, Cheshire WA15 0AN (email: crundell@compuserve.com).

RUSSELL, Anthony Patrick QC, MA (Oxon)

Positions: Queen's Counsel; Recorder.
Areas of Influence: Law.
Profile: *b.* April 11th, 1951.
Educated at The Kings School, Chester (King's Scholar) and Pembroke College, Oxford. Career profile: Called to the Bar, Middle Temple (1974); In practice at Bar on Northern Circuit (1974); Standing Counsel to Inland Revenue (1994-96); Editor, Newsletter of Northern Circuit Clubs and societies: Member of: Oxford and Cambridge Club; Choir, St.Ann's Church.
Interests: Music (especially singing), photography (still and video), countryside.
Contact details: Peel Court Chambers, 45 Hardman Street, Manchester M3 3PL (tel: 0161 832 3791, fax: 0161 835 3054).

RUSSELL, David

Position: Owner, Property Alliance Group.
Areas of Influence: Commerce, Finance.
Profile: *b.* September 15th, 1956; 3 sons; 1 daughter.
Educated at Balderstone School, Rochdale. After completeing a joinery apprenticeship, David Russell went into sales and marketing before founding Farouche Kitchens (1980) which manufactures, installs and sells kitchems direct to the public. In 1986-87 Farouche had 36 branches nationwide. It was then sold to BET Plc. David then founded DRPH (1987), building a large and varied property portfolio incorporating industrial, commercial, residential, and retail sites. In 2002 Property Alliance Group was formed inccorporating DRPH and Pentith Construction.
Interests: Rugby, football, go-karting, cycling.
Contact details: Alliance Property Group, Alliance House, Westpoint Enterprise park, Clarance Avenue, Trafford park, Manchester M17 1QS (tel: 0161 868 4300, fax: 0161 872 0290, email: julie@propertyalliancegroup.com).

RUSSELL, Kenneth Clifton, MCIBS

Positions: Director of Corporate Banking, Bank of Scotland, Manchester; Chairman, Manchester Merchant and International Bankers Association (1999 - present).
Areas of Influence: Finance.
Profile: *b.* January 14th, 1951; *m.* Elizabeth; 2 daughters.
Educated at Glasgow Academy; Trainee Quantity Surveyor (1969-72); various Glasgow branches of the Bank of Scotland (1972-79); British Linen Bank Ltd (1980-99); Assistant Manager, BLB, Glasgow (1981); Manager, BLB, London (1985); Senior Manager, BLB, Manchester (1991); Assistant Director BLB Manchester (1997); Director Corporate Banking, BoS, Manchester (1999). Clubs and societies: Member of Hazel Grove Golf Club, Glasgow Academical Club and Poynton 41 Club (chairman 1996-97); Member, Chartered Institute of Bankers Scotland (MCIBS).
Interests: Golf, rugby, reading, gardening, voluntary work.
Contact details: Bank of Scotland, 19/21 Spring Gardens, Manchester M2 1FB (tel: 0161 251 6377, fax: 0161 251 6374, email: kenneth_russell@bankofscotland.co.uk); 38 Chester Road, Poynton, Cheshire SK12 1EU (tel: 01625 859 823, email: kenneth@russell49.fsnet.co.uk).

RYDER, Ernest Nigel, TD (1996), QC (1997)

Positions: Deputy High Court Judge (2000 - present); Member, Deans Court Chambers (1999 - present); Recorder of the Crown and County Courts (1997 - present); Assistant Boundary Commissioner; Member of the Lord Chancellor's Advisory Group on Children's Act / Judicial Case management (2002 - present); Trustee, Duke of Lancaster's own Yeomanry; Council Member, RFCA (NW); Trustee of various Army Trusts.
Areas of Influence: Law, Public Sector.
Profile: *b.* December 9th, 1957; *m.* Janette; 1 daughter.
Educated at Bolton School (1962-76) and Peterhouse, Cambridge (1976-79). Career profile: William Brandt Merchant Bank (1979-80); Inns of Court School of Law (1980-81); Pupillage with His Honour Judge Hall, and His Honour Judge Tetlow, 601 The Royal Exchange, Manchester; Member, 8 King Street Chambers (1981-99). Publications: Editor, *Clarke Hall & Morrison on Children*, Butterworths. Military History: Commisioned into the Duke of Lancaster's own Yeomanry (1981), Squadron Leader (1989-92); Squadron Leader, Royal Mercian & Lancastrian Yeomanry in the North West (1992-94).
Contact details: Deans Court Chambers, 24 St John Street, Manchester M3 4DF (tel: 0161 214 6000, fax: 0161 214 6001, email: ryder@deanscourt.co.uk).

RYLE, Sallie Elizabeth

Positions: Head of Media Relations, Granada North (1998); Trustee, Eureka Museum for Children, Halifax.

Areas of Influence: Media, Arts, Public Relations.

Profile: *b.* November 14th; *m.* Nicholas; 1 son; 1 daughter.

Educated at Ilkley Grammar School and Horsforth College of Further Education. Career profile: Joined Yorkshire Television (1978); Head of Publicity (1984-87); Head of Publicity and Public Relations (1987-96); Chief Press Officer (1997), Granada Television. Member, Royal Television Society.

Interests: Equestrian sports, tennis, travel, television.

Contact details: Granada Television, Quay Street, Manchester M60 9EA (tel: 0161 827 2248, email: Sallie.Ryle@granadamedia.com).

SAATCHI, Roy, BA

Positions: Owner and Sole Trader, Roy Saatchi Associates; Visiting Professor of Broadcast Journalism, Liverpool John Moores; Member of the Board of Governors, Manchester Metropolitan University; Chairman, Estates and Services Committee; Council Member, The National Library for the Blind.
Areas of Influence: Education, Media.
Profile: *b.* November 17th, 1945; *m.* Joanna; 2 sons; 1 daughter.
Educated at The Welkin (Preparatory), Haberdashers' Aske's and University of Essex. Roy Saatchi began his broadcasting career in Liverpool in 1974 as one of the original members of the Radio City news team. In 1978, he joined the BBC working in Regional Television, Local Radio, Radio 4 and National News. He moved to Manchester in 1991 as Head of Local Programmes for North West England, managing Regional TV output and three Local Radio stations, and co-ordinating radio and TV journalism across the region. His executive roles have focused upon journalism, business planning and introducing new technology. Until recently, he was the project director of English Regions Open Access Centres. Roy is committed to training and development, having taken an active role in encouraging new talent and mentoring existing staff whilst at the BBC. In 2002 he left to set up his own consultancy business specialising in broadcast journalism training and development and project work. Publications: As a documentary maker with BBC Radio 4 he wrote and produced a number of programmes strands. Prizes and awards: Royal Television Society, Best Daily News Magazine (1989).
Interests: Travel, walking, scootering, computing including web design, transport - from model railways to the real thing, football, season ticket at Manchester United.

Contact details: 39 Castle Hill, Presbury, Cheshire SK10 4AS (tel: 01625 820 433, fax: 01625 829 835, email: roy.saatchi@saatchiassociates.com); tel: 01625 820735, email: roy.saatchi@zoo.co.uk.

SABBERWAL, Dr Amar Jit Parkash, BScENG, MScTECH, PhD, DSc, CENG, FIMECHENG, FIEE, FIMGMT

Positions: Executive Director, Molins Plc; Chief Executive, Molins Tobacco Machinery; Non-Executive Chairman, PAV Holdings Ltd; Non-Executive Chairman, Pinewood Associates Ltd; Non-Executive Director, University of Salford Enterprises; Member, North West Disability Consulting Group; Council Member, University of Salford.
Areas of Influence: Commerce, Education, Health.
Profile: *b.* November 25th, 1933; *m.* Jayasree.
Education: BScENG, Agra University; MScTECH, Manchester University; PhD, Manchester University; DSc, University of Salford. Career profile: Research Engineer, GKN Plc (1958-59); Senior Research Engineer, NRDC (UMIST) (1959-62); Works Manager, Indian Cable Company (1963-66); Group Leader, Stavely Plc (1966-67); Engineering Manager, Ferodo Ltd (1968-70); Engineering Director, Ferodo td (1970-73); Managing Director, Asbestos Cement Ltd (1974-77); Joint Managing Director, TAC Construction Materials (1977-81); Managing Director, TXN Materials Research (1981-85); Managing Director, BIP Chemicals (1986-89); Executive Director, TXN Plc (1989-96); Non-Executive Chairman, NHS Trust, Manchester Childrens Hospitals (1996-00).
Interests: Gardening, music, reading.
Contact details: Molins Plc, Haw Lane, Sauderton, High Wycombe, Buckinghamshire HP14 4JE (tel: 01844 343 211, fax: 01844 272 704, email: amar.sabberwal@molins.com); 10 Pinewood, Off Park Road, Bowden, Altrincham, Cheshire WA14 3JQ (tel: 0161 928 6788, fax: 0161 941 3667, email: ajps@cherry-trees.fsnet.co.uk).

SAINT, Alexandra, BA, MBA

Position: Chief Executive, Arts About Manchester.
Areas of Influence: Arts.
Profile: *b.* March 10th, 1965; *m.* Guy Pearson; 1 daughter, Sadie May.
Education: St. Michael's, Chorley, Lancashire; Queen Elizabeth's Grammar School, Blackburn; Bristol University; Durham University. Career profile: Administrator, Century Theatre; Head of Marketing and Development, Tyne and Wear Museum; Senior Consultant, Arts Business Ltd; Marketing Manager, English Heritage (London).
Interests: Arts, cycling, socialising with friends and family.

Contact Details: Chief Executive, Arts About Manchester, 2nd Floor Churchgate House, 56 Oxford Street, Manchester M1 6EU (tel:0161 238 4534, fax: 0161 237 8077, email: alex@aam.org.uk); 75 Beech Rd, Hale, Cheshire WA15 9HY (tel: 0161 927 9406, email: alex@alexsaint.com).

SANDERS Mark Henry, BSc, MBA, PG, Cert Ed

Position: Chief Executive, Bury MBC.
Areas of Influence: Public Sector, Education.
Profile: b. June 28th,1954; m. Bronwyn; 1 son; 1 daughter.
Education: Seldown Boys School, Poole; Poole Technical College; Southampton University; La Sainte Union College of Education. Career profile: Full time Official, National Union of Public Employees (1977-91); Project Manager, Leeds City Council (1991-97); Assistant Chief Executive/ Executive Director, Oldham MBC.
Contact details: Chief Executive, Bury Metropolitan Borough Council, Town Hall, Knowsley Street, Bury BL9 0SW (tel: 0161 253 5102, fax: 0161 253 5108).

SARWAR, Mohammed

Positions: Centre Manager, Multi Asian Arts Centre, Rochdale (1997 - present).
Areas of Influence: Arts, Education, Voluntary Sector.
Profile: b. July 31st, 1960.
Educated at Greenhill Upper School, Hopwood Hall College, Spring England, Yorkshire Arts / North West Arts Board and Huddersfield University. Career profile: Qualified Engineer, Robert Rileys and Smith Springs (1978-85); Instrumental Peripatetic Teacher, Bradford MBC (1987-89); Music Teacher for Performing Arts Students, Rochdale College (1988-89); Music Teacher, Greenhill Community College, Oldham (1989-91); Music Teacher, Sparrowhill Community School, Rochdale (1990-94); Music Teacher / Arts Coordinator, Cleveland Arts (1991-94); Asian Arts Development Coordinator, Multi Asian Arts Centre, Rochdale (1995-97); Offical Interpreter, GM Police. Clubs and societies: Asian Arts Appreciation; Advisor, North West Arts Board; Advisor, Arts Council; Music Borough Society, Rochdale MBC. Events: Bolton Mela (1999); Rochdale Summer Mela (1995 - present); Eid Mela, Rochdale Recreation & Community Services (1995); Middlesborough Mela (1992-93). Releases: *Qatra Shabnam Ka* (1998); *Munda Chad Ke Punjab* (1997). Publications: *Elements of Asian Music in the National Curriculum - Key stages 2 and 3* (1993-95); *Urdu Festival Songs for Children* (1993); *Tabla for Beginners* (1989). Mohammad Sarwar has also developed short educational courses in Asian music and has undertaken several research projects on the subject of culteral arts.
Interests: Cricket for South Lancashire, poetry, drama, health, fitness, pool table competitions, meeting people of various cultures.
Contact details: 129 Drake Street, Rochdale, Lancs OL16 1PZ.

SCHMIDT, Michael Norton, FRSL, BA, MA

Positions: Editorial and Managing Director, Carcanet Press Ltd; Editor, PN Review; Director, The Writing School, Manchester Metropolitain University.
Areas of Influence: Arts, Education, Media.
Profile: *b.* March 2nd, 1947; 2 sons; 1 daughter.
Education: The Hill School, Pottsum, PA, USA; Christ's Hospital, Horsham, Sussex; Harvard, USA; Cambridge; Wadham College, Oxford (exhibitioner). Michael Schmidt has written *Selected Poems, Lives of the Poets, The Story of Poetry* and various anthologies.
Contact details: Dept of English, Manchester Metropolitan University, Manton Building M15 6LL (tel: 0161 247 1732, email: schmidt@carcanet.u.net.com).

SCHOLES, Rodney James, QC (1987), BA, BCL

Positions: Queen's Counsel; Recorder of the Crown Court; Acting Deemster, Isle of Man.
Areas of Influence: Law.
Profile: *b.* September 26th, 1945; *m.* Katherin Elizabeth; 2 sons (1 deceased, 2000).
Education: Wade Deacon Grammar School, Widnes; St Catherines College, Oxford. Rodney Scholes was called to the Bar Lincoln's Inn in 1968 and became a Bencher of Lincoln's Inn (1997). He was awarded the David Blank Scholarship, St Catherines College in 1963, Hardwicke Scholar, Lincoln's Inn in 1964 and Mansfield Scholar, Lincoln's Inn in 1967. Mr Scholes is a member of both Burnage RUFC and Manchester RFC.
Interests: Rugby, football, dogs.
Contact details: Byrom Street Chambers, 12 Byrom Street, Manchester M3 4PP (tel: 0161 829 2100, fax: 0161 829 2101); 22 Old Buildings, Lincoln's Inn, London WC2A 3UJ (tel: 0171 831 0222); 442 Didsbury Road, Heaton Mersey, Stockport, Cheshire SK4 3BS (tel: 0161 442 9968, fax: 0161 442 9968).

SCHULTZ, John, MA, DipTCP, FCMI, MRTPI

Positions: Chief Executive, Stockport MBC; Lead Advisor, NW Regional Assembly.
Areas of Influence: Public Sector.
Profile: *b.* August 29th, 1951; *m.* Susan; 2 daughters.
Education: University of Oxford (1970-73); University of Manchester (1973-75). Career profile: Sefton Council; Merseyside County Council; Leicestershire County Council; Assistant Chief Executive, Warwickshire County Council.
Contact details: Chief Executive, Stockport Borough Council, Town Hall, Stockport SK1 3XE (tel: 0161 747 3000).

SCHWARZ, Pam, MA, FCIH, MBA, JP

Positions: Chief Executive, Mosscare Housing Ltd; Governor, Claremont Infant & Junior Schools, Moss Side; Secretary, Parochial Church Council, St James with St Clement, Moss Side.
Areas of Influence: Housing, Community Development, Ecology.
Education: Horsham High School; Aberdeen University, MA; Salford College, Chartered Institute of Housing Diploma; FCIH, Durham University Business School, MBA. Career profile: Maths teaching in Haywards Heath, Sussex (1968-69); Maths teaching in Mbabne, Swaziland as a volunteer with International Volunteer Service (1969-71); Trainee Housing Manager to Chief Executive, Mosscare Housing Ltd, first employee, involved in development of the housing association as a community development agency (1973 - present). Awarded the Millenium Award (2002). Member of Manchester Rambling Club, and Earthwatch.
Interests: Walking, allotment, theatre and the other arts.
Contact details: Mosscare Housing Ltd, 101 Great Western Street, Moss Side, Manchester M14 4AA (tel: 0161 226 4211, fax: 0161 226 8752, email: pam.schwarz@mosscare.org.uk); (tel: 07960 653 466, email: wpamms@hotmail.com).

SCOTT, David Ian, BA

Positions: Group Human Resources Director, United Utilities PLC; Non Executive Director, Whitehall and Industry Group (1998 - present).
Areas of Influence: Education, Arts.
Profile: *b.* May 2nd, 1953; *m.* Ingrid.
Career profile: University Cadetship, Royal Air Force (1971-74); British Telecommunications plc, ultimately Personnel Director, Group HQ (1975-95); Director of Personnel, HM Prison Service (1995-98); Chairman, Regional Advisory Committee, Duke of Edinburgh's Award North West; Chairman of Trustee's, Campus, University of Salford. Clubs and societies: NW Regional Council of the Prince's Trust; Director, Unity Theatre, Liverpool; Chairman, NW Regional Employment Group of Race for Opportunity.
Interests: Sport, motoring, walking.
Contact details: United Utilities PLC, Dawson House, Liverpool Road, Great Sankey, Warrington WA5 3LW (tel: 01925 237 007, fax: 01925 237 155, email: david.scott@uuplc.co.uk).

SCOTT, Robert Leslie, BA

Position: Acting Director, Museum of Science and Industry, Manchester.
Areas of Influence: Arts, Finance, Voluntary Sector.

Profile: *b.* April 5th, 1948; *m.* Nadine; 2 sons; 1 daughter.
Education: North Manchester Grammar School (1959-66); University of Leeds (1966-69). Career profile: Local Government (1970-83); Various Positions, Museum of Science and Industry, Manchester (1983 -).
Interests: Reading, gardening, football.
Contact details: The Museum of Science and Industry, Liverpool Road, Castlefield, Manchester M3 4FP (tel: 0161 606 0101, fax: 0161 606 0106, email: r.scott@msim.org.uk); Woodlands, Ravenhurst Drive, Bolton BL1 5DL (tel: 01204 845 778).

SCUDAMORE, Jeremy Paul, BA (Hons)

Position: Chief Executive Officer, Avecia.
Areas of Influence: Commerce, Finance, Health.
Profile: *b.* April 27th, 1947; *m.* Ruth; 1 son; 1 daughter.
Educated at Birkenhead School and Nottingham University. Career profile: Various commercial and planning jobs including secondments to Brazil and Japan, ICI Group; Business Director of Agrochemicals, Managing Director of Seeds and Bioscience, and Chief Executive of Specialities, Zeneca. Advisory Board Member, European Chemical News and Chemical and Engineering News, Washington USA; Non-Executive Chairman, Cyprotex plc; Member, North West Science Council; Member of DTI, Innovation and Growth Team for Chemicals; Board Member, Chemical Industry Association. Clubs and societies: MCC and FRSA.
Interests: Sport, music, gardening.
Contact details: Avecia, Hexagon House, Blackley, Manchester M9 8ZS (tel: 0161 721 2397, fax: 0161 721 5220, email: jeremy.scudamore@avecia.com).

SEAL, Michael Jefferson, MSI

Positions: Director, Brewin Dolphin Securities Ltd (2001 - present); Consultant, Brewin Dolphin.
Areas of Influence: Finance, Voluntary Sector, Arts.
Profile: *b.* October 17th, 1936; *m.* Julia Mary Seton; 1 son; 2 daughters.
Educated at Marlborough College, Wiltshire. Military Service: National Service, 3rd Royal Tank Regiment (1954-56); Major, Territorial Army, 41st RTR, Oldham (1956-67). Career profile: The Carborundum Co Ltd (1957-59); Partner, Jefferson Seal & Co (1960-68); Henriques Seal & Co (1972-74); Partner and Senior Partner, Charlton Seal Dimmock & Co (1974-90); Director, Benchmark GP Plc, Charlton Seal Ltd; Chairman, CST Emerging Asia Trust Plc (1991-98); Director, Wise Speke Holdings Ltd and Wise Speke Ltd (1998-01). Member, The Court of Victoria University of Manchester; Trustee / Director: The Clonter Farm Music Trust, The Greater Manchester Educational Trust, The Humane Society for the Hundred of Salford, Gaddum Centre,

Manchester Grammar School Trust, Manchester Midday Concerts Society, Wythenshawe Hospital Transplant Fund and Wood Street Mission. Clubs and societies: St James Club.
Interests: Country sports, game shooting, fishing, gardening, walking, music, opera, travel.
Contact details: Brewin Dolphin Securities Ltd, 36 St Ann Street, Manchester M60 2EP (tel; 0161 839 4222, fax: 0161 832 9092, email: michael.seal@brewin.co.uk); The Dene House, Great Budwirth, Northwich, Cheshire CW9 6HB (tel: 01606 891 555, email: sealsbudworth@freecall-uk.co.uk).

SELLERS, Rodney Horrocks (Rod), BSc, FCA, DpBA

Positions: Chairman, Ultraframe Plc and Manchester Business School Incubator Ltd; Non-executive Director, PZ Cussons Plc, James R Knowles (Holdings) Plc and Pets at Home Group Ltd; Chairman, Commonwealth Games Economic Benefits Initiative.
Areas of Influence: Commerce, Finance.
Profile: *b.* July 25th, 1946; *m.* Judith; 1 son; 1 daughter.
Education: Bacup and Rawtenstall Grammar School (1957-64); BSc (Econ) class I, London School of Economics (1967); Manchester Business School (1970-71). Career profile: Served Articles with Arthur Andersen in London (1967-70); Financial Comtroller / PA to CEO (1971-74), Financial Director (1974-91), Chief Executive (1990-96), Deputy Chairman (1996-97), British Vita Plc. In 1997 Rod Sellers formed his own Consultancy. He has served as Non-executive Director on four mainly North West Plc Boards in addition to his current positions. He also provides corporate consultancy for Seddon Group. Rod has a keen interest in the development of the NW economy and has been involved, over the past 10 years, in Manchester Chamber of Commerce Economics Committee, CBI Europe Committee, The MBS Incubator for Enterpreneurial Business Development, and Manchester Society of Chartered Accountants for whom he was President (2001-02). He is especially interested in the Commonwealth Games Economic Legacy. Received the Williams Deacons Bank Scholarship at Manchester Business School (1970). Clubs and societies: RSA; Bolton Golf Club.
Interests: Sport, travel.
Contact details: Thorncliffe, 551 Chorley New Road, Lostock, Bolton BL6 4JT (tel: 01204 491857, fax: 01204 847322, email: rodsellers@online.rednet.co.uk).

SELVAN, Fay, BA Hons, MSc

Positions: Chair, The Big Issue in the North; Proprietor, The Big Life Company; Chair, Trafford North PCT.
Areas of Influence: Health, Media, Public Sector.
Profile: *b.* August 20th, 1959; 1 daughter.

Education: Cranebourne Comprehensive (1970-75); St Mary's College (1975-77); BA Hons Politics, Sussex University (1977-80); MSc Strategic Leadership, Salford University (1996-99); Phd Network Relationships, Salford University (2001 - present). Fay Selvan established Diverse Resources (Previously CHRC) in 1991 and led its development from an unincorporated association with a turnover of just £17k per annum, to a group of companies and charities with a projected turnover of £2,5m. April 2002 saw the merger of Diverse Resources and The Big Issue in the North to form The Big Life Company and Fay became head of the Senior Management Team which oversees all the Companies in the group. Fay moved to Manchester in 1980, and has lived and worked in Hulme and Old Trafford for the past 20 years. She won the BIC Community Enterprise Award (1998).
Interests: Tai-Chi, reading.
Contact details: The Big Life Company, 135-141 Oldham Street, Manchester M4 1LN (tel: 0161 279 7839, fax: 0161 833 0200, email: fay.selvan@thebiglifecompany.com).

SEPHTON, Craig Gardner, QC (2001), MA, BCL

Positions: Queens Counsel; Recorder.
Areas of Influence: Law.
Profile: *b.* December 7th, 1957; 3 sons.
Education: The Ecclesbourne School, Duffield; Lincoln College, Oxford. Career profile: Called to the Bar (1981); Recorder (2001). Clubs and Societies: British Mountaineering Council; Hayfield Singers.
Interests: Computers; music; mountaineering.
Contact details: Deans Court Chambers, 24 St Johns Street, Manchester M3 4DF (tel: 0161 214 6000, fax: 0161 214 6001, email: sephton@deanscourt.co.uk).

SHAW, Michael Patrick, BA (Hons)

Positions: Managing Partner, Cobbetts (1996 - present).
Areas of Influence: Law
Profile: *b.* May 8th, 1956.
Educated at Dr Challoners Grammar School, Amersham and Manchester Polytechnic. Michael Shaw trained with Leak Almond & Parkinson, which was the predecessor firm to Cobbetts, before qualifying (1981), and then becoming Partner (1984).
Contact details: Ship Canal House, King Street, Manchester (tel: 0161 833 5267, fax: 0161 830 2688, email: michael.shaw@cobbetts.co.uk).

SHELDON, William

Position: Senior Clerk to Mr Jonathan Foster QC.
Areas of Influence: Law, Sport, Voluntary Sector.
Profile: *m.* Patricia; 1 daughter.
Educated to degree standard, William Sheldon has worked in Barristers Chambers over a period of 45 years and is a representative of the Manchester Barristers Clerks. He is a member of Northern Guild of Toastmasters and Bolton Sailing Club. He has devoted a great deal of time to Amateur Soccer i.e. F.A. Coach, treatment of sports injuries, organising charity events, and has a strong connection with the Manchester Football Association. He has passed Toastmaster exams set by the Officers of the National Association and is a Licenciate Member of the Northern Guild of Toastmasters.
Interests: Sailing, public speaking, calligraphy, voluntary work, soccer, rugby league, rugby union, boxing, walking, keep fit.
Contact details: Chambers of Jonathon Foster QC, 18 St John Street, Manchester M3 4EA (tel: 0161 278 1800, fax: 0161 278 8220, email: wsheldon@18stjohn.co.uk); Windy Ridge, 443 Bolton Road, Westhoughten, Bolton BL5 3BJ (tel: 01942 810024).

SHEPPARD, Elizabeth (Honor), FRMCM, ARMCM.

Position: Tutor in Vocal Studies, Royal Northern College of Music (1987 - present).
Areas of Influence: Arts, Education.
Profile: *b.* December 23rd, 1931; *m.* Robert Conyers Elliott (dec.); 1 son; 1 daughter.
Educated at Leeds High School for Girls and Royal Manchester College of Music (1952-56). Whilst still a student at the RMCM Honor Sheppard was auditioned and offered a place as a member of the BBC Northern Singers, and concurrently with this was invited to sing in concerts, oratorio and recitals in many parts of Britain. In 1960 she was invited to become the first soprano with the Deller Consort of London, and with them undertook many tours of Europe, Scandinavia, USA and South America until 1978. Honor has also made many recordings and has been a vocal tutor for Leeds and Manchester Universities. Received the Curtis Gold Medal for Singing at College. Member of the National Trust.
Interests: Gardening, reading.
Contact details: Royal Northern College of Music (tel: 0161 928 4727).

SHEPPARD, Lynn, BSc, MSc, MCIM

Position: Marketing Manager, Manchester Science Enterprise Centre.
Areas of Influence: Education, Public Sector, Media.
Profile: *b.* June 4th, 1953; *m.* Christopher; 1 son.
Education: Cheadle Hulme School for Girls (1964-72); Manchester Polytechnic (1972-

75); UMIST (1975-80). Career profile: Account Director, BDH; Strategic Marketing Consultant, Trafford Park Development Corporation; Director, Q2 Advertising and Marketing; Technology Marketing Manager, Manchester Science Enterprise Centre. Publications: *TQM Magazine*, Volume 7 Number 5 (1995). Clubs and societies: Manchester Publicity Association; Network North.
Interests: Reading, music, fashion, cinema, keep fit.
Contact details: Manchester Science Enterprise Centre, Fairbairn Building, UMIST, PO Box 88, Manchester M60 1QD (tel: 0161 955 8486, fax: 0161 955 8488, email: l.sheppard@msec.ac.uk).

SHERMAN, Colonel Thomas, OBE (1970), VRD (1960) with clasp (1970), DL (1977) MCAM

Positions: Deputy Lieutenant (1977 - present); Hon Life Vice President, Manchester Publicity Association; Hon Life Vice President, First Friday Club.
Areas of Influence: Media, Commerce, Voluntary Sector.
Profile: *b.* May 25th, 1919; *m.* Vera Blagbrough (dec. 1971); 1 son.
Educated at Liverpool Grammar School. Career profile: The Journal of Commerce & Shipping Telegraph (1946-51); Assistant Advertisement Manager, Odhams Press, Manchester (1951-61); Northern Advertisement Controller, Mirror Group Newspapers; High Sheriff of Greater Manchester (1985-86). Founder Member and Hon Secretary, Liverpool Publicity Association (1948); Chairman (1972-74), President (1975-77), Manchester Publicity Association (1951 - present); Chairman (1983), President (1996), First Friday Club (1961 - present). National Advertising Benevolent Society, Manchester Branch: Chairman (1986-91) and President (1991-98). Prizes and awards: Territorial Efficiency Medal (1945); Manchester Publicity Association Gold Medal for Services to Advertising and Publicity (1998). Military Service: The Kings Regiment, TA (1938); World War II: No 4 Independent Coy, Norway NWEF; No 2 Commando Vaagso Raid, St Nazaire Raid, RWAFF West Africa. Royal Marines Reserve (1950-70), Commanding Officer (1965-70), Honorary Colonel (1972-85).Vice Chairman (1978-84), Chairman of Publicity and Recruiting Committee (1975-84), NW England and Isle of Man TA and VR Association; Broughton House for Disabled Ex personnel (1985-99).
Interests: Geriatric swimming, cycling, walking.
Contact details: Christleton, 1B Fulshaw Park South, Wilmslow, Cheshire SK9 1QP (tel: 01625 583771).

SHIELDS, Michael, CBE (2002), DSc, BSc, DipTP, MRTPI, FRSA, FRGS

Positions: Chief Executive, North West Development Agency (1999 - present); Deputy Chairman of Governors, Salford University.
Areas of Influence: Public Sector.

Profile: *b.* January 23rd, 1943; *m.* Dorothy; 2 sons; 1 daughter. Educated at Durham Johnston Grammar School, Durham University and Newcastle University. Career profile: Planning Department, Newcastle upon Tyne Council (1964-65); Planning Department, Durham County Council (1965-69); Planning Department, Nottingham City Council (1969-73); Deputy Director of Planning, Leeds City Council (1973-78); City Technical Services Officer and Deputy Chief Executive, Salford City Council (1978-83); Chief Executive, Trafford Borough Council (1983-87); Chief Executive, Trafford Park Development Corporation (1987-98). Former Chairman, Altrincham Grammar School for Boys.
Contact details: PO Box 37, Renaissance House, Warrington, WA1 2XB (tel: 01925 400100, fax: 01925 400400).

SHIH, Chueh-Teng, MA

Position: Director, IBPS Stretford Road.
Areas of Influence: Education, Faith Groups, Voluntary Sector.
Profile: *b.* June 14th, 1969.
Contact details: Director, IBPS Stretford Road, Old Trafford, Manchester M16 9AF (tel: 0161 872 3338, fax: 0161 872 3334, email: ibps_man_uk@hotmail.com).

SHINDLER, Geoffrey Arnold, MA LLM (Cantab), MSI, SoLS, TEP

Positions: Partner, Head, Trust and Estate Department, Halliwell Landau (1986 - present); Vice-President, Society of Trust & Estate Practitioners; Chairman, Development Committee, Royal Exchange Theatre, Manchester; Trustee, Portico Library; Member, Trust Law Committee.
Areas of Influence: Law, Arts.
Profile: *b.* October 21st, 1942; *m.* Gay; 3 daughters.
Education: Bury Grammar School, Bury (1954-62); Gonville & Caius College, University of Cambridge (1962-66). Career profile: Articled Clerk, Solicitor, Partner, March Pearson & Skelton (1966-86). Publications: *Law of Trust*; Consulting Editor, *Trust and Estates Law Journal* and *Trusts and Estates Tax Found*; Member, Editorial Board, *Wills and Trust, Law Reports*. Clubs and societies: Marylebone Cricket Club; Lancashire County Cricket Club; Portico Library; Manchester Literary and Philosophical Society.
Interests: Drama, history, books, opera, sport.
Contact details: Halliwell Landau, St James Court, Brown Street, Manchester M2 2JF (tel: 0161 831 2699, fax: 0161 831 2843, email: gas@halliwells.co.uk); 10 Bury Old Road, Prestwich, Manchester M25 0EX (tel; 0161 740 2291, fax: 0161 740 1526).

SHINE, Jeremy, BA

Position: Joint Artistic Director, Manchester International Arts.
Areas of Influence: Arts.
Profile: *b.* September 18th, 1950.
Education: Kilburn Grammar School; University of Warwick. Career profile: Performer and Administrator, Action Space (1977-81); Founder and Director, The Green Room, Manchester (1980-86); Director, Manchester Festival (1984-86).
Interests: Horse riding, Spain Catalunya.
Contact details: Joint Artistic Director, Manchester International Arts, 3 Birch Polygon, Manchester M14 5HX (tel: 0161 224 0020, fax: 0161 248 9331, email: mia@streetsahead.org.uk).

SHORROCK, (John) Michael, QC (1988), MA

Positions: Practising Barrister; Head of Chambers (1992 - present), Peel Court; Recorder of the Crown Court; Member of Criminal Injuries Compensation Appeals Panel (1998 - present).
Areas of Influence: Law, Arts, Sport.
Profile: *b.* May 25th, 1943; *m.* Marianne; 2 daughters.
Educated at Packwood Haugh Prep. School, Clifton College Public School and Pembroke College, Cambridge University. Career profile: Called to the Bar (1967); Pupil to Patrick Russell, later Lord Justice Russell; Junior of Northern Circuit (1969); Secretary Circuit Executive Committee (1978-81); Recorder of Crown Court (1982); Member, Criminal Injuries Compensation Board (1996-01); Bencher, Inner Temple (1998).
Interests: Theatre, cinema, gardening, tennis, walking.
Contact details: Peel Court Chambers, 45 Hardman Street, Manchester M3 3PL (tel: 0161 832 3791, fax: 0161 835 3054).

SIM, Alistair

Position: Managing Director, Love.
Areas of Influence: Media, Commerce, Arts.
Profile: January 24th, 1973; *m.* Louise; 1 son; 1 daughter.
Education: Stockport Grammar School; Goldsmiths, University of London. Career profile: Junior Account Executive, Account Manager, Account Director, Director of Operations, Tucker Clarke Williams (1993-01). Awards: D&AD; Design Week; New York Festivals; Campaign Direct; Roses; Cream. Member of D&AD.
Interests: Film, music, football, cycling, making Manchester great again.
Contact details: Love.Creative, 72 Tib Street, Manchester M4 1LG.

SIMMONS, Jack, MBE (1990)

Positions: Chairman, Lancashire County Cricket Club
Areas of Influence: Sport, Finance.
Profile: *b.* March 28th, 1941; *m.* Jacqueline; 1 daughter; Kelly.
Educated at Accrington Technical School and Blackburn College; Jack Simmons was a professional cricketer (1961-89) and played for Lancashire (1969-89). He was one of Wisdons five cricketers of the year (1985), and captained Tasmania in Australia (1972-79). He is a member of Clitheroe Golf Club and MCC.
Interests: All sports.
Contact details: Jacmar, 16 Southcliffe, Gt Harwood, Blackburn, Lancs. (tel: 01254 883 369).

SIMPSON, Andrew Christopher, ACA, BA

Position: Assistant Director, NM Rothschild & Sons Ltd.
Areas of Influence: Finance, Commerce.
Profile: *b.* May 20th, 1968; 1 daughter.
Education: Guiseley School (1979-86); Sheffield University (1987-91). Career profile: LH Friskoff & Co, New York (1989-90); Price Waterhouse, Manchester (1991-95); NM Rothschild & Sons, Manchester/London/Leeds (1995 -). Andrew Simpson is a member of Stand Golf Club.
Interests: Golf, tennis, keep fit, travel, theatre.
Contact details: N M Rothschild & Sons, 82 King Street, Manchester M2 4WQ (tel: 0161 827 3800, fax: 0161 835 3789).

SIMPSON, Brian, MEP, CertEd

Position: Member of the European Parliament for North West England.
Areas of Influence: Public Sector, Politics.
Profile: *b.* February 6th, 1953; *m.* Linda; 1 son; 2 daughters.
Education: Golborne County Primary School; Golborne Secondary Modern for Boys; Golborne Comprehensive School; West Midlands College of Education. Career profile: Teacher, City of Liverpool (1971-89); County Councillor, Merseyside County Council (1981-86); Councillor, Warrington Borough Council (1987-91); Member of European Parliament for Cheshire East (1989-99); Deputy Chairman, Liverpool Airport (1981-86); Socialist Group Spokesperson, European Parliament for Transport and Tourism (1991 -); European PPS to the Deputy Prime Minister; Secretary, European Parliament's All Party Rugby League Group. Clubs and Societies: Golborne Sports and Social Club; RNLI; Heritage Railways Association; Lancashire County Cricket Club.
Interests: Rugby League, heritage railways, military history, keeping fit.

Contact details: Gilbert Wakefield House, 67 Bewsey Street, Warrington WA2 7JQ (tel: 01925 654074, fax: 01925 654077, email: briansimpson@la*b*.u-net.com).

SIMPSON, Richard Graham, GRSM, ARCM

Positions: Principal Oboe, BBC Symphony Orchestra with Sir Andrew Davis (1991 - present); Professor of Oboe, Guidhall School of Music and Drama.
Areas of Influence: Arts.
Profile: *b*. January 18th, 1951; *m*. Janet; 2 sons.
Educated at the Royal College of Music, London, studying with Sidney Sutcliffe. Career profile: Sub Principal Oboe, under Pierre Boulez, BBC Symphony Orchestra (1973); Principal Oboe, Hallé Orchestra (1974); Performed several concerts with the Hallé Orchestra and active in chamber music in the North West in my time with the Hallé . Attender of Religious Society of Friends (Quakers).

SIMPSON, William George (Bill), BA (Hons), FRSA, MCLIP

Positions: Director and University Librarian, John Rylands University Library of Manchester (2002 – present).
Areas of Influence: Education, Voluntary Sector.
Profile: *b*. June 27th, 1945; *m*. Margaret Pollard; 2 daughters.
Educated at The Liverpool Institute (1956-63), University of Liverpool (1963-67) and University of Aberdeen (1967-68). Career profile: Assistant Librarian, University of Durham (1969-73); Assistant Librarian, Sub Librarian, Senior Librarian, University of Manchester (1973-85); University Librarian, University of Surrey (1985-90); University Librarian, University of London (1990-94); Librarian and College Archivist, Trinity College, Dublin (1994-02). Publications: Various publications in library and information journals; edited CD-ROM version *Book of Kells*. Prizes and awards: Gilroy Scholarship in Semitric Languages, University of Aberdeen (1967); Jubilee Medal, Charles University, Prague (1998). Clubs and societies: Royal Society of Arts; Royal Asiatic Society.
Interests: Astronomy, archaeology, genealogy, travel, linguistics.
Contact details: John Rylands University Library of Manchester, Oxford Road, Manchester M13 9PP (tel: 0161 275 3700, fax: 0161 273 7488, email: bill.simpson@man.ac.uk).

SINGER, Harold Samuel, MA

Position: Circuit Judge, Northern Circuit.
Areas of Influence: Law, Voluntary Sector.
Profile: *b*. July 17th, 1935; m. Adele; 1 son; 2 daughters.
Education: Salford Grammar School; Fitzwilliam House, Cambridge. Career profile:

Called to the Bar, Gray's Inn (1957); Recorder, Crown Court (1981-84); Circuit Judge (1984 -).
Interests: Music, painting, books.
Contact details: The Court Service, 15 Quay Street, Manchester M60 9FD (tel: 0161 954 1800).

SINGER, Peta Doreen

Position: District Manager, Manchester Citizens Advice Bureau Service.
Areas of Influence: Voluntary Sector, Law.
Profile: *b.* July 30th, 1949; *m.* Neville; 1 son; 1 daughter.
Educated at Broughton High School.
Contact details: Manchester Citizens Advice Bureau Service, Swan Buildings, 20 Swan Street, Manchester M4 5JW (tel: 0161 839 , fax:0161 839 7750, email: cab-peta@mcr1.poptel.org.uk).

SINGH, Reuben

Positions: Chairman and CEO, alldaypa.com; Sole Shareholder and Chairman, Reuben Singh Group of Companies. Member, DTI's Competitiveness Council and the Small Business Council; Chairman, HRH Genesis Initiative.
Areas of Influence: Arts, Commerce, Finance.
Profile: *b.* September 20th, 1976.
Educated at Ramillies High School, William Hulme Grammar School, and Manchester Metropolitan University, Reuben Singh started his business at the age of 18. He has since received many accolades for his business achievements including UK Entrepreneur of the Year (2002), and has been labelled by The Times as the "British Bill Gates". In 1999 Reuben launched alldaypa.com, which today is the market leader in SME outsourced business support services and has developed worldwide patent telecommunications software. Reuben is keen on promoting the "cult of youth" and has devoted one of his investment companies to focus on concepts started by young entrepreneurs, in the form of a £25m, venture capital fund, "Dream on Attitude", investing up to £50,000 per project. RS Investments, another investment fund, was launched in 1999. Reuben also serves on a number of Government think tanks, and was one of six chosen to serve on the Governments 'peer reviews' to report on Government departments. He is an advisor on Entrepreneurship, being one of the country's appointed Ambassadors for Entrepreneurs, and is also involved in the Arts & Business of which HRH Prince Charles is the President. Reuben Singh has had his portrait hung in the National Portrait Gallery and was listed as 'World's Wealthiest Young Man' in Fortune Magazine's list, 'World Richest 40 under 40'.
Interests: alldayPA, cinema, film.

Contact details: alldayPA Ltd, Isher House, Michegan Avenue, Salford Quays, Manchester M50 2GY (tel: 0161 876 0990, fax: 0161 877 4207, email: danielle@freedman.alldaypa.com).

SLADE, Derek Harrison, FCA, ATII, JP (1971)

Positions: Bench Chairman, Manchester City Magistrates.
Areas of Influence: Finance, Commerce, Law.
Profile: *b.* August 23rd, 1933; *m.* Anne (dec. 2000); 1 son; 1 daughter; *m.* Margaret (2001).
Educated at Hulme Hall College. Career profile: Partner (retired), Ernst & Young; Treasurer and Member of Court, The University of Manchester; Chairman, St Anns Hospice; Vice Chairman, Central Manchester NHS Trust; General Commissioner of the Inland Revenue; Chairman of Governors, Cheadle Hulme School; President, Manchester Society of Chartered Accountants; President, Manchester Luncheon Club; Chairman, Board of Visitors, Manchester Prison; member of Council, Institute of Chartered Accountants in England and Wales; President, Manchester Junior Chamber of Commerce. Freeman of the City of London. Clubs and societies: St James's Club, Manchester; Army and Navy Club, London; MCC; RSPB; National Trust; English Heritage, Manchester Literary & Philosophical Society.
Interests: Walking, ornithology, gardening.
Contact details: Whitestone, 32 Ramillies Avenue, Cheadle Hulme, Cheshire SK8 7AL (tel: 0161 485 4001, email: dslade@globalnet.co.uk).

SLADE-LIPKIN, Heather, Bmus, GRSM, ARCM, ARMCM, PGCE

Positions: Professor of Keyboard; Concert Artist.
Areas of Influence: Arts, Education.
Profile: *b.* March 9th, 1947; E. Barry; 2 sons.
Education: Royal Northern College of Music; Liverpool University; Manchester Metropolitan University. Career profile: Professor, RNCM (1986-); Professor, Chetham's School of Music (2002-); Concert Artist, worldwide.
Interests: Reading, swimming, walking.
Contact details: Manor Lawn, 15 Normans Place, Altrincham, Cheshire WA14 2AB (email: heather@piano.u-net.com).

SMALLBONE, Tim, BSc, ACA, DipSIB

Position: Investment Director, Gresham, Manchester.
Areas of Influence: Finance.
Profile: *b.* October 1st, 1966; *m.* Therese; 1 daughter.
Education: Chiltern Edge School, Sonning Common, Oxon; King James College,

Henley-on-Thames; Manchester University. Career profile: Accountant, Price Waterhouuse, Manchester (1991); PW Corporate Finance (1991-93); Investment Manager, North West of England Ventures, Manchester (1993-96); Investment Manager, Granville Private Equity, Manchester (1996-98); Associate Director, KPMG Corporate Finance, Liverpool (1998-01).
Interests: Manchester City.
Contact details: Gresham Trust plc, 82 King Street, Manchester M2 4WQ (tel: 0161 935 8027, fax: 0161 935 8195, email: tim.smallborne@gresham.uk).

SMITH, Adrian Charles, LLB

Positions: Circuit Judge; Member, Mental Health Review Tribunal.
Areas of Influence: Law.
Profile: *b.* November 25th, 1950; 2 daughters.
Education: Blackpool Grammar School; Queen Mary College, London. Career Profile Barrister, Northern Circuit (1974-96); North West Mental Health Review Tribunal (1994-96); Restricted Pannel (2001 -); Circuit Judge (1996 -).
Interests: World travel, theatre, fell walking.
Contact details: The Court Service, 15 Quay Street, Manchester M60 9FD.

SMITH, Sir Cyril, MBE, LLD(hon), D.Ed(hon), DL

Positions: After Dinner Speaker, Hon Sec., Happy Hours Pensioners Club.
Areas of Influence: Public Sector, Education, Voluntary Sector.
Profile: *b.* June 28th, 1928.
Educated at Spotland Primary School, Rochdale and Rochdale Grammar School for Boys. Career profile: Councillor and Alderman, Rochdale Borough Council (1952-75); MP Rochdale (1972-92); Chief Whip, Liberal Party (1976-78); Mayor of Rochdale (1966-67); Managing Director, Smithsprings (Rochdale) Ltd (1963-88); Non-executive Director, United Industries (1988-92). Freeman of the Borough of Rochdale (1994). Sir Cyril is active within the Happy Hour Pensioners Club, Rochdale where 100 members meet weekly. He is a regular after dinner speaker at Luncheon Clubs and Dinners (humourous) and is still a party member of the Liberal Democrats for whom he was NW President (1994-98). Publication: *Big Cyril, Autobiography* (1979). Awarded Public Speaking Young Liberals Prize 1948!! Clubs and societies: National Liberal Club; Spotland Reform Club.
Interests: Music, brass bands, politics (listener), local government reading, TV - soaps and panorama.

SMITH, Dame Janet Hilary, DBE (1992), QC (1986)

Positions: High Court Judge (1992 - present) and Chairman of the Shipman Inquiry; Chairman of the Security Vetting Appeals Panel.
Areas of Influence: Law.
Profile: *b.* November 29th, 1940; *m.* Robin Mathieson.
Educated at Bolton School (1951-59). Career profile: called to the Bar, Lincoln's inn (1972). Honorary Doctorate of Law, Manchester Metropolitan University (2002).
Contact details: Royal Courts of Justice, Strand, London WC2A 2LL.

SMITH, John Bartlett, BA, MSc, PGDip

Position: Governor, HMP Manchester (1998 - present).
Areas of Influence: Public Sector, Law, Faith Groups.
Profile: *b.* May 19th, 1950; *m.* Anne; 2 sons; 1 daughter.
Education: BA Hons Theology, St Chad's College, Durham (1970-73); Cuddeson College, Oxford (1973-76); PGDip IR, Lancaster; MSc Distinction, Southbank; Oxford Certificate in Theology. Career profile: Ordained Deacon C of E (1976), Ordained Priest C of E (1977), Curate of St Martin's Group, Hereford. Joined prison service (1980): Assistant Govenor, Hewell Grange Borstal (1980); Assistant Governor, HMP Wormwood Scrubs (1984); Deputy Governor, HMP Haverigg (1988); Deputy Governor HMP Wandsworth (1992); Governor, HMP Coldingly (1995).
Interests: Non stipendary Ministry within C of E, English choral music, fell walking.
Contact details: HMP Manchester, Southall Street, Manchester M60 9AH (tel: 0161 834 8626 ex: 535, fax: 0161 833 3649).

SMITH, Lord Peter Richard Charles, MSc

Positions: Life Peer (1999); Leader, Wigan Council; Leader, Association of Greater Manchester Councils (2000 - present); Director, Manchester Airport (1986 - present)
Areas of Influence: Public Sector.
Profile: *b.* July 24th, 1945; *m.* Joy Lesley; 1 daughter.
Education: Bolton School (1956-64); BSc Econ, London School of Economics (1964-67); Cert. Ed. (f.e.), Garnet College, London University (1968-9); MSc Urban Studies, Salford University (1981-83). Career profile: Lecturer, Walbrooke College, London (1969-74); Lecturer, St Johns College, Manchester (1974-01); Councillor (1978 - present), Chairman of Finance (1982-91), Wigan MBC; Chairman, Manchester Airport (1989-95); Chair (1999-00), Leader (2001), North West Regional Assembly. Member of Hindley Green Labour Club.
Interests: Sport, rugby, jazz, gardening, reading, particularly political biography, relaxing with friends.
Contact details: Wigan Council, Town Hall, Library Street, Wigan WN1 1YW (tel:

01942 827 001, email: leader@wiganmbc.gov.uk); Myserin, Old Hall Mill Lane, Atherton, Manchester M45 0PG (tel / fax: 01942 676 127).

SMITH, Philip, M LLB

Positions: Senior Partner, SAS Lawyers, Stockport; Chairman, Greater Manchester Strategic Health Authority.
Areas of Influence: Health, Law.
Profile: *b.* May 6th, 1947; Hester; 1 son; 1 daughter.
Educated at Manchester University. Career profile: Solicitor, Stockport; Senior Partner, Higginbottom & White (1990-94); Senior Partner, Sinclair Smith (1994-99); Senior Partner, Sinclair Abson Smith (1999-02); Senior Partner, SAS Lawyers (2002 -); Non-executive Director, Stockport NHS Acute Trust (1994-98); Chairman, Stockport Health Authority (1998-02); Chairman, Greater Manchester Health Authority (2002 -).
Interests: Wine, cycling, sailing, travel, reading.
Contact details: 36 Greek St, Stockport SK3 8AW (tel: 0161 285 4921, fax: 0161 480 4246, email: philip@saslawyers.co.uk); Chair, Greater Manchester Strategic Health Authority, Gateway House, Piccadilly South, Manchester M60 7LP (tel: 0161 237 2595, email: philip.smith@gmha.nhs.uk).

SMITH, Quentin

Positions: Partner, Addleshaw Booth & Co, Solicitors (1996-97); Head of Sport & Media Unit; Head of Health & Safety Unit; Chairman, Sale Sharks.
Areas of Influence: Law, Sport.
Profile: *b.* October 20th, 1955.
Education: University College School (1964-74; BEcon (Hons), Victoria Manchester University (1974-77); CPE Hon, Law Society Final Course, Manchester Metropolitan University (1983-85). Career profile: Management in the Voluntary Sector (1978-83); Articled Clerk (1985-87), Solicitor (1987-89), Partner (1989-96), James Chapman & Co Solicitors, Manchester; Partner, Addleshaw Booth & Co (1996-present). Extensive freelance writing for a variety of publications since 1996 on mediation, health and safety issues, and sport. Also runs training courses and seminars. Member, Development Committee of Royal Exchange Theatre.
Interests: Rugby, cello, arts, sport.
Contact details: 100 Barbirolli Square, Manchester M2 3AB (tel: 0161 934 6566, fax: 0161 934 6060, email: quentin.smith@addleshawbooth.com); 23 Darley Avenue, West Didsbury, Manchester M20 2ZD (tel: 0161 445 2523).

SMITH, Steven James

Positions: Shareholder and Director of Cotton Traders.
Areas of Influence: Sport.
Profile: *b.* July 22nd, 1951; *m.* Sue; 2 daughters.
Educated at Kings School, Macclesfield and Loughborough College. Career profile: 28 England Caps (1973-83); Captain of England (1982-83); British Lion; Captain of Sale, Cheshire, Lancashire, North of England and Barbarians; Played in NW Counties Team who beat the All Blacks (1973); Played in North of England Team to beat All Blacks (1980); Part of Bill Beaumonts Grand Slam Team (1980); Played in world Winning England Team (1973); Started Cotton Traders with Fran Cotton 15yrs ago.
Contact details: Cotton Traders, Antlantic Street, Altrincham (tel: 0870 3333 038, fax: 0870 3333 039, email: steve@cottontraders.co.uk); 18 Barry Rise, Bowdon, Cheshire WA14 3JS (tel: 0161 929 0951).

SNYDER, Heath Lee

Positions: Director, Corporate Finance, PricewaterhouseCoopers, Manchester.
Areas of Influence: Finance.
Profile: *b.* February 3rd, 1969; *m.* Roslyn.
Educated at William Hulme Grammar School and Manchester University. Qualifications: BA(Hons) Accounting and Finance; ACA Chartered Accountant; FSI, Fellow of Securities Institute. Career profile: Kidsons Impey, Trainee Accountant (1990-93); Pricewaterhouse Finance, Manchester (1994-97); PricewaterhouseCoopers Securities LLC, New York, USA (1998-00).
Interests: Sport, travel, cinema.
Contact details: PricewaterhouseCoopers, 101 Barbirolli Square, Lower Mosley Street, Manchester M2 3PW (tel. 0161 245 2501, fax: 0161 245 2912, email: heath.l.snyder@uk.pwcglobal.com).

SODERSTROM, Berndt-Erik BSc (1956)

Positions: Member: Executive Committee, Manchester Consular Association; Executive Committee, Finn Guild, London; Social and Communications Committee, Finn Guild; Finnish Friendship Network, Finn Guild; Finland Society, Helsinki; Confederation of Scandinavian Societies in Great Britain; Federation Internationale des Corps et Associations Consulaires; Finnish Expatriate Parliament, Great Britain. Ambassador, Christies against Cancer Fundraising Appeal.
Areas of Influence: Commerce, Voluntary Sector.
Profile: *b.* October 10th, 1934, Turku, Finland; *m.* Madeleine Emily, née Burtwell; 2 sons; 1 daughter.
Career profile: Vice President, NW Counties Schoolboys Amateur Boxing

Association; President, Manchester Consular Association (1987); Founder/ President, Anglo-Nordic Society; Founder / Chairman, Nordik link. Vice Chairman, Finnish School at Manchester; Acting Consul of Finland at Liverpool (1978-92); Volunteer worker, Wigan Hospice; Accredited Blue Badge Tourist Guide, Wigan Metropolitan Borough. Clubs and societies: European Committee, Manchester Chamber of Commerce and Industry; Manchester Luncheon Club; St James Club, Manchester; Atheneum, Liverpool; Committee Scandinavian Seamen's Church, Liverpool; Ski Club of Great Britain; Finnish-British Trade Guild. Over 100 non-published essays on Finland and Finnishness used in connection with presentations, talks and lectures on Finland.

Interests: International co-operation, military history, books, sport, music, arts.

Contact details: Consulate of Finland, 22 Hullet Close, Appley Bridge, Wigan WN6 9LD (tel / fax: 01257 252684).

SORRELL, Stephen Terence LLB

Positions: Solicitor and Partner, Eversheds; Trustee, Manchester Art Gallery Development Trust.

Areas of Influence: Law, Public Sector.

Profile: *b.* October 5th, 1959; *m.* Jane; 2 daughters.

Education: Marple Hall Grammar School; Manchester University; Chester College of Law. Career profile: Trainee Solicitor, Abson Hall Solicitors, Stockport; Solicitor, Abson Hall Solicitors, Stockport; Partner, Abson Hall Solicitors, Stockport; Partner, Eversheds (1989 -). Clubs and societies: Law Society; Sponsor, Cornerhouse.

Interests: Arts, cinema, theatre, football.

Contact details: Eversheds, National Head of Property Development, Eversheds House, 70 Great Bridgewater Street, Manchester M1 5ES (tel: 0161 831 8300, fax: 0161 832 5337, email: stephen.sorrell@eversheds.com); 35 Ladythorn Road, Bramhall, Stockport, Cheshire SK7 2EX (tel: 0161 292 7957).

SPACKMAN, Stanley Harry, CStJ, TD, DL

Positions: Commander, St John Ambulance, Greater Manchester; Regional Representative, Priory of England & the Islands Order of St John; Vice-Chairman, NW RFCA; Chairman, NW Cadet Committee.

Areas of Influence: Voluntary Sector, Public Sector.

Profile: *b.* April 20th, 1937; *m.* Kathleen Ann; 4 sons.

Educated at Sudbury Grammar School. Career profile: Deputy Collector, HM Customs and Excise (Manchester Collection) (1993-95); Colonel of Volunteers, Royal Corps of Transport (1988-91); County Commandant, Greater Manchester Army Cadet Force (1992-96). Clubs and Societies: Army and Navy Club; Movement Control Officers Club; Institution of the RASC and RCT; Waggon Club; Manchester Naval

Officers Association.

Interests: Reading, travel, keeping fit, leadership training.

Contact details: 10 Roan House Way, Macclesfield, Cheshire SK11 7BY (email: stanannstpackman@aol.com).

SPENCER, Liam David, BA

Position: Artist.
Areas of Influence: Arts.
Profile: *b.* April 16th, 1964; *m.* Heather; 2 sons.
Education: Foundation Course, Burnley College of Arts and Technology (1982-83); Manchester Polytechnic (1983-86). Exhibitions: *Windows on the City*, Townley Hall Museum and Art Gallery Burnley (1996); *The Mancunian Way*, Royal Northern College of Music (1997-98); *Urban Panoramas*, The Lowry, Salford.
Interests: Fly fishing, football.
Contact details: 2nd Floor, Ferguson House, 11 Blackfriars Road, Salford M3 7AG (tel: 0161 832 3361, email: liam.spencer@lineone.net); 67 Albert Terrace, Cloughfold, Rossendale BB4 7PY (tel: 01706 221 948).

SPINOZA, Andrew Daniel, BA, AIPR

Positions: Managing Director, Spin Media Ltd; Vice-President, Community Foundation, Greater Manchester; Chairman, Manchester Digital Trade Association.
Areas of Influence: Media, Commerce, Public Sector.
Profile: *b.* July 24th, 1961; *m.* Lynne; 3 daughters.
Education: Minchenden Secondary School, Southgate, London; University of Manchester. Career profile: Founder, City Life, Manchester (1983); Arts and Features Editor, City Life, Manchester (1983-88); Curator, Sublime Exhibition, Cornerhouse, Manchester (1992); Diary Editor, Manchester Evening News (1993-98); Showbusiness Editor, Manchester Evening News (1998); Founder, Spin Media Public Relations Agency (1998).
Interests: Family, Manchester City Football Club.
Contact details: Spin Media, 2nd Floor, North Square, 11-13 Spear Street, Manchester M1 1JU (tel: 0161 236 9909, fax: 0161 236 8909, email: enquiries@spinmedia.co.uk).

SPOONER, John

Position: MD, Manchester Airport.
Areas of Influence: Commerce.

STACEY, Ed, BA, CertPR, DipPR, DipBC

Positions: Chief Executive, Oldham Chamber of Commerce; Director, Revolution Radio, Oldham Business Management School; Governor, Saddleworth School; Governor, Oldham VIth Form College.
Areas of Influence: Commerce, Media, Economic Regeneration.
Profile: *b.* June 4th, 1949; *m.* Lyn; 1 son, Robert; 1 daughter, Helen.
Education: Sheffield Polytechnic; Durham University Business School. Career profile: Sheffield Polytechnic Union of Students (1971-72); Public Relations and Economic Development, Corby, Leicester, Sunderland and Oldham Local Authorities; Private Sector Regeneration and Business Services, Oldham Enterprise and Oldham Chamber of Commerce. Clubs and societies: Labour Party, fund raiser; Scanner Appeal, fund raiser; Oldham Coliseum Theatre; Fund Raiser, School Bids for Specialist College Status; Linked with British Chamber of Commerce.
Interests: Sport, fund raising, politics, theatre, films, literature.
Contact details: Oldham Chamber of Commerce, The Oldham Business Centre, Cromwell Street, Oldham OL1 1BB (tel: 0161 620 0006, fax: 0161 620 0030, email: edstacey@oldchamber.co.uk,

STACEY, Glenys, BA (Hons), MBA

Positions: Justices' Chief Secretary (2000 - present); Chief Executive, Criminal Cases Review Commission (1997 - present).
Areas of Influence: Law, Public Sector, Finance.
Profile: *m.* Anthony; 1 son; 1 daughter.
Glenys Stacey's post arose from the amalgamation of the Magistrates Courts Committees for the City of Manchester, North & West Greater Manchester, Oldham, Stockport Tameside and Trafford and became effective in 2001, servicing the same area as the Greater Manchester Police Authority. As Justices' Chief executive, Glenys is responsible with the Magistrates Courts Committee for the delivery of an effective and efficient magistrates' Court Service throughout the county. The Committee employs some 700 staff and operates 10 couthouses, serviced by some 2000 lay Magistrates and five District Judges.The combined courts' caseload exceeds six percent of the total for England and Wales. Glenys is a solicitor and has worked both in private practice and for the Law Society. As an Area manager for the Legal Aid Board, she steered the Leeds regional office successfully through a period of considerable change. Clubs and societies: Law Society; Medico Legal Society; Association of Justices' Chief Executives.
Interests: Music, cycling.
Contact details: Sally Rogers, Press Officer and Executive Assistant to the Justices'

Chief Executive, GMCC Secretariat, Manchester City Magistrates Court, Third Floor Crown Square, Manchester M60 1PR (tel: 0161 832 7272, fax: 0161 834 2198, email: sally-anne.rogers@gmmcc.mcs.gov.uk).

STANLEY, Jeanette Letuina, DMS

Positions: Director, African and Caribbean Mental Health Services (1996 - present); Justice of the Peace.
Areas of Influence: Health, Women's Issues, Training.
Profile: *b.* June 22nd, 1949; 1 daughter.
Education: Excelsior High School, Kingston Jamaica; Claremont Secondary School; North Cheshire College; Burleigh Secretarial College; Manchester Polytechnic (1986-87); Manchester Metropolitan University (1991-93). Career profile: Medical Receptionist / Secretary (1982-81); Coordinator, Moss Side Office Skills Project (1981-83); Senior Administrator, Greater Manchester Council for Voluntary Services (1983-85); Project, Regional and Operations Manager, Fullemploy Training Ltd (1985-91); Manager, Moss Side & Hulme Community Development Trust Job Link (1991-96). Jeanette Stanley has been involved for 20 years in the provision of training for disadvantaged people, particularly those from the black and minority ethnic communities wishing to access education, training and employment opportunities. Equal Opportunities Committe at Forest Bank Prison.
Interests: Reading, listening to music, watching football and athletics.
Contact details: African and Caribbean Mental Health Services; Zion Community Resource Centre, 339 Stretford Road, Hulme, Manchester M15 4ZY (tel: 0161 226 9562, fax: 0161 226 7947, email: admin@acmhs-blackmentalhealth.org.uk); 18 Royston Road, Firswood, Stretford, Manchester M16 0EU (tel: 0161 286 6713), mob: 07930 357 122, email: jeanette.sankey@ntlworld.com).

STEPHEN, Dr Martin, BA DipEd, PhD, FRSA

Positions: High Master, The Manchester Grammar School (1994 - present); Visiting Lecturer, University of Manchester (2001 - present).
Areas of Influence: Education, Media.
Profile: *b.* July 18th, 1949; *m.* Jenny; 3 sons.
Education: Uppingham School (1962-66); University of Leeds (1967-70); University of Sheffield (1971-76). Career profile: Teacher, Uppingham School (1971-72); Teacher and Housemaster; Haileybury (1972-83); Second Master, Sedbergh School (1983-87); Headmaster, The Perse Scool, Cambridge (1987-94).
Interests: Writing, sailing, diving, field sports, art.
Contact details: High Master, Manchester Grammer School, Manchester M30 0XT (tel: 0161 224 7557, fax: 0161 257 2446, email: g.m.stephen@mgs.org); 9 Stanton Avenue, Didsbury, Manchester M20 2PG (tel: 0161 446 1210).

STEPHENSON, Alan, BA (Hons), MSc

Position: Chairman, Greater Manchester Ambulance Service, NHS Trust (1997 – present); Chairman, NHS Confederation Ambulance Service Working Group (1999 - present); National Trustee, NHS Confederation (2001 - present).
Areas of Influence: Health, Public Sector.
Profile: 45 years of age.
Education: Local Secondary Modern; Grammar School VIth Form; College of Higher Education. Career profile: Member, Greater Manchester Council (1981-86); Wigan Council (1988 - present). Clubs and societies: Lancashire County Cricket Club; St Helens Rugby League Club; Labour Party.
Interests: Health and Social Care, regeneration, politics, history.
Contact details: Chairman, Greater Manchester Ambulance Service NHS Trust, Bury Old Road, Whitefield, Manchester M45 6AQ.

STEPHENSON, Roger Francis, OBE (2001), BArch, Arb, RIBA

Positions: Director, Stephenson Bell Architects; Chairman, Manchester Conservation Areas & Historic Buildings Panel; Councillor, RIBA; Director, Castlefield Art Gallery.
Areas of Influence: Arts, Commerce, Education.
Profile: *b.* February 15th, 1946; *m.* Kate (separated); 2 sons; 1 daughter.
Education: Beckenham Grammar School, Kent (1959-72); Liverpool University (1964-69). Career profile: Building Design Partnership, Manchester (1969-72); Partner, Michael Hyde & Partners (1972-79); Founder Partner, Stephenson Bell (1979 -).
Publications: *Layers* (1999); *Stephenson Bell – projects*, by Kenneth Powell (2001).
Interests: Painting, drawing, skiing.
Contact details: Stephenson Bell, 43 Hulme Street, Manchester M15 6AW (tel: 0161 236 5667, fax: 0161 236 2010, email: roger.stephenson@stephenson-bell.com).

STEWART, Ian MP

Positions: Member of Parliament; PPS, Minister of State for Energy and Construction.
Areas of Influence: Public Sector.
Profile: *b.* August 28th, 1950; *m.* Merilyn; 2 sons; 1 daughter.
Education: David Livingstone Primary Meml. School, Blantyre; Calder Street Secondary, Blantyre; Alfred Turner Secondary Modern School, Salford; Stretford Technical College; Manchester Metropolitan University. Career profile: Regional Officer, TGWU (1978-97); Member, Deregulation Select Committee (1997-01); Member, Information Select Committee (1998-01); Member, PLP Employment and Training Committee (1997 -); Member, PLP Trade and Industry Committee (1997 -); Member, PLP Foreign Affairs Committee (1997 -); Member, PITCOM (1997 -); Vice-

Chairman, All Party China Group (1997 -); Member, GB China Centre Exec, (1997 -); Chairman, Parliamentary Group for Vaccine Damaged Children (1998-01); Joint Founder, European Foundation for Social Partnership and Continuing Trust Initiatives (1993). Clubs and societies: UK Society of Industrial Tutors (1980 -); Manchester Industrial Relations Society (1994 -); International Society of Industrial Relations (1996 -); Council European Informatics Market (1998 -); Fellow, Industry and Parliamentary Trust (1997); Visiting Fellow, Salford University (1998).
Contact details: House of Commons, London SW1A 0AA (tel: 020 7219 6175, fax: 020 7219 0903, email: ianstewartmp@parliament.uk).

STEWART, Stephen Paul QC (1996) MA

Positions: Queens Counsel; Recorder of the Crown Court; Deputy Judge, Technology and Construction Court.
Areas of Influence: Law.
Profile: October 9th, 1953; *m.* Dr. M. Felicity; 1 son; 1 daughter.
Education: Stand Grammar School, Whitefield; St Peters College, Oxford. Career profile: Barrister, 28 St John Street Chambers (1975-96); Barrister, 12 Byrom Street Chambers (1996 -). Stephen Stewart is a member of Alderley Edge Cricket Club.
Interests: Running, sport, wine, music.
Contact details: Byrom Street Chambers, 12 Byrom Street, Manchester M3 4PP (tel: 0161 829 2100, fax: 0161 829 2101, email: clerks@byromstreet.com).

STIRLING, Penny, FRNCM, GRSM, ARCM (Piano Teaching), ARCM (Violin Teaching), PGCE

Positions: Director, Junior Strings Project, Royal Northern College of Music.
Areas of Influence: Education, Arts, Music.
Profile: *b.* November 28th, 1954; *m.* Grahan Merriam; 2 stepsons.
Education: Sexey's Grammar School, Blackford, Somerset; Royal College of Music, London;
St Mary's College, Cheltenham. Career profile: Since 1991 Penny Stirling has been running the internationally renowned Junior Strings Project (JSP) at the Royal Northern College of Music in Manchester, which was awarded the Partnership Trust's Thorn EMI award for innovations in music teaching training (1995). In 1998 the RNCM became the first (and only) conservatoire to be awarded a Queen's Anniversary Prize for the Junior Strings Project. Penny has written articles for both *Music Teacher* magazine and *The Strad*. She is a member of the Manchester Music Service Management Committee and staff member of the Board of Governors of RNCM. In 2000 she was awarded Fellowship of the Royal Northern College of Music. Penny has also taught at the Chetham's School of Music and is currently teaching violin and viola at the Junior RNCM. She has always been keen to promote chamber

music playing with children and founded the Young String Venture course at Lake District Summer Music (1989). She also coaches for Pro Corda North. Penny is Course Leader for the Associated Board of the Royal Schools of Music's CT CBRSM course in Manchester, and she is a member of the Musician's Union, European String Teachers Association, National Trust, and Friends of the Earth.

Interests: Organic farming, sport.

Contct details: Royal Northern College of Music, 124 Oxford Road, Manchester M13 9RD (tel: 0161 907 5398, fax: 0161 272 7128, email: penny.striling@mcm.ac.uk); 159 Henrietta Street, Ashton-under-Lyne, OL6 8PH.

STOCK, The Right Reverend William Nigel BA DipTheol

Position: Bishop of Stockport.
Areas of Influence: Faith Groups.
Profile: *b.* January 29th, 1950; *m.* Carolyne; 3 sons.
Education: Durham Scool; Durham University; Ripon College, Cuddesdon. Career profile: Assistant Curate, Stockton-Tees (1976-79); Priest-in-Charge, Taraka, Lae, Papua New Guinea (1979-84); Vicar, Shiremoor, Newcastle-upon-Tyne (1985-91); Team Rector, North Shields (1991-98); Rural Dean of Tynemouth (1992-98); Honorary Canon, Newcastle Cathedral (1997-98); Residentiary Canon, Durham Cathedral (1998-00); Bishop of Stockport (2000 -)
Interests: Walking, photography, painting, reading, travel.
Contact details: Bishop of Stockport C of E, Bishp's Lodge, Dunham Town, Altrincham WA14 2SG (tel: 0161 928 5611, fax: 0161 929 0692, email: bpsockport@chester.anglican.org).

STOCKDALE, David Andrew, QC (1995), MA

Positions: Barrister, Deans Court Chambers; Recorder (1993 - present); Governor, Giggleswick School (1982 - present); Chairman of Governors, Giggleswick School (1997 - present); Governor, Terra Nova School (2000 - present).
Areas of Influence: Law, Education.
Profile: *b.* May 9th, 1951; *m.* Melanie; 1 son; 3 daughters.
Education: Giggleswick School (1960-69); Pembroke College, Oxford (1969-73), MA (Lit.Hum); The College of Law, London (1973-75). Career profile: Called to the Bar, Middle Temple (1975); pupillage with Keith Goddard QC, Deans Court Chambers, Manchester (1976); Junior of the Northern Circuit (1978); Assistant Recorder (1990); practising in common law, particularly personal injuries and professional negligence. Member, Sloane Club, London.
Interests: Family, the outdoors, remote Scotland.
Contact details: Deans Court Chambers, 24 St John Street, Manchester M3 4DF (tel: 0161 214 6000).

STOKES, Christopher Peter, Hon FTCl, BMus, FRCO.

Positions: Organist and Master of the Choristers (1996 - present), Manchester Cathedral; Head of Organ Studies, Chetham's School of Music (1994 - present); Member of Council, Royal College of Organists; Trustee, Organists Benevolent Fund. **Areas of Influence:** Arts, Education.
Profile; *b*. August 29th, 1952; *m*. Carolyn; 1 son; 1 daughter.
Educated at Royal Masonic School and Trinity College of Music. Career profile: Assistant Organist, St Martin in the Fields (1976-79); Organist and Master of Music, St Martin in the Fields (1979-89); Director of Music, St Margaret's, Westminster (1989-92); Organist, Manchester Cathedral (1992-96); Professor of Organ, Trinity College of Music, London (1978-94). Creative work: Sacred music for choirs. Awarded the Gertrude Norman Prize, Trinity College of Music.
Interests: Theatre, walking, eating, reading on the loo.
Contact details: Manchester Cathedral M3 1SX (tel; 0161 833 2220, fax: 0161 839 6226, email: christopherstokes@manchestercathedral.com).

STOLLER, Norman K, MBE (1976), OBE (1999), CStJ (1998), DL (1995)

Positions: Chairman, Stoller Charitable Trust; Non-executive Chairman, Mountain Goat Ltd; Lake Invest Ltd; Hon Life President, Oldham Chamber of Commerce.
Areas of Influence: Voluntary Sector, Commerce.
Profile: *b*. September 6th, 1934; divorced; 1 son, Martin (1964); 1 daughter, Linzi (1962).
Educated at Eccles High School. Career profile: Non-Commissioned Officer, Royal Air Force (1952-55); Joined Seton Products (1955). Managing Director, Seton Healthcare (1962-84); Chairman (1984-95); Seton Healthcare Group Plc Non Executive Chairman (1995-98); SSL International Plc, President (1998-99). High Sheriff County of Greater Manchester (1999-00). County President, St John Ambulance (1984-02). Founding Chairman Oldham Export Club; Pennine Chapter Young President's Association; Pennine Chapter World Presidents Association. CBI Daily Telegraph NW Businessman of the Year (1991). Member of the Royal College of Music (honoris Causa) (1999). Member of various Social Clubs and Windermere Golf Club.
Interests: Sailing, reading, wine, malt whiskey, golf.
Contact details: Inarush, Garsdale lane, Bolton BL1 5XD (tel: 01204 492312, email: nkstoller@hotmail).

STRACHAN, Anthony John (Tony)

Positions: Agent, Bank of England North West Agency (2000); Member, North West Industrial Development Board; Vice Chairman and Trustee, Museum of Science and

Industry in Manchester; Governor, Manchester Metropolitan University; Member of Court, University of Salford.
Areas of Influence: Finance, Commerce, Education.
Profile: *b.* September, 23rd, 1956, Chalfont St Giles, Bucks ; *m.* Sarah (1981); 1 son; 1 daughter.
Educated at Gayhurst School, Bucks (1963-69), Merchant Taylor's School, Northwood (1969-74) and Open University Business School (1995-9). Career profile: Bank of England, London (1974 - present): Exchange Control Department (1974-79); Pension Fund Administration (1979-83); International Division (1983-86); Banking Supervision Division (1986-88); Technical Assistant to Director, Banking and Banking Supervision (1988); Seconded to Takeover Panel (1989-90); Business Finance Division (1991-95); Appointed Agent in Manchester (1995). Publication: *The Governance and Role of Business Corporations in a Modern Society.* Clubs and societies: Portico Library; Liveryman of the Worshipful Company of Chartered Secretaries and Administrators; Freeman of the City of London.
Interests: Classical music, theatre, opera, ballet, walking, reading.
Contact details: Bank of England, North West Agency, PO Box 301, 82 King Street, Manchester M60 2HP (tel: 0161 834 6199, fax: 0161 839 1131, email: tony.strachan@bankofengland.co.uk).

STUART, Steven, FICA (1980), FACA (1977)

Position: Corporate Finance Partner, Ernst & Young.
Areas of Influence: Finance, Commerce.
Profile: *b.* July 4th, 1954; *m.* Susanne; 2 sons.
Education: Holt High School for Boys, Childwall, Liverpool. Career profile: Thompson Mclintock (1970); Cawoods Holdings; Arthur Young Mclelland Moores (1979). Clubs and Societies: Hillside Golf Club; Woolton Golf Club.
Interests: Liverpool Football Club, cooking, music.
Contact details: Ernst & Young, 100 Barbirolli Square, Manchester M2 3EY (tel: 0161 333 3000); Acrefield Cottage, Acrefield Road, Woolton, Liverpool L25 5JP (tel: 0151 428 1066, fax: 0151 421 1922).

STUNELL, Andrew MP OBE

Positions: Member of Parliament, Hazel Grove Constituencey; Chief Whip, Liberal Democrats.
Areas of Influence: Public sector, Law.
Profile: *b.* November 24th, 1942; *m.* Gillian; 3 sons; 2 daughters.
Education: Surbiton Grammar School; Manchester University; Liverpool Polytechnic. Career profile: Architecture Assistant (1965-85); Association of Liberal Democrat Councillors (1985-97); Member of Parliament, Hazel Grove (1997 -); Councillor,

Chester City Council (1979-90); Councillor, Cheshire County Council (1981-91); Vice-Chairman, Association of County Councils (1985-90); Councillor, Stockport Metropolitan Borough Council (1994-02).

Contact details: Liberal Democrat HQ, 68A Compstall Road, Romiley, Stockport SK6 4DE (tel: 0161 406 7070, fax: 0161 494 2425); 84 Lyme Grove, Romily, Stockport SK6 4DJ).

SuAndi, OBE (1999)

Profile: Freelance Cultural Director, Black Arts Alliance; Writer; Poet and Performance Artist.

Areas of Influence: Arts

Profile: *b.* October 17th, 1951.

Educated at Ardwick Technical High School and Bolton Technical College. Career profile: Board Member, NWAB, City of Drama, Akwaaba, National Disability Arts Forum, North West Playwrights, Arts Development Agency. Winston Churchill Fellow (1996). Clubs and societies: British Equity; NAWE; Circle Club, Manchester; AGIA, Atlanta GA; TAAC, USA. Publications: *Style*; *Nearly 40*; *There will be no tears*; *4 for More.*

Interests: Using the arts as a vehicle to widen the social and educational interests of all people and to help drive out biogotry.

Contact details: Black Arts Alliance, PO Box 86, Manchester M21 7BA (tel: 0161 832 7622, fax: 016 832 2276, email: baa@baas.demon.co.uk, web: www.baas.demon.co.uk /temp.html).

SUMMERS, John Heath, LTCL

Position: Chief Executive, Hallé Orchestra.

Areas of Influence: Arts.

Profile: *b.* June 5th, 1952; *m.* Jeanette; 3 sons; 1 daughter.

Education: Cranbrook School; St Olives Grammar School; Trinity College of Music. Career profile: Cellist (1977-81); Manager, Northern Sinfonia (1981-91); Chief Executive, Northern Sinfonia (1991-99); Chairman. Association of British Orchestras (1995-98); Chief Executive, Hallé Orchestra (1999 -).

Interests: Golf, cricket, fishing, food, wine.

Contact details: Chief Executive, Hallé Orchestra, Bridgewater Hall, Manchester M1 5HA (tel:0161 237 7000, fax: 0161 237 7014, email: john.summers@halle.co.uk).

SUMRA, Dr Ranjit Singh, MBBS (1963), MD (1966), BSc (1958), DM (1972)

Positions: Consultant Clinical Neurophysiologist, Tameside General Hospital, The Beaumont Hospital and Yale Hospital Wrexham; Medical Director, D-Medicine Ltd., Outline Medical Services; Chair, Council of Indian Language and Indo-British Collaboration; Representative, Sikhism in Interfaith Circuit;
Areas of Influence: Health, Education, Faith Groups.
Profile: *b.* July 5th, 1940; married with 2 children.
Career profile: Hospital Interpreter for Indian Languages (1979 - present); Counselling service for Ethnic Population for Education and Health Services (1990 - present); Represents Sikh Communities and Council of Indian Languages in the Local Strategic Partnership, Manchester City Council and other activities in support of Indian Languages, Sikhism and Cultural Diversity. Publications: Thirteen papers published in various professional journals, ten relating to Neurology and Clinical Neurophysiology, four to Internal Medicine, and a booklet on Aids (1990) for distribution in developing countries. Regular speaker on Clinical Governance. Clubs and societies: Association of British Clinical Neurophysiologists; Neurology Society of India; Hospital Consultants and Specialists Association UK; BMA; BMA Regional Consultant and Specialist Forum, Tameside General Hospital; GMC Specialist in Neuroscience.
Interests: Table tennis, badminton, activities relating to Indo-British collaboration.
Contact details: Tameside General Hospital, Ashton-u-Lyne, Greater Manchester (tel: 0161 331 5057 / 0161 282 8263).

SUTHERLAND, John, BCom, MA ,OBE

Position: Operations Director, British Red Cross, Manchester Merseyside and Lancashire.
Areas of Influence: Voluntary Sector.
Profile: *b.* July 2nd, 1938.
Education: University of Aberdeen (1956-59); University of Edinburgh (1959-61).
Career profile: Trainee Manager, Lewis's Department Store; Group Managing Director, Manchester (1981-88); Branch Director, British Red Cross, Merseyside (1993); Operations Director, British Red Cross, Manchester, Merseyside and Lancashire.
Interests: Opera, travel.
Contact details: British Red Cross Headquarters, Bradbury House, Ohio Avenue, Central Park, Salford Quays, Manchester M5 2GT (tel: 0161 888 8900, fax: 0161 877 7654, email: jsutherland@redcross.org.uk).

SUTTON, Michele, MSc

Position: Principal of Hopwood Hall College.
Areas of Influence: Education.
Profile: *m.* Jeff; 2 daughters.
Interests: Listening to Jazz, blues, rock and roll, reading, travelling, swimming.
Contact details: Hopwood Hall College, Rochdale Road, Middleton (tel: 0161 643 7560, fax: 0161 643 2114, email: michele.sutton@hopwood.ac.uk).

SWANTON, David

Positions: Director of Media and PR, Sale Sharks RUFC; BBC Radio Presenter.
Areas of Influence: Media, Sport.
Profile: *b.* March 24th, 1957; *m.* Carole; 2 sons.
Educated at High School and College. David Swanton has been involved in sport and music for almost 30 years. Publication: Central Park Years (1999). Prizes and awards: Tetleys Media manager of the Year (1999); Zurich Media Manager of the Year (2002).
Interests: Cricket, rugby, speedway, music.
Contact details: Sale Sharks, Heywood Road, Sale, M33 3WB (tel: 0161 610 0506, fax: 0161 969 4126, email: dave.swanton@salesharks.co.uk); 52 Lichen Close, Charnock Richard, Chorley (tel: 01257 791696).

SWEENEY, Vincent Anthony, BA (Hons)

Positions: Assistant Chief Constable (1994 - present).
Areas of Influence: Law, Public sector.
Profile: *b.* October 2nd, 1952; *m.* Sheila; 3 daughters.
Education: St Cuthberts Grammar School, Newcastle upon Tyne; BRNC, Dartmouth; BA (Hons) Criminal Justice Studies, New College, Durham. Career profile: Short Service Commission, Royal Navy (1971-76); Northumbria Police to rank of Chief Superintendent (1977 - 94).
Interests: Music, walking, golf.
Contact details: Greater Manchester Police HQ, PO Box 22, S West PDO, Chester House, Boyer Street, Manchester M16 0RE.

SWIFT, Caroline Jane, QC (1993), BA (Hons) (Dunelm)

Positions: Leading Counsel to the Shipman Inquiry (2001 - present); Recorder (1995 - present); Deputy High Court Judge (2000 - present). Governing Bencher of Inner Temple (1997 - present).
Areas of Influence: Law, Local Government.
Profile: *b.* May 30th, 1955; *m.* His Honour Judge C P L Openshaw; 1 son; 1 daughter.

Educated at Lancaster Girls Grammar School and University of Durham. Career profile: President, Durham Union Society (1975); President, Durham Riding Club (1975-76); Called to the Bar, Inner Temple (1977); Practised on Northern Circuit (1978 - present); Assistant Recorder (1992-95). Publications: *Ribchester: 100 Years in Photographs*; *Ribchester: a Millenium Record*.
Interests: Home and family, parish affairs, cooking, theatre, skiing.
Contact details: Byrom Chambers, 12 Byrom Street, Manchester M3 4PP (tel: 0161 829 2100, fax: 829 2101, email: peter@byromstreet.com).

SYKES, The Rev Canon John, BA

Positions: Team Rector and Vicar, Oldham; Chaplain, HRH Queen Elizabeth II.
Areas of Influence: Faith Groups, Education.
Profile: *b.* March 20th, 1939; *m.* Anne; 1 son; 1 daughter.
Education: Royd Hall Grammar School, Huddersfield; West Bridgford Grammar School, Nottingham; Manchester University; Ripon Hall, Oxford. Career profile: Curate, St Lukes, Heywood (1963-67); Priest in Charge, Holy Trinity, Bolton (1967-71); Lecturer, Bolton Institute of Technology (1967-71); Chaplain, Bolton Colleges of Further Education (1967-71); Rector, St Elisabeth, Reddish (1971-78); Vicar, Saddleworth (1978-87); Member, General Synod of CofE (1980-90); Council of The Care of Churches (1986-90); Vice-Chairman, Art and Design Committee (1988-90); Vicar and Team Rector, St Mary's with St Peter, Oldham (1987 -); Chaplain, Oldham Coliseum Theatre (1987 -); Honorary Canon, Manchester Cathedral (1991 -); Chaplain to High Sheriff, Greater Manchester (1993-94, 1996-97); Greater Manchester Police, Q Division (1995-99). Canon Sykes is a member of the Manchester Pedestrian Club.
Interests: Architecture, fine Arts, music, walking.
Contact details: Oldham Vicarage, 15 Grotton Hollow, Oldham OL4 4LN (tel: 0161 678 6767, fax: 0161 678 6767, email: j.sykes@rdplus.net).

SYKES, Sally Ann, MSc, BA (Hons), FRSA, MIPR

Positions: PR & Communications Director, AstraZeneca (Pharmaceuticals), Alderley Park, Cheshire; Director, Progress Trust Manchester and Centre for Corporate and Public Affairs, Manchester Metropolitan University; Board Member, Advisory Board, MMU PR Course.
Areas of Influence: Media, Commerce, Education.
Profile: *b.* February 16th, 1962; *m.* Paul.
Education: Altrincham Grammar School for Girls (1973-80); University of Leeds (1980-83); Distance Learning, University of Stirling (1992, 1996). Career profile: PR Manager, Scottish & Newcastle Breweries (1990-92); PR & Communications Manager, Littlewoods plc (1992-96); Head of Press & PR, Manchester Airport plc

(1996-2002); Guest Lecturer, PR Degree Programmes for undergraduates and post graduates, University of Central Lancashire, Leeds Metropolitan University, and Manchester Metropolitan University. Sally Sykes has produced many professional journal articles on Public Relations, the most recent of which was titled *Talent, Diversity, and Growing Expectations*, published in the Journal of Communications Management (2002). She was awarded North West of England PR Professional of the Year (2001) by the Institute of Public Relations. Clubs and societies: Network; Business Women's Network; Royal Society for Arts; Fellow of Manufacture and Commerce, Institute of Public Relations.

Interests: Arts, dance, theatre, music, visual art, entertaining, reading, travel, wine, motorcycling.

Contact details: AstraZeneca, Alderley Park, Alderley House, Macclesfield, Cheshire (tel: 01625 518 058, fax: 01625 585 405, email: sally.sykes@astrazeneca.com).

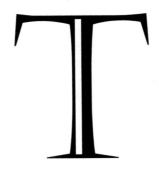

TAGGART, Paul William, BA

Positions: Professional Fine Artist; Author (1991 - present).
Areas of Influence: Arts, Media, Education.
Profile: *b.* February 27th, 1950; Eileen Tonnell (partner)
Education: Houghton le Spring Grammar School, Sunderland; Sunderland College of
Art; Manchester College of Art. Career profile: Exhibiting and selling Fine Arts (1973
- present); occasional private painting tutor offering painting holidays etc; Co-
founder and technical editor of Painting Magazines (1995-00); Occasional tutoring in
Public Sector (1974-98). Paul Taggart specialises in figurative genre work and
landscapes, whose signature feature is the quality of light. He works in all drawing
and painting media, plus some printing. He has had mainly solo exhibitions since
1974 plus some mixed exhibitions and showings across a wide spectrum of venues.
He has also produced original works of art in public and private collections in the
UK, Europe, USA and the Middle East. He is author and illustrator of over 10 art
instruction books.
Contact details: Paul Taggart, Fine Artist, 15 Lynwood Grove, Sale, Cheshire M33
2AN (tel: 0161 969 1987, email: mail@artworkshopwothpaul.com).

TALLIS, Professor Raymond Courtney, BA, BM, BCh, MRCP, FRCP

Positions: Professor of Geriatric Medicine, University of Manchester and Consultant
in Healthcare of the Elderly, Hope Hospital, Salford (1987).
Areas of Influence: Health, Medicine, Philosophy.
Profile: *b.* October 10th, 1946; *m.* Terry; 2 sons.
Education: Liverpool College (1954-64); Open Scholarship (Medicine), Keble College,
Oxford University; BA Animal Physiology, Oxford (1967); BM, BCh, Oxford

University and St Thomas' Hospital, London (1970); Doctor of Letters, Honoris causea, University of Hull (1997); Fellow of the Academy of Medical Sciences (2000); Doctor of Letters, Honoris causea, University of Manchester (to be conferred) (2002). Professor Tallis is responsible for acute needs and rehabilitation of in-patients. He also runs a unique epilepsy service for older people. Unlike may senior academic medics, he still covers acute services and participates in an on-call rota. Among his 150 or so publications are two major textbooks, *The Clinical Neurology of Old Age* (1988) and *Textbook of Geriatric Medicine and Gerontology* (2001). He has also published *Epilepsy in Older people* (1996). Fellow, Royal College of Physicians and Academy of Medical Sciences. Member of Athenaeum.

Interests: Family, music, Stella Artois.

Contact details: Hope Hospital, Clinical Science Building, Salford, M6 8HD (tel: 0161 787 7164, fax: 0161 787 5722, email: rtallis@FS1.HO.MAN.AC.UK; 5 Valley Road, Bramhall SK7 2NH (tel: 0161 439 2548).

TANDY, Virginia BA DipMuse

Positions: Director, Manchester City Galleries; Council Member, Museums Association.

Areas of Influence: Arts.

Profile: *b.* February 29th, 1956.

Education: Waterloo Park School for Girls, Liverpool; Newcastle upon Tyne Polytechnic; Manchester University. Career profile: Museums Officer, Tameside Borough Council (1979-84); Senior Exhibitions Officer, Cornerhouse (1984-86); Visual Arts Officer, North West Arts Board (1990-94); Director, Cornerhouse (1994-98); Director, Manchester City Galleries (1998 -).

Contact details: Manchester Art Gallery, Mosely St, Manchester M2 3JL (tel: 0161 235 8801, fax: 0161 235 8899, email: v.tandy@notes.manchester.gov.uk).

TARBUCK, Phil MA DipMan, CCETSW

Positions: Church Warden, Holy Innocents, Fallowfield; Management Committee, Voluntary Action Manchester; Management Committee, Partners of Prisoners and Families Support Group; Management Committee, Greater Manchester Imigration Aid Unit; Governor, Resurrection C of E Primary School.

Areas of Influence: Education, Faith Groups, Voluntary Sector.

Profile: *b.* March 14th, 1937.

Education: St Ambrose College, Hale Barns, Cheshire; Campion House, Osterley, Middlesex; St Josephs College, Malpas, Cheshire; Rainer House, Cromwell Road, London; University of Salford. Career profile: Apprenticeship, Ferranti Ltd; Pre-Ordination Studies, Sacred Heart Fathers; Youth Leader Certificate, Liverpool Education Committee; Home Office Qualification; Probation Officer. Clubs and

Societies: National Association of Probation Officers; British Institute of Social Workers.
Interests: Faith, politics, contemporary history, travel.
Contact details: 24 Mitford Court, Derby Road, Fallowfield, Manchester M14 6WD (tel: 0161 225 5967, fax: 0161 225 5967, email: p.tarbuck@btopenworld.com).

TATTERSALL, Geoffrey Frank, QC (1992), MA

Position: Barrister; Recorder, Crown Court; Judge of Appeal, Isle of Man.
Areas of Influence: Faith Groups, Law.
Profile: *b.* September 22nd, 1947; *m.* Hazel; 1 son; 2 daughters.
Education: Manchester Grammar School; Christ Church, Oxford. Career profile: Called to the Bar, Lincolns Inn (1970); In Practice, Northern Circuit (1970 -); Recorder, Crown Court (1989 -); QC (1992; Called to Bar, New South Wales (1992 -); Sc (1995); Bencher, Lincolns Inn (1997 -); Judge of Appeal, Isle of Man (1997 -); Lay Chairman, Bolton Deanery Synod (1993-02); Chairman, House of Law (1994 -); Vice-President, Manchester Diocesan Synod (1994 -); Member, General Synod (1995 -); Chairman, Standing Orders Committee (1999 -).
Interests: Travel, music, wine.
Contact details: Byrom Street Chambers, 12 Byrom Street, Manchester M3 4PP (tel: 0161 829 2100, fax: 0161 829 2101, email: gft@byromstreet.com).

TAVERNOR, Peter, BA, SocSc (Hons), PGCE

Positions: Principal, Manchester College of Arts and Technology; Member, Manchester Strategic Partnership; Member, Open and Distance Learning Quality Council; Member, Education Maintenance Working Party.
Areas of Influence: Education.
Contact details: Manchester College of Arts & Technology, Openshaw Campus, Ashton Old Road, Openshaw, Manchester M11 2WH (tel: 0161 953 2242, fax: 0161 953 3909, email: peter_tavernor@mancat.ac.uk); 109 The Fairway, Moston, Manchester.

TAYLOR, Anthony Roy, MA

Position: Chief Crown Prosecutor, Greater Manchester (1987 - present)..
Areas of Influence: Law.
Profile: *b.* February 1st, 1944; *m.* Angela; 2 sons; 1 daughter.
Education: Sedbergh School; Certificat d' Etudes Francaises Modernes, Université de Strasbourg; Cambridge University. Career profile: Solicitor, Manchester (1968-70); Travelling and Working, Africa (1970); Prosecuting, Manchester (1972-74); Prosecuting, Derbyshire (1974-77); Prosecuting, Manchester (1977-87). Clubs and Societies: Manchester and District Medico-Legal Society, Committee Member and

Former President; Committe Member, Manchester Law Society; Former President, Manchester Trainee Solicitors Group.

Interests: Family, vegetable patch.

Contact details: Chief Branch Crown Prosecutor, Crown Prosecution Service, PO Box 237, 8th Floor Sunlight House, Quay Street, Manchester M60 3PS (tel: 0161 827 4700, fax: 0161 827 4932); Hale Barns Cottage, Sunbank Lane, Ringway, Altrincham, Cheshire WA15 0PZ (tel: 0161 980 8718).

TAYLOR, Elisabeth, LLB, LSF

Position: Managing Partner, James Chapman & Co (1998 - present).

Areas of Influence: Law, Arts, Education.

Profile: *m.* Paul Lee; 2 sons; 1 daughter.

Educated at Bristol University and Liverpool Polytechnic (LSF). Elisabeth Taylor specialised in professional indemnity work for the past ten years and now heads the Professional Indemnity Department of James Chapman & Co. She handles professional negligence claims on behalf of solicitors, barristers, surveyors, valuers, architects, accountants, insurance brokers and other professionals. She also heads the general insurance team in claims such as policy disputes, product liability, fire and property damage. Clubs and societies: The Law Society.

Interests: Reading, music, theatre, sports, family.

Contact details: James Chapman & Co, 76 King Street, Manchester M2 4NH (tel: 0161 828 8000, fax: 0161 828 8018, email: profindemnity@james-capman.co.uk).

TAYLOR, Ian Donald, BA (Hons), Dip LA, MLI

Position: Centre Director, Community Technical Aid Centre.

Areas of Influence: Voluntary Sector, Regeneration.

Profile: *b.* March 8th, 1957; *m.* Dorcas Victoria; 2 twin sons.

Education: Salford Grammar School; Pendleton VIth Form College, Salford; Manchester Polythechnic; Manchester Metropolitan University. Career profile: Clerical Assistant, Manchester City Council, Housing Department; Clerical Officer, Manchester City Council, Housing Department; Rehousing Officer, Manchester City Council, Housing Department; Estate Manager, London Borough of Hackney, Comprehensive Housing Service; Senior Housing Officer, London Borough of Hackney, Comprehensive Housing Service; Estate Co-ordinator, London Borough of Hackney, Comprehensive Housing Service; Landscape Assistant, Community Technical Aid Centre, Manchester; Landscape Architect, Community Technical Aid Centre, Manchester.

Interests: Family; football, cricket, hill-walking, travel, food and drink.

Contact details: Centre Director, Community Technical Aid Centre, 2nd Floor, 3 Stevenson Square, Manchester M1 1JU (tel: 0161 236 5195, fax: 0161 236 5836, email: info@ctac.co.uk); 2 Barnsfold Court, Hayfield, High Peak SK22 2PB).

TAYLOR, Janet Elizabeth JP (1981 -)

Position: Chairman, Bolton Magistrates Court.
Areas of Influence: Education, Law.
Profile: *b.* July 19th, 1938; *m.* Robert Nicholas; 1 son; 3 daughters.
Educated at Bolton School. Career profile: Secretary; Teaching. Clubs and societies: Bolton Bridge Club; Bolton Golf Club.
Interests: Family, gardening, golf, bridge, British Show Pony Society.

TAYLOR, Kenneth Alan

Positions: Freelance Director; Actor.
Areas of Influence: Arts.
Profile: *b.* April 4th, 1937; *m.* Judith; 1 son, Jason; 1 daughter, Jessica.
Educated at St Francis Convent, Stratford and Stratford Grammar School. Career profile: Chief Executive, Oldham Coliseum (1997-02); Director, Nottingham Playhouse (1983-90). West End Productions: *One Night Stand; And then there were none....* National Tours: *House of Stairs; Feed; It's a Madhouse; Last Tango in Whitby; The Hobbit* etc. Various TV and Radio Roles as an Actor. Directed productions in Bolton, Sheffield Crucible, Hornchurch etc. Publications: Various pantomimes; Original musicals. Adaptaions: *Whistle Down the Wind; Spend. Spend. Spend; Christmas Carol.* Awards: MEN Best Production for *A Different way Home*; Horniman Award for Outstanding Achievment in Theatre. 2002 marks Kenneth Taylors nineteenth Pantomime at Nottingham Playhouse in *Beauty and the Beast*, which will also be presented at Oldham Coliseum. He is currently working on a book covering 13 years of his experiences in France, where he owns a property. Patron, Genesis, a cancer prevention charity.
Interests: Gardening, France, painting, writing, food and drink.
Contact details: Manor House, Oldham Road, Springhead, Oldham, Lancs OL4 4QJ (tel: 0161 652 5944).

TAYLOR, Michael BSocSc

Position: Editor, North West Business Insider.
Areas of Influence: Media.
Profile: *b.* July 9th, 1966; *m.* Clare; 2 sons.
Education: Lancaster Royal Grammar School; University of Manchester. Career profile: Journalist, Emap Business Communications; News Editor, Television Week

(1989-93); Researcher, Wire TV (1993-94); International Editor, Cable World (1994-95); Editorial Director, Creation Magazine (1996-00). Prizes and awards: Northern Jounalist Awards (2002); RICS Journalism Prize (2002). Publications: *Route One, A Guide to Careers in Film and TV*, MDI, 1998. Clubs and Societies: Blackburn Rovers FC; East Lancashire Railway Preservation Society; Old Lancastrians; Friends of Real Lancashire.

Interests: Family, true crime biography, travel, film, TV classics, Blackburn Rovers FC.

Contact details: Editor, Insider, 8th Floor, Boulton House, 17-21 Chorlton Street, Manchester M1 3HY (tel: 0161 907 9709, fax 0161 236 9862, email: michael.taylor@newsco.com).

TAYLOR, Michael John, DipManStu

Positions: General Manager, Granada Television Ltd; Managing Director, 3 Sixtymedia; Director, Gower St Estates; Director, North West Vision; Member, The Duchy of Lancaster's Advisory Committee for the Manchester Magistracy.
Areas of Influence: Media, Public Sector.
Profile: *b.* September 21st, 1956; *m.* Lynn; 2 sons.
Education: Cheadle Moseley Grammar School; Huddersfield Polytechnic; Manchester Polytechnic. Career profile: Trainee Accountant, Simon Carves Ltd; Assistant Management Accountant, Granada TV (1980); Production Accountant, Granada TV; Head of Design, Granada TV; Director of Resources, Granada Media Group; General Manager, Granada TV Ltd (1997); Managing Director, 3 Sixtymedia (2000 -). Clubs and societies: Stockport Golf Club; Bramhall Lane Lawn Tennis Club; BAFTA.
Interests: Media, sport.
Contact details: 3sixty Media, Quay St, Manchester M60 9EA (tel: 0161 827 2020, fax: 0161 832 8809, email: mike.taylor@3sixtymedia.com).

TAYLOR, Steve, BA (Hons)

Position: Managing Editor, BBC GMR (2001 - present).
Areas of Influence: Media.
Profile: *b.* December 12th, 1949; *m.* Cora; 2 daughters.
Educated at Stand Grammar, Whitefield, Manchester, and University of Warwick, English and American Literature; Reporter, Warrington Guardian (1972-74); Producer, BBC Radio Manchester (1974-78); News Editor, BBC Radio Carlisle (1978-80); News Editor, BBC Radio Lancashire (1980-84); News Editor, BBC Radio Manchester (1984-87); Northern Correspondent, BBC Network Radio (1987-89); Correspondent, BBC TV North West (1989-94); Managing Editor, BBC Radio Lancashire (1994-01).

Interests: Bury FC, horse racing (very unsuccessful small-time part owner).
Contact details: BBC GMR, PO Box 951, Oxford Road, Manchester, M60 1SD (tel: 0161 200 2000, fax: 0161 228 6110, email: steve.taylor@bbc.co.uk).

TEMPLE, Mollie, BA, MA

Positions: Principal, Bolton Institute; Board Member, Greater Manchester Learning and Skills Council; Governor, Bolton Community College; Member, HESDA; Member, NWUA; Chairman, HENW.
Areas of Influence: Education, Public Sector.
Educated at Leeds University. Career profile: Head, Student Office, Leeds University; Pro-Vice Chancellor, University of Sunderland.
Contact details: Principal, Bolton Institute, Dean Campus, Dean Road, Bolton BL3 5AB (tel: 01204 903 001, fax: 01204 521 920, email: mollie.temple@bolton.ac.uk).

TERRAS, Christopher Richard, MA (Oxon), FCA

Positions: Treasurer, University of Manchester (1999 - present); Chairman, North West Kidney Research Association (1992 - present).
Areas of Influence: Education, Finance, Public Sector.
Profile: *b.* October 17th, 1937; *m.* Janet; 1 son; 3 daughter.
Educated at Uppingham (1951-56) and University College, Oxford (1956-59). Career profile: Qualified as a Chartered Accountant (1962); Partner, Swanwick Terras & Co and Abbott & Son (1963-65); Partner, Arthur Andersen (1971-99); National Tax Director (1989-99). Clubs and societies: Free Foresters; MCC; Cheshire Gentlemen; The Manchester Literary and Philosophical Society; Portico Library; Lancashire County Cricket Club; Leicestershire Gentlemen; Vincent's; Forty; St James's Club, Manchester; Cheshire County Cricket; Alderley Edge Cricket Club.
Interests: Cricket (played for Cheshire).
Contact details: Frog Castle, Duck Lane, Macclesfield Road, Alderley Edge, SK9 7BH (tel: 01625 583832, fax: 01625 585 919).

THACKER, Martin Nicholas MPhil DipLib GTCL ARCO

Position: Librarian, Henry Watson Music Library, Manchester Public Libraries.
Areas of Influence: Education, Public Sector.
Profile: *b.* March 27th, 1952; *m.* Kathleen Janette; 2 daughters.
Education: Tottenham Grammar School; Trinity College of Music, London. Career profile: Assistant Librarian, Essex County Libraries (1977-79); Assistant Librarian, Britten-Pears Library, Aldeburgh (1979-81); Watson Music Librarian, Manchester Public Libraries (1981 -); Secretary, Manchester Musical Heritage Trust; Assistant Editor, Manchester Sounds. Clubs and Societies: Royal College of Organists;

Warrington Light Opera.

Interests: Music, amateur dramatics, computing, motorcycle restoration, caravanning.

Contact details: Central Library, St Peters Square, Manchester M2 5PD (tel: 0161 234 1976, fax: 0161 234 1961, email: mthacker@libraries.manchester.gov.uk); 24 Eagle Brow, Lymm, Cheshire WA13 0LY (tel: 01925 757 114, email: mthacker@care4 free.net).

THOMAS, Dr Duncan Andrew, BSC (Hons), ARCS, MSc, PhD

Positions: Chairman, Spiritual Assembly of the Baha'is of Manchester.
Areas of Influence: Faith Groups, Academia, Arts.
Profile: *b.* April 10th, 1974.
Education: BSc (Hons) ARCS Physics, Imperial College, London; MSc Technical Change and Industrial Strategy, University of Manchester; PhD (2002) *Water Policy and Technology Development in UK Water Industry*, United Utilities / University of Manchester. Career profile: Hotel Service / Hospitality; Playleader, Cwmbran Community Council; Research Engineer working on innovative prototypes of vehicles and aircraft lighting systems, fingerprint, EMI's Central Research Laboratories (1995-97); Telephone fundraising Manager, University of Manchester Alumni Annual Fund; Tutor, Technology Management; Contributing Editor, *Science Insight*; Research into Academic and Policy Dimensions of Science Enterprise. Publications: Paper on *Women, Science and Enterprise from Academic and Baha'i Persectives*; two short films; two original CDs; Colour photography published in corporate calenders; black and white photography in *Big Issue* Magazine. Member of United Nations Association.
Interests: Film Studies via numerous short courses.
Contact details: Manchester Baha'i Centre, 360 Wilmslow Road, Fallowfield, Manchester M14 6AB (tel: 0161 224 6490, email: manchester@bci.org).

THOMAS, Paul Alan, LLB

Position: Managing Partner, Halliwell Landau.
Areas of Influence: Law.
Profile: *b.* May 10th, 1954.
Education: John Bright Grammar School, Llandudno; Aberystwych University. Career profile: Partner, Halliwell Landau (1981); Head of Litigation, Halliwell Landau (1990); Managing Partner, Halliwell Landau (2000). Member of the RAC.
Interests: Rugby, France, food, wine.
Contact details: Halliwell Landau, St James's Court, Brown Street, Manchester M2 2JF (tel: 0161 835 3003, email: pathomas@halliwell.co.uk).

THOMAS of Macclesfield, Baron Terence James, CBE (1997), INSEAD, FCIB, FRSA, CIMgt, Hon D of letters (1996), Hon DBA (1998)

Positions: Life Peer; Chairman, Internexus Group (2002 – present).
Areas of Influence: Commerce.
Profile: *b.* October 19th, 1937; *m.* Lynda (1963); 3 sons.
Education: Queen Elizabeth Grammar School, Camarthen; Postgraduate Business Admin, University of Bath. Career profile: National Provincial later National Westminter Bank (1962-71); Joint Credit Card Company (1971-73); Marketing Manager (1973-77), Assistant General Manager then Joint General Manager (1977-83), Director (1984), Executive Director Group Development (1987), Managing Director (1988-97), The Co-operative Bank. Chairman, North West Development Agency (1988 - 2002): Director, Stanley Leisure Organisation plc (1994-98); Capita Group (1998-99); Rathbone CI (1998-99); Chairman, Venture Technic Ltd (1984-97); Director: English Partnerships (1998-99); Commn for the New Towns (1998-99); CDA. Chairman, NW Partnerships (1994-97). Member, Regional Economic Development Community, General Council CIB; President, International Cooperative Banking Association (1988-95); Chairman, NW Media Charitable Trust (1998-99). Visiting Professor, University of Stirling (1988-91). Member, Court of Governors UMIST (1996-02), Board of Trustees UNICEF (1998-99). Hon Fellow, University of Central Lancs (2000); University of Manchester (1999); UMIST (1999). Mancunian of the Year (1998).
Contact details: 51 Willowmead Drive, Prestbury, Cheshire SK10 4DD (tel: 01625 828092).

THOMPSON, Geoffrey Llewellyn, MBE (1995), ILAM

Positions: Executive Chairman, Youth Charter for Sport, Culture, and the Arts; International Sports Consultant; Board Member, New Opportunities Fund; Independent Assessor, Office of the Commission for Public Appointments.
Areas of Influence: Youth Culture, Sport, Social Inclusion.
Profile: *b.* February 3rd, 1958; *m.* Janice; 2 sons; 1 daughter.
In his role as Sports consultant, Geoffrey Llewellyn is currently advising corporate captains of Industry and Elite Performers on motivation, goal setting and team building. He has been five times World Karate Champion and holder of over 50 team and individual titles. He was a participant in the Government's 1988 Review of Sport in the Inner Cities, and was an ambassador for Manchester's 2000 Olympic Bid and the successful bid for the 2002 Commonwealth Games. Geoff was a member of Sport England between 1990 and 2001. Publication: *Karate - the Pursuit of Excellence.* Prizes and awards: Variety Club of Great Britian, Achievements in Sport; Commonwealth Sports Award, Humanitarian Services to Sport; Sports Writers Association, Outstanding Performance in Sport; Central Council of Physical Recreation, Arthur Bell Trophy for Services to Youth and the Community. Clubs and

societies: Martial Arts Hall of Fame.

Interests: All sports particularly martial arts and squash, reading, music, travel, philosophy.

Contact details: Youth Charter for Sport, Culture and The Arts, Ground Floor, The Atrium, Anchorage 2, Anchorage Quay, Salford Quay, Manchester M50 3YW (tel: 0161 877 8405, fax: 0161 877 8406, email: information@ycs.co.uk).

THOMPSON, Michael Edwin, LLB

Position: Partner, Eversheds, Manchester.
Areas of Influence: Law.
Profile: *b.* October 8th, 1965.
Education: Bishop Henshaw RC Upper School, Rochdale; Leeds University; Chester Law School. Career profile: Trainee Solicitor, Eversheds (1990); Solicitor, Eversheds (1992); Senior Solicitor/ Associate, Eversheds (1997); Partner, Eversheds (2000). Member of Manchester Golf Club.
Interests: Sport, football.
Contact details: Head of Employment, Eversheds, Eversheds House, 70 Great Bridgewater Street, Manchester M1 5ES (tel: 0161 831 8000, fax: 0161 832 5337, email: michaelthompson@eversheds.com).

THRELFALL, Stephen, GRNCM, Hon ARAM (2002), FRSA

Positions: Director of Music, Chetham's School of Music; President, Gorton Philharmonic Orchestra and Prestwich Music Society; Artistic Director, Brundibar Project for 2003.
Areas of Influence: Education, Arts.
Profile: *b.* February, 25th, 1956; *m.* Kathleen; 1 son; 1 daughter.
Educated at Parrswood High School and Royal Northern College of Music. Stephen Threlfall was for a number of years the sub-principal cello with the BBC Philharmonic Orchestra, having played also with many of this country's leading orchestras and ensembles, including the London Symphony Orchestra. He has been a cello teacher and coach for a number of years, both privately and at the University of Manchester, Chetham's School of Music and at the Royal Northern College of Music. He is a highly regarded conductor, with many CD recordings and broadcasts for BBC Classic FM, and Russian and South African Broadcasting Authorities. Stephen has been particularly associated with an ever growing number of concerts for charities. He recently devised and directed a large scale community and educational based project on Antartica. This included audiovisual performances and workshops and the premiere of *High on the Slopes of Terror* by Sir Peter Maxwell Davies. In 2002 the project was nominated for two prestigious Royal Philharmic Societies Education Awards. Stephen also works closely with a number of national and local musical and

artistic institutions and societies as an advisor and consultant. Prior to his appointment at Chethams, he was, from 1991, the Director of Music at Benenden School becoming Director of Music at Chetham's School of Music in 1995.
Interests: Cycling, history, Antarctic, soccer - Man City fan!
Contact details: Chetham's School of Music, Long Millgate, Manchester M3 1SB (tel: 0161 838 7229, fax: 0161 834 5861, email: stephenthrelfall@chetham's.com).

TIMMINS, Anthony George Patrick, BA

Positions: Senior Manager, PricewaterhouseCoopers; Joint Treasurer Manchester, Literary and Philosophical Society.
Areas of Influence: Finance, Voluntary Sector, Arts.
Profile: *b*. March 17th, 1955.
Education: The Campion School, Hornchurch; Wadham College, Oxford. Career profile: HM Inspector, Taxes (1978-84); Thompson McLintock/KPMG (1984-88); PricewaterhouseCoopers (1988 -). Clubs and societies: Manchester Literary and Philosophical Society; Botanical Society of the British Isles; Lancashire Cricket Club; Hallé Concerts Society; National Trust.
Interests: Performing and visual Arts, amateur botany, historic buildings, countryside, travel.
Contact details: PricewaterhouseCoopers, 101 Barbirolli Square, Manchester M2 3PW (tel: 0161 2452508, fax: 01612452903, email: antony.timmins@uk.pwcglobal.com); 8 Heaton Close, Stockport SK4 4DQ (tel: 0161 245 2903, fax: 0161 432 2388).

TIMMINS, Colonel John Bradford, KCVO (2002), OBE (1973), KStJ (1988), TD (1968), Hon LLD (2001); Hon DSc (1990), Hon RNCM (1991), Msc (1982), FRSA

Positions: Chairman, Warburton Properties Ltd; HM Lord Lieutenant for Greater Manchester (1987 - present); Honorary Colonel, Greater Manchester Army Cadet Force; County President, Order of St John (1988 – present); County President, Royal Society of St George (1987 – present); County President, SAAFA (1987 – present); President, Broughton House Home for Ex-service Personnel (1992 – present); Vice President, RFCA for NW England (1987 – present), President (1995-99); President, Greater Manchester West County Scouts (1987 – present).
Areas of Influence: Voluntary Sector, Reserve Forces, Construction and Property Industry.
Profile: *b*. June 23rd, 1932; *m*. Jean, nee Edwards; 5 sons; 1 daughter.
Educated at Dudley Grammar School, Wolverhampton Technical College, and University of Aston, Birmingham. Career profile: Management Construction Industry (1952-87); NW Regional President, Building Employers Confederation (1974-75). Military Service: Commissioned Royal Engineers (1954); Served East Lancs, Div. TA (1956-67); Second in Command and Commanding Officer, 75 Engineer

Regiment (V) (1967-73); Deputy Commander, 30 Engineer Brigade (1973-75); TA Colonel, North West District (1975-78); Honorary Colonel, 75 Engineer Regiment (1980-90), Honorary Colonel, Manchester & Salford UOTC (1990-98); Member TAVRA NW England (1968-87) (Vice Chairman 1983-87); Aide de Campe to HM The Queen (1975-80); High Sheriff of Greater Manchester (1986-87).
Interests: Sailing.
Contact details: Greater Manchester Lieutenancy, Byrom House, Quay Street, Manchester M3 (tel: 0161 834 0490, fax: 0161 835 1536); The Old Rectory, Warburton WA13 9SS (tel: 01925 753957, fax: 01925 756600).

TIMPSON, William John Anthony, BA

Positions: Chairman and Chief Executive, Timpson Ltd: Trustee, Uppingham School, Leicester; Trustee, Hatfield Trust, Hatfield College; Trustee, Childline; Court Assistant, Pattenmakers, Pattenmakers Company.
Areas of Influence: Commerce, Voluntary Sector.
Profile: *b.* March 24th, 1943; *m.* Alexandra Winkfield; 4 sons; 1 daughter.
Educated at Oundle School and University of Nottingham. After a Graduate Training Scheme with C&J Clark, John Timpson joined the family footwear retailing business William Timpson Limited, becoming the Director responsible for buying in 1970 and in 1975 became Managing Director. In 1987 he sold the shoe shops to George Oliver and has subsequently concentrated on building up the shoe repairing and key cutting business, which he has diversified into engraving and watch repairs. In 1995 he acquired the Automagic chain making Timpson the leader in its field. It is a private business, wholly owned by John and his family. Mr & Mrs Timpson have been foster parents for over 20 years during which time they have fostered over 60 children. Publications: *Columnist for Real Business Magazine; Dear James; Upside-down Management.* Prizes and awards: Mancunian of the Year, runner up; 6th place, Sunday Times Great Place to Work; 2nd place, Duke of Westminster Awards. Clubs and societies: Delamere Golf Club; Manchester Tennis & Raquet Club; Alderley Edge Cricket Club.
Interests: Golf, snooker, tennis, real tennis, squash.
Contact details: Timpson Ltd, Timpson House, Claverton Road, Wythenshawe, Manchester M23 9TT (tel: 0161 946 6225, fax: 0161 945 3987, email: barbara.mason@timpson.com).

TITLEY, Gary MEP, BA (Hons), PGCE

Positions: MEP, Labour's North West Euro Team (1999 - present); Leader, British Labour MEPs; Vice President of the Party of European Socialists in the European Parliament with special responsibility for Enlargement.
Areas of Influence: Public Sector.

Profile: *b.* January 19th, 1950; *m.* Charo; 1 son; 1 daughter.
Educated at York University. Following university Gary Titley worked in Spain for two years. After returning to Britain, he took up a number of teaching appointments, before he was made Campaign Manager to the late Terry Pitt in 1984. Since his election as MEP for Greater Manchester (1989), Gary has served on the European Parliament's Foreign Affairs, Social Affairs, Economic & Monetary, Legal Affairs & Internal Market, Environment and Petitions Committees. He played a key role in paving the way for enlargement in 1995. For his efforts, the Finnish Government made him a Commander of the White Rose, and the Austrian Government gave him the Gold Cross Award. Gary has acted as rapporteur for the European Parliament in many key areas of policy, including EU relations with South America and Ukraine, the NAFTA agreement, the European Economic Area, enlargement, association agreements with the countries of Central and Eastern Europe, Arms Export policy, the EU budget and the future of the European defence industry. In 1997, Gary was appointed European Parliamentary Private Secretary to the then British Foreign Secretary, Robin Cook. Until 1999 he was also Chief Spokeperson for the Socialist Group of MEPs on the powerful Foreign Affairs Committee.
Interests: Walking, watching football, cricket, rugby, reading, theatre.
Contact details: 16 Spring Lane, Radcliffe, Manchester M26 2TQ (tel: 0161 724 4008, fax: 0161 724 4009, email: contact @ gary-titley-mep.new.labour.org.uk, web: www.garytitley.eu.com).

TOPHAM, Charles Richard BSc

Positions: Chairman, Elite Homes Group Ltd; Director, Charles Topham Group Ltd; Chairman, Power Supply Group Ltd.
Areas of Influence: Commerce.
Profile: February 2nd, 1955; 2 sons; 1 daughter.
Education: North Cestrian Grammar School, Altrincham (1966-68); Westwoods Grammar School, North Leach, Glossop (1968-71); Urmston Grammar School, Trafford (1971-74); Salford University (1974-77). Career profile: Charles Topham Ltd (1977 -). Member of St James Club, Manchester.
Interests: Travel, sport, politics.
Contact details: Charles Topham and Sons Ltd, 14 Wynford Square, West Ashton Street, Salford, M5 2SN (tel: 0161 737 4900, fax: 0161 737 3727).

TRAVIS, David Joseph

Position: Northern Managing Partner, CLB (1997 - present).
Areas of Influence: Finance.
Profile: *b.* July 11th, 1963; *m.* Catherine; 1 son; 1 daughter.
Educated at Royton Crompton School, North Chadderton School, Manchester

Polytechnic, Accountancy Tuition Centre (FCA), and INSEAD Business School, Paris, France; Ernst & Whinney, Manchester (1982-87); Ernst & Whinney, New Zealand (1987-88); Ernst & Young, Manchester (1989-97). Involved in providing strategic and corporate finance advice to owner managers.
Interests: Golf (beginner), cars, family.
Contact details: CLB, Century House, 11 St Peters Square, Manchester M2 3DN (tel: 0161 245 1000, fax: 0161 245 1001).

TRIPPIER, Sir David, Kt (1992), RD (1983), JP (1975), DL (1994), OstJ (2000), MSI

Positions: Chairman, WH Ireland Group PLC, Murray VCT Plc and Precise Communications Ltd; Board Member, St Modwen Props plc, Murray Income Invested Trust plc, Nord Anglia plc and Unique Communications Group Ltd; Chairman of the Reserve Forces and Cadets in the North West of England; National Vice Chairman of the Council of RFCA; Chairman, of the Order of St John, Lancashire.
Areas of Influence: Commerce, Finance, Media.
Profile: *b.* May 15th. 1946; *m.* Lady Ruth; 3 sons.
Educated at Bury Grammar School. Career profile: Officer, Marines Reserve; Commando Course (1969) Parachutist, RAF Abingdon (1970); Company Commander; Staff College Course; he has served in Singapore, Malaysia, Malta and Norway; Hon Colonel Royal Marines Reserves Merseyside (1996); Director of a financial planning company; Stockbroker; elected to the Rochdale Metropolitan Borough Council (1969); Leader of the Conservative Group (1974); Leader of the Council and Magistrate (1975); MP for Rossendale (1979); Parliamentary Private Secretary to the Minister for Health (1982); Minister for Small Firms (1985-87); Minister for Inner Cities and Construction (1987); Minister of State for the Environment and Countryside (1989); Founder, Rossendale Enterprise Trust and Rossendale Groundwork Trust; Chairman, Marketing Manchester (1996-99); President, Manchester Chamber of Commerce and Industry (1999-00); National Chairman, Tidy Britain Group (1996). Publication: *Lend me Your Ears*, Biography (1999).
Interests: Gardening, reading, music.
Contact details: 19 Ralli Court, West Riverside, Manchester M3 5FT (tel: 0161 288 2884, fax: 288 2880, email: philipa@pendgragon-pr.co.uk); Dowry Head, Helmsmore, Rossondale, Lancs. BB4 4AE (tel: 01706 229370).

TUCKER, Anne, BA

Positions: Joint Artistic Director, Streets Ahead Events and Manchester International Arts (1988 - present); Freelance Arts Animateur (1985 - present).
Areas of Influence: Arts, Voluntary Sector.

Profile: *b.* July 7th, 1951.
Education: Badminton School, Bristol; Lycée Claud Monet, Ivry, Paris, France; University of Warwick. Career profile: Teacher (1974-77); Community Artist and Founder Member, Community Arts Workshop (1978-85); Arts Development Officer, Oldham; Chair of Arts Council of England Street Art Advisory Panel; Executive Member of Independent Street Arts Network. Organiser of 6 yearly *Streets Ahead* Festivals and subsequent special outdoor events.
Interests: Performing arts of all sorts, festivals, Southern European culture, gardening.
Contact details: MIA, 3 Birch Polygon M14 5HX (tel: 0161 224 0020, fax: 0161 248 9331, email: anne@streetsahead.org.uk).

TULLY, David John

Positions: Non-executive Chairman, Joseph Holt plc; President, St James's Club.
Areas of Influence: Law, Commerce.
Profile: *b.* March 13th, 1942; *m.* Susan Patricia; 1 son; 2 daughters.
Educated at Twyford School and Sherborne School. David Tully recently retired after 40 years with Addleshaw Booth & Co. His last position was that of Senior Partner. Other posts he has held include Past President of Manchester Law Society and Past Chairman of National Young Solicitors. He was also a former Governor of Manchester Grammar School. Prizes and awards: Ryland Fletcher Scholarship Prize (1961). Clubs and societies: Racquet; Ringway Golf Club; St James's.
Interests: Shooting, fishing, golf.
Contact details: The Cherries, 5 Greenside Drive, Hale WA14 3HX (tel: 0161 928 3029, fax; 0161 941 4864).

TUPHOLME, Andy, BA, ACA

Positions: Investment Manager, Gresham Trust plc (2001 - present).
Areas of Influence: Finance, Commerce.
Profile: *b.* September 5th, 1969; *m.* Joanna; 1 son.
Educated at Wales Comprehensive School, Sheffield and Durham University. Career profile: Ernst & Young, Sheffield (1991-95); Associate Director, PricewaterhouseCoopers Corporate Finance, Leeds (1995-01).
Interests: Football, rugby, golf, travel, fine wine, member of Sheffield United Supporters Club.
Interests: Gresham, 82 King Street, Manchester M2 4WQ (tel: 0161 833 7500, fax: 0161 833 7575); 151 Crimicar Lane, Fulwood, Sheffield S10 4FD (tel; 0114 2309 788, email: tupholme@IC24.net.

TURNBERG, Lord Leslie Arnold, KBt (1994), Peerage 2000, MD, FRCP, FMedSci, DSc (Hons)

Positions: Vice President, Academy of Medical Sciences. President: Medical Protection Society, Medical Council on Alcohol. Chair, Board of Health Quality Service; Advisor, Association of Medical Research Charities; Chairman, Public Health Laboratory Service; Member, House of Lords Select Committee on Science and Technology, (2001 - present).
Areas of Influence: Health, Education, Voluntary Sector.
Profile: *b.* March 22nd, 1934; *m.* Edna; 1 son; 1 daughter.
Educated at Stand Grammar School (1952-57) and Manchester University (1952-57, 1966). Career profile: Junior Doctor Training, Manchester Hospitals (1957-66); Lecturer in Medicine, Royal Free Hospital (1967); Research Fellow, Dallas, Texas (1967-68); Senior Lecturer, University of Manchester (1968) Professor of Medicine, University of Manchester (1973-97); Honorary Consultant Physician, Hope Hospital (1973-97); President, Royal College of Physicians (1992-97). Chairman: Conference of Medical Royal Colleges (1992-97), Specialist Training Authority (1996-97) and UK Forum for Genetics and Insurance (1999-02). Chair of Panel to review health services in London (1997); President, British Society of Gastroenterology (2000). Hon DSc. Salford (1996); Manchester (1997); London (2000). Hon. Fellow of 16 Medical Royal Colleges in UK and Abroad. Visiting Professor, USA, Canada, Australia, Israel, Singapore and Hong Kong.
Publications: Editor of 5 books on Gastroenterology and over 150 scientific papers on medical science. Prizes and awards: Arthur Hust Medal (1984); McKenna Medal (1996); Silver Medal, Indian Society of Gastroenterology (1986).
Interests: Reading, chinese ceramics, walking, talking.
Contact details: House of Lords, Westminster, London SW1A; 5 Broadway Avenue, Cheadle, Cheshire SK8 1NN (tel/fax: 0161 428 4237).

TURNER, John Brierley, MA, LLM, LRAM

Positions: Musician; Chairman: Manchester Musical Heritage Trust; The Ida Carroll Trust; The Douglas Steele Foundation.
Areas of Influence: Arts.
Profile: *b.* April 1st, 1943; *m.* Margaret Cordall, née Lister.
Education: Stockport Grammar School; The Northern School of Music; Senior Scholar, Fitzwilliam College, Cambridge. Until 1995 John Turner combined a career as a solicitor, acting particularly for many high profile musicians and musical organisations, with a career as a freelance musician specialising in the recorder. He has performed with the Early Music Consort of London and others of the UK's leading enembles and orchestras, as well as doing much solo work. Since then he has devoted himself to his musical career as a recorder player, writer, composer and

teacher. He has given premieres of over 300 works for the recorder, including concertos written for him by Leighton, Gilbert, Crosse, Dodgson, Pitfield, etc. and has performed as a soloist worldwide. His own recorder pieces are now part of the instrument's standard repertoire. He is a trustee of many musical trusts, including the Manchester Musical Heritage Trust which he founded. He has taught for the Universities of Manchester, Keele, Hull, Bangor, Liverpool and Sheffield as well as the Royal Northern College of Music and Chetham's School of Music. Compositions include: Four Diversions; Six Bagatelles; Serenade; numerous carols. Recordings include: *John and Peter's Whistling Book*; *English Recorder Music*; *Aspects of Nature*; *English Recorder Concertos*; *Rawsthorne McCabe Suite*. Publications: Many contributions to the *New Grove*, *Musical Times*, *Manchester Sounds*, *Recorder Magazine*, *British Music* and *Music and Letters*.

Contact details: email: recorderist@zoom.co.uk

TURNER, Mark George, QC (1998)

Positions: Barrister; Recorder (2000 - present).
Areas of Influence: Law.
Profile: *b.* August 27th, 1959; *m.* Caroline; 3 daughters.
Educated at Sedburgh School (1972-77), The Queen's College, Oxford (1977-80) and Inns of Court School of Law (1980-1981). Mark Turner joined Dean's Court Chambers in Manchester following pupillage commencing in 1981. He is involved professionally in claims arising out of the Hillsborough Disaster, The IRA Bombing of Central Manchester, The Fred and Rosemary West murdurs, The Birmingham Six, and the Achille Lauro cruiseship. Publications: *Industrial Disease Litigation*: *Occupational Asthma and Mucous Membrane Disorder* (1998); In preparation: *Neuropsychology and Brain Injury Claims*. Clubs and societies: Personal Injury Bar Association; Northern Circuit Commercial Bar Association; British Quiz Association; Mastermind Club; Patron of 'New Beginnings for Street Children' a charity for homeless children in the Ukraine.
Interests: Quizzes, classical music, history.
Contact details: Dean's Court Chambers, 24 St John Street, Manchester M3 4DF (tel: 0161 214 6000, fax: 0161 214 6001, email: turner@deanscourt.co.uk).

WADE, of Chorlton, Lord William Oulton, Kt (1982)

Position: Life Peer.
Areas of Influence: Commerce, Finance, Voluntary Sector.
Profile: *b.* December 24th, 1932; *m.* Gillian Margaret; 1 son; 1 daughter.
Educated at Birkenhead School, Wirral and Queen's University, Belfast. Career profile: Farmer; Landowner; Cheese Master; Company Director; Food Industry; Incubation; Investment; Technology. Clubs and societies: St James, Manchester; The Portico Library, Manchester; City Club, Chester.
Contact details: House of Lords, Westminster, London SW1A 0PW (tel: 0207 219 5499).

WAGG, Jimmy

Position: Broadcaster at BBC GMR, Oxford Road, Manchester.
Areas of Influence: Media.
Profile: *b.* October 24th, 1953; *m.* Debra; 1 son; 1 daughter;
Educated at St Wilfrids, Hulme; St Bede's Grammar School, Whalley Range; Sheffield University. Career profile: Worked 1 year in the Civil Service.
Interests: Golf, reading, comedy, playing with the children, Manchester City fan.
Contact details: BBC GMR, Oxford Road, Manchester (email: jimmy.wagg@bbc.co.uk).

WAIN, Neil, BA

Position: Superintendent, Greater Manchester Police.
Areas of Influence: Faith Groups, Law, Public Sector.

Profile: *b.* March 28th, 1962; *m.* Jane; 3 daughters.
Education: Two Trees School, Denton; Manchester University. Career profile: Constable (1981); Sergeant (1989); Inspector (1994); Chief Inspector (1998); Superintendent (2000). Neil Wain is a member of the Christian Police Association
Interests: Family, swimming, hiking, skiing.
Contact details: South Manchester Division, Brownley Road, Wythenshawe, Manchester M22 0DW (tel: 0161 872 5050, fax: 0161 437 6614, email: neil.wainegmp.police.uk).

WAINWRIGHT, John Peter, MA, FRICS

Position: Consultant, Lambert Smith Hampson.
Areas of Influence: Commerce, Education.
Profile: *b.* June 16th, 1938; *m.* Phoebe; 2 daughters.
Educated at Miss Bishop's, Terra Nova School, Charterhouse and Pembroke Cambridge. Career profile: Chartered Auctioneer, Chartered Surveyor then Director, W H Robinson & Co; Director then Consultant, Lambert Smith Hampton; Branch Chairman, Royal Institution of Chartered Surveyors; National President, General Practice; Director, Manchester Chamber of Commerce & Industry; Governor, Manchester Grammar School and Cransley Girls School; Member of Council, Manchester University; Trustee, Northern Rock Foundation and Manchester Guardian Society. Clubs and societies: International Dendrological Society; Portico Library; St James's; Manchester Tennis & Racquets.
Interests: Cricket, hockey, sports generally, horticulture, architecture, the arts, locomotives, music, opera.
Contact details: Lambert Smith Hampton, 79 Moseley Street, Manchester M2 3LQ (tel: 0161 228 6411, email: pwainwright@lsh.co.uk).

WALKER, Lynne, BA (Hons), LTCL

Positions: Freelance Journalist, Broadcaster, and Editor.
Areas of Influence: Arts, Media.
Profile: *b.* October 24th, 1956. *m.* Gerald Larner.
Education: The Mary Erskine School for Girls, Edinburgh (1961-73); Moray House Teacher Training College (1976-77); Huddersfield University (1977-80). Career profile: Marketing Officer, Royal Scottish National Orchestra (1980-87); Marketing Director, Royal Exchange Theatre (1987-94); Presenter, BBC Radio 4 Kaleidoscope (1995-98); Music and Theatre Critic and feature writer, Independent (2000 - present); Founding director, Edge-Wise (1990 - present), Britain's only arts programme material, copywriting and editing consultancy, with clients including arts organisations and festivals throughout Britain and abroad. As a broadcaster Lynne Walker has made several series for BBC Radio 4 as well as contributing regularly to

BBC Radio 3 and the World Service. She is a frequent presenter of previews and post-show events for a variety of arts organisations. Other significant freelance work includes contributing on all aspects of the arts for *The Herald* in Glasgow, and *In Scotland* and devising and presenting the BBC Philharmonic's Platform Preview series in the Bridgewater Hall (1998 - present). Member, Royal Philharmonic Society.
Interests: All aspects of the arts, European travel, walking, bird watching, wine, cooking.
Contact details: 38 Heyes Lane, Alderley Edge, Cheshire SK9 7JY (tel: 01625 585 378, fax: 01625 590 175).

WALKER, Professor Martin, BA, PhD

Positions: Dean, Faculty of Social Sciences and Law, University of Manchester.
Areas of Influence: Finance, Education.
Profile: *b.* January 17th, 1953; Carolyn Emma; 1 son.
Educated at Tadcaster Grammar School and University of Newcastle upon Tyne. Career profile: Reader, LSE; Professor, Dundee University.
Contact details: Manchester School of Accounting and Finance, University of Manchester,
Crawford House, Oxford Road, Manchester M13 9PL (tel: 0161 275 4028, fax: 0161 275 4023).

WALKER, Robin, B.A

Position: Freelance Composer.
Areas of Influence: Arts.
Profile: *b.* March 18th, 1953.
Educated at York Minster Song School (1961-67); St. Peter's School, York (1967-71); University of Durham (1972-75); University of Oxford (1975-78); Royal College of Music (1978-79); Career profile: Assistant Lecturer, King's College, London (1978-80); Tutor, Royal Academy of Music, London (1980); Lecturer in Music, University of Manchester (1981-87); Yorkshire Arts Young Composers Prize (1975); Clements Memorial Prize for Chamber Music (1985); Works performed by: The English Chamber Orchestra, The Hilliard Ensemble; Venues: Queen Elizabeth Hall, London, IRCAM, Paris, Bridgewater Hall, Manchester; Publications: Massey University Press; Forsyth Bros.; ASC Records; Riverrum Records; Articles in, *British Music Society Journal*; *Pianola Journal*.
Interests: Mountaineering, India, art galleries, cricket, tea shops.
Contact details: 41 Grains Road, Delph, Saddleworth OL3 5DS (tel: 01457 878 809).

WALL, Chris, BA (Hons), DMS, Mlex

Positions: International Business Consultant, Strategem Ltd (2001 - present); Honorary Consul for Brazil in Manchester.
Areas of Influence: Commerce, Education.
Profile: *b.* November 29th, 1957; *m.* Marcia; 2 sons.
Education: BA (Hons) Latin American Studies, Essex (1979); DMS International Management, Teeside (1983). Career profile: Volunteer with the YMCA of Sorocaba, Sao Paulo, Brazil on a social programme with shanty town dwellers and shoe-shine boys (1981-82); started a successful business English school in Brazil and worked as a Shipping and Export Manager for the Brazilian Forestry Company (1986-90); self employed export consultant specialising in trade with Brazil (1990-01). Chris Wall is very interested in UK / Brazil relations and trade development and is active in providing consular assistance to Brazilian nationals in Greater Manchester. Clubs and societies: Royton & Oldham Harriers and Athletic Club; Manchester Consular Association.
Interests: Marathon running, cross-country running, motorcycling.
Contact details: Strategem Ltd, Hough End Hall, Nell Lane, Manchester (tel: 0161 860 0344, fax: 0161 860 0888, email: cwall@strategem.co.uk); 100 Leander Drive, Castleton, Rochdale OL11 2XE (tel: 01706 860518, email: cm.wall@ntlworld.com).

WALLACE, Joanna Jane, BSc Hons, MBA

Positions: Chief Executive, The Christie NHS Trust; Member, Manchester University Court.
Areas of Influence: Health, Public Sector.
Profile: *b.* September 3rd, 1965. *m.* David Crowley. 1 daughter.
Educated at St. Helena High School for Girls, Chesterfield (1979-84); University College London, London University (1984-87); University of California, Berkeley, USA (1989-91); University of Keele, part-time (2001-03); Career profile: Management Consultancy (1987-89); Medical Services Planning and Planning Manager, Kaiser Permanente, Health Maintenance Organisation, San Francisco (1991-95); Director of Business Management, East Cheshire NHS Trust (1995-97); Chief Executive, St. Helens and Knowsley Health Authority (1997-2000).
Interests: Gardening, running, supporting Bolton Wanderers, botanical illustration.
Contact details: The Christie NHS Trust, Wilmslow Road, Withington, Manchester M20 3BX (tel: 01477 532 270, email: joanna.wallace@christie-tr.nwest.nhs.uk).

WALLER, Simon Thomas, BA (Hons)

Position: National Head of Corporate Recovery and Insolvency, Eversheds (2001 - present).
Areas of Influence: Law, Finance.
Profile: *b.* September 9th, 1964; *m.* Karen; 1 daughter.
Educated at St Cuthberts School, Newcastle upon Tyne and University of Durham. Career profile: Articled, Booth & Co, Leeds; Qualified as a solicitor (1989); Wilde Sarte, London (1991-96); Partner, Halliwell Landau, Manchester (1996-98); Partner, Eversheds, Manchester (1998 - present); Editor, *Receivers, Administrators and Liquidators Quarterly*.
Interests: Family, reading, travel.
Contact details: Eversheds, 70 Great Bridgewater Street, Manchester M1 5ES (tel: 0161 831 8203, fax: 0161 832 5337, email: simonwaller@eversheds.com).

WALSH, Chris, BSc

Positions: Chairperson of Manchester Environmental Resource Centre Initiative (MERCI); Director, North West Network and Fairfield Composting.
Areas of Influence: Voluntary Sector, Social Economy.
Profile: *b.* October 11th, 1971.
Education: BSc Physics with Environmental Science, UMIST; Postgraduate Diploma in Sustainable Development and Environmental Management. Career profile: Co-founder of MERCI, Chris Walsh is presently working to establish a number of social enterprises across Manchester. He also helped establish Manchester Progressive Enterprise Network.
Contact details: MERCI, Bridge Street Mill, 22a Beswick Street, Manchester M4 7HR (tel: 0161 273 1736, email: merci@gn.apc.org).

WALSH, John, OBE (1994)

Positions: Councillor, Bolton MBC; Mayor (2002-03)
Areas of Influence: Public Sector, Commerce.
Profile: November 7th, 1951; *m.* Christine.
Educated at Bolton School (1963-70). Career profile: Planning and Transport Consultant, Retained, Bolton Wanderers F.C, Reebok Stadium; Accountant, General Manager, various Motor Dealerships.
Interests: Politics, sport, football (especially Bolton Wanderers), local history, freemasonry.
Contact details: Mayor's Parlour, Town Hall, Bolton BL1 1RU (tel: 01204 331 057, fax: 01204 380 043, email: john.walsh@bolton.gov.uk) 52, New Hall Lane, Heaton, Bolton BL1 5LW (tel: 01204 840 188, fax: 01204 846 994, email: john.walsh@bolton.gov.uk).

WALTERS, Lord Mayor Councillor Roy, BEM, JP

Positions: Lord Mayor of Manchester; Magistrate; Councillor; Member of Court, Manchester University; Member of Hulme Deanery Synod; School Governor.
Areas of Influence: Education, Public Sector.
Profile: *b.* December 6th, 1937, Clarendon, Jamaica; *m.* Hylsa; 1 son; 3 daughters.
Councillor Walters settled in the UK in 1958. He was employed by Manchester Corporation Transport from 1960 to 1991 starting as a conductor and finally as Depot Operations Manager. In 1983 he was awarded the British Empire Medal for service to transport. Councillor Walters has served as a Magistrate since 1985. He is a life member of UNISON, a member of the Court for St James with St Clements Parish Church and a Deanery Synod Member of Hulme Deanery. Councillor Walters was elected for the Moss Side Ward in 1998. He has served on the Finance and Social Services Committees and is a former Chair of the Community Regeneration Overview and Scrutiny Committee. He is a former member of South Manchester Law Centre and the Greater Manchester Probation Committee. He has served as a non-executive director of Central Manchester Healthcare Trust and is a former Secretary of Mosscare Housing Limited. He is a past Chairman of the Jamaican Society and a Governor of Bishop Bilsborrow School.
Interests: Cricket, bowling, football.
Contact details: Lord Mayor's Office, Room 412, Town Hall, M60 2LA (tel: 0161 234 3180, fax: 0161 234 3230, email: lord.mayorsoffice@notes.manchester.gov.uk); 130 Great Western Street, Moss Side M14 4RA (tel: 0161 226 2225).

WANDER, Dr Philip Alan, BDS (1966), MGDSRCS (1980), DDHFHom (1990)

Positions: Dental Surgeon, Private Practice (1966 - present).
Areas of Influence: Health, Media, Sport.
Profile: *b.* November 13th, 1942; *m.* Jennifer; 2 sons; 2 daughters.
Education: Bowker Vale Primary School; Chetham Collegiate; Manchester Central Grammar; Batchelor of Dental Surgery, University of Liverpool (1962-66); Membership of The Royal College of Surgeons (1980); Diploma in Dental Homeopathy, Faculty of Homeopathy, London. Career profile: Founder Member and Chairman, British Dental Homeopathic Association; Lectures throughout UK on Dental Photography and Dental Homeopathy. Philip Wander has appeared regularly on Radio Manchester on Dental Topics and has treated many local celebrities in his practice. He has also appeared on Network TV on the dental topics *Virtual Dentistry* and *Use of Propolis in Dentistry*. He is an Honorary Dentist to the Royal College of Music and supports and lectures at Manchester Homeopathic Clinic, where he is also a Committee member. Publications: *Dental Photography*; many articles in Dental Journals and lay press. Prizes and awards: Postgraduate award in Dental Photography. Clubs and societies: Local Dental Committee; Chipping Norton Golf

Club; Manchester United Football Club; Manchester Homeopathic Clinic.
Interests: Golf, photography, football - an avid member of Manchester United Football Club.
Contact details: 20 St Anns Square, Manchester M2 7HG (tel: 0161 833 4658, fax: 0161 834 6494, email: philthetooth@onetel.net.uk); Chetwynd, 21 Knutsford Road, Wilmslow Sk9 6JB (tel: 01625 528 982).

WARD, District Judge Peter, LLB (Bristol)

Positions: District Judge (Magistrates' Courts), Manchester City Magistrates' Court (2001 – present).
Areas of Influence: Law
Profile: *b.* June 20th, 1943; *m.* Monica Stalker; 3 sons.
Educated at Bolton School and Bristol University. Career profile: Partner, Rothwell & Evans Solicitors, Salford (1969-94); Stipendiary Magistrate, Merseyside (1994-01).
Interests: Walking, reading, swimming.
Contact details: City Magistrates' Court, Crown Square, Manchester M60 1PR (tel: 0161 832 7272).

WARREN, Joelle Susan, BA, ACIB

Positions: Managing Director, Warren Partners Ltd; Governor, Manchester Metropolitan University; Churchwarden, Christchurch, Alsager.
Areas of Influence: Commerce, Faith Groups, Education.
Profile: *b.* 11th January, 1962; *m.* Andrew; 2 sons.
Educated at Withingtons Girl's School, Manchester and St Johns Colllege, University of Durham; After beginning her career in the city with Lloyds bank, Joelle spent 10 years in corporate and retail banking with Lloyds before moving back to the North west and joining a national search and selection firm in Manchester as a partner (1995). She then formed Warren Partners (1999), a business which is now becoming the search and selection business of choice in the North West, employing 14 people.
Interests: Church, family, entertaining, skiing, cycling, hill walking.
Contact details: Warren Partners Ltd, Edward House, 4 Royal Court, Knutsford, Cheshire WA16 6EN (tel: 01565 759800, fax: 01565 759801, email: mail@warrenpartners.co.uk).

WATKINS, Maurice, LLB, LLM

Position: Senior Partner, James Chapman and Co, Solicitors.
Areas of Influence: Law, Sport, Voluntary Sector.
Profile: Educated at Manchester Grammar School and University College London. Career profile: Commercial Lawyer, Sports Law; Director, Manchester United

Football Club, Manchester United PLC; President, British Association for Sport and Law; Member, FA Premier League Legal Working Party; UEFA Panel, External Legal Experts; Premier League Representative, Association of European Union Premier Professional Football Leagues; Member, FIFA, Dispute Resolution Chamber; Current Directorships, Manchester United Football Club Limited, Manchester United PLC, Regional Director for Coutts Bank, Company Secretary, MUTV. Clubs and societies: NSPCC, Sports Steering Group; Chairman, Tommy's Appeal; Chairman, MGS Bursary Appeal; The Law Society; British Association for Sport and Law; Lancashire Country Cricket Club; Northern Lawn Tennis Club; Governor, Manchester Grammar School.

Interests: Cricket, soccer, tennis.

Contact details: James Chapman and Co, 76, King Street, Manchester M2 4NH (tel: 0161 828 8000, fax: 0161 828 8012, email: sport@james-chapman.co.uk).

WATKINSON, Michael

Position: Cricketer; Draughtsman.
Areas of Influence: Sport.
Profile: *b.* August 1st, 1961, Westoughton; *m.* Susan (1986); 1 son, Liam (1991); 1 daughter, Charlotte (1989).
Educated at Rivington and Blackrod High School, Horwich.
Interests: Football, watching Bolton Wanderers

WATSON, Alan Arthur

Positions: Chairman, Diligencia Ltd; Chairman, South Manchester Accident Resue Team; Member of Council, Chester Zoo.
Areas of Influence: Finance.
Profile: *b.* May 19th, 1937; *m.* Moira; 1 son; 2 daughters.
Education: Liverpool College (1945-54). Career profile: Bank of England (1954-95); Several Non-executive Directorships; Governor, The Manchester Metropolitan University (1989-99); Trustee of several charities; Governor, Trinity Church of England School, Hulme (1993-01); Paul Harris Fellow, Rotary International. Fellow of Chartered Institute of Bankers; Honorary MA, University of Manchester and University of Salford.
Interests: Church activities, voluntary work, walking, gardening.
Contact details: Jenny Heyes, Heyes Lane, Alderley Edge, Cheshire SK9 7LH (tel: 01625 583479, email: alan@awatson98.freeserve.co.uk).

WATSON, Kevin, BA (Hons) (1980), PGCE (1981)

Position: Principal, Winstanley College, Wigan (1998 - present).
Areas of Influence: Education.
Profile: *b.* January 19th, 1958; divorced.
Education: Ashington High School, Ashington, Northumberland (1969-76); BA Honours Class I History, Clare College, Cambridge (1977-80); PGCE, University of York (1980-81). Career profile: Teacher of History and Social Studies, Cavendish School, Hemel Hempstead (1981-83); Lecturer and Senior Lecturer in History and Politics, Enfield College (1983-91); Head of Humanities and Science, Bridgwater College, Somerset (1992-97). Winstanley College was awarded Beacon status in 2001, and finished a record fourth in the college league table compiled by The Guardian. Kevin is one of a diminishing number of people who can trace their roots to being the son of a coal miner. Publications: various curriculum projects featured in Learning and Skills Development Agency Publications; National Audit Office Report (2002).
Interests: Range of sports both as participant and observer (lifelong supporter of Sunderland FC), literature, cinema, music, theatre, current affairs.
Contact details: Winstanley College, Winstanley Road, Billinge, Wigan WN5 7XF (tel: 01695 633 244, fax: 01695 633 409, email: kwatson@winstanley.ac.uk).

WATSON, Nenagh

Position: Co Artistic Director, doo-cot.
Areas of Influence: Arts, Lesbian & Gay.
Profile: *b.* November 24th, 1958; Rachael Field (partner).
Education: BA Hons class II div. 1, Combined Studies Creative Arts (Sculpture & Theatre), Crewe and Alsager College of Higher Education (1979-83); Institute de la Marionette, Charleville Mezieres, France, 'L'Animateur - Acteur et l'Objet Anime' (1985); Theatre of Objects (1989). Career profile: Freelance commissioned performances (1985-90); Drama Advisor, North West Arts Board (1986-00); Established doo-cot to create and access truly innovative theatre art which challenges both in form and content (1990); Advisor for *On the Brink of Belonging* a national enquiry into puppetry, published by Caloust Gulbenkian Foundation (1992). Publications: *Theatre of Animation, Contemporary Adult Puppet Plays in Context*; *The Rage of the Painter*; *The 5th Wall*. Received Barclays New Stages Award for *Odd if you Dare* (1994). Clubs and societies: ITC Independant Theatre Council; UNIMA Union International Marionnette; GALAS Gay & Lesbian Arts Group.
Interests: Gym, yoga, allotment gardening, contemporary music and jazz, reading.
Contact details: doo-cot@, Unit 4, 31 Range Road, Manchester, M16 8FS (tel: 07714 246 008, fax: 0161 232 0160, email: doo-cot@cssystems.net, web: www.doo-cot.com).

WEARNE, Mandy, RGN, RM, RHV, Dip. Nursing (Dist)

Positions: Director of Performance, Greater Manchester Strategic Health Authority (2002); Director, Manchester Care; Director, Connexions.
Areas of Influence: Health, Public Sector.
Profile: *b.* August 25th, 1961.
Mandy Wearne qualified as a nurse, midwife, and health visitor before gaining a Masters Degree in Public Health becoming England's first public health nurse. She then joined the primary care team at the former Mersey Regional Health Authority (1992), and was appointed senior nurse in primary and community care for NHS Executive North West. She is currently responsible for performance and service development within GMSHA.
Interests: Exploring Manchester (my new home), good food, having fun with friends, shopping.
Contact details: Greater Manchester Strategic Health Authority, Gateway House, Piccadilly South, Manchester (tel: 0161 237 2000, fax: 0161 237 2808, email: mandy.wearne@gmha.nhs.uk).

WEBB, Philip Ernest FCIB, FCCA, ACIS

Positions: Chairman, Admiral Leasing PLC; Director, Butterfly Holdings PLC.
Profile: *b.* April 25th, 1943; *m.* Gillian; 1 son; 1 daughter.
Educated at Altrincham Grammar School (1953 - 1959). Career profile: District Bank (1959-68); County Bank (1968 -71); Old Broad St Securities (1971-73); UDT (1974-78); ET Trust (1978-82); Mynshul Bank PLC (1982-89); Director, Wood St Mission. Stages the *Brass and Beatles* Annual Charity Concert. Clubs and societies: Rotary Club of Manchester; St James's Club; Bramhall Golf Club.
Interests: Grandchild, Rotary, golf.
Contact details: Admiral Leasing PLC, Admiral House, Parsons Street, Oldham OL9 7AH (tel: 0161 628 7008, fax: 0161 628 7132, email: philipw@admiral-leasing.co.uk); Chandlers Farm, Bollington Lane, Nether Alderley, Nr Macclesfield SK10 4TB (tel: 01625 861 342, fax: 01625 890 244, email: philipewebb@hotmail.com).

WEBSTER, Alistair Stevenson QC, B.A (Hons)

Positions: Deputy Head of Chambers, Lincoln House Chambers, Manchester; Recorder, Crown Court.
Areas of Influence: Law.
Profile: *b.* April 28th, 1953; *m.* Barbara; 2 daughters.
Educated at Hulme Grammar School, Oldham (1960-71) and Brasenose College, Oxford (1972-75). Career profile: Called to the Bar, Middle Temple (1976); Hon. Secretary, Northern Circuit (1986-93); Assistant Recorder (1991-96). Publications:

Contributed to the Criminal Law Review. Clubs and societies: Member, Rochdale Racquets Club.

Interests: Theatre, film, tennis, cricket, football, sailing, skiing.

Contact details: Lincoln House Chambers, 1 Brazennose Street, Manchester M2 5EL (tel: 0161 832 5701, fax: 0161 832 0839, email: websterq@aol.com).

WEINBERG, Rebecca Davida

Positions: Magistrate, Bury Bench (1990 - present); Student Services Manager, Langdon College (2002 -).

Areas of Influence: Voluntary Sector, Jewish Communal Issues.

Profile: *b.* July 7th, 1952; *m.* Robert; 1 son; 1 daughter.

Educated at Stand Grammar School for Girls (1963-70) and Froebel Institute College of Education (1970-73). Originally qualifying as a teacher, Rebecca Weinberg went on to complete a youth leadership course before working as a Residential Social Worker with young offenders (1974-79), and later as an Education Welfare Officer in Manchester and Bury (1975-79). Between 1984 and 1987 she held posts as an outreach worker, a tribunal representative and a deputy manager at Harpurhey CAB. She was then recruited by the Jewish Blind Society to set up and develop the Nicky Alliance Day Centre in 1987. Chair, then Executive Member, Voluntary Action Manchester (-2002).

Interests: Criminal Justice, gardening, travel, walking, cookery, family, voluntary choir, jewish emergency team.

WEST, Janice

Positions: Press Officer, Ridge Danyers College, Stockport; Tutor, Health & Social Care and Nursery Nursing; JWT Associates; Committee Member, Network North.

Areas of Influence: Media, Education.

Profile: *b.* August 10th, 1952; *m.* Alvin; 1 son.

Education: Fred Longworth CS School, Tyldesley (1964-70); Cert in Education, Elizabeth Gaskell College, Manchester (1970-73); Cert. in Management; Internal Verifier Award, and Assessor Award, RSA; City & Guilds Cert. in Further Education. Clubs and societies: Network North and Stockport Women in Partnership. Janice West is an experienced marketing communicator with a background in Business, Secondary and Higher Education. She has extensive knowledge of managing the press function, including press liaison and major event organisation, and is also a qualified teacher, whose career has adapted to a number of changing roles including Home Economics, Child Care and Education, Health Studies, Health and Social Care.

Interests: Walking, reading, riding, watching and listening to music, cooking.

Contact details: (tel/fax: 01663 765148, mob: 07885 465866, email: pr@jwtassociates .co.uk).

WESTMINSTER, 6th Duke of, (cr 1874); Gerald Cavendish Grosvenor, OBE (1995), TD (1994), DL (1982)

Positions: Royal Westminster Regiment; Honorary Colonel, 7 Regt AAC (1993 - present); Northumbrian University OTC (NUTOC), RMLY (2001 - present).
Areas of Influence: Public Sector.
Profile: *b.* December 22nd, 1951; *m.* Natalia Ayesha; 1 son, Earl Grosvenor (1991); 3 daughters, Lady Tamara Katherine (1979), Lady Edwina Louise (1981), and Lady Viola Georgina (1992).
Educated at Harrow. Career profile: Queens Own Yeo (1970), Commissioned (1973), Captain (1979), Major (1985), Lieut-Colonel (1992), Commanding Regiment (1992), Colonel (1995-97), DComd 143 (WM) Brigade (1997-99), Brigade TA HQ AAG (2000), Colonel in Chief. Sat as Conservative Peer, House of Lords until 1993; Landowner; Chairman, Grosvenor Group Holdings Ltd; Director: Grosvenor Estate Holdings, Deva Group Ltd, Deva Holdings Ltd, Grosvenor Ltd, Suttonridge Pty Ltd (Aust, Countryside Alliance, Claridges (1981-92), Marcher Sound Lts (1982-97), Harland & Woolfe (1984-87), Coutts & Co (1985), Business in the Community (1988-92), North West Business Leadership Team (1990-97), Royal & Sun Alliance Insurance Group plc (1995-99), Countryside Movement (1995-2000), The Royal Association of British Dairy Farmers (2000-01); Chairman of Trustees: TSB Foundation of England and Wales (1986-97), Royal Agricultural Society of the Commonwealth (1990-98), Thomas Cubbitt Memorial Trust, Falcon Trust, Westminster Foundation, Nuffield Trust for the Forces of the Crown; Trustee Westminster Abbey Trust; Chancellor: Manchester Metropolitan University, Keele University (1986-93); President and Vice President of various organisations.
Interests: Shooting, fishing, scuba diving.
Contact details: Eaton Hall, Chester, Cheshire CH4 9ET; Eaton Estate Office, Eccleston, Chester (tel: 01244 684400).

WEWER, Christian, BA (hons), BArch, RIBA

Positions: Managing Director, AEW Architects; Consul for Denmark in Manchester and North West (1986 - present).
Areas of Influence: Commerce, Arts, Education.
Profile: *b.* November 1st, 1948; *m.* Dian; 3 sons.
Educated at Epsom College, Epsom, Surrey and Manchester University, School of Architecture. Following qualification, Christian Wewer became the company architect for Simonbuild and was joint founding partner of AEW Architects (1992). He has been responsible for the design and involved in the procurement of several building projects in the North West such as Gadbrook Park, Northwich, Concord Business Park, Dakota 602, The Western Development, Broadway North stage and South stage, and 16 Total Fitness Projects. Christian was awarded 'Rider of Danebro'

from Denmark for consular services (1998), which is the Danish equivelent of the MBE. He is a memebr of the St James Club and Stockport RUFC.
Interests: Sailing, squash, travelling, cycling, music, reading.
Contact details: AEW Architects, Elizabeth House, St Peters Square, Manchester M2 3DF (tel: 0161 237 9695, fax: 0161 237 9694, email: cwewer@aewarchitects.com); 2 Pleasant Way, Cheadle Hulme, Cheadle, Stockport, Cheshire SK8 7PF (tel: 0161 439 5500, email: christian@wewer.freeserve.co.uk).

WHEATCROFT, Matthew, BA (Hons), HND

Position: Senior Creative Designer, Judgegill
Areas of Influence: Arts, Media.
Profile: *b.* September 20th, 1972.
Education: New Mills School (1984-90); HND Graphic Design Stockport College (1990-94); BA (Hons) Graphic Design, Kingston University (1994-96). Career profile: Attik, Huddersfield (1996-97), New York (1997), London (1997-00); Judgegill, Manchester (2000-02). Awards: STD Student Assessment Scheme (1996); Type Directors Club, Silver Award (1998); South African Annual Design Award (1999). Matthew Wheatcroft has designed on behalf of Parlaphone, First Direct Bank, Factory Records, PricewaterhouseCoopers, BBC, ITV, Sony Playstation, Princes Trust, Lend Lease, Bass, TBWA, Saatchi and Saatchi, Jobsports and Adidas.
Interests: The Great Outdoors! Likes everything except coconut, Marmite, heights, Manchester United and buses.
Contact details: Judgegill, 3 Cobourg Street, Manchester M1 3GY (tel: 0161 228 3066, fax: 0161 228 0137, email: mat@judgegill.co.uk); 5 Crestwell Grove, Didsbury, Manchester M20 2NH (tel: 07879 441 595).

WHEELDON, Richard Andrew, LLB (Hons)

Position: Partner, Addleshaw Booth and Co, Solicitors.
Areas of Influence: Law.
Profile: *b.* November 21st, 1961; *m.* Karen; 2 daughters.
Educated at Bradford Grammar School (1972-79), Manchester University.(1979-82) and Chester College of Law (1982-83). Career profile: Articled, Last Suddards, Bradford (1983-85); Qualified as a solicitor (1985); Assistant Solicitor, Last Suddards (1985-88); Booth and Co (1988-).
Contact details: 100 Barbirolli Square, Manchester M2 3AB (tel: 0161 934 6499, fax: 0161 934 6060, email: richard.wheeldon@addleshawbooth.com).

WHIBLEY, John, AGSM

Position: Director, John Whibley 'Holidays with music'.
Areas of Influence: Arts, Commerce.
Profile: *b.* May 11th, 1945; *m.* Helen; 5 sons; 1 daughter.
Educated at Worthing High School (1956-61), Dartington College of Arts (1961-63) and Guildhall School of Music (1963-67). Career profile: Cellist, Hallé Orchestra (1967-72); Cello Professor, Keele and Salford University (1972-75); General Manager, Manchester Camerata (1975-96); Deputy Chief Executive, Hallé Orchestra (1996-98).
Interests: Running in Derbyshire and the Pyrenees.
Contact details: Ash Lea, Longlands Road, New Mills, Derbyshire SK22 3BY (tel: 01663 746 578, fax: 01663 744 067, email: john@whibley.co.uk).

WHITBREAD, Neville Anthony, FCA

Positions: Managing Director, PBSI Ltd (1980 - present); Chairman, Friends of the Whitworth.
Areas of Influence: Arts, Commerce.
Profile: *b.* June 19th, 1938; *m.* Juliet; 1 son; 3 daughters.
Educated at West Downs (1948-52) and Eton (1952-56). Career profile: Commisioned Royal Horse Guards (1957-59); Qualified Audit Senior (1965-70), Deloitte Plendor Griffith, London (1960-65); Account Executive, Tozer Kemsley Williams (1971-74); Financial Controller, Miles Druce (1975-76); Financial Controller, H Brammer, Altrincham (1976-79). Member of Court Manchester University and UMIST. Clubs and societies: Friends of the Whitworth; City Art Gallery; National Trust; Historic Houses Association; Historic Churches; Delamere Forest Golf Club.
Interests: The arts generally, garden design, golf, tennis.
Contact details: PBSI Ltd, Bellevue Works, Boundary Street, Manchester M12 5NG (tel: 0161 223 5151, fax: 0161 230 6464).

WHITE, Alan, LLB, FCA

Positions: Chief Executive, N Brown Group.
Areas of Influence: Commerce, Finance.
Profile: *b.* April 15th, 1955; *m.* Helen; 1 son; 1 daughter.
Educated at Salford Grammar School and Warwick University. Career profile: Chartered Accountant, Arthur Anderson (1976-79); GM Finance, Sharp Electronics (1979-85); Group Finance Director, N Brown Group (1985-99); Group Finance Director, Littlewoods (1999-02). Member of Alderley Edge Cricket Club.
Interests: Tennis, squash, skiing, waterskiing, Manchester United.
Contact details: 53 Dale Street, Manchester (tel: 0161 238 2202).

WHITE, Graham, BA (Hons) (1988)

Positions: Superintendent, Greater Manchester Police; Sub Divisional Commander, South Trafford; Police Commander responsible for England Football Fixtures, International (2001 - present).
Areas of Influence: Public Sector, Sport.
Profile: *b.* August 1st, 1954; *m.* Christine; 2 sons.
Educated at Leigh Grammar School (1965-71) and Manchester Metropolitan University (1985-88). Career profile: Police Cadet, Lancashire (1971); Constable (1973); Sergeant (1979); Inspector (1989); Head, North West Regional Police Training (1992-94); Chief Inspector (1993); Superintendent (1996).
Interests: Gardening, theatre, cinema, music, Rugby League.
Contact details: Greater Manchester Police, Sub Divisional HQ, Barrington Road, Altrincham WA14 1HZ (tel: 0161 872 5050, fax: 0161 856 7560).

WHITE, Stephen John, LLB (Hons)

Position: Senior Partner, Cobbetts (1999 - present).
Areas of Influence: Law, Voluntary Sector.
Profile: *b.* May 9th, 1949; *m.* Anne; 1 son; 1 daughter.
Educated at The Manchester Grammar School and University College, London. Career profile: Articled Clerk (1972-74), Assistant Solicitor (1974-76), Partner (1976-87), Leak, Almond & Parkinson, Solicitors, Manchester; Partner, Cobbett Leak Almond, then Cobbetts (1987-1999). Council Member and Secretary, Pro Manchester; Council Member, Disabled Living; Vice President, Community Foundation for Greater Manchester. Member, St James's Club, Manchester.
Interests: Tennis, photography.
Contact details: Cobbetts, Ship Canal House, King Street, Manchester M2 4WB (tel: 0161 833 5222, fax: 0161 830 2788, email: stephen.white@cobbetts.co.uk).

WILDIG, Michael John, B.Sc, FCA, CTA

Position: Head of Tax, Ernst and Young, North Region.
Areas of Influence: Finance.
Profile: *b.* December 28th, 1953; *m.* Jane; 3 sons; 1 daughter.
Educated at King's School, Chester (1964-72) and Durham University (1972-75). Career profile: Ernst and Young (1975); Partner, Ernst and Young (1985); Member of Alderley Edge Cricket Club.
Interests: Squash, tennis.
Contact details: Ernst and Young, LLP, 100 Barbirolli Square, Manchester M2 3EY (tel: 0161 333 2532, fax: 0161 333 3013, email: mwildig@uk.ey.com).

WILKINSON, Stephen Austin, MBE (1992), MA, MusBac (Cantab), Hon MA (Manchester)

Position: Conductor, William Byrd Singers of Manchester (1970 - present) and Capriccio Young String Ensemble (1991 - present).
Areas of Influence: Arts, Media.
Positions: *b.* April 29th, 1919; *m.* Delyth; 3 sons; 3 daughters.
Educated at Christ Church Cathedral Choir School Oxford, St Edward's School Oxford and Queens' College Cambridge. Career profile: War Service in the Navy (1940-46): Lieutenent RNVR, Mine Disposal Officer, Faroe Islands (1941-43); Enemy Mining Staff, HMS Vernon, Portsmouth. Director, Hertfordshire Rural Music School, Hitchin (1947-53); Programme Producer, BBC Music Staff (1953-79); Conductor, BBC Northern Singers, appearing with them at major festivals such as Edinburgh and the Proms, and widely round the world. Publications: Numerous choral works, folk song arrangements and songs.
Interests: Composition, reading, walking, travel.
Contact details: 9 Harboro Road, Sale, Cheshire M33 5AE (tel: 0161 973 0392).

WILLIAMS, Barrie, LLB, AKC

Position: HM Coroner, Greater Manchester, North District (1993 - present).
Areas of Influence: Law, Public Sector.
Profile: *b.* May 28th, 1936; *m.* Judith; 1 son; 1 daughter.
Educated at QEGS, Wakefield and King's College, London. Barrie Williams qualified as a solicitor in 1961 and practised in a local high street firm of solicitors for over 30 years. He was appointed full time Coroner in 1993 by which time he had been a Non-executive Member of the Royal Oldham Hospital Trust Board, Vice Chairman of their Research and Ethics Committee and Vice Chairman of local Hulme Grammar School Board of Governors for many years. Clubs and societies: Local Civic Trust Society, Saddleworth Music Society.
Interests: Singing member of Huddersfield Choral Society, member of St Chad's Church, Uppermill.
Contact details: Telegraph House, Bailhe Street, Rochdale OL16 1QY (tel: 01706 649922, fax: 01706 641720); 133 Manchester Road, Greenfield, Oldham OL3 7HJ.

WILLIAMS, Bill, MA (Cantab)

Positions: Lecturer in Jewish Studies (1993 - present) and Fellow of the Centre for Jewish Studies, University of Manchester.
Areas of Influence: Arts, Faith Groups, Education.
Profile: *b.* August 21st, 1931; divorced; 2 sons; 1 daughter.
Education: Stonyhurst College; MA and Certificate in Education, Trinity College,

Cambridge. Career profile: Teacher of History in Cardiff and Malaysia (1954-64); Lecturer in History, Malayan Teachers College, Penang, Malaysia (1960-64); Lecturer in History, City of Birmingham College of Education (1964-67); Principal Lecturer in History, Department of Education, Manchester Polytechnic (1967-75); Trustee, Searchlight Educational Trust and Documentary Photographic Archive; Honorary President, Manchester Jewish Museum. Bill Williams is currently directing research at the University of Manchester into the lives of Jewish refugees into Manchester 1933 - 1941. He is an oral historian who has conducted interviews for the National Sound Archive, Manchester Jewish Museum and elsewhere. He is a member of the Strategic Vision Committee for Holocaust Memorial Day, Home Office and is currently writing a book, *The Jewish Immigrants in Manchester, 1875-1920*. Publications: *The Making of Manchester Jewry* (1976); *Manchester Jewry: a Pictorial History, 1788 - 1988* (1988); *Sir Sidney Hamburger and Manchester Jewry* (2000); numerous articles in press and learned journals.

Interests: Table tennis, snooker, cinema, theatre.

Contact details: Department of Religion and Theology, University of Manchester, Oxford Road, Manchester M13 9PL (tel: 0161 275 3614); 26 Park Avenue, Levenshulme, Manchester, M19 2EE (tel: 0161 224 1747).

WILLIAMS, The Revd Canon Michael Joseph, BA (Dunelm)

Positions: Vicar, Bolton Parish Church; Area Dean of Bolton.
Areas of Influence: Faith Groups.
Profile: *b*. February 26th, 1942; *m*. Mary Miranda; 1 son; 1 daughter.
Educated at West Bromwich Technical School, The Bernard Gilpin Society and St John's College, University of Durham. Career profile: Engineering Draughtsman, W&T Avery Ltd; Curate, St Philemon, Toxteth, Liverpool; Team Vicar, Toxteth Team Ministry, Liverpool; Director of Pastoral Studies, St John's College, Durham; Principal, The Northern Ordination Course, Manchester. Publication: *The Power and the Glory* (1989). Clubs and societies: Bolton Interfaith Council, Philosophy Research Seminar, Bolton Institute.
Interests: Cabinet making, hill walking.
Contact details: tel: 01204 533 847, email: vicar@boltonparishchurch.co.uk; The Vicarage, Silverwell Street, Bolton, BL1 1PS (tel: 01204 365 895).

WILLIAMS, John

Positions: Managing Director, Mason Williams Ltd; CEO, Muse Group; Managing Director, Arkitech; Board member, Public Relations Consultants Association, F 100.
Areas of Influence: Commerce, Media.
Profile: *b*. January 7th, 1948; Rita Rowe (partner); 1 daughter.
John Williams spent 12 years as a journalist from the Buxton Advertiser to the Daily

Mail before PR Agency Stringworth Williams in 1977 which was subsequently sold in 1986. He then founded Mason Williams with his partner Rita Rowe which now has offices in both Manchester and London. In 2002 he founded Muse Group to exploit his interest in new technology. Muse has offices in Manchester, London and Douglas, IOM, as well as licencees in Calgary, Canada. Clubs and Associations: British Racing Drivers Club; Royal Automobile Club.

Interests: International racing driver, sailing, all sports.

Contact details: Tanzaro House, Ardwick Green, Manchester M12 6FZ (tel: 0161 273 5923, email: john@mason-williams.com); Casa Lucem, Ruberts 07220 Pina, Mallorca, Balaeric Islands.

WILLIE, The Reverend David Frederick, MA (Cantab) (1968)

Position: Chairman, Manchester and Stockport District of the Methodist Church.
Areas of Influence: Faith Groups.
Profile: *b.* July 25th, 1939; *m.* Daphne; 2 sons; 1 daughter.
Educated at Jarrow Grammar School (1950-57) and University of Cambridge (1962-65). Career profile: Civil Service (1958-62); Methodist Minister (1965 - present). Member of Yorkshire Cricket Club.
Interests: Football, cricket, gardening, walking.
Contact details: 15 Woodlands Road, Handforth, Wilmslow, Cheshire SK9 3AW (tel/fax: 01625 523480, email: david@manstock.fsnet.co.uk).

WILMOT, Sir David, Kt (2002), QPM (1989), DL

Positions: Former Chief Constable, Greater Manchester Police (1991-02).
Areas of Influence: Public Sector.
Profile: *b.* March 12th, 1943 Fleetwood, Lancashire; *m.* Ann.
Educated at Baines Grammer School, Poulton-le-Fylde, and Southampton University. Career profile: Lancashire Constabulary (1974-81); Merseyside Police (1983-85); West Yorkshire Police
(1987-91); Member, International Association of Chief Constables.
Interests: Reading, gardening.

WILSON, Andrew James, DL (1998), MA

Positions: Under Sheriff of Greater Manchester (1977 - present); Consultant, Brabners Chaffe Street (2000 - present); Director, Cerberus Group Limited (2000 - present); Seal Keeper for the Duchy of Lancaster; Honorary Solicitor, The Lancashire Youth Association; Committee Member, Sheriffs Officers Association (2002 -); Chairman, Federation of Sheriffs of England and Wales (2001 - present).
Areas of Influence: Law, Commerce, Voluntary Sector.

Profile: *b.* December 5th, 1950; *m.* Tricia; 2 sons.
Educated at Malvern College Worcestershire, St John's College Oxford and The College of Law, Lancaster Gate, London. Andrew Wilson trained as a solicitor with Hall Brydon & Co, Manchester. He then joined the family firm of Wilson Wright & Ashcrofts following admission as a solicitor in 1975. He was a Committee member of the Under Sherifs Association from 1978 to 2002 for whom he held several posts, and Council Member of the Association of High Sheriffs from 1999 to 2001. Clubs and societies: Manchester Tennis and Racquet Club; Lansdowne Club, London.
Interests: Real tennis, walking, bee keeping.
Contact details: The Sheriff's Office, 26 Missouri Avenue, Salford, Manchester M50 2NP (tel: 0161 925 1800, fax: 0161 737 7799, email: andrew.Wilson@northern undersheriffs.com); The Cottage, 483 Garstang Road, Broughton, Preston PR3 5JA (tel/fax: 01772 866 306, email: ajwundersheriff@aol.com).

WILSON, Anthony Howard, BA (Hons) (Cantab)

Positions: Director, In the City Limited, Music33.com; Partner, Red Cellars, Livesey Wilson Associates; Presenter, Granada TV; Board Member, Museum of Science and Industry in Manchester, Manchester Science Park.
Areas of Influence: Media, Arts, Voluntary Sector.
Profile: *b.* February 20th, 1950; Yvette Livesey (partner); 1 son, Oliver (17); 1 daughter, Isabel (12).
Education: Martin House Prep. (1954-55); St Mary's Marple Bridge (1955-61); De La Salle College, Salford (1961-68); BA English, Jesus College, Cambridge University (1968-77). Anthony Wilson joined ITN as a Graduate Trainee (1971-73) before moving to Granada Television as an onscreen reporter. Program credits include *Granada Reports*, *Which Way*, *So it Goes*, *World in Action*, *Flying Start*, *Up Front*, and *The Other Side of Midnight*. Independent work included being a founder-presenter of Channel 4's legendary *After Dark* as well as fronting *The Amber Room*. Working as a TV Journalist in the arts field led to putting a variety of bands on televisions for the first time from the Sex Pistols to Steps. This led Wilson into, first, running a venue, The Factory, then a record label, Factory Records which released its first records in January 1979. He then opened the Hacienda in 1982 and finally, Dry, in Manchester's Northern Quarter. The Factory label had launched half a dozen platinum artists such The Happy Mondays. Wilson is currently busy relaunching Factory records under the new name, Red Cellars. Earlier this year a movie about the story of Factory records and the Hacienda was released called *24 Hour Party People*.
Interests: Reading and windsurfing, but he never has time for either.
Contact details: The Loft, 10A Little Peter Street, Manchester M15 4PS (tel: 07850 053333, email: ahw@factory.u-net.com).

WILSON, David Geoffrey OBE (1986), DL (1985), MA (1983), MA (1995) FCIB

Positions: Chairman, East Manchester Partnership. Director, Healthsure Group Ltd (1998 - present); Hon. Consul for Iceland (1981 - present); Deputy Chairman, Manchester Diocesan Board of Finance (1996 - present); Member of Council, Salford University (1996 - present); Founder Member (1968), Treasurer and now Vice President, St Ann's Hospice (1991 - present); Chairman, The Charity Service (1999 - present); Chairman, Manchester Settlement (1999 - present); Chairman of Governors, Nicholas Varley Community School, Miles Platting, Manchester.
Areas of Influence: Voluntary Sector, Public Sector.
Profile: *b.* April 30th, 1933; *m.* Dianne Elizabeth.
Educated at Leeds Grammar School and Hulme Grammar School, Oldham. Career profile: William Deacon's Bank (1953-70); Williams & Glyn's Bank (1970-82); Regional Manager, National Enterprise Board (1982-85); Regional Director, British Linen Bank (1985-91); Chairman, North Manchester Health Authority (1991-93); Chairman, North Manchester Healthcare NHS Trust (1993-97); Chairman, Manchester Business Link (1993-00); Chairman, Business Link Network Co Ltd (1998-01). High Sheriff, Greater Manchester (1991-92); President, Manchester Chamber of Commerce and Industry (1978-80); President, Manchester Luncheon Club (1981-82); President, Manchester Literary and Philosophical Society (1981-83); Treasurer, Hallé Orchestra (1986-92); Deputy Chairman, Hallé (1992-97); Clubs and societies: Manchester Literary and Philosophical Society; MCC; Lancashire County Cricket Club; St James's Club, Manchester; Army & Navy Club, London.
Interests: Gardening, music.
Contact details: 28 Macclesfield Road, Wilmslow SK9 2AF (tel: 01625 524133, fax: 01625 520605, email: wilsondg@talk21.com).

WILSON, Dianne Elizabeth

Positions: National Trustee and Chair, Turning Point, Northern Region (1997-).
Areas of Influence: Public Sector, Voluntary Sector.
Profile: *b.* April 30th, 1937; *m.* David Wilson.
Educated at Dore High School, Sheffield; Chesterfield College of Arts; London School of Fashion; Career profile: Management Trainee, Lewis's, Manchester; Buyer, William Timpson (Shoes) Ltd; Town Centre Co-ordinator, Wilmslow; Elected Councillor, Macclesfield Borough Council (1984-96); Chairman of Governors, Wilmslow High School (1988-95); President, Manchester Literary and Philosophical Society (1997-99); Chairman of Friends of Hallé (1991-97); Member of Manchester Literary & Philosophical Society.

Interests: People, making things happen.
Contact details: 28 Macclesfield Road, Wilmslow SK9 2AF (01625 524 133, fax: 01625 520 605, email: wilsondg@talk.com).

WILSON, Ronald Geoffrey Osborne, CStJ (1992), DL (1995)

Position: Non-executive Company Chairman.
Areas of Influence: Commerce.
Profile: *b.* September 19th, 1926; *m.* Barbara; 1 son; 2 daughters.
Educated at Oundle School, Queens University Belfast, O.T.S. Bangalore India; Army War Service (1944-48); Articled Clerk, Accountancy; Company Secretary, member of Board of Directors, CoE, Trafalgar Engineering Co. Ltd. (1952-70); Regional Advisor to the Board and Assistant Director, Samuel Montagu & Co (1970-85); Consultant, Edge Consultants Ltd. (1986-98); Chairman of several companies (1986-02); Member of Court, Salford University. Clubs and societies: Member, The Order of St John; Manchester Naval Officers Association; The Army & Navy Club; St James, London.
Interests: Music, gardening, reading the paper.
Contact details: 13 Heyes Lane, Alderley Edge, Cheshire SK9 7LA (tel: 01625 585121).

WINGATE-SAUL, Giles QC, LLB (Hons)

Positions: Queen's Counsel; Deputy High Court Judge; Deputy Judge, Technology and Construction Court; Bench of The Inner Temple.
Areas of Influence: Law.
Profile: *b.* March 9th, 1945; *m.* Dr Katherine Wynne; 1 son; 1 daughter.
Educated at Winchester College and Southampton University. Career profile: Called to the Bar (1967); Appointed Queen's Counsel (1983); Chairman, Northern Circuit, Commercial Bar Association (1996-2002). Clubs and societies: Rusland Valley Horticulural Society; Liverpool Ramblers A.F.C.
Interests: Church affairs, sport.
Contact details: Byrom Street Chambers, 12 Byrom Street, Manchester M3 4PP (tel: 0161 829 2100, fax: 0161 829 2101, email: clerks@byromstreet.com).

WINTON, Dr Malcolm, BA, MSc, PhD, FRSA

Positions: Registrar and Secretary, University of Salford.
Areas of Influence: Education, Faith Groups.
Profile: *b.* January 10th, 1947; *m.* Glynis; 2 daughters.
Educated at Stockport Grammar School, Christ's College Cambridge and University of Manchester. Malcolm Winton has worked in University Administration since 1972. Initially in personnel work at the Universities of Salford and Liverpool, but then returning to Salford in 1979 where he was appointed to his current posts in 1993. He

is also a Reader in the Church of England at St Mary's and St Cuthbert's Churches in Cheadle.
Interests: Music, theatre, gardening.
Contact details: University of Salford, Salford M5 4WT (tel: 0161 295 5411, fax: 0161 295 5545, email: m.d.winton@salford.ac.uk); 16 Huxley Drive, Bramhall, Stockport SK7 2PH.

WISEMAN, The Rev David John, MA

Position: Team Rector, Ashton-under-Lyne (2000 - present).
Areas of Influence: Faith Groups
Profile: *b.* August 31st, 1951; *m.* Mary; 2 sons.
Education: Master of Arts, University of Derby; Bachelor of Divinity, University of London; Diploma in Islam, University of Birmingham; Ordination Training, Cranmer Hall, St John's College, University of Durham. Career profile: Community Relations Officer for the Diocese of Manchester (1989-97).
Interests: Cycling, motorcycling, furniture restoration, Assyrian Church of the East.
Contact details: Holy Trinity Vicarage, Dean Street, Ashton-under-Lyne OL67HD (tel: 0161 344 0075).

WOLFE, Joy Sylvia, JP (1984)

Positions: President, Zionist Central Council of Greater Manchester; Life President, Manchester WIZO; Chairman, North Cheshire WIZO; Governor, North Cheshire Jewish Primary School; Publicity Officer, Combined Charity Card Shop; Justice of the Peace (1984 - present); Vice Chairman, Manchester Bench Probation Liaison Committee, Family Panel. Freelance Reporter, Jewish Chronicle
Areas of Influence: Voluntary sector, Media, Faith Groups.
Profile: *b.* January 4th, 1938; *m.* Brian; 1 son; 2 daughters.
Education: Hove County Grammar School; Extra Mural Oxford Certificate in Social Studies. Career profile: Joy Wolfe started life as a hairdresser before becoming a Public Relations Consultant in 1974; She went into journalism in 1979 and became a reporter, then Editor for *The Jewish Gazette*; Chairman, Manchester Balfour Trust; Vice Chairman of Governors, Langdon Special Needs College; Charity cards sales organiser, Stockport Multiple Sclerosis Society; Founder Member of Stockport MSS; Manchester correspondent, Jewish Chronicle; Executive member, Jewish Representative Council of Greater Manchester. Clubs and societies: Former Trustee, Manchester Jewish Museum; Volunteer visitor for Manchester Jewish Federation; Member of the Jewish Representative Central Council and of Zionist Central Council Speakers panels; Publications: Editor, *Manchester Justice*, the magazine of the Manchester bench; many articles in Jewish and wider community newspapers. Prizes and awards: Northern Jewish Woman of the Year (1994). Clubs and societies: David

Lloyd Club, Cheadle.

Interests: Tennis, travel, public speaking, occasional braodcasting and newspaper reviewing for BBC GMR.

Contact details: (tel: 0161 491 1350, fax: 0161 491 3192, email: j.wolfe@dial.pipex.com).

WOLSTENCROFT, The Venerable the Arch Deacon of Manchester, Alan, ULCI, GOE

Positions: Archdeacon of Manchester, Residentiary Canon of the Cathedral and Fellow of the College (1998 - present)
Areas of Influence: Faith Groups, Media.
Profile: *b.* July 16th, 1937; *m.* Christine; 1 son; 1 daughter.
Educated at Wellington Technical School, Altrincham, St John's College of Further Education and Cuddesdon College, Oxford. Career profile: Trainee Manager, W H Smith & Co (1953-60); RAF National Service, RAF Medical Branch and Mountain Rescue Service (1955-57); Regional Manager, Wine and Spirit Division, BASS Charrington (1960-67); Ordained Deacon, Curate St Thomas, Halliwell, Bolton (1969); Ordained Priest (1970); Curate, All Saints, Stand (1971); Vicar, St Martins, Wythenshawe and Chaplain at Wythenshawe Hospital and Forum Theatre (1973-80); Area Deacon of Withington (1978-91); Vicar, St John, Brooklands, Sale (1980-91); Hon. Canon of Manchester (1986); Vicar of Bolton (1991-98); Religious Advisor, Granada TV (2000). Publications: Parish / Diocesan Magazine Articles; Diocesan Reports. Clubs and societies: YMCA, Concord.
Interests: Squash, theatre, walking, reading, Bolton Wanderers, cinema, Freemasons.
Contact details: 2 The Walled Garden, Swinton, Manchester M27 0FR (tel: 0161 794 2401, fax: 0161 794 2411, email: archdeaconalan@wolstencrofta.co.uk).

WOLSTENCROFT, Edwina Maria

Positions: Executive Producer, BBC Radio 3, Manchester.
Areas of Influence: Arts, Media
Profile: *b.* August 20th, 1957; *m.* Peter Ratoff; 2 sons.
Education: Greenhead School, Huddersfield (1968-75); BA Honours 2:1 Music, Exeter University (1975-78). Edwina Wolstencroft joined the BBC in London in 1978 as a studio manager. Her first production experience was for Radio 3 in the early 1980's in Manchester. She then worked in London as a producer for Radio 4 on programmes such as *Kaleidoscope* and *Bookshelf.* She returned to Radio 3, producing *Third Ear* and special anniversary projects before returning to Manchester in 1991, She has since had a variety of posts at Senior and Executive levels for Radios 3 and 4. Prizes and awards: Sony Gold for *Symphonies and Silence*, a programme about Peter Maxwell Davis; BPS Journalism award for a programme about Anthony Burgess.

Interests: Playing the piano, reading, fashion, eating out, psychology.
Contact details: BBC, New Broadcasting House, Oxford Road, Manchester M60 1SJ (tel: 0161 244 4236, email: edwina.wolstencroft@bbc.co.uk).

WOOD, Professor Laurie, PhD, BA (Hons), CERTED, DipCIM

Positions: Director of Academic Enterprises, University of Salford (2001 - present); Chairman, Museum of Science and Industry in Manchester (2001 - present); Chairman of the Marketing Council (2000 - present); Trustee of the CAM Foundation (2000 - present); Director, CIM Holdings Ltd (1997 - present); Dfes National Training Awards Judge (1992 - present).
Areas of Influence: Education, Commerce, Arts.
Profile: *b.* December 25th, 1952; *m.* Derek Hurt; 1 daughter.
Education: BA class I, The Manchester Metropolitan University (1982); PGDip, Chartered Institute of Marketing (1982); PGCE, Victoria University of Manchester (1986); PhD, University of Salford (1993). Career profile: Assistant to Group Marketing Manager, CWS Packaging Technology Group (1971-73); Freelance Consultant, Finance & Marketing (1973-75); Marketing Service Manager, Natwest Bank, Manchester (1975-80); National Development Manager (1982-84); Senior Lecturer Marketing and Planning, Manchester Metropolitan University (1984-88); Senior Lecturer in Strategic Management, School of Management, University of Salford (1988-99); Associate Dean, Faculty of Business and Informatics, University of Salford (1999-01); International Chairman, Chartered Institute of Marketing (1999-00); Non-executive Director, Tameside and Glossop Acute Service NHS Trust (1997-00); Chairman, Arts About Manchester (1993-97). Over 40 publications, seminars, and presentations. Awarded Hon. Fellowship, CIM (2001). Clubs and societies: Freeman of the City of London; Fellow, Royal Society of Arts; Hon. Fellow, Chartered Institute of Marketing; Member, Institute of Directors.
Interests: Music, the arts, playing piano, keep fit, reading - English literature, DIY.
Contact details: Univerity of Salford, Faraday Building, Salford M5 HWT (tel: 0161 295 5998, fax: 0161 295 5954, email: l.wood@salford.ac.uk).

WOOD, Phil

Position: Presenter, BBC GMR.
Areas of Influence: Media.
Profile: *b.* 1994.
Career profile: Commercial Advertising; Commercial Radio; BBC Radio.
Interests: Restaurants, wine, winter sports, travel, films.
Contact details: BBC, Oxford Road, Manchester (tel: 0161 200 2000, email: phil.wood@bbc.co.uk).

WOODWARD, His Honour Judge

Position: Circuit Judge (1990 - present).
Areas of Influence: Law.
Profile: *m.* Patricia; 2 daughters.
Educated at Alderman Wraith Grammar School and Sheffield University. Career profile: Various teaching posts and research (1961-70); Called to the Bar (1970); Practised at the Bar on the Northern Circuit in Manchester (1970-84); Chairman of Industrial Tribunals (1984-90).
Interests: Skiing, golf, motor cycling, classic cars.
Contact details: Minshull Street Crown Court, Minshull Street, Manchester (tel: 0161 954 7500).

WOODWARD, Susan Lesley

Positions: Creative Director, Commonwealth Games (2002); Director of Broadcasting, Granada TV.
Areas of Influence: Media, Arts.
Profile: December, 22nd 1955; *m.* Brian Roberts; 1 son.
Education: Prescott Girls Grammar School, Merseyside; The Harris Institute, Preston; Business School, Preston Polytechnic Journalism School, The London Business School. Career profile: Newspaper Journalist, Liverpool Echo, Daily Mirror and Daily Mail; TV Reporter, Granada Television; TV Producer, Granada Television; Programme Editor, Channel 4; Executive producer, BBC1 and BBC2; Controller, Regional Television, Granada. Susan Woodward has published many newspaper articles and has been producing TV programmes for last 20 years across a wide base of genre such as TV News, current affairs, fiction, religion, and both the opening and closing ceremonies of the Commonwealth Games. She believes that "no mission is impossible"; 4 Royal Television Society Awards; 2 Plain English Campaign Awards; Member of the British Guild of Editors and the Royal Television Society.
Interests: New media, technology, reading, dining out, cinema, television.
Contact details: Granada TV, Quay St, Manchester M60 9EA (tel: 0161 832 7211, fax: 0161 793 0727, email: sue.woodward@granadamedia.com).

WOOLAS, Philip James MP, BA (Hons)

Position: Lord Commissioner to HM Treasury (WHIP) (2002 – present).
Areas of Influence: Politics, Public Policy, Media.
Profile: *b.* December 11th, 1959; *m.* Tracey Allen; 2 sons.
Educated at Nelson Grammar School (1971-76); University of Manchester, BA (Hons) Philosophy (1978-81); NUS President (1984-86); War On Want Fundraiser (1986); TVS Researcher (1987-88); BBC Newsnight Producer (1988-90); Channel 4 News Producer

(1990-91); GMB Head of Communications (1991-97); Member of Parliament for Oldham East and Saddleworth (1997-); PPS to Lord McDonald (1999-2001); Junior WHIP (2001-02).
Interests: Manchester United, photography, wine.
Contact details: House of Commons, London SW1A 0AA (tel: 020 7219 1149, fax: 020 7219 0992)

WRIGHT, Peter Duncan QC

Positions: Queens Counsel.
Areas of Influence: Law.
Profile: *b.* November 11th, 1957; *m.* Stephanie; 1 son; 2 daughters.
Educated at Chadderton Grammar School for Boys. Career profile: Called to the Bar (1981); Q.C (1999); Crown Court Recorder (2000); Prosecuting Counsel, Regina v Harold Shipman. Clubs and societies: Broughton Park R.U.F.C.
Interests: Sport, travel.
Contact details: Lincoln House, 1 Brazennose Street, Manchester M2 5 EL (tel: 0161 832 5701, fax: 0161 832 0839).

WROE, Chief Superintendent, Brian, BA (Hons)

Positions: Divisional Commander, Salford Division, GMP (2001 - present); Joint Chair, Salford Crime and Disorder Reduction Partnership; Deputy Chair, Salford Drug Action Team; Member, Local Strategic Partnership.
Areas of Influence: Law, Public Sector.
Profile: *b.* February 16th, 1954; *m.* Carol; 2 daughters.
Education: Thornleigh Salesian College, Bolton; BA (Hons) Politics and Contemporary History, University of Salford. Career profile: Constable, Bolton (1973); Sergeant, Wigan (1979); Inspector, Salford (1988); Chief Inspector, Training Branch (1995); Superintendent (1999). Member of the Police Superintendants Association.
Interests: Keep fit, season ticket holder at Bolton Wanderers FC, running, have successfully completed two marathon road races.
Contact details: Divisional Police Headquarters, The Crescent, Salford M5 4PD (tel: 0161 856 5405, fax: 0161 856 5427, email: brian.wroe@gmp.police.uk).

YATES, Andrew, BA (Keele 1972)

Position: Director of Trading Services, UMIST (1990 - present).
Areas of Influence: Education, Commerce.
Profile: *b.* October 31st, 1949; *m.* Elizabeth; 1 son; 1 daughter.
Educated at Kendal Grammar School (1961-66), Wilmslow County High (1966-68) and The University of Keele (1968-72). Career profile: Sales and Marketing, Ford Motor Company (1972-76); Conference manager, University of Essex (1976-78); Business manager, UMIST (1978-90);
Director, Stickups Ltd; Chairman, Open University Hosts Group; Founder member, Conference of University Business Officers; Member, Marketing Manchester Subvention Group. Responsible for the growth and development of Trading Services including the successful branding and development of the Manchester Conference Centre. Developed UMIST residences to be the first UK University to offer online telephony and IT in all student accommodation. Developed a unit to support academics from Greater Manchester Universities to attract and run international events: largest International Conference on Microbiology (1968), latest International Conference on Engineering Education (2002). Member of Prince Albert Angling Club, High Lane Conservative Club, and Trent Offshore Group. Advertising Secretary, St Mary's Parish Magazine, Disley.
Interests: Fishing, reading, walking, cartography, sailing.
Contact details: The Manchester Conference Centre, UMIST, PO Box 88, Manchester M60 1QD (tel: 0161 200 4065, fax: 0161 200 4090, email: andrew.yates@umist.ac.uk, web: www.netmeeting.co.uk); (email: andrew.yates@talk21.com).

YEAMAN, Angus George David, JP (1976), MIMechE

Position: President, The Manchester Literary & Philosophical Society (2001 - present).
Areas of Influence: Voluntary Sector.
Profile: *b.* July 3rd, 1928; *m.* Marguerite Faith.
Educated at Cheltenham College and Technical Colleges at Birmingham and Bristol. Career details: Technical Assistant to Assistant Engineer, SW Gas Board (1952-62); Assistant to Managing Director, Philblack Ltd, Bristol (1962-68); Senior Sales Engineer, Simon-Carves Chemical Engineering Ltd (1968-70); Regional Sales Manager, Sim-Chem Ltd (1970-82); Director, Vine Gardens Ltd (1983-89); Director, Manchester Literary and Philosophical Publications Ltd (1996-01). Justice of the Peace, Tameside PSD (1976-98), now on Supplemental list; Chairman, Marple CAB (1994-99). Member, National Farmers Union; Proprietor, The Portico Library. Clubs and societies: Council Member (1992-96), Manchester Lit and Phil Society; Hallé Concerts Society; Friends of the Whitworth; The Art Fund; Royal Agricultural Society; Multiple Sclerosis Society; Cheltonian Society; Chairman (1980-01), Marple Civic Society.
Interests: Gardening, painting, music.
Contact details: Tobits Farm, Werneth Low, Gee Cross, Hyde SK14 3AH (tel: 0161 367 8176).

YEAMAN, Marguerite Faith, JP (1973)

Position: Advisor on Tourism and Field Sports.
Areas of Influence: Voluntary Sector.
Profile: *b.* May 30th, 1932; Angus George David.
Educated at Cheltenham Ladies College (1942-49) and Bristol College of Commerce (1950-52). Career profile: Founder Member, League of Friends of Marple Hospitals (1970-75); Inaugurator, Multiple Sclerosis Society of Great Britain (1971-74); Member, Stockport Health Authority (1971-91); Proprietor, Faith Yeaman Organisation (1973-78); Administrator, University of Manchester (1979-81); Director, Vine Gardens Ltd (1983-89); Magistrate, Stockport (1973 - 2002); Retired Farmers wife. Clubs and societies: Manchester Lit and Phil (1981 - present); Marple Civic Society; Friends of Whitworth Art Gallery; National Art Collections Fund; Stockport Art Guild; Countryside Alliance; Scottish National Trust.
Interests: Reading, book collecting, field sports, painting, horticulture, political and literary history, making money.
Contact deatails: Tobits Farm, Werneth Low, Gee Cross, Cheshire SK14 3AH (tel: 0161 369 8176, mob: 07876 292632).

YEATES, Philip Michael, ACIB, FSA

Position: Director, NM Rothschild & Sons Limited (1994 - present).
Areas of Influence: Finance.
Profile: *b.* March 19th, 1964; *m.* Elaine; 1 son; 1 daughter.
Career profile: Manager, Specialist Finance Team, County Natwest Bank Limited (1992-94); Executive, Corporate Lending Team, Hill Samuel Bank Limited (1990-92); Executive, Regional Lending Department, TSB Bank plc (1989-90); Various roles as accelerated trainee (1982-89).
Contact details: 82 King Street, Manchester M2 4WQ (tel: 0161 827 3800, fax: 0161 839 2465, email: phil.yeates@rothschild.co.uk); (tel: 01625 531 244).

YEUNG, Kui Man (Gerry), BA (Hons)

Positions: Director, Yang Sing Restaurant; Secretary, Federation of Chinese Associations in Manchester; Director, Chamber Business Enterprises; Vice-President, MCCI and Bursary Appeal for Manchester Grammar School; Trustee, Museum of Science and Industry; Governor, Withington Girls School; Member, Manchester Asian Business Forum, SME Council of the CBI, Court of Manchester University and Lord Mayor's Charity Appeal Committee.
Areas of Influence: Commerce, Manchester.
Profile: *b.* August 5th, 1954; *m.* Yin Ling (Joanne); 1 son; 1 daughter.
With parents and elder brother, Harry, Gerry Yeung established the Yang Sing restaurant in 1977 in small basement premises in George Street, Manchester. It became a Limited Company in 1983 and over the last 25 years the restaurant has become a Manchester Institution. Clubs and societies: Manchester Luncheon Club; Portico Library; Manchester Lit & Phil; St James Club.
Interests: Reading, antique furniture, renovation of old properties.
Contact detail: (236 2200, fax: 0161 236 5934, email: info@yang-sing.com).

YEUNG, Kui Shum (Harry)

Positions: Chairman and Executive Chef, Yang Sing Restaurant.
Areas of Influence: Fusion Cooking, Chinese Community.
Profile: *b.* July 20th, 1953 (Canton, Southern China); *m.* Man Chang (Mandy); 2 sons (15, 10); 1 daughter (17).
Harry Yeung left school at 13 to begin his culinary career in Hong Kong under the watchful guidance of his father. He gained further experience in restaurants in London, other UK cities and in Manchester. The Yang Sing restaurant first featured in *Good Food Guide* in 1981 and in 1983 became the first ethnic restaurant to be awarded a *Pestle and Mortar*, their highest accolade. The present team of 30 chefs is under Harry's personal supervision, and he still goes to local market every day. The

Yang Sing was voted Best Oriental Restaurant of the year (2000) by the Observer. A series of five half hour television documentaries by Granada TV of the rebuilding of the Yang Sing after the fire in 1997 was shown in the North West and Hong Kong. Harry has also worked as a consultant on Marks and Spencer's Chinese Ready Meal range.

Interests: Staunch Manchester United Supporter, drives a 15 year old Bentley.

Contact details: Yang Sing Ltd, 34 Princess Street, Manchester M1 4JY (0161 236 2200, fax: 0161 236 5934, email: info@yang-sing.com).

YUILL, Major Chick, MA Hons

Position: Divisional Commander, Salvation Army, Central North Division.

Areas of Influence: Faith Groups, Voluntary Sector.

Profile: *b.* January 3rd, 1947; *m.* Margaret; 2 daughters.

Education: Glasgow University, MA (Hons) English Language and Literature. Career profile: Salvation Army Officer, 30 years; Staff of the Army's Officer Training College, London, 4 years; Leadership pf Pasadena Tabernacle, California, USA (1995); Publications: 3 books, *We need Saints*; *This means war*; *God created sex*.

Interests: Jazz, running, good coffee!

Contact details: 80 Eccles New Road, Salford M5 4DU (tel: 0161 743 3900, fax: 0161 743 3911, email: chick.yuill@salvationarmy.org.uk); 85 Blackcarr Road, Baguley, Manchester M23 1PW.

ZALUD, Rabbi Norman, APHS, FRSA

Positions: Rabbi: Chaplain for ten North West Prisons; North Manchester Reform Synagogue (2000 - present); Liverpool Progressive Synagogue (1976 - present); Blackpool Reform Synagogue (1986 - present).
Areas of Influence: Faith Groups.
Profile: *b.* October 5th, 1932; *m.* Barbara; 2 sons.
Educated at Grammar School Liverpool, Jews College London University, Guildhall School of Music and Leo Baeck Rabbinic College. Career profile: Minister, Birkenhead Hebrew Congregation (1952-57); Assistant Minister and Cantor, Allerton Hebrew Congregation (1957-61); Assistant Minister / Rabbi, Manchester Reform Congregation (1961-66). Clubs and societies: Chaplain and Officer, Jewish Lads and Girls Brigade; Philosophical Society; Jewish Ex-servicemen and Women.
Interests: Media, sports, horticulture, music - especially cantorial, education, youth work, working with special needs children.
Contact details: Sha'arei Shalom, North Manchester Reform Congregation, Elms Street, Whitefield, Manchester M45 8GQ (tel: 0161 796 6736); 256 Woolton Rd, Childwall, Liverpool L16 8NB (tel: 0151 722 4389).

ZOCHONIS, Sir John Basil, DL (1989), kt (1997), BA

Position: Trustee, Zochonis Charitable Trust; Council Member, British Executive Service Overseas (BESO).
Areas of Influence: Education, Health, Voluntary Sector.
Profile: *b.* October 2nd, 1929; *m.* Brigid Mary Evanson.
Educated at Rugby and Oxford. Career profile: Paterson Zochonis (1953); Director (1957); Chairman (1970-93); former High Sheriff, County of Greater Manchester

(1994-95). Clubs and societies: Carlton Travellers; MCC.
Interests: Reading, cricket.
Contact details: PZ Cussons, PZ Cussons House, Bird Hall Lane, Stockport SK3 0XN (tel: 0161 491 8000).

Arts

ALDERTON, Mark William
ALLEN, Professor John Charles
ALLEN, Charles Lamb
ANGLESEY, Natalie Ann
BALL, Michael,
BARNETT, Joel
BATTON, Carol Joyce
BEALE, James Robert
BEER, Professor Janet Patricia
BENSON, Stephen John
BISHOP, Sir Michael David
BLACKMORE, John Ashurst
BLOXHAM, Thomas Paul
BOYD, Douglas Gavin
BRACEGIRDLE, Cyril
BRASLAVSKY, Nicholas Justin
BROMLEY-DAVENPORT, John
BULLOCK, Alan David
BURNS, Josephine
BUTLER, Stella Vera Frances
BUTTERWORTH, Arthur Eckersley
CAMPBELL, Bill
CASEY, Ben
CASH, David Charles
CASKEN, Professor John
CEBERTOWICZ, Janina Dorota
CHAMPION, Sarah
CHAPMAN, Brian
CHEETHAM, Andrew
COOK, Ben
CURTIN, Liam
DAVID, Professor Ann Rosalie
DAVIES, His Honour Judge Sir Rhys
DERBY, Edward Richard William
DRIVER, Betty Mary
EAGLETON, Professor Terry
EAKIN, Michael George
ELDER, Mark
ELLIOTT, Marianne Pheobe
ELLIS, David
ESTEBANEZ, Salvador Dr
FALLOWS, David Nicholas
FAWCETT, Julia
FELL, Brian Stephen

FINLAY, Ian
FOLKMAN, Peter John
FORD, Anna
FORRESTER, Jim
FROST, Ronald
GARNER, Alan
GELDART, William
GILBERT, Dr Anthony John
GILLILAND, Judge James Andrew David
GODLEE, Richard Crosfield
GORB, Adam John Gideon
GOURLAY, James
GRANGE, Professor Philip Roy
GRANT, Len
GREEN, Lorna Leuw
GREEN, Gregory David
GREENWOOD, Michael John
GREGSON, Professor Edward
HALDER, Dr Ajit Kumar
HALL, Nigel Mark
HALL, Daniel Charles Joseph
HAZELWOOD, Colette
HEATHCOTE, Paul
HENSHALL, Nicholas Guy
HERSOV, Gregory Adam
HODGKISS, Susan Katrina
HONER, Chris
HOUGH, Stephen Andrew Gill
HOWITT, Basil William
HUSH, Gillian
JANSKI, Stefan
JARMAN, Professor Douglas
JELLICOE, Colin
JOHNSON, Trevor
JONES, Susan
JONES, Wendy Ann
KAUFMAN,.Gerald Bernard
KENNEDY, Michael
KENYON, Christopher George
KENYON, Margaret
KERSHAW, Walter
KEY, Geoffrey George Bamford
LARNER, Gerald
LATHAM, Glenys
LEE, Paul Anthony
LEVER, Lady Ray Rosalia
LIBESKIND, Daniel

LIVESEY, Philip Grimshaw
LIVINGSTONE, Jack
LONDON MORRIS, Hope
LUNNISS, Vivien
MALONE, Dr Kevin
MANSFIELD, Dr Nicholas Andrew
MANUELL, Sir John
MARIGLIANO, Emma
MARSH, Rosemary Caroline
MARSHALL, Wayne
MATHER, Elaine Grace
MAXWELL, Melinda Sara
McKINLAY, Donald Norval
McLACHLAN, Murray
MEACOCK, Lucy
MERRICK, Linda
MICHAEL, Richard
MITHA, Alnoor
MOAKES, Adrian
MORELAND, Claire Josephine
MOSCROP, Martin Richard
MOUTREY, David John
MURRAY, Braham Sydney
MURRAY, Jenni
MURREY, Martin
NEWSOME, Dr Roy
NICHOLLS, Susan Frances Harmar
O'NEAL, Eamonn Sean
O'NEILL, C J
O'ROURKE, Aiden
PASS, Anthony John Bradley
PATRIARCA, Stephen Richard
PICKSTONE, Professor John Victor
PIDGEON, Brian
PIKE, Fraser Jeremy
PIKE, Jennifer Elizabeth
POOLE, Dr Geoffrey
RANDALL, Jill Margaret
RARITY, Brian Stewart Hall
RAYNOR, Howard Kingsley
REGAN, Martin Peter
ROACHE, William Patrick
ROBERT-BLUNN, John
ROBERTS, Kieran
ROBSON, Andrew Edward
ROEBUCK, Valerie Jean
ROSE, Noah

ROWBOTHAM, Sheila
ROWLAND, Dr Christopher Selwyn
ROWLINSON, Geoffrey Mark
RUNDELL, Clark Eugene
RUSSELL, Anthony Patrick
RYLE, Sallie Elizabeth
SAINT, Alexandra
SARWAR, Mohammed
SCHMIDT, Michael Norton
SCOTT, Robert Leslie
SCOTT, David Ian
SEAL, Michael Jefferson
SHEPPARD, Elizabeth Honor
SHINDLER, Geoffrey Arnold
SHINE, Jeremy
SHORROCK, John Michael
SIM, Alistair
SIMPSON, Richard Graham
SINGH, Reuben
SLADE-LIPKIN, Heather
SPENCER, Liam David
STEPHEN, Dr Martin
STEPHENSON, Roger Francis
STIRLING, Penny
STOKES, Christopher Peter
SUMMERS, John Heath
TAGGART, Paul William
TANDY, Virginia
TAYLOR, Kenneth Alan
TAYLOR, Elizabeth
THRELFALL, Stephen
TIMMINS, Anthony George Patrick
TUCKER, Anne
TURNER, John Brierley
WALKER, Lynne
WALKER, Robin
WATSON, Nenegh
WEWER, Christian
WHEATCROFT, Matthew
WHIBLEY John
WHITBREAD, Neville Anthony
WILKINSON, Stephen Austin
WILLIAMS, Bill
WILSON Anthony Howard
WOLSTENCROFT, Edwina Maria
WOOD, Professor Laurie
WOODWARD, Susan Lesley

Commerce

ABBOTT, John Noel
AHMED, Iqbal
AHMED, Kabir
AINSCOW, Carol
AINSWORTH, Bernard
ALLEN, John Philip
ALLEN, Professor John Charles
ALLEN, Charles Lamb
ANGUS, Thomas
ARKLE, Richard
ARORA, Ashi
ASHTON, Michael
BALDWIN, Jonathan Francis
BARKWORTH, Glen Leigh
BARRETT, Professor Peter Stephen
BASHIR, Mazamil
BEAUMONT, Martin Dudley
BECKETT-HUGHES, Melinda Jane
BENZIE, Alan Athol Emslie
BERKLEY, David
BERNSTEIN, Howard
BERNSTEIN, David Alan
BISHOP, Sir Michael David
BLASKEY, Roger Waldo
BLOXHAM, Thomas Paul Richard
BOYERS, Jonathan Mark
BROWN, Robert Alexander Lindsay
BROWNSON, Susan Ann
BUCKLEY, John Spencer
BUCKLEY, Liam Joseph
BUTTERWORTH, Michael George
CADMAN, Major James Rodney
CASH, David Charles
CHAMBERLAIN, Dr Leslie Neville
CHAPLIN, Graeme Edgar
CLAVELL-BATE, Michael Frederick
CLEMENT, Roger
CLIFFORD, Chris
COLLIER, Professor Christopher George
COLLINS, Nicholas Frank
COLLINSON, Leonard
CONNOR, Bill
COOKE, Darryl John
COOMBS, Professor Roderick Wilson

DAUBNEY, Stephen Gordon
DAVENPORT, Colin
DAVIES, Jane
DERBY, Edward Richard William Stanley
DOHERTY, Ellie
DWEK, Joseph Claude
DYBLE, Michael
DYSON, Richard George
DYSON, Robert William
EGAN, Brigit Colleen
EINOLLAHI, Maghsoud
FAIRWEATHER, Eric
FAWCETT, Julia
FERGUSON, Mark William James
FITZWALTER, Raymond Alan
FOUNTAIN, Neil Taylor
FOX, Harry
FRASER, Ian Robert
GARTSIDE, Major Edmund Travis
GILLIES, Brian
GOLDSMITH, Professor Michael James
GOLDSTONE, Anthony Stewart
GOODDIE, Howard Rowsley
GOODEY, Felicity
GOODHAND
GOULD, John Roger Beresford
GRADWELL, Lorraine
GRAY, Bryan Mark
HADFIELD, Charles Alexander
HEALEY, Professor Nigel
HEALEY, Eric J G
HEGINBOTHAM, Peter
HODGKISS, Frank Lewis
HOUGH, Robert Eric
HOYLE, John Roger Horrocks
HUGHES, Richard Ian
HUGHES, Stephen
HUGHES, Eric
HUNTER, Mark James
HURST, Malcolm
INCARICO, Marcella
JEANES, Clive Frederick
JOHNSTON, T Keith
JONES, Sheila Margaret
JONES, Peter
JOSEPH, Rachel Jacqueline
KANARIS, Dr Andreas Demitri

KAPADIA, Babubhai
KEARY, Ged
KEATON, Dr James
KENNEDY, John Thomas
KENYON, Sir George Henry
KERSHAW, Walter
KIRKWOOD, Colonel David
LAWSON, Andrew Stuart
LEATHER, David William
LEE, K H
LEES-JONES, William George Richard
LEES-JONES, Simon Christopher
LEVY, Robert Adrian
LONDON MORRIS, Hope
LUPTON, Paul Nigel Carus
MAHMUD, Talat
MARSH, John
MARSTON, Allan Stewart
MARTIN, F A Peter
MARTIN, William Scott
MATHER, Elaine Grace
McGUIRE, John Charles
McKeith, David William
MEEUSS, John Francois Ferdinand
MELMOTH, Sir Graham John
MORAN, Andrew Gerard
MORRIS, David
MUIRHEAD, Geoffrey
MURRAY, Professor Richard
NEWTON, Paul Michael
NICHOLS, Rupert Henry Conquest
NIVEN, Alistair Edgar
O'BRIEN, Roger William
O'CALLAGHAN, Michael John
ORRELL, Susan
PEDELTY, Mervyn Kay
PETTY, Christopher R W
RAFFLE, Tim
RAFFLES, Ralph Leslie Stamford
RAYMOND, Peter
REGAN, Martin Peter
RINK, Paul J.E
ROBINSON, Angela Bridie
ROBSON, Andrew Edward
RUBINSTEIN, Shelly
RUSSELL, David
SABBERWAL, Dr Amar Jit Parkash

SCUDAMORE, Jeremy Paul
SELLERS, Rodney Horrocks
SHERMAN, Colonel Thomas
SIM, Alistair
SIMPSON, Andrew Christopher
SINGH, Reuben
SLADE, Derek Harrison
SODERSTROM, Berndt-Erik
SPINOZA, Andrew Daniel
SPOONER, John
STACEY
STEPHENSON, Roger Francis
STOLLER, Norman K
STRACHAN, Anthony John
STUART, Steven
SYKES, Sally Ann
THOMAS, Baron Terence James
TIMPSON, William John Anthony
TOPHAM, Charles Richard
TRIPPIER, Sir David
TULLY, David John
TUPHOLME, Andy
WADE, William Oulton
WAINWRIGHT, John Peter
WALL, Chris
WALSH, John
WARREN, Joelle Susan
WEBB, Philip Ernest
WEWER, Christian
WHIBLEY John
WHITBREAD, Neville Anthony
WHITE, Alan
WILLIAMS, John
WILSON, Ronald Geoffrey Osborne
WILSON, Andrew James
WOOD, Professor Laurie
YATES, Andrew
YEUNG, Kui Man
YEUNG, Kui Shum

Education

AL-HAFEEZ, Mahmood
ALLEN, Professor John Charles
ANDREWS, Anthony John David
ANGLESEY, Natalie Ann
APPLEGATE, The Venerable Dr John
ARNOLD, Professor John Andre
ASHTON, Michael
AVARI, Burjor
BAKER, Stephen Roy
BALDWIN, Jonathan Francis
BANISTER, Christopher Edward
BARRETT, Professor Peter Stephen
BATTERS, Royce
BAUME, Carole Diane
BEER, Professor Janet Patricia
BIANCHI, Adrian
BLACKMORE, John Ashurst
BODMER, Sir Walter (Fred
BOOTH, Arthur Thomas
BOWKER, Professor Peter
BOYD, Douglas Gavin
BRADFORD, Professor Michael Graham
BRADY Graham Stuart
BRAZIER, Professor Margot Rosetta
BROWNSON, Susan Ann
BRYANT, Christopher Gordon Alistair
BURGESS, Tim
BURNHAM, Andrew
BURSLEM, Alexandra Vivien
BUTLER, Stella Vera Frances
CAMPBELL, Colin
CARLISLE, Lord Mark of Bucklow
CARTER, B V
CASE, Professor Richard Maynard
CASEY, Ben
CASKEN, Professor John
CATLOW, Ronald Eric
CEBERTOWICZ, Janina Dorota
CHAMBERLAIN, Dr Leslie Neville
CHAUDHRY, Bashir Ahmed
CLAYTON, Judith Margaret
CLIFFORD, Chris
COLLIER, Professor Christopher George
COOK, Ben

COOMBS, Professor Roderick Wilson
COOPER, Professor Cary Lynn
CREWDSON, James
DAVID, Professor Timothy
DAVID, Professor Ann Rosalie
DAVIES, His Honour Judge Sir Rhys
DAVIS, Susan Elizabeth
DAWBER, Graham Derek
DAY, Michael Philip
DIXON, Paul
DONNACHIE, Professor Alexander
DUNN, Dennis
EAGLETON, Professor Terry
EGAN, Brigit Colleen
EJOH, Sonya
ELLIOTT, Marianne Pheobe
ELSTEIN, Professor Max
ESTEBANEZ, Salvador Dr
EVANS, Michael Norman Gwynne
EVANS, Gareth Antony
FALLOWS, David Nicholas
FAWCUS, Simon James David
FERGUSON, Mark William James
FINDON, The Rev Dr John Charles
FINNEY, Barbara Gill
FOLKMAN, Peter John
FORD, Anna
FORRESTER, Jim
FOX, David John
FROST, Ronald
FRCO, ARticts
FURBER, Professor Stephen Byram
GACESA, Professor Peter
GARNER, Alan
GARRITY, Michael
GARSIDE, Professor John
GIBSON, Alan David
GILBERT, Dr Anthony John
GILLESPIE, Professor Iain Erskine
GILLETT, The Rt. Revd. David Keith
GOLDSMITH, Professor Michael James
GOLDSTONE, Anthony Stewart
GOODDIE, Howard Rowsley
GORDON, Professor David
GOURLAY, James
GRANGE, Professor Philip Roy
GRANT, Lawrence Coleman

GREEN, Lorna Leuw
GREEN, Gregory David
GRIFFITHS, Elaine Christine
HACKETT, Cllr Mark
HALHEAD, Robert
HALL, Sir Iain Robert
HALL, Nigel Mark
HALLAM, Ian William
HANKINS, Harold Charles Arthur
HARFORD, Ian
HARLOE, Professor Michael Howard
HARNDEN, Professor David Gilbert
HARRIS, Professor Sir Martin Best
HAWORTH, Ian James
HAZELWOOD, Colette
HEALEY, Professor Nigel Martin
HEATHCOTE, Paul
HEATON, Stephen John
HENNESSEY, Jan
HENSHALL, Nicholas Guy
HIGGINS, Joan Margaret
HIGGINS, Geoffrey Paul
HINCHCLIFFE, Professor Tom Alan
HODGKISS, Susan Katrina
HOPKINS, Reverend Tim
HUMPHRIES, Gerard William
HUSH, Gillian
ISHERWOOD, Professor Ian
JANSKI, Stefan
JARMAN, Professor Douglas
JEANES, Clive Frederick
JOHNSON, Robert William Greenwood
JOHNSTON, T Keith
JONES, Peter Emerson
KANARIS, Dr Andreas Demitri
KEATON, Dr James
KENNEDY, John Thomas
KENYON, Christopher George
KENYON, Sir George Henry
KENYON, Margaret
KNOWLES, Janet Susan
KUSHNICK, Professor Louis
LATHAM, Glenys
LAWLEY, Janet M
LAWTON, Lawrence Duncan
LAYZELL, Paul John
LEE, K H

LEE, Paul Anthony
LEE-JONES, Christine
LEES-JONES, Christopher Peter
LEITCH, Dr Diana Mary
LEON, Anthony Jack
LEVER, Lady Ray Rosalia
LEWIS, The Right Reverend Michael
LI, Tyze Kai Tai
LIEBERMAN, Dr Brian Abraham
LONDON MORRIS, Hope
LOVELL, Alfred Charles Bernard
LOWRY, John Christopher
LUNNISS, Vivien
MACHELL, Raymond Donatus
MAHER, Christina Rose
MAKEPEACE, Christopher Edmund
MALLICK, Professor Sir Netar Prakash
MALONE, Dr Kevin
MANSFIELD, Dr Nicholas Andrew
MANUELL, Sir John
MARTIN, James
MAXWELL, Melinda Sara
McCABE, Terence
McCOMBS John
McCURDY, Cleveland
McKINLAY, Donald Norval
McLACHLAN, Murray Alexander Chree
McLEOD, Professor David
MELLOR, Ian
MERRICK, Linda
MILLAR, Professor Thomas Joseph
MILLER, Lucie Kathleen
MILLER, John
MILLS, William Stirling
MITHA, Alnoor
MOAKES, Adrian
MOGHAL, Nasrullah Khan
MOORE, Professor Stuart Alfred
MORAN, Terence Anthony
MORELAND, Claire Josephine
MORRIS, Margaret Ann
MOSCROP, Martin Richard
MOUNT, Peter William
MUIRHEAD, Geoffrey
MURRAY, Professor Richard
NEWCOMB, Edgar
NEWSOME, Dr Roy

O'BRIEN, Tamsin
OGLESBY, Professor Katherine Leni
LSBERG, Rev Leslie Mark
O'NEAL, Eamonn Sean
O'ROURKE, Aiden
PANNONE, Rodger John
PANTON, Elizabeth Jane
PATRIARCA, Stephen Richard
PICKERING, Janet D
PICKSTONE, Professor John Victor
PLUMB, Barry Sidney
POLLARD, Professor Brian James
POOLE, Dr Geoffrey
POPPLEWELL, Richard Ian
POWELL, Professor James Alfred
POWNALL, John Harvey
PRICE, Professor Patricia
PRIOR, Michael John
PULLEN, Professor Brian Sebastian
PURNELL, James Mark Dakin
QUAYLE, Robert Samual
RABBITT, Patrick Micheal Anthony
RAMSDEN, Professor Richard Thomas
RANDALL, Jill Margaret
RAYMOND, Peter
RAYNOR, Howard Kingsley
REES, Trevor Merion Emlyn
REID, Professor Steven Robert
RILEY, Harold Francis
ROBERTS, Professor Carole Alison
ROBERTS, Peter Lewis
ROBSON, Brian Turnbull
ROEBUCK, Valerie Jean
ROTHWELL, Professor Nancy Jane
ROWBOTHAM, Sheila
ROWLAND, Dr Christopher Selwyn
RUNDELL, Clark Eugene
SAATCHI, Roy
SABBERWAL, Dr Amar Jit
SANDERS Mark Henry
ARWAR, Mohammed
SCHMIDT, Michael Norton
SCOTT, David Ian
SHEPPARD, Lynn
SHEPPARD, Elizabeth
SLADE-LIPKIN, Heather
SMITH, Sir Cyril

STEPHEN, Dr Martin
STEPHENSON, Roger Francis
STIRLING, Penny
STOCKDALE, David Andrew
STOKES, Christopher Peter
STRACHAN, Anthony John
SUMRA, Dr Ranjit Singh
SUTTON, Michele
SYKES, The Rev Canon John
TAGGART, Paul William
TARBUCK, Phil
TAVERNOR, Peter
TAYLOR, Janet Elizabeth
TAYLOR, Elizabeth
TEMPLE, Mollie
TERRAS, Christopher Richard
THACKER, Martin Nicholas
THRELFALL, Stephen
TURNBERG, Lord Leslie Arnold
WAINWRIGHT, John Peter
WALKER, Professor Martin
WALL, Chris
WALLACE, Joanna Jane
WALTERS, Lord Mayor Councillor Roy
WARREN, Joelle Susan
WATSON, Kevin
WEST, Janice
WEWER, Christian
WILLIAMS, Bill
WINTON, Dr Malcolm
WOOD, Professor Laurie
YATES, Andrew
ZOCHONIS, Sir John Basil

Faith Groups

AHMED, Aaqil
ANDREWS, Anthony John David
APPLEGATE, The Venerable Dr John
AVARI, Burjor
BALLARD, The Venerable Andrew Edgar
BEALE, James Robert
BOOKBINDER, Alan Peter
BRAGARD, Dr Jean Claude
BRAIN, The Right Rev Terence

BRODIE, Rabbi Jeffrey
CARTER, Rev. Joseph
CHAUDHRY, Bashir Ahmed
COX, Edward Rawson
FOSS, The Rev Dr David Blair
FRISBY, Norman,
GARNER, The Reverend Keith Vincent
GIBSON, Alan David
GILLETT, The Rt. Revd. David Keith
GOKAL, Professor Ramanlal
GOULD, John Roger Beresford
GUTERMAN, Henry
HAIG, The Reverend Christopher Duncan
HALDER, Dr Ajit Kumar
HILL, Canon Roger Anthony John
HOPKINS, Reverend Tim
KAPADIA, Babubhai
KENT, The Rev Graham Richard
LASH, Very Rev. Christopher John
LEWIS, The Rt Rev Michael Augustine
LOWE, The Rt Revd Stephen Richard
McCULLOCH, Nigel Simeon
MIDGLEY, The Reverend John Andrew
OLSBERG, Rev Leslie Mark
O'REILLY, Very Rev Francis John
QUINLAN, Rt. Rev. Monsignor Michael
ROBINSON, Jason
ROEBUCK, Valerie Jean
RUBINSTEIN, Shelly
SHIH, Chueh-Teng
SMITH, John Bartlett
STOCK, The Rt Rev William Nigel
SYKES, The Rev Canon John
TARBUCK, Phil
TATTERSALL, Geoffrey Frank
THOMAS, Duncan Andrew
WAIN, Neil
WARREN, Joelle Susan
WILLIAMS, Canon Michael Joseph
WILLIAMS, Bill
WILLIE, The Reverend David Frederick
WINTON, Dr Malcolm
WISEMAN, The Rev David John
WOLFE, Joy Sylvia
WOLSTENCROFT, The Venerable Alan
YUILL, Major Chick
ZALUD, Rabbi Norman

Finance

AHMED, Riaz
ALCOCK, Graham Paul
ALLEN, John Philip
ANGUS, Thomas
ARKLE, Richard
ARNOLD, Professor John Andre
BAILEY, Richard
BAKER, Stephen Roy
BARNETT, Joel
BEAUMONT, Martin Dudley
BENZIE, Alan Athol Emslie
BERNSTEIN, Howard
BERNSTEIN, David Alan
BERRY, Grant
BIRD, Nicholas Charlton Penrhys
BLASKEY, Roger Waldo
BOLTON, M Clare
BOOTH, Arthur Thomas
BOYD, James Michael
BOYERS, Jonathan Mark
BRADY, Mark David
BROWNSON, Susan Ann
BURNETT, Paul
CHAPLIN, Graeme Edgar
CHUI, Peter Chee Keung
CLEMENT, Roger
COLLINSON, Leonard
CRAIG, Ian Alexander
DAVENPORT, Colin
DAWBER, Graham Derek
DONE, Frances Winifred
DYSON, Robert William
EINOLLAHI, Maghsoud
ENTWISTLE, Tim
EVANS, Richard David
FAIRWEATHER, Eric
FISH, David Thomas
FLYNN, Barry
GARSTON, Clive Richard
GARTSIDE, Major Edmund Travis
GILLESPIE, Colin Stephen
GILLIES, Brian
GILLILAND, Judge James Andrew
GRAHAM, Ronald Henry Joseph

GRANT, Lawrence Coleman
GREENWOOD, Michael John
HEALEY, Eric
HINDSHAW, Jennifer Mary
HUGHES, Richard Ian
HUGHES-LUNDY, Jacqueline Ann
HURST, Malcolm
HURST, Jonathon Paul Fenton
JOHNS, Peter Andrew
JOHNSON, Philip Michael
JONES, Sheila Margaret
KEARY, Ged
KELLY, Ruth
KIRKWOOD, Colonel David
LANE-SMITH, Roger
LAWSON, Andrew Stuart
LEATHER, David William
LEE, John Robert Louis
LEON, Anthony Jack
LIVESEY, Philip Grimshaw
LIVINGSTONE, Jack
LUPTON, Paul Nigel Carus
MARSTON, Allan Stewart
MARTIN, James
MARTIN, F A Peter
MARTIN, William Scott
MASTERS, Roger William
McCURDY, Cleveland
McGRATH, Eamonn John
McGUIRE, John Charles
McKeith, David William
McKIE, James Murray
MITCHELL, Paul
MORRIS, David
NEWTON, Paul Michael
O'CALLAGHAN, Michael John
PEDELTY, Mervyn Kay
PRIOR, Michael John
RACE, Robert Topham
RAFFLE, Tim
RARITY, Brian Stewart Hall
RICHENS, Nigel John
RICKITT, Peter Edward
RUSSELL, Kenneth Clifton
RUSSELL, David
SCOTT, Robert Leslie
SCUDAMORE, Jeremy Paul

SEAL, Michael Jefferson
SELLERS, Rodney Horrocks
SIMMONS, Jack
SIMPSON, Andrew Christopher
SINGH, Reuben
SLADE, Derek Harrison
SMALLBONE, Tim
SNYDER, Heath Lee
STACEY, Glenys
STRACHAN, Anthony John
STUART, Steven
TERRAS, Christopher Richard
TIMMINS, Anthony George Patrick
TRAVIS, David Joseph
TRIPPIER, Sir David
TUPHOLME, Andy
WADE, William Oulton, Lord of Chorlton
WALKER, Professor Martin
WALLER, Simon Thomas
WATSON, Alan Arthur
WEBB, Philip Ernest
WHITE, Alan
WILDIG, Michael John
WILSON, Ronald Geoffrey Osborne
YEATES, Philip Michael

Health

AHMED, Riaz,
AL-HAFEEZ, Mahmood
ALMOND, George Haylock
APPLEBY, Professor Louis
ASANTE-MENSAH, Evelyn Justina
ASHTON, Dr John Richard
BATTERS, Royce
BIANCHI, Adrian
BODMER, Sir Walter
BOWKER, Professor Peter
BRADLEY, Keith
BRADY Graham Stuart
BRASLAVSKY, Nicholas Justin
BRAZIER, Professor Margot Rosetta
BURNHAM, Andrew
BURNS, Professor Alistair

BUTTERS, Andrew Martin
CALTON, Patsy
CHAPMAN, Brian
CHISWICK, Professor Malcolm Leon
CREED, Professor Francis
CURT, John Reginald
Da-COCODIA, Louisa Adassa
DARROCH, Lit Colonel Peter Lyle Keith
DAS, Dr Bhagabat Charan
DAVID, Professor Timothy
DAVID, Professor Ann Rosalie
de VALDA, Michael Anthony Frederick
DEIRANIYA, Abdulilah Kheiro
DJANG, Alex Emmanuel
DOBBIN, Jim
DYER, Philip Arthur
EJOH, Sonya
ELSTEIN, Professor Max
ELTON, Dr Peter Joseph
FERGUSON, Mark William James
FIRTH, Mary
GALASKO, Charles Samuel Bernard
GARRITY, Michael
GARTSIDE, Major Edmund Travis
GILLESPIE, Professor Iain Erskine
GOKAL, Professor Ramanlal
GOODWIN, Dr Neil
GORDON, Professor David
HARNDEN, Professor David Gilbert
HARRISON, Jane Elinor
HEAGERTY, Professor Anthony Michael
HIGGINS, Joan Margaret
HOWELL, Professor Anthony
ISHERWOOD, Professor Ian
JOHNSON, Robert William Greenwood
JONES, Peter Emerson
KITCHENER, Professor Henry
LAWRENCE, Margaret Gillian
LEEMING, Marie Jennifer Jacqueline
LEON, Anthony Jack
LIEBERMAN
LIU YIN, Professor John Ahman
LOWRY, John Christopher
MALLICK, Professor Sir Netar Prakash
McCABE, Terence
McCOLLUM, Professor Charles Nevin
McLEOD, Professor David

MELLOR, Katherine Margaret
MILLER, Dr John
MONTGOMERY, Lady Joyce
MOORE, Professor Stuart Alfred
MORAN, Andrew Gerard
MORRIS, Margaret Ann
MORRIS, Peter John
MOUNT, Peter William
O'REILLY, Patrick Henry
PICKSTONE, Professor John Victor
POLLARD, John Stanley
POLLARD, Professor Brian James
POPPLEWELL, Richard Ian
POSTLETHWAITE, Dr Robert Joseph
PRICE, Professor Patricia
PROCTOR, Jean
RABBITT, Patrick Michael Anthony
RAFFLES, Ralph Leslie Stamford
RAMSDEN, Professor Richard Thomas
ROBERTS, Laura Patricia
ROBERTS, Peter Lewis
ROBINSON, Edna
RODEN, Angela
RUBINSTEIN, Shelly
SABBERWAL, Dr Amar Jit Parkash
SCUDAMORE, Jeremy Paul
SELVAN, Fay
SMITH, Philip M
STANLEY, Jeanette Letuina
STEPHENSON, Alan
SUMRA, Dr Ranjit Singh
TALLIS, Professor Raymond Courtney
TURNBERG, Lord Leslie Arnold
WALLACE, Joanna Jane
WANDER, Dr Philip Alan
WEARNE, Mandy
ZOCHONIS, Sir John Basil

Law

ADAMS, Shirley Meri
ALLAN, William Thomas
ALLWEIS, Martin Peter
ARORA, Ashi
ATHERTON, Robert Kenneth
AUSTIN, Jason Richard Alexander
BECKETT, Roy George
BENSON, Stephen John
BERG, Alan
BERKELEY, Leslie David
BERKLEY, David
BIRKETT, Peter Vidler
BLACK, Michael
BLOOM, His Honour Judge Charles
BOOTH, Michael John
BOYD, James Michael
BRASLAVSKY, Nicholas Justin
BRAZIER, Professor Margot Rosetta
BREEDON, Paul Heath
BRINNAND, John
BRODIE, Rabbi Jeffrey
BROMLEY-DAVENPORT, John
BROWN, Donald James
BUCKLEY, Liam Joseph
BURGESS, Tim
BURKE, John Kenneth
BURNS, Stephen Mark
CAMPBELL, Colin
CARLISLE, Lord Mark of Bucklow
CARTER, B V
CAWSON, Peter Mark
CHAN, Charles
CHUI, Peter Chee Keung
CLAVELL-BATE, Michael Frederick
COGLEY, Stephen William
CONRAD, Alan David
COOKE, Darryl John
CRAIG, Ian Alexander
CRAIG, Susan
DALE, Nigel Andrew
DANSON, Ann Elizabeth
DAVIES, Stephen
DAVIES, His Honour Judge Sir Rhys
DAWSON, Peter

DEVITT, Paul
DUNN, Dennis
EAGELSTONE, Diana Barbara
ECCLES, Frances Mary
EDWARDS
ELLERAY, Anthony, John
ELSTEIN, Professor Max
ENSOR, His Honour George Anthony
FAWCUS, Simon James David
FIELD, Patrick John
FIELDEN, John Anthony Haigh
FINESTEIN, Jonathon Eli
FINNEY, Barbara Gill
FIRTH, Mary Flora Mackinnon
FISH, David Thomas
FISHER, Catherine Jane
FISHWICK, Avril
FITZWALTER, Raymond Alan
FOSTER, Jonathan
FRASER, Vincent
GARSTON, Clive Richard
GILBART, Andrew James
GILLILAN, Judge James Andrew
GOLD, Antony
GOLDSTONE L Clement
GOODHAND, FLt Lt Brian
GOULTY, Ian Oliphant
GRAHAM, Ronald Henry Joseph
GRAY, David
GRIME, Mark Stephen Eastbourne
HALL, Daniel Charles Joseph
HAMILTON, Judge Iain McCormick
HAMMOND Robert Michael
HAWES, Roger
HAYDEN, Anthony
HEATON, Stephen John
HEGARTY Thomas Brendan
HEGINBOTHAM, Peter
HERWALD, Basil M
HEWISON, John E
HOLMAN, Richard Christopher
HORLOCK Timothy John
HOWARTH, Nigel John Graham
HUGHES, Chief Superintendent William
HUMPHRIES, Gerard William
HYTNER, Benet Alan
JESS, Dr Digby Charles

JOHNSTON, T Keith
KINGSLEY, Joy
KNIGHT, Brigid Agnes
KNOPF, Elliot Michael
KNOWLES, Janet Susan
LANCASTER, Roger
LANE-SMITH, Roger
LEE, Adrian
LEE, Paul Anthony
LEECH, Emma Jane
LEEMING, Marie Jennifer Jacqueline
LEES-JONES, Christopher Peter
LEVER, Judge Bernard Lewis
LEVY, Robert Adrian
LEWIS, His Honour Judge Jeffrey Allan
LOWCOCK, Judge Andrew Charles
LYON, Judge Adrian Pirrie
MACHELL, Raymond Donatus
MADDOCKS, Judge Bertram Catterall
MARKS, Richard Leon
MARTIN, William (Scott
MATTISON, Mark Robert
MAYER, Christine Alexander
McDERMOTT, Gerard Francis
McDONALD, James William Ian
MELLOR, Katherine Margaret
MOORE, Professor Stuart Alfred
MORAN, Andrew Gerard
MORGAN, Glyn
NICHOLS, Rupert Henry Conquest
O'BRIEN, Roger William
OLDROYD, James Colin
ORRELL, Susan
PANNONE, Rodger John
PATTERSON, Frances Sylvia
PETTY, Christopher R W
PIKE, Malcolm John
POLLARD, John Stanley
QUINLAN, Rt. Rev. Monsignor Michael
ROSS, Hilary Muriel
RUMBELOW, Judge Arthur Anthony
RUSSELL, Anthony Patrick
RYDER, Ernest Nigel
SCHOLES, Rodney James
SEPHTON, Craig Gardner
SHAW, Michael Patrick
SHELDON, William

SHINDLER, Geoffrey Arnold
SHORROCK, (John) Michael
SINGER, Peta Doreen
SINGER, Harold Sammuel
SLADE, Derek Harrison
SMITH Adrian Charles
SMITH, Dame Janet Hilary
SMITH, John Bartlett
SMITH, Dame Janet Hilary
SMITH, John Bartlett
SMITH, Quentin
SMITH, Philip
SORRELL, Stephen Terence
STACEY, Glenys
STEWART, Stephen Paul
STOCKDALE, David Andrew
STUNELL Andrew
SWEENEY, Vincent Anthony
SWIFT, Caroline Jane
TATTERSALL, Geoffrey Frank
TAYLOR, Janet Elizabeth
TAYLOR, Elizabeth
TAYLOR, Anthony Roy
THOMAS, Paul Alan
THOMPSON, Michael Edwin
TULLY, David John
TURNER, Mark George
WAIN, Neil
WALLER, Simon Thomas
WATKINS, Maurice
WEBSTER, Alistair Stevenson
WHEELDON, Richard Andrew
WHITE, Stephen John
WILLIAMS, Barrie
WILSON, Andrew James
WINGATE-SAUL, Giles
WOODWARD, His Honour Judge
WRIGHT, Peter Duncan
WROE, Chief Superintendent, Brian

Media

AHMED, Aaqil
ALDERTON, Mark William
ALLEN, Charles Lamb
ANGLESEY, Natalie Ann
BARKWORTH, Glen Leigh
BARNETT, Joel
BASHIR, Mazamil
BEALE, James Robert
BEER, Professor Janet Patricia
BESWICK, Allan
BISHOP, Sir Michael David
BOOKBINDER, Alan Peter
BOWDUR, Helen
BRACEGIRDLE, Cyril
BRAGARD, Dr Jean Claude
BROWN, Robert Alexander Lindsay
BURNS, Josephine
BURNS, Stephen Mark
BURSLEM, Alexandra Vivien
CAMPBELL, Darren Andrew
CATLOW, Richard
CHEETHAM, Andrew
CLIFFORD, Chris
COLLINSON, Leonard
CUMBES, Jim
DOHERTY, Ellie
DRIVER, Betty Mary
DYBLE, Michael
FAWCETT, Julia
FINLAY, Ian
FITZWALTER, Raymond Alan
FORD, Anna
FRISBY, Norman
GALE, Susie
GARVIE, Wayne
GELDART, William
GILLETT, The Rt. Revd. David Keith
GOODEY, Felicity
HALHEAD, Robert
HALL, Nigel
HANCOCK, Jim
HARRIS, Paul
HEATHCOTES, Paul
HENFIELD, Martin Owen
HENNESSEY, Jan
HENSHALL, Nicholas Guy
HERWALD, Basil M J
HICKMAN, James Paul
HORROCKS, Paul John
HUGHES, Stephen
HUNTER, Mark James
HUSH, Gillian
INCARICO, Marcella
JANSKI, Stefan
JONES, Donald Saunders
JONES, Bill
JOSEPH, Rachel Jacqueline
KAUFMAN, Gerald Bernard
KENNEDY, Michael
LARNER, Gerald,
LINDSAY, Sally
MANUELL, Sir John
MARTIN-SMITH, Nigel
MAXWELL, Melinda Sara
McLACHLAN, Murray Alexander Chree
MEACOCK, Lucy
MICHAEL, Richard
MOONEY, Claire
MOSCROP, Martin Richard
MURRAY, Braham Sydney
MURRAY, Jenni
NEWSOME, Dr Roy
NICHOLLS, Susan Frances Harmar
O'BRIEN, Tamsin
O'NEAL, Eamonn Sean
O'ROURKE, Aiden
PIDGEON, Brian
POWELL, Professor James Alfred
PURNELL, James Mark Dakin
RADCLIFFE, Mark
RARITY, Brian Stewart Hall
RAYNOR, Howard Kingsley
REGAN, Martin Peter
ROBERT-BLUNN, John
ROBERTS, Kieran
ROBINSON, Angela Bridie
ROBINSON, Jason
ROWBOTHAM, Sheila
RYLE, Sallie Elizabeth
SAATCHI, Roy
SCHMIDT, Michael Norton

SELVAN, Fay
SHEPPARD, Lynn
SHERMAN, Colonel Thomas
SIM, Alistair
SPINOZA, Andrew Daniel
STACEY, Ed
STEPHEN, Dr Martin
SWANTON, David
SYKES, Sally Ann
TAGGART, Paul William
TAYLOR, Steve
TAYLOR, Michael
TAYLOR, Michael John
TAYLOR, Steve
TAYLOR, Steve
TRIPPIER, Sir David
WAGG, Jimmy
WALKER, Lynne
WANDER, Dr Philip Alan
WEST, Janice
WHEATCROFT, Matthew
WILKINSON, Stephen Austin
WILLIAMS, John
WILSON Anthony Howard
WILSON, Dianne Elizabeth
WOLFE, Joy Sylvia
WOLSTENCROFT, The Venerable Alan,
WOLSTENCROFT, Edwina Maria
WOOD, Phil
WOODWARD, Susan Lesley
WOOLAS, Philip James

Public Sector

AGARD, Caryl Edward
ALMOND, George Haylock
ASANTE-MENSAH, Evelyn Justina
ASHTON, Michael
AVARI, Burjor
AXFORD, Colonel Arthur
BALDWIN, Jonathan Francis (Jon
BERKELEY, Leslie David
BERNSTEIN, Howard
BESTERMAN, Tristram Paul
BOOKBINDER, Alan Peter

BRADFORD, Professor Michael Graham
BRADLEY, Keith
BRAILSFORD, David
BRINNAND, John
BROWN, Donald James
BRYANT, Christopher Gordon Alistair
BURNS, Josephine
BURSLEM, Alexandra Vivien
BUTTERS, Andrew Martin
CALTON, Patsy
CAMPBELL, Colin
CARLISLE, Lord Mark of Bucklow
CATLOW, Ronald Eric
CHAMBERLAIN, Dr Leslie Neville
CHAPLIN, Graeme Edgar
CHAPMAN, Brian
CHAYTOR David Michael,
CHISWICK, Professor Malcolm Leon
COLLIER, Professor Christopher George
CRAIG, Susan
CREED, Professor Francis
DAVIES, Chris
DAVIS, Susan Elizabeth
DOBBIN, Jim
DONE, Frances Winifred
DYER, Philip Arthur
EAKIN, Michael George
ELLIS, Roger Martin
ELTON, Dr Peter Joseph
FINCH, David Francis
FISHWICK, Avril
FITZSIMONS, Lorna
FORRESTER, Jim
FOUNTAIN, Neil Taylor
FOX, David John
GLEAVE, Bill
GODDARD, Paul Frederick
GOGGINS, Paul
GOKAL, Professor Ramanlal
GOLDSMITH, Professor Michael James
GOLDSTONE, Anthony Stewart
GOODWIN, Dr Neil
GORDON, Professor David
GRADWELL, Lorraine
GRANT, Lawrence Coleman
GRAY, Bryan Mark
GREEN, Lorna Leuw

GREEN, Charles
GREENWOOD, Michael John
GUILLEMAIN Virginia
HACKETT, Cllr Mark
HAGUE, Gillian
HAIG, The Reverend Christopher Duncan
HALLAM, Ian William
HAMMOND Robert Michael
HARLOE, Professor Michael Howard
HARNEY, Marie
HARRIS, Professor Sir Martin Best
HAWORTH, Ian James
HEALEY, Professor Nigel Martin
HEGINBOTHAM, Peter
HEYES, David Alan
HIGGINS, Joan Margaret
HIGGINS, Geoffrey Paul
HOLLOWOOD, Philip John
HOWARTH, Councillor Robert Lever
HUGHES, Chief Superintendent William
HUNTER, Mark James
HUTCHINGS, Alan
IDDON Brian
INHELDER, Max
JONES Stephen Morris
KAUFMAN, Gerald Bernard
KILBURN Andrew
LAWTON, Lawrence Duncan
LEE, Adrian
LEESE, Richard Charles
LI, Tyze Kai Tai
LLOYD, Anthony Joseph
LOWRY, John Christopher
MAKEPEACE, Christopher Edmund
MALLICK, Professor Sir Netar Prakash
MARSH, John
MARTIN, F A Peter
MAYER, Christine Alexander
McCARTNEY, Ian
McDONALD, James William Ian
MCKERNAN, Vincent
MEACHER, Rt Hon MP, Michael
MENZIES, Walter Stuart
MILLS, William Stirling
MITHA, Alnoor
MONTGOMERY, Sir William Fergus
MOORE, Christopher

MORAN, Terence Anthony
MORRIS of Manchester, Baron Alfred
MORRIS, Margaret Ann
MORRIS, Peter John
MOUNT, Peter William
MURRAY, Braham Sydney
MURRAY, Jenni
MURRAY, Anthoney
ORRELL, Susan
PEDELTY, Mervyn Kay
PENDRY, Baron Thomas, of Stalybridge
PHILLIPS, Sheldon
POWELL, Professor James Alfred
POWNALL, John Harvey
PRIOR, Michael John
REES, Trevor Merion Emlyn
ROBERTS Geoffrey
ROBERTS, Professor Carole Alison
ROBERTS, Peter Lewis
ROBERTS, John Edward
ROBINSON, Edna J
ROBSON, Brian Turnbull
RODEN, Angela
RYDER, Ernest Nigel
SANDERS Mark Henry
SCHULTZ, John
SCHWARZ, Pam
SELVAN, Fay
SHEPPARD, Lynn
SHIELDS, Michael
SIMPSON, Brian
SMITH, Lord Peter Richard Charles
SMITH, John Bartlett
SMITH, Sir Cyril
SORRELL, Stephen Terence
SPACKMAN, Stanley Harry
SPINOZA, Andrew Daniel
STACEY, Glenys
STEPHENSON, Alan
STEWART, Ian
STUNELL Andrew
SWEENEY, Vincent Anthony
TAYLOR, Michael John
TEMPLE, Mollie
TERRAS, Christopher Richard
THACKER, Martin Nicholas
TITLEY, Gary

WAIN, Neil
WALSH, John
WALTERS, Lord Mayor Councillor Roy
WEARNE, Mandy
WESTMINSTER, Sir Gerald Cavendish
WHITE, Graham
WILLIAMS, Barrie
WILMOT, Sir David
WILSON, David Geoffrey
WILSON, Dianne Elizabeth
WROE, Chief Superintendant, Brian

SIMPSON, Brian
SIMPSON, Andrew Christopher
SMITH, Steven James
SMITH, Quentin
SWANTON, David
TAYLOR, Steve
THOMPSON, Geoffrey Llewellyn
WATKINS, Maurice
WATKINSON, Michael
WHITE, Graham

Sport

BECKHAM, David Robert Joseph
BERGIER, Jerzy Witold J
BERNSTEIN, David Alan
BREEDON, Paul Heath
BURNHAM, Andrew (Andy
CAMPBELL, Darren Andrew
CONDON, Allyn
COX, Sophie
CRAIG, Ian Alexander
DANSON, Ann Elizabeth
DIXON, Paul
GALASKO, Charles Samuel Bernard
HEWISON, John E
HICKMAN, James Paul
HOUGH, Robert Eric
HUGHES, Eric
LEATHER, David William
LEVER, Lady Ray Rosalia
LLOYD, David
MOORE, Christopher
PHILLIPS, Sheldon
QUEALLY, Jason Paul
RAPER, Stuart John
RATCLIFFE, Paul Andrew
RILEY, Harold Francis
ROBINSON, Jason
ROGERS, Michelle Mary
ROWLINSON, Geoffrey Mark
SHELDON, William
SHORROCK, John Michael
SIMMONS, Jack

Voluntary Sector

ABBOTT, John Noel
ADAMS, Shirley Meri
AGARD, Caryl Edward
AHMED, Riaz
AHMED, Aaqil
AL-HAFEEZ, Mahmood
ALMOND, George Haylock
ANDERSON, Farida Sharon
ANDERTON, Sir James (Cyril
APPLEGATE, The Venerable Dr John
ASANTE-MENSAH, Evelyn Justina
ASHBROOK, Viscount Michael Llowarch
BASHIR, Mazamil
BECKETT-HUGHES, Melinda Jane
BERKELEY, Leslie David JP
BERRY, Paul Karfoot
BIRD, Nicholas Charlton Penrhys
BOULTON, Francis Ann
BRAILSFORD, David
BRODIE, Rabbi Jeffrey
BROMLEY-DAVENPORT, John
BROWN, Donald James
BURTON, Khumi Tonsing
CADMAN, Major James Rodney
CARTER, Rev Joseph
CHAUDHRY, Bashir Ahmed
CHUI, Peter Chee Keung
CONN, Edith
COX, Edward Rawson
CRAIG, Susan
CURT, John Reginald Newstead
Da-COCODIA, Louisa Adassa

DARROCH, Lit Colonel Peter Lyle Keith
DAS, Dr Bhagabat Charan
DAVENPORT, Colin
DAVIS, Gregory Barrie
de COVERLEY-WILKINS, Col John Alfred
DERBY, Edward Richard William Stanley
DJANG, Alex Emmanuel
DOHERTY, Ellie
EJOH, Sonya
ELTON, Dr Peter Joseph
EVANS, Michael
FIELDEN, John Anthony Haigh
FINCH, David Francis
FINDON, The Rev Dr John Charles
FINLAY, Ian
FIRTH, Mary Flora Mackinnon
FOSS, The Rev Dr David Blair
FRISBY, Norman
GARNER, The Reverend Keith Vincent
GIBBS, Colonel Donald Edwin
GODDARD, Paul Frederick
GOULTY, Ian Oliphant
GREEN, Gregory David
GRIFFITHS, Elaine Christine
GUTERMAN, Henry
HADFIELD, Charles Alexander
HAIG, The Reverend Christopher Duncan
HALDER, Dr Ajit Kumar
HARFORD, Ian
HARRISON, Jane Elinor
HEYES, David Alan
HILL, Canon Roger Anthony John
HINDSHAW, Jennifer Mary
HODGKISS, Susan Katrina
HOPKINS, Reverend Tim
HUGHES-LUNDY, Jacqueline Ann
KAPADIA, Babubhai
KENNEDY, John Thomas
KENYON, Sir George Henry
KIRKWOOD, Colonel David
LAWRENCE, Margaret Gillian
LEE, K H
LEES-JONES, Christopher Peter
LEITCH, Dr Diana Mary
LEWIS, The Right Reverend Michael
Augustine Owen
LI, Tyze Kai Tai,

LIVINGSTONE, Jack
LOWE, The Rt Reverend Stephen Richard
MAHER, Christina Rose
MAHMUD, Talat
MANSFIELD, Dr Nicholas Andrew
MARSH, Rosemary Caroline
MASSEY, Nick
MATHER, Elaine Grace
McCURDY, Cleveland
McHUGH, Ian David
McMANUS, Catherine Mary
MEACOCK, Lucy
MEEUSS, John Francois Ferdinand
MENZIES, Walter Stuart
MILLER, Lucie Kathleen
MITCHELL, Lieut-Commander Noel
MONTGOMERY, Lady Joyce
MOORE, Christopher
MORGAN, Glyn
MURRAY, Anthoney
NICHOLS, Rupert Henry Conquest
OLSBERG, Rev Leslie Mark
PANNONE, Rodger John
PHILLIPS, Sheldon
PICKERING, Janet
PROCTOR, Jean
RAFFLES, Ralph Leslie Stamford
RINK, Paul
ROACHE, William Patrick,
ROBERTS Geoffrey
RODEN, Angela
ROSS, Hilary Muriel
SARWAR, Mohammed
SCOTT, Robert Leslie
SEAL, Michael Jefferson
SHELDON, William
SHERMAN, Colonel Thomas
SHIH, Chueh-Teng
SINGER, Peta Doreen
SINGER, Harold Sammuel
SMITH, Sir Cyril
SODERSTROM, Berndt-Erik
SPACKMAN, Stanley Harry
STOLLER, Norman K
SUTHERLAND, John
TARBUCK, Phil
TAYLOR, Ian Donald

TIMMINS, Anthony George Patrick
TIMMINS, Colonel John Bradford
TIMPSON, William John Anthony
TUCKER, Anne
TURNBERG, Lord Leslie Arnold
WADE, William Oulton, Lord of Chorlton
WALSH, Chris
WATKINS, Maurice
WEBB, Philip Ernest
WEINBERG, Rebecca Davida
WHITE, Stephen John
WILSON, David Geoffrey
WILSON, Dianne Elizabeth
WILSON, Andrew James
WOLFE, Joy Sylvia
YEAMAN, Angus George David
YEAMAN, Marguerite Faith
YUILL, Major Chick
ZOCHONIS, Sir John Basil

ABBREVIATIONS

A

AA	Architectural Association
AAF	Auxiliary Air Force
ABA	American Bar Association
ABCC	Association of British Chambers of Commerce
ABPS	Associate, British Psychological Association
ABRSM	Associated Board, Royal Schools of Music
ABS	Associate, Building Societies Institute
ABSI	Associate, Boot and Shoe Institute
ACA	Associate, Institute of Chartered Accountants
ACAS	Advisory Conciliation and Arbitration Service
ACBSI	Associate, Chartered Building Societies Institute
ACCA	Associate, Chartered Association of Certified Accountants
ACCS	Associate, Corporation of Secretaries
ACEA	Associate, Association of Cost and Executive Accountants
ACF	Army Cadet Force
ACGI	Associate, City and Guilds Institute of London
ACIArb	Associate, Chartered Institute of Arbitrators
ACIB	Associate, Chartered Institute of Bankers
ACII	Associate, Chartered Insurance Institute
ACIS	Associate, Institute of Chartered Secretaries and Administrators
ACM	Association of Computing Machinery
ACMA	Associate, Institute of Cost and Management Accountants
ACSD	Associate of the Central School of Speech & Drama
ACST	Associate of the College of Science and Technology
ACT	Association of Corporate Treasurers
ADB	Associate of the Drama Board
ADC	Aide-de-Camp

Adj	Adjutant
AdvCounDip	Advanced Counselling Diploma
AdvDip	Advanced Diploma
AdvDipSpEd	Advanced Diploma in Special Education
AEEU	Amalgamated Engineering & Electrical Union
AEU	Amalgamated Engineering Union
AFA	Associate, Institute of Financial Accountants
AFC	Association Football Club
AGSM	Associate, Guildhall School of Music
AHA	Area Health Authority
AI	Artificial Intelligence
AIA	Associate, Institute of Actuaries
AICE	Associate, Institute of Civil Engineers
AIDS	Acquired Immunity Deficiency Syndrome
AIEE	Associate, Institute of Electrical Engineers
AIIMR	Associate, Institute of Investment Management and Research
AIL	Associate, Institute of Linguistics
AIMSW	Associate Institute of Medical Social Workers
AIPD	Associate, Institute of Professional Designers
AIQS	Associate, Institute of Quantity Surveyors
AIT	Association of Investment Trusts
AKC	Associate, King's College, London
ALA	Associate of the Library Association
ALCD	Associate, London College of Divinity
ALI	Associate, Landscape Institute
ALS	Associate of the Linnaean Society
AMA	Associate of the Museums Association
AMBIM	Associate Member, British Institute of Management
AMCST	Associate, Manchester College of Science and Technology

AMCT	Associate, Manchester College of Technology	ASRE	American Society of Refrigeration Engineers
AMInstTA	Associate Member, Institute of Transport Administration	Assoc	Association(s)
		AssocMCT	Associate of the Manchester College of Technology
AMIPM	Associate Member, Institute of Personnel Management	Asst	Assistant
AMSPetE	Associate Member, Society of Petroleum Engineers	ATC	Air Training Corps *or* Art Teacher's Certificate
ANSM	Associate, Northern School of Music	ATCL	Associate, Trinity College of Music, London
AO	Officer, Order of Australia	ATD	Art Teacher's Diploma
AOF	Admiral of the Fleet	ATI	Associate, Textile Institute
APIL	Association of Personal Injury Lawyers	ATII	Associate of the Institute of Taxation
APMI	Associate, Pensions Management Institute	ATIT	Associate, Institute of Taxation
		AUA	American Urological Association
ARAM	Associate, Royal Academy of Music	AUMIST	Associate of UMIST
ARBS	Associate, Royal Society of British Sculptors *or* Association for the Recognition of Business Schools		

B

		b	born
		BA	Bachelor of Arts
ARCA	Associate, Royal College of Art	BA(Arch)	Bachelor of Architecture
ARCM	Associate, Royal College of Music	BA(Com)	Bachelor of Commerce
		BA(Econ)	Bachelor of Arts (Economics)
ARCO	Associate of the Royal College of Organists	BAcc	Bachelor of Accountancy
		BAFM	British Association of Friends of Museums
ARCS	Associate, Royal College of Science	BAFTA	British Academy of Film & Television Arts
ARIBA	Associate, Royal Institution of British Architects	BAO	Bachelor of Art of Obstetrics
ARICS	Associate, Royal Institution of Chartered Surveyors	BAOR	British Army on the Rhine
		BArch	Bachelor of Architecture
ARMCM	Associate, Royal Manchester College of Music	Bart	Baronet
		BAS	Bachelor of Agricultural Science
ARNCM	Associate, Royal Northern College of Music	BAS	Bachelor of Applied Science
ARSH	Associate, Royal Society for the Promotion of Health	BBA	British Bankers Association
		BBC	British Broadcasting Corporation
ARSM	Associate, Royal School of Mines	BCA	Bachelor of Commerce and Administration
ARTC	Associate, Royal Technical College, Glasgow	BCh	Bachelor of Surgery
ARTCS	Associate, Royal Technical College, Salford	BChir	Bachelor of Surgery
		BCL	Bachelor of Civil Law
ARVA	Associate, Incorporated Association of Rating and Valuation Officers	BCom	Bachelor of Commerce
		BComm	Bachelor of Commerce
		BCS	British Computer Society
ASA	Associate, Society of Actuaries	BD	Bachelor of Divinity
ASCA	Associate, Society of Company and Commercial Accountants	Bde	Brigade
		BDentSc	Bachelor of Dental Science
ASH	Action on Smoking and Health	BDS	Bachelor of Dental Surgery
		BDSc	Bachelor of Dental Science

BEC	Business Education Council
BEd	Bachelor of Education
BEM	British Empire Medal
BEng	Bachelor of Engineering
BFMPI	British Federation of Master Printers Institute
BGS	British Geriatric Society
BIM	British Institute of Management
BIMA	British Interactive Multi-Media Association
BJRULM	Bulletin of the John Rylands University Library of Manchester
BL	Bachelor of Law
BLA	Bachelor of Landscape Architecture
BLA	Bachelor of Liberal Arts
BLESMA	British Limbless Ex-Servicemen's Association
BLitt	Bachelor of Literature
BLL	Bachelor of Law
BM	Bachelor of Medicine
BMA	British Medical Association
BMet	Bachelor of Metallurgy
BMus	Bachelor of Music
Bn	Battalion
BNFL	British Nuclear Fuels Ltd
BPharm	Bachelor of Pharmacy
BPhil	Bachelor of Philosophy
BPS	British Psychological Society
BPsS	British Psychological Society
BRNC	Britannia Royal Naval College
BS	Bachelor of Science (US) or Bachelor of Surgery (US)
BSc	Bachelor of Science
BSc(Econ)	Bachelor of Science (Economics)
BSc(Optom)	BSc in Optometry
BScTech	Bachelor of Technological Science (UMIST)
BScSoc	Bachelor of Social Sciences
BSocSci	Bachelor of Social Sciences
BSS	Bachelor of Social Science
BTC	British Textile Confederation
BTEA	British Textile Employers Association
BTech	Bachelor of Technology
BTMA	British Textile MachineryAssociation
BUPA	British United Provident Association

C

(C)	Conservative
CA	Member, Institute of Chartered Accountants, Scotland
CAB	Citizens Advice Bureau
CAM	Communications, Advertising & Marketing
CAMPUS	Campaign to Promote the University of Salford
Capt	Captain
CArch	Chartered Architect
CB	Companion of the Bath
CBC	County Borough Council
CBE	Commander, Order of the British Empire
CBI	Confederation of British Industry
CBIM	Companion, British Institute of Management
CBiol	Chartered Biologist
CBSO	City of Birmingham Symphony Orchestra
CC	Cricket Club or County Council or County Court or Cycling Club
CCC	County Cricket Club
CChem	Chartered Chemist
CDCE	Centre for the Development of Continuing Educaiton
CE	Church of England
CEA	Cinema Exhibitors Association
CEGB	Central Electricity Generating Board
CEI	Council of Engineering Institutions
CEng	Chartered Engineer
CEO	Chief Executive Officer
CERN	Centre Européenne pour la Recherche Nucléaire
CertEd	Certificate in Education
CertInstMan	Certificate in Institutional Management
CertPA	Certificate in Public Administration
CertWM	Certificate in Works Management
CGeol	Chartered Geologist
CGLI	City and Guilds of London Institute
ChB	Bachelor of Surgery
CHC	Community Health Council
ChLNH	Chevalier de la Légion Nationale d'Honneur

ChM	Master of Surgery	CSD	Co-operative Secretaries Diploma
CIE	Companion, Order of the Indian Empire	CSS	Council of Social Services
CIEx	Companion, Institute of Export	CStJ	Commander of the Order of St John of Jerusalem
CIM	Companion, Institute of Management	CText	Chartered Textile Technologist
CIMF	Companion of the Institute of Mechanical Engineers	CTT	Chartered Textile Technologist
		CUP	Cambridge University Press
CIMgt	Companion, Institute of Management	CVCP	Committee of Vice-Chancellor & Principals
CIMUSET	International Committee of Museums of Science & Technology	CVM	Company of Veteran Motorists
		CVS	Council of Voluntary Services
		CWS	Co-operative Wholesale Society
CIP	Chartered Insurance Practitioner		

D

CIPD	Companion Institute of Personnel Development	DA	Diploma in Anaesthesia *or* Diploma in Art
CIPFA	Chartered Institute of Public Finance and Accountancy	DAA	Diploma in Archive Administration
CIPM	Companion, Institute of Personnel Management	DAAG	Deputy Assistant Adjutant-General
CIRP	Collège Interationale pour Recherche et Production	DAD	Deputy Assistant Director
		DAES	Division of Adult Education Service
CIT	Fellow, Chartered Institute of Transport	DArts	Doctor of Arts
CL	Contact Lens Diploma, Association of British Dispensing Opticians	DASE	Diploma in Admin Sports Education
		DBA	Doctor of Business Administration
CLASP	Consortium of Local Authority Schools Project	DBE	Dame Commander, Order of the British Empire
CLP	Constituency Labour Party	DBS	Diploma in Business Studies
CMath	Chartered Mathematician	DCH	Diploma in Child Health
CMC	Consortium of Management Consultantants	DCh	Doctor of Surgery
		DCM	Distinguished Conduct Medal
CMG	Companion of St Michael and St George	DD	Doctor of Divinity
CNAA	Council for National Academic Awards	DDSc	Doctor of Dental Science
		decd	deceased
CND	Campaign for Nuclear Disarmament	DEd	Doctor of Education
		DEng	Doctor of Engineering
CO	Commanding Officer	Dep	Deputy
COI	Central Office of Information	dept	department
CompTI	Companion of the Textile Institute	DES	Department of Education and Science
CP	County Primary	DFA	Doctor of Fine Arts
CPA	Chartered Patent Agent	DFBCS	Distinguished Fellow of the British Computer Society
CPhys	Chartered Physicist		
CPS	Crown Prosecution.Service	DFC	Distinguished Flying Cross
CPsychol	Chartered Psychologist	DFEE	Department for Education and Employment
CQSW	Certificate of Qualification in Social Work		
		DHSS	Department of Health & Social Security
CRE	Commission for Racial Equality		
CS	Civil Service		

425

DIC	Diploma, Imperial College, London	DipPhysEd	Diploma in Physical Education
Dip	Diploma	DipPrimEd	Diploma in Primary Education
DipAD	Diploma in Art and Design	DipRADA	Diploma, Royal Academy of Dramatic Art
DipAdEd	Diploma in Adult Education		
DipAdvStEd	Diploma in Advanced Studies in Education	DipRCM	Diploma of the Royal College of Music
DipAdvStud	Diploma in Advanced Studies	DipSocAdmin	Diploma in Social Administration
DipAdvStSci	Diploma in Advanced Studies in Science	DipSocSt	Diploma in Social Studies
DipAE	Diploma in Adult Education	DipTecSc	Diploma in Technical Sciences
DipArch	Diploma in Architecture	DipTheol	Diploma in Theology
DipBA	Diploma in Business Administration	DipTimbTech	Diploma in Timber Technology
		DipTP	Diploma in Town Planning
DipBibStud	Diploma in Biblical Studies	DipTrainingMgt	Diploma in Training Management
DipCD	Diploma in Civic Design		
DipCIM	Diploma of Chartered Institute of Management	DipURP	Diploma in Urban & Regional Planning
DipCommPrac	Diploma in Commercial Practice	DipWSEd	Diploma of the Wines & Spirits Education Trust
DipCouns	Diploma in Counselling	*diss*	dissolved
DipDA	Diploma in Dramatic Art	DL	Deputy-Lieutenant
DipEd	Diploma in Education	DLit	Doctor of Literature *or* Doctor of Letters
DipEdMgt	Diploma in Education Management		
DipEdPsych	Diploma in Educational Psychology	DLitt	Doctor of Literature *or* Doctor of Letters
DipEnvHlth	Diploma in Environmental Health	DM	Doctor of Medicine
		DMA	Diploma in Municipal Administration
DipFA	Diploma in Fine Art	DML	Diploma in Magisterial Law
DipFE	Diploma in Further Education	DMRD	Diploma in Medical Radiological Diagnosis
DipHE	Diploma in Higher Education		
DipHEIM	Diploma in Home Economics & Institutional Management	DMRE	Diploma in Medical Radiology and Electrology
DipHSM	Diploma in Health Services Management	DMS	Diploma in Management Studies
DipIM	Diploma in Industrial Management	DMus	Doctor of Music
		DObst	Doctor of Obstetrics
DipInstManAcc	Diploma of the Institute of Mangement Accounting	DoE	Department of the Environment
		DoH	Department of Health
DipLib	Diploma in Library and Information Studies	DPA	Diploma in Public Administration
DipLS	Diploma in Library Science	DPE	Diploma in Physical Education
DipM	Diploma in Marketing	DPH	Diploma in Public Health
DipManEd	Diploma in Management and Education	DPh	Doctor of Philosophy
		DPhil	Doctor of Philosophy
DipManSci	Diploma in Management Science	DPM	Diploma in Psychological Medicine
DipManStud	Diploma in Management Studies	DRCOG	Diploma of the Royal College Obstetricians and Gynaecologists
DipPA	Diploma in Public Administration		
DipPH	Diploma in Public Health	DRD	Diploma in Restorative Dentistry

DRSAMD	Diploma of the Royal Scottish Academy of Music & Drama	FAQMC	Fellow, Association of Quality Management Consultants
DSA	Diploma in Social Administration	FASA	Fellow, Australian Society of Accountants
DSC	Distinguished Service Cross	FASCE	Fellow, American Society of Civil Engineers
DSc	Doctor of Science		
DSIR	Department of Scientific and Industrial Research	FASME	Fellow, American Society of Mechanical Engineers
DSS	Department of Social Security	FAVLP	Fellow, Association of Valuers of Licensed Property
DStJ	Dame Commander, Order of St John of Jerusalem	*fax*	facsimile
DTech	Doctor of Technology	FBA	Fellow, British Academy *or* Federation of British Artists
DTI	Department of Trade & Industry	FBAM	Fellow, British Academy of Management
DTM & H	Diploma in Tropical Medicine and Health	FBCA	Fellow of the British-Caribbean Association
DU	Doctor of the University	FBCO	Fellow, British College of Ophthalmic Opticians
Dunelm	Dunelmis (of Durham)		
DUniv	Doctor of the University	FBCS	Fellow, British Computer Society

E

(Eng)	Engineering	FBDO	Fellowship Diploma, Association of British Dispensing Opticians
Ed	Edinburgh *or* Editor		
EDC	Economic Development Committee	FBIM	Fellow, British Institute of Management
Educ.	Educated		
EEC	European Economic Community	FBiol	Fellow, Institute of Biology
		FBKS	Fellow, British Kinematic Sound and Television Society
EETPU	Electrical, Electronic, Telecommunication & Plumbing Union	FBOA	Fellow, British Optical Association
EMMA	Europan Multi Media Association	FBPsS	Fellow, British Psychological Society
Eng	England *or* Engineering	FBS	Fellow, Building Societies Institute
ENO	English National Opera		
EPSRC	Engineering & Physical Sciences Research Council	FC	Football Club
		FCA	Fellow, Institute of Chartered Accountants
ERD	Emergency Reserve Decoration		
ESRC	Economic & Social Research Council *or* Electricity Supply Research Council	FCAnaesth	Fellow, College of Anaesthetists
		FCBSI	Fellow, Chartered Building Societies Institute
EU	European Union	FCCA	Fellow, Chartered Association of Certified Accountants
EuroFIET	International Federation of Commercial, Clerical & Technical Employees		
		FCCP	Fellow, College of Chest Physicians (US)
		FCCP(USA)	Fellow, College of Chest Physicians (USA)

F

FAAO	Fellow, American Academy of Optometry	FCGL	Fellow, Guild of Cleaners and Launderers
FACP	Fellow, American College of Physicians	FChemS	Fellow, Chemical Society
		FChS	Fellow, Society of Chiropodists

FCIArb	Fellow, Chartered Institute of Arbitrators	FFD	Fellow of the Faculty of Dental Surgeons
FCIB	Fellow, Chartered Institute of Bankers	FFDRCSI	Fellow, Faculty of Denistry, Royal College of Surgeons in Ireland
FCIBS	Fellow, Chartered Institute of Bankers of Scotland	FFOM	Fellow, Faculty of Occupation Medicine
FCIEH	Fellow, Chartered Institute of Environmental Health	FFPHM	Fellow, Faculty of Public Health Medicine
FCIH	Fellow, Chartered Institute of Housing	FFRRCSI	Fellow, Faculty of Radiologists, Royal College of Surgeons, Ireland
FCII	Fellow, Chartered Insurance Institute	FGCL	Fellow, Goldsmiths' College, London
FCIM	Fellow of the Chartered Institute of Marketing *or* Fellow, Institute of Corporate Managers (Australia)	FGCL	Fellow, Guild of Cleaners and Launderers
FCIOB	Fellow, Chartered Institute of Building	FGS	Fellow, Geological Society
		FHA	Fellow, Institute of Health Service Administrators
FCIPA	Fellow, Chartered Institute of Patent Agents	FHCIMA	Fellow, Hotel Catering and Institutional Management Association
FCIS	Fellow, Institute of Chartered Secretaries and Administrators	FHKSA	Fellow, Hong Kong Society of Accountants
FCIT	Fellow, Chartered Institute of Transport	FHSA	Family Health Services Authority
FCIWEM	Fellow, Chartered Institute of Water & Enviornmental Management	FIA	Fellow, Institute of Actuaries
FCMA	Fellow, Institute of Management Accountants	FIBF	Fellow, Institute of British Foundrymen
FCollP	Fellow, College of Preceptors	FIBiol	Fellow, Institute of Biology
FCP	Fellow, College of Preceptors	FICA	Fellow, Institute of Chartered Accountants in England & Wales
FCPath	Fellow, College of Pathologists		
FCS	Fellow, Chemical Society	FICE	Fellow, Institute of Civil Engineers
FCT	Fellow, Association of Corporate Treasurers	FIChemE	Fellow, Institute of Chemical Engineers
FDS	Fellow in Dental Surgery		
FDSCRCSEd	Fellow in Dental Surgery, Royal College of Surgeons Edinburgh	FICorr	Fellow of the Institute of Corrosion
		FICorrST	Fellow, Institution of Corrosion, Science & Tecnhnology
FDSRCS	Fellow in Dental Surgery, Royal College of Surgeons, England	FICW	Fellow, Institute of Clerks of Works of Great Britain
FE	Further Education	FID	Fellow, Institute of Directors
FEng	Fellowship of Engineering	FIDE	Fellow, Institute of Design Engineers
FFA	Fellow, Faculty of Actuaries		
FFAEM	Fellow, Faculty of Accident and Emergency Medicine	FIEE	Fellow, Institute of Electrical Engineers
FFARCS	Fellow, Faculty of Anaesthetists, Royal College of Surgeons, England	FIERE	Fellow, Institute of Electronic and Radio Engineers
FFB	Fellow, Faculty of Building	FIFireE	Fellow, Institute of Fire Engineers
FFCM	Fellow, Faculty of Community Medicine		

FIGasE	Fellow, Institution of Gas Engineers	FInstPI	Fellow, Institute of Patentees and Inventors
FIGD	Fellow, Institute of Grocery Distributors	FInstSM	Fellow, Institute of Sales Management
FIHE	Fellow, Institute of Health Education	FInstWM	Fellow, Institute of Waste Management
FIHSM	Fellow, Institute of Health Service Management	FIOP	Fellow, Institute of Printing
FIHT	Fellow, Institute of Highways and Transportation	FIPA	Fellow, Institute of Practitioners in Advertising
FIIC	Fellow, International Institute for Conservation	FIPD	Fellow, Institute of Personnel Development or Fellow, Institute of Practising Designers
FIIM	Fellow, Institution of Industrial Managers	FIPHE	Fellow, Institute of Public Health Engineers
FIInfSc	Fellow, Institute of Information Scientists	FIPM	Fellow, Institute of Personnel Management
FIIP	Fellow, Institute of Incorporated Photographers	FIProdE	Fellow, Institute of Production Engineers
FILEx	Fellow, Institute of Legal Executives	FIQS	Fellow, Institute of Quantity Surveyors
FIM	Fellow, Institute of Metallurgists	FISM	Fellow, Institute of Supervisory Management
FIMA	Fellow, Institute of Mathematics and its Applications	FIStructE	Fellow, Institute of Structural Engineers
FIMarE	Fellow, Institute of Marine Engineers	FITD and	Fellow, Institute of Training Development
FIMC	Fellow, Institute of Management Consultants	FITMA	Fellow, Institute of Trade Mark Agents
FIMechE	Fellow, Institute of Mechanical Engineers	FIWEM	Fellow, Institute of Water and Environmental Management
FIMF	International Federation of Physical Medicine	FIWES	Fellow, Institute of Water Engineers and Scientists
FIMgt	Fellow, Institute of Management	FIWM	Fellow, Institution of Works Managers
FIMI	Fellow, Institute of the Motor Industry	FIWPC	Fellow, Institute of Water Pollution Control
FIMS	Fellow, Institute of Management Specialists	FLA	Fellow of the Library Association
FIMunE	Fellow, Institute of Municipal Engineers	FLI	Fellow, Landscape Institute
FInstD	Fellow, Institute of Directors	FLS	Fellow, Linnaean Society
FInstE	Fellow, Institute of Energy	FMA	Fellow, Museums Association
FInstEHO	Fellow, Institution of Environmental Health Officers	FMSM	Fellow, Manchester School of Music
FInstEx, FIEx	Fellow, Institute of Export	FNAEA	Fellow, National Association of Estate Agents
FInstM	Fellow, Institute of Marketing	FNSM	Fellow, Northern School of Music
FInstMC	Fellow, Institute of Measurement and Control	FPC	Family Practitioner Committee
FInstMgt	Fellow, Institute of Management	FPMI	Fellow, Pension Management Institute
FInstP	Fellow, Institute of Physics	FPRI	Fellow, Plastics and Rubber Institute

FRACDS   Fellow, Royal Australian College of Dental Surgeons

FRAeS   Fellow, Royal Aeronautical Society

FRAI   Fellow, Royal Anthropological Institute

FRAM   Fellow, Royal Academy of Music

FRAS   Fellow, Royal Astronomical Society

FRCA   Fellow, Royal College of Anaesthetists

FRCA   Fellow, Royal College of Art

FRCAnaes   Fellow, Royal College of Anaesthetists

FRCGP   Fellow, Royal College of General Practitioners

FRCM   Fellow, Royal College of Music

FRCO   Fellow, Royal College of Organists

FRCOG   Fellow, Royal College of Obstetricians and Gynaecologists

FRCOphth   Fellow, Royal College of Opthalmologists

FRCP   Fellow, Royal College of Physicians

FRCPath   Fellow, Royal College of Pathologists

FRCPE   Fellow, Royal College of Physicians, Edinburgh

FRCPI   Fellow, Royal College of Physicians of Ireland

FRCPscyh   Fellow, Royal College of Psychiatrists

FRCR   Fellow, Royal College of Radiologists

FRCS   Fellow, Royal College of Surgeons

FRCSE   Fellow, Royal College of Surgeons, Edinburgh

FRCSEng   Fellow, Royal College of Surgeons of England

FRGS   Fellow, Royal Geographical Society

FRHistS   Fellow, Royal Historical Society

FRIBA   Fellow, Royal Institute of British Architects

FRIC   Fellow, Royal Institute of Chemistry

FRICS   Fellow, Royal Institution of Chartered Surveyors

FRINA   Fellow, Royal Institution of Naval Architects

FRIPHH   Fellow, Royal Institute of Public Health and Hygiene

FRMCM   Fellow, Royal Manchester College of Music

FRMS   Fellow, Royal Microscopical Society

FRNCM   Fellow, Royal Northern College of Music

FRPS   Fellow, Royal Photographic Society

FRS   Fellow, Royal Society

FRSA   Fellow, Royal Society of Arts

FRSAMD   Fellow, Royal Scottish Academy of Music and Drama

FRSC   Fellow, Royal Society of Chemistry

FRSE   Fellow, Royal Society, Edinburgh

FRSH   Fellow, Royal Society for the Promotion of Health

FRSM   Fellow, Royal Society of Medicine

FRSocMed   Fellow, Royal Society of Medicine

FRTPI   Fellow, Royal Town Planning Institution

FRTS   Fellow, Royal Television Society

FRVA   Fellow, Rating and Valuation Association

FSA   Fellow, Society of Antiquaries

FSCA   Fellow, Society of Company and Commercial Accountants

FSDC   Fellow, Society of Dyers and Colourists

FSS   Fellow, Royal Statistical Society

FSVA   Fellow, Incorporated Society of Valuers and Auctioneers

FT   Financial Times

FTCL   Fellow, Trinity College of Music, London

FTI   Fellow, Textile Institute

FTII   Fellow, Institute of Taxation

FUMIST   Fellow, Manchester Institute of Science and Technology

FWBO   Friends of the Western Buddhist Order

FWeldI   Fellow, Welding Institute

FZS	Fellow, Zoological Society

G

GAMTA	General Aviation Manufacturers and Trades Association
GB	Great Britain
GCE	General Certificate of Education
GCLJ	Grand Cross of St Lazarus of Jerusalem
GCSE	General Certificate of Secondary Education
GEC	General Electric Company
GM	Greater Manchester
GMB	General Municipal Boilermakers (Union)
GMC	General Medical Council *or* Greater Manchester Council
GMEDC	Greater Manchester Economic Development Corporation
GMP	Greater Manchester Police
GMPTE	Greater Manchester Passenger Transport Executive
GMR	Greater Manchester Radio
GMT	Greater Manchester Transport
GNSM	Graduate, Northern School of Music
GNVQ	General National Vocational Qualification
GP	General Practitioner
GradCertEd	Graduate Certificate of Education
GradDipBldCons	Graduate Diploma in Building Conservation
GradDipPhys	Graduate Diploma in Physiotherapy
GRNCM	Graduate of the Royal Northern College of Music
GRSM	Graduate of the Royal Schools of Music
Gtr	Greater

H

HA	Health Authority
HAA	Heavy Anti-Aircraft
hc	honoris causa
HM	Her Majesty's
HMC	Hospital Management Committee
HMC	Headmasters' Conference
HMSO	Her Majesty's Stationery Office

HNC	Higher National Certificate
HND	Higher National Diploma
Hon	Honorary
Hons	Honours
HQ	Headquarters
HUGO	Human Genome Organisation
HVCert	Health Visitors Certificate

I

IAAP	International Association for Applied Psychology
IBA	Independent Broadcasting Authority *or* International Bar Association
IBP	Institute for British Photographers *or* Institute for Business Planning
ICA	Institute of Chartered Accountants in England and Wales
ICAEW	Institute of Chartered Accountants in England & Wales
ICE	Institution of Civil Engineers
ICI	Imperial Chemical Industries
ICL	International Computers Ltd
ICom	International Council of Museums
IEE	Institution of Electrical Engineers
IFAAST	International Federation of Associations for the Advancement of Science & Technology
IHSM	Institute of Health Services Management
ILEA	Inner London Education Authority
IMC	Institute of Management Consultants *or* International Media Centre
IMechE	Institution of Mechanical Engineers
IMM	Institution of Mining & Metallurgy
IMS	Institution of Management Sciences
IMunE	Institution of Municipal Engineers
Inst	Institute
InstMechEng	Institution of Mechanical Engineers
Instn	Institution

IOD	Institute of Directors	KSS	Knight of St Silvester
IOM	Indian Order of Merit	KStG	Papal Knight of St Gregory
IoM	Isle of Man	KStH	Knight of the Order of St Hubert (Austria)
IPFA	Chartered Institute of Public Finance and Accountancy	KStJ	Knight of the Order of St John of Jerusalem
IPM	Institute of Personnel Management	Kt	Knight
IRRV	Member, Institute of Revenues, Rating and Valuation	**L**	
ISM	Incorporated Society of Musicians	(L)	Liberal
ISO	Imperial Service Order	(Lab)	Labour
ISOTC	International Organisation for Standardisation Technical Committee	LAC	London Athletic Club
		LAMSAC	Local Authorities' Management Services and Computer Committee
ISVA	Incorporated Society of Valuers and Auctioneers	LB	London Borough
ITA	Independent Television Authority	LCCC	Lancashire County Cricket Club
ITV	Independent Television	LCCI	Liverpool Chamber of Commerce and Industry
IUPAP	International Union of Pure and Applied Physics	LCH	Licentiate of the College of Homeopaths
		LDS	Licentiate in Dental Surgery
J		LGO	Local Government Officer
JCL	Licentiate of Canon Law	LGSM	Licentiate, Guildhall School of Music
JILA	Joint Institute for Laboratory Astrophysics	LHD	Literarum Humaniorum Doctor
JP	Justice of the Peace	LHSM	Licentiate, Institute of Health Service Management
JRULM	John Rylands University Library of Manchester	LIM	Licentiate of the Institute of Metals
		LitD	Doctor of Literature *or* Doctor of Letters
K		LittHum	Litterae Humaniores
KBE	Knight Commander, Order of the British Empire	LLAMDA	Licentiate, London Academy of Music and Dramatic Art
KCB	Knight Commander, Order of the Bath	LLB	Bachelor of Laws
KCMG	Knight Commander, Order of St Michael and St George	LLCM	Licentiate, London College of Music
KCSG	Knight Commander of St Gregory	LLD	Doctor of Laws
KCVO	Knight Commander, Royal Victorian Order	LLM	Master of Laws
		LMSSA	Licentiate in Medicine and Surgery, Society of Apothecaries
KG	Knight of the Order of the Garter	LRAM	Licentiate, Royal Academy of Music
KHS	Knight, Order of the Holy Sepulchre	LRCP	Licentiate, Royal College of Physicians, London
KLJ	Knight, St Lazarus of Jerusalem	LRSC	Licentiate of the Royal Society of Chemistry
KOSB	King's Own Scottish Borderers	LSE	London School of Economics & Political Science
KRRC	King's Royal Rifle Corps		
KSC	Knight of St Columba	LSO	London Symphony Orchestra
KSP	Knight of St Peter (Rome)		

LtCol	Lieutenant Colonel	MCIT	Member, Chartered Institute of Transport
LTI	Licentiate of the Textile Institute	MCom	Master of Commerce
		MConsE	Member, Association of Consulting Engineers
M		MCOptom	Member of the College of Optometrists
m	married		
M	Million	MCSP	Member, Chartered Society of Physiotherapy
M & A	mergers & acquisitions		
M/c	Manchester	MCT	Member, Association of Corporate Treasurers
MA	Master of Arts		
MAE	Member, Academia European	MD	Doctor of Medicine *or* Managing Director
MAFA	Manchester Academy of Fine Arts		
		MDC	Metropolitan District Council
Manc	Manchester *or* of University of Manchester	MDiv	Master of Divinity
		MDS	Master of Dental Surgery
MAP	Ministry of Aircraft Production	MDSc	Master of Dental Science
marr diss	marriage dissolved	ME	Mining Engineer
MASCE	Member, American Society of Civil Engineers	MEd	Master in Education
		Mencap	Royal Society for Mentally Handicapped Children & Adults
MASME	Member, American Society of Mechanical Engineers		
MB	Bachelor of Medicine	MEng	Master in Engineering
MBA	Master of Business Administration	MEP	Member of the European Parliament
MBBS	Bachelor of Medicine	MFCM	Member of the Faculty of Community Medicine
MBBS	Bachelor of Surgery		
MBC	Metropolitan Borough Council	MFOMRCP	Member of the Faculty of Occupational Medicine, Royal College of Physicians
MBCS	Member, British Computer Society		
MBE	Member, Order of the British Empire	MGDSRCS	Member in General Dental Surgery, Royal College of Surgeons
MBIM	Member, British Institute of Management		
		MGS	Manchester Grammar School
MBO	Management Buy Out	MHSM	Member, Institute of Health Services Management
MBS	Manchester Business School		
MBSc	Master of Business Science	MIA	Manchester International Arts
MC	Military Cross	MIBF	Member, Institute of British Foundrymen
MCC	Marylebone Cricket Club		
MCCI	Manchester Chamber of Commerce and Industry	MIBiol	Member, Institute of Biology
		MIBr	Member, Institute of Brewing
MCD	Master in Civic Design	MICE	Member, Institute of Civil Engineers
MCFA	Member, Catering and Food Association		
		MIChemE	Member, Institute of Chemical Engineers
MCFC	Manchester City Football Club		
MCh	Master in Surgery	MIConsE	Member, Institute of Consulting Engineers
MChir	Master in Surgery		
MCIBS	Member, Chartered Institute of Bankers in Scotland	MIDPM	Member, Institute of Data Processing Management
MCIM	Member, Chartered Institute of Marketing	MIEE	Member, Institution of Electrical Engineers
MCIOB	Member, Chartered Institute of Building	MIEEE	Member, Institute of Electrical and Electronic Engineers

MIEnergy	Member, Institute of Energy
MIEx	Member, Institute of Exports
MIFA	Member, Institute of Field Archeologists
MIFE	Member, Institute of Fire Engineers
MIH	Member, Institute of Housing
MIHE	Member, Institute of Heating Engineers
MIHT	Member, Institution of Highways and Transportation
MIIM	Member, Institution of Industrial Managers
MIInfSc	Member, Institute of Information Scientists
MILAM	Member, Institute of Leisure and Amenity Management
MILE	Member of the Institution of Locomotive Engineers
MILPA	Member, Institute of Licenced Practitioners in Advertising
MIM	Member, Institute of Metallurgists
MIMC	Member, Institute of Management Consultants
MIMechE	Member, Institute of Mechanical Engineers
MIMgt	Member, Institute of Management
MIMI	Member, Institute of the Motor Industry
MIMinE	Member, Institute of Mining Engineers
MIMT	Member, Institute of Muncipal Transport
MInstGasE	Member, Institution of Gas Engineers
MInstLAM	Member, Institute of Leisure and Amenity Management
MInstM	Member, Institute of Marketing
MInstMM	Member, Institution of Mining and Metallurgy
MInstP	Member, Institute of Physics
MInstPet	Member, Institute of Petroleum
MIOB	Member, Institute of Building
MIoD	Member, Institute of Directors
MIOP	Member, Institute of Printing
MIPA	Member, Insolvency Practitioners' Association
MIPD	Member, Institute of Personnel & Development
MIPLE	Member, Institute of Public Lighting Engineers

MIPM	Member, Institute of Personnel Management
MIPR	Member, Institute of Public Relations
MIQA	Member, Insititute of Quality Assurance
MIStructE	Member, Institution of Structural Engineers
MITA	Member, Industrial Transport Association *or* Institute of Transport Administration
MITMA	Member, Institute of Trade Mark Agents
MIWEM	Member, Institute of Water and Environmental Management
MIWHM	Member, Institution of Works and Highways Mangement
MIWM	Member, Institution of Works Managers
MLA	Master in Landscape Architecture
MLI	Member, Institute of Linguists
MLitt	Master of Letters
MLS	Master of Library Studies
MMA	Music Masters &·Mistresses Association
MMIGD	Master Member, Institute of Grocery Distribution
MMU	Manchester Metropolitan University (formerly Manchester Polytechnic)
MMus	Master of Music
MO	Medical Officer *or* Municipal Officer *or* Military Operations
MP	Member of Parliament
MPhil	Master of Philosophy
MPPS	Master of Public Policy Studies
MR	Magnetic Resonance (Scanner)
MRAeS	Member, Royal Aeronautical Society
MRAIC	Member, Royal Architectural Institute of Canada
MRC	Medical Research Council
MRCGP	Member Royal College of General Practitioners
MRCOG	Member, Royal College of Obstetricians and Gynaecologists
MRCP	Member, Royal College of Physicians
MRCPath	Member, Royal College of Pathologists.

MRCPE	Member, Royal College of Physicians, Edinburgh	NATO	North Atlantic Treaty Organisation
MRCPGlas	Member, Royal College of Physicians, Glasgow	NBT	Northern Ballet Theatre
MRCPsych	Member, Royal College of Psychologists	NCB	National Coal Board
		NDB	National Diploma in Baking (Denmark)
MRCS	Member, Royal College of Surgeons	NDD	National Diploma in Design
MRI	Manchester Royal Infirmary	NDN	National District Nurse Certificate
MRIA	Member, Royal Institute Academy	NEAB	Northern Examinations and Assessment Board
MRIN	Member, Royal Institute of Navigation	NEC	National Executive Committee
MRSC	Member, Royal Society of Chemistry	NEDC	National Economic Development Council
MRSH	Member, Royal Society for the Promotion of Health	NEDO	Nationl Economic Development Office
MRSM	Member, Royal Society of Medicine	NHS	National Health Service
		NSEAD	National Society for Education in Art & Design
MRST	Member, Royal Society of Teachers	NSM	Non-Stipendiary Minister
MRTPI	Member, Royal Town Planning Institute	NSPCC	National Society for the Prevention of Cruelty to Children
MS	Master of Surgery *or* Master of Science (US)	NSW	New South Wales
		NTDA	National Trade Development Association
MSC	Manpower Services Commission	NUT	National Union of Teachers
MSc	Master of Science	NVQ	National Vocational Qualification
MSI	Member of the Securities Institute	NW	North West
MSocSci	Master of Social Science	NWRHA	North West Regional Health Authority
MSPI	Member, Society of Practitioners of Insolvency		
MSST	Master of Science and Science Teaching	**O**	
		o/c	Officer Commanding
MTC	Music Teachers Certificate	OBE	Order of the British Empire
MTPI	Member, Town Planning Institute	OC	Officer Commanding
		OCA	Old Comrades Association
MUP	Manchester University Press	OCCA	Oil and Colour Chemists Association
MusB	Bachelor of Music		
MusBac	Bachelor of Music	OFWAT	Officer of Water Services
MusM	Master of Music	OHA	Oldham Health Authority
MVO	Member, Royal Victorian Order	OM	Order of Merit
		OMCS	Office of the Minister for the Civil Service
		ONC	Ordinary National Certificate
N		OPSS	Office of Public Service & Science
NADFAS	National Association of Decorative and Fine Arts Societies	OST	Office of Science and Technology
NATE	National Associate for the Teaching of English	OStJ	Officer of the Order of St John of Jerusalem

OUDS	Oxford University Dramatic Society
OUP	Oxford University Press

P

PA	Personal Assistant
Para	Parachute
pc	personal computer
PC	Privy Councillor
PE	Physical Education
PGCE	Post Graduate Certificate in Education
PGDAA	Post Graduate Diploma in Arts Administration
PgDip	Postrgraduate Diploma
PGDipIA	Post Graduate Diploma in Industrial Administration
PGRNCM	Post Graduate of the Royal Northern College of Music
PhD	Doctor of Philosophy
PhL	Licentiate of Philosophy
PIBA	Personal Injuries Barristers Association
PLC	Public Limited Company
PMD	Programme of Management Development
PPARC	Particle Physics and Astronomy Research Council
PPRNCM	Professional Performance Diploma, Royal Northern College of Music
PPS	Parliamentary Private Secretary
PR	Public Relations
PrD	Probate Divorce Admiralty Division
PREST	Policy Research in Engineering, Science & Technology
ProdEng	Production Engineering
PSD	Petty Sessional Division

Q

QC	Queen's Counsel
QCVSA	Queen's Commendation for Valued Service in the Air
QFSM	Queen's Fire Service Medal
QHP	Queen's Honorary Physician
QHS	Queen's Honorary Surgeon
QMG	Quarter Master-General
QPM	Queen's Police Medal
QSO	Queen's Service Order
QUB	Queen's University, Belfast

R

R&D	Research & Development
RA	Royal Academy *or* Royal Artillery
RAC	Royal Agricultural College
RAC	Royal Armoured Corps *or* Royal Automobile Club
RADA	Royal Academy of Dramatic Art
RAEC	Royal Army Education Corps
RAF	Royal Air Force
RAFA	Royal Air Force Association
RAFVR	Royal Air Force Volunteer Reserve
RAM	Royal Academy of Music
RAMC	Royal Army Medical Corps
RAOC	Royal Army Ordinance Corps
RAPC	Royal Army Pay Corps
RAS	Royal Astronomical Society
RASC	Royal Army Service Corps
RBA	Member, Royal Society of British Artists
RC	Roman Catholic
RCA	Royal College of Art
RCambA	Royal Cambrian Academy
RCOG	Royal College of Obstetricians and Gynaecologists
RCS	Royal College of Surgeons *or* Royal Corps of Signals
RCT	Royal Corps of Transport
RD	Naval Reserve Decoration
RE	Religious Education *or* Royal Engineers
Regt	Regiment
REME	Royal Electrical and Mechanical Engineers
retd	retired
Rev	Reverend
RFC	Rugby Football Club
RGN	Registered General Nurse
RGS	Royal Geographical Society
RIBA	Member, Royal Institute of British Architects
RICS	Royal Institute of Chartered Surveyors
RLPO	Royal Liverpool Philharmonic Orchestra
RM	Royal Mail
RMA	Royal Military Academy Sandhurst
RMCM	Royal Manchester College of Music

RMCS	Royal Military College of Science	SRP	State Registered Physiotherapist
RMO	Resident Medical Officer	SSAFA	Soldiers', Sailors' and Airmens' Families Association
RN	Royal Navy	STEP	Society of Trust & Estate Practitioners
RNAS	Royal Naval Air Service		
RNCM	Royal Northern College of Music	*stepd*	stepdaughter
		steps	stepson
RNLI	Royal National Lifeboat Institution	STL	Sacre Theologiae Lector (Reader *or* Professor of Sacred Theology)
RNSA	Royal Naval Sailing Association		
RNVR	Royal Naval Volunteer Reserve	**T**	
ROI	Royal Institute of Painters in Oils	TA	Territorial Army
		TAVR	Territorial Army Volunteer Reserve
RSA	Royal Society of Arts		
RSCM	Royal School of Church Music	TAVRA	Territorial Auxiliary and Volunteer Reserve Association
RSPB	Royal Society for the Protection of Birds	TBT	Training Based Technology
RTPI	Royal Town Planning Institute	TCD	Trinity College, Dublin
RTR	Royal Tank Regiment	TD	Territorial Decoration
RUFC	Rugby Union Football Club	TEC	Training and Enterprise Council
RWAFF	Royal West African Frontier Force		
		tel	telephone
RYA	Royal Yachting Association	TEng	Technician Engineer
		TEP	Trust & Estate Practitioner
S		TIE	Theatre in Education
S/sgt	Staff Sergeant	TSB	Trustee Savings Bank
ScD	Doctor of Science	TUC	Trades Union Congress
SCI	Society of Chemical Industry		
SCM	State Certified Midwife	**U**	
SCM	Student Christian Movement	UCH	University College Hospital (London)
SCYB	South Caernarvonshire Yacht Club	UCL	University College, London
SDI	Strategic Defence Initiative	UCW	Union of Communication Workers *or* University College of Wales
SDP	Social Democratic Party		
SPUR	Stockport Partnership for Urban Regeneration	UDC	Urban District Council *or* Corporation
Sec	Secretary		
SERC	Science & Engineering Research Council	UEMS	Union Européenne des Medicins Spécialistes
SFInstE	Senior Fellow, Institute of Energy	UGC	University Grants Committee
		UIA	Union Internationale des Avocats
SHO	Senior House Officer		
SHOT	Society for the History of Technology	UKAEA	United Kingdom Atomic Energy Authority
SLTC	Society of Leather Trade Chemists	UMIST	University of Mancheser Institute of Science and Technology
SOGAT	Society of Graphical and Allied Trades		
		Univ	University
SPSL	Society for the Protection of Science & Learning	USAAF	United States Army Air Force
		USDAW	Union of Shop Distributive and Allied Workers
SRC	Science Research Council		
SRN	State Registered Nurse		

USPHS	United States Public Health Service	**W**	
		WAAF	Womens' Auxiliary Air Force
V		WEA	Workers' Educational Association
V&A	Victoria and Albert	wef	with effect from
VAD	Voluntary Aid Detachment	WHO	World Health Organization
VAT	Value Added Tax	WPHA	West Pennine Health Authority
VLSI	Very Large Scale Integration (of electronic circuits)	WRNS	Women's Royal Naval Service
VRD	-Royal Naval Volunteer Reserve Officer's Decoration	WRVS	Women's Royal Voluntary Service
VSO	Voluntary Service Overseas	WWF	World Wide Fund for Nature
		Y	
		YMCA	Young Mens' Christian Association